Other Kaplan Books on Law School Admissions:

Law School Admissions Adviser
Two Real LSATs Explained

LSAT*

2000–2001

By the Staff of Kaplan Educational Centers

Simon & Schuster

SYDNEY • **LONDON** • **SINGAPORE** • **NEW YORK**

*LSAT is a registered trademark of Law School Admission Council, which is not affiliated with this product.

Kaplan Books
Published by Simon & Schuster
1230 Avenue of the Americas
New York, NY 10020

Copyright © 2000 by Kaplan, Inc.

"The Kaplan Advantage™ Stress Management System" by Dr. Ed Newman and Bob Verini, Copyright © 1996, Kaplan, Inc.

Bentley Boyd cartoons copyright © 1999 Kaplan, Inc.

"Hazardous Waste and Environmental Liability: An Historical Perspective," by Martin V. Melosi, *Houston Law Review*, Volume 25: 741, 1988. Reprinted by permission of the *Houston Law Review*.

"Pool Coverage, Press Access, and Presidential Debates: What's Wrong with This Picture?" by Wendy S. Zeligson, *Cardozo Law Review,* Vol. 9, 1988. Reprinted by permission of *Cardozo Law Review*.

"The Profit Motive in Medicine," by Dan W. Brock and Allen E. Buchanan. *Journal of Medicine and Philosophy,* Vol. 12, 1987. Reprinted by permission of *Journal of Medicine and Philosophy*.

"The Republic Reborn by Steven Watts, " by Fred Anderson, *American Historical Review*, vol. 94, no. 2 (April 1989), p. 516. Reprinted with permission of *American Historical Review*.

"Equal Pay for Jobs of Comparable Worth: An Analysis of the Rhetoric," by Judith Olans Brown, Phyllis Tropper Baumann, and Elaine Miller Melnick, *Harvard Civil Rights & Civil Liberties Review,* No. 1, Winter 1986. Copied with permission; copyright 1988 by the President and Fellows of Harvard College.

Contributing Editor: Trent Anderson
Project Editor: Eileen Mager
Production Editor: Maude Spekes
Interior Design: Krista Pfeiffer
Interior Production: Amparo Graf
Desktop Publishing Manager: Michael Shevlin
Managing Editor: David Chipps
Executive Editor: Del Franz

Special thanks to: Julie Schmidt, Grace Begany, Hugh Haggerty, Jan Gladish, Larissa Shmailo, and Ben Paris

Manufactured in the United States of America
Published simultaneously in Canada

March 2000
10 9 8 7 6 5 4 3 2

ISSN: 1090-9079
ISBN 0–684–87011–8

CONTENTS

DISCLAIMERS

This book was designed for self-study only and is not authorized for classroom use. For information on Kaplan courses, which expand on the techniques offered here and are taught only by highly trained Kaplan instructors, please call 1-800-KAP-TEST (within the U.S.A.) or 1-212-492-5990 (outside the U.S.A.).

The information in this book is up-to-date at the time of publication. The Law School Admission Council and Law School Data Assembly Service may have instituted changes after this book was published. Please read all material you receive from these organizations regarding the LSAT test and law school admissions carefully.

ABOUT THE AUTHORS

Trent Anderson is the Executive Director of Graduate Programs at Kaplan Educational Centers. He has worked extensively with LSAT and admissions consulting (for business school, law school, and graduate school). He has been teaching LSAT, developing innovative and effective pedagogy, and creating LSAT material since 1989. He has scored in the ninety-ninth percentile every time he has taken the LSAT and has helped tens of thousands of people get into law school. He received his B.A. from the University of California, Los Angeles and his J.D. and M.B.A. from the University of Southern California. He is a member of the California Bar, the Federal Districts Courts for the Central District of California, and the Ninth Circuit Court of Appeals.

Eric Goodman has been teaching the Kaplan LSAT course for nine years and works for Kaplan Educational Centers as a product consultant. When not teaching or writing for Kaplan, Eric works as a composer and musician in New York City.

Pat Harris, a 1993 graduate of the University of Michigan Law School in Ann Arbor, is currently employed as an assistant public defender in Nashville, Tennessee. When not in court, he travels the country, teaching seminars on law school admissions and interviewing law school admissions officers.

Benjamin Paris is a curriculum director responsible for the LSAT at Kaplan Educational Centers. He received his B.A. from Bowdoin College, completed the general course at the London School of Economics, and received his J.D. from New York University. He has taught thousands of students how to succeed on standardized tests.

Bob Verini is currently Director of Academic Development for the western United States and a national training associate for Kaplan Educational Centers. Since 1980, Bob has taught thousands of students how to ace the LSAT. He also trains new Kaplan instructors nationally, works in course development, and serves as an academic counselor in Kaplan's one-on-one Admissions Consulting program. He holds a B.A. from SUNY/Albany and an M.F.A. from Indiana University. When he takes a break from the LSAT, Bob is a writer, actor, and director, with several films and extensive stage experience to his credit. Bob is also one of the biggest money winners in the history of the game show *Jeopardy!*™ and was the winner of the 1987 Tournament of Champions.

PREFACE

Once upon a time, not so many years ago, a law degree was a sure-fire ticket to prosperity. With a J.D. or L.L.B. in hand, a person entering the job market could be virtually certain of finding a solid, well-paying position in the legal profession. Entry-level jobs were plentiful, and if you were a particularly hot prospect, you might even find yourself wooed by several big-name law firms, weighing their lucrative job offers over a late supper (on the firm's expense account, of course) at the best restaurants in town.

Well, in case you haven't heard, those glory days are over. In today's job market, some law-school graduates are forced to drive cabs and wait tables for a living. Others have to labor away for years in marginal positions that used to be filled by summer interns or first-year grads. Still others have to use their law degrees in nontraditional legal jobs, doing work they never pictured themselves doing when they first decided to go to law school.

Why the big change? Well, there are many reasons, but the main one is probably the age-old law of supply and demand. Nowadays, there are just too many newly minted lawyers every year and not enough starting positions in law. Yes, the top graduates can still command impressive salaries and prestigious positions, and job prospects have improved recently. But the great jobs are still few and far between, and there are more people than ever vying for each one.

As a prospective law school student facing this kind of competitive atmosphere, you really have only two choices. Either you can give up your dream of becoming a lawyer, or else you can make yourself a plan—a plan whose first step is getting into the very best law school you possibly can.

We respectfully suggest that you make the latter choice.

And that's where Kaplan comes in. We at Kaplan have had decades of experience getting people into great law schools, and one thing we've learned is that *you have to have a comprehensive strategy*. You can't approach law school admission in a casual, piecemeal way. If you want to maximize your likelihood of success, you have to take advantage of every opportunity at your disposal to strengthen your application. You can't afford to waste a single opportunity!

That's the philosophy behind this Kaplan guide. First, in our LSAT section, we'll tackle what's probably the single most important element in your application—your LSAT score. We'll give you a quick course in the legendary Kaplan LSAT strategies and techniques, and give you tips on how to relax and stay in top form as the day of the test approaches. Then, we'll give you Kaplan Practice Tests to prepare for the real thing, complete with full strategic explanations for every question.

Getting the highest possible LSAT score is only part of the battle; all other elements of your application have to be maximized as well. In our section on getting into law school, Kaplan's expert in law school admissions will take you step-by-step through the application process, with an eye to making yourself unrejectable. While every element of your application is an opportunity to present yourself in a favorable light, it's also an opportunity to screw up big time. But if you're in control, you won't make foolish mistakes. We'll show you how to avoid the common pitfalls and make your application stand out from the crowd.

This book will help you ace the LSAT and gain admission to the law school of your choice. But did you know that with Kaplan's free *Think About Law* forums, you can speak with our panel of legal experts who will advise you on applying to law school, the law school experience, and career options? They will share their experiences with you and help you make smart education and career choices. *Think About Law* will take place in select U.S. cities throughout the months of March and April. Seats are limited, so call us at 1-800-KAP-TEST or visit our Web site (www.kaptest.com) to register for this free event.

It's harder these days than it used to be to achieve the kind of law career to which you aspire. But keep in mind that tough times should be regarded as a challenge—an opportunity rather than an obstacle. It may be an academic jungle out there, but even in the harshest jungle, the smart and the savvy will thrive.

HOW TO USE THIS BOOK

We're confident that *LSAT 2000–2001* will serve as an indispensable resource for you in your quest to master the LSAT exam. What follows are some suggestions on how to most effectively use the various components of the book in your test preparation:

STEP ONE: Read the "Mastering the LSAT" Section

Kaplan's live LSAT course has set the industry standard for decades. In this section, we've distilled the main techniques and approaches from our course in a clear, easy-to-grasp format. We'll introduce you to the mysteries of the LSAT and show you how to take control of the test-taking experience:

LSAT Test Content
In the chapters dealing with the content of the LSAT, "Logical Reasoning," "Logic Games," "Reading Comprehension," and "The Writing Sample," we'll give you specific methods, strategies, and practice problems for every type of LSAT question you're likely to see.

Taking Control of the Test
The "Taking Control of the Test" chapter in the book offers item-specific techniques, as well as advice on how to pace yourself over the entire section and how to choose which questions to answer and which to guess on. The peculiarities of a standardized test can sometimes be used to your advantage; we can teach you how. Chapters six and seven will also provide you with the proper test attitude for executing all you've learned.

You'll also find the most important points regarding the LSAT in easy-to-read sidebars in the outer margins throughout the book.

STEP TWO: Take Kaplan's Practice Test One

Having trained in the Kaplan methods, you should then use Practice Test One—a full-length, simulated LSAT—as a test run for the real thing.

STEP THREE: Use the Strategic Explanations

These explanations for every test question will enable you to understand your mistakes, so that you don't make them again on the test. Try not to confine yourself to the explanations of the questions you've answered incorrectly. Instead, read all of the explanations—to reinforce good habits and to sharpen your skills so that you can get the right answer even faster and more reliably next time.

STEP FOUR: Review to Shore up Weak Points

Go back to the test content chapters to review the topics in which your performance was weak.

STEP FIVE: Repeat the Process with the Other Practice Tests

There are a total of three full-length practice tests in this book. Once you've gone through the steps outlined above with Practice Test One, repeat the steps with Practice Tests Two and Three. After you've completed all the practice tests and done all you can to master the concepts with which you continue to have difficulty, reread the "Taking Control of the Test" and "Kaplan Advantage™ Stress Management" chapters to make sure you're in top shape for the test.

Follow these five steps, and you can be confident that your application to law school will be as strong as it can be.

Special Bonus: Getting Into Law School Section

Sure, your LSAT performance is a very important criterion in your application, so the bulk of this book is devoted to test prep. But law schools base their admissions decisions on far more than just the LSAT. In fact, a host of other parts of your application can make or break your candidacy. So, to give you the very best odds, we provide expert advice to lead you through the parts of the application process before and beyond the LSAT. We'll give you an overview of the application process, drawing from our years of helping law school candidates, and outline a plan to make your application as strong as it can be. We've also included checklists and schedules to keep you on track.

A SPECIAL NOTE FOR INTERNATIONAL STUDENTS

In recent years, U.S. law schools have experienced an increase in inquiries from non-U.S. citizens, some of whom are already practicing lawyers in their own countries. This surge of interest in the U.S. legal system has been attributed to the spread of the global economy. When business people from outside the United States do business with Americans, they often find themselves doing business under the American legal system. Gaining insight into how the American legal system works is of great interest around the world.

This new international interest in the U.S. legal system is having an effect on law schools. Many schools have even developed special programs to accommodate the needs of this special population of lawyers and students from outside the United States. If you are an international student or lawyer interested in learning more about the American legal system, or if you are considering attending law school in the United States, Kaplan can help you explore your options.

Getting into a U.S. law school can be especially challenging for students from other countries. If you are not from the United States, but are considering attending law school in the United States, here's what you'll need to get started.

- If English is not your first language, start there. You will probably need to take the Test of English as a Foreign Language (TOEFL) or show some other evidence that you are proficient in English. Most law schools require a minimum TOEFL score of 600 (250 on the computer-based TOEFL) or better.
- You may also need to take the Law School Admissions Test (LSAT). All law schools in the United States require the LSAT for their J.D. programs. L.L.M. programs usually do not require the LSAT.
- Since admission to law school is quite competitive, you may want to select three or four programs you would like to attend and complete applications for each program.
- You need to begin the application process at least eighteen months in advance. Be aware that many programs only offer August or September start dates. Find out application deadlines and plan accordingly.
- Finally, you will need to obtain an I-20 Certificate of Eligibility in order to obtain an F-1 Student Visa to study in the United States.

For an overview of the law school admissions process, see the "Getting into Law School" section of this book.

Kaplan International Programs

If you need more help with the complex process of graduate school admissions, assistance preparing for the LSAT or TOEFL, or help building your English language skills in general, you may be interested in Kaplan's programs for international students.

Kaplan International Programs were designed to help students and professionals from outside the United States meet their educational and career goals. At locations throughout the United States, international students take advantage of Kaplan's programs to help them improve their academic and conversational English skills, raise their scores on the TOEFL, LSAT, and other standardized exams, and gain admission to the schools of their choice. Our staff and instructors give international students the individualized instruction they need to succeed. Here is a brief description of some of Kaplan's programs for international students:

General Intensive English

Kaplan's General Intensive English classes are designed to help you improve your skills in all areas of English and to increase your fluency in spoken and written English. Classes are available for beginning to advanced students, and the average class size is 12 students.

English for TOEFL and University Preparation

This course provides you with the skills you need to improve your TOEFL score and succeed in an American university or graduate program. It includes advanced reading, writing, listening, grammar and conversational English, plus university admissions counseling. You will also receive training for the TOEFL using Kaplan's exclusive computer-based practice materials.

LSAT Test Prep Course

The LSAT is a crucial admission criteria for law schools in the United States. A high score can help you stand out from other applicants. This course includes the skills you need to succeed on each section of the LSAT, as well as access to Kaplan's exclusive practice materials.

Other Kaplan Programs

Since 1938, more than 3 million students have come to Kaplan to advance their studies, prepare for entry to American universities, and further their careers. In addition to the above programs, Kaplan offers courses to prepare for the SAT, GMAT, GRE, MCAT, DAT, USMLE, NCLEX, and other standardized exams at locations throughout the United States.

Applying to Kaplan International Programs

To get more information, or to apply for admission to any of Kaplan's programs for international students and professionals, contact us at:

Kaplan International Programs
888 Seventh Avenue, New York, NY 10106 USA
Telephone: (212) 492-5990 Fax: (212) 957-1654
E-mail: world@kaplan.com Web: www.studyusa.kaplan.com

Note: Kaplan is authorized under federal law to enroll nonimmigrant alien students. Kaplan is authorized to issue Form IAP-66 needed for a J-1 (Exchange Visitor) visa. Kaplan is accredited by ACCET (Accrediting Council for Continuing Education and Training). Test names are registered trademarks of their respective owners.

MASTERING THE LSAT

By Eric Goodman

CHAPTER 1

AN INTRODUCTION TO THE LSAT

The LSAT is unlike any other test you've ever taken in your academic career. Most of the tests you've encountered in high school and college have probably been knowledge-based tests, that is, tests requiring you to recall and be conversant with a certain body of facts, formulas, theorems, or other acquired knowledge. The LSAT, on the other hand, is a skills-based test. It doesn't ask you to spit back memorized facts. It doesn't ask you to apply learned formulas to specific problems. In fact, all you'll be asked to do on the LSAT is think—thoroughly, quickly, and strategically. There's literally no content to study!

Sound too good to be true? Well, before you get the idea that you can waltz into the most important test of your life stone cold, let's clarify the very important distinction between study and preparation.

If you were taking the National Medical Boards, you would need to study things like anatomy beforehand, to make sure you were up-to-date on all of the required knowledge in that area. But the LSAT isn't designed to evaluate your grasp of this kind of field-specific knowledge. Instead, it's designed to test only the critical reading and analytical thinking skills that have been deemed necessary (by the governing body of law schools themselves) for success in the first year of law school. These are skills that you already possess to some extent; you've acquired them gradually over the decade-and-a-half (or more) of your education. But what you probably haven't yet acquired is the know-how to use these skills to best advantage in the rarified atmosphere of a standardized skills-based test.

And that's where test preparation—and this section of this book—comes in. In this section, we'll teach you to tailor your existing skills to the very specific and idiosyncratic tasks required by the LSAT. For example, you already know how to read; but we'll show you how to take your critical reading skills and use them most effectively to unlock the dense but highly structured arguments and passages on the LSAT. Similarly, while you've probably developed plenty of sound, logical ways of analyzing problems in everyday life, we'll teach you how to apply those natural deductive and analytical skills to the unusual demands of the Logic Games and Logical Reasoning sections of the LSAT.

So, while you can't technically study for a standardized skills-based test like the LSAT, you can and must prepare for it. And in the section that follows, we'll show you just how to do that.

Before launching into strategies, though, you need to know exactly what you're dealing with in the LSAT.

What Is the LSAT?

Let's start with the basics. The LSAT is, among other things, an endurance test. It consists of 175 minutes of multiple-choice testing, plus a thirty-minute writing sample. Add in the administrative details at both ends of the testing experience, plus a break of ten to fifteen minutes midway through, and you can count on being in the test room for at least four-and-a-half to five hours.

It's a grueling experience, to say the least. And if you can't approach it with confidence and rigor, you'll quickly lose your composure. That's why it's so important that you take control of the test, just as you've been taking control of the rest of your application process.

The LSAT consists of five multiple-choice sections—two Logical Reasoning sections (LR), one Logic Games section (LG), one Reading Comprehension section (RC), and one so-called "Experimental" section, which will almost certainly look exactly like one of the other multiple-choice sections. In addition to these five sections, there will be a Writing Sample section in which you'll have to write a short essay.

TAKE CONTROL

The LSAT should be viewed just like any other part of your application—as an opportunity to show the law schools who you are and what you can do. If you can take control of your LSAT experience, you can take the fullest advantage of that opportunity.

AN ESSENTIAL RESOURCE

If you plan to take the LSAT, you will need to obtain a copy of the *LSAT/LSDAS Registration & Information Book*. This book will provide you with the most up-to-date information on how to register for and take the LSAT and how to subscribe to the Law School Data Assembly Service. Call (215) 968-1001 or visit the LSAC Web site at www.lsac.org to order a copy.

Here's how the sections break down:

Section	Number of Questions	Minutes
Logical Reasoning	24–26	35
Logical Reasoning	24–26	35
Logic Games	23–24	35
Reading Comprehension	26–28	35
"Experimental"	24–28	35
Writing Sample	n/a	30

Some important things to note:

- The five multiple-choice sections can appear in any order, but the Writing Sample invariably comes last.
- The ten- to fifteen-minute break will come between the third and fourth sections of the test.
- The so-called "Experimental" section will look just like any other multiple-choice section, but it won't contribute to your score. (No, the test makers don't throw in the experimental section just to make you crazy; they do it to test out questions for use on future tests.)

We'll talk more about each of these question types in later chapters. But the big thing to take note of right now is this: You'll be answering roughly 125 questions (excluding the Writing Sample) over the course of three intensive hours. That's just a little over a minute per question, not counting the time required to read passages and set up games. Clearly, you're going to have to move fast. But you can't let yourself get careless. Taking control of the LSAT means increasing the speed of your work without sacrificing accuracy!

How Is the LSAT Scored?

You'll receive one and only one score for the LSAT (no separate scores for LR, LG, and RC, in other words). That one score will fall in a range of 120 to 180. Here's how they'll calculate it.

TIME IS OF THE ESSENCE

Many people could probably ace the LSAT if they had unlimited time. But they don't. To succeed on the LSAT, you've got to think smart and fast.

There are roughly 101 scored multiple-choice questions on each exam:

- About fifty from the two Logical Reasoning sections
- About twenty-four from the Logic Games section
- About twenty-seven from the Reading Comprehension section

(Remember, the Writing Sample doesn't receive a numerical score, while the Experimental section, no matter what question type it contains, doesn't count.)

The number of these 101 questions that you answer correctly is your "raw score." Your raw score will then be multiplied by a complicated scoring formula (which is different for each test, to accommodate differences in difficulty level) to yield the "scaled score"—the one that will fall somewhere in that 120–180 range. This scaled score is what is reported to the schools as your LSAT score.

Since the test is graded on a largely preset curve, the scaled score will always correspond to a certain percentile, which will also be given on your score report. A score of 160, for instance, corresponds roughly to the eightieth percentile, meaning that 80 percent of test takers scored at or below your level. The percentile figure is important because it allows law schools to get a sense quickly of where you fall in the pool of applicants.

All questions (except, again, those on the Experimental section) are worth the same amount—one raw point—and there's no penalty for guessing. That means that you should always fill in an answer for every question, whether you get to that question or not! Never let time run out on any section without filling in an answer for every question!

What's a "Good" LSAT Score?

Of course, what you consider a "good" LSAT score depends on your own expectations and goals, but here are a few interesting statistics:

If you got about half of all of the scored questions right (a raw score of roughly fifty), you would earn a scaled score of roughly 147, putting you in about the thirtieth percentile—not a great performance. But on the LSAT, a little improvement goes a long way. In fact, getting only one additional question right every ten minutes would give you a raw score of about sixty-four, pushing you into the sixtieth percentile—a huge improvement. That's why it's important to maximize your performance on every question. Just a few questions one way or the other can make a big difference in your score.

By the same token, however, you don't have to be perfect to do well. On most LSATs, you can get as many as twenty-eight wrong and still remain in the eightieth percentile—or as many as twenty-one wrong and still remain in the ninetieth percentile. Even students who receive perfect scaled scores of 180 usually get a handful of questions wrong.

SOME SAMPLE PERCENTILES

Percentile	Approx. Scaled Score (Range 120–180)	Approx. Raw Score
99th percentile	172	~91 correct out of 101
95th percentile	167	~84 correct out of 101
90th percentile	164	~80 correct out of 101
80th percentile	160	~73 correct out of 101
75th percentile	158	~69 correct out of 101
50th percentile	152	~59 correct out of 101

Note: Exact percentile-to-scaled-score relationships vary from test to test.

Although many factors play a role in admissions decisions, the LSAT score is usually one of the most important. And—generally speaking—being average just won't cut it. While the median LSAT score is somewhere around 152, you need a score of at least 163 to be considered competitive by most law schools. And if you're aiming for the top, you've got to do even better. According to *Careers 2000* (published by Kaplan/*Newsweek*), the median LSAT scores of the best law schools in the country, such as Yale, Stanford, and Columbia, range from the high 160s to the low 170s. That translates to a percentile figure of ninety-five and up.

What Kinds of Questions Are on the LSAT?

Now let's take a quick look at each question type you'll encounter on the test. We'll get into strategies and techniques later. For now, just familiarize yourself with the kinds of questions asked on each section.

Logical Reasoning

What It Is
Each of the two scored Logical Reasoning sections consists of twenty-four to twenty-six questions based on short passages we call "stimuli." Each stimulus takes the form of an argument—i.e., a conclusion based on evidence. You need to understand the stimulus argument to answer the one or two questions based on it. Although you don't need to know the technical terms of formal logic, you do need the critical reasoning skills that enable you to analyze an argument and make judgments accordingly.

Why It's on the Test
The law schools want to see whether you can understand, analyze, evaluate, and manipulate arguments, and draw reliable conclusions—as every law student and attorney must. It's important to note that this question type makes up half of your LSAT score, so you know that the law schools value these skills.

What It's Like
Here are the directions to the section, along with a sample question:

> Directions: This test is composed of questions that ask you to analyze the logic of statements or short paragraphs. You are to choose as the answer to each question the one choice you consider <u>best</u> on the basis of your common-sense evaluation of the statement and its assumptions. Although a question may seem to have more than one acceptable answer, there is only one <u>best</u> answer, and it is the one that does not entail making any illogical, extraneous, or conflicting assumptions about the question.

1. A study of twenty overweight men revealed that each man experienced significant weight loss after adding SlimDown, an artificial food supplement, to his daily diet. For three months, each man consumed one SlimDown portion every morning after exercising, and then followed

his normal diet for the rest of the day. Clearly, anyone who consumes one portion of SlimDown every day for at least three months will lose weight and will look and feel his or her best.

Which one of the following is an assumption on which the argument depends?

(A) The men in the study will gain back the weight they lost if they discontinue the SlimDown program.
(B) No other dietary supplement will have the same effect on overweight men.
(C) The daily exercise regimen was not responsible for the effects noted in the study.
(D) Women will not experience similar weight reductions if they adhere to the SlimDown program for three months.
(E) Overweight men will achieve only partial weight loss if they do not remain on the SlimDown program for a full three months.

Choice (C) is correct. We'll show you how to approach Logical Reasoning questions like this in a later chapter.

Logic Games

What It Is
There are twenty-three to twenty-four questions in the Logic Games (a.k.a. Analytical Reasoning) section, and these are almost always based on four games, with five to seven questions each. They require an ability to reason clearly and deductively from a given set of rules or restrictions, all under strictly timed conditions.

Why It's on the Test
The section exists to test your command of detail, your formal deductive abilities, your understanding of how rules limit and order behavior (which is the very definition of law itself), and your ability to cope with many pieces of data simultaneously in the course of solving problems.

What It's Like
What follows are directions to the Logic Games section as well as a shortened sample game and questions:

LOGIC GAMES AT A GLANCE

- Thirty-five minutes long
- Accounts for just under 25 percent of your score
- Twenty-three to twenty-four questions
- Usually four games (common types: sequencing, grouping, matching)
- Tests how rules create systems of order and limit possible outcomes
- Attention to detail is key, as is the ability to maintain awareness of multiple facts simultaneously
- Basic logic is important: *if* versus *only if*; the logical meaning of *or*; the contrapositive
- Often the most intimidating section initially
- Often shows rapid improvement with practice

Directions: Each group of questions is based on a set of conditions. You may wish to draw a rough sketch to help you answer some of the questions. Choose the _best_ answer for each question and fill in the corresponding space on your answer sheet.

Questions 1–2

Five workers—Mona, Patrick, Renatta, Saffie, and Will—are scheduled to clean apartments on five days of a single week, Monday to Friday. There are three cleaning shifts available each day—a morning shift, an afternoon shift, and an evening shift. No more than one worker cleans on any given shift. Each worker works exactly two cleaning shifts during the week, but no one works more than one cleaning shift in a single day.

Exactly two workers clean on each day of the week.
Mona and Will clean on the same days of the week.
Patrick does not clean on any afternoon or evening shifts during the week.
Will does not clean on any morning or afternoon shifts during the week.
Mona cleans on two consecutive days of the week.
Saffie's second cleaning shift of the week occurs on an earlier day of the week than Mona's first cleaning shift

1. Which one of the following must be true?

(A) Saffie cleans on Tuesday afternoon.
(B) Patrick cleans on Monday morning.
(C) Will cleans on Thursday evening.
(D) Renatta cleans on Friday afternoon.
(E) Mona cleans on Tuesday morning.

2. If Will does not clean on Friday, which one of the following could be false?

(A) Renatta cleans on Friday.
(B) Saffie cleans on Tuesday.
(C) Mona cleans on Wednesday.
(D) Saffie cleans on Monday.
(E) Patrick cleans on Tuesday.

M
M T W Th F
Ⓐ
Ⓔ

W → Night 2 days
w/ M (2 days in a row)

P → Morning, not w/ W
or M

M → 2 days in a row

S → 2 day occasion on
either day in the week than
M + W

R

(Note that there are only two questions accompanying this game; a typical logic game will have five to seven questions.)

For Question 1, the answer is (C); for 2 it's (E). Games are highly amenable to systematic technique and the proper use of scratchwork, which we'll discuss in detail later.

Reading Comprehension

What It Is
The Reading Comprehension section consists of four passages, each about 450 words long, with five to eight questions. These long excerpts of scholarly passages are reminiscent of the kind of prose found in law texts. The topics are chosen from the areas of social sciences, humanities, natural sciences, and law.

Why It's on the Test
The purpose of the section is to see whether you can quickly get the gist of long, difficult prose—just as you'll have to do in law school.

What It's Like
Here are the directions and a sample passage. Note that the passage below is just an excerpt from a full-length passage; standard passages are generally longer.

Directions: Each selection in this test is followed by several questions. After reading the selection, choose the best response to each question and mark it on your answer sheet. Your replies are to be based on what is stated or implied in the selection.

It has been suggested that post–World War II concepts of environmental liability, as they pertain to hazardous waste, grew out of issues regarding municipal refuse collection and disposal and industrial waste disposal in the period 1880–1940. To a great degree, the remedies available to Americans for dealing with the burgeoning hazardous waste problem were characteristic of the judicial, legislative, and regulatory tools used to confront a whole range of problems in the industrial age. At the same time, these remedies were operating in an era in which the problem of hazardous waste had yet to be recognized. It is understandable that an assessment of liability was narrowly drawn and most often restricted to a clearly identified violator in a specific

READING COMPREHENSION AT A GLANCE

- Thirty-five minutes long
- Accounts for just over 25 percent of your score
- Usually consists of twenty-seven questions (common types: main idea, detail, inference, logic, extrapolation)
- Usually consists of four passages (natural sciences, social sciences, humanities, law)
- Tests ability to read dense, scholarly material and ascertain the structure, purpose, and logic—just as you will do in law school
- Key skill is identifying main idea of a passage, "the gist" of the argument. This is not the way you're taught to read in school!
- Does not require outside knowledge
- Is very different from SAT Reading Comp: denser, more difficult prose, more difficult inferences
- Is not a test of memorizing details
- Requires learning a new reading "mindset": reading with different goals and employing different techniques

act of infringement of the property rights of someone else. Legislation, for the most part, focused narrowly on clear threats to the public health and dealt with problems of industrial pollution meekly if at all.

1. According to the passage, judicial assessments of liability in waste disposal disputes prior to World War II were usually based on

    (A) excessively broad definitions of legal responsibility
    (B) the presence of a clear threat to the public health
    (C) precedents derived from well-known cases of large-scale industrial polluters
    (D) restricted interpretations of property rights infringements
    (E) trivial issues such as littering, eyesores, and other public nuisances

The answer: (D). We'll show you how to approach the Reading Comp questions later.

The Experimental Section

The experimental (unscored) section allows Law Services to test questions for use on future tests. This section will probably look just like one of the others—either LR, LG, or RC—so don't try to figure out which section is experimental and then just cruise through that section. That's an extremely risky proposition. Just do as well as you can on every section, and you're covered.

The Writing Sample

What It Is
The Writing Sample comes at the end of your LSAT day. You'll be given a scenario followed by two possible courses of action, and you'll have thirty minutes to make a written case that one is superior.

Why It's on the Test
The writing sample shows the law schools whether you can argue for a position while breaking down the argument of an opponent. This essay is ungraded, but is sent to law schools along with your LSAT score.

DON'T TRY TO GUESS THE EXPERIMENTAL

The LSAT battlefield is littered with the bodies of those who've tried to outsmart the test by guessing (incorrectly) which section is experimental and then using that time to rest. Don't take the chance! Perform your best on every section.

What It's Like
Here's a sample topic for a Writing Sample:

The *Daily Tribune*, a metropolitan newspaper, is considering two candidates for promotion to business editor. Write an argument for one candidate over the other with the following considerations in mind:

- The editor must train new writers and assign stories.
- The editor must be able to edit and rewrite stories under daily deadline pressure.

Laura received a B.A. in English from a large university. She was managing editor of her college newspaper and served as a summer intern at her hometown daily paper. Laura started working at the *Tribune* right out of college and spent three years at the city desk covering the city economy. Eight years ago the paper formed its business section and Laura became part of the new department. After several years covering state business, Laura began writing on the national economy. Three years ago, Laura was named senior business and finance editor on the national business staff; she is also responsible for supervising seven writers.

Palmer attended an elite private college where he earned both a B.S. in business administration and an M.A. in journalism. After receiving his journalism degree, Palmer worked for three years on a monthly business magazine. He won a prestigious national award for a series of articles on the impact of monetary policy on multinational corporations. Palmer came to the *Tribune* three years ago to fill the newly created position of international business writer. He was the only member of the international staff for two years and wrote on almost a daily basis. He now supervises a staff of four writers. Last year, Palmer developed a bi-monthly business supplement for the *Tribune* that has proved highly popular and has helped increase the paper's circulation.

Obviously, there can be no right or wrong "answer" to the Writing Sample topic, but there are good and bad responses. We'll show you one possible response to this topic later, in the Writing Sample chapter.

THE WRITING SAMPLE AT A GLANCE

- Is thirty minutes long
- Is unscored
- Consists of one essay
- Task is to choose between two alternatives and make a sound argument for your choice. The alternatives are intentionally chosen to be equally valid, such that the decision to take one side or the other will not give any advantage
- Tests ability to write a clear, persuasive argument
- Does not require outside knowledge
- Is photocopied and sent to schools along with your score report
- Is read and used to evaluate applications more frequently than is commonly thought
- Helps schools choose between relatively equal candidates, decide on borderline candidates

How Do You Take Control of the LSAT?

Now that you have an idea of what the LSAT is and how it's set up, let's talk a little about how to approach the test in a general way. As we'll see, knowing the specific strategies for each type of question is only part of your task. To really do your best on the LSAT, you have to approach the entire test in the proper spirit. That spirit—and the proactive, take-control kind of thinking it inspires—is something we call the LSAT Mindset.

The LSAT Mindset

The LSAT Mindset is what you want to bring to every question, passage, game, and section you encounter. Being in the LSAT Mindset means reshaping the test-taking experience so that you are in the driver's seat. It means:

- Answering questions *if* you want to (by guessing on the most difficult questions rather than wasting time on them).
- Answering questions *when* you want to (by saving tough but doable games, passages, and questions for later, coming back to them after racking up points on the easy ones).
- Answering questions *how* you want to (by using our shortcuts and strategies to get points quickly and confidently, even if those methods aren't exactly what the test makers had in mind).

The following are some overriding principles of the LSAT Mindset that will be covered in depth in the chapters to come:

- Read actively and critically.
- Translate prose into your own words.
- Prephrase answer choices so you know what to look for.
- Save the toughest questions, passages, and games for last.
- Know the test and each of its components inside and out.
- Allow your confidence to build on itself.
- Take full-length practice tests the week before the test to break down the mystique of the real experience.
- Learn from your mistakes—it's not how much you practice, it's how much you get out of the practice.
- Look at the LSAT as a challenge, the first step in your legal career, rather than as an arbitrary obstacle to it.

THE LSAT MINDSET

Knowing strategies for each question type is only the beginning. You also have to approach the test with the proper attitude—a proactive, take-control kind of thinking we call the LSAT Mindset.

And that's what the LSAT Mindset boils down to: taking control. Being proactive. Being on top of the test experience so that you can get as many points as you can as quickly and as easily as possible.

To take control in this way, though, you have to be in command on all levels of the test. You may be great at individual Logical Reasoning questions, for instance, but that expertise won't do you much good unless you also have a plan for the entire LR section, so that you get a chance to use your expertise on as many LR questions in a section as possible. That's why we've developed a plan for integrating strategies and techniques on all levels of the test—from the microlevel of individual question strategies, to the midlevel of handling the mechanics of a whole section, to the macrolevel of bringing the right kind of thinking to the entire test as a whole. We call this plan "The Kaplan Master Plan for the LSAT."

The Kaplan Master Plan

Test Content

Here we'll talk about managing individual questions, games, and reading passages. For success on the LSAT, you'll need to understand how to work through the specifics of each section. What's the difference between assumption and inference questions? What are the best ways of handling each? What's a matching game and how do I approach it? How should I read a Reading Comp passage and what should I focus on? What essay formats are best for the Writing Sample? We'll provide you with all of the information, strategies, and techniques you'll need to lay the groundwork for your LSAT success.

Test Expertise and Test Mentality

Next, we'll move up the ladder from individual questions, passages, and games to discussing how to manage full sections within the specified time limit. We'll show you how to handle the test mechanics so that you have a framework in which to use the content strategies—and the time to use them. Then we'll show you how to pull it all together, marshalling the strategies and expertise with the right mindset, so that you're in control of the entire test. With good test mentality, you can have everything at your fingertips—from the contrapositive to gridding techniques, from sequencing game strategies to pacing methods. We'll outline all of the subtle attitudinal factors, often overlooked, that are nonetheless integral to tying together all of the disparate elements of your training, so that you can perform your absolute best on the test.

LSAT CHECKLIST

Before the Test

❑ **Get the LSAT/LSDAS Registration and Information Book.**
It's available at most colleges and law schools, and at all Kaplan Centers; you can also order it by phone from LSDAS (Law School Data Assembly Service). Keep in mind that the information in this book is up-to-date at the time of publication, but LSDAS may have instituted changes after this book was published.

❑ **Choose a test date.**
June is best, October second best.

❑ **Complete and send LSAT/LSDAS Registration Form.**
Parts A, B, and D apply to the LSAT.
Make sure you list a first- and second-choice test center.
Don't forget to sign the form and include payment!

❑ **Receive your LSAT admission ticket.**
Check it for accuracy.
Check out your test center.

❑ **Create a test-prep calendar to ensure that you're ready by the day of the test.**

The Day of the Test

❑ **Make sure you have your LSAT admission ticket.**

❑ **Make sure you have one form of acceptable ID.**

❑ **Make sure you have the "LSAT Survival Kit" described in chapter six of this book.**

CHAPTER 2

LOGICAL REASONING

The fact that Logical Reasoning comprises half of your LSAT score is actually good news, because you already have most of the Logical Reasoning skills you need for the test. In fact, we all do. But as we pointed out earlier, the LSAT tests your ability to use those skills thoroughly, quickly, and strategically in the context of a strictly timed, multiple-choice test.

On the LSAT, in law school, and in your law career, you'll need the ability to see and understand complex reasoning. It's not enough to sense whether an argument is strong or weak; you'll need to analyze precisely why it is so. This involves an even more fundamental skill, one that's called on by nearly every Logical Reasoning question—the ability to isolate and identify the various components of any given argument. And that brings us to the basic principles of Logical Reasoning.

The Seven Basic Principles of Logical Reasoning

Here are the basic things you must do to succeed on the LR sections.

Understand the Structure of Arguments

Success in Logical Reasoning depends on knowing the structure of arguments so that you can break an argument down into its core components.

First of all, let's clarify what's meant by the word *argument*. We don't mean a conversation in which two or more people are shouting at one another. No, the word *argument* in Logical Reasoning means any piece of text where an author puts forth a set of ideas and a point of view, and attempts to support it.

YOU HAVE WHAT IT TAKES

There's nothing bizarre or esoteric about the skills you need for Logical Reasoning. You just have to learn how to adapt those skills to the peculiar requirements of a timed, standardized test.

EVERYTHING'S AN ARGUMENT

Virtually every LR stimulus is an argument, consisting of two major parts—evidence and conclusion.

Every LSAT Logical Reasoning stimulus—that is, every argument—is made up of two basic parts:

- The conclusion (the point that the author is trying to make)
- The evidence (the support that the author offers for the conclusion)

Success on this section hinges on your ability to identify these parts of the argument. There is no general rule about where conclusion and evidence appear in the argument—the conclusion could be the first sentence, followed by the evidence, or else it could be the last sentence, with the evidence preceding it, or any sentence in between. Consider the following short stimulus.

> The Brookdale Public Library will require extensive physical rehabilitation to meet the new building codes passed by the town council. For one thing, the electrical system is inadequate, causing the lights to flicker sporadically. Furthermore, there are too few emergency exits, and even those are poorly marked and sometimes locked.

Let's suppose that the author of the argument above were allowed only one sentence to convey her meaning. Do you think that she would waste her lone opportunity on the statement: "The electrical system at the Brookdale Public Library is inadequate, causing the lights to flicker sporadically"? Would she walk away satisfied that she got her main point across? Probably not. Given a single opportunity, she would have to state the first sentence: "The Brookdale Public Library will require extensive physical rehabilitation. . . ." This is her conclusion. If you pressed her for her *reasons* for making this statement, she would then cite the electrical and structural problems with the building. This is the evidence for her conclusion.

But does that mean that an evidence-statement such as, "The electrical system at the Brookdale Public Library is inadequate" can't be a conclusion? No; we're saying that it's not the conclusion for this particular argument. Every idea, every new statement, must be evaluated in the context of the stimulus it appears in. Let's, for the sake of argument (no pun intended), see what a stimulus would look like in which the statement above serves as the conclusion:

The electrical wiring at the Brookdale Public Library was installed over forty years ago, and appears to be corroded in some places *(evidence)*. An electrician, upon inspection of the system, found a few frayed wires as well as some blown fuses *(evidence)*. Clearly, the electrical system at the Brookdale Public Library is inadequate *(conclusion)*.

To succeed in Logical Reasoning, you have to be able to determine the precise function of every sentence in the stimulus. Use structural signals, or keywords, when attempting to isolate evidence and conclusion. Words in the stimulus such as *because, for,* and *since* usually indicate evidence is about to follow, while words such as *therefore, hence, thus,* and *consequently* usually signal a conclusion.

The explanations of the Practice Test in the back of this book discuss the structure of all fifty LR arguments on the test, so read these carefully to shore up your understanding of this crucial aspect of Logical Reasoning.

Preview the Question Stem

Looking over the question stem before reading the stimulus tells you in advance what to focus on in your initial reading of the stimulus. In effect, it gives you a jump on the question. For example, let's say the question attached to the original library argument above asked the following:

The author supports her point about the need for rehabilitation at the Brookdale Library by citing which of the following?

If you were to preview this question stem before reading the stimulus, you would know what to look for in advance—namely, evidence, the "support" provided for the conclusion. Similarly, if the question asked you to find an assumption that the author is relying on, this would tell you in advance that there was a crucial piece of the argument missing, and you could begin to think about it right off the bat.

Previewing the stem allows you to set the tone of your attack on each particular question, and thus will help you save time in the long run. As you'll soon see, this technique will come in especially handy when we discuss approaches to the various question types.

STRUCTURAL SIGNALS

Certain clue words and phrases can help you isolate the conclusion and the evidence in a stimulus.

Clues that signal evidence include *because, since, for, as a result of,* and *due to.*

Clues that signal the conclusion include *consequently, hence, therefore, thus, clearly, so,* and *accordingly.*

KNOW WHAT YOU'RE LOOKING FOR

Previewing the question stem before reading the stimulus makes you a better, more directed reader. You'll know what you're looking for in advance.

IN YOUR OWN WORDS

It's much easier to understand and remember an argument if you restate it simply, in your own words.

Paraphrase the Author's Point

After you read the stimulus, you'll want to paraphrase the author's main argument, i.e., restate the author's ideas in your own words. Frequently, the authors in Logical Reasoning (and in Reading Comprehension, as we'll see) say pretty simple things in complex ways. But if you mentally translate the verbiage into a simpler form, you'll find the whole thing more manageable.

In the library argument, for instance, you probably don't want to deal with the full complexity of the author's stated conclusion:

> The Brookdale Public Library will require extensive physical rehabilitation to meet the new building codes just passed by the town council.

Instead, you probably want to carry a much simpler form of the point in your mind, something like:

> The library will need fixing up to meet new codes.

Often, by the time you begin reading through answer choices, you run the risk of losing sight of the gist of the stimulus. After all, you can concentrate on only a certain amount of information at one time. Restating the argument in your own words will not only help you get the author's point in the first place, but it'll also help you hold on to it until you've found the correct answer.

Judge the Argument's Persuasiveness

You must read actively, not passively, on the LSAT. An active reader is always thinking critically, forming reactions as he goes along. He constantly questions whether the author's argument seems valid or dubious. On a section where many of the questions deal with finding flaws in the author's reasoning, it's imperative to read with a very critical eye.

For instance, how persuasive is the argument in the library stimulus? Well, it's pretty strong, since the evidence certainly seems to indicate that certain aspects of the library's structure need repair. But without more evidence about what the new building codes are like, we can't say for sure that the conclusion of this argument is valid. So this is a strong argument, but not an airtight one.

Remember, part of what you're called on to do in this section is to evaluate arguments, so don't allow yourself to fall into the bad habits of the passive reader—reading solely for the purpose of getting through the stimulus. Those who read this way are clueless when it comes to answering the questions, and invariably find themselves having to read the stimuli twice or even three times. Then they wonder why they run out time on the section. Read the stimuli right the first time—with a critical eye and an active mind.

Make Sure You Answer the Question Being Asked

It's disheartening when you fully understand the author's argument, and then blow the point by supplying an answer to a question that wasn't asked. For example, when you're asked for an inference supported by the argument, it does you no good to jump on the choice that paraphrases the author's conclusion. Likewise, if you're asked for an assumption, don't be fooled into selecting a choice that looks vaguely like a piece of the author's evidence.

When asked why they chose a particular wrong choice, students sometimes respond by saying such things as, "Well, it's true, isn't it?" and "Look, it says so right there," pointing to the stimulus. Well, that's simply not good enough. The question stem doesn't ask, "Which one of the following looks vaguely familiar to you?" It asks for something very specific. It's your job to follow the test makers' line of reasoning to the credited response.

Also, be on the lookout for "reversers"—words such as *not* and *except*. These little words are easy to miss, but they change entirely what kind of statement you're looking for among the choices.

Try to Prephrase an Answer

This principle, which is really an extension of the last one, is crucial. You must try to approach the answer choices with at least a faint idea of what the answer should look like. This is not to say that you should ponder the question for minutes until you're able to write out your own answer—it's still a multiple-choice test, so the right answer is there on the page. Just try to get in the habit of instinctively framing an answer to each question in your own mind.

If you can come up with a hint of a possible answer, scan the choices. Sure, the correct answer will be worded correctly, will be grammatically correct, and will be more fleshed out than your little seed of an idea. But if it matches your thought, you'll know it in a second. And you'll find that there's no more satisfying feeling in Logical Reasoning than prephrasing correctly, allowing you to choose the correct answer quickly and confidently.

DON'T ANSWER A DIFFERENT QUESTION

You read the argument. You see a major weakness in it. You find an answer choice that points out this weakness. You choose that answer. And you miss the point. Why? Because the question stem was asking for a statement that strengthened the argument, not one that weakened it. Don't let this happen to you. Always double-check the question stem.

For instance, let's say a question for the library argument went like this:

> The author's argument depends on which of the following assumptions about the new building codes?

Having thought about the stimulus argument, an answer to this question may have sprung immediately to mind—namely, the assumption that the new codes apply to existing buildings as well as to new buildings under construction. After all, the library will have to be rehabilitated to meet the new codes, according to the author. Clearly, the assumption is that the codes apply to existing buildings. And that's the kind of statement you would look for among the choices.

By the way, don't be discouraged if not all questions are good candidates for prephrasing answers. Some questions just won't have an answer that jumps out at you. But if used correctly, prephrasing can work on many, many questions. It will really boost your confidence and increase your speed on the section when you can come up with a glimmer of what the right answer should look like, and then have it jump right off the page at you.

Keep the Scope of the Argument in Mind

One of the most important Logical Reasoning skills, particularly when you're at the point of actually selecting one of the five choices, is the ability to focus in on the scope of the argument. The majority of wrong choices on this section are wrong because they are "outside the scope." In everyday language, that simply means that these choices contain elements that don't match the author's ideas, or that simply go beyond the context of the stimulus.

Some common examples of scope problems are choices that are too narrow, or too broad, or literally have nothing to do with the author's points. Also, watch for and eliminate choices that are too extreme to match the argument's scope; they're usually signaled by words such as *all*, *always*, *never*, *none*, and so on. Choices that are more qualified are often correct for arguments that are moderate in tone, and contain words such as *usually*, *sometimes*, *probably*, etcetera.

To illustrate the scope principle, let's look again at the question mentioned above:

> The author's argument depends on which of the following assumptions about the new building codes?

SCOPE IT OUT

A remarkable number of wrong answers in LR have scope problems. Always be on the lookout for choices that are too extreme, that contain value judgments that are not relevant to the argument, or that don't match the stimulus in tone or subject matter.

Let's say one of the choices reads as follows:

(A) The new building codes are far too stringent.

Knowing the scope of the argument would help you to eliminate this choice very quickly. You know that this argument is just a claim about what the new codes will require—that the library be rehabilitated. It's not an argument about whether the requirements of the new codes are good, or justifiable, or ridiculously strict. That kind of value judgment is outside the scope of this argument.

Recognizing scope problems is a great way of eliminating dozens of wrong answers quickly. Make sure to pay special attention to the scope issues discussed in the Practice Test explanations.

The Nine Crucial LR Question Types

Now that you're familiar with the basic principles of Logical Reasoning, let's look at the most common types of questions you'll be asked. As we said earlier, certain question types crop up again and again on the LSAT, and it pays to be familiar with them. Of the types discussed below, the first three predominate on most LR sections, but try to become familiar with the others as well.

Assumption Questions

An assumption bridges the gap between an argument's evidence and conclusion. It's a piece of support that isn't explicitly stated, but that is required for the conclusion to remain valid. When a question asks you to find an author's assumption, it's asking you to find the statement without which the argument falls apart.

In order to test whether a statement is necessarily assumed by an author, therefore, we can employ the **Denial Test**. Here's how it works: simply deny or negate the statement and see if the argument falls apart. If it does, that choice is the correct assumption. If, on the other hand, the argument is unaffected, the choice is wrong. Consider, as an example, this simple stimulus:

Allyson plays volleyball for Central High School. Therefore, Allyson must be more than 6 feet tall.

THE MISSING LINK

Some arguments lack an important bridge between their evidence and their conclusion. That bridge is the necessary assumption—a key part of many arguments that remains unspoken.

ASSUMPTION QUESTIONS AT A GLANCE

- They are one of the most popular LR question types.
- They are unstated in the stimulus.
- They bridge the gap between evidence and conclusion.
- They must be true in order for the conclusion to remain valid.
- They can be checked by applying the Denial Test.

You should recognize the second sentence as the conclusion, and the first sentence as the evidence for it. But is the argument complete? Obviously not. The piece that's missing—the unstated link between the evidence and conclusion—is the assumption, and you could probably prephrase this one pretty easily:

All volleyball players for Central High School are more than 6 feet tall.

To test whether this really is an assumption necessary to the argument, let's apply the Denial Test, by negating it. What if it's *not true* that all volleyball players for Central High School are more than 6 feet tall? Can we still logically conclude that Allyson *must be* taller than 6 feet? No, we can't. Sure, it's possible that she is, but just as possible that she's not. By denying the statement, then, the argument falls to pieces; it's simply no longer valid. And that's our conclusive proof that the statement above is a necessary assumption of this argument.

As we've just seen, you can often prephrase the answer to an Assumption question. By previewing the question stem, you'll know what to look for. And stimuli for Assumption questions just "feel" like they're missing something. Often, the answer will jump right out at you, as in this case. In more difficult Assumption questions, the answers may not be as obvious. But in either case, you can use the Denial Test to check quickly whichever choice seems correct.

Sample Stems
Here are some of the ways in which Assumption questions are worded:

- Which one of the following is assumed by the author?
- Upon which one of the following assumptions does the author rely?
- The argument depends on the assumption that . . .
- Which one of the following, if added to the passage, will make the conclusion logical?
- The validity of the argument depends on which one of the following?
- The argument presupposes which one of the following?

Strengthen and Weaken Questions

Determining an argument's necessary assumption, as we've just seen, is required to answer assumption questions. But it also is required for another common question type—Strengthen-the-Argument and Weaken-the-Argument questions.

One way to weaken an argument is to break down a central piece of evidence. Another way is to attack the validity of any assumptions the author may be making. The answer to many Weaken-the-Argument questions is the one that reveals an author's assumption to be unreasonable; conversely, the answer to many Strengthen-the-Argument questions provides additional support by affirming the truth of an assumption or by presenting more persuasive evidence.

Let's take the same stimulus we used before, but look at it in the context of these other question types:

> Allyson plays volleyball for Central High School. Therefore, Allyson must be more than 6 feet tall.

Remember the assumption holding this argument together? It was that all volleyball players for Central High School are more than 6 feet tall. That's the assumption that makes or breaks the argument. So, if the question asked you to weaken the argument, you'd want to attack that assumption:

> Which one of the following, if true, would most weaken the argument?

> *Answer:* Not all volleyball players at Central High School are more than 6 feet tall.

We've called into doubt the author's basic assumption, thus damaging the argument.

But what about strengthening the argument? Again, the key is the necessary assumption:

> Which one of the following, if true, would most strengthen the argument?

> *Answer:* All volleyball players at Central High School are more than 6 feet tall.

Here, by making explicit the author's central assumption, we've in effect bolstered the argument.

STRENGTHEN/ WEAKEN QUESTIONS AT A GLANCE

- Weaken questions are very popular; strengthen questions are less so.
- They are related to assumption; strengtheners often shore up the central assumption, while weakeners often show the central assumption to be unreasonable.
- You must evaluate each choice as to the effect it would have on the argument if true.
- Correct choices don't prove or disprove argument, but simply tip the scale the most in the desired direction.

THE OLD BAIT AND SWITCH

A common LR trap is to have a statement that nicely weakens the argument hiding among the choices for a strengthen question (or the reverse—a great strengthener statement in the choices for a weaken question). Don't fall for this classic trap!

Extra Tips

Weaken questions tend to be more common on the LSAT than Strengthen questions. But here are a few concepts that apply to both question types:

- Weakening an argument is not the same thing as disproving it, while strengthening is not the same as proving the conclusion to be true. A strengthener tips the scale toward believing in the validity of the conclusion, while a weakener tips the scale in the other direction, toward doubting the conclusion.
- The wording of these question types always takes the form "Which one of the following, if true, would most [weaken or strengthen] the argument?" The *if true* part means that you have to accept the truth of the choice right off the bat, no matter how unlikely it may sound to you.
- Don't be careless. Wrong answer choices in these questions often have exactly the opposite of the desired effect. That is, if you're asked to strengthen a stimulus argument, it's quite likely that one or more of the wrong choices will contain information that actually *weakens* the argument. By the same token, weaken questions may contain a choice that *strengthens* the argument. So once again, pay close attention to what the question stem asks.

Sample Stems

The stems associated with these two question types are usually self-explanatory. Here's a list of what you can expect to see on the test:

Weaken:
- Which one of the following, if true, would most weaken the argument above?
- Which one of the following, if true, would most seriously damage the argument above?
- Which one of the following, if true, casts the most doubt on the argument above?
- Which one of the following, if true, is the most serious criticism of the argument above?

Strengthen:
- Which one of the following, if true, would most strengthen the argument?
- Which one of the following, if true, would provide the most support for the conclusion in the argument above?
- The argument above would be more persuasive if which one of the following were found to be true?

Inference Questions

Another of the most common question types you'll encounter on the LR section is the Inference question. The process of inferring is a matter of considering one or more statements as evidence, and then drawing a conclusion from them.

Sometimes the inference is very close to the author's overall main point. Other times, it deals with a less central point. A valid inference is something that must be true if the statements in the passage are true—an extension of the argument rather than a necessary part of it.

For instance, let's take a somewhat expanded version of the volleyball team argument:

> Allyson plays volleyball for Central High School, despite the team's rule against participation by nonstudents. Therefore, Allyson must be over 6 feet tall.

> *Inference:* Allyson is not a student at Central High School.

Clearly, if Allyson plays volleyball *despite* the team's rule against participation by nonstudents, she must not be a student. Otherwise, she wouldn't be playing *despite* the rule; she'd be playing in accordance with the rule. But note that this inference is not an essential assumption of the argument, since the conclusion about Allyson's height doesn't depend on it.

So be careful; unlike an assumption, an inference need not have anything to do with the author's conclusion—it may simply be a piece of information derived from one or more pieces of evidence. However, the Denial Test works for inferences as well as for assumptions: A valid inference always makes more sense than its opposite. If you deny or negate an answer choice, and it has little or no effect on the argument, chances are that choice is not inferable from the passage.

Sample Stems

Inference questions probably have the most varied wording of all the Logical Reasoning question stems. Some question stems denote inference fairly obviously. Others are more subtle, and still others may even look like other question types entirely. Here's a quick rundown of the various forms that Inference questions are likely to take on your test:

- Which one of the following is inferable from the argument above?
- Which one of the following is implied by the argument above?

INFERENCE QUESTIONS AT A GLANCE

- They are one of the most popular LR question types.
- The answer must be true if statements in the stimulus are true.
- They often stick close to the author's main point.
- The question stems vary considerably in appearance.
- They can be checked by applying the Denial Test.

STAY IN LINE!

A good inference:

- Stays in line with the gist of the passage
- Stays in line with the author's tone
- Stays in line with the author's point of view
- Stays within the scope of the argument or the main idea
- Is neither denied by, nor irrelevant to, the argument or discussion
- Always makes more sense than its opposite

FLAW QUESTIONS AT A GLANCE

- They ask: "What's wrong with this argument?"
- Some correspond to well-defined categories.
- Some are specific to individual arguments.
- Understanding structure of arguments is the key.

- The author suggests that . . .
- If all the statements above are true, which one of the following must also be true on the basis of them?
- The author of the passage would most likely agree with which one of the following?
- The passage provides the most support for which one of the following?
- Which one of the following is probably the conclusion toward which the author is moving?

Flaw Questions

This question type—known also by the moniker of Critique the Logic—asks you to recognize what's wrong with an argument. There are two basic types.

In the *general type* of Flaw question, the correct choice will critique the reasoning by pointing out that it contains a classic fallacy (e.g., "The argument attacks the source of an opinion, rather than the opinion itself"). In this case, the flaw falls into a general, well-defined category.

In the *specific type* of Flaw question, the correct choice won't refer to a classic fallacy, but rather will attack a specific piece of the argument's reasoning. An example of this would be: "It cannot be concluded that the number of male turtles has increased simply because the percentage of turtles that are male has increased."

Notice that the subject of the above statement isn't turtles; it's the author's faulty reasoning *about turtles.* Similar to many other question types, the required skill is the ability to identify the structure of the author's argument—specifically, where the argument goes wrong.

Method of Argument Questions

Method of Argument questions bear a similarity to Flaw questions. Once again, you'll be asked to demonstrate an understanding of how an author's argument is put together. However, unlike Flaw questions, Method of Argument questions don't always involve faulty logic. You're simply asked to pick the choice that describes how the author goes about presenting his or her case. The key skill—once again—involves being able to analyze the structure of an argument. If you can't identify the evidence and conclusion, you'll have difficulty describing how an argument works.

Also like Flaw questions, there are two distinct types of Method of Argument questions—one *general*, one *specific*. The first deals with classic arguments. These are the classic argumentative structures, such as, "arguing from a small sample to a larger group," or "inferring a causal relationship from a correlation." The other type of Method of Argument question gives you a description of the argument in much more specific terms. An example of this might read, "The author presents the case of his mother in order to show that not all astronauts are men."

Focus on the following: "What is the evidence? What is the conclusion? How does the author link the evidence and conclusion together?" These are the questions you have to ask yourself in order to determine the author's method of argument.

Parallel Reasoning Questions

Parallel Reasoning questions require you to identify the answer choice that contains the argument most similar, or parallel, to that in the stimulus in terms of the reasoning employed. To do this kind of question, you need to grasp the distinction between an argument's form and its content. "A causal relationship concluded from a correlation" is a form—a type—of reasoning. Any argument with this form can contain virtually any content. Your task is to abstract the stimulus argument's form, with as little content as possible, and then locate the answer choice that has the form most similar to that of the stimulus. Don't let yourself be drawn to a choice based on its subject matter. A stimulus about music may have an answer choice that also involves music, but that doesn't mean that the *reasoning* in the two arguments is similar.

A good approach to these questions is to see first if the argument can be symbolized algebraically, using X's and Y's. Take the following example:

> All cows eat grass. This animal eats grass. Therefore, it must be a cow.

This (flawed) argument can be symbolized in the following way:

> All X do Y. This does Y. Therefore, this must be an X.

If the stimulus can be symbolized this way, your job will be to search for the choice that can be symbolized in the same way. Your answer might look something like this:

Every politician *(all X)* tells lies *(does Y)*. Stegner is lying *(this does Y)*. So he must be a politician *(therefore, this must be an X)*.

Notice how the exact wording doesn't have to match ("all X" means "every X"), and notice that the subject matter doesn't have to match in the least. What's important is the parallel structure.

Sometimes, though, an argument's reasoning isn't amenable to symbolization. In such a case, see if you can put a label on the type of argument being used, such as "Arguing from a Part to a Whole," or "Circular Reasoning" (evidence and conclusion are identical). Naming the argument will often help eliminate two or three choices that don't even come close to this general form.

But whatever way you choose, as long as you can summarize the argument's form without including content, you're well on your way to finding the parallel argument among the choices.

Extra Tips

Here are a few more tips on parallel reasoning:

- *All* elements of the original argument must be present in its parallel. For example, if the original argument made a generalization to a specific case, a second argument, no matter how similar in structure otherwise, cannot be parallel unless it makes a comparable generalization.
- Stay away from answer choices written about the same subject matter as the original. This is an old trick of the test makers, intended to catch those who mistakenly try to mimic the content rather than the structure of the stimulus.
- Statements that are logically parallel don't have to have all logical elements in the same sequence. Provided all elements of the first argument exist in the second, even in a different order, the two arguments are parallel.

Paradox Questions

A paradox exists when an argument contains two or more seemingly inconsistent statements. You'll know you're dealing with a paradoxical situation if the argument ends with what seems to be a bizarre contradiction. Another sure sign of a paradox is when the argument builds to a certain point, and then the exact opposite of what you would expect to happen happens.

PARALLEL REASONING QUESTIONS AT A GLANCE

- They must mimic structure or form, not content, of stimulus.
- They are sometimes amenable to algebraic symbolization.
- The key is to summarize argument's overall form and match it to that of the correct choice.

In a typical Paradox question, you'll be asked either to find the choice that "explains the paradoxical result" or "resolves the apparent discrepancy." Basically, this will be the choice that reconciles the seemingly inconsistent statements that make up the argument while allowing them all to still be true.

Take the following question:

> Fifty-seven percent of the registered voters in this district claimed to support the Democratic candidate, and yet the Republican candidate won the election with 55 percent of the vote.

> Which of the following would resolve the apparent discrepancy above?

The stimulus seems paradoxical since the Republican won the election, even though more registered voters preferred the Democrat. But do all registered voters vote? No. So a correct answer for this question might read something like this:

> Because of an intensive get-out-the-vote effort in traditionally Republican neighborhoods, a disproportionate number of registered Republicans actually voted in the election.

This statement reconciles the seemingly contradictory elements of the argument by showing that the group of registered voters is not identical to the group of people who actually voted in the election.

Extra Tips
Here are a few tips for handling this question type:

- Before attempting to resolve a paradox, make sure you have a good grasp of what the paradox is. If it doesn't hit you right off the bat, look hard for an unexpected result, or what seems to be a blatant contradiction between the author's evidence and conclusion.
- Resolving paradoxes is often a matter of recognizing that two things that are being compared aren't really the same thing. Read critically to note these subtle distinctions.
- In Paradox questions, avoid choices that merely amplify points already raised in the argument.

THE OLD SIMILAR-CONTENT TRAP

On some parallel-reasoning questions, one of the wrong choices will be an unparallel argument that nonetheless has similar content to the original argument. Don't fall for the trap. The question is interested in structure, not content.

PARADOX QUESTIONS AT A GLANCE

- The correct choice will resolve apparent discrepancy or contradiction.
- The correct choice should have an intuitive "click."
- The correct choice will often involve realizing that two groups presented as identical are actually not.

- They're a relatively new question type.
- They are the closest question type to the actual workings of the law.
- The correct choices usually express author's key concepts and terms.

Principle Questions

Principle questions involve fitting a specific situation into a global generality (or, occasionally, vice versa). Usually, you'll be given an argument, and then asked to find the principle that seems to justify the author's reasoning. For example, suppose that an author's evidence leads to this conclusion in the final sentence of the stimulus:

> Therefore, Marvin should provide a home for his ailing grandmother until she gets back on her feet.

The question stem might read: "The author's position most closely conforms to which one of the following principles?" In other words, what principle best accounts for or justifies the author's position? The answer could sound like this:

> If a close relative is in need, one should always do his or her best to help that person, regardless of personal inconvenience.

On the other hand, the question stem might read: "Which one of the following principles would justify Marvin's refusal to follow the author's recommendation?" In this case, the answer may sound something like this:

> No person should be obligated to provide support for another person, even if that other person is a close relative.

Notice the general nature of both principles. While they don't specifically mention Marvin or his grandmother, or the exact conditions of the stimulus *per se*, the general situation (helping a relative in need) is addressed in both.

The correct answer to Principle questions is usually the one that expresses the key concepts and contains the key terms that the other choices leave out. Be extremely wary of choices that are outside the scope of the argument. Most of the wrong choices contain principles that sound very formal and look good on the page by themselves, but that don't address the author's main concern.

Formal Logic Questions

The manner in which formal logic is tested on the LSAT has evolved over the last few years. Gone (at least for now) are the days when the test makers would line up formal if/then and all/some/none statements and ask

KAPLAN

you what can, must, or cannot be true on the basis of them. Nowadays, the test makers bury formal statements in the context of a casual argument, asking for an inference that can be drawn from the passage. You may not easily recognize formal logic when you see it, and questions of this nature are fewer in number than in the past. But formal logic skills are tested in Logic Games as well, so it's best to get a solid handle on it now.

Let's look at an example:

> Ian will go to the movies only when his wife is out of town. He'll go to a matinee alone, but will see a movie at night only if accompanied by Ezra and Mabel.

This simple stimulus looks like any other casual argument in Logical Reasoning, but in fact, it's made up of a couple of formal logic statements, each fraught with its own implications. Formal logic statements resemble rules in Logic Games. Be on the lookout for Logical Reasoning stimuli that contain sentences that can be boiled down to such hard and fast rules. When you come across examples of these, you can apply the following principles of formal logic to help you arrive at the correct answer.

The Contrapositive

For any if/then statement—or a statement that can be translated into if/then form—the contrapositive of the statement will result in an equally valid second statement. This is a nice shortcut to employ when faced with formal logic on the test.

The contrapositive can be formed by reversing and negating the terms of any if/then statement. The general model goes like this:

> If X, then Y.

The contrapositive of this statement is:

> If *not* Y, then *not* X.

The contrapositive of a valid if/then statement will always be valid itself.

Let's illustrate this with a simple example. Consider the following strict formal statement:

> If the building has vacancies, then the sales office will be open.

To form the contrapositive, reverse and negate the terms, like so:

> If the sales office is NOT open, then the building does NOT have vacancies.

This would be a valid inference based on the original statement. The contrapositive, while quite a fancy term, is nothing more than everyday common sense.

Now let's apply the contrapositive to the first sentence of the earlier example. Here's the original:

> Ian will go to the movies only when his wife is out of town.

THE CONTRAPOSITIVE

The contrapositive is probably the most important rule of logic you need for LSAT success. It's essential that you learn what it is and how to use it.

This is a little trickier, because it's not stated in the form of a true if/then statement. But we can translate this statement into an if/then statement without changing its original meaning:

> *If* Ian goes to the movies, *then* his wife must be out of town.

If the statement above is true, which one of the following must be true on the basis of it? Why, the contrapositive of it, of course:

> If Ian's wife is *not* out of town, then Ian does *not* go to the movies.

Simple enough, right? One caveat: wrong answers often result from either forgetting to switch around the terms before negating them, or negating only one of the terms. For example, from the above example, if Ian doesn't go to the movies, we can't infer anything about whether his wife is in or out of town. Similarly, if Ian's wife *is* out of town, we can't tell for sure whether Ian goes to the movies or not.

If one part of the formal logic statement contains a compound phrase, then both parts of the phrase must be taken into account. For example, let's take the other part of the stimulus above:

> Ian will see a movie at night only if accompanied by Ezra *and* Mabel.

> *Translation:* If Ian sees a movie at night, then he's accompanied by Ezra *and* Mabel.

> *Contrapositive:* If Ian is *not* with Ezra *and* Mabel, then he does *not* see a movie at night.

Correct Interpretation: If either Ezra or Mabel is missing, then Ian's out of luck. If he's with only one of them, or neither of them, then he can't go to a night movie.

Finally, if one part of a formal statement is already in the negative, the same rules that apply to math apply to forming the contrapositive: negating a negative yields a positive.

If the sun is shining, then Samantha does not wear green.

Contrapositive: If Samantha *is* wearing green (if she's *not not* wearing green), then the sun is *not* shining.

Necessary versus Sufficient Conditions
For success in formal logic, it's crucial that you distinguish clearly between necessary and sufficient conditions. Here are examples of each:

Sufficient: If I yell loudly at my cat Adrian, he will run away.
Necessary: The TV will work only if it is plugged in.

My yelling loudly is a sufficient condition for Adrian to run away. It's all I need to do to get the cat to run; it's sufficient. But it's not necessary. My cat will run if I throw water at him, even if I don't yell loudly.

The TV's being plugged in, on the other hand, is a necessary condition of its working. My TV won't work without it, so it's necessary. But it's not sufficient. Other conditions must apply for the TV to work (for example, the electricity to the house must be on).

You must be clear on what kinds of deductions you can and can't make from statements of necessary and sufficient conditions. For instance, sufficient conditions are usually signaled by an if/then statement, which means that the contrapositive can be used.

If I yell loudly at my cat Adrian, he will run away.

Given that the above statement is true, which one of the following statements must also be true?

Not Valid: If I don't yell loudly at my cat Adrian, he will not run away.

Not Valid: If my cat Adrian has run away, then I yelled loudly at him.
Valid: If my cat Adrian has not run away, then I did not yell loudly at him.

The third statement is the contrapositive, and is the only one of the three statements that's inferable from the original. My yelling loudly is sufficient to make Adrian run away, but it's not necessary; that is, it'll do the trick, but it's not the *only* possible thing that will make him head for the hills. If I squirt him with a water gun, he'll also run away. This is why the first two statements are not inferable from the original statement.

Necessary conditions, on the other hand, are usually signaled by the word *only:*

The TV will work only if it is plugged in.

Given that the above statement is true, which one of the following statements must also be true?

Not Valid: If my TV is plugged in, it will work.
Not Valid: If my TV is not working, then it must not be plugged in.
Valid: If my TV is working, then it must be plugged in.
Valid: If my TV is not plugged in, then it won't work.

Plugging the TV in is necessary for the TV to work. To work, the TV needs to be plugged in. However, plugging in the TV is not sufficient to make the TV work. True, the TV won't work without plugging it in, but plugging it in is not a *guarantee* that the TV will work. What if other conditions interfere? Maybe the picture tube is broken. Maybe my electricity is out due to a hurricane. So the first two statements above are not inferable from the original statement, while the last two are.

The Kaplan Four-Step Method for Logical Reasoning

Now that you've learned the basic LR principles and have been exposed to the full range of question types, it's time to learn how to orchestrate all of that knowledge into a systematic approach to Logical Reasoning. We've developed a four-step approach that you can use to attack each and every question on the section.

NECESSITY VERSUS SUFFICIENCY

It's necessary that you learn the difference between necessary and sufficient requirements, but knowing that is not sufficient in and of itself to get a great score.

Here are the four steps:

1. Preview the question stem.
2. Read the stimulus.
3. Try to prephrase an answer.
4. Choose an answer.

1. Preview the Question Stem

As we mentioned in the discussion of basic principles, previewing the stem is a great way to focus your reading of the stimulus, so that you know exactly what you're looking for.

2. Read the Stimulus

With the question stem in mind, read the stimulus, paraphrasing as you go. Remember to read actively and critically, pinpointing evidence and conclusion. Also get a sense for how strong or weak the argument is.

3. Try to Prephrase an Answer

Sometimes, if you've read the stimulus critically enough, you'll know the answer without even looking at the choices. It will be much easier to find it if you have a sense of what you're looking for among the choices.

4. Choose an Answer

If you were able to prephrase an answer, skim the choices looking for something that sounds like what you have in mind. If you couldn't think of anything, read and evaluate each choice, throwing out the ones that are outside the scope of the argument. After settling on an answer, you may wish to briefly double-check the question stem to make sure that you're indeed answering the question that was asked.

Using the Kaplan Four-Step Method for Logical Reasoning

Now let's try this approach on a genuine Logical Reasoning item:

A study of twenty overweight men revealed that each man experienced significant weight loss after adding SlimDown, an artificial food supplement, to his daily diet. For three months, each man consumed one SlimDown portion every morning after exercising, and then followed his normal diet for the rest of the day. Clearly, anyone who consumes one portion of SlimDown every day for at least three months will lose weight and will look and feel his or her best.

Which one of the following is an assumption on which the argument depends?

(A) The men in the study will gain back the weight they lost if they discontinue the SlimDown program.
(B) No other dietary supplement will have the same effect on overweight men.
(C) The daily exercise regimen was not responsible for the effects noted in the study.
(D) Women will not experience similar weight reductions if they adhere to the SlimDown program for three months.
(E) Overweight men will achieve only partial weight loss if they do not remain on the SlimDown program for a full three months.

1. Preview the Question Stem

We see, quite clearly, that we're dealing with an Assumption question. Good—immediately we can adopt an "assumption mindset," which basically means that, before even reading the first word of the stimulus, we know that the conclusion will be lacking an important piece of supporting evidence. We now turn to the stimulus, already on the lookout for this missing link.

2. Read the Stimulus

The first sentence introduces a study of twenty men using a food supplement product, resulting in weight loss for all twenty. The second sentence describes how they used it: once a day, for three months, after morning exercise. So far so good; it feels as if we're building up to something. The structural signal word *clearly* usually indicates that some sort of conclusion follows, and in fact it does: the author concludes in the third sentence that anyone who has one portion of the product daily for three months will lose weight, too.

You must read critically! Notice that the conclusion doesn't say that anyone who follows the *same routine* as the twenty men will have the same results; it says that anyone who simply *consumes the product* in the same way will have the same results. You should have begun to sense the inevitable lack of crucial information at this point. The evidence in the second sentence describes a routine that includes taking the supplement after daily exercise, whereas the conclusion focuses primarily on the supplement and entirely ignores the part about the exercise. The conclusion, therefore, doesn't stem logically from the evidence in the first two sentences. This blends seamlessly into Step 3.

3. Prephrase an Answer

As expected, the argument is beginning to look as if it has a serious short-coming. Of course, we expected this because we previewed the question stem before reading the stimulus.

In really simplistic terms, the argument proceeds like so: "A bunch of guys did A and B for three months, and had X result. If anyone does A for three months, that person will experience X result, too." Sound a little fishy? You bet. The author must be assuming that A (the product), not B (exercise), must be the crucial thing that leads to the result. If not (the Denial Test), the conclusion makes no sense.

So, you might prephrase the answer like this: "Something about the exercise thing needs to be cleared up." That's it. Did you think your prephrasing had to be something fancy and glamorous? Well, it doesn't. All you need is an inkling of what the question is looking for, and in this case, it just seems that if we don't shore up the exercise issue, the argument will remain invalid and incomplete. So, with our vague idea of a possible assumption, we can turn to Step 4, which is . . .

4. Choose an Answer

Since we were able to prephrase something, it's best to skim the choices looking for it. And, lo and behold, there's our idea, stated in a very LSAT-like manner, in choice (C). (C) clears up the exercise issue. Yes, this author must assume (C) to make the conclusion that eating SlimDown alone will cause anyone to lose weight.

At this point, if you're stuck for time, you simply choose (C) and move on. If you have more time, you may as well quickly check the remaining choices, to find (we hope) that none of them fits the bill.

Of course, once you grasp the structure of the argument and have located the author's central assumption, you should be able to answer any question they throw at you. This one takes the form of an Assumption question. But it could just as easily have been phrased as a Weaken-the-Argument question:

THE ART OF PREPHRASING

Your prephrasing of an answer need not be elaborate or terribly specific. Your goal is just to get an idea of what you're looking for, so the correct answer will jump out at you.

Which one of the following, if true, casts the most doubt on the argument above?

Answer: Daily exercise contributed significantly to the weight loss experienced by the men in the study.

And here's a Flaw question that could have been based on the same stimulus:

The author's reasoning is flawed because it . . .

Answer: . . . overlooks the possibility that the results noted in the study were caused by daily exercise rather than by the consumption of SlimDown.

So there you have it—a quick demonstration of how to use the strategies and techniques outlined in this chapter to work through the complete Logical Reasoning process. Try to apply these techniques as best you can on the following practice set and in the Logical Reasoning sections of the three full-length Practice Tests in this book. Pay careful attention to all of the written explanations, even those for the ones you got right.

After you work through the practice set, we'll move on to another major section of the test: Logic Games.

Logical Reasoning Practice Set

<u>Directions:</u> This test is composed of questions that ask you to analyze the logic of statements or short paragraphs. You are to choose as the answer to each question the one choice you consider correct on the basis of your common-sense evaluation of the statement and its assumptions. Although a question may seem to have more than one acceptable answer, there is only one answer, and it is the one that does not entail making any illogical, extraneous, or conflicting assumptions about the question. These questions do not presuppose any knowledge of formal logic on your part. (The answer and explanation can be found at the end of each question.)

Question 1

In his long and epochal career, Beethoven was both synthesizer and innovator, the supreme classicist who startled the musical world of his time by his bold surges forward toward the chromaticism to come. But because his later music made so much use of unprecedented dissonance, a few cynical critics have suggested that the composer's progressively worsening deafness must have weakened his ability to imagine and produce consistently harmonious music. In other words, he was writing what he misheard, according to these critics. I maintain that, on the contrary, if the deaf Beethoven had been trying to create in a medium he had known intimately but could no longer manipulate successfully, he would have been all the more likely to _____.

Which one of the following best completes the passage above?

(A) depend heavily upon the rules of conventional harmony to produce predictable sounds
(B) compose dissonances from his inability to hear what he had written

(C) rely upon his own judgment in deciding what type of music to compose
(D) avoid cynical criticism by composing only consistently harmonious music
(E) suspect that his ear had become so untrustworthy that he should end his career before full maturation

Ⓐ Ⓑ Ⓒ Ⓓ Ⓔ

Answer and Explanation

In Question 1, you have to fill in the blank. You'll want to get an idea of the direction in which the passage is going, so that you can extrapolate to the most likely ending.

The passage begins by labeling Beethoven as two things. He was both an innovator—meaning he brought music forward, moving toward what the passage says was "the chromaticism to come" (whatever that is)—and a synthesizer, presumably not the Mogue variety but someone who "put it all together," that is, who also worked with classical forms. *But*—structural signal of contrast here—some critics have said that Beethoven's innovations (his work with dissonance) were *not* some kind of wonderful experimentation, but merely a manifestation of his increasing deafness—hence, they represent an unharmonious flaw in his later music.

The author doesn't hold with this interpretation. She does, after all, label them "cynical critics." And she says, "I maintain that, on the contrary. . . ," which is another signal of contrast announcing that the author is about to take issue. Her belief is that if Beethoven's deafness was (as is alleged) impairing his ability to handle his musical medium, then he would have been all the more likely to do . . . what? Well, she wants to finish with a statement of a contrary effect. Her argument is: If the cause the cynics describe were, in fact, the case (if deafness made Beethoven less competent), then there would be an opposite effect, an effect something like choice (A). A less competent

Beethoven would have played it safe by producing conventional, traditional music.

Choice (B) directly echoes or parallels the opinion of the cynical critics—it doesn't stand in contrast to it—so it's not an opinion that would be cited to bolster the author's own feelings about Beethoven. Jumping to choice (E)—by seeming to agree that Beethoven was losing his abilities towards the end of his career—you can see that choice (E), too, is more in line with the view of the cynical critics.

Choice (C)'s sentiment is somewhat in line with that of the author; it makes a bit of sense in that it suggests that Beethoven composed what he wanted to compose. But it doesn't act as a clear contrast to the notion that Beethoven composed dissonant music because his hearing was impaired and didn't know what sounds he was making, so it doesn't act in a satisfactory way to fill in the blank.

Finally, choice (D) brings up the issue of "harmonious music," which you want. But by assigning a motive to Beethoven—that he was trying to defuse critical response—choice (D) goes far afield. No such reference to motive has a place in the argument as written. Choice (A) best completes the paragraph in Question 1.

Question 2

Many factors affect the home-building industry, but the number of single-family homes under construction generally rises as interest rates decline. Contractors are able to plan their hiring schedules and order essential building materials in response to reliable predictors of the movement of prevailing interest rates.

It can be inferred from the passage above that

(A) the price of building materials rises when interest rates decline
(B) no factor affecting home building is as reliable a predictor as interest rates
(C) assessments of growth in the housing industry are sometimes based upon expected fluctuations of interest rates
(D) a contractor does not order building materials until a hiring schedule is set up
(E) most housing being built today is single-family housing

Ⓐ Ⓑ Ⓒ Ⓓ Ⓔ

Answer and Explanation

Question 2's stimulus isn't much of an argument, is it? It's little more than a series of flat statements on a topic. And that topic is interest rates, one of the major factors affecting the housing industry. Interest rates are cited as having an inverse relationship with the building of single-family dwellings: as rates go down, construction goes up, literally. In line with that (says the second sentence), contractors order building materials based on predictions of which way interest rates will go. This should make sense. If the contractors believed that rates were about to decrease, they would be likely to order more supplies in expectation of a greater demand for single-family homes. Conversely, an expected rise in interest rates would prompt a cutback in supply orders, in expectation of less demand.

All of this is in line with choice (C). And remember, when you're asked what can be inferred from the passage, you really want something that must be true—something in line with the scope and point of view. Choice (C) is just a broader rephrasing of the relationship cited in the stimulus and is thus the best answer. (Note that the choice is rendered even more reasonable by its use of the qualifier *sometimes*. Because it's not an extreme statement with no exceptions possible, it's easy to sign on to (C) as a reflection of the author's equally moderate views.)

Choice (A) brings up the cost of building materials, but since the passage says nothing at all about the costs of home building—there isn't a single reference to costs—it goes beyond the scope and must therefore be rejected quickly. You can't infer that those who sell building materials raise their prices in response to the greater demand they expect from the lower interest rates.

Choice (B) distorts the paragraph. Interest rates are cited as *a* good predictor. But are they the best? Who knows? And anyway, they're cited only in terms of one type of home—the single-family dwelling. Choice (B) evokes the entire industry—again, going beyond the scope.

As for choice (D), just because the author mentions hiring schedules before mentioning orders for new materials does not mean that one of those things must come first on the builder's agenda.

And (E) is an unwarranted inference since the author's only concern is one type of dwelling, the single-family home. You cannot fairly extrapolate from this paragraph to any statement about the home-building industry in general.

Again, it was choice (C) for Question 2.

Question 3

Critics of current commercial TV programming expect that Federal Communications Commission (FCC) rules restricting such popular items as children's adventure cartoons and sexually explicit motion pictures would result in more responsible programming, such as public affairs panel discussions, medical self-help series, and live productions of classic drama. But would they so fervently advocate government intrusion into broadcasting if they knew a little more about the real workings of the marketplace? Actually, enforced restrictions on programming would result in milder but still mindless offerings: more situation comedies about bewildered housewives, more coverage of obscure sporting events in minor cities, and more talk shows devoted to the private lives of forgettable "instant celebrities."

The author of the above passage assumes that

(A) current commercial TV programming is not irresponsible

(B) FCC restrictions of commercial TV programming will not necessarily be easy to enforce

(C) those who wish to restrict certain popular TV programs will dislike their popular replacements

(D) the FCC should have no control over the broadcast industry, which is likely to serve the public better if it is not regulated

(E) the marketplace is the true test of whether or not a new program idea is worthwhile

Ⓐ Ⓑ Ⓒ Ⓓ Ⓔ

Answer and Explanation

The speaker in Question 3 doubts that stricter FCC regulations will result in better quality television. Some expect that greater restrictions on kid's shows and dirty movies will prompt TV programmers to give us more, shall we say, elevating fare. But the speaker feels that stronger FCC rules will do no such thing—that the networks will be able to conform to the rules while continuing to provide the same vapid programming choices that have always been popular (that's the reference to the marketplace). The networks (it is predicted) will simply switch from controversial themes—that is, from sex and violence—to milder but still mindless shows. In other words, the networks won't attempt (as the proregulators predict) to put on more educational shows. They will just shift to whatever dopey (yet popular) fare is not restricted by the FCC.

You're to find an assumption, and the credited choice—the thing the speaker must be taking for granted as true—is (C). The speaker is taking for granted that the people who dislike TV as it is now will also dislike the shows that will be broadcast after the rules are instituted. After all, the speaker is essentially saying to the proregulators, "You're wrong in wanting to institute those rules because you'll get no better programming than before." But the speaker ignores the possibility that those in favor of the FCC rules will gladly greet the new dumb sitcoms and sports shows as a welcome change from the sex and violence that the rules are designed to reduce.

Choice (A) says that current TV is not irresponsible. But the speaker doesn't argue that the proposed rules are superfluous because current TV programming is responsible. Rather, the speaker argues that the rules won't make TV any better. In fact, the whole passage indicates that the author believes the opposite of (A): that much programming is irresponsibly mindless.

Choice (B) is not a necessary assumption either, since the speaker is not concerned with the ease or difficulty of enforcement but rather with how effective or ineffective the rules would be when enforced.

Choice (D) isn't assumed because the author doesn't argue that unregulated TV will be better, but rather that regulated TV will not be any better. The thrust here is that, because of the marketplace, TV will always be a vast wasteland.

Finally, choice (E) suggests that the true test of programming worth is the marketplace. Well, the speaker does believe that it's the marketplace that determines what we see on TV. But what the public sees is, to the speaker, execrable: sexy, violent, dopey, and worthless. Choice (E)'s rather democratic sentiment is completely at odds with the author's argument, and so it's not something that is assumed or built into that argument. Again, choice (C) is correct for Question 3.

Question 4

The federal government currently interferes blatantly in the relationship between parent and child. The Internal Revenue Service provides a child-care or dependent's deduction on the annual income tax return. In effect, the government, by rewarding some providers of support, determines which taxpayers are to be considered worthy enough to care for dependents.

Which one of the following, if true, weakens the argument above?

(A) A taxpayer need only attach the appropriate schedule to the tax form to apply for the deduction.
(B) The deduction is likely to offer a proportionately greater benefit to the lower income taxpayer.
(C) A child must be living at home with the provider of support in order to qualify as a dependent.
(D) The deduction actually affects a fairly small percentage of taxpayers.
(E) The deduction is available to anyone who supplies the principal support of a dependent.

Ⓐ Ⓑ Ⓒ Ⓓ Ⓔ

Answer and Explanation

Always watch for tone words! The charge in Question 4's stimulus that the government interferes "blatantly," wrongly using its bureaucratic power, alerts you immediately to the author's opinion.

It seems that the IRS gives a child-care deduction to certain people who provide support to a dependent. The complaint is that the government exercises unfair control in its choice of which people receive this deduction and which do not. The author believes that the government can have no justifiable basis on which to make this decision, and is in effect deciding which people are worthy of caring for dependents and which are not.

The choice that most weakens this argument is (E). If the tax deduction is, as choice (E) says, available to anyone who is the principal supporter of a dependent, then that answers the implicit charge that the government has arbitrarily set itself up as an authority, with the right to decide people's personal worth. If the IRS, in other words, is using an appropriate criterion that is applied equitably to all, then the charge that the deduction is being selectively used to decide people's worth is rendered groundless. If you provide someone's principal support, then you get the deduction. If not, you don't. So (E) really damages the reasoning.

Choice (A) might have fooled you, because it seems to be saying that anyone who wants the deduction can have it. But it really says that anyone who attaches the appropriate schedule may apply for the deduction; they won't necessarily get it. The fact that the IRS will consider anyone doesn't mean that it isn't (as the author alleges) making the final decision on inappropriate criteria, choosing people arbitrarily on the basis of what it deems to be their personal worth. So choice (A) is incorrect.

Choice (B) mentions the deduction but is otherwise beyond the argument's scope, going off on the interesting but irrelevant topic of the relative size of the deduction for lower-income taxpayers.

As for choice (C), even if it were true, the government might still be reaching its decision as to who gets the deduction based on improper criteria. All choice (C) gives us is one of those criteria—the requirement that a dependent be a coresident. But perhaps the other criteria are just as objectionable as the author seems to feel they are.

Finally, choice (D)'s implication that only a few people will get the deduction is another "error in scope," because choice (D) has nothing to do with the main issue, which is the government's methods or motives. The "weakener" you need has to somehow demonstrate that the government—contrary to what the author believes—is awarding the deduction based on proper criteria. Only choice (E) does that, and that's why it's correct for Question 4.

Question 5

Detective-adventure series and other action programming on prime-time television have been criticized for inciting some viewers, male adolescents in particular, to commit acts of violence. The most carefully engineered studies have not, however, supported this assumption. Rather, it seems likely that someone who is frustrated and resentful, and therefore prone to violence, is drawn to the kind of programming that shows characters who release their frustrations in acts of violence.

Which one of the following would provide the most logical concluding sentence for the paragraph above?

(A) In fact, action programming probably helps a frustrated viewer release his hostility without resorting to violence.

(B) Moreover, there are studies that indicate that male adolescents are more likely than other viewers to believe that the world shown in action programming is realistic.

(C) In other words, an unusual interest in action programming may be an indication of a violence-prone personality rather than an incitement to violence.

(D) Be that as it may, action programming continues to grow in popularity with the American TV audience.

(E) Therefore, the reasonable observer of the American scene will conclude that action programming should be banned from prime-time viewing hours.

Ⓐ Ⓑ Ⓒ Ⓓ Ⓔ

Answer and Explanation

In Question 5 the author counters the view that violent TV shows incite people to commit violent acts. Apparently a correlation has been noticed—and a correlation, of course, is an acknowledgment that two phenomena accompany each other, whether or not they're causally related. A correlation has been noted between watching TV violence and committing violent acts. Apparently it's true that people who watch violent shows are more likely to commit violent crimes than those who don't watch those shows. And this finding might well suggest that the TV shows are causing the viewers to commit the crimes. But the author believes that the correlation is better explained in another way—that violence-prone people tend to watch violent shows because they feel an affinity to the violence-prone characters of the shows. So to the author, the critics cited in the first sentence are guilty of confusing cause and effect. The TV shows don't make the viewer violence prone; rather, it's frustration and resentment that make people violence prone and make these people watch violent TV programs.

The passage ends abruptly without a proper conclusion—for obvious reasons, since you're asked to come up with that yourself. The best answer is (C), which takes the author's argument to its logical conclusion: A person's addiction to action TV shows may reveal something about that person's tendency towards violence, but it doesn't indicate an inducement to commit violence.

Choice (A) goes too far. It states that the effect of action shows is salutary, by helping the violence-prone viewer vent his hostility in a nonthreatening way. But that doesn't at all follow from the argument, which merely contends that the crime-and-TV-show correlation can be explained in an alternative way. To say, as choice (A) does, that TV violence can act as a corrective goes far afield.

Choice (B) raises the issue of who finds the action programs realistic. This issue comes from left field. You're looking for a summation of the given argument. (B) introduces a new point, and you really can't say what effect this new point has on the passage. It's certainly not a good conclusion.

Choice (D) is irrelevant—you would never expect a paragraph about whether action TV leads to violence to end with a quick reference to action shows' general popularity.

And it's more likely that the author would disagree with choice (E) than end her discussion with it. In a way her views are a defense of action programming against the charge of aiding and abetting violent crime. Therefore, choice (E)'s call for a ban on action shows is just plain uncalled for. In any case, the idea of a ban comes from left field, and cannot provide a logical concluding sentence. Once again, it was choice (C) for Question 5.

Questions 6–7:

Although the legislative process in our democratic government is based on the proposition that Congress must represent the interests of the majority of its constituents, this principle that the majority rules is frequently contradicted by the efforts of lobbyists. Minority interests with the wherewithal to finance hard-sell lobbying campaigns can distort an elected official's sense of public opinion, thereby exercising a destructive influence over political decisions.

Question 6

The argument above depends upon the truth of which one of the following assumptions?

(A) The democratic process is a reflection of our capitalist economic system.

(B) The democratic process requires that minority interests be protected by Constitutional amendment.

(C) Minority interests cannot be protected without spending large sums of money on lobbying activities.

(D) The democratic process cannot function properly unless the activities of big business are restrained.

(E) The democratic process depends on the ability of all members of society to have equal influence on the legislative process.

Ⓐ Ⓑ Ⓒ Ⓓ Ⓔ

Answer and Explanation

In the stimulus for Questions 6 and 7, the conclusion is expressed in the main clause of the first sentence: Lobbyists have a negative effect on the principle of "the majority rules" as practiced in Congress. The reason for that conclusion—the evidence or support—comes in the second sentence: Wealthy minority interests can afford to finance lobbyists, who pressure elected officials. These lobbyists make the officials believe that the opinions of the lobby are held by the people at large. So, the argument goes, some people (namely the rich interest groups) have a greater influence on decision making than do others. And this, it's alleged, thwarts majority rule.

Thinking about a key assumption connecting this evidence to that conclusion—and that's what Question 6 is asking for—you should note that the author jumps from the idea that lobbyists distort Congress's sense of public opinion, to the conclusion that lobbyists undermine the majority-rule concept. And in order to make this leap, the author must be assuming that all members of society have to have equal influence on legislation, in order for majority-rule to work. All the evidence says is that lobbyists distort Congress's sense of public opinion—it doesn't claim that the opinion of the majority is completely silenced. The majority-rule principle (according to this passage) implies that Congress should represent the interests of the majority of its constituents. So, by asserting that the lobbyists muck things up, the author must be taking for granted that all members of society have to be heard from, have to have equal influence, in order for the concept of majority-rule to work. That's what choice (E) is saying and why choice (E) is correct for Question 6.

Of the incorrect choices, (A)'s reference to capitalism takes it way, way beyond the scope of the argument. The only connection between money and the argument's content is a more or less tangential one—the idea that money helps the lobbyists distort Congress's sense of public opinion. Choice (A) blows that out of proportion. Choice (B), meanwhile, is too specific. To say that minority interests have to be protected by Constitutional amendment is to propose a specific solution to a problem floating around the argument, but the author need not be assuming or

signing on to that solution as he reasons. Choice (C) is off the point because the argument is concerned with protecting majority interests—the concept of majority-rule is what's allegedly in danger here. (This could be brought up as an objection to choice (B), as well.) Finally, choice (D) plays off your possible assumption that the minority interests in the passage are big-business fat cats, but as far as the passage goes it may be the case that other minority interests, ones not connected with big business at all, engage in lobbying, too. Once again, choice (E) is correct for Question 6.

Question 7

Which one of the following, if true, would most weaken the argument above?

(A) The majority opinion on many political issues is ill-informed and unconsidered.
(B) Elected officials are rarely influenced by pressures of lobbying campaigns.
(C) Interest groups can accumulate large sums of money through fund-raising activities.
(D) All groups and interests are entitled to hire professional lobbyists to represent their cause.
(E) There is no clear-cut majority position on many political issue facing Congress.

Ⓐ Ⓑ Ⓒ Ⓓ Ⓔ

Answer and Explanation

Now there's another major assumption at work here—it's not among the answer choices for Question 6, but it's the key to Question 7. The author is assuming that Congress, bullied and influenced by the lobbyists, goes about the act of legislating under that influence. He's assuming (in short) that lobbyists' efforts are, by and large, successful. But if, as choice (B) says, it's a rare day when an elected official is at all moved by a lobbying campaign, then the lobbyists are not successful. If (B) is true, if Congress gives these minority interests a deaf ear, then that denies the allegation (in the last sentence) that the lobbyists have destructive influence over decisions. That in turn categorically defuses the author's concerns about the danger to majority-rule. Thus choice (B) is an excellent weakener and the correct answer for Question 7.

Choice (A) is no good because the argument isn't about the quality of the majority opinion; the author is only concerned with whether the majority's opinion is being sufficiently represented, and doesn't care if that opinion is rather ignorant or foolish. Choice (C) supports the argument: If interest groups can (as it says) raise a lot of cash, they can then use the cash for lobbying purposes—the exact sort of situation that has the author all bent out of shape. So (C) lends fuel to the author's flame. As for choice (D), even if groups are entitled to employ lobbyists, it doesn't weaken the author's claim that the effect of lobbyists is dangerous. There are many things all of us are entitled or permitted to do that may not be good for us or for society. Finally, choice (E): there need not be any clear-cut majority position on any one issue in order for the argument to make sense. The point again is that lobbies obscure the majority position such that Congress can't even tell whether it is clear-cut, or even what it is. Even if the majority position were not, as (E) says, one definite position but a mush of many, the author wants Congress to be able to have a clear view that that is the case. Despite choice (E), the lobbyists may still muddy Congress's view, as the author alleges. But if choice (B) is true, then the lobbyists do not muddy the view, and that's why the answer to Question 7 is choice (B).

Question 8

If we reduce the rate of income taxation, people will spend a larger portion of their gross incomes on consumer goods. This will stimulate economic growth and result in higher salaries and thus in higher government revenues, despite a lower rate of taxation.

Which one of the following arguments most closely resembles the reasoning in the statements above?

(A) If we reduce the amount of overtime our employees work, production costs will decline and our total income will thus increase.
(B) If we make it harder to participate in the school lunch program, people will have to pay for more of their food and the farm income will therefore increase.
(C) If a movie is classified as obscene, more people will want to see it and the morals of the general community will be corrupted more than they would be otherwise.
(D) If we give our employees more paid holidays, their efficiency while actually on the job will improve and our total productivity will thus increase.
(E) If we give our children more spending money, they will learn to manage their finances better and will thereby realize the virtue of thrift.

ⒶⒷⒸⒹⒺ

Answer and Explanation

To look for an argument that "resembles" the stimulus is to find a parallel argument, one whose structure is as close as possible to that of the original. The stimulus says that if you lower taxes, people will buy more things. Doing so will stimulate economic growth, which in turn will raise salaries, which in turn will bring in more money for the government. Of course you're not concerned here with whether this is a sound program or a bogus one, but with how it's put together. And the bottom line is, what you have here is something of a paradox: begin by lowering taxes, which (you'd assume) would lower government revenues, and in the end, government revenues will increase. To abstract it further, it goes like so: engaging in a particular action will (in the end) give you a result that's the opposite of what you might have expected.

And that's what you get in correct choice (D). Though it would be reasonable to expect that more employee days off would reduce productivity (since they'd be spending less time on the job), in fact productivity will be greater, the exact opposite effect, because of the greater efficiency that (D) says will emerge. The chain of events described in the stimulus may be a little longer—it has more steps—than choice (D), but its overall shape is very similar.

Choice (A) presents no paradox at all. You would expect that reducing overtime would bring down costs and increase total income. Naturally it would. The course of action choice (A) outlines is predictable. But what you want in your answer is a surprising result from a course of action.

Choice (B) departs from the stimulus's pattern. The original gives you the government reducing income taxes and getting more money back because of it. (B) has the government changing the rules about the school lunch program and the farmers—a third party—reaping a benefit. This is a bit underhanded, but it's certainly not a paradox; more importantly, the benefit to a third party is not at all what happens in the stimulus.

Choice (C)'s plan certainly carries a bit of irony in its assertion that rating a movie "X" ends up corrupting the morals of the community. But as in choice (B)—and *unlike* correct choice (D)—the agent who performs the first action here (the censor) is not the one who reaps the ultimate benefit or, indeed, is directly affected by the action. Choice (E), meanwhile, may be even less of a paradox than choice (A). It is not at all surprising that a kid given more practice managing money ends up learning the value of thrift.

It is surprising that a company's giving employees more days off should make them better workers and bring the business more revenue, and that's why choice (D) is correct for question eight.

Question 9

If a judge is appointed for life, she will make courtroom decisions that reflect the accumulated wisdom inherent in this country's judicial history, relying upon the law and reason rather than upon trends in political thinking. If, on the other hand, the judge is appointed or elected for short terms in office, her decisions will be heavily influenced by the prevailing political climate. In sum, the outcome of many court cases will be determined by the method by which the presiding judge has been installed in her post.

Which one of the following, if true, does not support the argument in the passage above?

(A) Surveys indicate that judges enjoy their work and want to remain in office as long as possible.

(B) Judges appointed for life are just as informed about political matters as are judges who must run for reelection.

(C) The rulings of judges who must run for reelection are generally approved of by the voters who live in their elective districts.

(D) Most judges appointed for life hand down identical rulings on similar cases throughout their long careers.

(E) Only judges who are selected for short terms of office employ pollsters to read the mood of the electorate.

Ⓐ Ⓑ Ⓒ Ⓓ Ⓔ

Answer and Explanation

Four of the five answer choices in Question 9 support the logic, so you'll be looking for a statement that either weakens the logic or has no effect on it. The conclusion is that the way a judge came into his or her job, and thus how much job security he or she has, often determines how a case will come out—that judges decide differently depending on whether they were elected or appointed for life or only for a short term. How so? Short-term judges (it goes on to say) think about their cases in light of which way the political winds are blowing, whereas appointed-for-life judges don't care about political trends and rely solely on a long tradition of judicial theory. In the end, then, the author evidently believes that the wiser judge is the life-term judge.

Since the author provides nothing concrete to back up his claim that short-term judges keep looking back over their shoulders to politics, while life-term judges don't, the answer choices have many opportunities to support the reasoning. Choice (A), for instance, supports the idea that the short-term judges are likely to be moved by the prevailing political climate. If, as (A) says, they really want to keep their jobs, they will be more likely to decide the way the voters want them to decide in order to improve their election chances. Likewise, choice (C) supports that connection between the approval of the voters (which is necessary for re-election, of course) and the voters' view of the judge's decisions, by showing that short-term judges "happen" to rule in a way the voters approve of. And if you jump ahead to choice (E), here you get perhaps the strongest support for the allegation that short-term judges have one eye on the scales of justice and the other on the mood of the voters—according to (E) they're the only judges who use pollsters, whose sole purpose is to track public opinion.

So choices (A), (C), and (E) lend greater credence to the allegations about short-term judges.

Meanwhile, Choice (D) lends support to the other part of the argument—the view of lifelong judges—in its comment that appointed judges show great consistency in their thinking over the years. Choice (D) implies that those judges, as alleged by the author, do turn a blind eye to the vicissitudes of politics and decide based on fundamental, lasting principles.

You're left with choice (B), which may in fact weaken the argument. If (B) is right in its claim that long-term judges keep their ear to the political ground as much as short-term judges do, then that damages the distinction between judges raised in the argument. And when that distinction is hurt, so is the conclusion based on it. Even if long-term judges don't act on their political knowledge, choice (B) is simply irrelevant. You might have seen this directly—you might have picked (B) right from the start. But it was useful to go through this process and demonstrate how you could have answered it by process of elimination. Either way may be helpful for you on a given question on the LSAT. Certainly, either way gets you to choice (B) for Question 9.

Question 10

These so-called pacifists are either the victims or the propagators of a false logic. They claim that weapons reductions would result in a so-called climate of peace, thereby diminishing the likelihood of conflicts leading to war. But what are the facts? In the past ten years, during which time we have seen increased spending for such defense requirements as state-of-the-art weapons systems and augmented combat personnel, there have been fewer military actions involving our forces than in any previous decade in the twentieth century. Our own installations have not been attacked and our allies have rarely found it necessary to ask for our armed support. In other words, defense readiness is, in the real world, the most efficient peace-making tool.

Which of the following is an assumption underlying the conclusion of the passage above?

(A) Military actions involving our forces can be instigated by any of a number of different factors.

(B) Our buildup of weapons systems and combat personnel has prevented our adversaries from increasing their own spending on defense.

(C) The increased defense spending of the past ten years has lessened the need for significant military expenditure in future decades.

(D) At the present time, state-of-the-art weapons systems and the augmentation of combat personnel are equally important to a nation's resources.

(E) The number of military actions involving our forces would have been greater in the past decade if we had not increased our defense spending.

Ⓐ Ⓑ Ⓒ Ⓓ Ⓔ

Answer and Explanation

The author in Question 10 is refuting some "so-called pacifists" (that's his phrase) who, you learn by inference, have been calling for weapons reductions to create a climate of peace. The author, however, believes quite the opposite, that a "climate of peace" has been created by increased military spending on things like new weapons systems and more personnel. How does the author support this claim that a climate of peace exists, and exists because of the greater military spending? He does so by pointing to the number of attacks on this country and its allies. Fewer attacks, it is said, have occurred since military spending began to rise, and thus the author sees a causal connection between the "defense readiness" maintained by greater spending, and the low number of attacks.

Now the assumption underlying this causal connection is your goal in Question 10, and you find it in choice (E). It has to be true that had defense spending not gone up, the number of attacks on this country and its allies would have increased. Otherwise there would be no causal connection between the two phenomena, as the author claims. Remember the assertion is that high defense spending has caused fewer military engagements (and, in turn, a "climate of peace"). That assertion is true only if choice (E) is true, and that's what you need in a major assumption.

Choice (A), in its reference to the possible causes of military actions, is irrelevant. The author doesn't refer to what causes them, but simply asserts that military readiness can prevent them irrespective of the cause. With regard to choice (B), the author doesn't tell you how and why more defense spending has prevented military actions, just that it has done so. The so-called "climate of peace," in the author's view, is based on the greater spending on defense this country has engaged in, and is not necessarily attributable to any trends in defense spending on the part of this country's adversaries (which is choice (B)'s thrust). And the author makes no claim about the future of peace or of military spending, choice (C). The thrust of the argument is toward the past, and what past spending has done to peace in the past. Whether all this readiness can permit future cuts is a matter upon which the author doesn't speculate. Finally, choice (D)'s equation of weapons and personnel is silly, specious, and irrelevant. Both are mentioned as key elements of the current peace climate, and both have benefited from having more money available. But while the author might have an opinion as to which (weapons or personnel) are more valuable, he's keeping it to himself if he does. So you cannot ascribe choice (D)'s view to him. You can be sure he subscribes to choice (E), which makes it the best answer for Question 10.

Question 11

It is possible for a panhandler to collect a considerable amount of money from passersby if she can convince them that she is destitute and that begging is the only way for her to help herself. If, on the other hand, passersby get the impression that they are being conned or that the panhandler is just being lazy, they will not give her anything at all.

Which one of the following statements can be most reliably concluded from the passage above?

(A) Most panhandlers are unwilling to work.
(B) If someone begs when she does not need to, people will not give her any money.
(C) Most passersby would give a panhandler money if they thought that she was not conning them.
(D) Passersby often base their decision of whether or not to give money to a panhandler on their impressions of her and her honesty.
(E) People who give money to panhandlers are not influenced by how much change they have in their pockets when they decide the amount of money they will give.

Ⓐ Ⓑ Ⓒ Ⓓ Ⓔ

Answer and Explanation

In Question 11, you're asked for a conclusion. The stimulus argument basically describes some conditions and factors that influence whether or not, and how much, passersby will give to panhandlers.

There are two conditions here. First, if passersby find a panhandler to be destitute and forced to beg, they may give her quite a bit of money. Second, and on the other hand, if passersby think they are being conned, or that the panhandler is merely lazy, they won't give her anything at all.

So basically the passage is showing you how the perceptions that people have of panhandlers affect their reactions to them. Thus, the most reliable conclusion is choice (D). People decide whether to give to a panhandler based on how they perceive her—as sincere, or lazy and dishonest. It's choice (D) for Question 11.

As soon as you realize that the passage is describing only how people's perceptions influence their reactions, you can eliminate a couple of wrong answers. The passage never tells you whether most panhandlers are lazy or not; it merely speaks of what happens if people perceive them as lazy. Thus, (A) is incorrect.

The same problem exists in (B). You don't know that some beggars can't fool passersby. The stimulus speaks of people's perceptions, not the reality underneath those perceptions.

As for (C), it's a misreading of the first condition. Appearing truly needy is necessary for getting money from passersby; yet it need not be sufficient. Furthermore, (C) speaks of most passersby, which needn't be true at all. Perhaps most people never give money to panhandlers.

And finally, (E) concludes that a completely new factor, the amount of change one has, doesn't influence the decision making of passersby. There are no grounds for concluding this. The stimulus presents some factors in the decision making, but it never says that these are the only factors. So (E) could well be false, and the correct answer for Question 11 remains choice (D).

CHAPTER 3

LOGIC GAMES

Nothing inspires more fear in the hearts of LSAT test takers than Analytical Reasoning—affectionately known as Logic Games. Why? Partly, it's because the skills tested on the section seem so unfamiliar— you need to turn a game's information to your advantage by organizing your thinking and spotting key deductions, and that's not easy to do.

Games tend to give most trouble to students who don't have a clearly defined method of attack. And that's where Kaplan's basic principles, game-specific strategies and techniques, and Five-Step Method for Logic Games will help most, streamlining your work so you can rack up points quickly and confidently.

The following are the major analytical skills that the Logic Games section is intended to measure:

- **Organization**—the ability to efficiently assimilate, both in your head and on the page, the formidable amount of data associated with each game
- **Mental agility**—the ability to keep track of multiple pieces of information simultaneously, and still maintain enough flexibility to shuffle the pieces around in different ways for each question
- **Memory**—the ability to retain the work done in the setup stage while focusing on the new information in each question stem
- **Concentration**—the ability to keep focused on the task at hand and not let your mind wander

Let's now take a look at the major principles that should guide your work on this section.

DON'T BE A GAMEOPHOBE!

Many LSAT takers live in fear of the Logic Games section. But Logic Games are definitely manageable —if you take control of the test as we recommend.

The Four Basic Principles of Logic Games

The rallying cry of the Logic Games–impaired is: "If only I had more time, I could do these!" Well, this is no consolation on the day of the test, when you simply won't have any extra time. You can spend as much time on a game as you like when you're sitting in your own living room, but when your proctor says, "You have thirty-five minutes . . . begin," he or she is not kidding around. Remember, the test makers aren't testing just to see who can answer the twenty-three to twenty-four LG questions correctly, but also who can do so in thirty-five minutes.

Logic Games is perhaps the most speed-sensitive section of the test. The test makers know that if you (not to mention an intelligent ten-year-old) could spend hours methodically trying out every choice in every question, you'd probably get everything right. But what does that prove? Nothing. Who's going to get the sought-after legal position or win the important client—the person who can write the legal brief and prepare the court case in four days, or the person who can do the same job in four hours? It's all about efficiency, both on the test and in your future career.

And that brings us to the first, and somewhat paradoxical sounding, Logic Games principle:

First Principle: To Go Faster, Slow Down

To gain time in Logic Games, you must spend a lot of time thinking through and analyzing the setup and the rules. This is not only the most important principle for logic games success, it's also the one that's most often ignored, probably because it just doesn't seem right intuitively; people having timing difficulties tend to speed up, not slow down. But by spending a little extra time up front thinking through the stimulus, the "action" of the game, and the rules, you'll be able to recognize the game's key issues and make important deductions that will actually save you time in the long run.

Games are structured so that, in order to answer the questions quickly and correctly, you need to search out relevant pieces of information that combine to form valid new statements, called deductions. Now, you can either do this once, up front, and then utilize the same deductions throughout the game, *or* you can choose to piece together the same basic deductions—essentially repeating the same work—for every single question.

For instance, let's say that two of the rules for a Logic Game go as follows:

If Bob is chosen for the team, then Eric is also chosen.
If Eric is chosen for the team, then Pat will not be chosen.

You can, as you read through the rules of the game, just treat those rules as two separate pieces of independent information. But there's a deduction to be made from them. Do you see it? If Bob is chosen, Eric is, too. If Eric is chosen, Pat is not. That means that, if Bob is chosen, Pat is not chosen. That's an important deduction—one that will undoubtedly be required from question to question. If you don't take the time to make it up front, when you're first considering the game, you'll have to make it over and over again, every time it's necessary to answer a question. But if you *do* take the time to make this deduction up front, and build it into your entire conception of the game, you'll save that time later. You won't be doing the same work several times.

The choice is yours; we just find that the rush-to-the-questions method is inefficient, time-consuming, and stress-inducing.

So, always try to take the game scenario and the rules as far as you can before moving on to the questions. Look for common elements among the rules (like Eric in the rules above)—this will help you combine them and pull out major deductions. The stimulus creates a situation, and the rules place restrictions on what can and cannot happen within that situation. If you investigate the possible scenarios, and look for and find major deductions up front, you'll then be able to rack up points quickly and confidently.

Second Principle: Understand What a Rule Means, Not Just What It Says

If you're interested in demonstrating how well you can read a statement and then spit it back verbatim, you'd be better off training to be a legal secretary instead of a legal practitioner or scholar. That's why you'll never see this on the LSAT:

> RULE: Arlene is not fifth in line.
> QUESTION: Which one of the following people is not fifth in line?
> ANSWER: Arlene.

True, some LG questions are easy—but not that easy. The LSAT, after all, measures critical thinking, and virtually every sentence in Logic Games has to be filtered through some sort of analytical process before it will be of any use. You may have to use the information about Arlene to

NO PARROTS, PLEASE

To fully grasp a rule in Logic Games, you must know more than just what it says. You've got to know what the rule means in the context of the game and in combination with other rules.

ACCENTUATE THE POSITIVE

Always try to turn negative rules—"Box 2 does not contain any gumdrops"—into a positive statement—"Box 2 must contain chocolates and mints."

help you eliminate a choice or lead you to the right answer, but even in the simplest of cases, this will involve the application, as opposed to the mere parroting, of the rule.

So, getting back to the principle, it's not enough just to copy a rule off the page (or shorthand it, as we'll discuss momentarily); it's imperative that you think through its exact meaning, including any implications it might have. And don't limit this behavior to the indented rules; statements in the games' introductions are very often rules in and of themselves, and warrant the same meticulous consideration.

For instance, let's say a game's introduction sets up a scenario in which you have three boxes, each containing at least two of the following three types of candy—chocolates, gumdrops, and mints. Then you get the following rule:

Box 2 does not contain any gumdrops.

What does that rule say? That there aren't any gumdrops in Box 2. But what does that rule *mean*, when you think about it in the context of the game? That Box 2 *does* contain chocolates and mints. Each box contains at least two of three things, remember. Once you eliminate one of the three things for any particular box, therefore, you know that the other two things *must* be in that box.

Part of understanding what a rule means, moreover, is grasping what the rule *doesn't* mean. For example, take the rule we mentioned earlier:

RULE: If Bob is chosen for the team, then Eric is also chosen.
MEANS: Whenever Bob is chosen, Eric is, too.
DOESN'T MEAN: Whenever Eric is chosen, Bob is, too.

Remember the discussion of formal logic in the Logical Reasoning chapter? If I yell loudly at my cat Adrian, he will run away. That does mean that whenever I yell at him loudly, he runs away. But it *doesn't* mean that whenever he runs away, I've yelled at him.

GAME WISDOM

You must know the rules of a Logic Game cold—what they mean, how they impact on other rules, and what implications they have in the context of the game scenario.

Third Principle: Use Scratchwork and Shorthand

The proper use of scratchwork can help you do your best on Logic Games. As you may recall, the directions state: "You may wish to draw a rough sketch to help answer some of the questions." Notice that they use the wording *rough sketch*, not *masterpiece*, *work of art*, or *classic picture for the ages*. The LSAT is not a drawing contest; you get no points for creating beautiful diagrams on the page.

However, although some games aren't amenable to scratchwork, for most games you'll find that it is helpful to create a master sketch, one that encapsulates all of the game's information in one easy-to-reference picture. Doing so will not only give your eye a place to gravitate toward when you need information, but it will also help to solidify in your mind the action of the game, the rules, and whatever deductions you come up with up front.

Remember to keep your scratchwork simple—the less time you spend drawing, the more time you'll have for thinking and answering questions. Pay careful attention to the scratchwork suggestions in the explanations to the four games on the Practice Test in the back of this book.

Part of your scratchwork should involve jotting down on your page a quick and shortened form of most rules. Shorthand is a visual representation of a mental thought process, and is useful only if it reminds you at a glance of the rule's meaning. Whether you shorthand a rule or commit it to memory, you should never have to look back at the game itself once you get to the questions.

The goal of the entire scratchwork process is to condense a lot of information into manageable, user-friendly visual cues. It's much easier to remember rules written like so:

$B \rightarrow E$
No G in 2

than ones written like so:

If Bob is chosen for the team, then Eric is also chosen.
Box 2 does not contain any gumdrops.

This is helpful as long as you know, for instance, what the arrow from B to E means, and you're consistent in using it. If you can develop a personal shorthand that's instantly understandable to you, you'll have a decided advantage on the day of the test.

Fourth Principle: Try to Set off Chains of Deduction

When hypothetical information is offered in a question stem, try to use it to set off a chain of deductions. Consider the following question. (Since this question is excerpted without the accompanying introduction and rules, ignore the specific logic of the discussion; it's just presented to make a point.)

If the speedboat is yellow, which one of the following must be true?

(A) The car is green.
(B) The airplane is red.
(C) The train is black.
(D) The car is yellow.
(E) The train is red.

The question stem contains a *hypothetical*, which is an if-clause offering information pertaining only to that particular question. The wrong approach is to acknowledge that the speedboat is yellow, and then proceed to test out all of the choices. The muddled mental thought process accompanying this tragic approach might sound something like this:

> "All right, the speedboat's yellow, does the car have to be green? Well, let's see, if the speedboat's yellow, and the car is green, then the train would have to be yellow, but I can't tell what color the airplane is, and I guess this is okay, I don't know, I better try the next choice. Let's see what happens if the speedboat's yellow and the airplane is red. . . ."

Don't do this kind of dithering! Notice that the question doesn't ask: "What happens if, in addition to this, the car is green?" or "What happens if this is true and the airplane is red?" So why is the confused test taker above intent on answering all of these irrelevant questions? Never begin a question by trying out answer choices; that's going about it backwards. Only if you're entirely stuck, or are faced with a question stem that leaves you no choice, should you resort to trial and error.

Most Logic Games questions are amenable to a more efficient and systematic methodology. The correct approach is to incorporate the new piece of information into your view of the game, creating one quick sketch if you wish. How do you do this? Simple: Apply the rules and any previous deductions to the new information in order to set off a new chain of deductions. Then follow through until you've taken the new information as far as it can go. Just as you must take the game and rules as far as you can before moving on to the questions, you must carry the information in a question stem out as far as you can before moving on to the choices.

A Last Resort

Trial and error with the answer choices should be your last resort, not your first. It's much quicker to follow a chain of deduction until it leads you to the answer. In some cases, trial and error is necessary, but don't turn to it unless you have to.

So make sure to stay out of answer-choice land until you have sufficiently mined the hypothetical. If the question-stem contains a hypothetical, then your job is to get as much out of that piece of information as you can before even looking at the choices. This way, *you* dictate to the test, and not the other way around. You'll then be able to determine the answer and simply pick it off the page.

You'll have a chance to see these major Logic Games principles in action when you review the explanations to the games in the Practice Tests in the back of this book.

The Three Crucial LG Skills

Although the Logic Games section can contain a wide variety of situations and scenarios, certain skills are required again and again. These are the most common:

Sequencing

Logic Games that require sequencing skills have long been a favorite of the test makers. No matter what the scenario in games of this type, the common denominator is that in some way, shape, or form, they all involve putting entities in order. In a typical sequencing game, you may be asked to arrange the cast of characters numerically from left to right, from top to bottom, in days of the week, in a circle, and so on. The sequence may be a sequence of degree—say, ranking the eight smartest test takers from one to eight. On the other hand, the sequence may be based on time, such as one that involves the order of shows broadcast on a radio station. In some cases, there are two or even three orderings to keep track of in a single game.

Fixed and Unfixed Sequences

There are generally two types of sequence games: the fixed, or standard sequence, and the unfixed, or "free floating" sequence. In a fixed sequence game, the placement of entities is very strictly defined. We may be told, for example, that "A is third," or that "X and Y are adjacent," and so on. These are definite, concrete pieces of information, and the game centers around placing as many people into definite spots as possible. In contrast to this, in an unfixed or "free floating" sequence game, our job is to rank the entities only in relation to one another. We're usually never asked to fully determine the ordering of the cast of characters. Instead, the relationships *between* the entities constitute the crux of the game.

SEQUENCING AT A GLANCE

- It's historically the most popular game type.
- It involves putting entities in order.
- It comes in two varieties—fixed and unfixed ("free floating").
- Its orderings can be in time (the sequence of shows on a radio station), space (people standing next to one another in line), or degree (shortest to tallest, worst to best, etcetera).

Typical Issues

The following is a list of the key issues that underlie sequencing games. Each key issue is followed by a corresponding rule—in some cases, with several alternative ways of expressing the same rule. At the end, we'll use these rules to build a miniature Logic Game, so that you can see how rules work together to define and limit a game's "action." These rules all refer to a scenario in which eight events are to be sequenced from first to eighth:

- Which entities are concretely placed in the ordering?

    X is third.

- Which entities are forbidden from a specific position in the ordering?

    Y is not fourth.

- Which entities are next to, adjacent to, or are immediately preceding or following one another?

    X and Y are consecutive.
    X is next to Y.
    No event comes between X and Y.
    X and Y are consecutive in the ordering.

- Which entities *cannot be* next to, adjacent to, or immediately preceding or following one another?

    X does not immediately precede or follow Z.
    X is not immediately before or after Z.
    At least one event comes between X and Z.
    X and Z are not consecutive in the sequence.

- How far apart in the ordering are two particular entities?

    Exactly two events come between X and Q.

- What is the relative position of two entities in the ordering?
    Q comes before T in the sequence.
    T comes after Q in the sequence.

KAPLAN

How a Sequence Game Works

Let's see how rules like those above might combine to create a simple Logic Game.

Eight events—Q, R, S, T, W, X, Y, and Z—are being ordered from first to eighth.

> X is third.
> Y is not fourth.
> X and Y are consecutive.
> Exactly two events come between X and Q.
> Q occurs before T in the sequence.

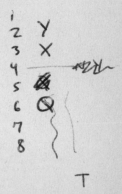

How would you approach this simplified game? Remember our third basic principle: use scratchwork and shorthand. With eight events to sequence from first to eighth, you'd probably want to draw eight dashes in the margin of your test booklet, maybe in two groups of four (so you can easily determine which dash is which). Then take the rules in order of concreteness, starting with the most concrete of all—Rule 1—which tells you that X is third. Fill that into your sketch:

Jump to the next most concrete rule, Rule 4, which tells you that exactly two events come between X and Q. Well, since Q can't obey this rule coming before X, it must come after X—in the sixth space.

$$ \underline{}\ \underline{}\ \underline{X}\ \underline{}\quad \underline{}\ \underline{Q}\ \underline{}\ \underline{} $$

Rule 5 says that Q comes before T. Since Q is sixth, T must be either seventh or eighth. To indicate this, under the sketch, write T with two arrows pointing to the seventh and eighth dashes.

Meanwhile, Rule 3 says that X and Y are consecutive. X is third, so Y will be either second or fourth. Rule 2 clears up that matter. Y can't be fourth, says Rule 2, so it will have to be second:

$$ \underline{}\ \underline{Y}\ \underline{X}\ \underline{}\quad \underline{}\ \underline{Q}\ \underline{}\ \underline{} $$
$$ \nwarrow T \nearrow $$

And this is how the rules work together to build a sequence game. The questions might then present hypothetical information that would set off the "chain of deduction" we mentioned in the basic principles section. You'll see how this works in the sequencing games on the Practice Tests. Those are full-strength sequencing games, so make sure to pay careful attention to the written explanations.

Grouping

All games begin with a set of entities. What sets grouping apart is the "action" of the game, or specifically, what you're asked to do with the entities. In a pure grouping game, unlike sequencing, there's no call for putting the entities in order. Instead, you'll usually be required to "select" a smaller group from the initial group, or "distribute" the entities in some fashion into more than one subgroup. As a distinct skill, grouping differs from sequencing in that you're not really concerned with what order the entities are in, but rather how they're grouped—who's in, who's out, and who can and cannot be with whom in various subgroups.

Grouping Games of Selection and Distribution
In "selection" games, you'll be given the cast of characters and told to select from them a smaller group, based, of course, on a set of rules. For example, a game may include eight musical cassettes, from which you must choose four. Sometimes the test makers specify an exact number for the smaller group, and other times they don't. A small variation of this type occurs when the initial group of entities is itself broken up in groups to begin the game. An example would be a farmer choosing three animals from a group of three cows and five horses.

In "distribution" games, we're more concerned with who goes where than we are with who's chosen and who isn't—who's in and who's out, in other words. Sometimes, every entity will end up in a group—an example is placing or distributing eight marbles into two jars, four to a jar. On the other hand, it's perfectly viable for a game to mandate the placement of three marbles in each jar, leaving two marbles out in the cold.

It's important for you to be aware of the numbers that govern each particular grouping game, because although all grouping games rely on the same general skills, you have to adapt these skills to the specific situations of each. Still, all grouping games revolve around the same basic questions. Is this entity in? Is it out? If it's not in this group, is it in that one?

Like sequencing games, grouping games have a language all their own, and it's up to you to speak that language fluently when you come across games that require this particular skill on your test.

GROUPING AT A GLANCE

- It's a very popular game type.
- It comes in two varieties—selection and distribution.
- The number element is often crucial (how many chosen, how many in each group, etcetera).
- Its action involves deciding if each entity is in or out; if it is in, you may then need to determine where (in distribution games).

Typical Issues—Grouping Games of Selection
The following is a list of the key issues that underlie grouping games of selection. Each key issue is followed by a corresponding rule—in some cases, with several alternative ways of expressing the same rule. At the end, again, we'll use these rules to build a miniature Logic Game.

These rules all refer to a scenario in which you are to select a subgroup of four from a group of eight entities—Q, R, S, T, W, X, Y, and Z:

• Which entities are definitely chosen?

Q is selected.

• Which entities rely on a different entity's selection in order to be chosen?

If X is selected, then Y is selected.
X will be selected only if Y is selected.
X will not be selected unless Y is selected.

Note: A common misconception surrounds the rule, "If X is selected, then Y is selected." This works only in one direction; if X is chosen, Y must be, but if Y is chosen, X may or may not be. Remember the discussion of the second principle above—understand what a rule means, but also what it doesn't mean!

• Which entities must be chosen together, or not at all?

If Y is selected, then Z is selected, and and if Z is selected, then Y is selected.
Y will not be selected unless Z is selected, and vice versa.

• Which entities cannot both be chosen?

If R is selected, then Z is not selected.
If Z is selected, then R is not selected.
R and Z won't both be selected.

How Grouping Games of Selection Work
We can combine these rules to create a rudimentary grouping game of selection:

A professor must choose a group of four books for her next seminar. She must choose from a pool of eight books—Q, R, S, T, W, X, Y, and Z.

> Q is selected.
> If X is selected then Y is selected.
> If Y is selected, Z is selected, and if Z is selected, then Y is selected.
> If R is selected, Z is not selected.

One good way of dealing with this kind of game is to write out the eight letters—four on top, four on the bottom—and then circle the ones that are definitely selected while crossing out the ones that are definitely not selected. Thus, Rule 1 would allow you to circle the Q:

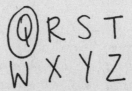

The other rules can't be built into the sketch just yet, since they describe eventualities (what happens if something else happens). Here's where you'd want to use shorthand:

- Rule 2 translates as, "If X, then Y" or "X ——> Y."
- Rule 3 might be rendered as, "YZ together" (as a reminder to choose them together, if at all).
- Rule 4 could be shorthanded as, "Never RZ" (since R and Z are mutually exclusive).

The rules would then be poised to take effect whenever a question would add new hypothetical information, setting off a chain of deduction. For instance, let's say a question reads like so:

> If R is selected, which of the following must be true?

This new information would put the rules into motion. R's inclusion would set off Rule 4—"Never RZ"—so we'd have to circle R and cross out Z:

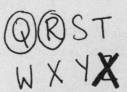

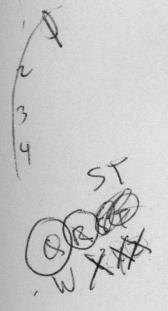

KAPLAN

This would in turn set off Rule 3—"YZ together." Since Z is out, Y is out, because they must be chosen together or not at all:

Now Rule 2 comes into play. "X ——> Y" means that if Y is not chosen, X can't be either (since X's inclusion would require Y's). So we can take the chain of deduction one step further:

A correct answer to this question, then, might be "X is not selected." And that, in a nutshell, is how a (simplified) grouping game of selection works.

Typical Issues—Grouping Games of Distribution
Here are the issues involved in the other kind of grouping game—grouping games of distribution—along with the rules that govern them. These rules, by the way, refer to a scenario in which the members of our old favorite group of eight entities—Q, R, S, T, W, X, Y, Z—have to be distributed into three different classes:

• Which entities are concretely placed in a particular subgroup?

    X is placed in Class 3.

• Which entities are barred from a particular subgroup?

    Y is not placed in Class 2.

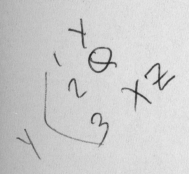

- Which entities must be placed in the same subgroup?

  X is placed in the same class as Z.
  Z is placed in the same class as X.
  X and Z are placed in the same class.

- Which entities cannot be placed in the same subgroup?

  X is not placed in the same class as Y.
  Y is not placed in the same class as X.
  X and Y are not placed in the same class.

- Which entity's placement depends on the placement of a different entity?

  If Y is placed in Class 1, then Q is placed in Class 2.

How Grouping Games of Distribution Work
The above rules, neatly enough, also can combine to form a miniature grouping game of distribution.

Eight students—Q, R, S, T, W, X, Y, and Z—must be subdivided into three different classes—Classes 1, 2, and 3.
    X is placed in Class 3.
    Y is not placed in Class 2.
    X is placed in the same class as Z.
    X is not placed in the same class as Y.
    If Y is placed in Class 1, then Q is placed in Class 2.

A good scratchwork scheme for games of this type would be to draw three circles in your booklet, one for each of the three classes. Then put the eight entities in the appropriate circles as that information becomes known.

Here again, start with the most concrete rule first, which is Rule 1, which definitively places X in Class 3. Rule 2 just as definitively precludes Y from Class 2, so build that into the scratchwork, too:

DON'T BE A MINDLESS DIAGRAMMER!

Remember, scratchwork should be an aid to thinking, not a substitute for thinking. Don't draw diagrams just because you think you have to. Use them only if and when they help you organize your work.

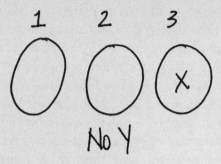

Rule 3 requires Z to join X in Class 3:

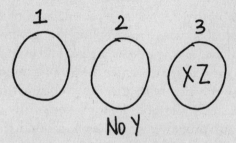

Rule 4, prohibiting Y from being in the same class as X, means that Y can't be in Class 3. But we already know that Y can't be in Class 2. We can deduce, therefore, that Y must go in Class 1. That in turn puts Rule 5 into play: if Y is in Class 1 (as it is here), Q is in Class 2:

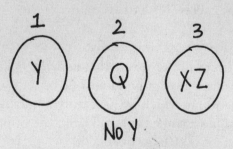

And that is the dynamic of most grouping games of distribution (though, again, in much simplified form). For more complex distribution games, check out the Practice Tests and Explanations in the back of this book.

Matching

The third skill we need to discuss is matching. Matching games have haunted LSAT test takers since they came into favor some years ago. As the name implies, matching games ask you to match up various characteristics about a group of entities. They often require you to distribute many characteristics at once. A game may involve three animals, each assigned a name, a color, and a particular size. It's no wonder test takers get bogged down in these types—there's often a lot to keep track of.

Some people dislike matching games because they feel as if they're being bombarded with information, and they don't know where to start. Organization, as in any game, is crucial for matching games. A table or grid can be helpful, but for some games you need to rely on your instincts to organize the information efficiently based on the particulars of the game. If you do use a sketch, and this goes for any game, remember that *thinking must always precede writing*. A visual representation of a mental thought process can be invaluable, whereas scribbling thoughtlessly for the sake of getting something down on the page is useless, and even detrimental.

One matching hint is to try to center the game around the most important characteristic—the one with the most information attached to it. Going back to the example above, don't necessarily assume that you should organize your thinking, or a sketch, around the animals—there may be a better attribute, one that you know more about, that should take center stage. An efficient test taker spends less time panicking and being intimidated by all of the information in a matching game, and more time visualizing the action and creating a mental picture or a sketch on the page that places the elements into a logical order. If you think through the scenarios and don't get scared off by their seeming complexity, you should find matching games accessible and even fun.

Typical Matching Game Issues

The following is a list of the key issues that underlie matching games. Each key issue is followed by a corresponding rule or set of rules. All of these rules refer to a situation in which we have three animals—a dog, a cat, and a goat. Each animal has a name (Bimpy, Hank, and Sujin), a color (brown, black, or white), and a size (large or small):

- Which entities are matched up?

  The dog is brown.
  The black animal is small.

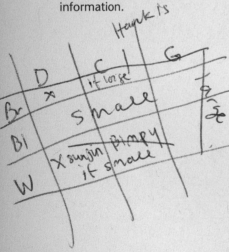

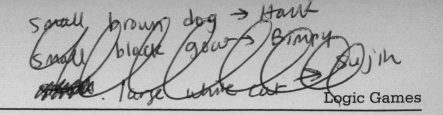

• Which entities are not matched up?

> Bimpy is not white.
> The goat is not large.

• Which entity's matchups depend on the matchups of other entities?

> If the cat is large, then Hank is brown.
> If the white animal is small, then Sujin is not the dog.

Notice that these last rules take the form of if/then statements, which, based on our discussion of Logical Reasoning in the previous chapter, means that the contrapositive can be employed. Whenever rules take this form, you should always work out the contrapositive and then add the result, as a valid deduction, to your view of the game. Remember, the contrapositive can be formed by reversing and negating the terms of an if/then statement. For the first, we get:

> If Hank is NOT brown, then the cat is NOT large.

Taking the contrapositive of the second rule results in this statement:

> If Sujin IS the dog, then the white animal is NOT small.

Both of these new pieces of information are just as powerful as any of the indented rules given in the game's introduction.

How Matching Games Work
You know the drill by now. Let's take some of the rules above and form them into a minilogic game:

> A rancher owns three animals—a dog, a cat, and a goat. The animals are named Bimpy, Hank, and Sujin, though not necessarily in that order. One of the animals is brown, one is black, and one is white. Two of the animals are large and one is small.
>
> The dog is brown.
> The black animal is small.
> Bimpy is not white.
> The goat is not large.
> If the cat is large, then Hank is brown.

THE CONTRAPOSITIVE REDUX

Use the contrapositive on all if-then rules in Logic Games. It will almost always yield an important deduction.

IT'S LIKE MATH

Like math questions, Logic Games questions have definite right and wrong answers. Once you find the answer that works, pick it and move on. There's no need to check out the other choices.

A good way to approach this game would be to set up a grid or chart to keep track of all of the attributes to be matched up:

(animal)	Dog	Cat	Goat
(name) BHS			
(size) LLS			
(color) br bl wh			

Notice that Rules 1 and 4—the most concrete rules—can be built into the sketch immediately.

(animal)	Dog	Cat	Goat
(name) BHS			
(size) LLS			not L
(color) br̶ bl wh	br		

But remember, think about what Rule 4 means, not just what it says. There are only two sizes here—small and large. If the goat is not large, it must be small, and since there are two large and only one small animal, we can deduce the size of the other two as well:

(animal)	Dog	Cat	Goat
(name) BHS			
(size) ~~LS~~	L	L	S not L
(color) ~~br~~ bl wh			

Once we know that the cat is large, moreover, Rule 5 kicks in, telling us that Hank is brown. And since we've already deduced that the brown animal is the large dog, we know that Hank is the large brown dog.

And that's how a simple matching game works. The third game of the Logic Games section on the Practice Test is a typical matching game for you to work on. Pay careful attention to the way in which it's set up, as outlined in the written explanations.

More Logic Game Tips

Here are some other points to keep in mind on the LG section:

Hybrid Games

Many games are what you might call "hybrid games," requiring you to combine sequencing, grouping, and/or matching skills (we'll have a look at one later on when we talk about the five-step method). Keep in mind that while we try to recognize games as a particular type, it's not necessary to attach a strict name to every game you encounter. For example, it really doesn't matter if you categorize a game as a sequencing game with a grouping element or as a grouping game with a sequencing element, as long as you're comfortable with both sets of skills.

LOOK FOR THE COMMON ELEMENT

Rules that deal with one or more of the same entities can often be combined to make important deductions.

No "Best" Choice

Unlike the answer choices in Logical Reasoning and Reading Comprehension, in which the correct answer is the "best" choice, the answers in Logic Games are objectively correct or incorrect. Therefore, when you find an answer that's definitely right, have the confidence to circle it and move on, without wasting time to check the other choices. This is one way to improve your timing on the section.

Common Elements and Deductions

Rules that contain common elements are often the ones that lead to deductions. Consider the following three rules:

> If Sybil goes to the party, then Edna will go to the party.
> If Jacqui goes to the party, then Sherry will not go to the party.
> If Edna goes to the party, then Dale will go to the party.

Rules 1 and 2 have no entities in common, which is a sure sign that we can't deduce anything from combining them. The same goes for Rules 2 and 3. But since Rules 1 and 3 have Edna in common, a deduction is possible (although not guaranteed). In this case, combining Rules 1 and 3 would allow us to deduce another rule: if Sybil goes to the party, then Dale will go also.

Focus on the Important Rules

Not all rules are equal—some are inherently more important than others. Try to focus first on the concrete ones and the ones that have the greatest impact on the situation, specifically the ones that involve the greatest number of the entities. These are also the rules to turn to first whenever you're stuck on a question and don't know how to set off the chain of deduction.

Know the Forms of Question Stems

You must have a solid command of the various forms of Logic Games question stems. When you take a few seconds to think through what kind of statements would be the right and wrong answers to a particular question, your work becomes more time efficient. You're also less likely to slip up at the last minute and pick the wrong thing. The following should clear up any misconceptions you may have regarding what the choices should look like for each of the major types of questions:

- If the question reads: Which one of the following statements *could be true*?—the right answer will be a statement that could be true, and

KAPLAN

the four wrong choices will be statements that definitely cannot be true (that is, statements that must be false).

- If the question reads: Which one of the following statements *cannot be true?*—the right answer will be a statement that cannot be true, and the four wrong choices will be statements that either must be true or merely could be true.

- If the question reads: Which one of the following statements *must be true?*—the right answer will be a statement that must be true, and the four wrong choices will be statements that either cannot be true or merely could be true.

- If the question reads: All of the following statements *could be true EXCEPT . . . ,* the right answer will be a statement that cannot be true, and the four wrong choices will be statements that either could be true or even must be true.

- If the question reads: All of the following statements *must be true EXCEPT . . . ,* the right answer will be a statement that either cannot be true, or merely could be true, and the four wrong choices will be statements that must be true.

- If the question reads: Which one of the following statements *could be false?*—the right answer will be a statement that cannot be true or could be true or false, and the four wrong choices will be statements that must be true.

- If the question reads: Which one of the following statements *must be false?*—the right answer will be a statement that cannot be true, and the four wrong choices will be statements that either must be true or merely could be true.

IS NOTHING CLICKING?

If you find you can't make a single important deduction by combining rules, you're probably missing something. Check the game introduction and rules again to make sure you're not misinterpreting something.

The Kaplan Five-Step Method for Logic Games

Now that you have some Logic Games background, it's time to see how you can marshall that knowledge into a systematic approach to games. The five steps of the Kaplan Method are as follows.

1. Get an Overview
Read carefully the game's introduction and rules to establish the "cast of characters," the "action," and the number limits governing the game.

2. Visualize and Map out the Game
Make a mental picture of the situation, and let it guide you as you create a sketch, or some other kind of scratchwork, if need be to help you keep track of the rules and handle new information.

3. Consider the Rules Individually
As you think through the meaning and implications of each rule, you have three choices. You can:

- Build it directly into your sketch of the game situation
- Jot down the rule in shorthand form to help you remember it
- Underline or circle rules that don't lend themselves to the first two techniques

4. Combine the Rules
Look for common elements among the rules; that's what will lead you to make deductions. Treat these deductions as additional rules, good for the whole game.

5. Work on the Questions Systematically
Read the question stems carefully! Take special notice of words such as *must, could, cannot, not, impossible,* and *except.* As always, use the hypothetical information offered in *if*-clauses to set off a chain of deduction.

Using the Kaplan Five-Step Method for Logic Games

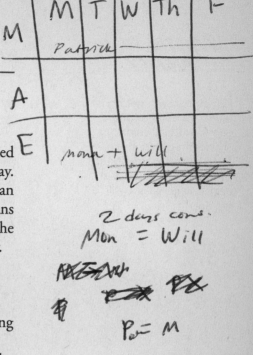

Here's how the approach can work with an actual Logic Game:

Questions 1–2

Five workers—Mona, Patrick, Renatta, Saffie, and Will—are scheduled to clean apartments on five days of a single week, Monday to Friday. There are three cleaning shifts available each day—a morning shift, an afternoon shift, and an evening shift. No more than one worker cleans in any given shift. Each worker cleans exactly two shifts during the week, but no one works more than one cleaning shift in a single day.

Exactly two workers clean on each day of the week.

Mona and Will clean on the same days of the week.

Patrick doesn't clean on any afternoon or evening shifts during the week.

Will doesn't clean on any morning or afternoon shifts during the week.

Mona cleans on two consecutive days of the week.

Saffie's second cleaning shift of the week occurs on an earlier day of the week than Mona's first cleaning shift.

1. Which one of the following must be true?

    (A) Saffie cleans on Tuesday afternoon.
    (B) Patrick cleans on Monday morning.
    (C) Will cleans on Thursday evening.
    (D) Renatta cleans on Friday afternoon.
    (E) Mona cleans on Tuesday morning.

2. If Will does not clean on Friday, which one of the following could be false?

    (A) Renatta cleans on Friday.
    (B) Saffie cleans on Tuesday.
    (C) Mona cleans on Wednesday.
    (D) Saffie cleans on Monday.
    (E) Patrick cleans on Tuesday.

WHAT'S IN A NAME?

Remember, you get no points for categorizing a game; you get points for answering questions correctly. Don't worry about what to call a game. Just decide what skills it will require.

(Note that there are only two questions accompanying this game; a typical logic game will have five to seven questions.)

1. Get an Overview

We need to schedule five workers, abbreviated M, P, R, S, and W, in a particular order during a five-day calendar week, Monday to Friday. The ordering element tells us we're dealing with a sequencing task, though there is a slight grouping element involved in that a couple of the rules deal with grouping issues—namely, which people can or cannot clean on the same day of the week as each other. That makes this a "hybrid" game—but remember, it doesn't matter what you call it, as long as you can do it.

Be very careful about the numbers governing this game; they go a long way in defining how the game works. There are to be exactly two workers per day (never cleaning on the same shift). Each worker must clean exactly two shifts, and since workers are forbidden to take two shifts in the same day, this means that each worker will clean on exactly two days. So, in effect, ten out of the fifteen available shifts will be taken, and five will be left untouched.

2. Visualize and Map out the Game

Go with whatever you feel is the most efficient way to keep track of the situation. Most people would settle on a sketch of the five days, each broken up into three shifts, like so:

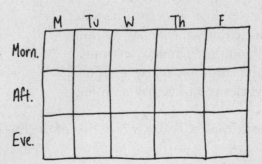

Into this sketch—one letter per box—each entity will have to go twice (each worker does two shifts, remember). So your pool of entities to place would be: MMPPRRSSWW. You might want to include five Xs (or Øs) for the five shifts that won't be taken by anyone.

3. Consider the Rules Individually

We've already dealt with some of the number-related rules hidden in the game's introduction. Now let's consider this statement from the intro:

> No more than one worker cleans in any given shift.

Make sure you interpret rules like this correctly. You may have to paraphrase, in your own words, its exact meaning. In this case: two workers per shift is no good, three is out of the question, etcetera. But it doesn't mean that any given shift *must* have a worker. If the test makers meant to imply that, they would have written, "Exactly one worker cleans on every given shift." Notice the difference in wording. It's subtle, but it has a huge impact on the game.

Let's consider the other rules:

1) We've already handled Rule 1. You may wish to jot down "2 a day," or something like that, to remind you of this important information.

2) Mona and Will clean on the same days, and that holds for both of the days they clean. Shorthand this any way that seems fitting (one suggestion is to draw MW with a circle around it on your page).

3) and 4) We can handle these two rules together because they're so similar. You can shorthand these rules as they are, but you'd be doing yourself a great disservice. Instead, first work out their implications, which is actually a pretty simple matter. If Patrick doesn't clean afternoons or evenings, he *must* clean mornings. If Will doesn't clean mornings or afternoons, he *must* clean evenings. Always take the rules as far as you can, and *then* jot down their implications on your page for reference.

5) This one is pretty self-explanatory; Mona's shifts must be on consecutive days, such as Thursday and Friday. MM might be a good way to shorthand this.

6) Here's another sequencing rule—you must place both Ss for Saffie on earlier days of the week than the two Ms, for Mona. That means that Saffie and Mona can't clean on the same day (although we already knew that from Rule 2), and that Mona's shifts can't come before Saffie's. Try shorthanding this as (S...S...MM).

4. Combine the Rules

This is the crucial stage for most games. Here, notice that Mona appears in three of the six indented rules; that's a good indication that combining these rules should lead somewhere useful. Combining Rule 2 and Rule 5 gives us two Mona/Will days in a row:

Will must be scheduled for evening shifts (remember, we turned Rule 4 into this positive statement). That means that Mona would take the morning or afternoon shift on these consecutive days.

Rule 6 concerns Mona as well: two Saffies before the two Monas. How is this possible? We need two S's on different days to come before the two consecutive M's. If Saffie's cleaning shifts are as early in the week as possible, she'll clean on Monday and Tuesday. That means that the earliest day that Mona can clean (and Will as well, thanks to Rule 2) is Wednesday. There's our first really key deduction:

> Mona and Will cannot clean on Monday and Tuesday;
> they must clean Wednesday, Thursday, or Friday.

Do we stop there? No, of course not. The difference between the Logic Games expert and the Logic Games novice is that the expert knows how to press on when further deductive possibilities exist. If you relate this deduction back to Rule 5, it becomes clear that Mona and Will must clean on Wednesday and Thursday, *or* on Thursday and Friday. This brings us to another big deduction:

> Either way, Mona and Will must clean on Thursday. Thanks to Rule 4, we can slot Will in for Thursday evening. Mona will then take Thursday morning *or* afternoon. The other Mona/Will day must be either Wednesday or Friday, to remain consecutive.

The following sketch shows what your completed sketch may look like, with as many of the rules built into it as possible.

KAPLAN

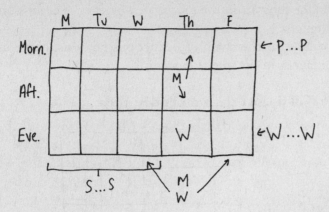

Now that we've combined the rules and have even uncovered a few big deductions, it's time to move on to the questions.

5. Work on the Questions Systematically

Now you'll see how all the work we did up front pays off. Question 1 offers no hypothetical information; it simply asks what must be true. And since we've already deduced a few things that must be true, we can scan the choices for one that matches any one of our newly discovered pieces of information. It doesn't take long to spot choice (C)—it's our big deduction staring us right in the face. You shouldn't even waste time checking the other choices. Instead, have the confidence that you've done the right work the right way, and circle (C) and move on. [Just for the record, for those of you who are curious, (A), (B), and (D) could be true, but need not be, while (E), as we discovered earlier, is an impossibility.]

Question 2 contains a hypothetical: no Will on Friday. One glance at our sketch tells us that the second Mona/Will cluster must therefore be placed on Wednesday, next to the Thursday Mona/Will group. Saffie must then clean on Monday and Tuesday, in order to satisfy Rule 6 (although we don't yet know the exact shifts she takes during those days).

That brings us to the two questions that test takers ask all too infrequently: "Who's left?" and more importantly, "Where can they go?" Two Ps and two Rs are left to place, with one spot on Monday, one spot on Tuesday, and two spots on Friday open to place them. How can this be done? Friday can't get both Ps or both Rs (from the last sentence in the introduction), so it will have to get one of each, with P in the morning and R in either the afternoon or evening. The other P and the other R will join S on Monday or Tuesday, in either order. Of course, whichever day P is on, he must be in the morning, whereas the exact shifts for R and S are ambiguous.

Look at how far the chain of deductions takes us, beginning with the simple statement in the question stem:

If Will doesn't clean on Friday, then . . .

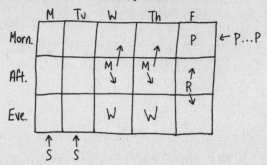

With all of this information at our disposal, there's not a question in the world we can't answer correctly. This one asks for a statement that could be false—which means that the four wrong choices will all be things that must be true. And in fact, choices (A) through (D) match the situation in this question perfectly, while (E) merely could be true: Patrick's first cleaning shift of the week *could be* on Tuesday, but it just as easily *could be* on Monday as well. (His second shift must be on Friday, of course.) (E) is therefore the only choice that could be false.

Conclusion

This concludes our general discussion of the Logic Games section. Try to use the Five-Step Method, and all of the techniques mentioned in this chapter, when you work through the following set of practice questions and the games in the Practice Tests.

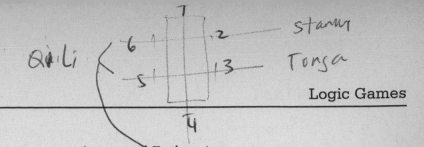

Logic Games Practice Set

<u>Directions:</u> Each group of questions is based on a passage or a set of conditions. You may wish to draw a diagram to answer some of the questions. Choose the <u>best</u> answer for each question. (The answer and explanation can be found at the end of each question.)

Questions 1–5: Six people—Matt, Ned, Qi Li, Stanley, Tonga, and Vladimir—are sitting around a rectangular table with six seats, one at the head of the table, one at the foot, and two on each long side of the table. The chairs are numbered 1 through 6 in a clockwise fashion, beginning with the chair at the head of the table, such that Chairs 1 and 4, 2 and 6, and 3 and 5 are directly across the table from each other.

Consecutively numbered chairs are considered adjacent. Chairs 1 and 6 are also considered adjacent.

Ned is sitting in chair 1 or chair 4.

Stanley and Tonga are sitting in adjacent chairs on one long side of the table.

Qi Li and Stanley are not sitting in adjacent chairs.

Question 1

Which one of the following could be the seating arrangement of the six people in Chairs 1 through 6, respectively?

(A) Ned, Vladimir, Tonga, Stanley, Matt, Qi Li
(B) Vladimir, Stanley, Tonga, Ned, Matt, Qi Li
(C) Qi Li, Matt, Ned, Stanley, Tonga, Vladimir
(D) Ned, Tonga, Qi Li, Vladimir, Stanley, Matt
(E) Qi Li, Vladimir, Matt, Ned, Tonga, Stanley

ⒶⒷⒸⒹⒺ

Answer and Explanation

This game involves placing people around a table, and it's pretty straightforward. The table is clearly described, maybe even too clearly. It's awfully wordy for all it has to say.

There is a rectangle in which Chair 1 and 4 are at opposite ends, the head and foot, with Chairs 2 and 3 adjacent to each other on one side, and Chairs 5 and 6 adjacent on the other. You go clockwise around the table, the rules tell you, and, although you might have figured it out for yourself, you're even told exactly which chairs are opposite which. So this all turns out to be pretty simple to sketch.

Rule 2 says Ned is in Chair 1 or 4. Of course, that means he is either at the head or foot of the table. You could have written a note to yourself at the top of the page: "N head or foot." And, as a result, each time you drew the table to answer a question, you would have seen that note and remembered right away to put Ned at the bottom or the top of the rectangular table.

Same thing for the other rules. You could have written in big letters "ST" at the top of the page to remind yourself that those two characters, Stanley and Tonga, have to be next to each other along one of the table's two long edges. Alternatively, you might have written "ST = 2 and 3 or 5 and 6." That's just another way of noting the relevant information. And there's no need to do much more with Rule 4 than write something like "Q not = S," a reminder always to separate Qi Li and Stanley.

Armed with all that information, you should be able to make short work of Question 1, which asks for the one and only one acceptable sequence. Ned has to be in Chair 1 or 4. That means that choice (C) is unacceptable since (C) puts him in Chair 3. Cross out (C); there's no point in ever looking at it again. Next, remember that Stanley and Tonga have to be adjacent, and that eliminates choice (D), which puts two people between S and T in either direction.

Moreover, they have to be adjacent along a long side of the table, that is, in Chairs 2 or 3 or 5 and 6. This eliminates choice (A), in which they are next to each other but Stanley is sitting in Chair 4, that is, at the foot of the table.

Nothing seems to have violated Rule 4 yet, but dollars to doughnuts, one choice will. And it turns out to be choice (E). You can't have Q in 1 and S in 6 because that, according to the first rule, counts as adjacency. You're left with choice (B), which must be okay since the other four choices violate rules. (B) is correct, although you needn't bother to check it at this point as long as you're sure the others are wrong. Just choose (B) and get out.

Question 2

If Vladimir is sitting in Chair 4, then which one of the following pairs must be sitting in adjacent seats?

(A) Matt and Ned
(B) Matt and Qi Li
(C) Ned and Qi Li
(D) Ned and Stanley
(E) Stanley and Vladimir

Ⓐ Ⓑ Ⓒ Ⓓ Ⓔ

Answer and Explanation

A quick sketch for Question 2 puts V in Chair 4, and should immediately put Ned in Chair 1. He has to be in one or the other, and since someone else is in 4, he has to be in Chair 1. On one side of the table, as always, you put Stanley and Tonga. You don't know which side right now. That leaves two people, Qi Li and Matt, and they, too, will be along one long side of the table. That's all that's left. So, when Question 2 asks who has to be next to each other, you should look

for Qi Li and Matt, and you'll find them in correct choice (B). All of the other pairs *could* be adjacent but needn't be. So it's choice (B), and you're done with that one almost as quickly as you started.

Question 3

If Qi Li is sitting in Chair 1, then which one of the following must be sitting adjacent to her?

(A) Ned
(B) Matt
(C) Stanley
(D) Tonga
(E) Vladimir

Ⓐ Ⓑ Ⓒ Ⓓ Ⓔ

Answer and Explanation

Question 3 can be done very quickly, too. Putting Qi Li in Chair 1, as you're told to do, means that Ned goes to Chair 4 this time. That leaves Stanley and Tonga, once again, along one of the long sides. But remember Rule 4: you have to separate Qi Li and Stanley. Therefore, Qi Li, who will have to sit next to either S or T, since she's at the head, will be next to Tonga for sure, choice (D). Ned, choice (A), is opposite Qi Li. Stanley, choice (C), can't be next to her. And, certainly, either Matt, choice (B), or Vladimir, choice (E), will have to be next to Qi Li, too, although you cannot choose between them. So it's Tonga, choice (D), for Question 3.

KAPLAN

Matt   Vladimir
Qili   } 6 |2 stanley|
          5 |3 Tonga|
                4
              Ned

Question 4

If Stanley and Vladimir are sitting in adjacent chairs, then Matt could be sitting in any of the following EXCEPT:

(A) Chair 1
(B) Chair 2
(C) Chair 3
(D) Chair 5
(E) Chair 6

Ⓐ Ⓑ Ⓒ Ⓓ Ⓔ

Answer and Explanation

Question 4 asks, "Where could Matt *not* be?" The rules tell you very little about Matt, so build on the concrete information you're given about the other characters and see where that leaves Matt at the end.

Stanley and Vladimir are next to each other, you're told to assume. Stanley and Tonga are likewise next to each other, right? So, both V and T will flank Stanley at the table. However, you specifically know that Stanley and Tonga take up one long side of the table. This means that Vladimir will have to end up at one end of the table or the other, either the head or the foot. Well, the other end, the head or the foot, is reserved for Ned. So if you look at the answer choices with the head and the foot going to Vladimir and Ned, there's no way that Matt or anyone else, besides those two, could occupy Chair 1 or Chair 4. The former has been chosen as the correct answer, choice (A). As for the others, Matt could take any of those. He and Qi Li will occupy 2 and 3 or 5 and 6, but more than that you don't know. So it's choice (A) for Question 4.

Question 5

If Stanley is sitting in Chair 3 and Matt is sitting in Chair 6, then which one of the following pairs CANNOT sit directly across the table from each other?

(A) Ned and ~~Qi Li~~
(B) Ned and ~~Vladimir~~
(C) ~~Qi Li and Stanley~~
(D) Qi Li and Vladimir
(E) Stanley and Vladimir

Ⓐ Ⓑ Ⓒ Ⓓ Ⓔ

Answer and Explanation

Question 5, in its exploration of who can or cannot sit across from whom, explicitly places two people in chairs and allows you to do likewise with a third. Specifically, if Stanley is in Chair 3, Tonga (who again has to be next to Stanley along a long side of the table) has to take the other chair along that side, Chair 2. Stanley in 3, Tonga in 2, and Matt in 6. Now, at this point, a lot depends on the placement of Ned. Both Chair 1, the head, and Chair 4, the foot, are available to him. If Ned is in Chair 1, the head, that is between Tonga on his left and Matt on his right, that leaves two chairs, 4 and 5, available to Qi Li and Vladimir. But Qi Li can't take Chair 4 while Stanley is in Chair 3. Rule 4 forbids it. So you would have to have Vladimir in 4 and Qi Li in 5. Under those circumstances, you would see choice (C), Qi Li and Stanley opposite each other in Chairs 5 and 3 respectively, and also choice (B), Ned and Vladimir opposite each other at the ends of the table.

But suppose Ned's in Chair 4 at the foot. With Matt in 6, Ned in 4, Stanley in 3, and Tonga in 2, the possibilities are slightly more numerous. Chairs 1 and 5 remain for Qi Li and Vladimir, with no restrictions as to which one is in which. Under those circumstances, you could certainly have Ned in 4 opposite Qi Li in 1, leaving Vladimir in 5 opposite Stanley in 3. And thus A and E must be rejected. Either is a possibility. But under no circumstances will you ever see Qi Li and Vladimir opposite each other (as it turns out, in none of these scenarios did you see that), and that makes choice (D) correct for Question 5.

Questions 6–11: A history teacher has administered two different tests—one on ancient history, one on modern history—to the five students in his honors class. The five students are Ken, Lea, Marc, Nell, and Otis. The ten exams were graded on the descending scale of A, B, C, D, and F, with A being the highest grade and F the lowest.

No student who received a B on the ancient history exam received lower than a C on the modern history exam.

Marc and exactly one other student each received an A on the modern history exam.

Exactly two students received Fs on the ancient history exam.

Ken and Otis each received a higher grade on the modern history exam than on the ancient history exam.

Lea received a B on her ancient history exam.

Question 6

If Nell and Marc each received an A on the ancient history exam, then which one of the following must be Ken's grade in the ancient history exam?

(A) A
(B) B
(C) C
(D) D
(E) F

Ⓐ Ⓑ Ⓒ Ⓓ Ⓔ

Answer and Explanation

In this game, you have to wade through some manipulations of two parallel grading scales. This is a grouping game of distribution. Five students each take two tests and receive a grade of A, B, C, D, or F on each test. You have to distribute the grades, and you're given five indented rules to help you figure out who got what grade.

The first rule can be best understood as a simple if/then statement. If a student got a B in ancient history, then that student got no lower than a C in modern history. Put another way, if a student got a B in ancient history, then that student got an A, B, or C in modern history. You could very well have written it that way at the top of the page. That way every time in the course of the game you saw someone get a B in ancient history, you could have referred to the note to see what follows.

Next you get a rule about someone's specific grade. You can keep track of that data as well as everything else you've learned about people's specific grades in a very simple way. Draw two columns, one labeled *ancient history* and the other *modern history,* and label them with the names of the five students. You can enter Marc's A under the modern history column, and at the bottom of that column you can note *one more A,* or something like that. In the same way, at the bottom of the ancient history column, you can note two Fs, and thus incorporate the information provided by Rule 3. You can also, skipping ahead to Rule 5, note Lea's B in ancient history. The point of jotting all this down, remember, is so that you can easily refer to it and access it in the course of the questions.

The remaining rule, the fourth one, is a little tougher to jot down. You could write *better grade* in the modern history column next to Ken's name, and do the same thing next to Otis's name in the same column. If you were to note for Ken and Otis that the better grade would fall in the modern history column, you would probably be able to remember that their ancient history grades are lower, and proceed accordingly. But again, it doesn't matter how you deal with a rule, whether you jot it down or write it in shorthand on the page, provided that you get the rule right, and that you are able to remember it during the course of the game.

By the way, you might have stopped at some point to note that, since Ken and Otis did better on the modern exam than the ancient, neither of them could have gotten an F in modern history. Right? You can't do worse than an F. This may not seem very significant as a deduction, but it is deducible, and it does prove to be a key element in a question coming up, as you'll see in a few minutes.

Okay, there's at least one more major thing you should realize. Lea is affected by Rule 1. Based on that rule, you can jot down A, B, or C next to Lea in the modern history column, because Lea must have received one of those three grades on that exam. Can you deduce anything else here? Not really. Anyone—Ken, Lea, Nell, or Otis—could get the remaining A in modern history. Any two of Ken, Marc, Nell, and Otis could get the two Fs in ancient history. And you have no idea of how anything else falls out. So it's time to move on to the questions.

Question 6 starts out very concretely by telling you to assume that Nell and Marc got As on the ancient history test. This works out pretty simply. You know from Rule 3 that there were exactly 2 Fs on that test. And you know already that Lea didn't get an F because she got a B. With Nell and Marc also eliminated from contention for those Fs, it has to follow that the only two people who remain, Ken and Otis, got the Fs. So not only did Ken get an F, choice (E), but so did Otis.

This sort of process of elimination is very important in Logic Games. Here, you have to keep thinking of the fact that once you've identified the grades of one or more students, the restrictions given in the rules may allow you to figure out some more grades. And in this game there are only five students involved, which also has an impact. Anyway, (E) is correct for Question 6.

Question 7

Which one the following students could possibly have received an F on the modern history exam?

(A) Ken
(B) Lea
(C) Marc
(D) Nell
(E) Otis

Answer and Explanation

Question 7 involves a little more thinking, but it's still pretty easy if you keep your cool. Who could have received an F in modern history? You should see immediately that it's impossible for Lea to get an F on a modern history exam, because she received a B on the ancient history exam, so, according to Rule 1, she must get at least a C on the modern history exam. Marc couldn't have received an F on the exam, either, because Rule 2 tells you that he got an A. So Marc is out. What about the remaining folks, Ken, Otis, and Nell? This was covered back in the discussion of Rule 4. Ken and Otis did worse on ancient history than on modern history, but if one of them had received an F on modern history, where could he go from there? If a student got an F in modern history there would be no room to do worse on ancient history, as the rule requires. Therefore, Ken and Otis did better than an F on modern history. This leaves you with Nell, choice (D), the correct answer to Question 7. Maybe no one got an F on that test, but only Nell *could* have done so.

Question 8

If exactly three of the students each received a D on the modern history exam, then all of the following must be true EXCEPT:

(A) Ken received an F on the ancient history exam.
(B) Lea received an A on the modern history exam.
(C) Marc received a B on the ancient history exam.
(D) Nell received a D on the modern history exam.
(E) Otis received an F on the ancient history exam.

Ⓐ Ⓑ Ⓒ Ⓓ Ⓔ

Answer and Explanation

Question 8 is one of those in which you're given four true statements and you have to find the one bad apple. The best way to approach this is to take the information you're given, plug it in, and see what happens. Do that first before you worry about eliminating all the answer choices. In this case, if three students got Ds on the modern history exam, then you have all the grades mapped out. Why? Because after those three Ds there are only two students unaccounted for, and you already know that Marc and one other student got As. Furthermore, you know that Lea must be the one who got the A with Marc because, having

received a B on the ancient history exam, she can't get less than a C on the modern exam. Therefore, Ken, Otis, and Nell must be the three students who, according to the stem, have received Ds on the modern exam. This means you've ruled out choices (B) and (D). You know that both of those choices must be true. What else can you conclude? Rule 4 comes in handy here. Ken's and Otis's Ds on the modern test mean that both of them got Fs on ancient history. Right? Their ancient history grade has to be lower than their modern history grade, and only F is lower than D. So choices (A) and (D) are also true. Ken and Otis must have received Fs. That leaves choice (C), which certainly may be true, but doesn't have to be. Marc might have received an ancient history B, but not necessarily, so it's choice (C) for Question 8.

Question 9

If Ken and Otis each received a C on the ancient history exam, and if Nell received an A on the modern history exam, then what is the maximum total number of Bs that could have been received by the five students?

(A) 3
(B) 4
(C) 5
(D) 6
(E) 7

Ⓐ Ⓑ Ⓒ Ⓓ Ⓔ

Answer and Explanation

Question 9 begins more concretely than any of the previous questions. You start by resketching your columns off to the side, a sketch that includes what you've learned from the rules and then puts in what you're told for this question: Ken's and Otis's ancient history Cs, and Nell's modern history A. The question: "What's the maximum number of Bs all around?"

Start with ancient history. You have to factor in the need for two Fs in the ancient history column, and with Ken, Lea, and Otis now variously getting Bs or Cs in ancient history, Marc and Nell have to bite the bullet and take those Fs. So only one B will come out of ancient history, the one bestowed on Lea by the original rule.

Look at the B grade in modern history. The As are set. According to this question and Rule 2, Marc and Nell get those As. Ken and Otis, according to Rule 4, have to improve on their ancient history Cs, and there are no As left. Therefore, Ken and Otis definitely get Bs here. Lea could get a modern history B, too. Rule 1 doesn't forbid it. So you have three definite Bs and one potential B for a total of four. There could be as many as four Bs here, so (B) is the correct choice for Question 9.

Question 10

Assume that each student was awarded 4 points for each A, 3 for each B, 2 for each C, 1 for each D, and no points for each F. If Otis received a total of 6 points for his two exams, then what is the maximum total number of points Ken could have received for his?

(A) 4
(B) 5
(C) 6
(D) 7
(E) 8

Ⓐ Ⓑ Ⓒ Ⓓ Ⓔ

Answer and Explanation

Question 10 tells you to understand and make use of a 0–4 grading point system, one that (happily enough) you are probably familiar with from everyday life. You're also told that Otis received a total of 6

points between his two exams. Given the system—4 points for an A, 3 for a B, 2 for a C, 1 for a D, and 0 for an F—without too much trouble you can figure out exactly what Otis's two grades were. Why? Because there's only one combination of grades that can give Otis 6 points while abiding by Rule 4. He must have received a C on the ancient history exam and an A on the modern—2 plus 4. Of course, 3 plus 3 is impossible, because one of the grades has to be better than the other. Now, the big impact of all this is determining that you're out of As to give in modern history. The only As go to Marc and someone else, and in this question you've just deduced that the other A belongs to Otis. Therefore, the best grade Ken can possibly get in modern history is a B for 3 points. And since his ancient history grade has to be inferior to his modern history grade, the best he can possibly do in ancient history is a C for 2 points. His points add up to 5, so that's the best possible point total Ken can get. And 5 points is correct—choice (B) for Question 10.

Question 11

Assume that each student was awarded 4 points for each A, 3 for each B, 2 for each C, 1 for each D, and no points for each F. If Lea and Marc received the same total number of points for the two exams, and if Nell received an A on both exams, then what is the maximum number of points Otis could have received for his two exams?

(A) 3
(B) 4
(C) 5
(D) 6
(E) 7

Ⓐ Ⓑ Ⓒ Ⓓ Ⓔ

Answer and Explanation

This same point system is in effect for Question 11. The length of Questions 10 and 11 might have seemed a little daunting at first until you realized that both of them make use of the same familiar, logical point system. Anyway, your goal is a decision about Otis's maximum score.

Nell gets two As. The net effect of that is, once again, all the available modern history As have been given. As noted several times, only Marc and one other person get As on the test. Here, that other person is Nell. You're to assume that Lea, with 3 points for her B in ancient history, and Marc with 4 points for his A in modern history, end up with the same point total. You should investigate what that total is or could be and remember, thanks to Rule 1, the only possibilities for Lea's modern history grade are A, B, and C.

But wait a minute. A grade of A is out—there are no modern history As left. So Lea's total is either 6 based on receiving two Bs or 5 points for a B in ancient history and a C in modern. Marc, too, will have a total of 5 or 6, and since he already has 4 points from modern history, it follows that in ancient history Marc got either a C for 2 points or a D for 1 point.

Now think a little more about ancient history. You need 2 Fs there. They don't belong to Lea, Marc, or Nell, so it's Ken and Otis who get Fs or 0 points. And that makes Otis's best possible total 3, choice (A). With an F in ancient history and no more As available in modern, the best Otis can hope for is a 3-point B in modern history, so it's choice (A) for Question 11.

CHAPTER 4

READING COMPREHENSION

Reading Comprehension is the only question type that appears on all major standardized tests, and the reason isn't too surprising: no matter what academic area you pursue, you have to make sense of dense, unfamiliar prose. Law, of course, is no exception. The topics for LSAT Reading Comp passages are taken from four areas:

- Social sciences
- Natural sciences
- Humanities
- Law

These passages tend to be long, densely worded, and difficult—not unlike at least some of the material you'll face in law school. So right now is a good time to start shoring up your reading skills, both for the test and for your future study and practice of law.

A Word about Outside Knowledge

On the LSAT, no outside knowledge on your part is presupposed, and that holds for the Reading Comp section, too. It's not necessary to know anything about the topics covered in the passages; everything you'll need to answer every question is included in the passages themselves. However, the passages are always logical, and always reflect ideas that you have heard about and can understand. Don't read in a vacuum—relate what you read to your world, and recognize the common sense of

THE PERILS OF OUTSIDE KNOWLEDGE

Certainly knowing a little about the topic discussed in a Reading Comp passage can be helpful. If you can relate the ideas in the passage to what you know of the world, you'll be more confident. But remember to answer the questions based on what's in the passage, not on what you may have learned elsewhere about the topic.

the text. One warning, though: The questions test your understanding of the author's points, not your previous understanding or personal point of view on the topic.

So use your own knowledge to help you understand the passages, but be careful not to let it infer with answering questions correctly.

The Seven Basic Principles of Reading Comprehension

Improvement at Reading Comprehension requires practice and patience. You may not see dramatic improvement after taking only one section. But with ongoing practice, the principles below will help to increase your skill and confidence on this section by the day of the test.

1. Read the First Third of the Passage Carefully

The first third of any passage usually introduces the topic and scope, the author's main idea/primary purpose, the author's tone, and almost always hints at the structure that the passage will follow. Let's take a closer look at these crucial elements of a Reading Comp passage.

Topic, Scope, and Purpose

Topic and *scope* are both objective terms, meaning they include no specific reference to the author's point of view. The difference between them is that the topic is broader; the scope narrows the topic. Scope is particularly important because the (many) answer choices that depart from it will always be wrong. The broad topic of "The Battle of Gettysburg" would be a lot to cover in 450 words. We should ask, "What *aspect* of the battle does the author take up?"—and, because of length limitations, it's likely to be a pretty small chunk. Whatever that "chunk" is—the prebattle scouting, or how the battle was fought, or the effects of the battle on the U.S. political scene—that will be the passage's scope. Answer choices that deal with anything outside of this narrowly defined chunk will be wrong.

The topic/scope distinction ties into the all-important author's purpose. The author deliberately chooses to narrow the scope by including certain aspects of the broader topic and excluding others. Why the author makes those choices has to do with why the passage is being written in the first place. We can say that the topic is broadly stated and objective (for instance, a passage's topic might be "solving world hunger"). Scope is also objective, but narrower (a new technology for solving world hunger) and

ZOOMING IN

Reading the first third of the passage is a zooming-in process. First, you get a sense of the general topic. Then you pin down the more specific scope of the passage. Finally, you glean the author's purpose in writing the passage—and the main idea that he or she is trying to get across about that particular subject.

leads rather quickly to the author's subjective purpose (the author is writing in order to describe a new technology and its promising uses). And this is what turns into the author's main idea, which will be discussed at greater length in the next principle.

All this leads to a clear point of attack. Don't just "read" the passage; instead, try to do the following three things: identify the topic; narrow it down to the precise scope that the author includes; and make a hypothesis about why the author is writing and where he or she is going with it. A clear conception of these three things translates directly into points.

Structure and Tone

In a quest to master the content side of the passages—namely, *what* the author says—test takers are notorious for ignoring the less glamorous, but just as important, structural side—namely, *how* the author says it. One of the keys to success on this section is to understand not only the purpose, but also the structure of each passage. Why? Simply because the questions ask both what the author says, *and* how he or she says it. The following is a list of the classic LSAT passage structures:

- Passages based on a strong opinion
- Passages based on a serious problem or situation
- Passages based on differing opinions
- Passages based on significant new findings (often science passages)

Many LSAT passages have been based on one of these classic structures, or a variation thereof. You've most likely seen these structures at work in passages before, even if unconsciously. Your task is to seek them out actively as you begin to read a passage—usually, the structure is announced within the first third of the passage. Let these classic structures act as a "jump start" in your search for the passage's "big picture" and purpose.

As for "how" the author makes his or her point, try to note the author's position within these structures, usually indicated by the author's tone. For example, in the third structure, the author may simply relate the two sides of the story, or may at some point jump in and take a side, or even reject the conflicting opinions in favor of her own. In the first structure, the opinion could be the author's, in which case the author's tone may be opinionated, argumentative, heated, or passionate. On the other hand, the author could simply be describing the strongly held opinions of someone else. This author's writing style would be more descriptive, fac-

DON'T BE TONE DEAF

Some passages have a strong tone—i.e., the author has a definite viewpoint on the topic and is expressing it with emotion. Other passages have a more even tone—they report information without much emotion or a discernible angle. Distinguishing one from the other is an important skill in Reading Comprehension.

tual, and even-handed. His or her method may involve mere storytelling, or the simple relaying of information, which is altogether different from the former case.

Notice the difference in tone between the two types of authors. Correct answer choices for a primary purpose question in the former case would use terms like *argue for, propose,* and *demonstrate,* whereas correct choices for the same type of question in the latter case would use terms like *describe* and *discuss.* Correct answers are always consistent with the author's tone, so noting the author's tone is a good way to score points.

2. Focus on the Main Idea

Almost every passage boils down to one big idea. We discussed above how topic leads to scope, and then in turn to the author's purpose in writing the passage. An author's primary purpose and main idea are forever intertwined. Take, for example, the hypothetical passage stated above, in which the author had the following purpose.

> The author is writing in order to describe a new technology and its promising uses.

The main idea is simply a restatement of this without the active verb structure:

> Biochemical engineering (or whatever new technology is discussed) can help solve world hunger.

Your job is to cut past the fancy wording and focus on this big idea. Most often, the main idea will be presented in the first third of the passage. But occasionally the author will build up to it gradually, in which case you may not have a solidified conception of the author's purpose or big idea until the very end.

In any case, the main idea must appear somewhere in the passage, and when it does, you must take conscious note of it. For one thing, the purpose of everything else in the passage will be to support this idea. Furthermore, many of the questions—not only "main idea" or "primary purpose" questions, but all kinds of questions—are easier to handle when you have the main idea in the forefront of your mind. Always look for choices that sound consistent with the main idea. Wrong choices often sound inconsistent with it.

WHAT'S THE BIG IDEA?

You should always keep the main idea in mind, even when answering questions that don't explicitly ask for it. Correct answers on even the detail questions tend to echo the main idea in one way or another.

3. Get the Gist of Each Paragraph

The paragraph is the main structural unit of any passage. After you've read the first third of the passage carefully, you need only find the gist, or general purpose, of each succeeding paragraph, and then attempt to relate each paragraph back to the passage as a whole. To find the gist of each paragraph, ask yourself:

- Why did the author include this paragraph?
- What shift did the author have in mind when moving on to this paragraph?
- What bearing does this paragraph have on the author's main idea?

This process allows you create a "mental roadmap" of the passage, which ties in strongly with the structure and main idea. When questions arise that require you to look back into the passage, having a roadmap will help you locate the place in the text that contains the answer. For example, it's helpful to know that, say, the author's critique of a recommendation is in paragraph three. Doing so will allow you to zero in on the relevant information quickly. The art of *not* trying to understand every little thing in the passage brings us to our next principle.

4. Don't Obsess over Details

There are differences between the reading skills required in an academic environment and those useful on standardized tests. In school, you probably read to memorize information for an exam. This kind of reading most likely includes taking note of and memorizing details as well.

But this is not the type of reading that's good for getting points on LSAT Reading Comprehension. On the test, you'll need to read for short-term, as opposed to long-term, retention. When you finish the questions on a certain passage, that passage is over, gone, done with. You're free to promptly forget everything about it.

What's more, there's certainly no need to memorize details—it's an open-book test, after all. You always have the option to relocate details if a particular question requires you to do so. If you have a good sense of a passage's structure and paragraph topics, and your mental roadmap is clear in your mind, then you should have no problem navigating back through the text when the need arises.

5. Attack, Don't Just Read, the Passages

Always remember that you get no points for just "getting through" the passage. Don't be the kind of test taker who views reaching the end of a

MAKE A MAP

Try labeling each paragraph, so you know what's covered in each and how it fits into the overall structure of the passage. This will help you get a fix on the passage as a whole, and it will help you locate specific details later.

HEY, IT'S AN OPEN BOOK TEST

Don't feel that you have to memorize or understand every little thing as you read the passage.

Remember, you can always refer back to the passage to clarify the meaning of any specific detail.

passage as a moral victory—this type of victory is short-lived when you find you can't answer any questions.

No, you must *attack*—not simply read—the passages. The former embodies the winning mindset: you're entering the passage for the sole purpose of picking up the author's key ideas that will enable you to rack up points. By thinking in terms of attack, you're less likely to be diverted from this mission or to let the densely worded prose distract you.

Attacking a passage involves the application of all of the strategies mentioned in the previously stated principles. It also means reading actively. Active readers keep their minds working at all times, while trying to anticipate where the author's points are leading. Typically when we read—say a newspaper—we start with the first sentence and read the article straight through. The words wash over us and are the only things we hear in our minds. This is typical of the passive approach to reading.

Active reading, on the other hand, involves doing more than just reading the words on the page—it means thinking about what you're reading as you read it. It means paraphrasing the complicated-sounding ideas and jargon. It means asking yourself questions as you read:

- What's the author's main point here?
- What's the purpose of this paragraph? of this sentence?

When you read actively, there's a running commentary going on in your mind as you read. You may want to jot down notes or underline. When you read actively, you don't absorb the passage, you attack it!

6. Beware of Classic Wrong Answers

Knowing the most common types of wrong answer can help you eliminate wrong choices quickly, winning you extra time. Of course, ideally, you want to have prephrased an answer choice in your mind before looking at the choices. But in cases where that technique doesn't apply, you'll have to go to the choices and eliminate the bad ones to find the correct one. In such cases, you should always be on the lookout for:

- Choices that go beyond the author's scope
- Choices that are "half-right, half-wrong"
- Choices that use the wrong verb
- Choices that distort the passage's ideas
- Choices that say the exact opposite of what you are looking for

Being sensitive to these classic wrong choices will make it that much easier to zero in on the correct choice quickly and efficiently.

7. Read Critically

The single most important factor in Reading Comp success is the basic skill that underlies each of the preceding principles, as well as the rest of the test: critical reading.

Critical reading involves perspective—the ability to step back from a piece of prose and carefully evaluate it. On the Reading Comp section, critical reading echoes all of the principles we've been talking about, including:

- **Reading for purpose and idea**
  Why is the author writing? What's his or her point of view or main idea?

- **Reading for structure**
  How is the passage put together?

- **Reading between the lines**
  What is implied by the text?

The following are ways in which you can improve the specific critical reading skills necessary for success on Reading Comprehension:

- **Get a handle on the "spirit" of the passage.**
  Is it passionate? Neutral? Is it academic, conversational, or poetic in tone? What does the author favor? Disapprove of?

- **Keep paraphrasing key ideas.**
  Make sure you can put the author's most important concepts into your own words.

- **Keep anticipating where the author is going.**
  Each step of the way, ask yourself: "What could or must follow?"

- **Don't let complex-sounding words and sentences scare you.**
  Most passages consist of pretty simple ideas, written to sound impressive.

- **Connect abstract ideas to your own experience.**
  Visualize the subject matter if you can.

- **Read carefully for the gist or main point.**
  Read loosely for everything else—details, etcetera.

- **Remember that authors are repetitious.**
  Not every sentence they write adds a new idea.

- **Use keywords.**
  Like LR arguments, RC passages are full of structural signals—words or phrases whose main function is to help the author string ideas together logically. They allow you to infer a great deal about content, even if that content is obscure or difficult. Conclusion signals (*therefore, consequently, thus*) and evidence signals (*because, since*) are extremely helpful, as are contrast signals (*but, however, although, by contrast*) which indicate an opposition or shift in ideas.

The Three Crucial RC Question Types

While it might be convenient to break down the Reading Comprehension section into the types of *passages* that typically appear on it, Kaplan feels that that's not the best way to master the section. In Logic Games, categorizing the games is helpful because Sequencing games and Matching games, for instance, have their own sets of peculiarities, making a distinction between them useful. However, the same types of differences don't separate a humanities RC passage from a social science one, or even a natural science passage from a law passage. Their topics differ, but we read them in the same way, employing the same critical reading techniques for each.

For that reason, we find it more efficient to break the section down into the three main question types that accompany each passage: Global, Explicit Text, and Inference. Let's look at each of these more closely.

Global Questions

A Global question asks us to sum up the author's overall intentions, ideas, or passage structure. It's basically a question whose scope is the entire passage. Global questions account for 25 to 30 percent of all Reading Comp questions.

In general, any Global question choice that grabs onto a small detail—or zeros in on the content of only one paragraph—will be wrong. Often, scanning the verbs in the Global question choices is a good way to take a first cut at the question. The verbs must agree with the author's tone and way in which he or she structures the passage, so scanning the verbs can narrow down the options quickly. The correct answer must be consistent with the overall tone and structure of the passage, whereas the wrong choices will go beyond the scope or focus on a detail or be inconsistent with the author's tone. You'll often find Global questions at the beginning of question sets, and often one of the wrong choices will play on some side issue discussed at the tail end of the passage.

Main Idea and Primary Purpose Questions

The two main types of Global questions are main idea and primary purpose questions. We discussed these types a little earlier, noting that main idea and purpose are inextricably linked, because the author's purpose is to convey his or her main idea. The formats for these question types are pretty self-evident:

- Which one of following best expresses the main idea of the passage?
- The author's primary purpose is to . . .

Title Questions

A very similar form of Global question is one that's looking for a title that best fits the passage. (This question type disappeared for a while from the LSAT, but has started to make a comeback.) A title, in effect, is the main idea summed up in a brief, catchy way. This question may look like this: "Which of the following titles best describes the content of the passage as a whole?"

Be sure not to go with a choice that aptly describes only the latter half of the passage; a valid title, like a main idea and primary purpose, must cover the entire passage.

Structure Questions

Another type of Global question is one that asks you to recognize a passage's overall structure. Here's what this type of question might sound like: "Which of the following best describes the organization of the passage?"

Answer choices to this kind of Global question are usually worded very generally; they force you to recognize the broad layout of the passage as opposed to the specific content. For example, here are a few possible ways that a passage could be organized:

GLOBAL QUESTIONS AT A GLANCE

- GQs represent 25–30 percent of Reading Comp questions.
- GQs sum up author's overall intentions or passage structure.
- Nouns and verbs must be consistent with the author's tone and the passage's scope.
- Types of GQs: main idea, primary purpose, title, structure, logic, and tone.

• A hypothesis is stated and then analyzed.
• A proposal is evaluated and alternatives are explored.
• A viewpoint is set forth and then subsequently defended.

When choosing among these choices, literally ask yourself: "Was there a hypothesis here? Was there an evaluation of a proposal, or a defense of a viewpoint?" These terms may all sound similar, but in fact, they're very different things. Learn to recognize the difference between a proposal, a viewpoint, and so on. Try to keep an eye on what the author is doing as well as what the author is saying, and you'll have an easier time with this type of question.

Logic Questions

Logic questions are those that ask why the author does something—cite a source, bring up a detail, put one paragraph before another, etcetera. Choices that discuss the content or a detail will be wrong for these questions.

Tone Questions

The last type of Global question is the tone question, which asks you to evaluate the style of the writing or how the author sounds. Is the author passionate, fiery, neutral, angry, hostile, opinionated, low-key? Here's an example: "The author's tone in the passage can best be characterized as. . . ."

Make sure you don't confuse the nature of the content with the tone in which the author presents the ideas—a social science passage based on trends in this century's grisliest murders may be presented in a cool, detached, strictly informative way. Once again, it's up to you to separate what the author says from how he or she says it.

Inference Questions

Inference questions make up 55 to 60 percent of the Reading Comprehension section, and are very similar to those found in Logical Reasoning. An inference is something that is almost certainly true, based on the passage, but that is contained "between the lines." The answer is something that the author strongly implies or hints at, but does not state directly. Furthermore, the Denial Test, which was introduced earlier for Logical Reasoning assumption and inference questions, works for inference questions on Reading Comp as well. The right answer, if denied, will contradict or significantly weaken the passage. So in those two respects,

Logical Reasoning and Reading Comp inferences are similar. The differences?

- RC Inference questions can be on major points or small, whereas LR Inference questions tend to focus on major elements of the stimulus.
- In RC, we can't always be sure where in the passage to look for the answer to an Inference question.
- RC text is tougher to get through than LR prose, which is much briefer, so RC Inference questions are tougher.

The same rules that apply to inferences in Logical Reasoning also apply to inferences in Reading Comp. A good inference:

- Stays in line with the gist of the passage
- Stays in line with the author's tone
- Stays in line with the author's point of view
- Stays within the scope of the passage and its main idea
- Is neither denied by, nor irrelevant to, the ideas stated in the passage
- Always makes more sense than its opposite

Extracting valid inferences from Reading Comp passages requires the ability to recognize that information in the passage can be expressed in different ways. The ability to bridge the gap between the way information is presented in the passage and the way it's presented in the correct answer choice is vital. In fact, Inference questions often boil down to an exercise in translation.

Standard Inference Questions
The most common type of Inference question simply asks what can be inferred from the passage, but does so in a variety of different ways:
- It can be inferred from the passage that . . .
- The passage/author suggests that . . .
- The passage/author implies that . . .
- The passage supports which one of the following statements . . .

Usually, some specific information will complete these question introductions, so you'll almost always have a clue as to which idea or set of ideas from the passage is the key to the answer. When evaluating the answer choices, keep the relevant ideas firmly in mind. The farther you stray from them to endorse a choice, the more likely it is that this choice

INFERENCE QUESTIONS AT A GLANCE

- IQs represent 55–60 percent of Reading Comp questions.
- IQs are similar to Logical Reasoning inferences.
- IQs test ability to read between the lines.
- The Denial Test works to test choices.
- IQs often boil down to translating the author's points.
- The IQ question stem usually provides a clue as to where in the passage the answer will be found.
- IQs will ask for either something that can be inferred from a specific part of the passage, or else for something with which the author would agree.

will be wrong. Occasionally, the stem won't contain specific information, in which case you simply have to work your way through the choices until you find the one that's most consistent with the passage.

Agreement Questions
Another common form of Inference question is one that asks you to find a statement that the author (or some character or group mentioned in the passage) would agree with. Once again, the question stem will usually provide a hint as to in which part of the passage the answer can be found.

Explicit Test Questions

The third major category of Reading Comprehension questions is the Explicit Test question. As the name implies, an Explicit Test question is one whose answer can be directly pinpointed and found in the text. This type makes up roughly 10 to 20 percent of the questions on the section. It's fairly simple to identify an Explicit Text question from its stem:

* According to the passage/author . . .
* The author states that . . .
* The author mentions which one of the following as . . .

Often, these questions provide very direct clues as to where an answer may be found, such as a line reference or some text that links up with the passage structure. (Just be careful with line references—they'll bring you to the right area, but usually the actual answer will be found in the lines immediately before or after the referenced line.) Detail questions are usually related to the main idea, and correct choices tend to be related to major points.

You may recall that we advised you to skim over details in Reading Comp passages in favor of focusing on the big idea, topic, and scope. So what do you do with a question type that's specifically concerned with details? The fact is, most of the details that appear in a passage aren't tested in the questions. With the few that are, you'll do one of the following:

* Remember them from your reading
* Be given a line reference to bring you right to them
* Simply have to find them on your own in order to track down the answer

EXPLICIT TEST QUESTIONS AT A GLANCE

* ETQs represent 10–20 percent of Reading Comp questions.
* ETQ answers can always be found in the text.
* ETQs sometimes include line references to help you locate the relevant material.
* ETQs are concrete, and therefore the easiest RC question type for most people to answer.

If that's the case—if your mental roadmap and understanding of the purpose of each paragraph are both in the forefront of your mind—it shouldn't take long to locate the relevant detail and then choose an answer. And if even that fails, as a last resort, you have the option of putting that question aside and returning to it later, if and when you have the time to search through the passage. The point is, even with the existence of this question type, the winning strategy is still to note the purpose of details in each paragraph's argument, but not to attempt to memorize the details themselves.

Most students find Explicit Test questions to be the easiest type of Reading Comp question, since they're the most concrete. Unlike inferences, which hide somewhere between the lines, explicit details reside in the lines themselves. For this reason, we suggest placing Explicit Test questions high on your list of priorities, above Inference questions but below Global questions, when choosing the order in which you tackle the questions.

And speaking of setting priorities, this brings us to our next major topic, which should help bring all of these principles and strategies together.

The Kaplan Three-Step Method for Reading Comprehension

Now that you have the basics of LSAT Reading Comp under your belt, you'll want to learn our three-step method that allows you to orchestrate them all into a single modus operandi for RC questions:

1. Attack the first third of the passage.
2. Read the rest of the passage.
3. Do the questions in an efficient order.

1. Attack the First Third of the Passage

As outlined in the Basic Principles section, read the first part of the passage with care, in order to determine the main idea and purpose (via the zooming-in process we talked about earlier). Keep in mind two caveats, however. First, in some passages, the author's main idea doesn't become clear until the end of the passage. Second, occasionally a passage won't include a main idea, which in itself is a strong hint that the passage is more of a descriptive, storytelling type of passage, with an even-handed

ALL QUESTIONS ARE NOT CREATED EQUAL

Those who always answer the questions in the order in which they appear are not taking control of the test. It does matter which questions you choose to do first.

tone and no strong opinions. Bottom line: don't panic if you can't immediately pin down the author's main idea and purpose. Read on.

2. Read the Rest of the Passage

Do so as we described in the Basic Principles section, making sure to take note of paragraph topics, location of details, etcetera.

3. Do the Questions in an Efficient Order

Quickly scan the question stems for Global questions, specifically main idea or primary purpose questions. Doing these questions first will often help you solidify your conception of the author's main idea and purpose, and you're more likely to answer them correctly now, while the passage is still fresh in your mind.

If there are any other global types, such as questions regarding the author's overall tone or the organization of the passage, you may benefit from seeking out and handling those next. Explicit Text questions, especially those with line references, are good candidates to tackle after that. Many test takers benefit from leaving the more difficult Inference questions for last.

This, of course, is only a rough order based on question type. You may want to revise this order to account for the difficulty level of each individual question. For example, on any given passage, some Inference questions may be easier than some Explicit Text questions. So, for each question, quickly ask yourself: "Can I answer this question quickly?" Shop around—tackle the questions that you think will get you quick points first, and leave the others for later. This reinforces the all-important LSAT mindset—your conscious decision to take control of the test.

Using the Kaplan Three-Step Method for Reading Comprehension

Now let's try the three-step method on an actual LSAT-strength RC passage. For the time being, we've just included the question stems of the questions attached to this passage, since you don't want to get into individual choices until later:

It has been suggested that post–World War II concepts of environmental liability, as they pertain to hazardous waste, grew out of issues regarding municipal refuse collection and disposal and industrial waste disposal in the period 1880–1940. To a great
(5)   degree, the remedies available to Americans for dealing with the burgeoning hazardous waste problem were characteristic of the judicial, legislative, and regulatory tools used to confront a whole range of problems in the industrial age. At the same time, these remedies were operating in an era in which the problem of haz-
(10) ardous waste had yet to be recognized. It is understandable that an assessment of liability was narrowly drawn and most often restricted to a clearly identified violator in a specific act of infringement of the property rights of someone else. Legislation, for the most part, focused narrowly on clear threats to the public
(15) health and dealt with problems of industrial pollution meekly if at all.

Nevertheless, it would be grossly inaccurate to assume that the actions of American politicians, technologists, health officials, judges, and legislators in the period 1880–1940 have had little
(20) impact on the attempts to define environmental liability and to confront the consequences of hazardous waste. Taken as a whole, the precedents of the late nineteenth through the mid-twentieth century have established a framework in which the problem of hazardous waste is understood and confronted today. Efforts at
(25) refuse reform gradually identified the immutable connection between waste and disease, turning eyesores into nuisances and nuisances into health hazards. Confronting the refuse problem and other forms of municipal pollution forced cities to define public responsibility and accountability with respect to the envi-
(30) ronment. A commitment to municipal services in the development of sewers and collection and disposal systems shifted the burden of responsibility for eliminating wastes from the individual to the community. In some way, the courts' efforts to clarify and broaden the definition of public nuisance were dependent on
(35) the cities' efforts to define community responsibility itself.

The courts retained their role as arbiter of what constituted private and public nuisances. Indeed, fear that the courts would transform individual decisions into national precedents often contributed to the search for other remedies. Nonetheless, the
(40) courts remained an active agent in cases on the local, state, and

national level, making it quite clear that they were not going to be left out of the process of defining environmental liability in the United States. In the case of hazardous waste, precedents for behavior and remedial action were well developed by 1940. Even

(45) though the concept of *hazardous waste* is essentially a post–World War II notion, the problem was not foreign to earlier generations. The observation that the administrative, technical, and legal problems of water pollution in the 1920s were intertwined is equally applicable to today's hazardous waste problem.

1. According to the author, the efforts by cities to define public responsibility for the environment resulted in which of the following?

2. Which of the following, if substituted for the word *immutable* (line 25), would LEAST alter the author's meaning?

3. With which one of the following statements would the author be most likely to agree?

4. The author's primary purpose is to discuss . . .

5. The tone of the author's discussion of early attempts to deal with waste and pollution problems could best be described as . . .

6. According to the passage, judicial assessments of liability in waste disposal disputes prior to World War II were usually based on . .

7. The passage suggests that responses to environmental problems between 1880 and 1940 were relatively limited in part because of . . .

1. Attack the First Third of the Passage Carefully

The first few sentences introduce the topic: hazardous waste. The scope, as you recall, is the specific angle the author takes on the topic, and this seems to be the post–World War II concept of environmental liability associated with hazardous waste. The author points out that it's been suggested that this concept of liability has some connection to issues from the time period 1880–1940; latterday remedies for hazardous waste are "characteristic of the judicial, legislative, and regulatory tools used to confront a whole range of problems in the industrial age." Since hazardous waste

liability concepts of the postwar era had their roots in an era that predat-
ed the recognition of hazardous waste problems, the author finds it understandable that liability assessment and the ensuing legislation regarding
hazardous waste were both "narrowly drawn."

All of this comes out of the first paragraph. In some cases, this would
be enough to cover the "first third of the passage" reading. However, the
keyword *nevertheless* at the beginning of the next paragraph indicates that
it may be helpful to include this sentence in your initial reading as well.
This sentence harks back to and solidifies the connection between the
actions and policies from the period 1880–1940 and the concept of environmental liability associated with hazardous waste. This connection is the
author's main idea.

2. Read the Rest of the Passage

The sentence from lines 21 to 24—"Taken as a whole. . . ."—is simply
another restatement of the main idea. It's followed by a description of the
gradual recognition of the hazardous waste problem, and some of the
repercussions of the cities' and courts' efforts to define the problem and to
assign responsibility for it. Note that there's some talk in the paragraph
about individual versus community responsibility, and the role of cities,
but don't fuss over the specifics. If there's a question on these issues, you'll
know where to look.

The first part of the last paragraph deals mainly with the courts' role in
defining environmental liability. The last three sentences of the passage
reinforce the main idea; namely that there's a historical context for the
ways in which hazardous waste problems are viewed today.

3. Do the Questions in an Efficient Order

Let's look again at the seven question stems attached to this passage:

1. According to the author, the efforts by cities to define public responsibility for the environment resulted in which of the following?

2. Which of the following, if substituted for the word *immutable* (line
   25), would LEAST alter the author's meaning?

3. With which one of the following statements would the author be most
   likely to agree?

4. The author's primary purpose is to discuss . . .

5. The tone of the author's discussion of early attempts to deal with waste and pollution problems could best be described as . . .

6. According to the passage, judicial assessments of liability in waste disposal disputes prior to World War II were usually based on . . .

7. The passage suggests that responses to environmental problems between 1880 and 1940 were relatively limited in part because of . . .

Global Questions

Quickly scan the question stems for Global questions, specifically main idea or primary purpose. Upon inspection, if you come across the following question, you should attempt it at this point while the author's big idea is fresh in your mind:

4. The author's primary purpose is to discuss

(A) contrasts in the legislative approaches to environmental liability before and after World War II
(B) legislative trends which have been instrumental in the reduction of environmental hazardous wastes
(C) the historical and legislative context in which to view post–World War II hazardous waste problems
(D) early patterns of industrial abuse and pollution of the American environment
(E) the growth of an activist tradition in American jurisprudence

Choice (C) has the elements of a right answer: the connection (denoted by "the historical and legislative context . . . to view . . . waste problems") that represents the author's main idea, and the correct topic and scope—hazardous waste, post–World War II.

Choice (B) is tempting; legislative trends were discussed, but not in enough depth to constitute the author's primary purpose. More damaging to (B) is the fact that the discussion hinges on defining liability for hazardous wastes, and doesn't specifically discuss any factor "instrumental in the *reduction of environmental wastes.*"

Meanwhile, (A) misinterprets the passage structure—there is no such contrast presented, while (D) and (E) both violate the topic and scope of the passage (notice that neither one even mentions the topic of hazardous wastes).

Question 5, focusing on tone, is another Global question that you may wish to answer early on. Continuing to scan the question stems, the one with the line reference, question 2, may have caught your eye. This type simply tests your understanding of a certain word in a particular context, and since it tells us exactly where in the passage the word is, you'd be justified in trying this one next. Questions 1 and 6 are clearly Explicit Text questions, so you should do those next, beginning with the one that seems the most familiar. Questions 3 and 7, the Inference questions, are good candidates to be saved for last.

We've already discussed one of the Global questions, question 4, so let's now conclude this discussion with a brief look at one Explicit Text question and one Inference question:

Explicit Text Question
Here's the complete form (with answer choices) of question 6:

6. According to the passage, judicial assessments of liability in waste disposal disputes prior to World War II were usually based on

(A) excessively broad definitions of legal responsibility
(B) the presence of a clear threat to the public health
(C) precedents derived from well-known cases of large-scale industrial polluters
(D) restricted interpretations of property rights infringements
(E) trivial issues such as littering, eyesores, and other public nuisances

Pre–World War II judicial assessments of liability should ring a bell—they were discussed in the first paragraph. The correct answer, choice (D), is a direct paraphrase of the passage: ". . . an assessment of liability was narrowly drawn and most often restricted to a clearly identified violator in a specific act of *infringement of the property rights* of someone else."

Choice (E) is a common type of wrong answer; it consists of wording taken straight from the passage, but unfortunately, the wrong *part* of the passage. Don't choose an answer simply because you recognize some of the words or phrases in it; this is a common trap that snags many careless test takers.

Choice (B) is another classic wrong answer—the *au contraire* choice. This choice actually represents the *opposite* of what's stated or implied in the passage. According to the author, pre–World War II was "an era in which the problem of hazardous waste had yet to be recognized."

WATCH FOR TRAPS

Same-wording and *au contraire* wrong choices are common. Recognize them and avoid them.

Inference Question

Finally, let's take a quick look at question 3, a complete Inference question:

3. With which one of the following statements would the author be most likely to agree?

(A) The growth of community responsibility for waste control exemplifies the tendency of government power to expand at the expense of individual rights.

(B) Although important legal precedents for waste control were established between 1880 and 1940, today's problems will require radically new approaches.

(C) While early court decisions established important precedents involving environmental abuses by industry, such equally pressing matters as disposal of municipal garbage were neglected.

(D) Because environmental legislation between 1880 and 1940 was in advance of its time it failed to affect society's awareness of environmental problems.

(E) The historical role of U.S. courts in defining problems of hazardous waste and environmental liability provides valuable traditions for courts today.

Remember the basic rule for inferences: An inference must stay in line with the author's tone as well as the passage's topic and scope. The author's tone in this passage—factual, evenhanded—doesn't seem to fit with choices (A) and (B).

Choice (A) offers a judgment taken from the community/individual responsibility issue, something the author never does; he or she simply says that the burden shifted from one to the other.

There's no reason to believe that the author would agree with (B), either. While he or she would certainly agree with the first part, there's nothing that indicates that the author would advocate radical new approaches for today's problems. Both of these choices fail to match the author's tone, and are slightly outside the scope of the passage as well.

Notice how correct choice (E) sounds like an offshoot of the author's main idea. The first sentence of the second paragraph says that it would be wrong to assume that the actions of judges and legislators, among others, had little impact on defining liability and confronting the issue of hazardous waste. This implies that the courts had a positive impact, which is bolstered by lines 39 to 43. Combine that with the statement in lines 21 to 24: "Taken as a whole, the precedents of the late nineteenth through the mid-twentieth century have established a framework in which the problem of hazardous waste is understood and confronted today." All of this points towards (E) as a statement that the author would agree with, and therefore the answer to this Inference question.

After you work through the following set of Reading Comp practice questions, we'll address the last section of the LSAT: the Writing Sample.

Reading Comprehension Practice Set

Directions: Each passage in this test is followed by several questions. After reading the passage, choose the best answer to each question. Your replies are to be based on what is *stated* or *implied* in the selection. (The answer and explanation can be found at the end of each question.)

Passage for Questions 1–7:

Various factors influence voter preference in United States presidential elections, but perhaps none is so persuasive as a candidate's performance on nationally televised debates just prior to the
(5) election. Newspapers and television news programs generally attempt to provide thorough coverage of the debates, further augmenting the effect of good or bad candidate performances. In this way, the news media fulfill the traditional
(10) role of educating the public and enabling voters to make better informed decisions about elected officials. However, the same media that bring live debates into millions of living rooms across the nation also limit the availability of debate cover-
(15) age by use of "pool" coverage, the sharing of news coverage with other news organizations. When typical pool situations arise, one of the major networks covers the event, and a "feed" is created so other broadcasters may have access to the same
(20) coverage. Individual broadcasters are unable to convey a unique account to their viewers. The pool system limits the news-gathering ability of television news organizations and denies viewers an opportunity to gain maximum insight from
(25) the debate. The First Amendment freedoms afforded the press exist largely to ensure that the public benefits from the free flow of information.

Some commentators suggest that the purpose of a free press is to inform citizens about matters of
(30) public concern. Others, however, believe that the value of free press lies in its ability to foster a marketplace of ideas in which the best options prevail. Presidential debates embody all these considerations. Not only do candidates provide infor-
(35) mation about matters of utmost interest, they also offer diverse views on how to approach the major issues. Given television's ability to further informational and marketplace-of-ideas goals of the First Amendment, debate coverage should be
(40) diverse as possible.

What difference does it make whether viewers saw a "tight shot" of one candidate or a "two-shot" of both candidates at a given time? The answer depends on what happens, when it
(45) happens, and whether the pool director anticipated it or was fortunate enough to have captured it anyway. It may be argued that none of this matters. The important thing, the argument goes, is that viewers will know generally what happened.
(50) According to this line of reasoning, the number of news organizations covering an event—and even which ones—would be irrelevant. But courts have held differently: "It is impossible to treat two news services as interchangeable, and
(55) . . . it is only by cross lights from varying directions that full illumination can be secured." Undoubtedly, there are some circumstances in which pool coverage is the only way to cover an event. But these few situations must not foster a
(60) casual acceptance of pool implementation in other situations.

Question 1

It can be inferred that the author's primary objection to the pool system of covering presidential debates is that it

(A) restricts the public's access to a diversity of ideas and information •
(B) limits the number of people who have access to debates on television
(C) undermines candidates' ability to persuade voters
(D) dissuades voters from exercising their right to choose between candidates
(E) contributes to an overreliance by the public on televised accounts of political issues

Ⓐ Ⓑ Ⓒ Ⓓ Ⓔ

Answer and Explanation

The first passage is pretty straightforward. It revolves around the author's argument that "pool" coverage of presidential debates stifles the news media's ability to gather and present news. Why does the author find such a limitation on the media so alarming? She feels that it denies viewers an opportunity to gain maximum insight from presidential debates—that is, it sets limits on the amount and variety of information that the public receives. That's the passage's main point. Be aware that the author is talking about the actual "shooting" of a news event—the visual image broadcast to the viewer. She feels that a diversity of images is needed to fully illuminate an event. Although she concedes at the end of the passage that pool coverage may be the only way to cover *some* events, she cautions against the indiscriminate use of such coverage.

Question 1 asks for the author's primary objection to pool coverage of presidential debates. As noted, the author is primarily concerned with the way pool coverage limits the public's exposure to a variety of view-points and information. Choice (A) says exactly that, and is the correct answer. The author never charges the pool coverage system with limiting the *number* of people who have access to televised debates. Her point is that it limits the number of *versions* of a debate being offered to people, so choice (B) is wrong. The author discusses the impact of a candidate's debate performance in the first paragraph. But when examining the effects of pool coverage, the author clearly is thinking of the effect on the public's ability to judge, not on the candidates' ability to persuade, so choice (C) is out. Choice (D) involves a similar distortion of the passage's contents. The author claims that pool coverage, by limiting the information viewers receive, hampers the public's ability to choose between candidates, not its right to choose. As for choice (E), the author salutes TV's ability to bring live debates into millions of living rooms across the country. She sees this as an important factor in enabling voters to make better informed decisions about candidates. Her argument doesn't include a discussion of the dangers of an "overreliance" by the public on television, as choice (E) incorrectly suggests. Again, it's (A) for Question 1.

Question 2

The author would probably assert that the opinion of the court presented in the second paragraph is

(A) useful but biased
(B) reflective of an unfortunate trend •
(C) overly permissive •
(D) substantially correct
(E) commendable but ineffective

Ⓐ Ⓑ Ⓒ Ⓓ Ⓔ

Answer and Explanation

Take a look at the second paragraph and see what motivates the author's reference to court opinion. The author begins the paragraph by anticipating a possible counterargument—that it doesn't matter what specific images people see as long as they know generally what happened. This argument would lead a proponent of pool coverage to say that the number of news organizations covering an event is irrelevant. At the end of the paragraph, the author attacks this counterargument by quoting a court decision. That is, she's using the words of the court to defend her own views. If you realize this, you don't even have to look at the quote to infer the author's opinion of the court's findings. She must agree with them to a large extent, right? The only answer choice that reflects this level of agreement is choice (D)—"substantially correct." Choices (B) and (C) are way too negative, and choices (A) and (E) are not positive enough. So choice (D) is the answer for Question 2.

Question 3

In the first paragraph, the author cites two opinions concerning the benefits provided to society by a free press primarily in order to

(A) suggest the range of benefits that potentially would be provided by competitive coverage of presidential debates
(B) indicate that some of the defenses of pool coverage contradict one another
(C) criticize the assumptions held by some commentators on journalism
(D) contend that First Amendment freedoms do not apply to presidential debates
(E) reconcile different points of view in an effort to reach a more acceptable definition of press freedom

Ⓐ Ⓑ Ⓒ Ⓓ Ⓔ

Answer and Explanation

To answer Question 3, you need to take a close look at the second half of the first paragraph. The two benefits of a free press cited there are (1), its ability "to inform citizens about matters of public concern," and (2), its ability "to foster a marketplace of ideas in which the best options prevail." The author presents these not as contradictory benefits but as complementary ones. Both benefits are involved when television airs a presidential debate, and the author argues that diversity of coverage would maximize these benefits. Choice (A) paraphrases this argument, and is the correct choice. The author doesn't mention these benefits as proposed "defenses" of pool coverage and they certainly don't contradict each other, so choice (B) is off the mark. (C) is wrong—you more or less know this as soon as you see the verb *criticize*—it just doesn't fit what the author is doing in the first paragraph. The author is in no way critical of the benefits of a free press or of the commentators who have suggested them. The same goes for (E); the author does not "reconcile" anything here. In fact, there's no need to—the different views on free press benefits are presented here as being complementary. Finally, choice (D) is dead wrong—the point of this paragraph is that First Amendment freedoms have a whole lot to do with presidential debates. Once again, it was (A) for Question 3.

Question 4

It can be inferred from the passage that a proponent of the pool system of debate coverage would be most likely to defend her viewpoint with which of the following remarks?

(A) Broadcasters rarely betray their political preferences in debate coverage.
(B) Although imperfect, pool coverage is the only practical means of reporting most political events.
(C) Presidential debates are too complex to be covered thoroughly by any one broadcaster.
(D) Broadcasters are prevented by public opinion from presenting biased coverage.
(E) Small differences in style of coverage do not significantly affect the amount of information conveyed to viewers.

Ⓐ Ⓑ Ⓒ Ⓓ Ⓔ

Answer and Explanation

Question 4 asks how a proponent of the pool system would defend her viewpoint. Since the author argues that pool coverage limits the information provided to viewers, you need a choice that would challenge the author's point of view. Choice (A) doesn't address this position. So what if broadcasters only rarely betray their political preferences in debate coverage? Pool coverage still limits viewers to coverage by only one of these broadcasters. (B) could be tempting, too, but it also doesn't attack the author's main argument. The author already concedes that pool coverage may be the only way to cover some events. But the drawbacks of such coverage still exist for nonpolitical events—and you might have to forgo "practicality" at some point in deference to larger issues. Choice (C) only serves to strengthen the author's argument. If presidential debates are so complex that one broadcaster cannot cover them properly, pool coverage should be eliminat-

ed, allowing coverage by a number of broadcasters. Choice (D) is similar to choice (A) and is wrong for the same reason. (By the way, when you see that two or more answer choices on the LSAT are very similar, it's a strong signal that these choices are wrong. After all, there should be only one "right" answer to a given question.) Choice (E) is your last chance—and it's the right answer. If small differences in style of coverage don't affect the amount of information conveyed to viewers, then the premise to the author's argument is blown out of the water. (E) would be the best remark for a proponent of pool coverage to make in its defense.

Question 5

The author warns that the use of pool coverage in situations in which it may be needed may lead to other situations in which

(A) public events covered by the media are subjected to undue analytical scrutiny
(B) broadcasters accept further limitation of their First Amendment freedoms
(C) the informational content of news events is diminished
(D) pool coverage is relied upon when it is in fact undesirable '
(E) broadcasters suffer increasing erosion of their capacity for news gathering

Ⓐ Ⓑ Ⓒ Ⓓ Ⓔ

Answer and Explanation

Question 5 is a detail question. The authorial warning occurs in the last paragraph. There the author expresses the hope that the few situations in which pool coverage is necessary will not "foster a casual acceptance of pool implementation in other situations." Unnecessary pool coverage translates to undesirable pool coverage for the author—so choice (D) is your answer. (A) comes out of left field—the author never mentions the dangers of analysis-crazed media. (Who knows, she might even welcome such a situation. It would provide the public with a lot of information, wouldn't it?) (B) calls attention to the author's fleeting reference—back in the first paragraph—to the First Amendment freedoms afforded the press. But in her discussion of these freedoms, the author never makes the specific argument that pool coverage violates them. So expanded use of pool coverage couldn't be referred to as a "further limitation."

Choice (C) could have been tempting if you made things difficult for yourself. If you thought, "Well, gee, the author thinks pool coverage limits the informational content of presidential debates, so she probably would claim that expanded use of pool coverage would reduce the informational content of other news events, too." But such logical gymnastics shouldn't be necessary on the LSAT. And remember, this is a specific-detail question—you've got to stick to what the author is doing in the last paragraph, where her warning occurs. The same thing goes for (E). The author does think pool coverage limits news gathering, but this point never arises in her final warning to you. Once again, it was (D) for Question 5.

Question 6

The author's argument that the pool system "denies viewers an opportunity to gain maximum insight from the debate" (lines 23–25) would be most WEAKENED if it could be shown that

(A) candidates' debate performances rarely make a difference of more than a few percent in voting results
(B) most debate viewers form their opinions primarily on the basis of post-debate commentary presented separately by each network
(C) candidates' posture and mannerisms during debates are as important in forming voter opinion as their actual words
(D) few viewers of televised debates bother to read followup commentary in newspapers and magazines
(E) competitive coverage would provide viewers with a wider variety of interpretations on which to base their opinions

Ⓐ Ⓑ Ⓒ Ⓓ Ⓔ

Answer and Explanation

Question 6 calls your attention to a specific part of the passage, namely lines 23–25, but you're actually dealing once again with the author's overall argument. The author feels that the pool system "denies viewers an opportunity to gain maximum insight from the debate" because the sharing of news coverage means that viewers are receiving only one set of images—only one version of the debate—not a wide variety representing various viewpoints. According to the author, this prevents individual broadcasters from conveying a unique account of the debate to their viewers. The question asks you to find an answer choice that would weaken the author's contention that this limitation adversely affects viewers' ability to make voting decisions.

Choice (A) might be tempting at first. If debate performances don't sway many voters one way or another, what difference does it make what version of the debate they saw? But choice (A) doesn't address the author's specific argument concerning the effects of the pool system on voter insight. It doesn't matter if a debate doesn't have a major impact on the outcome of an election. What matters—to the author at least—is that the public has access to as much information as possible when deciding how to vote. So (A) wouldn't weaken the author's argument. Choice (B) reveals a way to alleviate—if not make irrelevant—the limits that the pool system places on the public's access to a

KAPLAN

variety of ideas. If networks were to wrap up a debate with their own followup commentary, providing the public with a diversity of ideas that they then use as a basis for making voting decisions, then the author's objections to the pool system would be weakened. So (B) looks pretty good, but go on to the other choices. (C), (D), and (E) would all strengthen, not weaken, the author's argument. If (C) is correct, then the author's objections to pool coverage are right on the mark—no amount of postdebate coverage could make up for viewers' having access to only one visual version of a debate. If (D) is correct, the importance of televised coverage—and a variety of it—is emphasized all the more. Finally, (E) just restates the author's argument. "Competitive coverage" means the same thing as elimination of pool coverage. So it was choice (B) for Question 6.

Question 7

Which of the following titles best describes the content of the passage?

(A) Debate Coverage: How It Changes Voters' Opinions

(B) The "Pool" System: A Limitation on Public Access to Information

(C) The "Pool" System: Its Benefits Versus Its Impracticalities

(D) First Amendment Press Rights: How They Conflict with Presidential Politics

(E) Televised Debates: Their Role in Presidential Politics

Ⓐ Ⓑ Ⓒ Ⓓ Ⓔ

Answer and Explanation

Question 7 asks for the title that best describes the content of the passage. Wrong answer choices in such questions usually involve titles that are either too general or too specific—or those that are totally outside

the passage's scope. Take choice (A), for example. The author doesn't discuss how debate coverage changes voters' opinions, does she? Throw it out! The author also doesn't discuss the benefits or impracticalities of the pool system. Throw (C) out! Does the author discuss how First Amendment press rights conflict with presidential politics? Nope—forget (D). How about (E)? In the first paragraph, the author does touch on the influence exercised by televised presidential debates. But the brunt of the passage involves the pool system and the limitations it imposes on public access to information. That's (B), your answer—the only choice that accurately reflects the author's main concerns.

Passage for Questions 8–10:

It is crucial to question the assumption that for-profit health care institutions have special obligations to help subsidize care for the needy over and above their general obligation as taxpayers. As the (5) for-profits are quick to point out, supermarkets are not expected to provide free food to the hungry poor, and real estate developers are not expected to let the poor live rent free in their housing. Yet food and housing, like health care, (10) are basic necessities for even minimal subsistence. If there are basic human rights to some adequate level of health care, it is reasonable to think there are such rights to food and shelter as well.

Whose obligation is it, then, to secure some (15) basic health care for those unable to secure it for themselves? Assuming that private markets and charity leave some without access to whatever amount of health care that justice requires be available to all, there are several reasons to believe (20) that the obligation ultimately rests with the federal government. First, the obligation to secure a just or fair overall distribution of benefits and burdens across society is usually understood to be

a general societal obligation. Second, the federal
(25) government is the institution society commonly
employs to meet societywide distributive requirements. With its taxing power, it has the
revenue-raising capacities to finance what would
be a massively expensive program for an adequate
(30) level of health care to be guaranteed to all. This
taxing power also allows the burden of financing
health care for the poor to be spread fairly across
all members of society and not to depend on the
vagaries of how wealthy or poor a state or local
(35) area happens to be. The federal government also
has the power to coordinate programs
guaranteeing access to health care for the poor
across local and state boundaries. This is necessary both for reducing inefficiencies that allow
(40) substantial numbers of the poor to fall between
the cracks of the patchwork of local and state
programs, and for ensuring that there are not
great differences in the minimum of health care
guaranteed to all in different locales within our
(45) country.

If we are one society, a *United* States, then the
level of health care required by justice for all citizens should not vary greatly in different locales
because of political and economic contingencies.
(50) It is worth noting that food stamp programs and
housing subsidies, also aimed at basic necessities,
similarly are largely a federal responsibility. These
are reasons for the federal government having the
obligation to guarantee access to health care for
(55) those unable to secure it for themselves. It might
do this by directly providing the care itself, or by
providing vouchers to be used by the poor in the
health care marketplace. *How* access should be
guaranteed and secured—and in particular, to
(60) what extent market mechanisms ought to be uti-
lized—is a separate question.

Question 8

The author's primary concern in the passage is to
discuss

(A) the level of expenditures required to ensure equi-
table access to health care for all
(B) measures that might be enacted to carry out a program of subsidized health care
(C) differences among states and localities in the provision of basic social services
(D) whether a national commitment to health care
can be reconciled with the federal structure of the
United States
(E) which institutions bear the obligation for assuring
adequate health services for the poor

Ⓐ Ⓑ Ⓒ Ⓓ Ⓔ

Answer and Explanation

The main topic of this passage isn't immediately
apparent. The first paragraph leaves you expecting the
author to examine the obligations of for-profit health
care or the basic human rights to food and shelter.
The author's real topic becomes clear only when you
reach the second paragraph and its introductory
question—"Whose obligation is it to secure basic
health care for those unable to secure it for themselves?" According to the author, it's the federal government's obligation; the rest of the passage serves to
back up this claim. The second paragraph outlines the
powers that enable the federal government to guarantee access to health care for all those who need it.
Finally, the third paragraph reiterates the basic right to
an adequate level of health care and the government's
responsibility to provide it. The author ends by introducing the problem of how the federal government
should guarantee access to health care.

Question 8 is a main idea question that takes you
back to the beginning of the second paragraph.
Remember, that's where the author first introduces his

main topic—the question of whose obligation it is to secure basic health care for those unable to secure it for themselves. That's this passage's big idea, and choice (E), the correct choice, captures it well. Turning now to the wrong answers, choice (A) is way too specific. The author mentions in the second paragraph that the government's taxing power enables it to raise the money required for health care expenditures, but he doesn't delve into specifics, like the exact level of expenditures that would be required. The same goes for choices (B) and (C). In the last paragraph, the author only fleetingly discusses the how of his argument, choice (B). He also mentions that differences among various states and localities in the provision of basic social services could arise, choice (C), but these differences aren't specifically described, and they don't take up the bulk of the discussion. As for choice (D), the author's argument presupposes that a national commitment to health care can be reconciled with the federal structure of the United States. Indeed, the author's whole argument is that the federal structure is ideal for assuring access to health care. Again, the correct answer is choice (E).

Question 9

The author mentions federal "food stamp programs and housing subsidies" (lines 50–51) primarily in order to

(A) modify a previous point in response to new information

(B) support his argument by mentioning a comparable situation

(C) argue that these programs should be modified

(D) make a concession to a contrasting opinion

(E) acknowledge that not all programs would benefit from the approach he favors

Ⓐ Ⓑ Ⓒ Ⓓ Ⓔ

Answer and Explanation

Look at lines 50–51, where the author mentions federal food stamp programs and housing subsidies. Why are these mentioned? The author notes that the food stamp programs and housing subsidies, both of which are aimed at basic necessities, are largely a federal responsibility. He mentions these two already established federal programs in order to support his argument that the federal government should start a *similar* program involving access to health care—another basic necessity. Now, keeping that in mind, you probably could have picked the correct answer, choice (B), by looking solely at the verbs of the answer choices.

But take a closer look at the wrong answers. As for (A), the author certainly doesn't modify a previous point—in fact, he reiterates his main argument wholesale. And he doesn't argue for the modification of the aforementioned programs, either. He just wishes that a federal health care program would join them, so (C) gets eliminated. The author's reference to food stamp programs and housing subsidies does not involve a "contrasting opinion." As you know, the author sees the existence of these programs as support for his own argument. Since no contrasting opinion is presented, no "concession" can be made to it, and choice (D) is wrong. The "approach" favored by the author is federal support of programs involving basic human necessities. Food stamps and housing subsidies are examples of programs that have already benefited from this approach, so (E) doesn't make sense. Again, choice (B) is the answer.

Question 10

According to the passage, the federal government possesses all the following powers in regard to health care EXCEPT the power to

(A) raise the revenue to finance health care expenditures

(B) distribute the costs of health care equitably among different sectors of the country

(C) ensure that the poor have access to health care regardless of state and local boundaries

(D) compel private businesses and charities to assume greater responsibility for financing health care for the needy

(E) set comparable standards for the minimum level of health care in different areas

Ⓐ Ⓑ Ⓒ Ⓓ Ⓔ

Answer and Explanation

This is a detail question, and the second paragraph provides you with all the information you need. It is there that the author lists the federal government's powers regarding health care. If you managed to remember the nature of these powers, it might have been fairly easy for you to run down through the choices and pick out the one that looked suspicious. Assuming you didn't, compare each choice with the information in the second paragraph. Choice (A) corresponds to the first power cited—the federal government's ability to tax. This power enables it to raise the revenue needed to finance health care expenditures. Choice (B), conveniently enough, corresponds to the second power cited. The government's taxing power ensures that the burden of financing health care would be spread equitably across all members of society. Choice (C) corresponds nicely to the third power— the power to coordinate programs guaranteeing access to health care for the poor across local and state boundaries. The ability to ensure that there are not great differences in the minimum of health care guaranteed to all is the last power cited and one that is paraphrased in choice (E). This leaves you with choice (D). Nowhere does the author mention a state power that can compel private businesses and charities to assume greater responsibility for financing health care for the needy. By virtue of being wrong, choice (D) is the answer to Question 10.

KAPLAN

CHAPTER 5

THE WRITING SAMPLE

The Writing Sample comes at the end of your LSAT day. Typically, it consists of a scenario followed by two possible courses of action. You'll have thirty minutes to make a written case that one of the two courses of action is superior.

This section tests your ability to write a clear, concise, persuasive argument. No outside knowledge whatsoever is required.

You'll receive a pen to write the essay, as well as scrap paper to plan out your response before you actually write it. Your essay must be confined to the space provided, which is roughly the equivalent of one sheet of standard lined paper. You won't be given additional paper, so you'll have to keep your argument concise. Usually, two or three paragraphs will be enough. Note that there's really no time or space to change your mind or radically alter your essay once you've begun writing, so *plan your argument out carefully before beginning to write*. Make sure to write as legibly as you can.

The Writing Sample is ungraded, but it is sent to law schools along with your LSAT score. Many law schools use the Writing Sample to help make decisions on borderline cases, or to decide between applicants with otherwise comparable credentials. Granted, it may not carry the same weight as the scored sections of the test, but since it can impact on your admission chances, your best bet is to take it seriously.

Sample Topic

The structure of every Writing Sample topic is the same: a brief introduction first outlines the choice to be made. That's followed by two

DOES IT REALLY MATTER?

The Writing Sample may not matter in some admissions decisions, but in others, it will be crucial. If you take it seriously, therefore, you'll be covered either way.

bullet-pointed criteria that should guide your decision. Finally, the two alternatives that you're to choose from are described in a paragraph each. The following is an example of a Writing Sample topic:

The *Daily Tribune,* a metropolitan newspaper, is considering two candidates for promotion to business editor. Write an argument for one candidate over the other with the following considerations in mind:

- The editor must train new writers and assign stories.
- The editor must be able to edit and rewrite stories under daily deadline pressure.

Laura received a B.A. in English from a large university. She was managing editor of her college newspaper and served as a summer intern at her hometown daily paper. Laura starting working at the *Tribune* right out of college and spent three years at the city desk covering the city economy. Eight years ago the paper formed its business section and Laura became part of the new department. After several years covering state business, Laura began writing on the national economy. Three years ago, Laura was named senior business and finance editor on the national business staff; she is also responsible for supervising seven writers.

Palmer attended an elite private college where he earned both a B.S. in business administration and an M.A. in journalism. After receiving his journalism degree, Palmer worked for three years on a monthly business magazine. He won a prestigious national award for a series of articles on the impact of monetary policy on multinational corporations. Palmer came to the *Tribune* three years ago to fill the newly created position of international business writer. He was the only member of the international staff for two years and wrote on almost a daily basis. He now supervises a staff of four writers. Last year, Palmer developed a bimonthly business supplement for the *Tribune* that has proved highly popular and has helped increase the paper's circulation.

NOBODY CARES

The admissions officers don't care what you think here; they care *how* you think. Make your choice of alternative quickly and then stick with it.

The Eight Basic Principles of Writing Sample Success

Here are the most important rules-of-thumb to remember when attacking the Writing Sample:

1. Use Scrap Paper to Plan Your Essay

The proctors give you scrap paper for a reason. Use it! Make yourself a rudimentary outline, listing the points you want to make in each paragraph. Ideally, you should know what you want to say and how you want to say it before putting pen to paper.

2. Don't Obsess over Making Your Choice of Alternative

Nobody really cares which choice you make (for example, whether you choose to support Laura or Palmer in the sample above). What's important is how well you support the choice you make. Generally, the alternatives are written to be pretty evenly matched, so there's no right or wrong answer, just a well-supported or ill-supported position.

3. Get Right to the Point

The first sentence should immediately offer a solid endorsement of one choice over the other. Assume that the reader is already familiar with the situation; there's no need to waste time describing the scenario and the alternatives.

4. Use a Clear, Simple Essay Format

Since all the essay topics have the same structure, you can decide in advance how you will structure your response. One possibility is the "winner/loser" format, in which the first paragraph begins with a statement of choice and then discusses the reason why your choice (the winner) is superior. The next paragraph focuses on why the other alternative (the loser) is not as good, and should end with a concluding sentence reaffirming your decision. Another possibility is the "according to the criteria" format, in which the first paragraph would discuss both the winner and the loser in light of the first criterion, and the second paragraph would discuss them both in light of the second criterion.

Whether you adopt one of these formats or use one of your own, the most important thing is that your essay be coherent in its reasoning. The more organized your essay is, the more persuasive it will be.

NO POINTS FOR SPONTANEITY

Since the Writing Sample topic always takes the same basic form, you can decide in advance exactly how you will structure your response to that topic. That will save time, giving you more time to devote to your deathless prose.

5. Mention, but Downplay, the Loser's Strengths and the Winner's Weaknesses

Use sentence structures that allow you to do this, such as, "Even though Palmer won a prestigious national award. . ." and then attempt to demonstrate why this is really no big deal. This is an example of mentioning yet downplaying one of the loser's strengths. Try to do the same thing for at least one of the winner's obvious weaknesses. Doing so demonstrates that you see the full picture. Recognizing and dealing with possible objections makes your argument that much stronger.

6. Don't Simply Repeat Facts about the Candidates

Try instead to offer an *interpretation of the facts in light of the stated criteria*. If you're arguing for Laura in the topic above, you can't state simply that "Laura was named senior business and finance editor on the national business staff" and expect the reader to infer that that's a good thing. For all we know, being in that position may be a detriment when it comes to the criteria—training new writers and working under daily deadline pressure. It's up to you to indicate why certain facts about the winner are positive factors in light of the criteria, and vice versa for facts about the loser. Merely parroting what's written in the topic won't win you any points with the law schools.

7. Write Well

It sounds obvious, of course, but you should try to make your prose as clean and flawless as you can. Some people get so entangled in content that they neglect the mechanics of essay writing. But spelling, grammar, and writing mechanics are important. Use structural signals to keep your writing fluid and clear, and use transitions between paragraphs to keep the entire essay unified. Above all, write legibly. Nothing annoys essay readers more than an illegible essay.

8. Budget Your Time Wisely

We suggest spending roughly five to seven minutes reading the topic, making a decision, and planning out your essay. As we suggested, use the scrap paper provided to jot down a quick outline of the points you intend to make. Then spend about twenty minutes writing the essay. This should be plenty of time; remember, we're only looking at two or three paragraphs at the most. This schedule will leave about three to five minutes at the end to proofread your essay for spelling and grammar.

BUT DOCTORS HAVE BAD HANDWRITING . . .

If you don't think your poor handwriting will work against you, guess again. Many people will be prejudiced against your Writing Sample if it's hard to decipher.

KAPLAN

Sample Essay

At this point, you'll probably want to try your hand at writing an essay on the above-mentioned topic. Please do so (observing the thirty-minute time limit, of course). Then check your essay, making sure it observes the basic principles outlined above.

The following is a sample response to the essay topic above:

Both candidates are obviously qualified, but Laura is the better choice. For one thing, Laura has been working at the *Tribune* for eleven years, and has therefore had plenty of opportunity to learn the workings of the paper. For another, her experience has been in national rather than international business, and national business will certainly be the focus of the *Tribune*'s financial coverage. In her current capacity, she is responsible for writing and editing articles while simultaneously overseeing the work of a staff of seven. Clearly, then, Laura can work under deadline pressure and manage a staff, a capability she demonstrated at an early age as the managing director of her college newspaper. Although Laura's academic credentials may not measure up to Palmer's, her background in English, her history of steady promotions, and her work as senior national business writer—combined with a solid business knowledge and obvious drive for accomplishment—will certainly spur the department to journalistic excellence.

Palmer's résumé is admirable but is nonetheless inferior to Laura's. True, Palmer has evidently done a fine job managing the international section, but his staff numbers only four, and the scope of the venture is smaller than Laura's. True, Palmer's articles on the impact of monetary policy did win an award in the past, but since he has been working for the *Tribune* no such honors have been forthcoming. Not only does Palmer lack the English literature background that Laura has, but he also lacks her long experience at the *Tribune*. Furthermore, Palmer's editing experience seems slight, considering the length of his current tenure and the size of his staff, and while he demonstrates competence in the area of international business, he has little experience in the national business area.

In light of these circumstances, the newspaper would meet its stated objectives best by promoting Laura to the position of business editor.

SO CLEARLY THE JOB MUST BE GIV . . .

Don't let yourself get cut off. It's a big mistake to leave the Writing Sample unfinished. Be strict with yourself, so that you'll have at least a few minutes left at the end to read over what you've written.

This generally well-reasoned and well-written essay would be an asset to any applicant's law school admissions file. The writer states his choice in the first sentence and then substantiates this choice in a paragraph on the winner and a paragraph on the loser. Notice the way this writer acknowledges, yet rebuts, the winner's flaws and the loser's strengths. Whether or not one agrees with the choice of Laura over Palmer, the essay definitely makes a strong, well-reasoned case for the choice—and that, after all, is what the law schools will be looking for.

A Note on Finishing

Before leaving the topic of the Writing Sample, we want to make one more important point—make sure you finish your essay. Some students find that time is called while they're still writing. Bad move. Not only does that leave you with an incomplete essay, it also hints to the admissions officers that your organization and time-management skills aren't stellar.

So don't make this classic error. Give yourself plenty of time to finish the essay.

CHAPTER 6

TAKING CONTROL OF THE TEST

The first year of law school is a frenzied experience for most law students. In order to meet the requirements of a rigorous work schedule, they either learn to prioritize and budget their time or else fall hopelessly behind. It's no surprise, then, that the LSAT, the test specifically designed to predict success in the first year of law school, is a time-intensive test, demanding excellent time-management skills as well as that *sine qua non* of the successful lawyer—grace under pressure.

As we saw, it's one thing to answer a Logical Reasoning question correctly; it's quite another to answer twenty-five of them correctly in thirty-five minutes. And the same goes for Reading Comp and Logic Games—it's a whole new ballgame once you move from doing an individual game or passage at your leisure to handling a full Logic Games or Reading Comp section under actual timed conditions. In fact, the only section of the test that's not very time intensive is the Writing Sample; most test takers find they have ample time to write the essay. But when it comes to the scored sections, time pressure is a factor that affects virtually every test taker.

So when you're comfortable with the content of the test, namely, the type of material discussed in the previous chapters, your next challenge will be to learn how to manage the all-important time element of the test.

IT'S NOT JUST ABOUT CORRECT ANSWERS

For complete LSAT success, you've got to get as many correct answers as possible in the time you're given. Knowing the strategies is not enough. You've got to perfect your time management skills so that you get a chance to use those strategies on as many questions as possible.

Test Expertise

On most of the tests you take in school, you wouldn't dream of not taking at least a try at every single one of the questions. If a question seems particularly difficult, you spend significantly more time on it, since you'll probably be given more points for correctly answering a hard question. Not so on the LSAT. Remember, every LSAT question, no matter how hard, is worth a single point. And since there are so many questions to do in so little time, you'd be a fool to spend three minutes getting a point for a hard question and then not have time to get a couple of quick points from two easy questions later in the section.

Given this combination—limited time, all questions equal in weight—you've got to develop a way of handling the test sections to make sure you get as many points as you can as quickly and easily as you can. Here are the principles that will help you do that:

Attack the Questions in Any Order That Strikes You as Logical

One of the most valuable strategies to help you finish the sections in time is to learn to recognize and deal first with the questions, games, and passages that are easier and more familiar to you. That means temporarily skipping those that promise to be difficult and time consuming. You can always come back to these at the end, and if you run out of time, you're much better off not getting to questions you may have had difficulty with, rather than missing potentially doable material. Of course, since there's no wrong-answer penalty, always fill in an answer to every question on the test, whether you get to it or not.

Learn to Recognize and Seek out Questions You're Good At

Another thing to remember about managing the sections is that LSAT questions, games, and passages, unlike items on the SAT and other standardized tests, are not presented in order of difficulty. There's no rule that says that you have to work through the sections in any particular order; in fact, the test makers scatter the easy and difficult questions throughout the section, in effect rewarding those who actually get to the end. Don't lose sight of what you're being tested for along with your reading and thinking skills—efficiency and cleverness. If you find sequencing games particularly easy, for example, seek out the sequencing game on the LG section and do it first. Similarly, if you just love formal logic questions, head straight for such questions when you first turn to the LR sections.

BE A TEST EXPERT

In order to meet the stringent time requirements of the LSAT, you've got to cultivate the following elements of test expertise:

- A sense of timing
- An ability to skip around without getting mixed up
- An ability to assess the difficulty level of a question or passage or game
- A cool head

POP QUIZ

Every question is worth exactly one point. But questions vary dramatically in difficulty level. Given a shortage of time, which questions should you work on—easy or hard?

KAPLAN

Know That the Test Questions Are Written at Different Levels of Difficulty

It's imperative that you remain calm and composed while working through a section. You can't allow yourself to be rattled by one hard logic game or reading passage, so that it throws off your performance on the rest of the section. Expect to find at least one difficult passage or game on every section, but remember, you won't be the only one to have trouble with it. The test is curved to take the tough material into account. Having trouble with a difficult logic game isn't going to ruin your score—but getting upset about it and letting it throw you off-track will. When you understand that part of the test maker's goal is to reward those who keep their composure, you'll recognize the importance of not panicking when you run into challenging material.

Control Time Instead of Letting Time Control You

Of course, the last thing you want to happen is to have time called on a particular section before you've gotten to half the questions. It's essential, therefore, that you pace yourself, keeping in mind the general guidelines for how long to spend on any individual question, passage, or game (we'll give you those guidelines below). No one is saying that you should spend, for instance, exactly one and a quarter minutes on every Logical Reasoning question. But you should have a sense of how long you have to do each question, so you know when you're exceeding the limit and should start to move faster.

Keeping track of time is also important for guessing. Remember, there's no penalty for a wrong answer on the LSAT! So it pays to leave a little time at the end to guess on the questions you couldn't answer. For instance, let's say you never get a chance to do the last logic game on an LG section. If you just leave the grids for those questions blank, you're going to get no points for that entire game. If, on the other hand, you give yourself a little time at the end to fill in a guess for each of those questions, you'll have a very good chance of getting lucky on at least one or two questions. That would up your raw score by one or two points—which translates into a higher scaled score.

So, when working on a section, always remember to keep track of time. Don't spend a wildly disproportionate amount of time on any one question or group of questions. Also, give yourself thirty seconds or so at the end of each section to fill in answers for any questions you didn't get to. After all, a correct guess is worth just as much as any other correct answer.

DON'T BE MACHO!

It's difficult for some of us to give up on a tough, time-consuming question, but it must be done occasionally. Remember, there's no point of honor at stake here, but there are LSAT points at stake.

GUESS!

We've said it before and we'll say it again: If you can't do a question or can't get to it, guess! Fill in an answer—any answer—on the answer grid. There's no penalty if you're wrong, but there's a big fat point if you're right.

LOGICAL REASONING EXPERTISE

Here are some of the important LR time techniques to remember:

- Spend an average of one and a quarter minutes per item.
- Save question types that traditionally give you trouble for last.
- Always do the double-questions, and get two points for the time-price of one.

Section-Specific Strategies

Let's now look at the section-specific timing requirements and some tips for meeting them.

Logical Reasoning

Time Per Question

Twenty-four to twenty-six questions in thirty-five minutes works out to roughly a minute and a quarter per question. Keep in mind that this is only an average; there are bound to be some questions that take less time and some that take more. It's okay if the occasional question takes you two minutes, if you're able to balance it out with a question that takes forty-five seconds. Remember, too, that every question is worth the same, so don't get hung up on any one question. No single point on this section is worth three minutes of your valuable time, that's for sure. And think about it—if a question is so hard that it takes you that long to answer it, chances are you may get it wrong anyway. In that case, you'd have nothing to show for your extra time but a lower score.

Managing the Section

What kind of Logical Reasoning questions should you skip? Certainly questions containing stimuli that are indecipherable to you after a quick reading. Questions containing extra-long stimulus arguments may be good to skip initially as well, especially if you're running behind on time. But don't automatically be intimidated by the sheer length of a stimulus; often, the long ones are uncomplicated and easy to understand.

If you adhere to our strategy of reading the question stem first, you may be able to single out questions to postpone based solely on question type. This is a matter of recognizing your own strengths and weaknesses. For example, if a question involves finding a principle that lends credence to an argument, and you know historically that principle questions are a problem for you, then that's a good question to postpone.

A good stimulus is one that comes with two questions attached. There are usually anywhere from two to four double-question stimuli on each Logical Reasoning section. Working through these, as opposed to single question arguments, saves a little time, as you can potentially rack up two points for reading only one stimulus.

KAPLAN

Logic Games

Time Per Game

There are four games to get through in thirty-five minutes, which works out to roughly eight and a half minutes per game. Remember, just as in Logical Reasoning, this is an average—some games may take a little more time, while some may take a little less.

Managing the Section

There are definitely some things to keep in mind when it comes to working through an entire Logic Games section. First, and most important, is the necessity of previewing the section. By this, we mean that you should literally flip through the pages, having a glance at each game in order to decide which games look the easiest and most familiar to you. Previewing, of course, is not foolproof; a game that looks fairly straightforward at first glance could easily turn out to be a killer. But it works more often than not.

The ideal goal is to tackle the games in order of difficulty, from easiest to hardest. But if you achieve nothing more than saving the hardest game for last, then the strategy is a winner.

So how do you tell which games may be difficult? The best way is to know the game types discussed in the Logic Games section cold, and to have a feeling for which types you're strong in and which ones you should avoid like the plague (until the end, of course). A game that doesn't look familiar at all could simply be an oddball game—a good candidate to postpone. And don't necessarily be scared off by games with a lot of rules; sometimes, this works to your advantage. The more rules they give you, the more definite and concrete the game situation is, and the easier it will be to answer the questions. It's the games with few rules that often turn out to be tough, because they're inherently ambiguous.

If you have several Logic Games to practice on, you may wish to build gradually to the point where you're ready to take full-length sections. Begin by attempting one game in eight or nine minutes. Next, try two games in seventeen minutes. When you're ready to move on, try three games in about twenty-six to twenty-seven minutes, until finally you can handle a full four-game section in thirty-five minutes.

Finally, remember what we said about the way the test makers test efficiency. They're crafty—they'll sometimes throw an intentionally time-consuming question at the end of a game, possibly one involving a rule change that requires you to backtrack and set the game up all over again. Bear in mind that when this happens, they may not be testing who's smart

---

LOGIC GAMES EXPERTISE

Here's how best to manage your time on the LG section:

- Spend about eight and a half minutes per game.
- Preview the section so you know what you're up against.
- Do the easiest game first; save the toughest for last.
- Skip rule-change questions and others that promise to be especially time consuming.

enough to get the right answer, but who's clever enough to skip the killer question in order to devote their precious time to the next game, with a possible payoff of six or seven new points.

If you apply the principles regarding making deductions and working through questions discussed earlier, and combine that with these tips on how to approach a full Logic Games section, you'll be well on your way to an excellent Logic Games performance on the day of the test.

Reading Comprehension

Time Per Passage

The Reading Comp section format is similar to that of the Logic Games section: four passages in thirty-five minutes, which means about eight and a half minutes per passage. The Reading Comp strategies and techniques in the previous chapter should help you to get through each passage as quickly as possible, but here are a few additional points about tackling a full section.

Managing the Section

It's a little more difficult to preview the Reading Comp section than it is to preview a Logic Games section, but it is possible to know that it's time to move on if the first third of a passage is extraordinarily confusing or simply really boring to the point of distraction. Concentration is a major key in Reading Comp, and if you simply can't "lock into" the ideas in a particular passage, then it's time to put that one aside and look for friendlier territory. As in Logic Games, the goal is to save the most difficult stuff for last.

Quite often, you'll encounter Reading Comprehension passages that contain a preponderance of technical details or difficult concepts, only to find that few if any questions deal with the part of the passage that's so dense. Just as in the Logic Games example above, the test makers aren't necessarily testing to see who's smart enough to understand that section of the passage; they may be looking to see who's clever enough to skim past those details and focus on the more important aspects of the passage instead. If you keep this in mind, you'll be less likely to get mired in extraneous details.

READING COMP EXPERTISE

Some suggestions for maximizing your time on the RC section:

- Spend about eight and a half minutes per passage (including questions).
- Preview the section, as in LG, to assess difficulty levels.
- Save any passages that look daunting for last.
- Remember not to get mired in details. Read for structure and main idea and come back for the details if necessary to answer questions.

Answer Grid Expertise

An important part of LSAT test expertise is knowing how to handle the answer grid. After all, you not only have to pick the right answers; you also have to mark those right answers on the answer grid in an efficient and accurate way. It sounds simple, but it's extremely important: *Don't make mistakes filling out your answer grid!* When time is short, it's easy to get confused going back and forth between your test book and your grid. If you know the answer, but misgrid, you won't get the points. Here are a few methods of avoiding mistakes on the answer grid.

Always Circle Questions You Skip

Put a big circle in your test book around the number of any question you skip (you may even want to circle the whole question itself). When you go back, such questions will then be easy to locate. Also, if you accidentally skip a box on the grid, you can more easily check your grid against your book to see where you went wrong.

Always Circle Answers You Choose

Circle the correct answers in your test booklet, but don't transfer the answers to the grid right away. That wastes too much time, especially if you're doing a lot of skipping around. Circling your answers in the test book will also make it easier to check your grid against your book.

Grid Five or More Answers at Once

As we said, don't transfer your answers to the grid after every question. Transfer your answers after every five questions, or at the end of each Reading Comp passage or Logic Game (find the method that works best for you). That way, you won't keep breaking your concentration to mark the grid. You'll save time and improve accuracy. Just make sure you're not left at the end of the section with ungridded answers!

Save Time at the End for a Final Grid Check

Make sure you have enough time at the end of every section to make a quick check of your grid, to make sure you've got an oval filled in for each question in the section. Remember, a blank grid has no chance of earning a point, but a guess does.

Now let's turn our attention to test mentality, and put the finishing touches on your comprehensive LSAT approach.

DON'T UNDERESTIMATE THE IMPORTANCE OF GRID TECHNIQUE

Yes, it's pure bookkeeping, but you won't get the points if you put your answers in the wrong place, or if you waste time searching for the right place to put your answers. Take the time now to develop some good answer grid habits.

Test Mentality

We've already armed you with the weapons you need to do well on the LSAT. But you must wield those weapons with the right frame of mind and in the right spirit. This involves taking a certain stance toward the entire test. Here's what's involved:

1. Test Awareness

To do your best on the LSAT, you must always keep in mind that the test is like no other test you've taken before, both in terms of content and in terms of scoring system. If you took a test in high school or college and got a quarter of the questions wrong, you'd probably receive a pretty lousy grade. But on the LSAT, you can get a quarter of the questions wrong (about twenty-five) and still score higher than the eightieth percentile! The test is geared so that only the very best test takers are able to finish every section. But even these people rarely get every question right. As mentioned earlier, you can get a "perfect" score of 180 and still get a handful of questions wrong.

What does this mean for you? Well, just as you shouldn't let one bad game or passage ruin an entire section, you shouldn't let what you consider to be a below par performance on one section ruin your performance on the entire test. A lousy performance on one single section will not by itself spoil your score (unless you miss almost every question). However, if you allow that poor section to rattle you, it can have a cumulative negative effect, setting in motion a downward spiral. It's the kind of thing that could potentially do serious damage to your score. Losing a few extra points won't do you in, but losing your head will.

Remember, if you feel you've done poorly on a section, don't sweat it. Who knows, it could be the experimental. And even if it's not, chances are it's just a difficult section—a factor that will already be figured into the scoring curve anyway. The point is, you must remain calm and collected. Simply do your best on each section, and once a section is over, forget about it and move on.

While we're on the topic of the experimental section, we'd like to reiterate an important point: never, never try to figure out which section is unscored. This practice has caused trouble for countless test takers. They somehow convince themselves that a certain section is the one that doesn't count, and then don't take it seriously. And they're pretty upset when they find out they guessed wrong. You can't know which section is the experimental section, so handle each section as if it counts. That way, you're cov-

WHAT MAKES FOR GOOD TEST MENTALITY?

We're glad you asked. The important elements are:

- Test awareness
- Stamina
- Confidence
- The right attitude

NOBODY'S PERFECT

Remember that the LSAT isn't like most tests you've taken. You can get a lot of questions wrong and still get a great score. So don't get rattled if you miss a few questions. Even those with "perfect" scores of 180 get some questions wrong.

ered no matter what. If a section you had trouble with turns out to be experimental, it's gravy. If it turns out to be scored—well, think how much worse you'd have done if you blew it off entirely.

2. Stamina

The LSAT is a fairly grueling experience, and some test takers simply run out of gas before it's over. To avoid this, take as many full-length practice tests as possible in the week or two before the test. That way, five sections plus a writing sample will seem like a breeze (well, maybe not a breeze, but at least not a hurricane).

One option is to buy PrepTests, which are the actual released exams published by Law Services. The available PrepTests are listed in the *LSAT Registration and Information Book*, which is available at most colleges and law schools, or you can call Law Services at 215-968-1001 for information. (Try to send away for them early, since they take two to three weeks for delivery.)

Another option, if you have some time, would be to take the full Kaplan course. We'll give you access to every released test plus loads of additional material, so you can really build up your LSAT stamina. As a bonus, you'll also have the benefit of our expert live instruction in every aspect of the LSAT. If you decide to go this route, call 1-800-KAP-TEST for the Kaplan Center location near you.

3. Confidence

Confidence feeds on itself, and unfortunately, so does self-doubt. Confidence in your ability leads to quick, sure answers and a sense of well-being that translates into more points. If you lack confidence, you end up reading sentences and answer choices two, three, or four times, to the point at which you confuse yourself and get off-track. This leads to timing difficulties, which only perpetuate the downward spiral, causing anxiety and a tendency to rush in order to finish sections.

If you subscribe to the LSAT mentality we've described, however, you'll gear all of your practice toward the major goal of taking control of the test. When you've achieved that goal—armed with the principles, techniques, strategies, and methods set forth in this book—you'll be ready to face the LSAT with supreme confidence. And that's the one sure way to score your best on the day of the test.

BE COOL

Losing a few extra points here and there won't do serious damage to your score, but losing your head will. Keeping your composure is an important test-taking skill.

GET TOUGH

You wouldn't run a marathon without working on your stamina well in advance of the race, would you? The same goes for taking the LSAT.

4. The Right Attitude

Those who approach the LSAT as an obstacle, and who rail against the necessity of taking it, usually don't fare as well as those who see the LSAT as an opportunity to show off the reading and reasoning skills that the law schools are looking for. Those who look forward to doing battle with the LSAT—or, at least, who enjoy the opportunity to distinguish themselves from the rest of the applicant pack—tend to score better than do those who resent or dread it.

It may sound a little dubious, but take our word for it: attitude adjustment is a proven test-taking technique. Here are a few steps you can take to make sure you develop the right LSAT attitude:

- Look at the LSAT as a challenge, but try not to obsess over it; you certainly don't want to psyche yourself out of the game.
- Remember that, yes, the LSAT is obviously important, but this one test will not single-handedly determine the outcome of your life.
- Try to have fun with the test. Learning how to match your wits against the test makers can be a very satisfying experience, and the reading and thinking skills you'll acquire will benefit you in law school as well as in your future legal career.
- Remember that you're more prepared than most people. You've trained with Kaplan. You have the tools you need, plus the know-how to use those tools.

Global Principles

Let's conclude with a recap of some of the most important global principles and strategies for success on the LSAT:

- The test questions are not necessarily presented in order of difficulty. Answer the questions in any order that seems effective.
- There is no penalty for wrong answers on the LSAT. *Always guess if you can't answer a question*, or if you can't get to it! Never leave a question blank.
- All questions are worth the same amount, so don't spend an excessive amount of time on any one question.
- You are rewarded for correctly identifying the "credited answer." Learn to think like the test maker—follow the test maker's reasoning to that credited answer.

Tips for the Final Week

Is it starting to feel like your whole life is a buildup to the LSAT? You've known about it for years, worried about it for months, and now spent at least a few weeks in solid preparation for it. As the test gets closer, you may find your anxiety is on the rise. You shouldn't worry. After the preparation you've received from this book, you're in good shape for the test.

To calm any pretest jitters you may have, though, let's go over a few strategies for the days before the test.

The Week Before Test Day

In the week or so leading up to the test, you should do the following:

- Recheck your admission ticket for accuracy; call Law Services if corrections are necessary.
- Visit the testing center if you can. Sometimes seeing the actual room where your test will be administered and taking notice of little things—like the kind of desk you'll be working on, whether the room is likely to be hot or cold, etcetera—may help to calm your nerves. And if you've never been to the campus or building where your test will take place, this is a good way to ensure that you don't get lost on the day of the test. Remember, you must be on time—the proctors won't wait for you.
- Practice getting up early and working on test material, preferably a full-length test, as if it were the real day of the test.
- Time yourself accurately, with the same device and in the same manner in which you plan to keep track of time on the test.
- Evaluate thoroughly where you stand. Use the time remaining before the test to shore up your weak points, rereading the appropriate sections of this book. But don't neglect your strong areas; after all, this is where you'll rack up most of your points.

The Day Before the Test

Try to avoid doing intensive studying the day before the test. There's little you can do to help yourself at this late date, and you may just wind up exhausting yourself and burning out. Our advice is to review a few key concepts, get together everything you'll need for test day, and then take the night off entirely. Go to see a movie or watch some TV. Try not to think too much about the test.

THE FINAL DAYS OF YOUR PREPARATION ARE KEY

The tendency among students is to study too hard during the last few days before the test, and then to forget the important practical matters until the last minute. Part of taking control means avoiding this last-minute crush.

The Day of the Test

Get up early, leaving yourself plenty of time. Read something to warm up your brain—you don't want the LSAT to be the first written material your brain tries to assimilate that day.

Dress in layers for maximum comfort. That way, you'll be able to adjust to the testing room's temperature.

In traveling to the test center, leave yourself enough time for traffic and mass transit delays.

Be ready for a long day. Total testing time, remember, is three hours and twenty-five minutes. When you add the administrative paperwork before and after, and the ten- to fifteen-minute break in the middle, you're looking at an experience of four and a half to six hours.

Don't get flustered when they fingerprint you as you enter the testing room—this is standard operating procedure and is not intended for your FBI file. The test administrators do this because occasionally they have reason to believe that some test takers are not exactly who they say they are. If you're on the up and up, you'll have nothing to worry about.

After the test booklets are handed out, and you've filled out all of the required information, the test will begin. Your proctor should write the starting and ending time of each section on a blackboard in front of the room, and will usually announce the time remaining at specified intervals, such as when there's ten minutes remaining, five minutes remaining, and one minute remaining.

Most test centers have a clock on the wall that the proctor will use to time the test, but don't take anything for granted—your test center may not (stranger things have been known to happen). You should definitely bring along your own timing device, such as a watch or a stopwatch, so long as it doesn't make any noise (devices that beep on the hour or sound an alarm at specified times are prohibited from the testing site).

It's also best to practice using a timing routine that you'll follow during the real test. For example, some students find it helpful to set their watches at twenty-five past the hour for the scored sections, often 11:25. This way, they know that the section will end exactly when their watch says 12:00. Others reset their watches exactly on the hour at the beginning of each section, and know that every section will end at thirty-five minutes after the hour (except for the Writing Sample, of course, which will end on the half-hour). Still others synchronize their watches with the room clock and follow the proctor's timing guidelines. It doesn't matter which one of the these procedures you adopt, or even if you come up with one of your own that you're comfortable with, just as long as you use it consistently, so that keeping track of time during test is second nature.

Here are some other last-minute reminders to help guide your work on the test:

- Read each question stem carefully, and reread it before making your final selection. Also, to make sure your answer sheet is gridded accurately, say the question number and choice to yourself (silently, of course) as you grid.
- Give all five choices a fair shot in Logical Reasoning and Reading Comp, time permitting. For Logic Games, go with the objectively correct answer as soon as you find it and blow off the rest.
- Don't get bogged down in the middle of any section. At the end of *every* section are questions that may be really easy and manageable. Make sure that you get to them! Conversely, don't be alarmed if you run across extra-tough questions at the beginning, especially in Logical Reasoning. It happens. Skip past tough ones and come back to them later, making sure to circle them in the test booklet so you can find them fast.
- Preview the LG and RC sections before you launch into them. The third or fourth game or reading passage could be the easiest one. Take a brief look at all four before you decide where to begin.
- Don't bother trying to figure out which section is unscored. It can't help you, and you might very well be wrong. Instead, just determine to do your best on every section.
- Confidence is key. *Accentuate the positives, and don't dwell on the negatives!* Your attitude and outlook are crucial to your performance on test day.
- During the exam, try not to think about how you're scoring. It's like a baseball player who's thinking about the crowd's cheers and the sportswriters and his contract as he steps up to the plate. There's no surer way to strike out. Instead, focus on the question-by-question task of picking (A), (B), (C), (D), or (E). The correct answer is there. You don't have to come up with it; it's sitting right there in front of you! Concentrate on each question, each passage, each game—on the mechanics, in other words—and you'll be much more likely to hit a home run.

Test Rhythm

Between sections 1 and 2, 2 and 3, and 4 and 5, the proctor will say only: "Time's up on this section. Go on to the next section." Notice that there's no break here—you must go immediately from one section to the next. Also, if you finish a section early, you're not allowed to

DON'T RELY ON PROCTORS

Hey, they're usually nice people, but nobody's perfect. Be your own timer.

I AM NOT A CROOK

No, they don't fingerprint you because they expect you to cheat. They do it to have some way of making sure you're who you say you are.

DON'T HEED THE INTERMISSION PUNDITS

During the break, there will undoubtedly be those who want to talk about the test—how hard or easy it is, which section is "definitely experimental," etcetera. Don't listen to these people. They will probably be wrong, for one thing. And their comments will just hurt your concentration on the rest of the test.

DO YOU REALLY WANT TO CANCEL?

The key question to ask yourself when deciding whether to cancel is this, "Will I really do significantly better next time?"

move on to another section. They're pretty strict about this one, so watch your step. If you have extra time, spend it looking back over your work on that section alone.

After section 3, you'll be instructed to close your test booklets and take a ten- to fifteen-minute break. Pay no attention to people's nervous chatter during the break. Some will say it's the hardest test since the dawn of time; others will say it's so easy they can't believe it. Either kind of comment can rattle you. Instead, bring a Walkman, headphones, and some tunes that'll pump you up and some that'll relax you, to use as needed.

After the break, you'll return to the testing room for the remaining sections. Then, after section 5, your test materials will be collected and the Writing Sample materials and pens to write the essays will be handed out (no pens are allowed on the scored sections).

After the Writing Sample is collected, the test ends and you're free to get on with your life. For most of you, this means getting back to the rest of the application and admission process we talked about earlier. In the short term, however, this signals the beginning of a well-deserved night out to unwind.

After the Test

Cancellation and Multiple Scores Policy

Unlike many things in life, the LSAT allows you a second chance. If you walk out of the test feeling that you've really not done as well as you could have, you have the option of canceling your score—as long as you notify Law Services within five business days after the day of the test. Canceling a test means that it won't be scored. It will just appear on your score report as a cancelled test. No one will know how well or poorly you really did—not even you.

There's been a recent change in the LSAT cancellation policy. Previously, in order to cancel a test, you had no option except to mail or fax the signed cancellation form to Law Services within five business days. While you still have that option, it's now possible to cancel your score immediately after the test, right at the test center. However, we strongly advise against this. When deciding whether to cancel your score, a good rule of thumb is to make an honest assessment of whether you'll do better on the next test. Wishful thinking doesn't count; you need to have a valid reason to believe that the next time would be different. Remember, no test experience is going to be perfect. If you were distracted by the proctor's hacking cough this time around, next time you may be even more distracted by construction noise, or a cold, or the hideous lime-green sweater of the person sitting in front of you.

Two legitimate reasons to cancel your test are illness and personal circumstances that cause you to perform poorly on that particular day. Also, if you feel that you didn't prepare sufficiently, then it may be advisable to cancel your score and approach your test preparation a little more seriously the next time.

But keep in mind that test takers historically underestimate their performance, especially immediately following the test. They tend to forget about all of the things that went right, and focus on everything that went wrong. So unless your performance is terribly marred by unforeseen circumstances, don't cancel your test immediately—at least sleep on the decision for one or two nights, and if you still feel you want to do it again, then send in the form. Just remember, cancellations are permanent. Once the form is sent, you can't change your mind.

What the Schools Will See

If you do cancel your test and then take it again for a score, your score report will indicate that you've canceled a previous score. Since it won't be scored, you don't have to worry about this score showing up on any subsequent score report. If you take more than one test without canceling, then all the scores will show up on each score report, so the law schools will see them all. Most law schools average LSAT scores, although there are a few exceptions. Check with individual schools for their policy on multiple scores.

Post-LSAT Festivities

After all the hard work you've done preparing for and taking the LSAT, you want to make sure you take time to celebrate afterwards. Plan to get together with friends the evening after the test. Relax, have fun, let loose. After all, you've got a lot to celebrate. You prepared for the test ahead of time. You did your best. You're going to get a good score.

So start thinking about all of the great parties you'll be attending at the law school of your choice!

ABOUT CANCELING

While we hope you won't find it necessary to cancel your LSAT score, here are a few points to keep in mind:

- Scores can be canceled on the spot or within five working days after the test date.
- To avoid anxiety, use a mailgram, telegram, fax, or overnight letter.
- A form is provided at the test site, or write your own letter with name, address, social security number, signature, test date, test center name, test center code number.
- Send to: Law Services Score Cancellation, Box 2000-T, 661 Penn St., Newtown, PA 18940-0995, or fax (215) 968-1277.
- Scores can now be canceled at the site of the test. But we recommend that you not do so except in extreme cases of performance disaster. Better to sleep on it and cancel later if necessary.

CHAPTER 7

THE KAPLAN ADVANTAGE™ STRESS MANAGEMENT SYSTEM

The countdown has begun. Your date with THE TEST is looming on the horizon. Anxiety is on the rise. The butterflies in your stomach have gone ballistic. Perhaps you feel as if the last thing you ate has turned into a lead ball in your stomach. Your thinking is getting cloudy. Maybe you think you won't be ready. Maybe you already know your stuff, but you're going into panic mode anyway. Worst of all, you're not sure of what to do about it.

Don't freak! It is possible to tame that anxiety and stress—before and during the test. We'll show you how. You won't believe how quickly and easily you can deal with that killer anxiety.

Making the Most of Your Prep Time

Lack of control is one of the prime causes of stress. A ton of research shows that if you don't have a sense of control over what's happening in your life you can easily end up feeling helpless and hopeless. So, just having concrete things to do and to think about—taking control—will help reduce your stress. This section shows you how to take control during the days leading up to taking the LSAT—or any other test.

STRESS TIP

Don't forget that your school probably has counseling available. If you can't conquer test stress on your own, make an appointment at the counseling center. That's what counselors are there for.

Identify the Sources of Stress

The first step in gaining control is identifying the sources of your test-related stress. The idea is to pin down that free-floating anxiety so that you can take control of it. Here are some examples:

- I always freeze up on tests.
- I'm nervous about the Logic Games section (or the Logical Reasoning section or the Reading Comprehension section).
- I need a good/great score to go to Acme Law School.
- My older brother/sister/best friend/girl- or boyfriend did really well. I must match their scores or do better.
- My parents, who are paying for school, will be really disappointed if I don't test well.
- I'm afraid of losing my focus and concentration.
- I'm afraid I'm not spending enough time preparing.
- I study like crazy but nothing seems to stick in my mind.
- I always run out of time and get panicky.
- I feel as though thinking is becoming like wading through thick mud.

Take a few minutes to think about your own particular sources of test-related stress. Then write them down in some sort of order. List the statements you most associate with your stress and anxiety first, and put the least disturbing items last. As you write the list, you're forming a hierarchy of items so you can deal first with the anxiety-provokers that bug you most. Very often, taking care of the major items from the top of the list goes a long way toward relieving overall testing anxiety. You probably won't have to bother with the stuff you placed last.

Take Stock of Your Strengths and Weaknesses

Take one minute to list the areas of the test that you are good at. They can be general (Logical Reasoning) or specific (inference questions). Put down as many as you can think of, and if possible, time yourself. Write for the entire time; don't stop writing until you've reached the one-minute stopping point.

Next, take one minute to list areas of the test you're not so good at, just plain bad at, have failed at, or keep failing at. Again, keep it to one minute, and continue writing until you reach the cutoff. Don't be afraid to identify

VERY SUPERSTITIOUS

Stress expert Stephen Sideroff, Ph.D., tells of a client who always stressed out before, during, and even after taking tests. Yet she always got outstanding scores. It became obvious that she was thinking superstitiously—subconsciously believing that the great scores were a result of her worrying. She also didn't trust herself, and believed that if she didn't worry she wouldn't study hard enough. Sideroff convinced her to take a risk and work on relaxing before her next test. She did, and her test results were still as good as ever—which broke her cycle of superstitious thinking.

and write down your weak spots! In all probability, as you do both lists you'll find you are strong in some areas and not so strong in others. Taking stock of your assets *and* liabilities lets you know the areas you don't have to worry about, and the ones that will demand extra attention and effort.

Now, go back to the "good" list, and expand it for two minutes. Take the general items on that first list and make them more specific; take the specific items and expand them into more general conclusions. Naturally, if anything new comes to mind, jot it down. Focus all of your attention and effort on your strengths. Don't underestimate yourself or your abilities. Give yourself full credit. At the same time, don't list strengths you don't really have; you'll only be fooling yourself.

Every area of strength and confidence you can identify is much like having a reserve of solid gold at Fort Knox. You'll be able to draw on your reserves as you need them. You can use your reserves to solve difficult questions, maintain confidence, and keep test stress and anxiety at a distance. The encouraging thing is that every time you recognize another area of strength, succeed at coming up with a solution, or get a good score on a test, you increase your reserves. And, with a plan to strengthen a weak area or get a good score on a practice test, there is absolutely no limit to how much self-confidence you can have or how good you can feel about yourself.

What Do You Want to Accomplish in the Time Remaining?

The whole point of this next exercise is sort of like checking out a used car you might want to buy. You'd want to know up front what the car's weak points are, right? Knowing that influences your whole shopping-for-a-used-car campaign. So it is with your conquering-test-stress campaign: Knowing your weak points ahead of time helps you prepare.

So let's get back to the list of your weak points. Take two minutes to expand it just as you did with your "good" list. Be honest with yourself without going overboard. It's an accurate appraisal of the test areas that give you troubles.

Facing your weak spots gives you some distinct advantages. It helps a lot to find out where you need to spend extra effort. Increased exposure to tough material makes it more familiar and less intimidating. (After all, we mostly fear what we don't know and are probably afraid to face.) You'll feel better about yourself because you're dealing directly with areas of the test that bring on your anxiety. You can't help feeling more confident

STRESS TIP

Don't work in a messy or cramped area. Before you sit down to study, clear yourself a nice, open space. And make sure you have books, paper, pencils—whatever tools you will need—within easy reach before you sit down to study.

LINK YOUR THOUGHTS

When you're committing new information to memory, link one fact to another, much as elephants are linked trunk to tail in a circus parade. Visualize an image (preferably a bizarre one) that connects the thoughts. You'll remember them in the same linked way, with one thought easily bringing the next to your mind.

THE "NEW AGE" OF RELAXATION

Here are some more tips for beating stress:

- Find out if massage, especially shiatsu, is offered through your school's phys ed department, or at the local "Y."
- Check out a book on acupressure, and find those points on your body where you can press a "relax button."
- If you're especially sensitive to smells, you might want to try some aromatherapy. Lavender oil, for example, is said to have relaxing properties. Health food stores, drug stores, and New Age bookstores may carry aromatherapy oils.
- Many health food stores carry herbs and supplies that have relaxing properties, and they often have a specialist on staff who can tell you about them.

STRESS TIP

If you want to play music, keep it low and in the background. Music with a regular, mathematical rhythm—reggae, for example—aids the learning process. A recording of ocean waves is also soothing.

when you know you're actively strengthening your chances of earning a higher overall test score.

Imagine Yourself Succeeding

This next little group of exercises is both physical and mental. It's a natural followup to what you've just accomplished with your lists.

First, get yourself into a comfortable sitting position in a quiet setting. Wear loose clothes. If you wear glasses, take them off. Then, close your eyes and breathe in a deep, satisfying breath of air. Really fill your lungs until your rib cage is fully expanded and you can't take in any more. Then, exhale the air completely. Imagine you're blowing out a candle with your last little puff of air. Do this two or three more times, filling your lungs to their maximum and emptying them totally. Keep your eyes closed, comfortably but not tightly. Let your body sink deeper into the chair as you become even more comfortable.

With your eyes shut you can notice something very interesting. You're no longer dealing with the worrisome stuff going on in the world outside of you. Now you can concentrate on what happens inside you. The more you recognize your own physical reactions to stress and anxiety, the more you can do about them. You may not realize it, but you've begun to regain a sense of being in control.

Let images begin to form on the "viewing screens" on the back of your eyelids. You're experiencing visualizations from the place in your mind that makes pictures. Allow the images to come easily and naturally; don't force them. Imagine yourself in a relaxing situation. It might be in a special place you've visited before or one you've read about. It could be a fictional location that you create in your imagination, but a real-life memory of a place or situation you know is usually better. Make it as detailed as possible and notice as much as you can.

If you don't see this relaxing place sharply or in living color, it doesn't mean the exercise won't work for you. Some people can visualize in great detail, while others get only a sense of an image. What's important is not how sharp the details or colors, but how well you're able to manipulate the images. If you can conjure up finely detailed images, great. If you have only a faint sense of the images, that's okay—you'll still experience all the benefits of the exercise.

Think about the sights, the sounds, the smells, even the tastes and textures associated with your relaxing situation. See and feel yourself in this special place. Say you're special place is the beach, for example. Feel how warm the sand is. Are you lying on a blanket, or sitting up and looking out at the water? Hear the waves hitting the shore, and the occasional seagull. Feel a comfortable breeze. If your special place is a garden or park, look up and see the way sunlight filters through the trees. Smell your favorite flowers. Hear some chimes gently playing and birds chirping.

Stay focused on the images as you sink farther back into your chair. Breathe easily and naturally. You might have the sensations of any stress or tension draining from your muscles and flowing downward, out your feet and away from you.

Take a moment to check how you're feeling. Notice how comfortable you've become. Imagine how much easier it would be if you could take the test feeling this relaxed and in this state of ease. You've coupled the images of your special place with sensations of comfort and relaxation. You've also found a way to become relaxed simply by visualizing your own safe, special place.

Now, close your eyes and start remembering a real-life situation in which you did well on a test. If you can't come up with one, remember a situation in which you did something (academic or otherwise) that you were really proud of—a genuine accomplishment. Make the memory as detailed as possible. Think about the sights, the sounds, the smells, even the tastes associated with this remembered experience. Remember how confident you felt as you accomplished your goal. Now start thinking about the upcoming test. Keep your thoughts and feelings in line with that successful experience. Don't make comparisons between them. Just imagine taking the upcoming test with the same feelings of confidence and relaxed control.

This exercise is a great way to bring the test down to earth. You should practice this exercise often, especially when the prospect of taking the exam starts to bum you out. The more you practice it, the more effective the exercise will be for you.

Exercise Your Frustrations Away

Whether it is jogging, walking, biking, mild aerobics, pushups, or a pick-up basketball game, physical exercise is a very effective way to stimulate both your mind and body and to improve your ability to think and concentrate. A surprising number of students get out of the habit of regular exercise, ironically because they're spending so much time prepping for exams. Also, sedentary people—this is medical fact—get less oxygen to

OCEAN DUMPING

Visualize a beautiful beach, with white sand, blue skies, sparkling water, a warm sun, and seagulls. See yourself walking on the beach, carrying a small plastic pail. Stop at a good spot and put your worries and whatever may be bugging you into the pail. Drop it at the water's edge and watch it drift out to sea. When the pail is out of sight, walk on.

TAKE A HIKE, PAL

When you're in the middle of studying and hit a wall, take a short, brisk walk. Breathe deeply and swing your arms as you walk. Clear your mind. (And don't forget to look for flowers that grow in the cracks of the sidewalk.)

CYBERSTRESS

If you spend a lot of time in cyberspace anyway, do a search for the phrase *stress management*. There's a ton of stress advice on the Net, including material specifically for students.

NUTRITION AND STRESS: THE DOS AND DON'TS

Do eat:

- Fruits and vegetables (raw is best, or just lightly steamed or nuked)
- Low-fat protein such as fish, skinless poultry, beans, and legumes (like lentils)
- Whole grains such as brown rice, whole wheat bread, and pastas

Don't eat:

- Refined sugar; sweet, high-fat snacks (simple carbohydrates like sugar make stress worse, and fatty foods lower your immunity)
- Salty foods (they can deplete potassium, which you need for nerve functions)

the blood and hence to the head than active people. You can live fine with a little less oxygen; you just can't think as well.

Any big test is a bit like a race. Thinking clearly at the end is just as important as having a quick mind early on. If you can't sustain your energy level in the last sections of the exam, there's too good a chance you could blow it. You need a fit body that can weather the demands any big exam puts on you. Along with a good diet and adequate sleep, exercise is an important part of keeping yourself in fighting shape and thinking clearly for the long haul.

There's another thing that happens when students don't make exercise an integral part of their test preparation. Like any organism in nature, you operate best if all your "energy systems" are in balance. Studying uses a lot of energy, but it's all mental. When you take a study break, do something active instead of raiding the fridge or vegging out in front of the TV. Take a five- to ten-minute activity break for every fifty or sixty minutes that you study. The physical exertion gets your body into the act which helps to keep your mind and body in sync. Then, when you finish studying for the night and hit the sack you won't lie there, tense and unable to sleep, because your head is overtired and your body wants to pump iron or run a marathon.

One warning about exercise, however: It's not a good idea to exercise vigorously right before you go to bed. This could easily cause sleep-onset problems. For the same reason, it's also not a good idea to study right up to bedtime. Make time for a "buffer period" before you go to bed: For thirty to sixty minutes, just take a hot shower, meditate, simply veg out.

Get High . . . Naturally

Exercise can give you a natural high, which is the only kind of high you can afford right now. Using drugs (prescription or recreational) specifically to prepare for and take a big test is definitely self-defeating. Except for the drugs that occur naturally in your brain, every drug has major drawbacks—and a false sense of security is only one of them.

You may have heard that popping uppers helps you study by keeping you alert. If they're illegal, definitely forget about it. You're just wasting your time. Amphetamines make it hard to retain information. So you'll stay awake, but you probably won't remember much of what you read. And, taking an upper before you take the test could really mess things up. You're already going to be a little anxious and hyper; adding a strong stimulant could easily push you over the edge into panic. Remember, a little anxiety is a good thing. The adrenaline that gets pumped into your bloodstream helps you stay alert and think more clearly. But, too much anxiety and you can't think straight at all.

Mild stimulants, such as coffee, cola, or over-the-counter caffeine pills can sometimes help as you study, since they keep you alert. On the down side, they can also lead to agitation, restlessness, and insomnia. Some people can drink a pot of high-octane coffee and sleep like a baby. Others have one cup and start to vibrate. It all depends on your tolerance for caffeine.

Alcohol and other depressants are out, too. Again, if they're illegal, forget about it. Depressants wouldn't work, anyway, since they lead to the inevitable hangover/crash, the fuzzy thinking, and lousy sense of judgment. These are not going to help you ace the test.

Instead, go for endorphins—the "natural morphine." Endorphins have no side effects and they're free—you've already got them in your brain. It just takes some exercise to release them. Running around on the basketball court, bicycling, swimming, aerobics, power walking—these activities cause endorphins to occupy certain spots in your brain's neural synapses. In addition, exercise develops staying power and increases the oxygen transfer to your brain. Go into the test naturally.

Take a Deep Breath . . .

Here's another natural route to relaxation and invigoration. It's a classic isometric exercise that you can do whenever you get stressed out—just before the test begins, even *during* the test. It's very simple and takes just a few minutes.

Close your eyes. Starting with your eyes and—*without holding your breath*—gradually tighten every muscle in your body (but not to the point of pain) in the following sequence:

1. Close your eyes tightly.
2. Squeeze your nose and mouth together so that your whole face is scrunched up. (If it makes you self-conscious to do this in the test room, skip the face-scrunching part.)
3. Pull your chin into your chest, and pull your shoulders together.
4. Tighten your arms to your body, then clench your hands into tight fists.
5. Pull in your stomach.

STRESS TIP

Don't study on your bed, especially if you have problems with insomnia. Your mind may start to associate the bed with work, and make it even harder for you to fall asleep.

THE RELAXATION PARADOX

Forcing relaxation is like asking yourself to flap your arms and fly. You can't do it, and every push and prod only gets you more frustrated. Relaxation is something you don't work at. You simply let it happen. Think about it. When was the last time you tried to force yourself to go to sleep, and it worked?

6. Squeeze your thighs and buttocks together, and tighten your calves.
7. Stretch your feet, then curl your toes (watch out for cramping in this part).

At this point, every muscle should be tightened. Now, relax your body, one part at a time, in reverse order, starting with your toes. Let the tension drop out of each muscle. The entire process might take five minutes from start to finish (maybe a couple of minutes during the test). This clenching and unclenching exercise should help you to feel very relaxed.

And Keep Breathing

Conscious attention to breathing is an excellent way of managing test stress (or any stress, for that matter). The majority of people who get into trouble during tests take shallow breaths. They breathe using only their upper chests and shoulder muscles, and may even hold their breath for long periods of time. Conversely, the test taker who by accident or design keeps breathing normally and rhythmically is likely to be more relaxed and in better control during the entire test experience.

So, now is the time to get into the habit of relaxed breathing. Do the next exercise to learn to breathe in a natural, easy rhythm. By the way, this is another technique you can use during the test to collect your thoughts and ward off excess stress. The entire exercise should take no more than three to five minutes.

With your eyes still closed, breathe in slowly and deeply through your nose. Hold the breath for a bit, and then release it through your mouth. The key is to breathe slowly and deeply by using your diaphragm (the big band of muscle that spans your body just above your waist) to draw air in and out naturally and effortlessly. Breathing with your diaphragm encourages relaxation and helps minimize tension.

As you breathe, imagine that colored air is flowing into your lungs. Choose any color you like, from a single color to a rainbow. With each breath, the air fills your body from the top of your head to the tips of your toes. Continue inhaling the colored air until it occupies every part of you, bones and muscles included. Once you have completely filled yourself with the colored air, picture an opening somewhere on your body, either natural or imagined. Now, with each breath you exhale, some of the colored air will pass out the opening and leave your body. The level of the air (much like the water in a glass as it is emptied) will begin to drop. It will descend progressively lower, from your head down to your feet. As you continue to exhale the colored air, watch the level go lower and lower, farther and farther down your body. As the last of the colored air passes out of the opening, the level will drop down to your toes and disappear. Stay quiet for just a moment. Then notice how relaxed and comfortable you feel.

Thumbs Up for Meditation

Once relegated to the fringes of the medical world, meditation, biofeedback, and hypnosis are increasingly recommended by medical researchers to reduce pain from headaches, back problems—even cancer. Think of what these powerful techniques could do for your test-related stress and anxiety.

Effective meditation is based primarily on two relaxation methods you've already learned: body awareness and breathing. A couple of different meditation techniques follow. Experience them both, and choose the one that works best for you.

Breath Meditation

Make yourself comfortable, either sitting or lying down. For this meditation you can keep your eyes open or close them. You're going to concentrate on your breathing. The goal of the meditation is to notice everything you can about your breath as it enters and leaves your body. Take three to five breaths each time you practice the meditation, which should take about a minute for the entire procedure.

Take a deep breath and hold it for five to ten seconds. When you exhale, let the breath out very slowly. Feel the tension flowing out of you along with the breath that leaves your body. Pay close attention to the air as it flows in and out of your nostrils. Observe how cool it is as you inhale and how warm your breath is when you exhale. As you expel the air, say a cue word such as *calm* or *relax* to yourself. Once you've exhaled all the air from your lungs, start the next long, slow inhale. Notice how relaxed feelings increase as you slowly exhale and again hear your cue words.

Mantra Meditation

For this type of meditation experience you'll need a mental device (a mantra), a passive attitude (don't try to do anything), and a position in which you can be comfortable. You're going to focus your total attention on a mantra you create. It should be emotionally neutral,

THINK GOOD THOUGHTS

Create a set of positive, but brief affirmations and mentally repeat them to yourself just before you fall asleep at night. (That's when your mind is very open to suggestion.) You'll find yourself feeling a lot more positive in the morning. Periodically repeating your affirmations during the day makes them even more effective.

repetitive, and monotonous, and your aim is to fully occupy your mind with it. Furthermore, you want to do the meditation passively, with no goal in your head of how relaxed you're supposed to be. This is a great way to prepare for studying or taking the test. It clears your head of extraneous thoughts and gets you focused and at ease.

Sit comfortably and close your eyes. Begin to relax by letting your body go limp. Create a relaxed mental attitude and know there's no need for you to force anything. You're simply going to let something happen. Breathe through your nose. Take calm, easy breaths and as you exhale, say your mantra (*one, ohhm, aah, soup*—whatever is emotionally neutral for you) to yourself. Repeat the mantra each time you breathe out. Let feelings of relaxation grow as you focus on the mantra and your slow breathing. Don't worry if your mind wanders. Simply return to the mantra and continue letting go. Experience this meditation for ten to fifteen minutes.

Quick Tips for the Days Before the Exam

DRESS FOR SUCCESS

When you dress on the day of the test, do it in loose layers. That way you'll be prepared no matter what the temperature of the room is. (An uncomfortable temperature will just distract you from the job at hand.)

And, if you have an item of clothing that you tend to feel "lucky" or confident in—a shirt, a pair of jeans, whatever—wear it. A little totem couldn't hurt.

- The best test takers do less and less as the test approaches. Taper off your study schedule and take it easy on yourself. You want to be relaxed and ready on the day of the test. Give yourself time off, especially the evening before the exam. By that time, if you've studied well, everything you need to know is firmly stored in your memory banks.
- Positive self-talk can be extremely liberating and invigorating, especially as the test looms closer. Tell yourself things such as, "I choose to take this test" rather than "I have to"; "I will do well" rather than "I hope things go well"; "I can" rather than "I cannot." Be aware of negative, self-defeating thoughts and images and immediately counter any you become aware of. Replace them with affirming statements that encourage your self-esteem and confidence. Create and practice doing visualizations that build on your positive statements.
- Get your act together sooner rather than later. Have everything (including choice of clothing) laid out days in advance. Most important, know where the test will be held and the easiest, quickest way to get there. You will gain great peace of mind if you know that all the little details—gas in the car, directions, etcetera—are firmly in your control before the day of the test.

- Experience the test site a few days in advance. This is very helpful if you are especially anxious. If at all possible, find out what room your part of the alphabet is assigned to, and try to sit there (by yourself) for a while. Better yet, bring some practice material and do at least a section or two, if not an entire practice test, in that room. In this case, familiarity doesn't breed contempt; it generates comfort and confidence.

- Forego any practice on the day before the test. It's in your best interest to marshal your physical and psychological resources for twenty-four hours or so. Even race horses are kept in the paddock and treated like princes the day before a race. Keep the upcoming test out of your consciousness; go to a movie, take a pleasant hike, or just relax. Don't eat junk food or tons of sugar. And—of course—get plenty of rest the night before. Just don't go to bed too early. It's hard to fall asleep earlier than you're used to, and you don't want to lie there thinking about the test.

Handling Stress During the Test

The biggest stress monster will be the day of the test itself. Fear not; there are methods of quelling your stress during the test.

- Keep moving forward instead of getting bogged down in a difficult question or passage. You don't have to get everything right to achieve a fine score. So, don't linger out of desperation on a question that is going nowhere even after you've spent considerable time on it. The best test takers skip (temporarily) difficult material in search of the easier stuff. They mark the ones that require extra time and thought. This strategy buys time and builds confidence so you can handle the tough stuff later.

- Don't be thrown if other test takers seem to be working more busily and furiously than you are. Continue to spend your time patiently but doggedly thinking through your answers; it's going to lead to higher-quality test taking and better results. Don't mistake the other people's sheer activity as signs of progress and higher scores.

WHAT ARE "SIGNS OF A WINNER," ALEX?

Here's some advice from a Kaplan instructor who won big on *Jeopardy!*™ In the green room before the show, he noticed that the contestants who were quiet and "within themselves" were the ones who did great on the show. The contestants who did not perform as well were the ones who were fact-cramming, talking a lot, and generally being manic before the show. Lesson: Spend the final hours leading up to the test getting sleep, meditating, and generally relaxing.

- *Keep breathing!* Weak test takers tend to share one major trait: they forget to breathe properly as the test proceeds. They start holding their breath without realizing it, or they breathe erratically or arrhythmically. Improper breathing hurts confidence and accuracy. Just as importantly, it interferes with clear thinking.

- Some quick isometrics during the test—especially if concentration is wandering or energy is waning—can help. Try this: Put your palms together and press intensely for a few seconds. Concentrate on the tension you feel through your palms, wrists, forearms, and up into your biceps and shoulders. Then, quickly release the pressure. Feel the difference as you let go. Focus on the warm relaxation that floods through the muscles. Now you're ready to return to the task.

- Here's another isometric that will relieve tension in both your neck and eye muscles: Slowly rotate your head from side to side, turning your head and eyes to look as far back over each shoulder as you can. Feel the muscles stretch on one side of your neck as they contract on the other. Repeat five times in each direction.

With what you've just learned here, you're armed and ready to do battle with the test. This book and your studies will give you the information you'll need to answer the questions. It's all firmly planted in your mind. You also know how to deal with any excess tension that might come along, both when you're studying for and taking the exam. You've experienced everything you need to tame your test anxiety and stress. You are going to get a great score.

PRACTICE TESTS AND ANSWERS

HOW TO TAKE THE PRACTICE TESTS

Before taking each test, find a quiet place where you can work uninterrupted for about two and a half hours. Make sure you have a comfortable desk and several No. 2 pencils.

Each Practice Test includes four scored multiple choice sections. Keep in mind that on the actual LSAT, there will be an additional multiple-choice section—the experimental section—that will not contribute to your score, plus an unscored Writing Sample.

Use the grid on the following page to record your answers for Practice Test One. You may record your answers for Practice Tests Two and Three on the grids immediately preceding each test.

Once you start a Practice Test, don't stop until you've gone through all four sections. Remember, you can review any questions within a section, but you may not go back or forward a section.

You'll find answer keys and explanations following each test. Use the score converter on pages 155 and 156 to calculate your score for each Practice Test.

Good luck!

HOW TO CALCULATE YOUR SCORE

Step 1

Add together your total number correct for all four sections.
This is your raw score.

Section 1   _____
(# correct)

Section 2   _____
(# correct)

Section 3   _____
(# correct)

Section 4   _____
(# correct)

_____

Total Correct   _____
(raw score)

Step 2

Find your raw score on the table below and read across
to find your scaled score and your percentile.

Raw Score	Scaled Score	Percentile Rank	Raw Score	Scaled Score	Percentile Rank
0	120	0	19	129	1
1	120	0	20	130	2
2	120	0	21	130	2
3	120	0	22	130	2
4	120	0	23	131	2
5	120	0	24	132	3
6	120	0	25	133	3
7	120	0	26	133	3
8	121	0	27	133	3
9	122	0	28	134	4
10	122	0	29	135	5
11	123	0	30	136	6
12	124	0	31	136	6
13	124	0	32	137	8
14	125	0	33	137	8
15	126	1	34	138	9
16	126	1	35	138	9
17	127	1	36	139	10
18	128	1	37	140	13

Raw Score	Scaled Score	Percentile Rank	Raw Score	Scaled Score	Percentile Rank
38	140	13	70	157	74
39	140	13	71	158	77
40	141	15	72	158	77
41	142	17	73	159	80
42	142	17	74	159	80
43	143	20	75	160	83
44	144	23	76	160	83
45	144	23	77	161	86
46	144	23	78	162	88
47	145	26	79	162	88
48	146	29	80	162	88
49	146	29	81	163	90
50	147	33	82	164	92
51	147	33	83	164	92
52	148	37	84	165	93
53	148	37	85	166	95
54	149	41	86	166	95
55	150	45	87	167	96
56	150	45	88	167	96
57	150	45	89	168	97
58	151	50	90	169	97
59	151	50	91	170	98
60	152	54	92	170	98
61	153	58	93	171	98
62	153	58	94	172	99
63	153	58	95	173	99
64	154	62	96	174	99
65	155	66	97	175	99
66	155	66	98	176	99
67	156	70	99	177	99
68	156	70	100	179	99
69	156	70	101	180	99

PRACTICE TEST ONE
SECTION I
Time—35 minutes

25 questions

Directions: This test is composed of questions that ask you to analyze the logic of statements or short paragraphs. You are to choose as the answer to each question the one choice you consider <u>best</u> on the basis of your common-sense evaluation of the statement and its assumptions. Although a question may seem to have more than one acceptable answer, there is only one <u>best</u> answer, and it is the one that does not entail making any illogical, extraneous, or conflicting assumptions about the question. These questions do not pre-suppose any knowledge of formal logic on your part.

1. If we must refrain from liberating the conquered islands simply because the lives of some civilians would be endangered, then we must never engage in any kind of armed conflict near populated areas.

    The author of the argument above assumes that

    (A) armed conflict invariably endangers the lives of civilians
    (B) the conquered islands can be liberated without conflict
    (C) one cannot engage in armed conflict near popu-lated areas without endangering civilians
    (D) the liberation of the conquered islands is less important than the lives of a few civilians
    (E) the conquered islands should be liberated despite the risk to civilians

2. Marybeth will go shopping only when she has her mother's permission. Her mother allows her to go shop-ping alone at the mall down the street, but she insists that Marybeth take Sue and Desiree along for any shop-ping expeditions to the downtown department stores.

    Which one of the following conclusions can be logically inferred from the statements above?

    (A) If Marybeth is shopping alone, then she is not shopping at a department store.
    (B) If Marybeth is shopping, then Sue and Desiree are with her.
    (C) If Desiree is not with Marybeth, then Marybeth is not shopping.
    (D) If Marybeth is shopping at the downtown department stores, then Sue is with her.
    (E) If Desiree and Sue are with her, then Marybeth is shopping at the downtown department stores.

3. The owners of an Italian bicycle manufacturing compa-ny, unhappy that 20 percent of their new "Street Fleet" bicycles came back for repair within six months of pur-chase, recalled every "Street Fleet" bicycle and altered them to make them less susceptible to ordinary wear and tear. They improved the construction by switching to an equally lightweight but sturdier metal, and by increasing the number of spokes supporting the rim. The company renamed the new bikes "Rough Rider," and in six months sold roughly the same number of these as the original "Street Fleets." Despite the improvements, 50 percent of the "Rough Riders" came back for repairs within six months of purchase.

    Which one of the following, if true, most helps to explain the unexpected results noted in the passage?

    (A) The higher costs of the new manufacturing process have forced the owners to close one of their two service centers.
    (B) The company's new promotional literature on the "Rough Rider" now appeals to customers more apt to ride the bikes on unusually rough terrain.
    (C) The company has broadened its warranty on the "Rough Rider" so that it now covers parts as well as labor.
    (D) The aerodynamic design, initially suspected to cause the "Street Fleet" to veer slightly left-ward at top speeds, was not corrected in the "Rough Rider."
    (E) The bikes still use a braking system that puts an unusually large amount of pressure on both the front and back rims.

GO ON TO THE NEXT PAGE.

Questions 4–5

Ms. Maloney: Drug X is effective only when its cumulative effects are allowed to work on the body over several months. Drug Y, however, works much more quickly and is just as powerful as drug X. I know that drug Y has side effects, but it will cure my daughter more quickly, so it's the best thing for her. I demand that you replace her current dosage of drug X with the same dosage of drug Y.

Doctor Ortiz: Yes, drug Y is as effective as drug X, but it has not yet been thoroughly tested for use with children. Side effects that are merely inconvenient for adults may prove to be very harmful for children. Drug X has been very successful so far, and it's a better choice in this case.

4. Which one of the following is the main point at issue between Ms. Maloney and Dr. Ortiz?

(A) whether the use of drug Y should be discontinued for use in treatment because of its side effects

(B) whether the patient's current dosage of medicine is inappropriate for children

(C) whether it is justifiable to try a drug that may be harmful when a safer drug is available

(D) whether the patient would be a viable test subject for an experiment on drug Y's effects on children

(E) whether parents should be able to recommend changes in medication prescribed for their children

5. Doctor Ortiz's position most closely conforms to which one of the following principles?

(A) Doctors are more qualified to prescribe treatment than are even the most well-informed parents.

(B) When there is a choice between two similar treatments, the patient's potential safety should be the primary factor in the decision.

(C) Adults and children have very different medical needs, and doctors must base treatment recommendations on the age of the patient in question.

(D) If a certain treatment is found to be effective, it is unwise to change to another treatment without a valid medical reason.

(E) Drugs that work by accumulating in the body are less jarring to a patient's immune system than are quick-acting drugs.

6. Botanists have found that a certain wildflower that is known to have bordered the cart paths of New England in colonial times does not grow on the modern roadsides that cover the same tracts of land. Obviously, the botanists have concluded, these particular flowers could not tolerate the auto emissions, since other wildflower species have continued to flourish on roadsides without any perceptible change in number.

The argument above presupposes which of the following?

(A) No disease specific to the wildflowers in question could have caused their disappearance, while leaving other species intact.

(B) Pollution has been shown to be the cause of the demise of many botanical species since the invention of the automobile.

(C) The flowers are not found in areas of New England that are sheltered from auto emissions.

(D) Auto emissions have grown steadily more toxic as the evolution of the automobile has progressed.

(E) Most botanical species are able to adapt to changing environments without undergoing drastic evolutionary change.

7. Vegetables, in the proper combinations, can provide all of the nutrients necessary for human life. A mixture of whole grains and legumes, for instance, contains protein of a quality at least as high as that of animal protein, and the major vitamin and mineral groups can easily be represented in an all-vegetable diet. What's more, a little culinary imagination can make a vegetarian feast as varied and interesting as any meal based around meat. Given these facts, it's certainly time that we outlaw the raising and slaughtering of domestic livestock and turn to the wider cultivation of high-nutrition crops.

Which one of the following is a major flaw of the argument above?

(A) The author does not provide a full definition of the terms used in the argument.

(B) The author bases the conclusion on an inappropriate analogy.

(C) The evidence provided by the author does not sufficiently support the conclusion.

(D) The author does not demonstrate that a wider cultivation of high-nutrition crops is feasible.

(E) The author employs circular reasoning in making the argument.

GO ON TO THE NEXT PAGE.

Questions 8–9

Public speaker: When Daphne LaBranche was caught littering in the state park she was given a stiff fine, which the judge said would go toward the park's upkeep. When Ewell McTavish was caught doing the same thing, he was let off with a reprimand and a nominal fine. Granted, Daphne's litter spread out over a wider area and was harder to pick up, but that was only because it was a windy night when she littered, not because she dumped more litter. The offenses were virtually identical. The judge only gave Daphne a stiffer fine because she's wealthy, and he was using a court case to do a little fund raising. That's patently unjust. The judge punished Daphne for her wealth rather than for her crime.

8. Which one of the following best describes the function performed in the argument by the statement that Daphne's litter was harder to pick up than Ewell's?

   (A) It presents additional evidence that directly supports the argument's conclusion that Daphne was treated unfairly.
   (B) It shows the author is aware of a reason for a possible objection to his contention that Daphne and Ewell deserved equal punishment.
   (C) It deliberately characterizes the judge's position in an opposing argument in an unfair way so as to discredit it.
   (D) It explains the reasoning that led the judge to impose a harsher fine on Daphne.
   (E) It emphasizes the difference between the seriousness of Daphne's offense and Ewell's offense.

9. Which one of the following principles, if established, would do most to justify the speaker in concluding from the evidence presented that Daphne was treated unfairly?

   (A) A judge should not treat crimes against state property more severely than crimes against public property.
   (B) The desire to do good often causes a judge to violate the letter of the law.
   (C) The only consideration in punishing a criminal should be the seriousness of his or her crime.
   (D) A person cannot be held legally responsible for natural phenomena and "acts of God."
   (E) The primary purpose of a legal sentence should be deterrence of future crime rather than punishment of the convicted criminal.

10. Delgado's hiring policy is fundamentally unsound for a large corporation like our own. She insists that we should fill executive positions with recent business school graduates because "their grasp of theory more than makes up for a lack of hands-on experience, even though they may not yet be presidential material." That kind of thinking is extremely dangerous. Readers of flying manuals may know a lot about flying, but that hardly qualifies them to pilot a jumbo jet.

Which one of the following methods of argumentation is most central to the passage above?

   (A) using a specific example in order to illustrate and support a general principle
   (B) illustrating a judgment by drawing an analogy between two situations
   (C) attacking an opponent's belief by impugning the motives of that opponent
   (D) showing that an existing policy will lead to a conflict of interest
   (E) making a judgment about one type of situation by alluding to findings in another type of situation

11. In seeking indisputable proof that the continents as we know them today are in fact the result of millions of years of drift and collision, one scientist noted that marsupials are generally found only in South America and Australia. In fact, even the parasites of marsupials on the two continents are the same. He concluded that at one time these two great land masses were joined, with Antarctica as the link, and that marsupials and other mammals migrated to Australia from South America.

Which one of the following, if true, would most probably be cited by a scientist wishing to dispute the claim that marsupials came to Australia from South America?

   (A) Its present ice and snow cover make travel across Antarctica difficult at best.
   (B) An Australian marsupial captured in the wild and flown to a South American country is unlikely to thrive there.
   (C) Years of intensive work on the rich fossil fields of Antarctica have yielded many kinds of bones, but none of marsupials.
   (D) The oldest known marsupial fossil is of a North American animal that resembles today's opossum.
   (E) Marsupial bones discovered in Antarctica resemble neither those of South American nor those of Australian marsupials.

GO ON TO THE NEXT PAGE.

12. Student: Dismissing Ms. Geschwitz because of her known advocacy of drug legalization amounts to a denial of her constitutional rights. Her personal views are her own business and have nothing to do with her work as a guidance counselor.

School administrator: Ms. Geschwitz is free to proclaim her views in private. As an administrator, it is my responsibility to balance her rights against those of the parents of our students, who do not want their children unduly influenced by someone whose views they do not agree with.

Which one of the following would be most relevant to investigate in evaluating the validity of the school administrator's position?

(A) whether Ms. Geschwitz could be persuaded to take another position at the school that would require no contact with students
(B) whether Ms. Geschwitz has ever used her authority to convince students to adopt her views
(C) what the student population thought of Ms. Geschwitz's work as a guidance counselor
(D) whether Ms. Geschwitz is the only school employee who espouses controversial opinions
(E) whether any parents of the students share Ms. Geschwitz's controversial views regarding drug legalization

13. Director: I know that our bylaws prohibit the inclusion in the festival of plays that have received more than five full productions, but I think we should make an exception in the case of *The Green Light Revue*, since all seven of its productions were short runs staged in tiny theaters with very small audiences.

The bylaws are most probably intended to ensure that the festival includes plays that

(A) have already proven their appeal in previous productions
(B) are actual narrative plays rather than revues
(C) have not already received wide exposure
(D) are suitable for production in small theaters
(E) are not running elsewhere simultaneously

14. Advertisement: The residents of East Hollow, New Jersey, were given free samples of Treegro feed for their oaks. As a result of this distribution of Treegro over the past ten years, the oaks in East Hollow are 4 inches taller than the average New Jersey oak. For taller oaks, try Treegro today.

Which one of the following, if true, is the strongest criticism of the suggestion made in the above advertisement that the product will cause oaks to grow taller?

(A) Most oaks in East Hollow were already ten years old when the distribution of Treegro was begun.
(B) Half of the trees in New Jersey were recently planted under a federally sponsored reforestation program.
(C) Many New Jersey residents living outside of East Hollow also used Treegro on their oaks.
(D) Many oaks in New Jersey grow in heavily industrialized towns.
(E) The average age of East Hollow oaks is substantially greater than that of other New Jersey oaks.

15. Polychlorinated biphenyls, a versatile group of chemicals used in Michigan in recent years to aid in the cultivation of animal feed grain, should be banned immediately lest they cause more harm to humans. Residual traces of the biphenyls used in the cultivation of feed grain have been found in the cow feed distributed to hundreds of Michigan farmers over the past ten years.

Which one of the following, if true, most conclusively strengthens the argument above?

(A) Scientists have observed an unusually high rate of intestinal cancer among consumers of Michigan dairy products over the past two years.
(B) Traces of polychlorinated biphenyls have been found in the blood and urine of many Michigan cows.
(C) Michigan has one of the highest cancer rates in the country.
(D) Industrial scientists who contributed to the research and development of polychlorinated biphenyls conducted extensive tests to ascertain the safety of the chemicals.
(E) The rate of sterility among Michigan cows greatly exceeds the national average.

GO ON TO THE NEXT PAGE.

Questions 16–17

Esmeralda: According to environmentalists, personality traits are determined and molded by the growing child's home environment. Yet identical twins who are separated at birth and reared by adoptive families of different socioeconomic and educational levels are often found later in life to have the same tastes, temperaments, and patterns of behavior. Obviously, environment has little to do with the development of personality.

Lothar: Environment is a factor that must work upon the genetic material at hand, and the significant aspect of environment is not so much the family's socioeconomic and educational background as its level of commitment to nurturing the individual child.

16. Lothar's response has which one of the following relations to Esmeralda's views?

(A) It presents a logical consequence of her views.
(B) It strengthens her views by pointing out supporting evidence that had not been mentioned.
(C) It supplies a premise for Esmeralda's argument that had not been stated explicitly.
(D) It cannot be true if Esmeralda's assertion concerning the development of adoptive identical twins is true.
(E) It weakens Esmeralda's argument by pointing out its lack of precision.

17. The point at issue between Esmeralda and Lothar is

(A) whether genetics or environment plays more of a role in the development of personality
(B) whether Esmeralda's evidence about adopted identical twins necessarily demonstrates that environment has little effect on personality development
(C) whether families of less privileged educational and socioeconomic backgrounds are as capable of nurturing their children as are families of more privileged educational and socioeconomic backgrounds
(D) whether personality traits predetermined by genetics can be overcome through the proper environmental influences
(E) whether families are as committed to nurturing their adopted children as they are to nurturing their biological children

18. If Larry studied harder, he would have more confidence in his abilities. He would feel better about himself, and he would be glad that he had made the decision to study harder. His whole outlook on school would improve. Clearly, then, Larry's increase in study time will lead to increased confidence.

Which one of the following arguments contains flawed reasoning that most closely parallels the flawed reasoning in the argument above?

(A) If voters were to research our candidate's background, they would understand why she is the best person for the job. She has made great strides in the area of human rights, she has lowered taxes, and she has improved our school system. Clearly, therefore, if voters make a well-informed choice, they will probably choose our candidate.
(B) If students with difficulties in specific subject areas seek tutoring, they will probably improve. Tutoring also allows superior students to review their own work while helping classmates to learn. Tutoring leads to overall scholastic improvement. Thus, all schools should implement tutoring programs.
(C) If television were made more educational, more parents would approve of it. Parents would recommend programs for their children, and let them choose their own viewing patterns. Their entire opinion of TV would be revised. Obviously, therefore, a rise in educational programming will lead to an increase in parental approval of television.
(D) If historians want to know how people lived, they should stage reenactments of historical events. They would learn more about customs, while coping with some of the same hardships that historical personages had to cope with. Therefore, reenactments are one of the most powerful tools that historians can use.
(E) Obviously we should pay more attention to the effects of workplace pollutants on our employees. Not only will the number of insurance claims rise if we continue to ignore health hazards, but we will also be faced with an increasing number of lawsuits. Clearly, therefore, we should form a committee to investigate the sources of workplace pollutants.

GO ON TO THE NEXT PAGE.

19. Four out of five people who filled out our questionnaire about solar energy indicated that they would strongly support any decision to direct more federal resources toward solar energy research, even if it involved cutting funds to synthetic fuel research. How, then, can the Administration claim that interest in solar energy is waning? The direction of public opinion is clear.

The argument above would be most conclusively weakened if it could be demonstrated that

(A)   people who oppose solar energy research are far less likely to fill out a questionnaire than are people who support it

(B)   synthetic fuel is a cheaper and cleaner source of energy than is solar power

(C)   those who filled out questionnaires were not knowledgeable about energy issues

(D)   the Administration has never been known in the past to willfully mislead the public

(E)   the need for alternative energy sources will increase significantly in the future

20. Newspapers have completely overemphasized Dalyville's rate of violent deaths for this year. One isolated incident, a bus crash, was the cause of more than three-fourths of the violent deaths in the city this year. Meanwhile, papers are printing headlines like, "Violent Death Rate Skyrockets in Dalyville This Year!" This is hurting our tourism industry and making some citizens of Dalyville afraid to walk the streets at night.

If the statements above are true, which one of the following conclusions is most strongly supported by them?

(A)   Dalyville has never before had an accident as major as this year's bus crash.

(B)   Newspapers should never print statistics without the prior approval of city tourism associations.

(C)   Citizens of Dalyville are apt to react strongly to statistics published by the news media.

(D)   The term "violent death" is too vague to allow for appropriate interpretation of these statistics.

(E)   Misuse of statistics on the part of news media has given Dalyville an undeservedly poor reputation.

21. Barbara Weston is a travel agent whose agency deals exclusively with business travel packages. Her agency had advertised only in *People and Places,* a monthly magazine, since its beginning, but she realized that this magazine did not reach many of her potential clients. Therefore, she changed all of her advertising to *Paper Money,* a weekly newspaper. Many of *Paper Money*'s readers are international business travelers, and it has lower advertising rates than *People and Places*. After one year, however, she discovered that the amount of revenue generated by advertising for her business had plummeted.

Which one of the following, if true, does most to explain the steep drop in revenue generated by advertising?

(A)   *People and Places* has a much higher total readership and serves a more diverse population than does *Paper Money*.

(B)   The ad in *People and Places* would be seen by many people who take frequent family trips to resorts and amusement areas.

(C)   The amount of money spent on a business trip by a *People and Places* reader is likely to be far greater than the amount spent by a reader of *Paper Money,* a "budget" travel publication.

(D)   The circulation of *People and Places* has risen steadily for the last five years, and will probably surpass that of *Paper Money* within two years.

(E)   Although *People and Places* has higher advertising rates, the cost of advertising over a year would work out to be approximately the same as that of advertising in *Paper Money* for a year.

GO ON TO THE NEXT PAGE.

KAPLAN

Questions 22–23

A study of women between the ages of thirty and fifty-five found that even those who are moderately overweight run a substantially higher risk of heart disease. Of the women observed, even the moderately overweight were at an 80 percent higher risk than were the thinnest women. Thus, at weights considered average on the height-and-weight charts issued by insurance companies, there was an increased risk of heart disease. This is the first time that being moderately overweight has been alleged to be a health risk.

22. If all of the statements in the passage are true, which one of the following must also be true on the basis of them?

   (A) Insurance premiums for moderately overweight women will rise.

   (B) Weights listed as average on insurance company charts may in fact be in excess of what is healthy.

   (C) Obesity poses as serious a risk to health as do heavy smoking and excessive alcohol consumption.

   (D) Overweight women are at as great a risk for heart disease as are comparably overweight men.

   (E) Overweight women aged thirty to fifty-five are more likely to suffer from heart disease than are overweight women in any other age group.

23. A group of doctors is deciding whether to recommend that their overweight female patients aged thirty to fifty-five lose weight. In addition to the information in the passage, it would also be useful for the doctors to consider which one of the following?

   (A) the risk, if significant, of heart disease for women aged fifty-five and older

   (B) the risk, if significant, of heart disease for women between the ages of fifteen and thirty

   (C) the percentage of women between the ages of thirty to fifty-five who are overweight

   (D) the risk of heart disease for women between the ages of thirty to fifty-five who are very overweight

   (E) the benefits, if any, of a woman aged thirty to fifty-five being slightly overweight

24. If human beings attempt to understand their lives, then they will be faced with certain unanswerable questions. That will lead them to admit the uncertainty underlying all things. If they make that admission, they will conclude that their lives are necessarily without meaning. Thus, if human beings attempt to understand their lives, they will conclude that their lives are without meaning.

Which one of the following uses reasoning most similar to that used in the argument above?

   (A) If people believe that their lives are meaningful, they must admit that life itself has a discernible purpose, and thus that life itself can be understood. If people believe that life can be understood, they will never give up trying to understand their lives. As a result, if people believe that their lives are meaningful, they will never give up trying to understand their lives.

   (B) If human beings attempt to answer unanswerable questions, they will be faced with a decision between admitting that their understanding is limited or that the world is unknowable. If they decide the former, they must admit that their lives are meaningless; if the latter, that the world is meaningless.

   (C) Because human beings attempt to understand their lives, they ask themselves unanswerable questions. Because they ask themselves unanswerable questions, they conclude that the world is unknowable and therefore meaningless. Thus, human beings should not attempt to understand their lives.

   (D) If human beings attempt to understand that which is incomprehensible, they will have to admit defeat. If they admit defeat, they will soon regard their lives as meaningless. If they regard their lives as meaningless, they will no longer attempt to understand that which is incomprehensible. Therefore, it is impossible to attempt to understand that which is incomprehensible.

   (E) Whenever people attempt to find meaning in their lives, they ask unanswerable questions. When they ask unanswerable questions, they must provide themselves with false answers. False answers, therefore, are incompatible with the attempt to find meaning in life.

GO ON TO THE NEXT PAGE.

25. Between November and April, Fairvale's city pound collected an average of twenty-five stray animals per month. Yet between May and October the average dropped to seven strays per month. It's clear that fewer animals roam the streets of Fairvale during the warmer months from May to October than during the colder months, November through April, since the pound employs the same number of people all year long.

For the conclusion that fewer animals roam the streets of Fairvale during the warmer as opposed to the colder months to be valid based on the evidence cited, the author must assume which one of the following?

(A) The pound facilities have room to handle at least thirty-five animals at a time, including those who remain there for several months.

(B) The pound does not have any temporary or seasonal employees who substitute for employees on leave or vacation.

(C) Diseases such as rabies and distemper tend to be more prevalent in Fairvale during the summer months.

(D) The drop in the number of animals impounded was not caused by a change in animal impoundment regulations.

(E) A similar drop in impoundings during the summer months has been observed in many other pounds across the country.

STOP
IF YOU FINISH BEFORE TIME IS CALLED, YOU MAY CHECK YOUR WORK ON THIS SECTION ONLY. DO NOT WORK ON ANY OTHER SECTION IN THE TEST.

SECTION II
Time—35 minutes
27 questions

<u>Directions</u>: Each selection in this test is followed by several questions. After reading the selection, choose the <u>best</u> response to each question and mark it on your answer sheet. Your replies are to be based on what is <u>stated</u> or <u>implied</u> in the selection.

The War of 1812 has been a curiosity in American history—an inconclusive, mostly inglorious conflict that contemporaries insisted was of the utmost importance to new nation but one that even they had difficulty explaining.
(5) The historiography of the war has been small in quantity and disproportionately concerned with the war's causes. Steven Watts's ambitious but flawed book aims to explain why contemporary Americans said what they did about the war and to recast it as a central event in the formation of the
(10) nineteenth-century republic.

Watts argues that between 1790 and the first decade of the nineteenth century many Americans worried about the evident contradictions between republican ideology, which emphasized patriotic devotion to public good, and their own
(15) individualistic economic behavior-a contention he illustrates with numerous sketches of prominent political, intellectual, literary, and religious figures, most of whom favored war as a means of establishing the "national character" of the United States. By probing their personal experiences and public
(20) pronouncements, Watts concludes that their views-and those of the nation large-emerged from attempts to resolve inner doubts over the disparity between the austere prescriptions of republicanism and the reality of their personal lives. The war promised these and other Americans a release from guilt,
(25) an opportunity to demonstrate the kind of self-sacrifice shown by the Founding Fathers, and a means of validating their own liberal political and economic behavior. The war's brought an emotional purgation and established the hegemony of a new political economy, liberal republicanism,
(30) in America.

This robust formulation is not without problems. Most seriously, the thesis that war crystallized an emergent American culture and defined its future course is more asserted than proved. Although Watts faults previous
(35) historians for not clarifying "vital connections between economic change, transforming social values, developing political ideology, and the actual circumstances of the war," he devotes only one section of his last chapter to analyzing these conditions. The rest of the book examines how
(40) Americans viewed the prospect of conflict and the prevailing psychological "compulsion to war." Thus, despite its stated intent to analyze "the complicated function of war in

American society," the book mostly adds to the old debate on the war's causes.
(45) Beyond this, some may find Watts's insistence on psychological explanations for his witnesses' behavior to be reductionist in character, since it can make all other meanings subordinate. Others may object that his attribution of great transforming power to "liberalization" is
(50) too arbitrary-little different from other scholars' similar claims for modernization. Such judgments will depend on readers' ideological commitments and personal tastes. Individual preferences aside, however, Watts's book merits the attention of anyone interested in the transition from
(55) republican to liberal political and economic culture in postrevolutionary America.

1. The author of the passage is primarily concerned with

   (A) recommending an approach
   (B) establishing a historical perspective
   (C) evaluating an interpretation
   (D) describing a traditional viewpoint
   (E) contrasting scholarly explanations

2. It can be inferred from the passage that Watts believes that the attitudes toward the War of 1812 displayed by many of the figures cited in his book were

   (A) more favorable than most Americans
   (B) more ambivalent than most Americans
   (C) at odds with the views of the Founding Fathers regarding war
   (D) shaped to a large degree by personal considerations
   (E) indicative of a general opposition to liberal republicanism

GO ON TO THE NEXT PAGE.

3. According to the passage, which one of the following has characterized most histories of the War of 1812?

(A) an exaggeration of the republican loyalties of supporters of the war

(B) a preoccupation with explaining the antecedents of the war

(C) appraisals of the economic and political consequences of the war

(D) studies of the links between the war and the new national culture

(E) analyses of the 'compulsion to war' then prevalent in American society

4. The author suggests that the "psychological explanations" (line 46) given by Watts for the actions of many of the witnesses cited in his book

(A) add significantly to previous studies of the war's cultural impact

(B) are among the least controversial aspects of Watts's study

(C) may be viewed as offering unsatisfactory accounts of those actions

(D) ignore the economic and political motivations of those witnesses

(E) overlook apparent inconsistencies in the recorded statements of those witnesses

5. The passage suggests that Watts would be most likely to agree with which of the following?

(A) The attitudes of prominent national figures are a reliable indicator of the general sentiments of the American public.

(B) The connection between historical events and the development of American political culture cannot be precisely determined.

(C) The Founding Fathers favored going to war as a means of ridding the nation of its collective guilt.

(D) The experiences of ordinary people provide historians with little information of real value about the era in which they lived.

(E) The most useful insights into historical events are provided by books that ignore cultural developments.

6. Which of the following best expresses the author's main point?

(A) Watts's book contributes several new insights to an emerging debate over the causes of the War of 1812.

(B) American leaders were preoccupied with the inconsistencies between their political philosophy and their social and economic status in the decades before the War of 1812.

(C) Watts's book focuses more on the causes of the War of 1812 than on the connections between the war and the rise of liberal republicanism in America.

(D) Watts's belief that the national character of the United States was reshaped by developments leading up to and following the War of 1812 is incorrect.

(E) Historians have neglected the links between the War of 1812 and liberal republicanism because they have been too concerned with examining the causes of the war.

7. The author of the passage would most likely agree with which of the following statements about Watts's study of the War of 1812?

(A) It provides an interesting but ultimately unpersuasive analysis of the war's consequences.

(B) It provides a compelling explanation of the war's effects but neglects many of its significant causes.

(C) It is likely to be a major influence on the work of future historians of the war.

(D) It represents a notable advance over previous studies of the war.

(E) It is primarily useful for its psychological interpretations of public attitudes toward the war.

GO ON TO THE NEXT PAGE.

Until quite recently, the pattern of early marine animal evolution seemed to be fairly well established. It was believed that most present-day animal groups had appeared during the "Cambrian explosion," an extraordinary burgeoning of
(5) multicellular life in the warm seas of the Cambrian period, between 570 and 500 million years ago. It was assumed that, despite the very large number of species that appeared during the Cambrian explosion, nearly all fit into the same small number of phyla that exist today. Each phylum—a
(10) group of organisms with the same basic pattern of organization, such as the radial symmetry of jellyfish and other coelenterates or the segmented structure of worms and other annelids—was seen as evolutionarily stable. While countless numbers of species have arisen and died out,
(15) development and extinction were assumed to have occurred within existing phyla. The elimination of entire phyla was thought to be extremely rare.

Nonetheless, a diverse group of marine fossils, known as the Problematica, always posed difficulties for this
(20) interpretation. The Problematica show patterns of organization so unique that it is hard to fit them into present-day phyla. Notable examples are the banana-shaped *Tullimonstrum* and the spiny *Hallucigenia*. The Ediacaran fauna, which respired, absorbed nutrients, and eliminated
(25) wastes directly through their external surfaces, are other odd examples. The developmental approach taken by this extinct subgroup appears in just a very few modern creatures (such as tapeworms), which are otherwise totally dissimilar.

Several theorists now feel that the Problematica are not
(30) just hard to classify; they supply evidence that the conventional view of the Cambrian explosion is wrong. These researchers argue that the Cambrian explosion represented the simultaneous appearance of a far larger number of animal phyla than exists today. Each phylum was
(35) essentially a separate "experiment" in basic body design, and the Cambrian seas teemed with phyla, each represented by just a few species. Today the number of phyla has fallen drastically, but each surviving phylum contains a much larger number of species—there are at least 20,000 species of
(40) fish alone. The Problematica, according to the new view, were not bizarre and unsuccessful variants within present-day phyla. Rather, each represented a distinct phylum in its own right.

While all theorists agree that species develop through
(45) natural selection, the revisionists recognized that the selection process has eliminated not only individual traits, but entire body plans, entire approaches to survival. The Ediacaran fauna, for instance, developed a unique solution to the problems of gas and fluid exchange with their
(50) environment, but their approach to body engineering was lost when the group died out. Given the improbability of duplicating an entire body plan through chance mutation, it was unlikely that the approach would ever be tried again.

8. The author implies that the theorists discussed in the third paragraph view efforts to classify the Problematica in present-day phyla with

(A) complete enthusiasm
(B) cautious optimism
(C) considerable skepticism
(D) substantial indifference
(E) growing ambivalence

9. The description in lines 23–26 of the Ediacaran fauna suggests that they

(A) may not belong in any present-day phylum
(B) were entirely unlike any other known organisms
(C) could only absorb or excrete fluids with difficulty
(D) were probably members of the same phylum as *Tullimonstrum*
(E) may be closely related to modern tapeworms

10. The passage implies that present-day phyla contain

(A) a relatively small number of species each
(B) species more dissimilar than many phyla in the Cambrian period
(C) many species showing basic structural similarities
(D) species that have undergone little evolutionary change
(E) a very large number of species that existed during the Cambrian period

GO ON TO THE NEXT PAGE.

11. Coelenterates and annelids are mentioned in paragraph one in order to give examples of

(A)   phyla that disappeared because their body plans were not viable

(B)   the structural patterns characteristic of some modern phyla

(C)   phyla that are closely related to the Problematica

(D)   phyla that have evolved since the Cambrian period

(E)   groups of organisms that do not fit into conventional evolutionary models

12. The passage implies that conventional and revisionist theorists differ about all the following EXCEPT

(A)   the general pattern of marine animal evolution in the Cambrian period

(B)   the probable number of marine animal phyla during the Cambrian period

(C)   the likelihood of an entire phylum becoming extinct

(D)   whether large numbers of species appeared during the Cambrian period

(E)   whether the Problematica can be assigned to present-day phyla

13. The passage contains information that can be used to answer which of the following questions?

(A)   In what period did the majority of modern species evolve?

(B)   What marine animals existed prior to the Cambrian explosion?

(C)   Why did many Cambrian organisms eventually become extinct?

(D)   How do some Cambrian species differ from modern species?

(E)   Why did marine animal life proliferate during the Cambrian period?

14. Which of the following most accurately summarizes the author's view of the argument that evolution has involved variation within a small number of stable phyla?

(A)   It is supported by the discovery that *Hallucigenia* occupy a phylum of their own.

(B)   It is probably accurate but requires more evidence to be accepted.

(C)   It has weaknesses but is superior to any other theory.

(D)   It does not explain why most present-day species appeared within a relatively brief period.

(E)   It rests on questionable assumptions and fails to explain important data.

GO ON TO THE NEXT PAGE.

KAPLAN

Given his visionary and increasingly abstract interpretations of landscape, the English artist J.M.W. Turner (1775–1851) is often called an artistic forerunner of Impressionism. Yet Andrew Wilton argues that Turner is at (5) the same time rooted in an older aesthetic tradition, that of the "sublime." Before landscape painting was accepted in the nineteenth-century as an artistic rendering of reality—a materialistic notion that led eventually to Impressionism—it was seen as an aesthetic expression of a universal spiritual (10) ideal.

The roots of the aesthetic notion of the sublime, Wilton argues, can be found in Aristotelian concepts of art as mimicking or otherwise expressive of the universe. In the first century A.D., the Greek writer Longinus observed (15) (according to an eighteenth-century paraphrase of his treatise *On the Sublime*) that "the effect of the sublime is to lift the human soul toward the splendor of divinity." For centuries, the sublime in all forms of art was understood as elevating the human toward unity with the divine.

(20) The sublime was originally associated with literary rather than visual art, as its connotations of mystery and power were more readily evoked in words. Its subject matter was epic, historical, or religious, and its focus on the human condition was explicit. To eighteenth-century thinkers, (25) Homer's epics, the stories of the Bible, and Milton's poems were all quintessentially sublime. As the concept was gradually applied to painting, the original narrative emphasis continued. Thus, for the eighteenth-century English portrait painter Joshua Reynolds, Michelangelo's *Last Judgment* (30) exemplified the sublime. For this reason, landscape painting, which lacked the human presence (except incidentally), was viewed as distinctly inferior.

The conceptual transition that led to public recognition of Turner's achievement in landscape had several sources. (35) One was the eighteenth century's enthusiasm for scientific studies of nature. A second was the rise of an educated, affluent English middle class possessing the leisure to travel, which created a demand for artistic renderings of the natural vistas of Wales, Scotland, and the European continent. (40) Another was the popularity of nature epics such as Thomson's "The Seasons," which applied blank verse, with its own connotations of the sublime, to the portrayal of nature's vastness.

By the end of the century there was a well-defined (45) contemporary notion of the sublime which emphasized nature. According to Burke's essay of 1757, the sublime was most closely linked to vastness, lack of habitation and cultivation, and danger. In Turner's landscapes, these qualities appear in a series of sub-genres that, as Wilton

(50) shows, encompass the major themes in Turner's body of work: the "picturesque" sublime, the "terrific," or terrifying, sublime, the sublime of the mountains, sea, and darkness, and, surprisingly, even the "architectural," or urban, sublime.

15. The author's primary purpose in the passage is to

(A) argue that Turner's art has been experienced in multiple and often contradictory ways
(B) discuss the idea of the sublime as related to the development of Turner's art
(C) examine the sources of nineteenth-century landscape painting
(D) compare the concept of the sublime in literature and painting
(E) dispute the view of Turner as a precursor of Impressionism

16. According to the author, Burke contributed to the development of the concept of the sublime specifically by

(A) defending landscape painting as a genre worthy of recognition
(B) broadening the concept of the sublime to include nature
(C) giving a clearer definition of the sublime than earlier writers
(D) defining qualities in nature that could be considered sublime
(E) rejecting a traditional identification of the sublime with religious experience

17. The author suggests that as the concept of the sublime developed

(A) it eventually lost its universal implications
(B) historical and epic subjects became more common
(C) traditional connotations were applied to natural scenes
(D) its appeal to writers gradually declined
(E) it was separated from the idea of vastness

GO ON TO THE NEXT PAGE.

18. The author suggests which of the following about the "rise of an educated, affluent English middle class" (lines 36–37)?

    (A)   It increased the popularity of Impressionism.

    (B)   It led to a declining popular interest in the sublime.

    (C)   It reinforced traditional notions of the sublime.

    (D)   It influenced cultural sensibilities regarding nature.

    (E)   It created a market for Turner's paintings.

19. According to the passage, landscapes were not originally seen as embodying the sublime because

    (A)   the conception of the sublime was human-centered

    (B)   only religious subjects were seen as embodying the sublime

    (C)   the sublime was originally a literary rather than a pictorial concept

    (D)   landscape painting was traditionally viewed as realistic

    (E)   nature was not considered awe-inspiring

20. With which of the following statements about Turner would the author most probably agree?

    (A)   Turner was an underappreciated artist during his own lifetime.

    (B)   Turner had little regard for earlier artists such as Michelangelo.

    (C)   Turner's paintings appealed more to middle- than upper-class buyers of art.

    (D)   Turner's landscapes should not be seen as having influenced Impressionist painters.

    (E)   Turner's landscapes encompass a variety of different images of the sublime.

21. The author mentions Joshua Reynolds primarily in order to

    (A)   emphasize the connection between the sublime and the narrative tradition in painting

    (B)   illustrate the impact of Homer's epics on eighteenth-century portrait painting

    (C)   explain some of the literary and visual sources of nineteenth-century landscape painting

    (D)   clarify the relationship between eighteenth-century English portrait painting and contemporary nature epics

    (E)   suggest ways in which literary and visual concepts of the sublime differed

GO ON TO THE NEXT PAGE.

KAPLAN

In order to understand the hostility that has surrounded the idea of comparable worth, it is necessary to examine the opponents' arguments. These involve three related contentions: the male-female earnings gap results, largely, (5) from factors unrelated to discrimination by particular employers; comparable worth analysis is logistically impossible since there is no objective basis for establishing comparisons between different jobs; and, third, pay equity based on comparable worth would cripple the free market.

(10) The argument that the male-female wage gap results from non-discriminatory factors is clearly expressed in a report by the U. S. Civil Rights Commission. The Commission essentially argues three propositions: women choose low-paying jobs because of sociological predisposition; women (15) make educational choices which lead to low-paying jobs; and the interrupted participation of women in the labor force leads to lower pay. Each contention is misguided or flawed, but the report's most serious shortcoming is that it mistakenly assumes that the validity of comparable worth (20) theory depends upon a demonstration that discrimination accounts for the entire wage gap between men and women workers. The issue in comparable worth litigation is not some generalized assertion about any overall wage gap, but a specific complaint that particular disparities between men (25) and women, working for one employer, in enumerated positions, are the result of discrimination.

The second major argument mounted against comparable worth is that no objective technique exists for comparing jobs that are not identical in content. The Civil Rights (30) Commission contends that job evaluations are inherently subjective and cannot establish jobs' intrinsic worth. This objection, though partially valid, goes too far. While evaluation techniques are not absolutely objective, job evaluation is a well-established technique in American (35) industry for determining relative wage levels. Even a cursory examination of industrial relations practice demonstrates that business and industry have long used specific techniques to determine the relative wage rates of jobs which are dissimilar in content.

(40) The third argument raised against comparable worth is that it requires an unwarranted intrusion into the market. This argument's proponents insist that supply and demand curves create the wage disparity at issue. Thus, comparable worth theory is not a legitimate response to discrimination (45) but rather a specious definition of discrimination. If there is no discrimination, there is no justification for interference with market forces. This argument would cloak impermissible sex-based discrimination in the putative legality of "market operation." Yet the argument sidesteps (50) the contention of comparable worth proponents that, despite a pay differential, the jobs are equivalent according

to a rational standard. The market-based argument is instructive in that it links criticisms of the allegedly spurious nature of comparable worth with antipathy to the remedy—(55) interference with the market. It is this connection which is critical to an understanding of judicial opinions in the comparable worth area, since judges often defer to the operation of the market.

22. Which of the following, if true, would most strengthen the author's belief about the relationship between discrimination and the male/female wage gap?

(A) An experienced female patent attorney employed by a law firm earns less money than an inexperienced male patent attorney employed by a rival firm.

(B) A female computer programmer working for an engineering company earns less money than her junior male co-worker.

(C) A female airline pilot with ten years on the job earns less money than her male counterpart with twenty years on the job.

(D) A female corporate vice president earns less money than the male corporate president, even though she must work longer hours.

(E) A highly regarded female plastic surgeon in private practice earns less money than a mediocre male vascular surgeon employed by the local hospital.

23. The author's assertion that job evaluation is a justifiable technique for comparing dissimilar jobs is qualified by an admission that

(A) risks to a company's economic health cannot be ruled out

(B) the technique can cause divisiveness among a company's employees

(C) subjectivity cannot be entirely avoided in making the evaluations

(D) the technique is a recent, relatively untested procedure

(E) objectivity is not desirable in establishing comparable worth

GO ON TO THE NEXT PAGE.

24. It can be inferred that opponents of the idea of comparable worth have concluded which of the following?

    (A) Interference with market forces is involved in all social reform.
    (B) Application of the idea would be economically beneficial, but socially harmful.
    (C) The legal opinions of judges often reflect an unwillingness to interfere with market forces.
    (D) Sex-based wage discrimination is a widespread phenomenon that should be dealt with by individual employers.
    (E) Wage disparities between men and women result primarily from sociological factors and the effects of supply and demand.

25. According to the author's argument, opinions of the Civil Rights Commission in regard to comparable worth have included all of the following assertions EXCEPT:

    (A) The unequal pay of women does not stem primarily from discriminatory practice on the part of employers.
    (B) It is not feasible to measure the relative value of dissimilar jobs.
    (C) Women are paid at lower rates because their participation in the labor force is intermittent.
    (D) Women are predisposed to choosing poorly paying employment positions.
    (E) There can never be justification for judicial interference with the functioning of a free market.

26. The author suggests that the argument that wage disparities are a legitimate result of supply and demand fails to take into account the

    (A) notion that a job's intrinsic worth can only be measured subjectively
    (B) possibility that two jobs with dissimilar pay can be determined to possess equal value
    (C) idea that market forces should never be manipulated for political purposes
    (D) legitimate role of the courts in shaping an appropriate response to wage disparities
    (E) occurrence of social injustice in America

27. The author's attitude toward the U.S. Civil Rights Commission finding that discrimination is not a factor in the male-female wage gap can best be described as

    (A) totally dismissive
    (B) fervently enthusiastic
    (C) somewhat bewildered
    (D) quietly opposed
    (E) politely supportive

S T O P
**IF YOU FINISH BEFORE TIME IS CALLED, YOU MAY CHECK YOUR WORK ON THIS SECTION ONLY.
DO NOT WORK ON ANY OTHER SECTION IN THE TEST.**

SECTION III
Time—35 minutes
24 questions

Directions: Each group of questions is based on a set of conditions. You may wish to draw a rough sketch to help you answer some of the questions. Choose the best answer for each question and fill in the corresponding space on your answer sheet.

Questions 1–6

A basketball coach is forming two three-person teams to play against each other in a scrimmage game. The coach can choose from the following players: Charles, Edna, Greg, Jerrod, Katya, Mort, Paulina, and Terence. Each person chosen for a team plays opposite a specific player chosen for the other team. Those not chosen sit on the bench.

Charles, Edna, Katya, and Paulina are tall; the rest of the players are short.
A tall player can play only opposite another tall player.
If Paulina is chosen, Charles is chosen to play opposite her.
If Terence is chosen, Charles is chosen and plays on the same team as Terence.

1. Which one of the following players must be chosen for a team?

   (A) Edna
   (B) Terence
   (C) Katya
   (D) Charles
   (E) Jerrod

2. Which one of the following is an acceptable team?

   (A) Paulina, Jerrod, Charles
   (B) Charles, Jerrod, Mort
   (C) Jerrod, Mort, Greg
   (D) Mort, Paulina, Greg
   (E) Edna, Katya, Charles

3. Which one of the following pairs of players CANNOT sit together on the bench?

   (A) Edna and Katya
   (B) Jerrod and Paulina
   (C) Mort and Jerrod
   (D) Paulina and Edna
   (E) Greg and Terence

4. Paulina can play on the same team as any one of the following EXCEPT:

   (A) Edna
   (B) Greg
   (C) Katya
   (D) Terence
   (E) Mort

5. If one team consists of Katya, Charles, and one other player, how many possible combinations are there for the other team?

   (A) 1
   (B) 2
   (C) 3
   (D) 4
   (E) 5

6. Which one of the following CANNOT be true?

   (A) Paulina and Mort are chosen for different teams, while Edna sits on the bench.
   (B) Paulina is chosen while Greg sits on the bench.
   (C) Paulina and Edna are chosen for different teams, while Jerrod and Greg sit on the bench.
   (D) Charles is chosen for the same team as Mort and Terence, while Paulina sits on the bench.
   (E) Terence and Edna are chosen for the same team, while Katya sits on the bench.

GO ON TO THE NEXT PAGE.

Questions 7–12

A laboratory is testing six chimps for acquisition of communication skills. The six chimps are Alonzo, Bobo, Carlo, Dingo, Elmo, and Frank. A technician will work with one chimp at a time for a single time slot—defined as an entire morning or an entire afternoon. Each chimp will be tested exactly once. Time slots not filled by chimp testing are considered free. The tests will be conducted during a single week from Monday to Friday.

Alonzo is tested on Thursday morning.
Bobo, Elmo, and Frank sleep late, and can be tested only in the afternoon.
No testing is conducted on Monday morning.
Elmo is not tested on Monday or Tuesday.
The time slot immediately preceding that in which Alonzo is tested is free.
Alonzo is tested after Dingo but before Frank.
Carlo is tested on Tuesday.

7. Which one of the following must be true?

   (A)   Bobo is tested on Monday.
   (B)   Alonzo is the fourth chimp tested.
   (C)   Carlo is the second chimp tested.
   (D)   Alonzo is tested immediately before Frank.
   (E)   There are exactly three free morning time slots.

8. Which one of the following pairs of chimps CANNOT be tested on the same day?

   (A)   Bobo and Dingo
   (B)   Carlo and Dingo
   (C)   Carlo and Bobo
   (D)   Alonzo and Elmo
   (E)   Alonzo and Frank

9. If Dingo is tested on Tuesday morning, which one of the following must be true?

   (A)   Elmo is tested on Thursday.
   (B)   Frank is tested on Friday.
   (C)   Bobo is tested on Monday.
   (D)   There are exactly two free morning time slots.
   (E)   There are exactly two free afternoon time slots.

10. If Frank is tested two days after Bobo is tested, which one of the following can be false?

   (A)   Frank is tested immediately after Alonzo.
   (B)   Bobo is tested immediately after Carlo.
   (C)   The free time slots are only on Monday, Wednesday, and Friday.
   (D)   Elmo is the last chimp tested.
   (E)   Dingo is the first chimp tested.

11. If Dingo is tested in the afternoon, in how many different ways can the chimps be scheduled for testing?

   (A)   1
   (B)   2
   (C)   3
   (D)   4
   (E)   5

12. If at least one chimp is tested each day, and if Elmo is tested on the same day as another chimp, which one of the following must be true?

   (A)   Bobo is tested in the time slot immediately preceding the time slot in which Carlo is tested.
   (B)   Elmo is tested on the day after Dingo is tested.
   (C)   Carlo is tested in the time slot immediately preceding the time slot in which Dingo is tested.
   (D)   No other chimp is tested between Bobo and Dingo.
   (E)   Exactly one other chimp is tested between Carlo and Elmo.

GO ON TO THE NEXT PAGE.

Questions 13–18

A teacher instructs her class to create four separate pictures to be used as scenery for a school play. There are to be one dog picture, one house picture, and two tree pictures. Each picture is done in one of two media, paint or crayon. Each picture is done in one of three colors—blue, red, or yellow.

There is exactly one blue and one yellow picture.
The two tree pictures are done in different colors but in the same medium.
The blue and yellow pictures are not done in the same medium.
The dog picture is done in crayon.
One tree picture is done in red.

13. Which one of the following is an acceptable group of four pictures?

(A) Blue crayon dog, red painted house, red painted tree, yellow crayon tree
(B) Yellow crayon dog, red painted house, blue painted tree, red crayon tree
(C) Blue crayon dog, red painted house, red painted tree, yellow painted tree
(D) Yellow crayon dog, blue painted house, red crayon tree, red crayon tree
(E) Yellow painted dog, red painted house, blue crayon tree, red crayon tree

14. If the maximum number of pictures is done in crayon, which one of the following must be true?

(A) A tree is done in blue.
(B) A tree is done in yellow.
(C) The dog is done in red.
(D) The house is done in blue.
(E) The house is done in yellow.

15. If the dog picture is done in blue, which one of the following must be FALSE?

(A) There are more crayon pictures than painted pictures.
(B) There are more painted pictures than crayon pictures.
(C) The house is done in crayon.
(D) The house is done in paint.
(E) One tree is done in yellow.

16. If the house is done in yellow, which one of the following CANNOT be true?

(A) The trees are done in paint.
(B) The trees are done in crayon.
(C) There is an equal number of pictures done in crayon and in paint.
(D) Both red pictures are done in paint.
(E) The yellow picture is done in crayon.

17. If neither of the tree pictures is done in yellow, and if there are more painted pictures than those done in crayon, then which one of the following is true?

(A) The dog picture must be done in blue paint.
(B) The house picture could be done in red crayon.
(C) The house picture could be done in yellow paint.
(D) The dog picture must be done in red crayon.
(E) The house picture must be done in red paint.

18. Which one of the following pieces of additional information would make it certain that the dog picture is done in blue or yellow?

(A) Exactly three pictures are done in crayon.
(B) Exactly three pictures are done in paint.
(C) The house is done in blue.
(D) A tree is done in blue.
(E) The house is done in yellow.

GO ON TO THE NEXT PAGE.

Questions 19–24

Nine chairs are arranged in a circle, with each chair facing the center of the circle. Lisa, Marvin, Naomi, Oliver, Pam, Randi, and Sybil each sit in one of the chairs. The other two chairs are empty.

> Sybil sits immediately to Marvin's left.
> Randi sits three chairs to Sybil's right.
> Neither Randi nor Sybil sits next to empty chairs.
> Lisa sits in a chair immediately next to Oliver.

19. Which one of the following must be true?

    (A) Pam sits next to Randi.
    (B) Naomi sits next to Randi.
    (C) Lisa sits next to an empty chair.
    (D) The empty chairs are immediately next to each other.
    (E) Oliver sits next to Sybil.

20. If Oliver sits two chairs to the right of Randi, which one of the following could be false?

    (A) Randi sits three chairs away from an empty chair.
    (B) Oliver sits next to an empty chair.
    (C) Lisa sits next to Randi.
    (D) Exactly two people sit between Pam and Naomi.
    (E) Pam sits next to Sybil.

21. Which one of the following CANNOT be true?

    (A) Pam sits next to neither Randi nor Sybil.
    (B) Oliver sits next to neither Randi nor Sybil.
    (C) Pam sits immediately between Randi and Marvin.
    (D) Sybil sits next to Lisa.
    (E) Sybil sits next to Naomi.

22. If Lisa sits next to an empty chair, how many different arrangements of people in chairs are possible?

    (A) 2
    (B) 3
    (C) 4
    (D) 5
    (E) 6

23. Which one of the following statements would allow one to determine the exact positions of all seven people?

    (A) Exactly two people sit between Lisa and Pam.
    (B) Oliver sits next to Sybil.
    (C) Exactly one person sits between Lisa and Naomi.
    (D) Lisa sits next to Randi.
    (E) Exactly two people sit between Oliver and Naomi.

24. If Sybil sits two chairs to Marvin's right, but all of the other conditions remain the same, which one of the following statements CANNOT be true?

    (A) Marvin sits next to an empty chair.
    (B) Pam sits next to an empty chair.
    (C) Randi sits next to Oliver.
    (D) Naomi sits exactly three chairs away from Lisa.
    (E) Sybil sits exactly three chairs away from Lisa.

S T O P
**IF YOU FINISH BEFORE TIME IS CALLED, YOU MAY CHECK YOUR WORK ON THIS SECTION ONLY.
DO NOT WORK ON ANY OTHER SECTION IN THE TEST.**

SECTION IV
Time—35 minutes
25 questions

Directions: This test is composed of questions that ask you to analyze the logic of statements or short paragraphs. You are to choose as the answer to each question the one choice you consider <u>best</u> on the basis of your common-sense evaluation of the statement and its assumptions. Although a question may seem to have more than one acceptable answer, there is only one <u>best</u> answer, and it is the one that does not entail making any illogical, extraneous, or conflicting assumptions about the question. These questions do not presuppose any knowledge of formal logic on your part.

1. Mass public education in the past half-century has clearly failed at the most basic level. In fact, it has been detrimental to the public welfare. Recent studies show that only about half of the country's graduating high school seniors can compose a simple business letter.

    Which one of the following, if true, gives the strongest support to the author's argument?

    (A) A larger percentage of high school seniors than ever before are able to write a business letter correctly.

    (B) At least 15 percent of today's high school seniors speak English as a second language.

    (C) Fewer than half of the high school seniors graduating today can do the math necessary to complete an income tax return.

    (D) More accurate data show that only 46 percent of the nation's high school seniors can compose a simple business letter.

    (E) A survey taken five decades ago showed that four out of five graduating seniors could write an acceptable business letter.

2. Editorial: Residents who accept miserable air quality and dangerous levels of pollution as unavoidable concomitants of living in a city the size of Eastchester should consider recent history. Five years ago we all accepted a crumbling infrastructure and hopeless traffic congestion as inevitable, until Mayor Angel made transportation his top priority and spent the necessary money to fix the system. The mayor doesn't seem to place the same value on clean air, but there is a candidate who has promised to make it her top priority. Those citizens who share her concern should remember what determination can accomplish and should vote for Inge Schwartz.

    Which one of the following best describes the argumentative strategy employed by the editorial?

    (A) It draws a causal connection between the city's former inefficient transportation system and its current problem with air pollution.

    (B) It contrasts Schwartz's willingness to spend money on programs she considers to be important with the mayor's unwillingness to do the same.

    (C) It demonstrates that air pollution in Eastchester is not an inevitable result of the city's size, but instead is a correctable problem.

    (D) It exhorts the readers to place clean air at the top of their list of priorities and therefore to vote for Schwartz.

    (E) It compares Eastchester's pollution problem to its former transportation problem in order to imply that the current problem can be solved by city government.

GO ON TO THE NEXT PAGE.

3. Wisdom does not come from a life of untrammeled ease but only from adversity. Constanza is a very wise old woman—therefore she must have suffered a great deal in her life.

Which one of the following most closely parallels the reasoning in the above argument?

(A) Character is a result of early training in patience and fortitude. Leon is a man of exemplary character, so he must have had dutiful parents.

(B) Denise won the gold medal at the Olympics, so she must have had an excellent coach, since such a high level of performance can come only with the very best training and preparation.

(C) Good health cannot develop without attention to proper nutrition. Farley will remain healthy throughout his life since he is a fanatic about eating a healthy diet.

(D) Francois is a brilliant musician; he must have been surrounded by other excellent musicians from the day he was born, since musical ability flourishes only among people who have some steady exposure to good music.

(E) A society that does not provide for its poor stands condemned as a failure, despite its other political and cultural achievements. Therefore our own society will be judged harshly by history.

4. Economists can directly compare how effectively different economic systems perform specific tasks—for example, the number of automobiles or tons of steel produced at what cost in labor—simply by referring to the relevant statistics. Assuming the statistics are accurate, one system then can be fairly judged better or worse than others in terms of its operational effectiveness. In comparing systems as a whole, however, the difficulty of comparing their unquantifiable aspects—such as what constitutes an acceptable level of unemployment or a fair distribution of income—may produce widely diverging opinions among economists who otherwise concur in their analyses of the systems' relative operational merits.

If all of the statements in the passage are true, which one of the following must also be true on the basis of them?

(A) An economic system's effectiveness in performing specific tasks cannot be accurately determined by statistical analysis alone.

(B) The statistics on unemployment and income distribution within a given economic system are frequently considered unreliable by economic analysts.

(C) In comparing economic systems as a whole, economists must inevitably make value judgments about certain aspects of the systems' performances.

(D) Most economists would agree that the relative merits of different economic systems should not be assessed on the basis of their productive capabilities.

(E) Comparative analysis of different economic systems depends on agreement among economists about how statistics should be correctly interpreted.

GO ON TO THE NEXT PAGE.

KAPLAN

5. Although we tend to measure the phenomenon of aging in a casual way by referring to the passing of chronological time, this really provides an incomplete description of an animal's or a human being's real physiological age. Physiological, or "true," age relates the physiological changes brought about in the animal by the passing of chronological time to the whole aging process of its species. A fifteen-year-old cat could aptly be described as "very old," which would not be true of a horse younger than twenty years, while a fifty-year-old human being nowadays could be considered still relatively young.

    It can be most properly inferred from the above that

    (A)   people are better able to make an accurate determination of another person's age than of an animal's age
    (B)   the idiosyncrasies of animal physiology preclude any meaningful use of words such as old or young in descriptions of age
    (C)   evaluating an animal's physiological condition is not the most accurate way of determining its true age
    (D)   definitions of the adjectives "old" and "young" depend on whether they are applied to humans or to other animals
    (E)   knowing the chronological age of any animal is meaningful as a measure of true age only when its species' life span is also known

6. The city council's policy of granting contracts for construction projects to companies filing the lowest bid is an invitation to disaster. The effect of the policy is that bridges, buildings, and other public works are built with inferior materials and workmanship, creating a situation which is not only dangerous but financially self-defeating. Extra maintenance costs on poorly constructed projects are excessive, often negating within a few years the savings on original building costs. This misguided policy must be changed if we are to maintain a safe and efficient infrastructure in this city.

    Which one of the following, if true, would significantly weaken the argument above?

    (A)   The need to rebuild poorly constructed buildings provides many jobs for the city's residents.
    (B)   The city's building contracts rarely specify the quality of the materials or workmanship to be employed.
    (C)   The policy requires that the city entertain bids only from firms whose plans meet very stringent standards of workmanship and materials.
    (D)   Even buildings that are constructed with the finest materials and workmanship can be dangerous if their architectural design is faulty.
    (E)   The city is already operating with an enormous budget deficit and cannot afford to spend more money on the construction and maintenance of the projects in question.

GO ON TO THE NEXT PAGE.

7. Evidently, the director's intention here was to draw a contrast between the social status of the military and that of the working classes during the second World War. The drab, simple clothing of the charwomen and chimney sweeps indicates a debased socioeconomic position, whereas the crisp, neat, colorful uniform of General Von Vandt denotes the respect and honor accorded to German fighting men. We must not allow the conversational allusions to social equality to blind us to the film's powerful visual message.

The author's argument presupposes which one of the following?

(A) Film is fundamentally a visual medium.
(B) Moviegoers are frequently misled by filmmakers' subtle messages.
(C) Viewers are prone to ignore the visual aspects of a film.
(D) A film's true message can be conveyed visually rather than verbally.
(E) Social distinctions between working people and the military were unique to Germany during the second World War.

8. The government is considering two different sites—one on the Abaco River and one on the Bornos River—for the multibillion dollar hydroelectric plant. Although the technical expertise exists to build roughly the same plant in either place, producing roughly the same amount of electricity per hour, building the plant on the Abaco site will cost over twice as much money. With the federal budget currently in deficit, it is clear why they should choose to build the dam at the Bornos site.

Which one of the following would be most useful in explaining the difference in building costs for the two proposed dam sites?

(A) Many farms along the lower Bornos River valley would benefit from the controlled flow of water a dam would make possible.
(B) The Abaco site is in an inaccessible area, requiring the building of new roads and the importation of nonlocal labor.
(C) The Bornos site is near a large city whose residents could use the resulting lake for inexpensive recreation.
(D) The Abaco site is in an area that contains many endangered species that would be threatened by the new dam.
(E) The Abaco River has a relatively low volume of flow, making it impossible to expand an Abaco plant to meet future electricity needs.

GO ON TO THE NEXT PAGE.

Questions 9–10

Menendez: My mother stated in her living will that she would refuse life-saving treatment if she became terminally ill. Yet when she stopped breathing, you attached her to a respirator. Your refusal to let her die despite her repeated requests to be taken off the machine amounts to a breach of your duty as a physician.

Doctor: Although this state honors living wills, my duty as a physician is nonetheless to intervene, if necessary, in order to save lives. I cannot "play God," even if it means acting against patients' wishes.

9. Which one of the following principles, if established, would determine that attaching Mrs. Menendez to a respirator was the right decision or instead would determine that her wishes should have been heeded?

   (A) If a patient whose life is being artificially sustained has expressed the desire to die, the physician is morally obliged to facilitate that desire.
   (B) If a terminally ill patient has expressed the desire to die, the physician is obliged to intervene medically to facilitate that desire.
   (C) When a patient with a living will is in a persistent vegetative state, the physician is obliged to carry out the desires expressed in that will, regardless of the family's wishes.
   (D) When a terminally ill patient has expressed a clear wish to die, the physician is obliged to honor that request, regardless of when the request was originally expressed.
   (E) If a terminally ill patient's desires contradict what she originally expressed in her living will, the physician is obliged to carry out the wishes of the patient's closest living relative.

10. Which one of the following characterizations of the doctor's response would contribute most to a defense by Menendez against the doctor's position?

    (A) It leads to the further but unacceptable conclusion that only those who can afford life-saving treatment should be eligible to receive it.
    (B) It draws a false distinction between the patient's desire and the physician's professional obligation.
    (C) It is imprecise in that it fails to demonstrate that artificially prolonging someone's life is different from "playing God."
    (D) It overlooks the possibility that the patient could later change her mind regarding her desire to die.
    (E) It assumes without warrant that the patient did not make her request when she was mentally competent.

11. A single remark can mean many different things in different contexts, its connotations changing with the situation in which it is uttered and the person uttering it. However, most remarks contain objective information that is not subject to interpretation.

    Which one of the following is most similar in principle to the situation described above?

    (A) Many athletes compete to be the best in their sport, but only one can actually win that honor.
    (B) A particular tie can look different with many different suits, but most ties have definite, individual traits.
    (C) A single work of art can provoke many different reactions from different people, but most artwork cannot easily be classified as good or bad.
    (D) A particular person may behave differently in different situations, but most people find that consistency is a desirable character trait.
    (E) A comment that was intended as praise can sometimes be interpreted as criticism by an individual, but most people wouldn't misinterpret the comment.

GO ON TO THE NEXT PAGE.

12. In order to promote off-season business, Mt. Dunmore Lodge made the following "Welcome Back" offer to their winter guests: guests who rent a room for at least a week during ski season can come back during the summer and get 25 percent off the standard summer price of any room they rent. After the summer passed, the owners of the lodge determined that the majority of their guests had taken advantage of the "Welcome Back" offer and paid the reduced rates. However, they were surprised to find they still managed to rent more rooms at full price than they did at the discount rate.

Which one of the following, if true, most helps to explain the apparent discrepancy in the passage?

(A) Most of the guests who stayed at Mt. Dunmore Lodge during the winter did not stay for a full week.

(B) Those guests taking advantage of the "Welcome Back" discount were more likely to bring their families with them than were those guests who were paying full price.

(C) Some of the guests who received the "Welcome Back" discount also received a 10 percent rate reduction through their auto club.

(D) In order to pay for the construction of a new gymnasium and a new pool, the owners of the lodge raised their summer prices considerably.

(E) On average, guests who took advantage of the "Welcome Back" discount spent more money at the hotel on additional goods and services than guests who paid full price for their rooms.

13. The weather this year was so poor, and last year's crop yield so unproductive, that many farmers in this county have had to take out loans just to make ends meet. To make matters worse, many farmers have had to sell some of their best farm equipment at auction, because many of the local lending institutions have regulations that allow loans only if a farmer's equipment is valued at less than a certain limit. Farmers whose equipment exceeded that value limit had to sell some of it in order to meet the lending requirements. Now, these farmers must harvest their crops without necessary equipment. The real problem, however, is that banks do not base their lending practices on how much farmers need, or even how much they produce, but on how much their tractors and combines are worth.

Which one of the following conclusions can most reasonably be drawn based on the information in the passage above?

(A) Local banks are paying less money for crops and more for farming machinery.

(B) Local farmers are being hurt by illegal banking practices.

(C) Local farmers are being forced to sell their assets in order to qualify for necessary loans.

(D) If they can endure present hardships, local farmers will eventually succeed.

(E) Unless the banks agree to subsidize local farmers, crop yields will be even lower this year than last.

GO ON TO THE NEXT PAGE.

14. When Euripides lived and wrote in ancient Athens, Greece was constantly in danger of civil war, and revolts among the slave class occasionally disrupted Greek society. The country of Erewhon is today in danger of civil war because of its unrelenting suppression of economically deprived classes, and guerrilla operations continually upset life in that country. It is surprising, therefore, that a dramatist of Euripides' stature has not appeared in Erewhon.

Which one of the following assumptions is most essential to the argument above?

(A) The behavior of guerrillas in Erewhon is very similar to that of the Greek slaves.
(B) Dramatists like Euripides can be expected to emerge during periods of civil war and social unrest.
(C) Greece was constantly plagued by civil wars as a result of its mistreatment of slaves.
(D) Ancient Greece and modern Erewhon have many similarities.
(E) The turmoil in Erewhon will produce a greater writer than Euripides.

15. Considering the current economy, the introduction of a new brand of cereal is unlikely to expand total sales of cereal, but rather will just cause some existing buyers of cereal to switch brands. So it makes no sense for the Coolidge Corporation to introduce another brand of cereal, since it will only hurt sales of the brands of cereal it already produces.

Which one of the following, if true, would most seriously weaken the argument above?

(A) Total sales of cereal will increase as the total population increases.
(B) Many new brands of cereal sell extremely well for the first year of their existence.
(C) Coolidge Corporation currently produces fewer brands of cereal than do its competitors.
(D) Some cereal buyers regularly switch from brand to brand, even when no new brands have been introduced.
(E) Research indicates that the new brand will attract more buyers of competitors' cereals than buyers of other Coolidge brands.

16. Betty: My opponent for the office of scout superintendent opposes a rule that would require all Wilderness Scout troop leaders to lead their scouts in the loyalty pledge before all meetings. How can my opponent claim she will represent the high moral standards of the Wilderness Scouts when she would forbid troop leaders from leading the pledge that proclaims our most important virtue?

Which one of the following points would be most useful to a person disputing the reasoning of the argument above?

(A) Some Wilderness Scouts also oppose the loyalty pledge rule.
(B) Loyalty is only one of many virtues espoused by the Wilderness Scouts.
(C) The opponent's position on the loyalty pledge rule may be atypical of her positions in general.
(D) Refusing to require an activity like the loyalty pledge is not the same thing as forbidding it.
(E) Opposing loyalty to an organization does not necessarily mean that one is disloyal to that organization.

17. No one can deny that, "This story is true," is a very different utterance from, "This story is long." A potential Bachelor of Philosophy does not, at the moment in which his degree is conferred, lose one attribute (potentiality) and gain a new one (actuality). Words like *true* and *potential* do not denote tangible, concrete qualities. Our minds cannot then learn them in the same way they learn words like *rectangular* or *blue*.

The author of the above passage is making which one of the following assumptions?

(A) Our minds can learn only tangible, concrete qualities.
(B) Attributes cannot be lost and gained.
(C) Abstract concepts are more difficult for the mind to grasp than are tangible qualities.
(D) Our minds are structured according to the types of words we learn.
(E) The process of learning words varies with the types of words learned.

GO ON TO THE NEXT PAGE.

Questions 18–19

Are we an active or a reactive society? Do we attempt to shape the world to our desires or do we merely respond by reflex to the harms that the world deals us? Most people would claim that we define ourselves as the former kind of society. Why, then, do many of these same people advocate capital punishment, a totally reactive response to crime? To execute violent criminals is to admit defeat, to assert that people cannot be changed or rehabilitated. Is it not better to be constructive rather than destructive, to regard criminals as flawed elements in our society that can be corrected, rather than irrevocable failures who must be written off?

18. Which one of the following best describes the point made by the author above?

(A) The execution of criminals is not consistent with the idea of an active, constructive society.

(B) Capital punishment does not deter other criminals from committing violent crime.

(C) We should reconsider our conception of ourselves as an active society.

(D) Our professed image of ourselves as a society is often at odds with our actions as a society.

(E) We should outlaw capital punishment because it violates the spirit of our laws.

19. The author of the above argument would most likely agree with which one of the following principles?

(A) Capital punishment makes a society as culpable as the criminals it executes.

(B) Violent criminals are flawed human beings who cannot be held responsible for their actions.

(C) A society that admits defeat in the matter of violent crime will not survive.

(D) Destroying human life is inappropriate for a society in any situation.

(E) Our society's treatment of criminals should be more rehabilitative and less punitive.

20. A recent survey found that all death row convicts in state penitentiaries who file petitions believe that there will be a substantial delay in the courts' processing of the paperwork attendant to their execution, and a more favorable outcome if the pardoning authority is made aware of the existence of the petition.

Which one of the following inferences can be most reliably drawn from the passage above?

(A) Most death row convicts in state penitentiaries who believe that there will be a dilatory effect if they file petitions do file petitions.

(B) All death row convicts in state penitentiaries who believe that there will be a dilatory effect if they file petitions do file petitions.

(C) If any death row convicts in state penitentiaries believe that routine petitions will have little or no effect, these convicts have not been among those prisoners filing petitions.

(D) Prisoners who file petitions have no sense of remorse for their actions.

(E) Most death row convicts in state penitentiaries who do not file petitions believe that there will be no benefit attached to filing a petition.

GO ON TO THE NEXT PAGE.

21. Jason: I found money-saving coupons for half of the items on your food list for the party. I know that the coupons are for brands that you don't usually buy, but if we use them for our party shopping, we'll save money.

    Twyla: No, in order to buy everything we need for the party, we'll spend more money if we use your coupons than if we don't.

    Each of the following would help support Twyla's assertion that more money would be spent if the coupons were used than if they were not used EXCEPT:

    (A) The coupons can be redeemed only at a store that charges much higher prices overall than the store that Twyla was planning to patronize.
    (B) Each couponed brand has a much lower net weight than the brands on Twyla's original list, thus requiring that they purchase much more of each product.
    (C) Exactly half of the couponed items are specially priced so that the final price, including the savings, equals the price of the corresponding products on Twyla's original list.
    (D) The prices of the couponed brands are much more expensive than the original brands on Twyla's list, thereby outweighing the savings from the coupons.
    (E) Twyla included on her list only products she knew to be on sale.

22. Since the new board of directors was elected at the beginning of the last financial quarter, a higher percentage of our potential clients have decided to purchase our competitor's system. As a result, two out of ten of our engineers have been let go, and our company's financial future is at risk. New strategies are on the agenda for the next board meeting.

    If the statements in the above passage are true, which one of the following must also be true?

    (A) Current sales are at their lowest level since the company was founded.
    (B) The competition's product is better than the company's.
    (C) Since the beginning of the last quarter, more clients have purchased the competitor's system than have purchased the company's system.
    (D) Since the beginning of the last quarter, the company has been less competitive than it had been in the past.
    (E) Most purchasers of systems think the competitor's system is better than the company's system.

23. In friendship one sees one's friend as another "self." One cares about him or her in the same way that one cares about oneself. Since each of us desires to know that we exist and are in good circumstances, each of us also wishes to know that our friends are likewise alive and well. Thus, true friendship requires that one live with or near one's friends.

    Which one of the following, if true, would most weaken the argument above?

    (A) Most people care for themselves much more than they care for their friends.
    (B) Technologies like the telephone allow us to confirm that our friends are alive and well even when we are separated from them by vast distances.
    (C) It is possible to live near and even with a friend without knowing for certain that he or she is in good circumstances.
    (D) Merely living near or with a friend will not necessarily ensure that the friend remains alive and in good circumstances.
    (E) Often circumstances dictate that one friend must move far away, and for him instead to remain among his friends would be so inconvenient that it would place too much strain on the friendship.

GO ON TO THE NEXT PAGE.

Questions 24–25

Duane: Over half the homicides that took place in this country last year were committed by means of handguns. It's misguided to talk about the "right" to own a handgun; a more important right is the right to live in safety. It's difficult to see why anyone other than handgun manufacturers would continue to argue against strict handgun controls. Such strict controls will reduce the number of guns in criminals' possession, and a reduction of guns will bring down the murder rate. Anything else is simply ineffective.

Sylvia: Even if one accepts such a casual dismissal of our time-honored right to bear arms, there's still no evidence that laws against carrying handguns will reduce homicides. Criminals can't be expected to obey anti-handgun laws of their own free will, and the supply is so plentiful and cheap that it will always be easy for criminals to find guns, no matter how strict the law; only honest people will find themselves disarmed.

24. Which one of the following is the main point at issue between Duane and Sylvia?

(A) whether the strongest opposition to the passage of strict handgun control laws comes from the manufacturers of handguns

(B) whether a reduction of the number of handguns in the hands of criminals would actually bring about a reduction of the homicide rate

(C) the likelihood that stringent punishments for the possession of handguns will actually deter criminals from carrying handguns

(D) whether strict anti-handgun laws can significantly reduce the number of handguns in the hands of criminals

(E) whether handguns can be strictly controlled without an illegal violation of the right to bear arms

25. Sylvia adopts which one of the following strategies in criticizing Duane's position?

(A) She undermines his analysis of the cause of the problem he is trying to solve.

(B) She relies on sarcasm in order to make the proposed solution appear ridiculous.

(C) She suggests that the proposed solution may result in exacerbating the problem instead of contributing to its solution.

(D) She denies that the course of action proposed by Duane will bring about the situation that he has identified as being necessary to the solution of the problem.

(E) She suggests that Duane has exaggerated the seriousness of the problem, in order to dismiss possible legal concerns about his proposed solution.

STOP
**IF YOU FINISH BEFORE TIME IS CALLED, YOU MAY CHECK YOUR WORK ON THIS SECTION ONLY.
DO NOT WORK ON ANY OTHER SECTION IN THE TEST.**

PRACTICE TEST ONE ANSWER KEY

Section 1 Logical Reasoning	Section 2 Reading Comprehension	Section 3 Logic Games	Section 4 Logical Reasoning
1. C	1. C	1. D	1. E
2, D	2. D	2. D	2. E
3. B	3. B	3. B	3. D
4. C	4. C	4. D	4. C
5. B	5. A	5. C	5. E
6. A	6. C	6. E	6. C
7. C	7. A	7. B	7. D
8. B	8. C	8. A	8. B
9. C	9. A	9. C	9. A
10. B	10. C	10. E	10. C
11. C	11. B	11. D	11. B
12. B	12. D	12. B	12. B
13. C	13. D	13. C	13. C
14. E	14. E	14. C	14. B
15. A	15. B	15. A	15. E
16. E	16. D	16. D	16. D
17. B	17. C	17. E	17. E
18. C	18. D	18. B	18. A
19. A	19. A	19. D	19. E
20. E	20. E	20. E	20. C
21. C	21. A	21. A	21. C
22. B	22. B	22. C	22. D
23. E	23. C	23. C	23. B
24. A	24. E	24. E	24. D
25. D	25. E		25. D
	26. B		
	27. A		

PRACTICE TEST ONE EXPLANATIONS

Section I: Logical Reasoning Explanations

1 (C) Conclusion: If civilians are to be kept out of harm's way, then any kind of armed conflict near populated areas is unacceptable. If the conclusion is to stand, it must be assumed that there's no way to simultaneously engage in armed conflict near populated areas and maintain civilian safety.

(A) Scope error: The issue is armed conflict near populated areas, not armed conflict in general.

(B) Liberating the conquered islands will endanger the lives of civilians, which implies that conflict is inevitable.

(D) The author begins with the word *if*, suggesting that holding off on liberation in favor of civilian safety isn't a foregone conclusion. The author may, in fact, favor liberation, civilians be damned.

(E) The author may be leading to this conclusion, but that doesn't mean that the argument depends on its being true.

Remember:

- An assumption bridges the gap between evidence and conclusion. It's a piece of information that the argument depends on for the conclusion to remain valid.

- The Denial Test can be used to check answers to Assumption questions. Deny or negate your choice and see if the argument falls apart. If it does fall apart, the answer is correct. If the conclusion is unaffected, the choice is wrong.

- Read choices critically with meticulous attention to detail. Choices (A) and (C) are virtually identical but for the phrase *populated areas,* which alone is the difference between a point and a wrong answer.

2 (D) Translation of the first sentence: "*If* Marybeth is shopping, *then* she has her mother's permission." So if her mother doesn't give her permission, Marybeth can't go shopping. She can shop alone at the mall down the street, but downtown she has to go with Sue and Desiree. Thus *if* Marybeth is shopping at the downtown department stores, *then* both Sue and Desiree must be with her.

(A) She can shop alone at other department stores, just not the ones downtown.

(B), (C) Neither can be inferred, since we know that there are circumstances when Marybeth can shop alone.

(E) The three girls can be together in many places other than the downtown department stores.

Remember:

- The test makers test formal logic by burying formal statements in the context of a casual argument. Be on the lookout for sentences that you can boil down to hard and fast rules.
- For any if/then statement, the contrapositive can be formed by reversing and negating the terms. The general model is: Original statement, "If X, then Y." The contrapositive, and valid inference, "If not Y, then not X."

3 **(B)** The "unexpected result" is that a far greater percentage of "new and improved" bicycles came back for repair than did the original bicycles that prompted the recall in the first place. Only something that has a major impact on the bicycle will effectively resolve this paradox, and (B) introduces the notion of the bicycle being used in a radically different way.

(A) Irrelevant. Which service center is in operation doesn't affect the overall percentage of bicycles coming back for repairs.

(C) A better warranty may be incentive for a few extra people to bring their bikes back for repair, but a marked change in the way the bicycle is used (B) explains the dramatic increase in repairs much better.

(D) This flaw is part of both models, and considering the improvements in the metal and the rims, (D) doesn't come close to explaining the bizarre results.

(E) First, the rims were improved; second, a factor consistent in both models can't account for the repair rate soaring from 20 to 50 percent.

Remember:

- A paradox is a seeming contradiction, an unexpected result contained in the argument. The correct answer will be the one that resolves this apparent contradiction.
- In Paradox questions, the question stem may use the word *paradox* itself or can take the form of the stem of question 3.

4 **(C)** Ms. Maloney demands that Dr. Ortiz replace her daughter's current dosage of drug X with the same dosage of drug Y, because even though Y has side effects, it works faster. Dr. Ortiz argues to stay with drug X, because Y's side effects may prove harmful for children. Clearly the disagreement centers around the issue of the side effects. Is it worth taking a chance on Y when X is safely doing the job?

(A) Too broad; the doctor's position is that Y simply hasn't been tested for use with children, which isn't the same as saying that it should be discontinued altogether.

(B) Neither disagrees that X is effective in its current dosage.

(D) The issue of her daughter's viability as a test subject is never broached.

(E) This is a global issue that the two people ignore, focused as they are on the single, specific case of Ms. Maloney's daughter.

Remember:

- In LSAT dialogue format questions, try to boil down each argument to its simplest terms. That will help you avoid wrong answers that sound as if they relate to the argument but are extraneous in some way.

5 **(B)** Dr. Ortiz's position is based on the safety of the patient, so the "most closely conforming principle" has to highlight that issue, and (B) hits the nail on the head: If two different yet equally effective treatments are available to choose between, safety should be the determining factor.

(A) The speaker's credentials aren't at issue here.

(C) Inferably, if an adult were in a similar situation and an alternative drug were available that hadn't yet been tested on adults, the doctor's treatment recommendation would be the same.

(D) Ignores the safety issue that's crucial to the doctor's position.

(E) The doctor's position focuses on a fear of the potential side effects of a drug, whereas (E) relates to the general working mechanisms of the two types of drugs in question.

Remember:

• Principle questions involve fitting a specific situation into a global generality (or, occasionally, vice versa). The answer is usually the choice that expresses the key concepts and contains the key terms that the other choices leave out.
• Try not to skip stimuli that come with two questions attached. Often the second question can be answered quickly after you've invested time in the first.

6 **(A)** Conclusion: The wildflower in question died away due to auto emissions. Their evidence is that the wildflower flourished during colonial times, before cars, but doesn't grow now on modern roadsides built on the same land where other wildflower species continue to thrive. The assumption is that no other factor was responsible for wiping out this particular species, and choice (A) plays off this. If disease caused the demise of the particular wildflower, the conclusion linking their disappearance to auto emissions falls apart.

(B) Since the argument is about wildflowers and auto emissions, the author needn't assume anything about pollution or botanical species in general.

(C) Areas sheltered from auto emissions are outside the scope of the botanists' argument.

(D) and (E) are both irrelevant. If the growing toxicity of auto emissions were a factor, then why aren't the other species affected? And the behavior of "most" botanical species has no bearing whatsoever on the argument.

Remember:

• Be aware of the various ways that Assumption questions are worded: "which is *assumed*," "the argument *presupposes* which of the following," "the conclusion *relies on* which of the following," etcetera.

7 **(C)** Evidence: 1) Vegetables can provide all the nutrients necessary for life (followed by an example), and 2) A vegetarian meal can be as varied and interesting as a meat-based meal. Then the author kicks into overdrive: She advocates banning the raising and slaughtering of livestock in favor of wider cultivation of high-nutrition crops. This sudden jump from a few words on the merits of veg-

etables to the extreme conclusion in the last sentence should come as somewhat of a surprise to you, and lead you to (C). The author simply doesn't give enough support for the conclusion.

(A) No terms warrant additional explanation, and the author *does* define what she means by the proper combinations of vegetables.

(B) There's no analogy in the argument, inappropriate or otherwise.

(D) It's not the author's responsibility to demonstrate the feasibility of her plan. The argument is strictly about what we *should* do, not what we *can* do.

(E) There is no circular reasoning employed: The conclusion, unwarranted as it may be, is not a restatement of the evidence.

Remember:

- Reading the question stem before the stimulus is a good strategy for all Logical Reasoning questions, but is even more applicable to Flaw and Weaken questions—your job is easier when you know in advance that there's something wrong with the reasoning in the stimulus.
- Be alert when you read; try to put the text into a real-life context. Evaluate the reasoning as you go along, and trust your instincts. For example, after reading the last line, it should be natural for you to think, "Whoa, where did that come from?" Then the answer becomes obvious.
- Use structural signals to help you sort out the key parts of the argument. The phrase *for instance* in the second sentence lets you know that what follows is not a new thought, but an example of the statement made in the previous sentence.

8 (B) The question, phrased another way, asks: "What's the point of the line, 'Daphne's litter was harder to pick up than Ewell's'?" By "granting" this, the speaker concedes that Daphne's act had a worse result, knowing full well that this is the most obvious point the court could use to justify the difference in punishment. By arguing that the worse result of Daphne's offense was due to the wind, not a difference in the severity of their crimes, the speaker is acknowledging and countering a possible objection to his claim that the offenders deserve equal punishment.

(A) The statement actually damages the author's claim when taken by itself, so it certainly couldn't be used as additional evidence to support the claim.

(C) The speaker attempts to discredit the judge's position later in the argument, and on other grounds.

(D) The speaker alleges that Daphne's wealth, and not the greater difficulty of picking up her litter, was the reason the judge imposed a harsher fine on her.

(E) The speaker actually uses the line in question to emphasize the opposite—that there is no difference between the seriousness of the two offenses, only between the seriousness of the two results.

Remember:

- When a question stem seems unwieldy, try to rephrase it in your own words. You'll never get the right answer if you're answering a question different from the one that's asked.

- When asked for the role a statement plays in an argument, make sure to relate the statement to the overall context. Stay away from choices that simply evaluate the statement unto itself.

9 (C) The principle that most justifies the speaker's position is the one that speaks to the most important elements of the speaker's argument—that the crimes were identical, and that mitigating circumstances (such as the wealth of the accused) shouldn't be factors in the judge's rulings.

(A) State versus public property is a nonissue. There's no such comparison to be made, since both offenders littered in a state park.

(B) Too vague. What "good" is the judge doing?

(D) According to the speaker, Daphne's punishment didn't stem from this but from her wealth. (C) addresses the entire issue better.

(E) Deterrence of future crime plays no part in the argument, so a principle based on this wouldn't help the speaker's position at all.

Remember:

- In Principle questions, look for a choice that most completely addresses the author's major concerns. Many choices seem to present principles that fit nicely around the specifics of the given argument, but the right answer is invariably the only one that fits perfectly, by ignoring irrelevancies and sticking to the author's main concepts.

10 (B) The argument is found right there in the first sentence: Delgado's hiring policy is unsound. The evidence: Her policy of hiring recent business school grads for executive positions is dangerous. To the author, trying to make up for a lack of corporate experience with a solid grasp of theory is like trying to pilot a jumbo jet by simply reading flying manuals. No two ways about it—that's an analogy.

(A) The author's argument is not geared towards a general principle, but rather towards a very specific judgment.

(C) Delgado's motives are never brought into the picture. The author disagrees with Delgado's policy because he finds the policy unsound and its underlying thinking dangerous, not because its underlying motives are suspect.

(D) The author doesn't like the policy because it's fundamentally unsound; no conflict of interest is mentioned or inferred.

(E) The author does allude to another situation, flying a plane, but solely for the point of creating an analogy. No findings are included in the plane reference.

Remember:

- Read the stimulus differently when looking to identify an author's method of argument. Your focus should not necessarily be on *what* the point is, but rather on *how* the point is made.
- In a Method-of-Argument question, test a choice by trying to come up with an example of what the situation would sound like if the method in question were employed. For

example, for (C) to be correct, the stimulus would have to include a motive on the part of Delgado—for example, a suggestion that she hired her friends over more qualified applicants. Since the argument doesn't include anything like this, (C) must be incorrect.

11 (C) The claim is that marsupials migrated from South America to Australia, inferably by way of the Antarctic link between the two. Any information casting doubt that the marsupials passed through Antarctica would serve to weaken this claim. If marsupials had to pass through Antarctica on their way from South America to Australia, it's hard to believe that the rich fossil fields could be searched extensively without yielding one marsupial bone. So (C) could be cited by a scientist wishing to dispute the author's claim.

(A) Present day Antarctic conditions are irrelevant, since the events of the stimulus obviously take place long in the past.

(B) The argument isn't contingent on the interchangeability of South American and Australian marsupials.

(D) This is totally irrelevant. Who cares how old marsupials are, or that the oldest one is from North America?

(E) It's possible that the lack of resemblance between marsupial bones in the Antarctic and those from the other two continents is the result of time and (frigid) weather.

Remember:

• Get familiar with the most common Logical Reasoning question types, and recognize them

even when the stem seems to go off into unfamiliar territory. If you cut away all the fancy wording, this one simply asks you to weaken the argument.

• To weaken an argument doesn't require positive evidence that blows the conclusion to kingdom come. Just as often, pointing out a lack of crucial evidence can make the author's point less believable.

12 (B) Since the school administrator assumes that Ms. Geschwitz communicates her views to her students, an evaluation of this position should center on whether this assumption is valid. If it's not, then the student has a good point and Ms. Geschwitz's views have nothing to do with her work as a guidance counselor.

(A) Whether they can find a way to employ Ms. Geschwitz in another capacity has no bearing on the school administrator's position.

(C) Ms. Geschwitz's popularity and reputation are irrelevant to the charge of whether she is exerting "undue influence" on her pupils.

(D) The number of other "offenders" on the faculty is irrelevant to whether this particular teacher has been out of line.

(E) The administrator seems to assume that some parents, at least, don't share Ms. Geschwitz's views, but the argument doesn't hinge on that assumption, because the administrator's position could be logically sound even if a lot of the parents see eye to eye with her.

Remember:

• Once again, previewing the question stem is

a winner. Here, it tells you to concentrate primarily on the second person in the dialogue.

- When asked to evaluate an author's position, pay careful attention to assumptions the author may be making. If there is a central assumption, the choice that questions it usually offers the best "relevant information."

13 (C) Even though the *Green Light Revue* was produced seven times, the director wishes to make an exception to the bylaws and include it because all seven productions were "short runs" in front of "small audiences." The exception, then, evidently is based on the fact that not many people saw the play, which means that the intention of the bylaws was inferably to ensure that the selected plays haven't been seen by many people.

(A) It seems that the opposite may be true; if they were looking for plays with proven appeal, the bylaws would probably encourage the inclusion of plays with more, not fewer previous productions.

(B) The director gives no consideration to the type of plays chosen, so it can't be inferred that the bylaws deal with this, either.

(D) From this context, it can be inferred that *tiny theaters* is intended to emphasize the small number of people who actually saw the play, not to suggest that an exception should be made for this revue based on its applicability to the small theater setting.

(E) The bylaws deal strictly with the number of times a play has been produced, but where this number comes from—one company performing it five times, five companies performing it once simultaneously, etcetera—isn't specified.

Remember:

- Inference questions are one of the most popular types of Logical Reasoning questions. Be on the lookout for words and phrases in question stems that tell you that you're dealing with inference: *most probably, suggests, provides evidence for, implies.*
- A good inference always stays in line with the author's point of view and tone, as well as the passage's scope and main idea.
- Choices that contain ideas that are neither contradicted nor supported by the passage are usually irrelevant and therefore wrong.

14 (E) Conclusion: Using Treegro will result in taller oaks. Evidence: Treegro was used in East Hollow over the past ten years, and now the East Hollow oaks are 4 inches taller than the average New Jersey oak. The easiest way to weaken this argument is to show that the oaks in East Hollow are taller for a reason totally unrelated to Treegro. If the trees in East Hollow are many years older than the trees in the rest of the state, the argument is damaged.

(A) This doesn't rule out a comparison to other New Jersey trees the same age, which could still demonstrate that the Treegro trees have the height advantage.

(B) We're not told which trees were planted under this program, so (B) does nothing to help us differentiate East Hollow trees from those in the rest of the state.

(C) Too vague. We're not told how long they've been using Treegro, so it's possible that Treegro is also helping the trees of non–East Hollow residents grow, but that the East Hollow trees are taller on average because they've been exposed to it for much longer.

(D) Too general. Fails to make a distinction between the oaks in East Hollow and the others in the state, so it does nothing to damage the validity of the claim.

Remember:

- Some stimuli are prime candidates for paraphrasing an answer. Try to react to this as if it were a real-life advertisement. Would it seem plausible? Would you rush out to buy Treegro, or recommend it to a friend (assuming either of you has a need for such a product)?
- The active test taker reads critically and questions the validity of reasoning, asking himself or herself such things as, "Does this make sense?" and "Am I convinced?"
- To weaken an argument, you can introduce another factor that could be responsible for the results in a passage. Such a statement undercuts the evidence and thus damages the conclusion.

15 (A) The argument, as it stands, is incomplete. The conclusion is, "Ban this chemical before it causes more harm to humans!" But the final sentence, presumably the evidence, concerns only the appearance of traces of the chemical in cow feed. In order to strengthen the conclusion, we need a connection—some additional information that identifies some extraordinary health-related problem in humans that could be reasonably linked to the biphenyls in cow feed. That's what (A) provides.

(B) This ignores the issue of harm to humans altogether.

(C) This is a general fact that provides no link between cancer rates and biphenyls or cows.

(D) If anything, this would *weaken* the argument, as it provides support for the notion that the chemicals are, in fact, safe.

(E) This fails to make any connection between the cows' misfortunes and harm to humans.

Remember:

- One common way to strengthen an argument is to shore up a basic assumption. Here, the author's conclusion necessarily depends on an unstated yet implied connection, and the correct answer is the one that supplies it.
- Don't carelessly choose "opposite" answer choices, such as choice (D), a weakener. Glance over the question stem quickly before settling on your choice, to ensure that you're answering the question posed.

16 (E) Esmeralda's conclusion, that environment has little to do with the development of personality, appears in her last sentence. Her evidence is that identical twins reared in totally different environments nonetheless exhibit similar personality traits later in life. Lothar contests Esmeralda's concept of environment, stating that the significant aspect of environment is not socioeconomic and education levels, but the level of commitment to nurturing. This damages her argument by calling into question one of her key terms as ill defined, or imprecise.

(A), (B), (C) These hinge on the idea that Lothar's argument somehow supports Esmeralda's point, when in fact Lothar takes issue with it.

(D) Lothar's response and Esmeralda's evidence on the development of adopted identical twins are not mutually exclusive concepts; they can both be true.

Remember:

- When dealing with one person's response to another's argument, take it one step at a time. First, make sure you have a good grasp of the argument in question. Only then can you clearly assess what relation the other's response has to it.
- Sometimes wrong choices fall into the same category; that is, they're wrong for the same overall reason, such as (A), (B), and (C) here. Choices like these that play on similar themes are easy to eliminate as a group.

17 (B) Esmeralda feels that her evidence fully supports her point, but Lothar disagrees with her concept of environment and therefore appears to be skeptical of her conclusion. Which aspects of environment are deemed as relevant to the issue will determine whether or not Esmeralda's evidence sufficiently proves her point. Therefore, the point at issue is whether Esmeralda's evidence adequately supports her thesis.

(A) They never get into the nature/nurture controversy per se. Lothar questions the validity of her evidence, but stops short of venturing an opinion.

(C) Outside the scope. Lothar argues that these aspects of environment are insignificant.

(D) Lothar questions Esmeralda's use of the concept of environment, but never hits on the issue of environment as a factor in overcoming genetic traits.

(E) Lothar believes that the most important aspect of environment related to personality development is the family's level of commitment to nurturing a child. Which children (adopted or biological) are better nurtured, however, falls outside the scope.

Remember:

- Zero in on what's actually said and weed out faulty interpretations. Lothar basically says one and only one thing to Esmeralda: "Your evidence stinks because you're neglecting the most important aspect of environment." That's it. Recognizing that this is negative rules out most of the choices in question 16. And for all of the choices in 17, you can ask yourself: "Does Lothar care about this?" A statement can't be a point at issue if one of the speakers is indifferent to it.

18 (C) Since the author is trying to assert that if Larry studied harder, he would have more confidence, the evidence should back this up by showing how studying leads to confidence. Instead, the evidence (Larry is feeling better about himself, is glad he decided to study more, and has a better outlook) are effects caused by the increased confidence—which, of course, is the conclusion the author's trying to establish. This is called circular reasoning—when the evidence and conclusion are, for all intents and purposes, identical. Likewise, in (C), if TV were made more educational, more parents would approve, but the first piece of evidence (parents recommending programs for their kids) depends on parents approving of TV.

(A) Although this sales pitch may not work on everyone, the reasoning is certainly not circular.

(B) The merits of tutoring seem plausible, and the conclusion seems justified based on the evidence. No flaw, no parallel.

(D) The evidence doesn't fully support the conclusion, but not any flawed choice will do. The correct answer has to be goofy in the same way as the original, which in this case means it must be circular.

(E) Not circular. It begins by concluding that something needs to be done, and ends with a specific recommendation for how to go about it.

Remember:

- Parallel reasoning involves mimicking the structure of an argument. Try not to get caught up with specifics; it's the general framework of the original that you're looking to locate in one of the answer choices.
- Stay away from answer choices written about the same subject matter as the original. This is an old trick of the test makers, intended to catch those who are not aware that they are to mimic the structure, not the content, of the stimulus.
- Due to its sheer length, this is a good question to skip and return to later (if time permits; if not, guess).

19 (A) The conclusion is based on the opinions not of random people, but rather of people "who filled out our questionnaire." This presents the possibility that only those who have an interest in solar energy filled out the questionnaire, which would tend to skew the results. If people who oppose solar energy refuse to take part, then the conclusion holds even less water.

(B) So what if it is? The argument is based on the results of the questionnaire, and therefore needs to be challenged on those grounds.

(C) The key issue is the number of people who support solar energy research. The knowledge level of the respondents in regard to their stated positions is irrelevant.

(D) The author and the Administration believe different things, but by simply stating that the Administration has never willfully mislead the public does not imply that the Administration in this case is right and the conclusion based on the questionnaire is wrong.

(E) Totally irrelevant, playing no part in breaking down the evidence or the path from the evidence to the conclusion.

Remember:

- The concept of the nonrepresentative sample comes up often in Logical Reasoning. Whenever a stimulus includes a poll, or a survey, check to see whether the people involved belong to a certain group or share a common belief. If so, the findings are probably suspect.

20 (E) One single bus crash and the town is virtually branded by the newspapers as a death trap, which in turn has negatively affected tourism and the citizen's perceived safety. This is an indictment of media misuse of data.

(A) The argument doesn't preclude in any way the occurrence of worse accidents in Dalyville; it simply focuses on the ramifications of this particular crash.

(B) Too extreme. The passage doesn't suggest that newspapers should check with the tourism people for any kind of statistic they wish to print.

(C) It's not the publication of statistics that is scaring the wits out of residents of Dalyville, but the hysterical headlines.

(D) There's nothing vague about the term *violent death*, especially since the bus crash is offered as an example. And the issue isn't the appropriate interpretation of statistics, but whether the statistic in question—one favorable to Dalyville—can be heard, given the noise of the shocking headlines.

Remember:

- Inferences tend to stick very close to the important phrases in the passage. Note that in correct choice (E), *misuse of statistics* refers to the bus crash and *poor reputation* is another way of saying that tourism and the citizens' confidence in their town are both sagging.
- Be wary of choices that use extreme words, such as *never, always, all,* and *none*. Such statements are by nature very strict and thus harder to infer. More often, correct choice are ones that are more qualified in tone.

21 (C) Barbara switches her advertising to a vehicle that offers two major advantages, yet her revenue from advertising plummets. Finding an unforeseen factor about *Paper Money* that negatively impacts on revenue would explain away this paradox, which is essentially what (C) does. If *Paper Money* readers spend much less than *People and Places* readers, then the drop in ad revenue would make sense in spite of the positive factors.

(A) Since *Paper Money* should reach more of Barbara's potential clients, it's therefore irrelevant that *People and Places* has a higher overall readership or serves a more diverse population.

(B) Family trips? Phooey. We're talking business travel here.

(D) Irrelevant. Even if true, it does nothing to counter the current advantages of *Paper Money,* so it fails to explain the strange result.

(E) Even if the yearly rates came out exactly even, this still negates only one of *Paper Money's* advantages. It's still a mystery how *Paper Money* is doing a worse job for Barbara even though it reaches many more of her potential clients.

Remember:

- Learn to recognize Paradox questions even when they don't actually use the word *paradox* itself. If a stimulus ends with a strange, bizarre, seemingly contradictory result, and you're asked to explain how it's possible, then you know what kind of question you're up against.

22 (B) It seems that the moderately overweight category from the study overlaps with the average-weight category on the insurance charts. So even some average-weight people, according to the insurance charts, have an increased risk of heart disease, which is the essence of (B).

(A), (C), and (D) Insurance premiums, heart disease versus smoking and alcohol, and overweight men? Outside the scope.

(E) There's no information about women in other age groups and their risk of heart disease, relative to the women in the study aged thirty to fifty-five.

Remember:

- In questions involving a study, look to quickly cross off choices that don't stay within the confines of the study. A correct inference is always consistent with the tone and scope of the passage, and often sounds very similar to the author's key concept or main idea.

23 (E) The question seeks information that would be most useful for the doctors to consider before recommending that the overweight women in the study lose weight. It would help to know, of course, whether there are any advantages of being slightly overweight—advantages that, if sacrificed, would somewhat offset or negate the health benefits related to a decreased risk of heart disease.

(A), (B), (C) Who cares about women aged fifty-five and older, or women between the ages of fifteen and thirty? And even within the correct age group, who cares about the overall percentage of women who are overweight? Certainly not the doctors; the information in these choices would be of little value to them.

(D) If even the moderately overweight run a high risk of heart disease, it's a safe bet that the very overweight are at risk as well. Still, this information has no bearing on the doctors' decision.

Remember:

- In a two-question stimulus, often the work you do in the first question can help you answer the second. In this case, many of the choices in the second question suffer the same weakness as the wrong choices in the first: they're outside the scope of the argument.
- It's very difficult to prephrase an answer to a relevant-information question, so your best line of attack is to move right to the choices and evaluate each until you find the one that has the greatest impact on the issue in question.

24 (A) If we represent each statement with variables, the argument breaks down to this: if A, then B; if B, then C; if C, then D. Thus (here's the conclusion), if A, then D. Stated in words: "One thing leads to another, which leads to another, which leads to another, which leads to the conclusion that the first thing leads to the last." The correct answer must incorporate every facet, including a conclusion that ties the first statement to the last.

(B) If A, then a choice between B and C, followed by the results of B and C.

(C) Because A, then B; because B, then C. This is followed by a judgment about A. No good.

(D) If A, then B; if B, then C; if C, then *not* A. Therefore, A is impossible. This one circles back on itself, creating somewhat of a paradoxical situation, something the original doesn't do.

(E) When A, then B; when B, then C. C, therefore, is incompatible with A. This isn't even close.

Remember:

- Some parallel reasoning stimuli lend themselves well to algebraic representation. If you can condense the structure to letters, do so, and then look for the choice with the same exact structural breakdown.

25 (D) Conclusion: Fewer animals roam the streets of Fairvale during the warmer as opposed to the colder months. Evidence: During the warm months, the city pound collected an average of 25 strays per month, but the average went down to seven when it got cold. A possible alternative explanation for the drop is a conscious decision to impound fewer animals, and so the author must assume that no such decision was made. Had the drop been caused by a change in impoundment regulations, of course, it would no longer be valid to conclude that the drop was due to fewer animals on the streets.

(A) The specifics of the pound facilities don't matter. The argument holds up fine without this piece of information.

(B) The seasonal substitution of employees doesn't alter the total manpower available for catching animals, so this piece of information is not a necessary assumption on the part of the author.

(C) The relation between diseases and the number of animals on the streets is ambiguous at best.

(E) Outside the scope. At best, this information could slightly strengthen the argument, if interpreted as support for the notion that fewer animals roam the streets in warmer weather. Still, this is quite a reach and the argument stands just fine without it.

Remember:

- The logic in some Assumption questions bears a similarity to that in Weaken-the-Argument questions. If this question asked for a weakener, choice (D)—stated in the positive—would suffice. Therefore, another way to come up with an argument's necessary assumption is to recognize a possible weakener and negate it, thus shoring up the conclusion.
- Once again, we see why it's so useful to get into the habit of reading each question stem first. This one literally gives away the conclusion, and that means less work for you.

Section II: Reading Comp Explanations

PASSAGE 1—War of 1812

Topic and Scope
The war of 1812; specifically, the merits and weaknesses of Watts's book.

Purpose and Main Idea
Author wants to argue that Watts's book is "ambitious but flawed."

Paragraph Structure
Paragraph 1 identifies the author's critical attitude. Paragraph 2 outlines the book's content: It analyzes the experiences of well-known figures in the period and generalizes about a new direction in U.S. culture toward liberal republicanism.

In paragraphs 3 and 4, the author levels her criticisms. The book, despite its ambitious claims, "mostly adds to the old debate on the war's causes." Watt's focus on the psychological motives of his witnesses may be "reductionist in character," and "his attribution of great transforming power to 'liberalization' is too arbitrary. . . ."

The Big Picture
LSAT history passages often focus on a recent book. When that happens, orient to the broad strokes of the author's review. Is it basically positive, critical, or mixed? In this psassage, despite her recommendation in the last sentence, the author is critical—she asserts that Watt's doesn't prove his thesis. Keep that main point in mind as you tackle the questions.

The Questions

1 **(C)** Abstractly worded global questions shouldn't be a problem. Only one choice will supply a precise fit. Focus on the appropriateness of verbs and nouns. Both verb and noun in (C) are precisely right. The author is *evaluating* Watts's *interpretation* of the War of 1812. This also jibes with the fact that this is a book review.

(A) and (E) Note the inappropriateness of the verbs in (A) and (E). The author's not recommending nor contrasting anything.

(B) The author is not establishing a historical perspective.

(D) The author is not describing a traditional point of view.

2 **(D)** corresponds to information in the middle of paragraph 2: Watts thought that the views of his witnesses "emerged from attempts to resolve inner doubts over the disparity between the austere prescriptions of republicanism and the reality of their personal lives."

(A) and (B) conflict with the idea that the witnesses' views represented those of Americans.

(C) is not suggested.

(E) contradicts the passage.

3 **(B)** paraphrases information from paragraph 1: Most historians have been "concerned with the war's causes."

(A) is not suggested.

(C) and (D) both seem inconsistent with the passage. It's Watts, not other historians, who tries to explain the war's consequences and its importance in national culture.

(E)'s "compulsion to war" is Watts's term, and more narrow than the broader idea of the war's causes.

4 **(C)** is consistent with the bigger purpose of the passage: One of the problems with Watts's book, according to paragraph 4, is that psychological explanations of his witnesses' motives may be seen as "reductionist in character. . . ."

(A) ignores the criticism and the distorts the content of previous studies.

(B) and (D) are *au contraire* choices.

(E) is never suggested.

5 **(A)** is directly implied in paragraph 2, and it also fits the whole logic of Watts's book as the author describes it: Watts probed these leaders' "personal experiences and public pronouncements" in order to draw conclusions about America's national character. Once you've found (A), go through the remaining choices if time permits and if you want insurance that you're right.

(B) and (E) are inconsistent with Watts's thesis.

(C) The Founding Fathers' view of war are never actually mentioned.

(D) is beyond the scope of the passage; it's not suggested, and it also seems inconsistent (Watts clearly feels that people's personal concerns *do* yield insight).

6 **(C)** The whole passage hinges on the idea that Watts's book is "ambitious but flawed," and choice (C) zeroes in on exactly how Watts's book, according to the author, goes wrong.

(A), by applauding Watts unequivocally, has a whiff of the *au contraire* choice about it.

(B) and (E) both pick up on details, (B) from paragraph 2, and (E) from paragraph 1.

(D) is half-right in the sense that the author is critical of Watts, but it distorts the author's point. The author never objects to Watts's thesis; rather, she simply asserts that he doesn't prove it.

Remember:

• Questions frequently narrow down to 2 or 3 choices, like (C) and (D) in this question. Keep in mind that one—(D) in this case—will have a *serious* problem. The answer is always the qualititatively superior idea.

7 **(A)** echoes the gist of the whole argument: As the author says in paragraph 1, Watts's books is "ambitious but flawed." Then she concludes that despite its problems, it "merits the attention" of those interested in the period.

(B) and (E) get things backwards: The book falls short on the war's effects and is too strong on its causes; it also overstresses psychological interpretations.

(C) and (D) are laudatory—inconsistent with the idea that the book is flawed.

PASSAGE 2—Cambrian Explosion

Topic and Scope
The "Cambrian explosion"; specifically, why the traditional classification of marine organisms that appeared during this period should be revised.

Purpose and Main Idea
The author wants to show that theorists have mounted a convincing argument that the traditional view of early marine evolution is incorrect and should be changed.

Paragrah Structure
Paragraph 1 supplies background info, explaining that the traditional view of the Cambrian explosion "assumed that, despite the very large number of species that appeared during the Cambrian explosion, nearly all fit into the same small number of phyla that exist today."

Paragraph 2 cites the problem with that view: The group of fossils called the Problematica—unique in body structure—never fit neatly into today's phyla.

Paragraph 3 introduces the theorists who see the Problematica as evidence that the number of Cambrian phyla was much larger than that existing today.

Paragraph 4 reiterates and suggests strongly that the author sides with the new viewpoint.

The Big Picture
The argument of this science passage fits an established pattern on the LSAT. It identifies a traditional way of thinking and then shifts to an updated viewpoint that, to a greater or lesser degree, discredits the old.

The Questions

8 **(C)** The theorists cited in the stem are challenging the old hypothesis which classified the Problematica in present-day phyla. According to paragraph 3, the theorists think the old view is wrong; thus, their attitude is one of *considerable skepticism* (C).

(A), (B) and (D) contradict the passage.

(E) is not critical enough.

9 **(A)** The bigger point of paragraph 2, where the Ediacaran fauna are mentioned, is that the Problematica (including the Ediacaran fauna) are "hard to fit . . . into present-day phyla" (A).

(B) doesn't work because the fauna bear a very limited resemblance to a few organisms like tapeworms.

(C), (D) and (E) are all inconsistent with information in the same paragraph.

10 **(C)** combines information in paragraphs 1 and 3. A phylum is defined in paragraph 1 as "a group of organisms with the same basic pattern of organization." And in paragraph 3: "Today the number of phyla has fallen drastically, but each surviving phylum contains a much larger number of species."

(A) and (B) are inconsistent with the passage.

(D) and (E) are never suggested.

11 **(B)** The two animal groups are mentioned in paragraph 1 to support the point that each phylum existing today is notable for its distinctive body structure (or patterns). (B) picks up on that general idea.

(A) and (D) miss the point.

(C) and (E) conflict with the passage.

12 **(D)** Neither group of scientists questions the large number of species that existed during the Cambrian period. All the other choices are true. With "EXCEPT" questions, avoid wading slowly through all the "true" choices by hunting aggressively for the choice that outright contradicts the passage.

(A), (B), and (E) are all central points of difference: Scientists disagree about evolutionary patterns in the Cambrian period, with revisionists saying that there was a much larger number of phyla than exists today; conventional theorists put the Problematica in present-day phyla.

(C) is another point of disagreement: The last sentence of paragraph 1 states that the conventional belief has been that "the loss of entire phyla was considered extremely rare." Revisionists say that the most phyla of the Cambrian period have disappeared (see paragraph 3).

13 **(D)** echoes the gist of paragraph 2: Organisms from the Problematica—*Tullimonstrum, Hallucigenia,* and the Ediacaran fauna—differ from modern species in their unique body structures (note the specific info about the Ediacaran fauna). If you read for paragraph content—for the gist of the detail—then (D) snaps into place more quickly, and time spent with wrong choices is reduced.

(A) The passage never says when most modern species evolved.

(B) Nothing is said about life before the Cambrian explosion.

(C) We're not told why many Cambrian organisms died out (probably for a variety of reasons).

(E) Nor are we told why the Cambrian explosion took place.

14 **(E)** The thrust of the author's ideas throughout is that the questions left unanswered by the older view pose serious problems. In paragraphs 1 and 2 she maintains a degree of neutrality, but her emphasis shifts to the new view in paragraph 3, and in paragraph 4 her attitude becomes clearer: "revisionists *recognize* that natural selection has eliminated not only single traits, but entire body plans, entire approaches to survival." In other words, revisionists are answering questions about the Problematica that the conventional do not (E).

(A), (B), and (C) are inconsistent with the author's support of the revisionists.

(D) is beyond the scope: The author never suggests that "most present-day species appeared within a relatively brief period."

PASSAGE 3—Turner's Landscapes

Topic and Scope
Turner's landscape paintings; specifically, Wilton's thesis that Turner's landscapes are rooted in the aesthetic tradition of the sublime.

Purpose and Main Idea
The author wants to outline Wilton's argument that landscape painting—Turner's landscape in partiuclar—found public acceptance because of a shift in public attitudes towards nature.

Paragraph Structure
Paragraph 1 cites Wilton as locating Turner in the tradition of the sublime, defined as "an aesthetic expression of a universal spiritual ideal." Paragraph 2 traces the roots of the sublime to ancient Greece. Paragraph 3 explains that the sublime was first expressed in literature, and later spread to painting. Paragraph 4 explains how landscape painting came to be accepted in the 18th century. Paragraph 5 mentions different expressions of the sublime in Turner's work.

The Big Picture
The series of 5 short paragraphs do a lot of the work for you by grouping details into manageable chunks. Give each paragraph just enough time (say, 30 seconds each) to gather up the gist. Return for the details later, to score points.

The Questions

15 **(B)** is easily the best choice: The sublime is discussed in every paragraph, and it's linked to Turner's painting in paragraphs 1, 4, and 5.

(A) refers to a detail in paragraph 1.

(C) is far too broad and unspecific.

(D) refers narrowly to paragraph 3.

(E) is too narrow, and its verb distorts the passage.

16 **(D)** Burke is cited in paragraph 5 as writing an essay that defined qualities in nature—"vastness, lack of habitation and cultivation, and danger"—which he linked to the sublime.

(A) He's not mentioned as defending landscape painting.

(B) tempts, but paragraph 4 hints that identification of the sublime with nature was under way before Burke's essay. Also, the word "specifically" in the stem points to (D).

(C) His definition of the sublime isn't mentioned as clearer than that of earlier writers.

(E) Burke isn't cited as rejecting a connection between the sublime and religious experience.

17 **(C)** fits the scope of the passage: Traditional motions of the sublime—its focus in the human and the divine, its mystery and power as expressed in literature—were gradually extended to nature and finally to landscape painting.

(A), (B), and (D) are never implied.

(E) is an *au contraire* choice. The idea of vastness in nature was stressed by Burke.

18 **(D)** paraphrases the thrust of paragraph 3: Changing social conditions led to rising interest in nature, which was linked to developments in painting and literature.

(A) mixes things up: Impressionism came after Turner; changing social patterns began earlier.

(B) and (C) are both *au contraire*.

(E) is beyond the scope—no market for Turner's paintings is mentioned.

19 **(A)** paraphrases info in paragraphs 2 and 3: The sublime was originally a concept that focused on the link between humanity and the divine. "Its focus on the human condition was explicit," says paragraph 3.

(B) is never suggested.

(C) confuses things: People denigrated landscape for its lack of human presence, not because it wasn't literary.

(D) cites an irrelevant detail from paragraph 1.

(E) is never implied.

20 **(E)** echoes the last paragraph's description of the various types of subject matter in Turner's landscapes. (E) is waiting there, buried at the bottom—an easy point. Be aggressive with choices that don't immediately click.

(A) There's no support for the contention that Turner was unappreciated.

(B) There's no support for the idea that he disliked Michaelangelo's art.

(C) There's no support for the idea that his work had less appeal for upper-class buyers.

(D) There's no support for the contention that he didn't influence Impressionists.

21 **(A)** is the answer. Reynolds is mentioned as exemplifying an older attitude toward the sublime, which stressed the human condition

relative to the divine—the "narrative" tradition, according to paragraph 3.

(B) and (D) confuse things: Portrait painting is not the issue.

(C) Landscape painting is not the issue, either.

(E) contradicts the passage: Reynolds would have seen literary and visual expressions of the sublime as similarly narrative.

PASSAGE 4—Comparable Worth

Topic and Scope
Comparable worth; specifically, the arguments against the policy of paying men and women the same money for jobs in the same company that are comparable if not identical.

Purpose and Main Idea
The author asserts a desire to "examine" the anti-comparable worth arguments, but it becomes clear that the purpose is to shoot them down.

Paragraph Structure
Paragraph 1 announces the topic and scope but fails to identify where the author stands (and even fails to define *comparable worth* for those unfamiliar with the phrase, who have to be patient until lines 21–26). Each of the remaining paragraphs takes up one of the anti–comparable worth arguments mentioned in paragraph 1, and you have to hang in there until you see the author align herself against the "antis" through phrases like, "Each contention is misguided or flawed"; "This objection . . . goes too far"; and "Yet the argument sidesteps . . . ."

The Big Picture

- As soon as the passage raises a controversy or question, you must immediately seek to identify which position, if any, the author takes.
- If the author remains neutral, recognize that. In some cases, the author simply describes the different sides of the controversy, without actually weighing in with an opinion.
- When the author's viewpoint seems obscure, hang in there—if he or she intends to profess an opinion, that opinion will be made clear by the end of the passage. There's no point in reading deeper into the text, or answering questions, until the task of pinpointing the author's position is successfully completed.

The Questions

22 **(B)** strengthens the claim made in paragraph 2 (the wage gap paragraph) that the question of gender discrimination should come into play when differently paid men and women hold similar jobs in the same firm, like the programmers in (B). The disparity between the woman and the man, who is her junior, smacks of just that kind of discrimination.

(A) and (E) depart from the scope of the author's discussion in that they involve men and women working for different employers. The author frames the discussion of comparable worth around the necessary condition that the employees share the same employer.

(C) doesn't spell out that the pilots work for the same airline, but nonetheless is wrong because in this instance the woman has ten years less seniority, which would explain the disparity in pay. (B), rather than (C), is a much more likely case of discrimination as the author describes it.

(D) does not present two people working in "comparable" jobs, a necessary condition for comparable worth to be at issue.

23 **(C)** This one refers to paragraph 3, whose topic is job evaluation and whose point is that one can fairly compare dissimilar jobs for the purpose of setting wages. The qualification is hinted at by the phrase *though partially valid* (line 32) and is then immediately spelled out: The comparison is never completely objective, synonymous with (C).

(A) comes from the wrong paragraph. The health of companies comes up in paragraph 4.

(B) is a plausible outcome of comparable worth, but the issue never comes up in the passage.

(D) and (E) are *au contraire* choices—choices that propose the opposite of what's stated. Job evaluation is "well established" (line 34), and objectivity is exactly what is "desirable" in comparable worth; it's just not 100 percent achievable.

Remember:

- It's inevitable that some questions will hinge on knowing which paragraph is at issue, especially when (as here) each building block has such a different topic. Know your paragraphs!

24 **(E)** The premise of the anti-comparable worth argument in paragraph 2 is that gender discrimination isn't the cause of the male-female wage gap—personal choice is the cause (lines 12–17). A bit later, advocates of the contention in paragraph 4 assert that "supply and demand curves create the wage disparity" (lines

42–43). (E) satisfactorily paraphrases both.

(A) goes way beyond the scope to cover "all social reform."

(B) On the evidence, those opposed to comparable worth find it economically crippling rather than helpful, and its social impact goes unmentioned (although opponents probably aren't too optimistic on that score, either).

(C) is a true statement made at lines 57–58, but it qualifies as a statement of fact, not as a conclusion drawn by opponents.

(D) is closer to the author's view. It hardly sums up the view of opponents, who basically deny sex-based wage discrimination altogether.

Remember:

- When more than one person's or group's viewpoints figure in a passage, read each question carefully to determine which person or group to focus on.

25 (E) The four wrong choices—the positions that are "rightly" called U.S.C.R.C. positions—can come from either paragraph (2 or 3) that mentions the agency by name. Happily (E) comes from paragraph 4, where no hint is made that the C.R.C. has signed on to a 100 percent hands-off attitude on the part of the courts with regard to market intervention.

(A) is the conclusion ascribed to the C.R.C. in lines 10–11.

(B) is cited in lines 29–31.

(C) is cited in lines 15–17.

(D) comes from lines 13–15.

Remember:

- Proper names stand out more than other words. When questions pick up on them, that may make it easier to decide where to focus your attention.

26 (B) The reference to "supply and demand" should direct your attention to market-centered paragraph 4. Then your search for something that sounds like "fails to take into account" should fix on "the argument sidesteps," and what it sidesteps is (B), the possible equivalence of jobs that are nevertheless paid differently.

(A) Paragraph 3 makes it clear that the author wouldn't subscribe to (A)'s idea that jobs "can only be measured subjectively."

(C) makes up the issue of political manipulation out of whole cloth.

(D) This choice, which refers to the judiciary, points to the proper paragraph. But the author turns to the topic of how judges have dealt with comparable worth only after concluding the assessment of whether supply and demand are at the heart of wage differentials. The last two sentences must be seen as parenthetical, a sidelong glance at another aspect of comparable worth but one essentially tangential to the passage's main thrust.

(E) A broad sociological issue unrelated to the author's topic and scope in general, let alone the paragraph in which supply and demand comes up.

Remember:

• When a question stem sends a strong hint about where in the passage the answer can be found, follow it. (You may want to target such questions to answer early on—often they are among the easiest.)

27 (A) There is no ambivalence at all in the author's opinion about the C.R.C.'s deeming discrimination to be unrelated to the male/female wage gap: "Each contention" supporting that position is "misguided or flawed" (line 17).

(B) is, of course, the exact opposite of the author's view.

(C) No hint of bewilderment, qualified or otherwise, can be seen in the author's text.

(D) The author's "opposition" is strongly argued, hardly quiet.

(E), like (B), is the opposite of the author's position—not that the author is impolite, just opposed.

Remember:

• A long or complex-sounding question stem needs to be read carefully, but the question need not be especially difficult once unpacked.

Section III: Logic Games Explanations

GAME 1—Basketball Teams

The Action

Choosing six out of eight people to play basketball, and breaking up the six players into two teams of three players each. The only unusual twist on this "grouping game of distribution" (meaning that it's a game in which you're putting the entities into subgroups), is that each player on a team plays opposite of a specific player on the other team. Here are the *Key Issues* that you should anticipate the questions will be based on:

- Which players are chosen and which ones sit on the bench?
- Which players can or must play together?
- Which players cannot play together?
- Which players can and cannot play opposite each other?

The Initial Setup

If you were the coach for this situation in real life, how might you use pencil and paper to keep track of it all? Here's a simple, intuitive way:

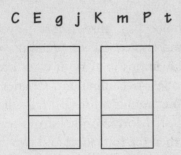

C E g j K m P t

There's nothing concrete to fill in yet, so let's move on to the rules.

The Rules

1) Rule 1 simply breaks the players into two groups: C, E, K, and P are tall, and the others— g, j, m, and t—are short.

2) Rule 2 says that the tall players can only play opposite each other. From that you can deduce that the short players are left to play opposite each other. This rule also implies that *there must be either two or four tall players chosen*. There's no way to match them up with each other if an odd number is chosen.

3) Rule 3 is straightforward enough: if P, then C opposite her. Just don't make the lethal mistake of inferring that the reverse is true, because it isn't. If C is chosen, P *can*, but does not *have to*, play opposite him.

4) Rule 4 is similar: If t is chosen, then C is chosen to play with t. Once again, the rule can't go backwards: Choosing C implies nothing about choosing t.

Key Deductions

The Key Deduction in this game involves the breakdown of tall and short players chosen. One of the implications of rule 2 is that there has to be either two or four tall players chosen. Taken one step further, this means that the coach has to choose either all four tall players and two short players, or all four short players and two tall players. One more deduction stems from this, but it's not as obvious, and therefore it's not a tragedy if you don't see it up front. In fact, it's tested for specifically in question 1, so we'll cover it there.

The Final Visualization

Here's everything we're armed with going into the questions.

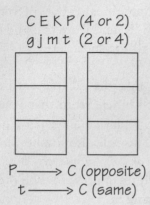

C E K P (4 or 2)
g j m t (2 or 4)

P ———> C (opposite)
t ———> C (same)

The Big Picture

- One way to latch onto the action of a game is to place the game in a real-life context. How would you handle this if you were the coach? Break down the mystique. If you approach the games as ordinary everyday situations, they won't be as baffling and you'll be able to think through them more clearly.
- When the entities are broken down into two distinct groups, you may find it helpful to differentiate them by using capital and lower-case letters.
- A good way to grasp the meaning of a rule is to ask yourself, "What would violate this rule?" Take a second, if it helps, to try out a concrete example that tests your understanding of the rule. Otherwise the rule will continue to be abstract, unclear, unhelpful.
- When a game involves numbers, always see if you can deduce specific number breakdowns. Keeping these firmly in mind gives you a distinct advantage when it comes to working through the questions.

The Questions

1 **(D)** The deductions made during the game overview pay off right away—there are only two ways to combine tall and short players to get the required six, and Charles is chosen in both of them. If the coach chooses all four tall players and two short players, then obviously Charles, a tall player, must be chosen. If, on the other hand, the coach chooses all four four short players and only two tall players, then short Terence must be chosen, and Charles as well, thanks to rule 4.

As for the others: Edna, choice (A), and Katya, choice (C), can both be bench-warmers if Charles and Paulina are chosen along with all four short players. However, Terence, choice (B), and Jerrod, choice (E), can sit out if Greg and Mort play along with all four tall players.

Remember:

- When a question offers no hypothetical information (no *if* clause), it means that it must be possible to deduce the answer from the rules alone. Build the new piece of information (in this case, the fact that Charles must be chosen) into your global view of the game.

2 **(D)** Choice (C), three short players on one team, and choice (E), three tall players on one team, are both impossible. Both cases break rule 2. (A) violates rule 3—Paulina and Charles can never be on the same team. As for (B), tall Charles, short Jerrod and short Mort cannot form a team: If they were a team, then the four short and two tall scenario would be in effect, placing Terence and Greg on the other team. But that contradicts rule 4, so it's no good. The players in the remaining choice, choice (D), form an acceptable team; the opposing team would have to include Charles, Jerrod, and Terence.

KAPLAN

Remember:

- When facing an Acceptability question, simply check the choices against each rule, eliminating the ones that violate the rules until you're left with only one choice.

3 **(B)** Since the roster must be four tall/two short or four short/two tall, the two bench players must be in the same category: if one were tall and the other short, then the four/two split would be impossible to achieve. Specifically, choice (B) is the only one that places one tall and one short player on the bench, leaving three tall and three short players for the game, which we've already deduced is an impossibility.

Remember:

- You can often find a shortcut by focusing on the categories that the entities fall into rather than the entities themselves.

4 **(D)** In questions like this, scan the list of choices for entities that seem suspicious. Terence is a good bet because he has a whole rule dedicated to him, which by nature restricts him more than the players in the other choices. Paulina can't play on the same team as Terence, because according to rule 4, Charles would have to be on that team, but that would violate rule 3. All of the players in the other choices make fine teammates for Paulina.

5 **(C)** According to rule 2, if Katya and Charles, two tall players, are one team, Paulina and Edna must play on the other team. The third player on that team can't be Terence (rule 4), but could be any of the other three short players, giving us PEg, PEj, and PEm as possibilities. The correct answer is therefore three, choice (C).

6 **(E)** In questions that offer no hypothetical information, sometimes the only way to proceed is to work out each choice, which could be time-consuming. A question like this is therefore a good candidate to skip and come back to later if time permits. However, if you had the time . . . here's how four of the choices are possible:

(A)—P, g, j versus C, t, m. Bench: E, K.

(B)and (C)—P, K, m versus C, E, t. Bench: g, j.

(D)—C, m, t versus K, g, j. Bench: P, E.

As for (E)—this is the one that's impossible. If t is chosen, then C must play on his team, resulting in a team of t, E and C. Thanks to rule 2, the other tall players, P and K, must play on the other team to oppose E and C, so it's impossible for K to sit on the bench.

GAME 2—Chimp Testing

The Action
Scheduling six chimps for language testing into ten time slots during a five-day week. The *Key Issues* for this sequencing game are:

- Which chimps are tested on which days, and in which time slot (morning or afternoon)?
- Which chimps are tested before and after which other chimps?
- Which chimps are tested on the same day?
- Which time slots are free?

The Initial Setup
In a sequence game with a calendar aspect, a days-of-the-week sketch may come in handy, as it does in everyday life when we need to keep track of a week's events:

```
          A B C D E F
  M        Tu        W        Th        F
┌────────┬────────┬────────┬────────┬────────┐
│        │        │        │        │        │
├────────┼────────┼────────┼────────┼────────┤
│        │        │        │        │        │
└────────┴────────┴────────┴────────┴────────┘
```

The Rules

1) Put an "A" in the Thursday morning slot.

3) Put an "X" (or whatever you feel will do the job) in the Monday morning slot to indicate that that time slot is free.

7) Jot down that Carlo is tested either Tuesday morning or afternoon.

   (Note: See "The Big Picture" below to see why we recommend handling the rules in this order.)

2) You can jot down the info on the three late risers, but there's no way to narrow down their placement further. Yet.

4) This helps clarify Elmo's place in the ordering. Combined with the previous rule, we know that Elmo has to be tested in the afternoon of Wednesday, Thursday, or Friday.

5) Alonzo is tested on Thursday morning, which means that according to this rule, Wednesday afternoon must be free.

6) Dingo, Alonzo and Frank must be tested in that order, from earliest to latest. Since Alonzo is tested on Thursday morning, Dingo must be tested Monday, Tuesday, or Wednesday, and Frank must be tested on either Thursday or Friday afternoon (taking rule 2 into account). Jot that stuff down.

Key Deductions

Elmo has to be tested in the afternoon, but not on Monday or Tuesday, and we now know that Wednesday afternoon is off limits. So Elmo must be tested on either Thursday or Friday afternoon, the same as Frank, which we deduced by combining rules 1, 2, and 6. So: Elmo and Frank must be tested on Thursday and Friday afternoon, in either order. The other heavy sleeper, Bobo, therefore will be tested on Monday or Tuesday afternoon. No chimp is left for Friday morning, so this time slot must be free.

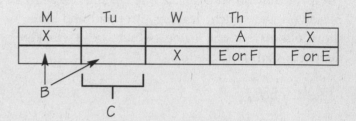

The Final Visualization

Putting all of this information into one sketch will allow us to dispose of the questions quickly.

The Big Picture

- You don't have to take the rules in order. Seek out and incorporate the most concrete rules first, in order to build a solid foundation.

- Always turn negative information around to the positive. For example, in rule 4, it's easy to figure out (and more powerful to know) when Elmo can be tested than when he can't be.

- Always search for the implications of rules. Don't recopy rule 5 on your page, but rather think it through and then build it into your visualization of the game.

- Don't be intimidated by games that contain many rules. The more the merrier. That's because, in general, the more information you're given to work with, the more structured

KAPLAN

the game is and the more restricted the entities are. This is good for you. Games with few rules tend to be the tough ones, as they involve much more ambiguity.

The Questions

7 **(B)** When you are asked, which must be true, then the four incorrect choices either might be true, or are outrightly false. With this in mind, look for ways to disprove each answer choice. If you can't disprove it, it must be true. Starting with (A)— Bobo could go on Tuesday. When you get to (B)— with Bobo, Carlo, and Dingo before Alonzo, and Elmo and Frank after, Alonzo must be fourth, so (B) is correct. If this was test day, you'd mark (B) and move on. But for completeness, let's consider the rest of the choices. (C)—Carlo could be third, after Bobo and Dingo. (D)—Alonzo could be tested immediately before Elmo, leaving Frank for Friday. (E) is false—if Carlo and Dingo are tested on Tuesday and Wednesday morning, respectively, then there would only be two free morning time slots.

Remember:

• The first question can solidify your conception of a game. Answering this one helps to reinforce, and show the value of, all the work we did up front.

8 **(A)** We deduced that Bobo must be tested on Tuesday or Wednesday afternoon, and Dingo must be tested Monday, Tuesday, or Wednesday. There's only room for one chimp on Monday and Wednesday, so Tuesday is the only common day open to both. But testing both Bobo and Dingo on Tuesday would violate rule 7, as this would leave Carlo hanging (possibly literally). So Bobo and Dingo are the chimps that can't be tested on the same day, which is choice (A).

Days that the pairs in the wrong choices can be tested: (B) Tuesday, (C) Tuesday, (D) Thursday, (E) Thursday.

Remember:

• Logic Games answers are objectively correct, so once you find an answer that works, even if it's (A) or (B), have the confidence to choose it and move on. This saves valuable time on a highly speeded section.

9 **(C)** Start with what you are given, and add to it what you already know. If Dingo goes on Tuesday morning, then Carlo must go on Tuesday afternoon (rule 7), leaving unfortunate Bobo in the first open slot, Monday afternoon (remember, Bobo's choices are limited to Monday or Tuesday afternoon). Elmo and Frank are unaffected, so as we deduced, either could be on Thursday or Friday, killing choices (A) and (B). With Bobo, Carlo, and Dingo placed, Wednesday morning must be free, resulting in three free time slots in the morning and only one in the afternoon, eliminating (D) and (E) as well.

Remember:

• You can sometimes save time by scanning the choices for the entities that are the most affected by the *if* clause. In this case, Dingo's actions directly impinge upon the placement of Bobo and Carlo, and scanning the choices for either of these chimps brings us quickly to choice (C).

10 **(E)** When the question asks which can be false, that means the four incorrect choices must be true. So, take the information given, and focus on placing as many of the chimps into slots as you can definitely place. That will eliminate the "true" choices.

Frank's choice of days is limited to Thursday and Friday, while Bobo must take either Monday or Tuesday. The only way to satisfy the stem is if Frank takes Thursday afternoon and Bobo takes Tuesday afternoon. Then Carlo must sneak in on Tuesday morning (rule 7), and Elmo gets the last slot, Friday afternoon.

That leaves Dingo as the only chimp not precisely slotted in: she can be tested on Monday afternoon OR Wednesday morning. Therefore, choice (E) *could* be true, but need not be (in other words, *can be false*): she could be tested Wednesday morning, which would place her third behind Carlo and Bobo. The other choices conform perfectly to the arrangement outlined above.

11 (D) Dingo in the afternoon must happen on either Monday or Tuesday. If it's Monday afternoon, Bobo must be Tuesday afternoon, and Carlo Tuesday morning. Elmo can be tested Thursday and Frank on Friday, or vice versa. So there are two schedules possible if Dingo goes on Monday. However, if Dingo is tested on Tuesday, then Bobo must be tested Monday afternoon, Carlo on Tuesday morning, and Elmo and Frank can still float between Thursday and Friday. This adds another two possibilities to the mix, resulting in a grand total of four.

Remember:

- When asked for the number of possible arrangements, start with a key entity and determine the number of possibilities for it. Then build as many arrangement around each of these possibilities as you can.

12 (B) Elmo's time slots are limited to Thursday or Friday afternoon, so if Elmo is tested on the same day as another chimp, it must be on Thursday, the same day as Alonzo. This puts Frank in the Friday afternoon spot. We're told that at least one chimp is to be tested each day. The only chimp available for Wednesday morning is Dingo. Carlo can only be tested on Tuesday (in this case, morning or afternoon), leaving Bobo on Monday afternoon. (B) is correct, with Elmo on Thursday and Dingo on Wednesday.

As for the others: (A) need not be true. Carlo could be tested on Tuesday afternoon, and we know Bobo's on Monday. However, Carlo could be tested Tuesday morning, in which case (C) bites the dust. (D) and (E) are both out-and-out false; Carlo on Tuesday comes between Bobo and Dingo, and two chimps, Dingo and Alonzo are tested between Carlo and Elmo.

Remember:

- When a question stem contains more than one hypothetical, focus on the one that seems to be more concrete first.

GAME 3—Four Pictures

The Action
This game centers around matching four pictures with the color and medium in which each picture will be created. The *Key Issues* here are fairly straightforward:

- What color is used for each picture?
- What medium is used for each picture?

KAPLAN

The Initial Setup

For matching games like this, a grid or a list that places the entities on one line and their properties underneath will generally be most helpful. A simple sketch, for starters, might look like this:

	Dog	House	Tree	Tree
paint or crayon				
B or R or Y				

The Rules

1) By telling us that exactly one picture will be blue and one will be yellow, we know that the remaining two must be red. Next to the "color" line of the list, you may wish to write "B Y R R" to represent this.

2) Here we learn that the two tree pictures share the same medium but have different colors. It might be helpful to note this directly on the sketch, perhaps by placing an equals sign between the two T's on the "medium" line and a separation or unequals sign between them on the "color" line.

3) Basically, this says that if the blue picture is done in paint, the yellow picture must be done in crayon, and vice versa. This doesn't result in any great deduction at this level, but will be critical when we move on to the questions.

4) and 5) These are the most concrete rules, the kind that can go directly into your sketch. As in the previous game, you could have jumped to these two first to get off to a good concrete start. Place a C in the "medium" line under dog, and an R in the "color" line under one of the trees.

Key Deductions

Combining rules 2 and 5, we now know that the other tree picture must be either blue or yellow, since one tree is red and the two trees can't be the same color.

The Final Visualization

After incorporating these rules into the sketch we developed earlier, here's what we can now use to attack the questions:

	Dog	House	Tree	Tree
paint or crayon	crayon		≠	
B Y R R			R ≠	B or Y

If B paint, then Y crayon, and vice versa.

The Big Picture

- Sometimes a key deduction breaks open an entire game, while other times a deduction is somewhat helpful, but not really a major factor. In this case, focus on the rules that don't play a big part in the setup (rule 3 and the second half of rule 2). Lacking major deductions, these are the kinds of rules that the questions will hinge on.

- As the name implies, matching games involve matching up various characteristics about a group of entities. Resolve right now to: 1) learn how to recognize a "matching" game, and 2) decide which, if any, form of sketch (such as a grid or a list) you're most comfortable using to keep track of matching information.

The Questions

13 **(C)** For this Acceptability question, four choices violate one or more rules, and one choice violates none of them. Compare each rule to the choices, throwing out violators. In (B), the two tree pictures are in different media (rule 2). (D) also violates rule 2, which requires the tree pictures to be of different colors.(A) can be eliminated because both the blue and yellow pictures are drawn in the same medium (rule 3). Finally, (E) can be knocked out since the dog must be in crayon, not paint (rule 4).

Remember:

- In Acceptability questions, try to focus on a rule and then scan the choices to find the ones that don't conform. This saves time.

14 **(C)** Since all the answer choices deal with color, first ascertain what the maximum number of pictures done in crayon is, and then see whether certain picture's colors can be determined. All four pictures can't be done in crayon because the blue and the yellow pictures must be in different media. What about three pictures in crayon? The dog is always crayon (rule 4), and since the two tree pictures must be in the same medium, let's make those two crayon as well. The house must therefore be done in paint.

What about color? One tree will be red and that the other tree must be blue or yellow. Since the latter is in crayon, the other picture done in blue or yellow must be painted (rule 3), which in this case is the house. Since the second red is all that is left, we can mark the dog as red and the answer as (C). The house and one of the trees will be the blue and yellow pictures, although we don't know which is which. The other four choices, therefore, all could be true, but need not be.

Remember:

- Whenever you figure out any new piece of information, and the question asks "what must be true," it's worth taking a few seconds to scan

the choices looking for your deduction. Sometimes you're rewarded with a quick and easy point.

15 **(A)** If the dog is blue, the second tree will be yellow (rule 1 and rule 2). This leaves red for the house (and the first tree—rule 2). The blue dog and the yellow tree must be done in different media, and since the dog is always done in crayon, the yellow tree (and the red tree) must be done in paint. The only information we're missing is whether the red house is in paint or crayon.

(A) must be false. At best, the house is crayon and there's an equal number of paint and crayon pictures, but there can't be more crayon pictures than painted ones. As for the others: (B), (C) and (D) all could be true, while (E) is a statement that must be true.

Remember:

- When testing if a choice must be false, attempt to make it true. If you can make it true, in even one case, then cross it off. If you fail to find a way to make it true, then you've found the answer.

16 **(D)** By making the house yellow, our Key Deduction tells us that tree number two must be blue, which makes the dog red. So far, we know nothing about the media of the house or the trees. As with question 15, we're asked to find the choice that cannot be true or, in other words, that must be false. Once again, test to see if you can make each choice true. This time it's (D) that's impossible, as the red dog must be done in crayon. (A) and (B) could be true, as the trees could be done in paint or crayon. Likewise, (C) and (E) could be true if the house was done in crayon and the trees in paint.

17 **(E)** The first *if* clause tells us, essentially, that the second tree will be blue. The second hypothetical is a roundabout way of telling us that there will be three pictures done in paint and one in crayon—and we know which one that is: the dog. So the trees and the house must be done in paint. The blue picture, in this case a painted tree, must be done in a different medium than the yellow picture, so the yellow picture must be the crayon dog, once again leaving the house as the second red picture. This supports correct choice (E).

(A) and (D) bite the dust because the dog is done in yellow crayon. The house, on the other hand, must be done in red paint, killing both (B) and (C).

Remember:

• When a question stem contains more than one hypothetical, focus on the one that seems to be more concrete first.

18 **(B)** This is a good question to skip and return to later if time permits, since you must employ backwards reasoning that may be time-consuming. We want to force the dog to be blue or yellow, so let's search the choices for the one that brings about the desired result. Exactly three crayon pictures? The house could still be the other blue/yellow picture, instead of the dog. Three paint pictures? Since the dog is in crayon, this means that the house and both trees must be paint. Could the house still be the other blue/yellow picture? No; this would violate rule 3, because both blue and yellow pictures would be done in paint. So (B), in fact, does force the dog to be done in blue or yellow. (C), (D) and (E) all result in situations where the house and one tree could make up the blue/yellow pictures.

GAME 4—The Nine Chair Circle

The Action
Arranging seven people and two empty chairs in a circle. The *Key Issues* on which the questions will be based are:
• Who can sit next to whom?
• Who must sit next to whom?
• How far away are some entities from other entities?
• Where are the entities with respect to the empty chairs?

The Initial Setup
Before attacking the rules, it should be helpful to create a sketch representing the circle of nine chairs. Anytime you have an odd number of entities to place, you can't draw a standard circle sectioned off like pieces of a pie, because this will always come out even. So instead, try drawing nine dots spaced out in a circle, and number the seats one through nine, making number one at the top and working clockwise for seats two through nine, like so:

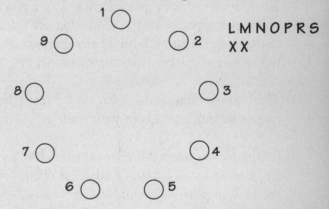

(Note: Assigning actual seat numbers is, in fact, a step beyond what you would normally do in this type of game—they're included solely as convenient reference points for the following explanations.)

Since this game specifies how people will be seated in terms of being to the left or right of one another, we must also take into account which way is left and right. In circle sequence games, people always sit facing the center of the circle; those sitting at the top of the circle, therefore, will have their left and right reversed from those on the bottom, who perceive left and right as you do. (Try to picture yourself sitting at the top of the circle, facing the center, and again at the bottom; you'll see how left and right reverse themselves). Make a mental note that left always points clockwise and right always points counterclockwise.

The Rules

1) With any circle sequencing game, we start by picking one of the entities and placing him/her at some point on the circle. Since we see S mentioned in most of the rules, we will start by placing her in a seat, let's say number 1, with M to her immediate right in seat number 9 (remember, right is counterclockwise).

2) Since Sybil's already placed, rule 2 is a good one to incorporate next: Counting off three chairs to the right of Sybil (remember—counterclockwise!) places R in chair number 7.

3) This means that seats 2, 6, and 8 can't be empty, so indicate this in your sketch.

4) If L and O sit immediately next to each other, we need to locate a pair of adjacent chairs for them. The possible candidates are: seats 2–3, seats 3–4, seats 4–5 and seats 5–6. Seats 3–4 and seats 4–5 won't work since each of those cases would necessitate placing an empty chair next to Randi or Sybil, which violates the previous rule. So, we know that the L–O pair will sit in either seats 2–3 or seats 5–6. Note that

even if we determine which of those pairs L and O actually sit in, we still don't know which person will sit in which chair.

Key Deductions

If L and O sit in numbers 2–3, the two empty chairs must be number 4 and number 5. Similarly, if L and O are in numbers 5–6, the empties must be numbers 3–4. (Incidentally, this answers question 19.) In any event, we can now ascertain that chair number 4 MUST be empty. Also, in either case one of the two remaining people, P or N, must sit in chair number 8.

The Final Visualization

The placements of S, M and R are determined; L and O are restricted to two pairs of chairs; the empty chairs are next to each other in one of two ways (numbers 3–4, or numbers 4–5); and N and P, the people not mentioned in any rules, are left to fill in the spaces as necessary. Here's what a sketch encompassing all of this info might look like:

L M N O P R S
X X

1 S

9 M   2 (no X)

8 (no X)   3

7 R   4

(no X)

6   5

L and O = #2 – 3 or #5 – 6
X and X = #3 – 4 or #4 – 5

The Big Picture

- In circle sequence games, always begin by placing the most prominent entity (the one connected to the most rules) into the circle first, and then build around it.
- It doesn't matter where in the sketch you place the first entity; the relationships between the entities is the crucial thing, which will remain consistent whether you begin by placing S in seat number 1 or seat number 6, for example.
- Check to see if the game cares about left and right. Some games will simply say "next to" and "across from." Others, like this one, care about direction.
- If left/right is an issue, make absolute certain which way is left and which way is right from any chair. If the entities are facing inward, as is usually the case, right will be counterclockwise and left will be clockwise.

The Questions

19 **(D)** We deduced that the two empty chairs must be either chairs 3 and 4, or chairs 4 and 5. Either way, the two empties are adjacent.

Neither (A) nor (B) needs to be true, as Pam and Naomi could sit in chair number 2. Although L *could* sit next to an empty chair, L in number 6 and O in number 5 proves that L doesn't *have to*, so (C) is out. The same example shows that (E) ain't necessarily so.

Remember:

- When the first question offers no hypothetical information, the answer will be something that will hold true for the entire game, so build it into your visualization and treat it as a valid rule for the rest of the game.

20 **(E)** When the question asks, which can be false, the other four choices must be true and therefore can be deduced. So first determine the precise location of as many people as possible. Based on the stem's description, O is in seat 5, and L is next to O in seat 6 (via rule 4). The empties must therefore take seats 3 and 4. N and P are free to float between seats 2 and 8, so while Pam could sit in seat 2, next to Sybil, she could also sit in seat 8. (E) can be false and is therefore correct. As for the others: (A) must be true, since three seats away from R is empty seat number 4. Furthermore, O, in seat 5, is next to empty seat number 4, so (B) can't be false, either. We can rule out (C) since in this case L does sit next to R. (D) gets thrown out because regardless of which of N and P sits in number 2 and which sits in number 8, there in fact must be exactly two people (S and M) between them.

21 **(A)** Let's test each choice by trying to make each one true. When we find the one that can't be made to work, then that's our winner. Luckily, the answer comes immediately in choice (A): If L and O take seats 2 and 3, Pam must sit in either number 6 or 8, next to Randi. If the other scenario exists (L and O in numbers 5 and 6), then Pam must sit in seat 2, next to Sybil, or seat 8, next to Randi. We remind you that logic games are objective, so once you come to an answer that works, stop and move on to the next question. But for completeness: By placing O in seat 3 or 5, we can make (B) true. The fact that P can sit between R and M rules out (C). (D) and (E) are out as well since seat 2 can be occupied by L or N.

Remember:

- If you can't decide where to begin in a question or to test out a choice, work with the entities that take up the most space—in this case, the

L/O combo. When major entities are limited to two possibilities, simply try out each and see what happens.

22 **(C)** Lisa can sit next to an empty chair if she sits in seat number 3, with O in number 2, or if she sits in seat number 5, with O in number 6. In the first case, P and N must sit in seats 6 and 8, in either order. So there are actually two possible arrangements attached to the first case. The same holds true for the second case, the scenario with L and O in numbers 5 and 6, respectively. P and N could then float between seats 2 and 8. So, there are two general ways to place Lisa next to an empty seat, each containing its own two variations, resulting in four different possible arrangements overall.

Remember:

- When asked for the number of different possible arrangements, simply try each variation of the seating until you've exhausted all possibilities.

23 **(C)** In order to determine the exact locations of everyone, we need to resolve the ambiguities—the uncertainty as to where N and P sit, and the question of placing the L/O twosome. The intuitive approach to this problem, therefore, is to look for a choice that mentions the people in each of these pairs. (A), (C), and (E) look like good candidates, so let's begin with those.

If Pam sits in seat 8, we can take care of (A) in two ways: L in seat 2 or L in seat 5. (E) can be discarded in the same way, by simply substituting O for L and N for P. (C), however, does the trick: The only way to get exactly one person between L and N is if N sits in seat 8 and L sits in seat 6. This forces O into seat 5, P into seat 2, with seat 3 and seat 4 left

empty. As for (B) and (D), neither one allows for a definitive placement of N and P.

Remember:

- When looking for a statement that'll precisely determine the placement of every entity, scan the list of choices for one that deals with the game's most ambiguous characters, and test those out first.

24 **(E)** The best approach here is to quickly create a fresh sketch for this question (and reapply the rules. Continue to keep S in seat number 1. Now, instead of being in number 9, M will be in seat number 3. Following original Rule 2, R remains in seat 7. Reapplying rule 3 tells us that now seats 2, 6, 8, and 9 can't be empty, so the only remaining seats, number 4 and number 5, must be the empties. Applying rule 4 tells us that L and O must share the only two remaining adjacent seats, number 8 and number 9, (in either order), while N and P are left to float between number 2 and number 6.

Now it's easy to see that (A) through (D) can all be true (choice (A) in fact must be true), while choice (E) can't possibly be true: The chairs that are three chairs away from Sybil are number 4, which is empty, and number 7, which is Randi's.

Remember:

- Questions that involve rule changes are good questions to skip, if you're pressed for time.

Section IV: Logical Reasoning Explanations

1 (E) Conclusion: Public education has deteriorated in the last 50 years. Evidence: The inability of high school seniors to compose a business letter. (E) strengthens the argument by adding meaning to the evidence. If 80 percent of seniors could write acceptable business letters 50 years ago, and only 50 percent of today's seniors can do so, then the conclusion is more believable.

(A) Contradictory. If the seemingly poor statistic was actually an improvement, then one might conclude that public education has succeeded, and not failed, in recent years.

(B) Nothing indicates whether the students who aren't native English speakers are among the 50 percent who can write the letters or the 50 percent who cannot.

(C) No way to know whether this represents an increase or a decrease in math capabilities.

(D) simply clarifies the evidence by giving us a more precise statistic. We are still left with the question of whether this represents improvement or deterioration in the students' skills.

Remember:

- The choices that best support an argument will be those that add additional support for the conclusion or forge a stronger link between support and conclusion.

2 (E) By describing how the seemingly "crumbling infrastructure and hopeless traffic congestion" problem was rectified by a mayor who put the money into a solution, the writer draws a parallel with the current air pollution problem. A mayor who makes this current problem a priority and invests money in it, the writer implies, will be able to fix it, and those people who are currently settling for the status quo need not do so.

(A) At no point are we told that there is any causal link between the transportation and pollution problems.

(B) The incumbent mayor has proven himself willing to spend money on programs he considers important, as evidenced by the transportation example.

(C) The ability to correct the air pollution problem is implied, but there's no actual demonstration that the problem can be fixed, just that Schwartz will give it a shot.

(D) The argument does not suggest that voters should alter their priorities; it merely exhorts those who already share her concern about air pollution to vote for Schwartz.

Remember:

- When an argument relies on an analogy, be wary of choices that infer an unwarranted connection, or causal link, between the two analogous situations.

3 (D) The argument can be broken down algebraically (X, wisdom, needs Y, adversity; Constanza is wise, X, therefore she must have suffered adversity, Y), or verbally ("someone with a particular trait must have another specific trait, because the latter is a prerequisite for the former"). By noting that Constanza is wise, the writer concludes that she shares an experience common to all wise folk. Similarly, by noting that Francois is "a brilliant musician," the writer of (D) concludes that he must, therefore, share an experience common to all excellent musicians.

(A) "Character requires training" follows the basic model, but then an extra leap to the source of the attribute is made: The training must have come from Leon's parents. This extra leap ruins the parallel.

(B) Winning a gold medal requires the "very best training and preparation." While good coaching might fall within this realm, it is not necessarily so.

(C), (E)   In these, the conclusion is a prediction.

Remember:

- Parallel logic tip: Whenever possible, try to translate the argument into simple content-neutral words, or even algebraic letters. This will help you avoid the trap of letting the content of the answer choice become confused with the content of the original argument.
- Many times, the elements of an argument will be mirrored in an answer choice, although not in the same order. The order is unimportant, provided that the correct elements exist.

4 (C) The passage refers to the use of statistics to judge economic systems in two ways: with respect to operational effectiveness, and "as a whole." When judging operational effectiveness, the passage suggests that the statistics speak for themselves. However, when looking at the big picture, economists need to determine the significance—or "value"—of unquantifiable aspects. Choice (C) stays consistent with the passage's theme, recognizing that economists must use some subjectivity in analyzing systems as a whole.

(A) Contradictory to the first sentence of the passage, this is the area in which statistical analysis can be used with reliability.

(B) The issues here comprise the "unquantifiable aspects" of systems as a whole, so statistics aren't relevant.

(D) The passage strongly implies that productivity is a good way of comparing economic systems, and the author doesn't address what "most economists would agree" upon.

(E) calls for a consensus among economists that is not dealt with in the passage.

Remember:

- In Inference questions, the correct choice is often one that's closely related to the passage's main idea. Wrong choices often focus on points that are either tangential or wholly irrelevant to the passage.
- Read carefully to separate the viewpoint of the author from that of other people whom the author may mention.

5 (E) The difference between chronological age and physiological age is that the latter is a more complete descriptor, because it places the chronological age of a species into the context of the life span of that species. (E) sticks very closely to this theme and is reinforced by the illustration in the last sentence.

(A) Off the mark. The passage deals with the issue of how to assign meaning to a particular "age"; ascertaining that age is not discussed.

(B) The words *old* and *young* have meaning, but those meanings merely vary from one animal to another.

(C) Beyond the scope. At no point is anything said about an animal's physiological condition.

(D) raises a distinction the author never makes, between humans and "other animals." To the author, the two different types of ages are applicable to both.

Remember:

- The opposite of a good inference will make little or no sense in light of the main idea. The best inferences actually tend to be restatements of a passage's gist.
- As with Reading Comprehension passages, don't focus on specific details or examples when approaching an inference question.

6 (C) The author argues that giving grants to the lowest bidder results in substandard and dangerous construction, a point (C) attacks by attacking the assumption that a low bidder must necessarily demonstrate shoddy workmanship and materials. If (C) is true, then all bidders, high or low, demonstrate high standards to begin with.

(A) at best suggests that concerns other than inferiority and safety ought to be considered when evaluating the city council's policy, but since this falls outside the scope, the conclusion remains untouched.

(B) may tend to strengthen the argument, by implying that contractors lack one particular "oversight mechanism" for keeping standards high.

(D) suggests another factor (design flaws) that can result in dangerous buildings, but fails to speak to the critical issue, namely whether going to the lowest bidder will result in dangerous buildings.

(E)'s message is merely, "We can't afford to do better," which doesn't address the argument at all.

Remember:

- The most important step in weakening an argument is actually defining the argument itself. Break it down as simply as you can. The correct choice will directly challenge the premises or conclusion of the argument, whereas wrong choices will often dwell on tangential points.

7 (D) The author argues that the visual message is the true one and that we shouldn't be distracted by the verbal themes. Thus the author must be assuming that a film's true message can, in fact, be conveyed by visual means only. If it can't, then the whole argument falls apart.

(A) may be true, but isn't a presupposition to the argument. In fact, the author admits that the verbal component of the film is a significant factor—insofar as he is fearful of the viewer's being distracted by the conversational elements.

(B) What "moviegoers frequently do" isn't an essential part of this argument.

(C) The author isn't troubled because audiences "are prone to ignore the visual" as a habit, but because in the case of this particular film the verbal elements send a different signal from the visual ones.

(E) Whether this is true (and it's doubtful) is irrelevant. The visual message of the film doesn't hinge on this insight.

Remember:

- Be careful not to let the specifics of a stimulus cause you to stray from the argument itself. The main issue here is films, not World War II.
- Stay away from choices that talk about what most (or all) members of a group do or want, particularly when such tendencies are never identified in the passage.

8 (B) Two courses of action could be taken to achieve the same result, and the author argues that the cheaper one should be chosen. We're asked to find a possible explanation for the disparity in costs. (B) provides a simple scenario whereby more costs would be incurred in building at the Abaco site than the Bornos site.

(A) This choice is an added argument in favor of Bornos but makes no mention of the disparity in cost.

(C) merely offers a long-term benefit to building on Bornos, whereas we're looking to explain the difference in building costs.

(D) A good argument against Abaco, but it fails to address the cost issue. We can't be sure that even if (D) were true, a single dollar would be spent on species protection.

(E) We can infer that the issue of future expandability isn't factored into the cost estimates of the two plants, so again, we're given information that does nothing to explain the cost discrepancy.

Remember:

- Read the question, and don't embrace choices that don't address the question at hand. If you're asked for an explanation, look for choices that explain. If you're asked for a counter argument, look for one of those. Don't confuse the two.

9 (A) In search of a principle, we must find a choice into which the specific facts of the stimulus will fit snugly. (A) states that if a patient is in a situation such as Mrs. Menendez's, the doctor's obligation is crystal clear. Under this principle, the doctor's argument against terminating life support would clearly fail.

(B), (D) Unlike the stimulus, these choices focus on any terminally ill patient, which is too broad. (B) also implies that such a patient may compel a doctor to act ("intervene") medically to kill her, which is pretty extreme for this situation.

(C) We're not told that Mrs. Menendez is in a vegetative state, and there is no disparity between family wishes and those of the patient.

(E) This choice focuses on resolving a discrepancy which does not exist. Here, the patient, her living will, and her nearest relative are all in accordance with each other.

Remember:

• When asked to reconcile a dispute, always look for choices that most closely mirror the facts in the dispute. Most often the correct answer is a choice custom-tailored to the fact scenario.

10 (C) Since the doctor relies on the statement that he cannot "play God" to provide a moral ground for his position, Menendez can counter the doctor's position by showing that the doctor's actions in fact constitute "playing God" whether he realizes it or not.

(A) The issue of who can afford life-saving treatment goes beyond the scope of the passage.

(B) On the contrary, the distinction between the two is clear; the doctor simply argues that, despite patient wishes, his obligations do not permit him to honor those wishes.

(D) The doctor's argument is centered around his obligation to preserve life, which would still exist regardless of the possibility that the patient would change her mind.

(E) The patient's mental capacity is way beyond the scope of the passage.

Remember:

• Read past the wordiness of complex question stems. This one simply asks how to weaken the doctor's argument.

11 (B) All this author is saying is that most statements can be interpreted both subjectively and objectively. (B) echoes this theme by pointing out both the varying "looks" of a tie (subjective) and the "definite individual traits" that aren't subject to interpretation (objective).

(A) fails to address the subjective. Fact: many compete to be the best. Fact: only one can wear the crown. There is no room for interpretation on either of these issues.

(C) focuses only on the reactions (subjective) people will have to artwork.

(D) The only interpretation discussed here is the subjective opinion of "most people" of a particular character trait (consistency).

(E) The objective, concrete thing here is that a comment was intended as praise, and is followed by the possibility (but not likelihood) of a subjective misinterpretation of it. In the original, the objective aspect isn't subject to interpretation.

Remember:

• When looking for a parallel principle or situation, make certain that the full point is covered in the choice; going halfway isn't enough.

12 (B) The discrepancy is in how most winter guests availed themselves of discounted pricing but the lodge nevertheless rented more rooms at full price. And if the discounted folks (B) were comprised mainly of families, packing in more guests per room, while the full-price guests tended to come solo with fewer guests per room, then it's easier to explain how there could be lots of discounted guests wandering around the hotel but more rooms rented at full price.

(A) These guests aren't even eligible for the summer discount, so they play no part in the argument or the confusing result.

(C) That some people got an added discount doesn't serve to explain the paradox. If anything, it makes even more mysterious the increase in full-price rooms.

(D) The argument centers on a full versus discounted rate. What that rate is is irrelevant.

(E) goes beyond the scope of the passage. Other charges above and beyond room rates are never discussed and are therefore not an issue.

Remember:

- When resolving a paradox, look for elements in the evidence and conclusion that appear to be similar, but are in fact totally different things (in this case, number of guests versus number of rooms). Usually, this will be at the heart of the seeming contradiction.
- As in Logic Games, feel free to work out an example to clarify your understanding of a concept. Imagine, for instance, that the hotel has ten rooms, and rents three at a discount and seven at full price. Now suppose that the discounted rooms contain five people per room, while the full-price rooms each contain one person. Voilà! More full-priced rooms than discounted, but more discounted guests than full-priced ones.

13 (C) The passage describes a cycle whereby farmers have a poor crop, need additional money, apply for loans, sell off expensive, quality equipment in order to qualify for loans, and are then left with fewer resources with which to harvest their crops, since their good equipment is now gone. Correct choice (C) follows this pattern, and indeed can be derived directly from the passage's second sentence.

(A) The passage doesn't address the issue of banks paying for crops or equipment; it simply cites the value of equipment as a factor in the bank's decision to approve a loan.

(B) While the passage implies that the farmers are hurting as a result of the banking practices, nothing suggests that these practices are illegal.

(D) Whether the farmers will succeed in the future is beyond the scope of this passage.

(E) The passage doesn't argue for banks to subsidize farmers. The author merely points out that the regulations surrounding lending are causing problems for farmers.

Remember:

- Don't confuse questions that ask you to find the author's conclusion (implying that it's somewhere in the passage) with questions that ask which conclusion "can most reasonably be drawn." The latter is usually looking for the next logical step of the statements in the passage.
- Sometimes the answer to this type of conclusion question is nothing more than an inference staring you in the face.

14 (B) Drawing a parallel between the turbulent times in Athens and Erewhon, and noting a causal link between the emergence of Euripides and the civil war in Athens, the author generalizes that a comparable dramatist should emerge in Erewhon. The argument lacks evidence—information to back up this generalization—but (B) forges the necessary link.

(A) So what? This may increase the chances of civil war, but we still know nothing about why we should expect another Euripides.

(C) So what? Where's the link to Erewhon? What about the emergence of a dramatist?

(D) is too broad in scope. We know some of the specific similarities, just not the one on which the argument depends.

(E) merely says that a greater writer than Euripides will emerge, but we're still missing the vital link, the essential assumption that explains why it is we should expect a fine dramatist to appear at all.

Remember:

- In an Assumption question, the author will have taken a "logical leap" in formulating the conclusion. Your job will be to find where that leap occurs and then find the choice that bridges the gap.
- To test a choice in an Assumption question, ask yourself, "If this is true, is the conclusion made more believable? Without this, does the argument fall apart?" If you can answer "yes" to both, you have a winner.
- Unlike inferences, assumptions don't come directly from the passage, nor will they be mere expansions of statements made in the argument. Remember that an assumption refers to that which is not explicitly stated.

15 (E) Coolidge, it's argued, won't benefit from introducing a new cereal since doing so will merely "steal" its own customers away from other Coolidge brands. Anything that demonstrates that Coolidge may actually benefit from introduc-

ing a new brand will weaken this argument, and (E) does exactly that. If introducing a new brand will attract buyers of competitors' cereals, Coolidge will have succeeded in increasing its overall customer base without cannibalizing its own product.

(A) The relation between cereal sales and population increase is irrelevant.

(B) While the first year may produce great sales for Coolidge's new brand, that might still be at the expense of its older brands, in which case the argument still stands.

(C) has no bearing on the argument, as it does nothing to suggest who will actually switch to Coolidge's new product.

(D) Be this as it may, this still fails to address the fundamental issue in the argument: the effect of Coolidge introducing a new brand of cereal to the market.

Remember:

- An LSAT argument about the predicted success or failure of a sales plan is no less speculative than it would be in real-life business. Use your common sense about real-life customer behavior to help you zero in on a plan's weak points.

16 (D) Betty opens by saying that her opponent opposes a rule requiring the leading of the loyalty pledge. Later, however, she attacks the opponent for trying to forbid the pledge. The opponent may see the pledge as merely optional, so it's unfair to jump from that to the claim that the opponent will out and out forbid the pledge (D).

(A) While this might be a good campaign point to argue on the opponent's behalf, others' opposition to the rule doesn't address the flaw in Betty's reasoning.

(B) Betty describes loyalty as the scouts' "most important virtue." The mere fact that there are other virtues doesn't undermine any part of her argument.

(C) Like (A), potentially a good campaign point in favor of Betty's opponent, but whether her position is out of character doesn't deal with the substance of Betty's reasoning.

(E) implies that Betty is accusing her opponent of disloyalty to the Wilderness scouts, but Betty doesn't go that far.

Remember:

• When reading a question stimulus, circle words that jump out as being inconsistent with each other. Often, the question will center around that discrepancy.

17 (E) The substance of the argument is found in the last two sentences. We're told that some words don't refer to concrete qualities and, consequently, they're learned differently from words that do represent the tangible. The assumption that learning varies with the type of word is, therefore, crucial to the argument.

(A) Contradictory. We're told that the intangible can be learned, albeit differently.

(B) Beyond the scope. The issue of gaining and losing attributes is only mentioned with respect to the given example. The point of that example was simply to show the difference between two words.

(C) At no point is it suggested that it's more difficult to learn the abstract than the tangible. All we're told is that the two are learned differently.

(D) The structure of our minds has no bearing on the argument.

Remember:

• Don't let the language in somewhat philosophical examples throw you off track. It's still just one main point supported by evidence.
• If an argument is loaded down with examples up front, it may make sense to skim down to the end and locate the conclusion that the examples are leading to. Then you can return to the evidence with a firmer grasp of the author's purpose.

18 (A) The author wants to point out an apparent hypocrisy, and to call on society to reconcile this hypocrisy in accordance with the author's beliefs. We say we're an "active" society, but going by the author's definitions, advocating capital punishment is more a part of a "reactive" society.

(B) The author doesn't deal with the idea of punishment as a means to deterrence. Instead, he argues against capital punishment by saying that we should work to reform criminals rather than execute them.

(C) The author would rather we retain the concept of being "active," and change our view of capital punishment to fit that mold.

KAPLAN

(D) This is too broad to be the author's main point, which, of course, is the issue of capital punishment.

(E) According to the author, capital punishment doesn't violate the spirit of our laws — the laws permitting capital punishment violate our image of our society.

Remember:

- When an argument deals with a political issue or a high-profile debate or controversy, be careful not to let your own personal views influence your thinking.
- Rhetorical questions are those whose answers are meant to be self-evident. It's easier when the author says flat-out what he means, so rhetorical questions can be difficult under LSAT time pressure. Consider saving arguments that employ rhetorical questions until later in the section.

19 (E) The last sentence and choice (E) say essentially the same thing: An active society, for which the author argues, would work to "correct the flawed elements in society" or, in other words, rehabilitate criminals rather than simply react and punish them.

(A) Too extreme. The author simply argues that there are better, more productive routes to take than capital punishment.

(B) The author never discusses whether criminals should be held responsible for their actions.

(C) Too extreme. The author does believe that the use of capital punishment is an admission of

defeat, but that doesn't mean he'd agree that a society with this mindset won't survive.

(D) Too vague. War, for example, involves the destruction of human lives, which the author may feel is okay in some situations.

Remember:

- "Agreement with principles" questions follow the same general rules as inferences. However, note that a correct choice may relate to a point much more narrow than the overall passage.
- Learn to recognize extreme-sounding choices like "will not survive" and "inappropriate in any situation." Unless the author's tone is extreme, these choices are often wrong.

20 (C) This is essentially a formal logic statement disguised as a casual one. Translation: *if* a death row convict in a state pen filed a petition, *then* that convict believes there will be a delay, and a more favorable outcome if the pardoning authority knows about the petition. The contrapositive is stated in choice (C): If an inmate were to be pessimistic about the effect of filing a petition, we can safely conclude that that inmate did not actually file one.

(A), (B) These are backward. The original states, "If you file, then you believe, etcetera." The structure of (A) and (B) is, "If most or all believe, then they file."

(D) Remorse is way outside the scope, and since the argument is tailored around a very specific type of prisoner (the death row inmate in state pens), we can't deduce anything about petition-filing convicts in general.

(E) The scope of the passage is limited to those who have filed petitions. Those who didn't file are irrelevant.

Remember:

• For any true if–then statement, its contrapositive must also be true, and it's formed by reversing and negating the terms. The general model is: Original statement—if X, then Y. The contrapositive, and valid inference—if not Y, then not X. This is very important for LSAT Logical Reasoning.

21 (C) Although Jason believes that coupons will save money, Twyla counters that more will be saved if they don't use the coupons. The "odd man out" statement is (C), because while half of the products would cost the same, the other half could very well be cheaper if Jason's coupons are used.

(A) furthers her argument by explaining why, even after using coupons, the money spent would be greater than what Twyla would otherwise have paid.

(B) If using the couponed brands requires buying more of each product, then the net result would likely be a higher bottom line.

(D) That the higher prices of the couponed brands outweigh the savings from the coupons clearly strengthens Twyla's argument.

(E) If Twyla has already taken the trouble to find bargains, then it's reasonable to believe that less money could be spent on her sale items than on Jason's couponed items.

Remember:

• As in Logic Games, read the question stem carefully, and always take note of the word *except*.
• When you're asked, "Which choice does *not* support the argument?" understand that the right answer will either weaken the argument or have no effect on it.

22 (D) Within the last quarter, the company lost customers to a competitor, which rather readily leads to the conclusion that the company simply isn't as competitive as it once was.

(A) At no point are sales figures discussed, particularly with respect to the company's history.

(B), (E) Not necessarily true. Perhaps customers left because the treatment they received from the company wasn't as good as that which they could receive elsewhere.

(C) A greater percentage of potential clients are buying the competitor's system, but that doesn't mean that more actual clients are doing so.

Remember:

• Learn to recognize the difference between percentages and actual numbers. The test makers love to play on this distinction, in wrong choices and in questions demonstrating faulty logic.
• Use real, simple numbers to help clarify numerical relationships for yourself.

23

(B) Anything alleging the possibility of keeping abreast of friends' well-being at a distance would seriously weaken the argument. (B) presents a way in which friends can live apart from one another and still keep in contact.

(A) seems to attack the second sentence of the argument. It doesn't really, because "the same way" is different from "the same amount," but even if it did it wouldn't injure the claim that friendship means physical proximity.

(C), (D) The argument doesn't say that proximity guarantees knowing that everything is OK. It merely implies that without proximity, such knowledge is impossible. As for (D), the author doesn't claim that living near or with a friend will guarantee the friend's well-being, so this doesn't damage the argument either.

(E) brings up a new and unrelated situation, and fails to address the key points raised in the argument. It therefore can't be a weakener.

Remember:

- Recognize and cross off choices that sound damaging, but, in fact, damage an argument other than the one the author is making.

24

(D) The point common to both Duane and Sylvia's arguments is the effect gun control will have on the number of guns possessed by criminals. Duane argues that strict measures will reduce that number, while Sylvia argues that gun control will not alter that number. (D) is the only choice that stays within the scope and isolates this issue that's critical to both arguments.

(A) Only Duane mentions the opposition by handgun manufacturers.

(B) Duane seems to support this notion, and Sylvia doesn't disagree. She merely bases her counterargument on other grounds—whether gun control laws will be effective in actually reducing the number of handguns in the possession of criminals.

(C) In neither argument is the effect of strict punishments explored.

(E) Neither suggests that gun control is a constitutional violation. Only Sylvia hints at it, and even so she puts that issue aside for the purpose of making her main argument.

Remember:

- When reconciling two arguments, limit yourself to choices that center around facts or points mentioned in both arguments.
- Don't get sidetracked by tangents.

25

(D) Duane presents a course of action (gun control) that will lead to a situation (fewer guns in the hands of criminals) that will in turn bring about a desired result (decrease in the murder rate). Sylvia attacks the middle piece: She asserts that the "fewer guns for criminals" scenario will not result from the proposed course of action, namely gun control.

(A) At no point does Sylvia argue against Duane's claim that guns are a cause of the homicide problem.

(B) There is no use of sarcasm by either person.

(C) Sylvia does suggest that even with gun control laws, the bad situation will continue, and that honest people may find themselves disarmed. However, she doesn't suggest that the homicide problem will get worse.

(E) Way outside the scope. Sylvia never suggests that Duane engages in exaggeration to make his point, and besides, legal concerns are not raised by either person.

Remember:

• When choices employ abstractions (*course of action, the situation, the problem*), try to be conscientious in relating back to the specifics of the stimulus. You can't evaluate such choices until you understand the general framework in the context of the passage.

PRACTICE TEST TWO

Remove or photocopy this answer sheet and use it to complete Practice Test Two.
See the answer key immediately following the test to correct your answers when you're finished.
Then use the score converter on pages 155 and 156 to calculate your score and percentile rank.

Start with number 1 for each new section. If a section has fewer questions than answer spaces, leave the extra spaces blank.

SECTION 1	SECTION 2	SECTION 3	SECTION 4
1 (A)(B)(C)(D)(E)	1 (A)(B)(C)(D)(E)	1 (A)(B)(C)(D)(E)	1 (A)(B)(C)(D)(E)
2 (A)(B)(C)(D)(E)	2 (A)(B)(C)(D)(E)	2 (A)(B)(C)(D)(E)	2 (A)(B)(C)(D)(E)
3 (A)(B)(C)(D)(E)	3 (A)(B)(C)(D)(E)	3 (A)(B)(C)(D)(E)	3 (A)(B)(C)(D)(E)
4 (A)(B)(C)(D)(E)	4 (A)(B)(C)(D)(E)	4 (A)(B)(C)(D)(E)	4 (A)(B)(C)(D)(E)
5 (A)(B)(C)(D)(E)	5 (A)(B)(C)(D)(E)	5 (A)(B)(C)(D)(E)	5 (A)(B)(C)(D)(E)
6 (A)(B)(C)(D)(E)	6 (A)(B)(C)(D)(E)	6 (A)(B)(C)(D)(E)	6 (A)(B)(C)(D)(E)
7 (A)(B)(C)(D)(E)	7 (A)(B)(C)(D)(E)	7 (A)(B)(C)(D)(E)	7 (A)(B)(C)(D)(E)
8 (A)(B)(C)(D)(E)	8 (A)(B)(C)(D)(E)	8 (A)(B)(C)(D)(E)	8 (A)(B)(C)(D)(E)
9 (A)(B)(C)(D)(E)	9 (A)(B)(C)(D)(E)	9 (A)(B)(C)(D)(E)	9 (A)(B)(C)(D)(E)
10 (A)(B)(C)(D)(E)	10 (A)(B)(C)(D)(E)	10 (A)(B)(C)(D)(E)	10 (A)(B)(C)(D)(E)
11 (A)(B)(C)(D)(E)	11 (A)(B)(C)(D)(E)	11 (A)(B)(C)(D)(E)	11 (A)(B)(C)(D)(E)
12 (A)(B)(C)(D)(E)	12 (A)(B)(C)(D)(E)	12 (A)(B)(C)(D)(E)	12 (A)(B)(C)(D)(E)
13 (A)(B)(C)(D)(E)	13 (A)(B)(C)(D)(E)	13 (A)(B)(C)(D)(E)	13 (A)(B)(C)(D)(E)
14 (A)(B)(C)(D)(E)	14 (A)(B)(C)(D)(E)	14 (A)(B)(C)(D)(E)	14 (A)(B)(C)(D)(E)
15 (A)(B)(C)(D)(E)	15 (A)(B)(C)(D)(E)	15 (A)(B)(C)(D)(E)	15 (A)(B)(C)(D)(E)
16 (A)(B)(C)(D)(E)	16 (A)(B)(C)(D)(E)	16 (A)(B)(C)(D)(E)	16 (A)(B)(C)(D)(E)
17 (A)(B)(C)(D)(E)	17 (A)(B)(C)(D)(E)	17 (A)(B)(C)(D)(E)	17 (A)(B)(C)(D)(E)
18 (A)(B)(C)(D)(E)	18 (A)(B)(C)(D)(E)	18 (A)(B)(C)(D)(E)	18 (A)(B)(C)(D)(E)
19 (A)(B)(C)(D)(E)	19 (A)(B)(C)(D)(E)	19 (A)(B)(C)(D)(E)	19 (A)(B)(C)(D)(E)
20 (A)(B)(C)(D)(E)	20 (A)(B)(C)(D)(E)	20 (A)(B)(C)(D)(E)	20 (A)(B)(C)(D)(E)
21 (A)(B)(C)(D)(E)	21 (A)(B)(C)(D)(E)	21 (A)(B)(C)(D)(E)	21 (A)(B)(C)(D)(E)
22 (A)(B)(C)(D)(E)	22 (A)(B)(C)(D)(E)	22 (A)(B)(C)(D)(E)	22 (A)(B)(C)(D)(E)
23 (A)(B)(C)(D)(E)	23 (A)(B)(C)(D)(E)	23 (A)(B)(C)(D)(E)	23 (A)(B)(C)(D)(E)
24 (A)(B)(C)(D)(E)	24 (A)(B)(C)(D)(E)	24 (A)(B)(C)(D)(E)	24 (A)(B)(C)(D)(E)
25 (A)(B)(C)(D)(E)	25 (A)(B)(C)(D)(E)	25 (A)(B)(C)(D)(E)	25 (A)(B)(C)(D)(E)
26 (A)(B)(C)(D)(E)	26 (A)(B)(C)(D)(E)	26 (A)(B)(C)(D)(E)	26 (A)(B)(C)(D)(E)
27 (A)(B)(C)(D)(E)	27 (A)(B)(C)(D)(E)	27 (A)(B)(C)(D)(E)	27 (A)(B)(C)(D)(E)
28 (A)(B)(C)(D)(E)	28 (A)(B)(C)(D)(E)	28 (A)(B)(C)(D)(E)	28 (A)(B)(C)(D)(E)
29 (A)(B)(C)(D)(E)	29 (A)(B)(C)(D)(E)	29 (A)(B)(C)(D)(E)	29 (A)(B)(C)(D)(E)
30 (A)(B)(C)(D)(E)	30 (A)(B)(C)(D)(E)	30 (A)(B)(C)(D)(E)	30 (A)(B)(C)(D)(E)

PRACTICE TEST TWO
SECTION I
Time—35 minutes

24 questions

Directions: Each group of questions is based on a set of conditions. You may wish to draw a rough sketch to help you answer some of the questions. Choose the best answer for each question and fill in the corresponding space on your answer sheet.

Questions 1–5

A designer will select exactly two appliance designs and exactly two cabinet designs for the renovation of a house. The available appliance designs are H, J, K, L, and M, and the available cabinet designs are T, V, and W. The selections of appliances and cabinets must be made in accordance with the following conditions:

H is selected only if J and W are selected.
M cannot be selected unless J is selected.
If V is selected, then H is selected.

1. If V is selected, which one of the following must be selected?

   (A) K
   (B) L
   (C) M
   (D) T
   (E) W

2. Which one of the following pairs of designs cannot be selected together?

   (A) H and J
   (B) H and M
   (C) J and K
   (D) J and L
   (E) J and M

3. If J is not selected, which one of the following must be true?

   (A) H and T are selected.
   (B) K and L are selected.
   (C) K and M are selected.
   (D) L and V are not selected.
   (E) M and W are not selected.

4. If L is selected, how many distinct combinations of designs can be selected?

   (A) 1
   (B) 2
   (C) 3
   (D) 4
   (E) 6

5. If the conditions are altered such that H can be selected without selecting J, but all of the other conditions remain in effect, then which one of the following is a pair of designs that may be selected together?

   (A) H and M
   (B) K and M
   (C) K and V
   (D) M and V
   (E) T and V

GO ON TO THE NEXT PAGE.

Questions 6–12

A committee is scheduling the events for a town's Summer Festival. The festival lasts three days, from Friday to Sunday. The eight events to be scheduled are a bake sale, a craft show, a dance contest, a fireworks display, an obstacle course, a parade, a relay race, and a softball game. Each event will be held during a single time period—morning, afternoon, or evening—on a single day, and no two events will be held during the same time period. The following conditions must also be met:

The softball game must be held after the parade.
The relay race must be held in the morning.
The fireworks display must be held on Saturday evening.
The bake sale must be held in the evening and before the parade.
The dance contest must not be held on Friday.
The craft show is the first event held.

6. If no event is held on Sunday morning, then which one of the following events must be held on Friday afternoon?

(A)   the bake sale
(B)   the dance contest
(C)   the obstacle course
(D)   the relay race
(E)   the softball game

7. Which one of the following is a complete and accurate list of the events that could be held on Saturday morning?

(A)   dance contest, obstacle course, parade
(B)   dance contest, parade, softball game
(C)   dance contest, obstacle course, parade, relay race
(D)   dance contest, obstacle course, parade, relay race, softball game
(E)   obstacle course, parade, relay race

8. If the softball game is held on Sunday morning, then which one of the following is held on Saturday afternoon?

(A)   no event
(B)   the dance contest
(C)   the obstacle course
(D)   the parade
(E)   the relay race

9. If the relay race is held on the same day as the softball game, then which one of the following must be true?

(A)   No event is held between the fireworks and the relay race.
(B)   Exactly one event is held between the craft show and the obstacle course.
(C)   The craft show is held on the same day as the obstacle course.
(D)   The dance contest is held on Sunday afternoon.
(E)   The parade is held on Saturday afternoon.

10. If the softball game is held a day before the dance contest and at the same time of day, then which one of the following must be true?

(A)   The dance contest is held on Saturday.
(B)   The fireworks display is held before the relay race.
(C)   The obstacle course is held on Sunday.
(D)   The parade is held in the afternoon.
(E)   The softball game is held after the obstacle course.

11. If exactly two events are held between the craft show and the softball game, then the scheduling of how many events can be precisely determined?

(A)   3
(B)   4
(C)   5
(D)   6
(E)   7

12. Each of the following is an acceptable schedule of events held on Sunday EXCEPT:

	Morning	Afternoon	Evening
(A)	no event	softball game	obstacle course
(B)	parade	softball game	no event
(C)	relay race	no event	dance contest
(D)	relay race	softball game	dance contest
(E)	softball game	obstacle course	dance contest

GO ON TO THE NEXT PAGE.

Questions 13–17

Five sled dogs—Gakido, Hira, Jinook, Kini, and Leinheit—occupy five positions on a racing team. The positions are numbered one through five, and exactly one sled dog occupies each position. The sled dogs are hitched to harnesses as shown below:

The assignment of sled dogs to positions is subject to the following conditions:

> Each harness connects exactly two sled dogs, and sled dogs connected by harnesses are considered adjacent to one another.
> Exactly two sled dogs are experienced and exactly three sled dogs are inexperienced.
> An experienced sled dog must occupy the first position.
> Jinook is an experienced sled dog.
> Gakido is an inexperienced sled dog.
> The experienced sled dogs cannot be adjacent to one another.
> Kini is not adjacent to Leinheit.

13. Which one of the following is an acceptable list of the positions in a single team that could be occupied by inexperienced sled dogs?

(A) first, second, fifth
(B) first, third, fourth
(C) second, third, fourth
(D) second, fourth, fifth
(E) third, fourth, fifth

14. If Jinook occupies the fifth position, which one of the following must be true?

(A) Gakido occupies the second position.
(B) Hira occupies the third position.
(C) Leinheit occupies the fourth position.
(D) The sled dog occupying the third position is experienced.
(E) The sled dog occupying the fourth position is inexperienced.

15. If Leinheit and Hira occupy the fourth and fifth positions, respectively, then which one of the following must be false?

(A) Gakido is adjacent to Jinook.
(B) Gakido is adjacent to Kini.
(C) Gakido is adjacent to Leinheit.
(D) Gakido is adjacent to Hira.
(E) Jinook is adjacent to Kini.

16. If Kini occupies the fifth position, which one of the following would guarantee that an experienced sled dog occupies the fourth position?

(A) Gakido occupies the second position.
(B) Gakido occupies the third position.
(C) Hira occupies the third position.
(D) Jinook occupies the first position.
(E) Leinheit occupies the second position.

17. If Jinook is adjacent to both Kini and Leinheit, then Hira must be

(A) adjacent to Gakido
(B) adjacent to Jinook
(C) adjacent to Kini
(D) adjacent to Leinheit
(E) adjacent to either Jinook or Leinheit

GO ON TO THE NEXT PAGE.

Questions 18–24

A veterinarian has scheduled seven animals—Porter, Quint, Rocky, Slacker, Tammy, Venus, and Willoughby—to be examined on a single day, from first to seventh. Each animal will be examined exactly once during the day, and no two animals will be examined at the same time. The order of examinations must conform to the following restrictions:

Porter is examined immediately before Tammy is examined.
If Quint is examined fifth, Venus is examined sixth.
If Slacker is examined second, Porter is examined third.
Willoughby is examined either fourth or sixth.
Venus is not examined first or fifth.

18. Which one of the following is an acceptable ordering of animal examinations?

(A) Quint, Slacker, Porter, Tammy, Venus, Willoughby, Rocky
(B) Quint, Venus, Slacker, Willoughby, Porter, Tammy, Rocky
(C) Rocky, Slacker, Venus, Willoughby, Porter, Tammy, Quint
(D) Slacker, Porter, Tammy, Quint, Willoughby, Rocky, Venus
(E) Slacker, Rocky, Porter, Tammy, Quint, Willoughby, Venus

19. If Slacker is examined second, which one of the following animals must be examined fifth?

(A) Porter
(B) Quint
(C) Rocky
(D) Tammy
(E) Willoughby

20. If Quint is examined fifth and Rocky is examined before Willoughby is examined, then which one of the following must be true?

(A) Porter is examined first.
(B) Rocky is examined third.
(C) Slacker is examined seventh.
(D) Tammy is examined second.
(E) Willoughby is examined sixth.

21. If Porter is examined third, which one of the following is a complete and accurate list of animals who can be examined fifth?

(A) Quint
(B) Slacker
(C) Quint, Slacker
(D) Rocky, Slacker
(E) Quint, Rocky, Slacker

22. If Willoughby is examined immediately after Quint is examined, and Slacker is examined immediately after Venus is examined, then Rocky must be examined

(A) third.
(B) fourth.
(C) fifth.
(D) sixth.
(E) seventh.

23. If Tammy and Venus are both examined sometime after Willoughby is examined, then the number of possible orderings of animal examinations is

(A) 1
(B) 2
(C) 3
(D) 4
(E) 5

24. If Rocky is examined fourth, which one of the following could be true?

(A) Porter is examined third.
(B) Quint is examined first.
(C) Slacker is examined second.
(D) Slacker is examined seventh.
(E) Tammy is examined seventh.

S T O P
**IF YOU FINISH BEFORE TIME IS CALLED, YOU MAY CHECK YOUR WORK ON THIS SECTION ONLY.
DO NOT WORK ON ANY OTHER SECTION IN THE TEST.**

SECTION II
Time—35 minutes
25 questions

<u>Directions:</u> This test is composed of questions that ask you to analyze the logic of statements or short paragraphs. You are to choose as the answer to each question the one choice you consider <u>best</u> on the basis of your common-sense evaluation of the statement and its assumptions. Although a question may seem to have more than one acceptable answer, there is only one <u>best</u> answer, and it is the one that does not entail making any illogical, extraneous, or conflicting assumptions about the question. These questions do not presuppose any knowledge of formal logic on your part.

1. Researchers in the harbor town of Osceola have determined that the channeling of recycled wastewater into the harbor is endangering the health of the town's residents. A sharp increase in cases of the intestinal illness giardia has been directly attributed to bacteria that began to appear in drinking water supplies immediately following the implementation of the wastewater recycling program. The researchers have proposed adding the synthetic enzyme tripticase to the water during recycling. The addition of this enzyme would solve the health problem by eliminating the bacteria that causes giardia.

   Which one of the following statements, if true, most weakens the researchers' argument?

   (A) The tripticase enzyme also acts to break down bacteria causing intestinal conditions other than giardia.

   (B) Giardia is one of the least common and the least severe of all known illnesses related to the consumption of contaminated drinking water.

   (C) No other illnesses aside from giardia have increased significantly in Osceola since the wastewater recycling program began.

   (D) Giardia may be caused by the ingestion of contaminated food as well as contaminated drinking water.

   (E) The tripticase enzyme also breaks down chlorine that is essential to maintaining a safe drinking water supply.

2. Toy Manufacturer: This rubber ball is costly to make. We should switch to a less costly brand of rubber for this product.

   Marketing Analyst: But the ball sells so well because of its superior bouncing properties. No other material performs as well. We should stick with what we know we can sell.

   The speakers above disagree over which one of the following issues?

   (A) Whether the rubber used for this ball is more expensive than other available materials.

   (B) Whether this product regularly meets its sales quotas.

   (C) Whether the company should make the rubber ball from a different brand of rubber.

   (D) Whether customer priorities should factor into product development decisions.

   (E) Whether other rubber materials perform as well as the material currently used.

GO ON TO THE NEXT PAGE.

Questions 3–4

Salesman: The revolutionary new Shepherd's Gate Protection System represents the latest in sheep-tending technology. The built-in sensors recognize the scent of predators from miles around. When your flock is in danger of attack, the electronic gates surrounding the flock will quickly slam shut, keeping any unwanted animals away and your flock safer than ever. Sure, the system is prone to false alarms, but you know what they say: "Better safe than sorry."

3. Which one of the following, if true, most strengthens the salesman's argument?

    (A)   Sheep cannot be injured by the electronic gates when they quickly slam shut.
    (B)   Similar electronic protection systems are currently used to protect cattle from attack from predators.
    (C)   Roughly half of the incidents in which the gates are activated are triggered by false alarms.
    (D)   Some sheep predators have been hunted almost to extinction.
    (E)   Flocks of sheep are rarely attacked by predators.

4. The phrase "better safe than sorry" plays which one of the following roles in the argument above?

    (A)   It illustrates how a supposedly problematic aspect of the Gate Protection System is actually beneficial.
    (B)   It provides additional evidence of the mechanical efficacy of the Gate Protection System.
    (C)   It reinforces the notion that false alarms from the Gate Protection System are relatively rare.
    (D)   It attempts to diminish the magnitude of a deficiency of the Gate Protection System.
    (E)   It introduces a further reason for the need for sheep-tending technology.

5. Administrator: Sandra would not make an effective teacher. She is too lenient to fail students and too critical to reward any students with high marks.

An assumption central to the argument above is that

    (A)   effective teachers fail a certain percentage of their students and reward the rest with high marks
    (B)   a teacher must be capable of either rewarding students with high marks or failing students in order to be an effective teacher
    (C)   in order to fail or reward her students, Sandra must be an effective teacher
    (D)   it is impossible to fail a student and then later reward the same student with high marks
    (E)   if Sandra were less critical, she would reward students with high marks

GO ON TO THE NEXT PAGE.

6. The financial burden imposed by job-related costs is greatest for individuals who make a salary of $30,000 to $40,000 per year, and less for those who make much lower or much higher salaries. The reason for this is that individuals in low-paying entry-level positions making far less than $30,000 per year generally have fewer costs associated with maintaining their jobs, such as wardrobe costs, dry-cleaning, and medical bills due to work-related stress. The burden of these costs increases as one is promoted to higher-ranking positions, but lessens as the salary levels commensurate with further promotions become more than adequate to offset such costs. Jenny, who now makes $40,000 per year as an administrative director, will therefore be less financially burdened over the coming years by costs related to this job.

The argument above depends on which one of the following assumptions?

(A) Jenny will be promoted in the years to come.
(B) Over the next several years, Jenny's employer will provide benefits that help reduce stress-related medical costs.
(C) $40,000 is not considered an entry-level salary for Jenny's position.
(D) None of Jenny's co-workers who earn the same salary as Jenny is as burdened as she is by job-related costs.
(E) The costs related to Jenny's previous job were not as high as the costs related to her current position.

7. An individual may become more personally appealing as he or she becomes more physically beautiful. At the same time, however, the positive attention brought on by greater beauty may make the person vain or arrogant, which may decrease his or her personal appeal.

Which one of the following statements is best illustrated by the situation described above?

(A) The link between beauty and personal appeal is entirely superficial.
(B) Traits that appear positive are usually negative.
(C) A characteristic may be both enhanced and reduced by a single factor.
(D) Negative traits can only be balanced by positive traits of equal importance.
(E) Beauty is in the eye of the beholder.

8. Educational consultant: Most school districts today do not provide adequate educations for their students. Teachers do not receive quality training. Moreover, after-school academic programs are limited by tight budgets, and parental involvement in the classroom is at an all-time low. The Prentice school district, however, is looking up; parents and community volunteers are spending more time assisting in classrooms than in previous years.

Which one of the following statements below is best supported by the education consultant's argument if the information in that argument is accurate?

(A) The education provided by the Prentice school district displays at least one component of adequate education more so than it has in the past.
(B) The education provided by the Prentice school district can be considered adequate.
(C) The Prentice school district surpasses others in terms of the quality of education that its students receive.
(D) Many schools currently offer fewer after-school academic programs than do the schools in the Prentice school district.
(E) There is less parental involvement in other school districts than there is in the Prentice school district.

GO ON TO THE NEXT PAGE.

Questions 9–10

A consumer survey of independent feature films revealed that the percentage of action films that received the survey's highest rating was greater than the percentage of romance films that received the highest rating. Yet, the survey organizers were probably erroneous in their conclusion that subject matter determines a feature film's popular appeal, since the action films were all directed by filmmakers with at least one hit film to their credit, while the romance films were directed by newer filmmakers, many of whom had not produced a previous film.

9. The statements above, if true, support which one of the following inferences?

(A) Fewer romance films than action films received the survey's highest rating.

(B) There is no relationship between the popular appeal of the feature films evaluated in the survey and any previous successes of the directors of those films.

(C) If consumers were surveyed regarding their impressions of big-budget mainstream films, the percentage of romance films that would receive the survey's highest rating would be lower than the percentage of action films that would receive the highest rating.

(D) Experienced filmmakers are more likely to produce hit films than are new filmmakers.

(E) Among directors with the same number of hit films to their credit, differences in the subject matter of their feature films may not affect the way the films are popularly rated.

10. Each of the following, if true, supports the author's contention that the organizers misinterpreted the survey data EXCEPT:

(A) The fact that one has directed a previous hit film is a positive indicator of that director's filmmaking talent.

(B) Consumer ratings of a new film are influenced by the previous history of success of the film's director.

(C) Action films generally require larger budgets than romance films and are thus prohibitive for many first-time film directors.

(D) It is rare for the films of first-time directors to attain the popular appeal of films directed by filmmakers with at least one hit film to their credit.

(E) Directors who have produced a previous hit film generally obtain the largest budgets and attract the most talented and well-known actors for their subsequent films.

11. Candidate: I am worried about the effects that the recent media coverage of my personal life will have on my chances of gaining office. Even though the reports are untrue, some voters interviewed on television, in response to these reports, have already expressed doubts regarding my ability to lead.

Campaign manager: Your concern is unfounded. Of 1,000 people in this city randomly surveyed by e-mail, only 25 have responded that their perception of your ability to lead has been negatively impacted by the recent media coverage.

The campaign manager's argument is most vulnerable to criticism on the ground that it fails to acknowledge the possibility that

(A) future media reports that follow up on the story of the candidate's personal life will further damage the public's perception of the candidate's ability to lead

(B) the candidate's main opponent will use the opportunity created by the recent media coverage to conduct her own survey to assess the damage done to her opponent's credibility

(C) the voting public would understand that its reaction to the recent media coverage of the candidate's personal life was the intended primary focus of the survey

(D) opinions expressed in television interviews are not always the most reliable indicator of how interviewees are likely to act in given situations

(E) many of those surveyed who are skeptical of the candidate's ability to lead due to the recent reports did not actually respond to the survey

GO ON TO THE NEXT PAGE.

12. Sarah's Principal: Sarah's teacher should spend more individual time with Sarah instead of generating more vocabulary charts for her to memorize. Sarah makes a large number of usage mistakes when she writes and does not seem to have a grasp of basic phonetics. She has yet to memorize one of the vocabulary charts entirely, and she continues to misuse in her writing words she has already learned. Research shows that individual attention is more effective in helping students learn than is rote memorization, so Sarah's teacher is not displaying good judgment in continuing to rely on vocabulary charts to improve Sarah's writing.

Which one of the following statements best describes the function served by the principal's proposal that Sarah's teacher should personally provide Sarah with additional help?

(A) It represents a central assumption of the argument.

(B) It is a claim that is supported by evidence in the passage, while at the same time it also supports another conclusion in the passage.

(C) It is a hypothesis that is not supported by evidence in the passage.

(D) It is the conclusion that the rest of the argument upholds.

(E) It is a piece of evidence designed to support the ultimate conclusion of the argument.

13. If too much pressure is exerted on the bottom shelf of a bookcase, the entire bookcase will collapse. Sherry's bookcase has collapsed. Therefore, too much pressure must have been exerted on its bottom shelf.

Which one of the following criticisms best describes a weakness in the argument above?

(A) It supports its conclusion with irrelevant evidence.

(B) It contains a shift in the meaning of the word "collapse" from "partial collapse" to "full collapse."

(C) It concludes that an outcome has been caused by a particular factor that may be only one possible cause of the outcome in question.

(D) It overlooks the possibility that some bookshelves have only one shelf.

(E) It draws an overly broad conclusion from contradictory evidence.

14. College Dean: Parker College provides a great deal of financial aid to its students. This year, every registered student is receiving either a student loan or a scholarship.

Financial Aid Officer: Then all of our registered students have loans this year, because every student who received a scholarship this year also received a student loan.

In which one of the following dialogues below does the pattern of reasoning most closely parallel the reasoning presented in the dialogue above?

(A) Florist: We are pleased with the mixed bouquets that your company delivered. Every bouquet that was delivered this week contained either beautiful orchids or vibrant red roses.
Flower Wholesaler: Then most of the bouquets delivered also contained a silver rose, because most of the bouquets delivered containing orchids this week also contained a silver rose.

(B) Grandmother: I am so proud of this family! Every member of our immediate family has attended either Branston College, the school you attend, or Browning College.
Grandson: Then I may be the first to attend both, because I am thinking of transferring to Browning.

(C) Psychiatrist: The patients on Ward A are generally improving. Each patient now receives either an antidepressant drug or an anti-schizophrenic drug.
Nurse: Then patients on Ward B must also be improving, because those patients also receive either an antidepressant or anti-schizophrenic drug.

(D) Margaret: The hospital is encouraging all patients to eat more vegetables. Tonight every patient ordered either brussel sprouts or corn.
Cafeteria Worker: Every patient who ordered corn tonight also ordered brussel sprouts. So every patient in the hospital ordered brussel sprouts tonight.

(E) Contractor: The architect's design calls for ornate crown moldings to be added to either the West wing or East wing, but not both.
Foreman: The moldings will be more obtrusive on the smaller West wing, so we will have to add them to the East wing.

GO ON TO THE NEXT PAGE.

15. A passenger vehicle is defined as any fully enclosed four-wheeled vehicle with room to transport at least one other passenger in addition to the driver. A semi truck, though it may have enclosed room to transport one non-driving passenger, always has more than four wheels. A jeep, though it may have four wheels and room to carry a driver and additional passengers, is rarely fully enclosed. A postal van, though it may be enclosed and have four wheels, usually does not have room to transport passengers other than the driver.

If the statements in the passage above are true, which one of the following must also be true?

(A) If an automobile is neither a semi truck, nor a jeep, nor a postal van, then it is not a fully enclosed four-wheeled vehicle.

(B) If an automobile is not a semi truck, or a jeep, or a postal van, then it is a passenger vehicle.

(C) If a jeep is fully enclosed with four wheels and room to carry non-driving passengers, then it is both a jeep and a passenger vehicle.

(D) Postal vans are more like passenger vehicles than are semi trucks.

(E) Some postal vans may be considered to be jeeps.

16. Superintendent: Teachers in our district must refrain from intervening in student conflicts in order to encourage students to hone their social interaction skills, except for cases in which physical violence is involved.

Which one of the following is an application of the Superintendent's principle of teacher intervention?

(A) A gym teacher watches while students break up a fist-fight between the players of two teams that was ignited over a disputed call.

(B) An English teacher takes the side of one student in an argument concerning a school locker, and sends the other student to the principal's office.

(C) A parent instructs her child who is having difficulty getting along with certain schoolmates to work it out on his own.

(D) A philosophy teacher instigates a heated debate between students holding radically different opinions on a controversial topic.

(E) A math teacher allows a group of students to tease another student about her new haircut.

17. Over the past seven years, private college tuition rates have increased, resulting in a large decrease in private college attendance across the country. Private college revenues, however, have progressively increased in each of the seven years during this period, and researchers predict further increases in the years to come.

Which one of the following, if true, offers the best explanation for the situation described above?

(A) Most private colleges increase tuition rates approximately once every two years.

(B) Attendance at vocational schools generally exceeds attendance at private colleges in most cities.

(C) The increase in tuition rates at private colleges has influenced many prospective students to seek a state scholarship to attend a public university.

(D) The decrease in students attending private colleges over the last seven years has been more than offset by the increases in tuition.

(E) Private colleges gain a larger percentage of their revenue from alumni contributions than do public universities.

GO ON TO THE NEXT PAGE.

KAPLAN

18. Children never develop strong self-esteem if they are guided by critical adults. Therefore, if children are guided by uncritical adults, they will develop strong self-esteem.

The flawed pattern of reasoning in which one of the following arguments is most similar to that in the argument above?

(A) Even though Hannah studies hard, she does not make good grades. Therefore, Hannah should not try to make good grades by studying hard.

(B) Telephone solicitors who have bad phone manners do not sell any products. Therefore, telephone solicitors with low sales records must have bad phone manners.

(C) Using the store's new knitting machine, the knitting store owner made twice as many sweaters yesterday as she did the day before. Therefore, if she uses the knitting machine again tomorrow, she will make twice as many sweaters as she did today.

(D) Puppies who are not well-socialized with humans do not interact comfortably with a large group of people. Therefore, the more a puppy is socialized with humans, the more comfortably the puppy will interact with a large group of people.

(E) Individuals who take calcium supplements do not increase their risk of heart disease. Therefore, it stands to reason that individuals who do not take calcium supplements will increase their risk of heart disease.

19. Some sports historians claim that professional tennis players develop unique playing styles that result from a combination of the peculiarities of each player's physical attributes and the influence of coaches during their early adaptation to the game. But when the increase in strength and endurance of modern players is discounted, it becomes readily apparent that the playing styles of the current crop of professional tennis players are no different from the styles of players from previous generations. Clearly, there is a universally efficient tennis style to which all professional tennis players conform.

The argument above is most weakened by which one of the following statements?

(A) The differences in physical attributes among tennis players are even more pronounced than the sports historians believe.

(B) Few current professional tennis players are familiar with the professional tennis players of fifty years ago.

(C) The increased strength of current tennis players contributes more to the development of individual playing styles than does increased endurance.

(D) All of the early coaches of today's professional tennis players were professional tennis players themselves earlier in their lives.

(E) Weight training and greater attention to diet are the primary factors in the increased strength and stamina of the current generation of professional tennis players.

GO ON TO THE NEXT PAGE.

20. Recently, the research and development departments at major pharmaceutical companies have been experimenting with new injections that provide the boost in iron that anemic children need to reverse their condition. These companies have expressed confidence that children who are suffering from anemia will be cured relatively simply through the use of such biochemical supplements.

In concluding that the biochemical remedy being developed will have its desired effect, the pharmaceutical companies assume that

(A) major pharmaceutical companies have the primary responsibility to cure childhood anemia

(B) a low iron level in the body is the major factor influencing the incidence of anemia in children

(C) a diet rich in iron cannot improve the conditions of children suffering from anemia to the point that biochemical supplements would become unnecessary

(D) children afflicted with anemia will find out about and submit to injections that can reverse their conditions

(E) the use of biochemical supplements is the safest way to cure anemia in children

21. When choosing pilots to participate in outer space missions, mission commanders subject applicants to challenging isolation tests. Commanders argue for the necessity of these tests by pointing out that performance on an isolation test may well indicate how safely a pilot could operate a craft during a long voyage home in the event that his or her crewmates were killed during a mission. But an individual's ability to withstand isolation may also arise from an antisocial personality disorder. Therefore, mission commanders should not use this test in selecting pilots.

The argument above is flawed because it fails to consider each of the following possibilities EXCEPT:

(A) Isolation tests may give applicants a more realistic idea of the dangers of an actual space mission, prompting some to reevaluate their decision to apply.

(B) Mission commanders may select more qualified pilots if the pilot tests are not subject to specific limitations.

(C) An applicant's ability to withstand isolation may indicate a capacity to cope with pressure.

(D) Good performance in isolation testing may indicate a high level of stamina and endurance in an applicant.

(E) Applicants who may not perform well under actual isolation conditions may nonetheless perform well in a simulated isolation test.

GO ON TO THE NEXT PAGE.

22. When Harry expressed frustration over the disarray of his baseball card collection, his older brother suggested that he organize the cards in a display album containing special pages to showcase his most valuable cards. After investigating albums available on the market, Harry concluded that his brother's suggestion would not help organize his collection because none of the albums with the special showcase pages were big enough to hold all of his cards.

Which one of the following assumptions is central to the reasoning behind Harry's dismissal of his brother's recommendation?

(A) Larger showcase display albums produced in the past were big enough to hold all of Harry's cards.

(B) Albums without showcase pages are never as effective for organizing baseball cards as are albums containing such pages.

(C) Any album large enough to hold all of Harry's cards would contain enough special showcase pages to display all of his most valuable cards.

(D) Harry's baseball card collection would not be well-organized if displayed in several showcase albums.

(E) Harry's baseball card collection is in disarray because he has more cards in his collection than he did last year.

23. A free press always informs the public of all aspects of a country's current military operations except for cases in which the safety of troops or the success of a mission would be jeopardized by the public's right to know.

Which one of the following adheres most closely to the principle set forth above?

(A) A free press would publish editorials supporting a current military campaign, but could repress dissenting opinions regarding the campaign.

(B) An unfree press would release information on the country's prisoners of war taken during a current military campaign, unless such information would hamper efforts to secure the prisoners' release.

(C) A free press would accurately report the number of casualties suffered on both sides of a battle, but could withhold information regarding the possible targets for a future military strike.

(D) An unfree press would print inflammatory accounts of an international event in order to garner public support for an unpopular war.

(E) A free press would reveal any new information regarding the country's past involvement in secret military operations as soon as that information became available.

GO ON TO THE NEXT PAGE.

24. Lillian has expressed concern about maintaining cohesion in her drug addiction recovery group that she leads at her youth center. She has worked to develop cohesion by encouraging group members to share their experiences openly with the group. But some of the group members take advantage of this opportunity for openness by sharing long violent stories primarily intended to shock the others. Aversion to these stories has caused some members to quit the group. These violent lengthy stories also take time away from other members, preventing them from sharing their experiences. To ensure cohesion in the group, then, Lillian should delineate a specific time slot for each member to speak during each session.

Which one of the following best describes the logical flaw in the argument above?

(A) Two actions that merely occur simultaneously are presented as actions that are causally related.

(B) A hypothesis is presented that runs counter to a proposal related to that hypothesis.

(C) A course of action is proposed to resolve a problem that would in actuality address only one cause of the problem.

(D) A conclusion is based on evidence that is unrelated to the issue at hand.

(E) A conclusion is supported by evidence that contradicts the conclusion.

25. The kuva weave fabric, produced by American Synthetics Inc., was once thought to be a miraculous invention due to its properties of strength and durability. However, industrial accidents over the past three years have proven that the material is extremely flammable. This discovery dealt a large blow to manufacturers who use the fabric in their products, as the fabric provided an excellent alternative to weaker textiles implicated in many product failures. Since the kuva weave fabric can no longer be used, manufacturers must eliminate all American Synthetics materials from their inventories.

The argument's conclusion is best justified if which one of the following statements is assumed?

(A) Early trial runs that testified to the safety of the kuva weave fabric have subsequently been shown to be incomplete.

(B) All materials produced by American Synthetics contain some form of the kuva weave fabric.

(C) The incidence of industrial fires in manufacturing plants that use the kuva weave fabric is relatively high compared to plants that do not use the fabric.

(D) Kuva weave fabrics are not as durable as originally believed.

(E) Manufacturers are likely to incur product liability lawsuits stemming from accidents caused by flammable products containing the kuva weave fabric.

STOP
**IF YOU FINISH BEFORE TIME IS CALLED, YOU MAY CHECK YOUR WORK ON THIS SECTION ONLY.
DO NOT WORK ON ANY OTHER SECTION IN THE TEST.**

SECTION III
Time—35 minutes
25 questions

<u>Directions:</u> This test is composed of questions that ask you to analyze the logic of statements or short paragraphs. You are to choose as the answer to each question the one choice you consider <u>best</u> on the basis of your common-sense evaluation of the statement and its assumptions. Although a question may seem to have more than one acceptable answer, there is only one <u>best</u> answer, and it is the one that does not entail making any illogical, extraneous, or conflicting assumptions about the question. These questions do not presuppose any knowledge of formal logic on your part.

1. John's Father: John has complained frequently that his psychoanalysis sessions are not helpful. But John has no knowledge of psychology, and he cannot accurately judge his analyst's techniques. His dissatisfaction in no way indicates that his analyst's methods are unsound, and is therefore no reason for him to discontinue his counseling sessions.

   John's Mother: But the purpose of his therapy is to help him adjust to our divorce. While it is true that John is not qualified to assess the analyst's methods, the only way to know if John is being helped by the therapy is through his evaluations of his own progress. If he believes that the sessions are a waste of time, he should stop seeing the analyst.

   Which one of the following is an assumption upon which John's mother's argument depends?

   (A) John's father is correct in concluding that John is unhappy with his counseling sessions.
   (B) Involvement in the therapeutic process does not hamper John's ability to perceive the value of his counseling sessions.
   (C) Psychoanalysts do not need to have extensive qualifications in order to be helpful to their clients.
   (D) If a psychoanalyst employs a sound method, then his or her clients will perceive the counseling sessions as helpful.
   (E) John is entitled to act on any belief concerning his own well-being, regardless of the origin or merits of that belief.

2. Harriet's husband: My wife Harriet has long desired to vacation in a region that is culturally rich. According to this travel brochure, income from the manufacture of industrial documentaries makes Sunshine Valley the second wealthiest region in the state. I have therefore decided to surprise Harriet with accommodations for a two week trip to Sunshine Valley.

   Which one of the following best characterizes a flaw in Harriet's husband's method of reaching his decision?

   (A) He displays circular reasoning in his attempt to justify his decision.
   (B) He equivocates with respect to a key factor in his decision.
   (C) He uses unreliable and potentially biased evidence as support for his decision.
   (D) He makes a major decision without consulting each party that the decision will affect.
   (E) He fails to demonstrate that his decision is economically feasible.

GO ON TO THE NEXT PAGE.

3. Chocolate is derived from the beans of the tropical New World tree *Theobroma cacao*. When chocolate arrived in Europe around 1500, it was consumed only as a hot drink. In the mid-1800s, however, the Swiss invented the first method for producing it in a solid edible form. Today, millions more pounds of chocolate are produced for eating than for drinking.

Which one of the following can be inferred from the statements above?

(A) Today, Theobroma cacao is grown only in the tropical New World.

(B) When chocolate was introduced to Europe, it was most commonly used in a solid form.

(C) The number of pounds of chocolate made for eating today is greater than the number of pounds of chocolate that were made for drinking during the 1800s.

(D) Chocolate was not consumed in a solid form in the New World during the 1500s.

(E) If the Swiss had not invented a method for producing chocolate in a solid edible form, chocolate would not have become as popular as it is today.

4. Nuclear physicist: *The Fairmarch Times* should make an effort to include the protestors' views in their stories on the nuclear reactor controversy. The *Times* has covered the controversy for a week now, but so far they have presented only the industry side of the issue. No effort has been made to cover the protestors' side. Stories regarding that perspective are completely lacking.

Plant engineer: The protestors' views do not need to be included. The *Times* coverage is fine as is.

Which one of the following statements, if true, most effectively counters the plant engineer's position?

(A) Newspaper reporting must present the views of both sides of a controversy in order to be truly effective.

(B) The *Times* is well known for the quality of its reporting and has presented a number of stories on controversies similar to the nuclear reactor controversy.

(C) Newspaper accounts of the nuclear reactor controversy are read by industry representatives as well as by members of the protest movement.

(D) One of the *Times* reporters covering the nuclear reactor controversy is a former member of the group that has organized protests against the reactor.

(E) Industry groups typically receive more media coverage than do protest organizations.

5. Botanists once claimed that plants of the Faura species required a balanced fertilizer comprised of the following elements to grow: nitrogen, boron, copper, and iron. This approach, however, inhibited Faura propagation.

The conclusion above is supported by each of the following EXCEPT:

(A) Advocating that Faura plants required a balanced composition of the four elements gave the impression that these elements would be sufficient for plant growth, but the plants cannot grow without an appropriate percentage of soluble potash as well.

(B) The omission of zinc from the list of necessary elements conveys the false impression that zinc is less essential to Faura plant growth than are the other four elements.

(C) The emphasis on balance between the four fertilizer elements suggests that the elements should be present in the same amounts, but nitrogen and iron are more essential to Faura plant growth and thus should be present in larger quantities.

(D) The recommendation that the growth-promoting fertilizer should contain copper overlooks the fact that in order for the copper to function effectively, Faura plants must also be fertilized with extremely small amounts of molybdenum.

(E) The inclusion of the element boron in the list served to remind botanists to include this less well-known element in their fertilizer treatment for Faura plants.

GO ON TO THE NEXT PAGE.

6. Three years ago, Ron and Crystal agreed that they would open a restaurant only when they both were prepared to put in the necessary long hours. At the beginning of this year, Ron assumed that Crystal was prepared to make this time commitment, but this erroneous belief was most likely the product of wishful thinking: Crystal just took on a new year-long project at her current job that requires a great deal of travel and takes up most of her focus and energy.

The argument above is structured to lead to which one of the following conclusions?

(A) Ron was mistaken when he assumed that Crystal was ready for the time commitment required to open the restaurant.
(B) Opening a restaurant requires a great deal of personal focus and energy.
(C) Opening the restaurant would involve even longer hours than Crystal's current job.
(D) Crystal was never truly interested in opening a restaurant with Ron.
(E) Ron and Crystal will not open their restaurant this year.

Questions 7–8

Center director: The number of volunteer applications for our elderly care center has doubled over the past five years. This clearly shows that community members are taking a greater interest in working with their aging parents.

Nurse: Unfortunately, my research indicates that just the opposite is true. If you look closely at our records, applications from patients' family members have decreased by 20% over the past five years. This would indicate that, contrary to your conclusion, community members' interest in working with their elderly parents has actually decreased.

7. If the statistics cited by both the center director and the nurse are correct, which one of the following must be true?

(A) The center has had a decline in its patient population over the past five years.
(B) The quality of care provided to patients at the facility has improved over the past five years.
(C) The center has received volunteer applications from individuals who are not related to patients at the center.
(D) The cost of maintaining adequate staff to care for the center's patients has risen enough to warrant the need for additional volunteers.
(E) Only a small percentage of all the people who apply to volunteer at the center actually assume volunteer positions.

8. Which one of the following, if true, would most seriously weaken the nurse's argument?

(A) Many community members living near the center have moved into newly-constructed housing developments on the outskirts of town.
(B) Over the past five years, center funding for family-oriented activities has decreased significantly.
(C) Volunteering in elderly care facilities requires training for which most individuals do not have the time.
(D) Due to a recent change in policy, many family members who volunteer at the elderly care center do not fill out formal applications.
(E) The time commitment required by volunteers at elderly care centers is relatively modest compared to other volunteer opportunities in the region.

9. Angie: If Bernard decides to allow his dog Pepe to sleep at the foot of his bed, Pepe will become spoiled and his current disciplinary problems will worsen.

Theresa: On the contrary, the dog's behavior would improve. Julian's dog used to chew his furniture at night just like Bernard's dog does now. When Julian followed a trainer's advice and allowed the dog to sleep in his bedroom, at the foot of his bed, his dog calmed down and stopped destroying the furniture within weeks. Similarly, if Bernard allowed his dog to sleep near his bed, the dog's destructive chewing would soon stop.

In her argument, Theresa does which one of the following?

(A) She provides a reinterpretation of evidence against a plan by pointing out how that evidence supports the plan.
(B) She offers a general recommendation to resolve a specific problem.
(C) She gives a rationale for why following a particular plan would cause difficulties for those who adhere to it.
(D) She claims that the results of one course of action would be similar to the results of a different course of action.
(E) She forecasts the results of following a plan in one instance by comparing that situation to a similar situation from the past.

GO ON TO THE NEXT PAGE.

10. A study sponsored by the Association of Educational Consultants has found that students learn and retain 20 percent of material they hear in class, 30 percent of material from written assignments, and 90 percent of material they teach to others. Based on these findings, the principal of Clarkstown Elementary School, interested in enhancing her students' learning and retention of typical grade-school material, has proposed the creation of a new curriculum in which the students conduct all of the teaching.

Which one of the following best characterizes the flaw in the principal's proposal above?

(A) It fails to take into account the fact that under the new curriculum students would still be required to listen in class much of the time.

(B) It mistakenly assumes that written assignments are as valuable a teaching aid as hearing material discussed in the classroom.

(C) It fails to demonstrate how the new curriculum would directly lead to higher test scores.

(D) It overlooks the possibility that the study's findings may be motivated in part by the self-interest of the sponsoring association.

(E) It ignores the fact that most elementary school children are limited in the number of typical grade-school subjects they are qualified to teach.

11. Most students at Carmine University feel overwhelmed by the elective choices available to them in their course offering handbook. This could be because the elective courses are not properly categorized, or because the descriptions of the elective courses are too extensive. A review of the lengths of typical elective course descriptions shows that each description is far less lengthy than the length that most students can absorb in any given reading. So it must be that the elective courses are not properly categorized.

Which one of the following is an assumption upon which the argument above depends?

(A) Improper categorization of elective course offerings makes it impossible to choose between those courses.

(B) Some students are overwhelmed by the length of the coursedescriptions.

(C) Some students find that the coursebook is not well-organized.

(D) The number of elective course offerings provided in the handbook is not the reason the students are overwhelmed.

(E) Most students can absorb rather lengthy course descriptions.

12. Due to a rash of behavioral problems among a particular group of high school students, the principal has canceled all school extracurricular activities for the next month. The organizers of a pep rally scheduled to take place during this period have made the case that this event should be allowed, because the increase in school spirit brought about by the pep rally will bond the participants together, which in turn will result in a decrease in aberrant behavior among the students in the long run.

The organizers of the pep rally assume which one of the following in making their argument?

(A) The principal did not intend to include the pep rally among the group of extracurricular activities canceled for the next month.

(B) The students exhibiting behavioral problems will take part in the pep rally.

(C) No other extracurricular activities besides the pep rally should be allowed to take place during the next month unless it can be determined that such activities would bond the students together.

(D) A pep rally is the most effective type of extracurricular activity to deal with the problem of aberrant school behavior.

(E) The principal will allow other canceled events to take place once she sees the beneficial effect that the pep rally has on the students.

GO ON TO THE NEXT PAGE.

13. Some individuals believe that attending cooking school in Southern France teaches one all there is to know about French cooking. All branches of La Terrelle Cooking Academy are located in Southern France. Yet, a recent graduate of La Terrelle did not know how to make bechamel sauce, a sauce widely used in French gourmet cooking.

If the statements above are true, which one of the following must also be true?

(A) Attending cooking school in Southern France does not always teach one all there is to know about French cooking.

(B) No graduate of La Terrelle Cooking Academy has learned all there is to know about French gourmet cooking.

(C) At least one branch of La Terrelle Cooking Academy is located outside of Southern France.

(D) La Terrelle Cooking Academy does not provide an effective education in French gourmet cooking.

(E) Cooking schools located in Southern France teach their students less about French gourmet cooking than do schools located in other parts of the country.

14. Tsumi bats are a rare breed of omnivorous bat found only in highly temperate climates. Most Tsumi bats living in captivity develop endocrine imbalances from their normal zoo diets, which consist mostly of fruits and berries. The healthiest way to feed the bats, therefore, is to provide them primarily with nuts, grubs, and vegetables, and only minimal amounts of fruits and berries.

Which one of the statements below does NOT reflect an assumption upon which the argument depends?

(A) Tsumi bats living in captivity will consume diets that consist of nuts, grubs, and vegetables, but no fruits or berries.

(B) Tsumi bats living in captivity will not be malnourished on diets that contain minimal fruits and berries.

(C) Those who care for Tsumi bats in captivity should avoid feeding them diets that produce endocrine imbalances.

(D) Tsumi bats living in captivity will be adequately nourished on a diet that consists primarily of nuts, grubs, and vegetables.

(E) For Tsumi bats living in captivity, no health problem stemming from diets consisting mostly of nuts, grubs, and vegetables would surpass in severity the health problems associated with endocrine imbalances.

15. Before the advent of writing, each of the isolated clans of the Comaquogue tribe contained master storytellers whose function was to orally transmit the tradition of each clan from one generation to the next. When writing was developed within certain clans of the tribe, the master storytellers of these clans disappeared within a few generations. This stands to reason, considering that the availability of written records obviated the need for masterful oral communicators to keep the tradition of literate clans alive. What has puzzled anthropologists, however, is the total lack of masterful storytellers in modern illiterate Comaquogue clans.

Which one of the following, if true, best helps to explain the puzzling situation mentioned above?

(A) Modern illiterate Comaquogue clan members display personality characteristics that resemble their ancestors more closely than they resemble the characteristics of modern literate Comaquogue clan members.

(B) Modern illiterate Comaquogue clans participate in more ritual gatherings than most modern literate Comaquogue clans do, but they participate in fewer ritual gatherings than did their common ancestors.

(C) Modern illiterate Comaquogue clans are recently descended from long-time literate clans that failed to pass on the skills of reading and writing due to a devastating 75-year war.

(D) The celebrations of modern illiterate Comaquogue clans involve a great deal of singing and dancing, and children are taught clan songs and dances from a very young age.

(E) The traditions of modern illiterate Comaquogue clans are an amalgamation of the cumulative experiences of previous generations plus innovations to the heritage added by the current generation of clan members.

GO ON TO THE NEXT PAGE.

16. Playing in a rock band during college has caused Matthew's grades to suffer, which in turn has decreased his chances of being accepted to a prestigious graduate program. But being active in extracurricular activities such as music can in some cases compensate for bad grades and help a candidate's chances for admission to graduate school by demonstrating that one is a well-rounded individual with varied interests. However, the dean of Wentworth Business School refuses to allow Matthew's participation in the band to positively impact on his acceptance chances.

Which one of the following principles best justifies the dean's position?

(A) The consequences of an action can only be evaluated with respect to the possible consequences of an opposing alternative action.

(B) Nothing that causes a condition can be used to compensate for the consequences of that condition.

(C) The overall value of an activity must not be overridden by a negative result of a single aspect of that activity.

(D) A decision that affects the future of an individual must not discount any factor relevant to that decision.

(E) A factor that eliminates a candidate from consideration in one instance should not be used to eliminate that candidate from consideration in a dissimilar situation.

17. Computer scientists have discovered two particularly insidious computer viruses known as the alphatron and b-scan viruses. These viruses typically infiltrate a computer's systems files and prevent files from being stored properly, namely by storing them in incorrect locations. Fortunately, at present there is no evidence to prove that the alphatron and b-scan viruses erase computer files entirely, so computer users who detect one or both of the viruses can rest assured that their files will not be erased.

The argument above is flawed because it

(A) fails to consider the fact that causal relationships that cannot be proven may nonetheless influence people who assume that these relationships exist

(B) fails to consider the possibility that a cause-and-effect relationship may exist even where it has not been demonstrated to exist

(C) neglects to explain the technical mechanisms by which computer files may be erased by viruses

(D) equivocates with respect to a key term

(E) supports its conclusion with evidence that merely restates the conclusion

18. If foods that require refrigeration are not kept at the proper temperature, they can become fertile environments for the growth of bacteria that invariably cause food poisoning in those who ingest it. Since the number of customers stricken with food poisoning at the Panhandler Restaurant rose significantly last month, the Panhandler must have served food that was not stored at the proper temperature.

Which one of the arguments below contains flawed reasoning similar to that in the argument above?

(A) Men over 65 with high blood pressure are at high risk for heart disease. Men over 65 from the Tonare tribe do not have high blood pressure, so they must not be at high risk for heart disease.

(B) Magelli is the only cabinet maker who could have crafted a cabinetsimilar to this one. But the records show that Magelli died 15 years ago. This cabinet must therefore be a copy.

(C) PaintAll paint is sold at Decorator Outlet stores. PaintAll paint is very popular among housepainters because of its brilliant pigment and its stain-resistant finish. Therefore, Decorator Outlets must sell more cans of PaintAll than any other kind of paint.

(D) Relief-O! is a new pain reliever that has been known to cause blurred vision in some people who take it. When Molly took a pain reliever last week to relieve a migraine headache, she experienced a bout of blurred vision. So the pain reliever Molly took last week must have been Relief-O!

(E) If tigermint is allowed to grow out of control in a garden, it can overrun other plants and kill them. Sally recently noticed that a number of plants in her garden looked better than ever. Clearly, her tigermint problem must be under control.

GO ON TO THE NEXT PAGE.

19. The paintings of French painter Trianne Déjère sold best in the period following the production of *La Triumph*, now Déjère's most famous piece. In the 12-month period preceding the unveiling of this piece, Déjère sold 57 percent of the works she produced in this period, a far greater percentage than in previous years. In the 12-month period following a glowing review of *La Triumph* in a popular magazine, however, Déjère sold 85 percent of the paintings she produced. Interestingly, Déjère's revenue from painting sales was roughly the same in both periods, since she sold the same number of paintings in the 12 months before presenting *La Triumph* as she did in the 12 months following the favorable review.

Which one of the following statements can be properly concluded from the passage, if the information above is true?

(A) Due to the positive review, Déjère was able to charge substantially more for the works produced after *La Triumph* than the works produced before it.

(B) Déjère was more concerned with positive reviews than with increasing the prices of her paintings.

(C) The positive review of *La Triumph* brought Déjère's work to the attention of more art collectors than were previously aware of her work.

(D) Déjère painted fewer works in the 12-month period following the review of *La Triumph* than she had in the 12-month period preceding its unveiling.

(E) Déjère paid more attention to marketing her paintings after *La Triumph* received such a positive reception.

20. Most of the time, Doug has no stomach problems whatsoever when he eats dairy products. So it is unreasonable to claim that he has an allergy to dairy foods solely based on the fact that he has had stomachaches after eating dairy products on several occasions.

The argument above is most similar in reasoning to which one of the arguments below?

(A) A significant number of artists who take this fine arts program are later selected for fellowships to pursue their art. It is therefore unreasonable to believe that there is no connection between taking the program and receiving an art fellowship, even though many artists who attend the program never receive such fellowships.

(B) In some cases, dogs will display anxiety in the moments before an earthquake strikes. But it is unreasonable to conclude on this basis that dogs have the ability to sense earthquakes before they strike. In the vast majority of cases in which dogs display anxiety, no earthquake follows.

(C) Many people who try this diet show no long-term weight loss. So it is unreasonable to believe that this diet is effective for weight loss, even though many people have lost weight on the diet.

(D) Most theories must apply to a large number of cases before they are considered valid theories. It is therefore unreasonable to believe that a theory is valid when it has been applied to only a few cases, even if it has been applied successfully to those cases.

(E) Even though many businesses with decentralized operational structures earn a profit, it is unreasonable to believe the success of these businesses is solely attributable to their choice of operational structure. Only businesses with extensive capital resources can adopt a decentralized operational structure.

GO ON TO THE NEXT PAGE.

21. Membership in the Theta Delta Psi fraternity is easily obtained by those who have previously had strong social connections with existing fraternity members before college. However, one must have attended high school with one or more of the members in order to forge such strong social connections. People who lack these social connections because they have not attended high school with one or more current fraternity members will therefore find it difficult to join the fraternity.

This argument displays flawed reasoning because it neglects to consider the possibility that

(A) many of those who went to high school with Theta Delta Psi fraternity members did not themselves become members of the fraternity

(B) it is more important in the long run to socialize with non-fraternity members than to develop strong connections with fraternity members

(C) it is more difficult to forge social connections with fraternity members than with non-fraternity members

(D) one may easily obtain membership in the fraternity through means other than having strong social connections with existing fraternity members

(E) some current members of the fraternity did not go to high school with other members

22. The advantages of the new farm subsidy laws enacted last year do not warrant their continued enforcement. While these laws have enabled farmers to maintain their incomes despite overproduction and have at the same time stabilized the agricultural market, they will inevitably have negative long-term results stemming from the fact that they will encourage the production of surplus goods and lessen the need for competitive developments in agricultural technology.

In the argument above, the statement about the negative results of the farm subsidy laws plays which one of the following roles?

(A) It is used to disprove evidence cited in support of the laws.

(B) It is used to imply that the laws may not have actually stabilized the agricultural market to the degree previously believed.

(C) It is used to offset plausible reasons for supporting the laws.

(D) It is used to prove that in the absence of the laws the development of agricultural technology will remain a high priority.

(E) It is used as evidence for the claim that market stabilization is less important to the agricultural industry than the development of competitive technology.

GO ON TO THE NEXT PAGE.

KAPLAN

23. Participants in Smallville's Annual Easter Egg Hunt search for special plastic Easter eggs containing valuable prizes. The top prize in the contest is an egg containing a three-carat diamond ring. The only way to locate the hidden eggs is by using clues provided to participants by the contest organizers. If every participant receives a complete list of clues for locating the eggs, then no participant will have any more information than any other participant about the whereabouts of the eggs. If no participant has any more information than any other participant, then no participant has a better chance of finding the diamond ring. However, the contest organizers did not provide a complete list of clues for locating the eggs to every participant. Therefore, some participant has a better chance of finding the diamond than all of the other participants.

Which one of the following statements is consistent with the facts of the above argument in such a manner that it points to a flaw in the argument's reasoning?

(A) Even if one participant received a more extensive clue list than all of the other participants, that participant might not necessarily find the diamond ring.
(B) None of the participants received a complete list of clues.
(C) Some participant may share a particular clue with other participants who did not receive that clue.
(D) All of the participants received identical clue lists.
(E) Some participants who did not receive a complete list of clues will nonetheless be able to locate the egg containing the diamond ring.

24. Judges in the Fair Valley Children's Essay Contest disqualified an entry by student Samuel Carter on the grounds that Samuel's entry broke one of the contest rules. The rules specified that entrants should place their names only on the cover page of their essays, and not on any other page, to allow for unbiased judging. Samuel's name was included on each page of his essay. In contesting the judges' decision, Samuel's teacher argued that Samuel's essay should be allowed to qualify because Samuel had recently undergone the traumatic and difficult experience of his parents' divorce.

Samuel's teacher's argument presents a flawed response to the judges' decision because it

(A) presents a conclusion without providing supporting evidence
(B) treats a factor that may cause a certain outcome as if that factor always causes that particular outcome
(C) focuses only on a trivial aspect of the judges' argument
(D) misrepresents evidence presented in the judges' argument
(E) appeals to the judges' emotions instead of addressing their reason for disqualifying Samuel

GO ON TO THE NEXT PAGE.

25. For healthy individuals who wish to improve their overall fitness, cross-training in several sports is more beneficial than training with a single activity. Cross-training develops a wide range of muscle groups, while single-sport training tends to isolate a select few muscles. Single sport activities, especially those that target slow-twitch muscles, tend to increase the tonic muscle fibers in the body. Cross-training works instead to increase the body's phasic muscle fibers, which burn more calories than tonic muscle fibers.

Which one of the following, if true, best supports the argument above?

(A)   In healthy persons, overall fitness increases in proportion to the number of calories burned by the body.

(B)   Overall fitness is most effectively improved through athletic training.

(C)   Tonic muscle fibers are of greater value to overall fitness than are phasic muscle fibers.

(D)   Strenuous physical exertion on a single sport is not recommended for those recovering from a serious illness.

(E)   Some slow-twitch muscles contain many phasic muscle fibers.

STOP
**IF YOU FINISH BEFORE TIME IS CALLED, YOU MAY CHECK YOUR WORK ON THIS SECTION ONLY.
DO NOT WORK ON ANY OTHER SECTION IN THE TEST.**

KAPLAN

SECTION IV
Time—35 minutes
27 questions

Directions: Each selection in this test is followed by several questions. After reading the selection, choose the best response to each question and mark it on your answer sheet. Your replies are to be based on what is stated or implied in the selection.

The Frankenstein monster is the most recognizable character in the horror genre, if not in all of fiction. Beneath the endless Hollywood adaptations and campy TV shows lies one of the great philosophical and prophetic works of
(5) the nineteenth century. While present generations associate the name Frankenstein with the image of Boris Karloff's movie portrayal of the monster, Mary Shelley's story of the mad doctor Victor Frankenstein is best known to serious readers as a cautionary tale of the danger of man's scientific
(10) hubris.

I saw—with shut eyes, but acute mental vision—I saw the pale student of unhallowed arts kneeling beside the thing he had put together. I saw the hideous phantasm of a man stretched out, and
(15) then, on the working of some powerful engine, show signs of life, and stir with an uneasy, half-vital motion. Frightful must it be; for supremely frightful would be the effect of any human endeavor to mock the stupendous mechanism of
(20) the Creator of the world.

From this horrifying dream during the summer of 1816, Shelley conceived the story in which Victor Frankenstein creates a man from body parts gathered from the dead. The clear clash of science and nature ensues. The book is
(25) structured to refute science and technology's attack on nature, and the most eloquent arguments come from the mouth of the monster himself. For seven brilliant and captivating chapters he tells his story and pleads his case for a companion. His point is clear: man should not create that
(30) for which he is not ready to take responsibility. The mad doctor ultimately refuses to create a mate for the monster, and Shelley portrays the horrifying consequences of man's abdication of responsibility and of arrogantly overstepping the bounds of nature.

(35) How a 19th century young woman crafted the timeless tale that has resonated through every successive generation is still a great mystery. For many years the book was published anonymously, as society could not yet cope with the fact that such a ghastly story was the work of a young woman.
(40) Yet if Frankenstein were merely the story of a monster run amok, we likely wouldn't know of it today. Its enduring appeal can best be attributed to the relevance of the themes

infused throughout the narrative: alienation of the outcast; the role of visual appearance in society; science versus
(45) nature; and technology as man's salvation. These themes have only grown in importance since the novel's publication in 1818. The seriousness and complexity of these issues, so magically and prophetically synthesized in Shelley's tale of terror, account for the inability to capture in cinematic form
(50) the deep philosophical richness of the book. It can only be hoped that the visual adaptations will not entirely eclipse in the public's mind the genius of the original masterpiece.

1. The passage suggests that the author would most likely agree with which one of the following statements?

(A) No artistic work can be successfully adapted from one medium into another.

(B) An artistic work that is likely to shock the sensibilities of its original audience should be presented anonymously.

(C) An artistic work that does not gain critical acclaim during its period of origin cannot appeal to successive generations.

(D) The resonance of thematic elements can contribute to the current relevance of an artistic work.

(E) The complexity and seriousness of an artistic work is directly related to its prophetic capabilities.

GO ON TO THE NEXT PAGE.

2. According to the author, "The clear clash of science and nature" (lines 23–24)

    (A) is one of the major elements of *Frankenstein* that is mainly responsible for the current popularity of the cinematic adaptations of that work
    (B) is one of the major elements of *Frankenstein* that is absent from the cinematic adaptations of that work
    (C) is one of the major elements of *Frankenstein* that forced its author to publish that work anonymously
    (D) is one of the major elements of *Frankenstein* that is less relevant today than it was at the time that work was first published
    (E) is one of the major elements of *Frankenstein* that has contributed to the enduring appeal of that work

3. The passage implies that each of the following are relevant aspects of the current era EXCEPT:

    (A) the belief in the power of technology to aid the human condition
    (B) the appreciation of artistic seriousness and complexity
    (C) the opposition between science and nature
    (D) the physical appearance of societal members
    (E) the isolation of individuals from society

4. The author views the cinematic adaptations of Mary Shelley's *Frankenstein* with

    (A) unbounded appreciation for their artistic merit
    (B) biting derision regarding the motivations of their producers
    (C) concern for the effect they may have on the appreciation of their literary precedent
    (D) guarded optimism as to the likelihood that they will spawn future efforts that will approach the philosophical richness of the original book
    (E) unreserved condescension towards the public's demand for such unsophisticated reworkings of literary masterpieces

5. The author's mention of "Hollywood adaptations" in the first paragraph serves which one of the following functions in the passage as a whole?

    (A) It provides a contrast that will resurface later as the basis of the author's central concern.
    (B) It introduces the background of a debate that the author will attempt to settle.
    (C) It reflects the main criticism of a work of art that the author will seek to deflect.
    (D) It offers an example of a form of art that the author will argue is the inevitable successor to literature.
    (E) It forms the basis of an artistic movement that the author will argue can never embody the seriousness and complexity of rich philosophical themes.

6. The passage is primarily concerned with

    (A) praising a work of art and voicing concern over its possible obsolescence
    (B) describing the process by which works of art are degraded when adapted to different forms
    (C) outlining the origin of a masterpiece of world literature
    (D) arguing that the human race will face serious consequences for arrogantly overstepping the bounds of nature
    (E) paying tribute to an art form that has been overshadowed by a more recent art form

GO ON TO THE NEXT PAGE.

KAPLAN

Max Weber's work is traditionally viewed as supporting a strictly objective, or value-neutral, approach to investigating social science issues. In many respects, Weber does uphold the notion of scientific objectivity throughout his writings. If
(5) we look at both his writings and his academic philosophies more carefully, however, it becomes clear that Weber's perspective on objectivity is more complicated than the traditional interpretation would have us believe.

The term "objectivity" is used to denote that which lies
(10) outside the framework of subjective perception or bias. It is traditionally defined as that which "exists as an object or fact, independent of the mind." Indeed, Weber does appear to believe in the concept of strict objectivity concerning questions of reality and truth. Weber postulates that there
(15) exists a true reality that is independent of individuals' viewpoints. This position is illustrated through his use of the concept of "ideal types." Ideal types are theoretical constructions that can be used to help the social scientist analyze, investigate, and uncover reality. If ideal types can
(20) help the scientist uncover true reality, then it stands to reason that "true reality" must itself exist.

In discussing our ability to investigate objective reality, however, Weber moves away from the notion of strict objectivity. While he postulates that an objective reality
(25) exists, he seems to believe that our knowledge of this reality cannot be totally objective. According to Weber, individuals can only know truths insofar as we share communal presuppositions about particular realms of knowledge. Our methods of investigating truths are limited to, and
(30) necessarily conditioned by, the value frameworks through which we approach issues. Thus individuals who investigate issues can generate only knowledge that is based upon assumptions and perspectives shared by the community of scholars within which they work. Knowledge may not be
(35) purely subjective, or influenced by individual bias, but it is only "objective" insofar as the scientific community upholds its presuppositions.

Weber goes even further afield from the traditional interpretation when discussing how individuals should use
(40) scientific knowledge to guide their actions. On this issue, Weber's stance approaches the purely subjective. He tells us clearly that each person should be free to choose how he or she acts upon the reality discovered by science. This position is put forth in his essay "Science as a Vocation," in which
(45) Weber argues that teachers must avoid personally imposing their own stances on their students, and must rather help students to account for the ultimate meaning of their own conduct. In Weber's view, a professor must sit back and allow his students to reach their own conclusions. When it
(50) comes to action, Weber believes that individuals must make their own decisions and that not even a teacher can assert the truth for another person.

7. Which one of the following best expresses the main idea of the passage?

(A) Weber's theory on the topic of objectivity is more complicated than most other theories of objectivity.

(B) Weber's views on objectivity are useful in supporting arguments against the notion of absolute truth.

(C) Weber never clearly lays out his views on objectivity in his works.

(D) Weber's views on the topic of objectivity are not as straightforward as is typically supposed.

(E) Weber's views on objectivity are inconsistent and therefore cannot provide a reliable foundation for a belief in objective reality.

8. Based on the information in the passage, which one of the following statements would Weber most likely support?

(A) Scientific knowledge about reality can never be completely free of subjective perceptions or biases.

(B) The use of ideal types enables the scientist to perceive his or her own subjective biases concerning reality.

(C) Teachers should refrain from imposing their personal views on students unless students are incapable of reaching their own conclusions.

(D) The concept of objective reality is misleading because reality cannot exist apart from the value frameworks through which reality is perceived.

(E) Ideal types are the only reliable method for investigating objective reality.

9. The primary purpose of the passage is to

(A) resolve a debate over an author's theory
(B) summarize the complexities of an author's view
(C) reconcile two differing views of an author's works
(D) argue against an author's perspective
(E) present and test an author's hypothesis

GO ON TO THE NEXT PAGE.

10. According to the passage, which one of the following is true about Weber's views on how individuals should use scientific knowledge to guide their actions?

   (A) Individuals may choose their own courses of action freely unless they are unable to account for the ultimate meaning of their own conduct.

   (B) Individuals should distrust scientific knowledge when making decisions that will determine their personal actions.

   (C) Individuals should be encouraged to determine their own courses of action based upon discovered scientific truth.

   (D) If a teacher determines that a particular course of action would be most beneficial for a given student, he or she should direct the student towards this course of action.

   (E) Teachers should follow their students' leads in determining the most appropriate course of action for themselves.

11. Which one of the following best describes the organization of the passage?

   (A) An explanation is put forth and then rejected in favor of a second explanation.

   (B) An author's viewpoint is first criticized and then reclaimed for its redeeming values.

   (C) An argument is put forth and then negated by the presentation of conflicting evidence.

   (D) A hypothesis is advanced and then strengthened through empirical testing.

   (E) An interpretation of a view is presented and support for this interpretation is provided.

12. Which one of the following is mentioned in the passage as evidence for the assertion that knowledge of reality cannot be totally objective?

   (A) Scientific methods of investigation are always influenced by the subjective biases of the community of scholars within which the scientist operates.

   (B) Scientific methods of investigation are not legitimate unless they can be proven to be strictly objective.

   (C) Scientific investigations use ideal types, which at best help to approximate reality.

   (D) In order for truth to be objective, it must be independent of the mind of the investigating scientist.

   (E) The concept of objective reality is illusory.

13. The author presents the traditional interpretation of Weber's view of objectivity in the first paragraph primarily in order to

   (A) dismiss the relevance of all previous scholarship on Weber that does not accord with the author's line of reasoning

   (B) argue that the concept of objective reality has been historically misunderstood by social scientists

   (C) provide background for a contrasting interpretation of Weber's beliefs central to the argument that follows

   (D) show how critics think that Weber's value-neutral approach to the notion of objectivity is more complicated than is traditionally believed

   (E) illustrate the gist of a notion under attack that the author will subsequently attempt to vindicate

GO ON TO THE NEXT PAGE.

KAPLAN

If one always ought to act so as to produce the best possible circumstances, then morality is extremely demanding, perhaps overly so. No one could plausibly claim that at every moment of their lives they have acted with (5) maximum efficiency to improve the condition of the world. Since it would seem strange to punish those intending to do good by sentencing them to an impossible task, some ethical philosophers have concluded that morality has an "overdemandingness" problem.

(10) From an analytic perspective, the potential extreme demands of morality are not a "problem." A theory of morality is no less valid simply because it asks great sacrifices. In fact, it is difficult to imagine what kind of constraints could be put on our ethical projects. Shouldn't (15) we reflect on our base prejudices, and not allow them to provide boundaries for our moral reasoning? Thus, it is tempting to simply dismiss the "overdemandingness" objection. However, in *Demands of Morality*, Liam Murphy takes this objection seriously.

(20) Murphy does not tell us what set of "firm beliefs" we ought to have. Rather, he speaks to an audience of well-intentioned but unorganized moral agents, and tries to give them principles that represent their considered moral judgments. Murphy starts with an initial sense of right and (25) wrong, but recognizes that it needs to be supplemented by reason where our intuitions are confused or conflicting. Perhaps Murphy is looking for the best interpretation of our convictions, the same way certain legal scholars try to find the best interpretation of the U.S. Constitution.

(30) This approach has disadvantages. Primarily, Murphy's arguments, even if successful, do not provide the kind of motivating force for which moral philosophy has traditionally searched. His work assumes and argues in terms of an inner sense of morality, and his project seeks to deepen (35) that sense. Of course, it is quite possible that the moral viewpoints of humans will not converge, and that some humans have no moral sense at all. Thus, it is very easy for the moral skeptic to point out a lack of justification and ignore the entire work.

(40) On the other hand, Murphy's choice of a starting point avoids many of the problems of moral philosophy. Justifying the content of moral principles and granting a motivating force to those principles is an extraordinary task. It would be unrealistic to expect all discussions of moral philosophy to (45) derive such justifications. Projects that attempt such a derivation have value, but they are hard pressed to produce logical consequences for everyday life. In the end, Murphy's strategy may have more practical effect than its more traditional counterparts, which do not seem any more likely (50) to convince those that would reject Murphy's premises.

14. The passage is primarily concerned with

(A) highlighting the disadvantages in adopting a philosophical approach
(B) illustrating a philosophical debate by comparing two current theories
(C) reconciling the differences between two schools of philosophical thought
(D) reviewing scholarly opinions of an ethical problem and proposing a new solution
(E) evaluating the merits of a model of ethical inquiry

15. The author suggests which one of the following regarding Murphy's philosophy?

(A) The application of Murphy's philosophy to the situations of two different groups would help to solve the problems of one group but not of the other.
(B) The application of Murphy's philosophy to the situations of two different groups could result in the derivation of two radically different moral principles.
(C) The application of Murphy's philosophy to the situations of two different groups would be contingent on the two groups sharing the same fundamental beliefs.
(D) The application of Murphy's philosophy to the situations of two different groups could reconcile any differences between the two groups.
(E) The application of Murphy's philosophy to the situations of two different groups would not provide definitive recommendations for either group.

16. The passage implies that a moral principle derived from applying Murphy's philosophy to a particular group would be applicable to another group if

(A) the first group recommended the principle to the second group
(B) the moral viewpoints of the two groups do not converge
(C) the members of the second group have no firmly held beliefs
(D) the second group shares the same fundamental beliefs as the first group
(E) either group has no moral beliefs at all

GO ON TO THE NEXT PAGE.

17. According to the passage, the existence of individuals who entirely lack a moral sense has which one of the following consequences?

(A) It confirms the notion that moral principles should be derived from the considered judgments of individuals.

(B) It suggests a potential disadvantage of Murphy's philosophical approach.

(C) It supports Murphy's belief that reason is necessary in cases in which intuitions are conflicting or confused.

(D) It proves that more traditional approaches to ethical theorizing will have no more influence over the behavior of individuals than will Murphy's philosophical approach.

(E) It is a necessary consequence of the "overdemandingness" problem.

18. The passage suggests that Murphy would agree that the application of reason is necessary for forming moral principles when

(A) the beliefs of one group supersede the beliefs of another

(B) people's firmly held beliefs are conflicting or confused

(C) the belief system of a group conflicts with an overriding ethical principle

(D) individuals have no moral sense at all

(E) the demands of morality seem too extreme

19. A school board is debating whether or not to institute a dress code for the school's students. According to Murphy, which one of the following actions would constitute the best way to come to an ethical decision regarding the matter?

(A) consulting the fundamental beliefs of the board members

(B) analyzing the results of dress codes instituted at other schools

(C) surveying the students as to whether or not they would prefer a dress code

(D) determining whether or not a dress code has ever been instituted in the school's history

(E) determining the best interpretation of the guarantees found in the U. S. Constitution

20. The primary purpose of the last paragraph of the passage is to

(A) describe the method of determining the best interpretation of an individual's firmly held beliefs

(B) explain the origin of the "overdemandingness" objection

(C) identify advantages associated with Murphy's approach to ethics

(D) reconcile two opposing schools of philosophical thought

(E) characterize Murphy's response to the "overdemandingness" objection

21. The passage suggests that the author would be most likely to agree with which one of the following statements?

(A) Arguing from a set of firmly held beliefs is an important element of traditional moral philosophy.

(B) Philosophical works that attempt to discover a motivating force behind moral principles have no value.

(C) No one who lacks a moral sense can make a significant contribution to an ethical debate.

(D) Those who are not well-intentioned are unlikely to be influenced by traditional approaches to moral philosophy.

(E) The "overdemandingness" objection does not represent a serious problem for traditional moral philosophy.

GO ON TO THE NEXT PAGE.

One of the many remarkable properties of water is the unwillingness of bodies of water of substantially different temperature to mix together. This property is responsible for the formation in freshwater lakes of a phenomenon known
(5) as the thermocline, a phenomenon that can play an important role in a lake's summertime ecology. Consider the annual temperature fluctuations in a typical deep-water impoundment in the southern United States. In late winter, usually sometime in February or March, whatever ice may
(10) have previously formed at the surface of the lake melts, and the water temperature measures a uniform 38–42 degrees. Wave action stirs oxygen into the water at the lake's surface, and the temperature uniformity allows distribution of this dissolved oxygen to all depths. With oxygen plentiful, many
(15) of the reservoir's fish species, both predator and forage, are found throughout the water column.

The windy, sunny days of early spring quickly warm the lake's surface. As the surface temperature increases, that water expands. Because 50-degree water is lighter than 40-
(20) degree water, a layer of warmer water builds at the surface of the lake, resting like a pillow on the mass of colder water below. The pillow of warm surface water slowly increases in thickness, as heat is transferred into the depths by the limited stirring of wave action.

(25) By early summer, a remarkable stratification has occurred. A sharp boundary separates two independent bodies of water within the lake. The boundary is a temperature gradient called the thermocline, and it acts as a barricade to prevent any further mixing of oxygen into the
(30) chilly depths. The depth of the thermocline fluctuates with air temperatures and the prevailing winds. On July 1, the water temperature might be 86 degrees at the surface, 84 degrees at 10 feet, and 82 degrees at 20 feet—but at 24 feet, the temperature has plunged to 65 degrees. When winter
(35) ended, the depths were well-oxygenated and populated with fish. But as the thermocline set up in late spring, the supply of oxygen to the depths was abruptly shut off. In summer, the temperature barrier prevents oxygen from circulating downward from the surface to replace the oxygen consumed
(40) by fish and dying zooplankton. In order to survive, fish are forced upward into the relatively narrow zone between the thermocline and the surface.

The cold nights of autumn reverse the trend, as the surface cools to the point that it is heavier than the water
(45) below the thermocline. This initiates a process known as the turnover: A current of richly oxygenated water plunges to the bottom of the reservoir, forcing stagnant water back to the surface. The lake reaches equilibrium by early winter and remains there until the process repeats itself the following
(50) spring.

22. The passage suggests that which one of the following can be inferred about dissolved oxygen in a lake?

(A) The colder the water, the less dissolved oxygen it can hold.

(B) There is always more dissolved oxygen within six feet of the surface than at 60 feet beneath the surface.

(C) The formation of ice can completely block the supply of dissolved oxygen.

(D) Dissolved oxygen is not necessary for organisms other than fish and zooplankton.

(E) Wave action at the surface is a significant source of dissolved oxygen.

23. Which one of the following most accurately describes the organization of the passage?

(A) A problem is described, its potential effects are summarized, and a possible solution is critiqued.

(B) A property is introduced, a process resulting from the property is described, and an effect is explored.

(C) A process is outlined and then described in greater detail, and its benefits are explained.

(D) A problem is defined, and its implications are considered and generalized.

(E) A chronology is described, various events are fit into the chronology, and predictions are made.

24. The author states in the second paragraph that 50-degree water is lighter than 40-degree water primarily in order to

(A) refute a commonly-held theory regarding the effects of temperature increases in the water near lake surfaces

(B) explain why warmer water tends to sink below layers of colder water in lakes of the southern United States

(C) prove that the number of fish occupying different water levels in freshwater lakes is directly related to the formation of the thermocline

(D) show how the decreased oxygen level in the depths of freshwater lakes during certain seasons could lead to the death of zooplankton

(E) supply background information relevant to an explanation of a step in the lake stratification process

GO ON TO THE NEXT PAGE.

25. The passage suggests that the effects of temperature stratification

   (A) would be relevant to the interests of fisheries managers
   (B) cannot be predicted on an individual lake
   (C) represent the most important factor influencing a lake's ecology
   (D) become more pronounced as a lake gets older
   (E) are most severe in the lakes of the southern United States

26. Which one of the following is not mentioned in the passage as a step in the yearly lake stratification process?

   (A) Fish congregate in the water layer above the thermocline in the summer.
   (B) Water temperatures achieve a general uniformity by late winter.
   (C) The thermocline reaches its maximum depth by early summer.
   (D) Oxygen levels decline in the layer beneath the thermocline.
   (E) The fall turnover replaces stagnant water in the depths with oxygen-rich water.

27. The author is primarily interested in discussing

   (A) the effect of fish and other aquatic organisms on a phenomenon known as the thermocline
   (B) the relationship between a lake's ecology and water purity
   (C) the contribution of the thermocline to overfishing in Southern lakes
   (D) an effect of the seasonal warming and cooling of water in freshwater lakes
   (E) the changes in a lake's water temperature caused by fluctuating oxygen levels

STOP
IF YOU FINISH BEFORE TIME IS CALLED, YOU MAY CHECK YOUR WORK ON THIS SECTION ONLY. DO NOT WORK ON ANY OTHER SECTION IN THE TEST.

PRACTICE TEST TWO ANSWER KEY

Section I Logic Games	Section II Logical Reasoning	Section III Logical Reasoning	Section IV Reading Comprehension
1. E	1. E	1. B	1. D
2. B	2. C	2. B	2. E
3. B	3. A	3. D	3. B
4. B	4. D	4. A	4. C
5. C	5. B	5. E	5. A
6. C	6. A	6. E	6. A
7. C	7. C	7. C	7. D
8. D	8. A	8. D	8. A
9. A	9. E	9. E	9. B
10. B	10. C	10. E	10. C
11. C	11. E	11. D	11. E
12. A	12. D	12. B	12. A
13. C	13. C	13. A	13. C
14. E	14. D	14. A	14. E
15. D	15. C	15. C	15. B
16. A	16. E	16. B	16. D
17. A	17. D	17. B	17. B
18. B	18. E	18. D	18. B
19. C	19. D	19. D	19. A
20. C	20. D	20. B	20. C
21. D	21. E	21. D	21. D
22. C	22. D	22. C	22. E
23. D	23. C	23. D	23. B
24. B	24. C	24. E	24. E
	25. B	25. A	25. A
			26. C
			27. D

PRACTICE TEST TWO EXPLANATIONS

Section I: Logic Games Explanations

GAME 1—Design Selections

The Action

A designer picks two out of five appliance designs and two out of three cabinet designs. So this a Grouping game of selection, with the minor wrinkle that we'll have to keep track of appliances and cabinets, too. The *Key Issues* are:

- Which appliance designs can, must, and cannot be selected?
- Which cabinet designs can, must, and cannot be selected?
- Which designs can, must, and cannot be selected with which other designs?

The Initial Setup

A list of entities with two columns—one for those that are selected and one for those that aren't—will do just fine. We can distinguish appliance from cabinet designs by writing the former in ALL CAPS.

H J K L M	t v w
pick 2	pick 2
IN	OUT

The Rules

1) Be careful when you see "only if." When translated into a standard "if-then," the term that follows "only if" will follow the "then." So Rule 1 means that if H is selected, then both J and w must be selected. Taking the contrapositive, if either J or w is absent, we cannot have H.

2) "M cannot be selected unless J is selected" means that if M is selected, then J is selected. So if J isn't selected, then M isn't selected, either.

3) Rule 3 is a little easier: v implies H, and not H implies not v.

Key Deductions

There really isn't much we can deduce for sure. All the rules are hypothetical, so this isn't a great game to plumb the depths looking for deductions. We can combine Rules 1 and 3 to deduce that if v is selected, the selected designs must be v, H, J, and w. But this isn't such a big deal. Having done some investigation, we can hit the questions, keeping in mind that we're picking two of each design type.

The Final Visualization

H J K L M	t v w
pick 2	pick 2
IN	OUT

H → J and w
no w or no J → no H
M → J
no J → no M
V → H, J, w
no w or no J or no H → no V

The Big Picture

- The first game in a section isn't always the easiest, but as it happens, this was a good place to start. A straightforward grouping game can help you gain some quick points and boost your confidence.

- Never forget about the numbers governing a grouping game. This game seems wide open until you remember that the initial paragraph specifies that the designer selects exactly two of each type.

- Know how to interpret and manipulate formal logic statements! "X cannot be selected unless Y is selected" simply means that X —> Y. The contrapositive of Rule 1 offered another challenge. Remember that the negation of "A and B" is "not A or not B." In other words, if it isn't the case that they are both selected, then it must be the case that one or the other (or both) is not selected.

The Questions

1 **(E)** First up is a straightforward hypothetical. Combining Rules 1 and 3, as we did in the Key Deductions, we see that if v is selected, then the complete group is v, H, J, and w. So choice (E) is correct. The others are impossible.

Remember:

- If you can handle formal logic statements, questions like this one are easy. But if you can't, Logic Games will be impossible. Make sure you have the basics under control before test day.
- Always save your work. The correct answer to a

hypothetical question is a scenario that could be true. So we know now that v, H, J, and w can be selected together. Having an acceptable scenario on hand often helps to eliminate wrong choices later on.

2 **(B)** There's not much to do here except hit the choices one by one. But there's no need to handle this question second. Chances are, if we hit it last, we'll be able to eliminate most of the wrong choices by using our previous work. But, if you attacked this question right away, you might have done something like this:

Choice (A) could be true and thus must be wrong, since we saw H and J together in the last question. (B), however, is impossible. If we have H and M, then we can select no more appliance designs. But Rule 1 says that when we select H we need to select J. So (B) doesn't work and must be correct. For the record, (C), (D), and (E) are out, because if we select t and w as our cabinet designs, we can select any of these choices without violating any rules.

Remember:

- It's always worth seeing if your previous work can help you knock off a few choices.
- You don't have to answer the questions in the order in which they appear on the page! Here, the question wasn't too brutal, anyway. But in another game, this strategy could be a real time-saver.

3 **(B)** Without J, we can't have either H or M (contrapositives of rules 1 and 2). Having eliminated three of the five appliance designs, we must select the remaining two. So K and L must be selected. Since we've rejected H, we must also reject v (contrapositive of rule 3). Now we must select the only two cabinet designs left: t and w. That's the entire set. (B) must be true, while the other choices are impossible.

Remember:

- Always work out the contrapositive of if-then rules, and then use those contrapositives to help you answer the questions quickly.

4 **(B)** If L is selected, then we can select only one more appliance design. But if we select H, we must select J. And if we select M, we must select J. Either way, we'd select three appliance designs, so we can select neither H nor M. Having rejected H, we must also reject v, which in turn means we must select both t and w. So there are two possibilities: LKtw and LJtw. (B) has it right.

Remember:

- As you go through a game's questions, you should become familiar with the way the rules work. By now, you should be used to selecting t and w when you reject H, since that's what happened in the previous question.

5 **(C)** For this one question, part of rule 1 doesn't apply. Selecting H still requires us to select w, but now we can have H without J. Let's look at the choices.

(A) and (B) have the same problem. If we select M, we must select J, and so these two choices force us to select three appliance designs. (C), however, is possible. Selecting v means we must select H and therefore w. Now that we can select H without selecting J, HKvw is an acceptable arrangement, and so (C) is correct.

For the record, (D) is out, since selecting v means we must select H, selecting M means we must select J, and we have three appliance designs again. Selecting v means we must select H, which means we must select w, and now we have three cabinet designs, and so (E) doesn't work, either.

Remember:

- Questions that change a rule should be handle last, if at all. You wouldn't want your work on this question to pollute your thinking on the other questions.

GAME 2—Summer Festival

The Action
We have eight events for nine time slots—morning, afternoon, and evening—for each of three days. So this is a Sequencing game, though it is a complicated one. The *Key Issues* are:

- When is each event scheduled?
- Which events can, must, and cannot be scheduled after which other events?
- Which events can, must, and cannot be scheduled on the same day as which other events?
- Which time period is blank?

The Initial Setup
Writing a list of entities is always a good start. From there, a 3 × 3 grid will help us keep track of all the time periods, just as it does on a real calendar.

B C D F O P R S

	Fri	Sat	Sun
Morn			
Aft			
Eve			

The Rules

1) First up is a standard sequencing rule. S is after P, so we'll have P . . . S somewhere. Be careful not to get rules like this backwards!

2) R is in the morning. We can build this into the sketch directly. For example, we can place an R in the "Morn" row.

3) Rule 3 is a concrete rule. We can now place F definitively.

4) B is in the evening, and before P. So B can't possibly be on Sunday evening, since that would leave no room for P. But wait! Given that F is on Saturday evening, the only available evening is Friday evening. So B is on Friday evening. You could have made this deduction here, and you could have made it at Step 4, but if you didn't see it at all, this was probably a very long game.

5) Rule 5 places D on either Saturday or Sunday. This one, too, can be built in directly, with arrows pointing to both valid days.

6) Careful! This doesn't mean that C is on Friday morning, since the first time period could be blank. But nothing is before C.

Key Deductions

To answer the questions in time, you really needed to make the most of this setup. The big deduction concerns B. As we indicated above, the only evening that allows B to precede P is Friday evening, so *B is on Friday evening*. We can also make a deduction concerning R. R is in the morning (rule 2) but cannot be the first event (rule 6). So *R is on either Saturday morning or Sunday morning*.

Note also that while B and C are on Friday, every remaining event other than O is on Saturday or Sunday. So if the empty slot's not on Friday, then O must join B and C on that day. Not a great breakthrough, but something that's probably worth noticing.

The Final Visualization

	Fri	Sat	Sun
Morn	C?	R?	R?
Aft	C?		
Eve	B	F	

P . . . S   D

The Big Picture

- Even given the deductions to be made here, this was a tough game. There's a lot to keep track of, and the questions were pretty complicated. So this one was worth postponing. Game 4, for example, offered easier points.
- Read critically in Logic Games! Rule 6 is an example of a rule that's easy to misinterpret.
- To find deductions, make the abstract concrete. Rule 4 tells you that B must be in the evening, but it's up to you to ask, "Which evening?"
- Tough games often have big deductions to make them manageable. So don't panic if a game looks like a killer. There will probably be something in there that the savvy test takers can find to help them get through in one piece.
- Sometimes you can find a deduction by recognizing that only one or two entities can occupy a given space. Here, it helps to recognize that the only event that can join C and B on Friday is O.

The Questions

6 **(C)** With the empty slot on Sunday, C, O, and B are the only events that can go on Friday. So C is in the morning (rule 6), B is in the evening (Key Deductions), and O is in the afternoon. (C) is correct. Boom.

Remember:

- Every battle is won or lost before the first shot is fired, and every Logic Game battle is won or lost before the first question is answered. This is another game that reinforces the importance of strong work in Steps 1–4 of the Kaplan Method. But don't stress if this game gave you fits. Instead, commit to focusing on the right issues before you get to the questions.

7 **(C)** This question is surely worth postponing, since we're likely to find possible scenarios in other questions that will help us eliminate wrong choices. In questions 6 and 8, R is on Saturday morning, so (A) and (B), which don't include R, must be wrong. In question 9, D could be on Saturday morning, so (E), which doesn't include D, must be wrong. That leaves (C) and (D), and the only thing that distinguishes them is that (D) includes S. Could S be on Saturday morning? No way, since that would force P before B, in violation of rule 4. So (C) is correct.

Remember:

- Postpone working on "complete and accurate" questions. Chances are, you'll be able to make short work of them if you use your work from the other questions.

8 **(D)** If S is on Sunday morning, then the only morning available for R is Saturday morning.

Now we have to place P before S but after B. The only available slot: Saturday afternoon! That's (D).

Remember:

- Improving your speed in Logic Games is a result of making better decisions, and not a result of crunching through more scenarios per minute. Deduce as much as you can before you hit the choices, and see if you can scan for the correct answer. Once you find it, don't check the other choices. Use that time to tackle other questions.

9 **(A)** If R and S are on the same day, which day could that be? Neither one can go on Friday, but how about Saturday? No way. If R and S join F on Saturday, we'll have no room for P. So R and S are on Sunday, with R in the morning (rule 2). That's all we know for sure going into the choices.

(A) must be true, so it's correct. F is on Saturday evening, and R is on Sunday morning. But just for the record:

(B) C and O could occupy the first two slots, leaving no event between them, so (B) need not be true.

(C), (D), and (E) The following acceptable arrangement proves that C and O need not be on the same day, (C); D need not be on Sunday afternoon, (D); and P need not be on Saturday afternoon, (E).

	Fri	Sat	Sun
Morn	C	P	R
Aft	empty	D	O
Eve	B	F	S

Remember:

- Making the abstract concrete helps you find deductions and helps you answer the questions. If two entities are on the same day, ask "which day could that be?"

10 **(B)** Here's another abstract question stem that you must translate. If S is on the day before D, and we know that S is on either Saturday or Sunday, then S must be on Saturday and D must be on Sunday. On to the second part of the stem. S and D are at the same time of day. What time is that? It can't be evening, since F is on Saturday evening. It can't be morning either, since R is on either Saturday or Sunday morning. So S and D must be on Saturday and Sunday afternoons, respectively. Now the only place for P is Saturday morning, and the only place for R is on Sunday morning. On to the choices:

(A) is impossible. The events on Saturday are P, S, and F.

(C), (E) O could be on Friday (C), but O could be on Sunday, too, which would place it after S, so (E) need not be true, either.

(D) is impossible. P is on Saturday morning.

(B) must be true, since F is on Saturday evening and R is on Sunday morning.

Remember:

- Keep making deductions as long as they are coming to you. But when you don't see what else you can deduce, check the choices.

11 **(C)** Here's another toughie. Two events are between C and S. Well, P must be before S (rule 1) and so if S were on Sunday, then at least three events would come between C and S—B, P, and F. So P and S must both be on Saturday, P in the morning and S in the afternoon. Now what happens? Well, the empty time slot must be on Friday, since C must be the first event and we can't have anything breaking up our C-B-P-S combination, lest we violate the mandate in the stem. P on Saturday morning places R on Sunday morning, leaving O and D to float between the afternoon and evening slots on Sunday. Here's what we have so far:

	Fri	Sat	Sun
Morn	C/empty	P	R
Aft	C/empty	S	O/D
Eve	B	F	O/D

So what *don't* we know? O and D split the last two slots, but we can't tell their order. We also can't place C definitively. C could be either first or second, depending on where the empty slot goes. So five events can be precisely determined, choice (C).

Remember:

- Translate question stems just as aggressively as you translate rules. Sometimes the hard part in answering a question is determining exactly what it's asking.

12 **(A)** Yick. This may be a good one to come back to if time permits. For the sake of continuity, however, let's work through it here. The correct answer will be the choice that couldn't be the list of events on Sunday, but there's no obvious rule violation. So the correct answer will force a violation on another day.

(A) As it happens, the violator is the first choice. Placing the empty slot, S, and O on Sunday forces R, P, and D onto Saturday, but F is already on Saturday, so there isn't room for all of them. (A) is the winner.

(B) The only available morning slot for R is on Saturday, the only available post-Friday slot for D is Saturday afternoon, and C and O occupy the first two slots. That's OK, so (B) is wrong.

(C) would force P and S into the first two slots on Saturday, with C and O in the first two slots on Friday. That's OK.

(D) leaves us more acceptable options. P and O can split the first two slots on Saturday, and C goes on Friday with the empty slot, in either order.

(E) Again, the only available morning slot for R is on Saturday, the only available post-Friday slot for P is Saturday afternoon, and C and the empty time period occupy the first two slots. That's OK, so (E) is wrong.

Remember:

- Don't forget that every question is worth the same! Don't worry about taking a quick guess on a killer question (or an easier question that's just too time-consuming). Here, the test maker took some mercy on us by making the correct answer (A), but that needn't be the case next time.

GAME 3—Sled Dogs

The Action
Five sled dogs are hitched together as the diagram indicates. We have to keep track of the positions of the sled dogs, so this game isn't too different from a Sequence game; it's just that the entities are arranged in an odd formation instead of in a line. If we had to assign a game type here, we'd call this a spatial Sequence game, but that's not important. What is important is that you identify the *Key Issues*:

- Which sled dogs can, must, and cannot occupy which positions?
- Which sled dogs can, must, and cannot be adjacent to which other sled dogs?

The Initial Setup
When the testmaker gives you a picture, use it! The picture provided is a good framework for organizing your work. Add a list of entities, and you're set.

G H J K L

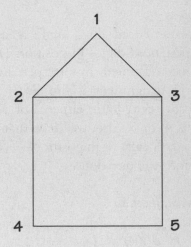

The Rules
1) This rule just defines "adjacency." This is pretty intuitive: sled dogs that are connected to the same harness are adjacent.

2) Rule 2 brings in a new distinction: experienced

and inexperienced. So now the game has become a bit more complicated. We can keep track of the experienced/inexperienced distinction by making a note under our list of entities. "2 XP, 3 non-XP" is one way to do this.

3) Here's one we can build in directly. We can fill in an "XP" to remind us that the dog in position 1 is experienced.

4) and 5) These rules can also be built in directly, by adding an "XP" to J and a "non-XP" to G.

6) Rule 6 is straightforward enough. The two experienced dogs cannot be adjacent. "No XP adjacent" is one way to represent this.

7) Rule 7 is similar to rule 6: K and L aren't adjacent. "No KL adjacent" will do.

Key Deductions

Since the experienced dogs aren't adjacent, and since an experienced dog is in position 1, positions 2 and 3 are occupied by inexperienced dogs. Therefore, J's assignment is limited. J is experienced, and so J can't be in either 2 or 3, and so J must be in 1, 4, or 5. Also, we know that since G is inexperienced, G can't be in position 1. That's plenty heading into the questions.

The Final Visualization

G(non-XP) H J(XP) K L

2 XP, 3 non-XP
No XP adjacent
No KL adjacent

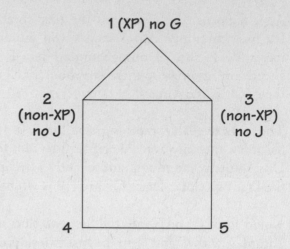

The Big Picture

- This wasn't an easy game, but it was easier than the previous game. This game was probably best handled third, after games 1 and 4.
- Games that require you to arrange characters in an odd formation aren't common on the LSAT, but they have appeared from time to time. Expect that your sequencing skills will help you with such games. You're still putting things in order, even though the order may not be a straight line.
- When the entities themselves are broken up into different categories, make sure you recognize the distinction. You can bet that most of these questions will require you to recognize who must be experienced.
- To find deductions you must translate the rules to find out what they mean in the context of the game. If the experienced dogs aren't adjacent, and we know that an experienced dog is in 1, what must be true? This is the kind of active thinking that leads to points.

The Questions

13 **(C)** This question is a quick battle if you've done good work up front. We can't have an inexperienced dog in position 1, so (A) and (B) are wrong. Positions 2 and 3 must be occupied by inexperienced dogs, so (D), which omits the third position, and (E), which omits the second position, must be wrong. (C) is the only choice that remains, and yes, positions 2, 3, and 4 could all have inexperienced dogs.

Remember:

- Don't do more work than necessary! If you can eliminate four choices, pick the next one without further delay.

14 (E) With J in 5, we have the experienced/inexperienced breakdown set. J is experienced, and position 1 has an experienced dog, and so positions 2, 3, and 4 must all have inexperienced dogs. The rest of the setup is pretty wide open, but (E) is inferable. Position 4 has an inexperienced dog, and so (E) is correct.

(A), (B), and (C) are all eliminated by this scenario:

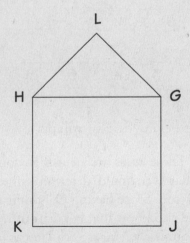

(D) is impossible. As we deduced above, position 3 is always occupied by an inexperienced dog.

Remember:

- As long as the deductions are coming to you, keep making them. But as soon as you're stuck, consult the choices. You may have deduced the correct answer.

15 (D) With L and H in 4th and 5th, J is forced into position 1, since otherwise J would be adjacent to an experienced dog in 1. That leaves G and K to be placed, but we know that K and L can't be adjacent, and so K must be in 3 and G must be in 2.

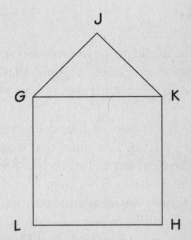

So all the choices must be true except (D). G and H aren't adjacent.

Remember:

- To make deductions, think about which rules and entities might be relevant. With slots 4 and 5 taken, you should think about where you can place J. With G and K yet to be placed, you should remember rule 7, which states that K and L are not adjacent. Knowing where to look is often half the battle.

16 (A) If K is in 5, what would guarantee that an experienced dog is in 4? From here, trying the choices is just as fast as anything else, and luckily, we don't have far to search. We have to separate K and L, so if G were in 2, then L would have to go in 1. That means J must go in 4, and so (A), if true, would guarantee that an experienced dog (i.e., Jinook) would be in 4.

(B), (C), (D), and (E) If J were first, L were second, and either G or H were third, then the other of the G/H pair must be fourth. Either way, K could be an experienced dog, and since we have only 2 experienced dogs (and one is first), all these choices fail to guarantee that the dog in position 4 is experienced.

Remember:

• Don't be afraid to postpone work on a tough question. Sometimes, a game that isn't that tough contains a killer question or two.

17 (A) If J is next to K and L, where could J be? J can't be first, since that would place K and L in 2 and 3, next to each other. So J must be in either 4 or 5. If J is in 4, then K and L occupy the only positions adjacent to J: positions 2 and 5. That leaves G and H to place. G can't be in 1 (rules 3 and 5), so G would go in 3, and H would go in 1. If J is in 5, we get much the same story: K and L split positions 3 and 4, G still can't go in 1 and so must go in 2, and H again goes in 1. So either way, Hira is adjacent to G, and choice (A) is correct.

(B) is impossible, since H is in 1 and J is in either 4 or 5.

(C) and (D) both could be true, but need not be true—both K and L could be in either 4 or 5.

(E) also need not be true, since J and L could occupy positions 4 and 5.

Remember:

• Sometimes, you can't make any solid deductions, but you can break down a question into two distinct scenarios. That's okay Work out those scenarios and you'll know what must, could, and cannot be true.

GAME 4—Animal Examinations

The Action
We have seven animals being examined, one at a time. Sounds like another basic sequence game. The familiar *Key Issues* are:

• What is the order of the examinations?
• Which animals could, must, and cannot be examined before and after which other animals?

The Initial Setup
Seven slots representing the seven exams, plus a list of entities, will do just fine:

P Q R S T V W

___ ___ ___ ___ ___ ___ ___
 1   2   3   4   5   6   7

The Rules
1) P is right before T. "PT" will do.

2) and 3) These rules are in if-then form, which means that we should determine their contrapositives, too. Since having Q 5th means that V is 6th, we also know that if V isn't 6th, Q cannot be 5th. Similarly, since S 2nd means that P is 3rd, we also know that if P isn't 3rd, then S isn't 2nd.

4) This is easy enough to build in directly, with arrows pointing to both the 4th and 6th positions.

5) Rule 5 can also be built in directly. "No V" in the 1st and 5th positions will do.

Key Deductions

This one stays pretty wide open. There aren't major blocs of entities, the rules aren't too concrete, and lots of stuff is possible. A little time spent here wasn't wasted, but in general, simple sequencing games tend not to have Big Deductions that fill in large chunks of the picture.

The Final Visualization

P Q R S T V W

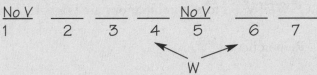

PT

If Q 5th then V 6th

If V not 6th then Q not 5th

If S 2nd then P 3rd

If P not 3rd then S not 2nd

The Big Picture

- Never rush through the rules. Take your time to avoid sloppy mistakes that can make the entire game impossible.
- Whenever you see an if-then rule, determine its contrapositive. Make sure you know what conditions would bring a rule into play. Here, for example, rule 2 comes into play whenever Q is 5th, but rule 2 also comes into play whenever V cannot be 6th.
- Don't worry if you can't find a deduction on a game that's relatively simple. Simple games are less likely to contain Big Deductions. Check the most likely candidates, but then move on.

The Questions

18 **(B)** The question set begins with the usual acceptability question, so we can use the familiar Kaplan strategy of using the rules to eliminate choices. Rule 1 is violated by no choice, but rule 2 is violated by (E) which has Q fifth without V sixth. Rule 3 kills (C), which has S second without P third. Rule 4 axes (D), which has W fifth. Finally, rule 5 eliminates (A), which has V fifth. Choice (B) remains and is correct.

Remember:

- Acceptability questions give you a shot at an easy point and give you the opportunity to practice applying the rules. That practice with the game's mechanics often helps on harder questions.

19 **(C)** If S is second, then P is third (Rule 3), and thus T must be fourth (rule 1). Since W isn't fourth, W must be sixth (rule 4). Now who could be fifth? V is never fifth (rule 5), and since V cannot be sixth, Q cannot be fifth either. So R is the only animal that can be fifth, and therefore (C) is correct.

Remember:

- When the stem provides concrete information in an "if clause," build the new information into a little picture and see where the new information takes you. If you don't see where to go, use the choices to help you.

20 **(C)** If Q is fifth then V is sixth (rule 2). Since W isn't sixth, W must be fourth (rule 4). Only slots 1, 2, 3, and 7 are open, and so the PT pair will have to go either first and second or second and third. Joining them in the first three slots is R (as the stem indicates) and so the only entity that could be seventh is S. So (C) must be true.

(A), (B) and (D) could be true, but R could be first, placing P second and T third.

(E) is impossible. W is fourth here.

Remember:

- When you're able to definitely place a number of entities, ask yourself "who's left?"

21 **(D)** If P is third, T is fourth (rule 1), and so W is sixth. Since V isn't sixth, Q isn't fifth, and we can eliminate (A), (C), and (E). The only difference between (B) and (D) is that (D) includes R. Could R be fifth? Sure. SVPTRWQ is one such acceptable arrangement. So R belongs on our list, and (D) is correct.

Remember:

- Don't do more work than necessary! Use the choices to help you answer "complete and accurate" questions more efficiently. Look to eliminate several choices at once, and never check entities that appear in all the remaining choices.

22 **(C)** If W is right after Q, where could they be? W cannot be sixth, since that would place Q fifth which in turn would force V to be sixth. So W must be fourth, and Q must be third. Now where can we place the VS pair mandated by the stem? Placing them first and second would violate rule 3, and V can never be fifth (rule 5), so V and S must be sixth and seventh, respectively. Now the only place for the PT pair is first and second. So R, the only animal left, must be fifth, the only space left. (C) is correct.

Remember:

- When you're working with a bloc of entities, see where it could go. You may be surprised to see that it can go in only one place.

23 **(D)** If P, T, and V all are examined after W, then W must be fourth and not sixth. V can never be fifth (rule 5), and if we placed V sixth we'd have to break up the PT pair. So V is seventh and P and T are fifth and sixth, respectively. Now we have to work out the possibilities for the first three slots. The only restriction that applies comes via rule 3. We know that S cannot be second because we know P cannot be third. If S is first, then the arrangement is either SQRWPTV or SRQWPTV. If S is third, the arrangement is either QRSWPTV or RQSWPTV. So four combinations are possible.

Remember:

- Straightforward sequencing games are usually quick and easy points, but not this time. The questions here were fairly complicated, so don't worry if you found them time-consuming. Just remember, an easy game can be made harder by asking tough questions. But sometimes the test makers make a hard game easier by including easier questions.

24 **(B)** If R is fourth, then W is sixth, but not much follows immediately from there. On to the choices:

(A) P can't be third, since that would force T into the fourth position, and the stem places R fourth. So (A) is impossible.

(B), however, could be true. If Q is first, we could place P and T second and third, respectively. S could be fifth, and V seventh, and presto! QPTRSWV is an acceptable arrangement. So (B) could be true and is therefore correct.

(C) If S is second we have no place for our PT pair.

(D) is nastier. If S is seventh, then who could be fifth? Not P or T, since they have to be together. Not Q, since V isn't sixth. Not V (rule 5). So if S is seventh, then no one could be fifth, and so (D) is impossible. Technically, we could have deduced that S must be fifth before we consulted the choices, but that deduction was pretty subtle, so there's nothing wrong with discovering it here.

(E) is impossible since P immediately precedes T, and we already know that W is sixth.

Remember:

- If you don't see the next deduction, hit the choices. You may still be able to find the correct answer quickly.

Section II: Logical Reasoning Explanations

1 **(E)** The problem: Channeling recycled waste-water into the harbor seems to have brought dangerous bacteria into this town's drinking water. The solution: Researchers recommend adding the enzyme tripticase to the water to eliminate those pestilent bacteria, which in turn will "solve the health problem." Since you're looking to weaken this argument, ask yourself if there could be a problem with this solution. It removes the bacteria, which will only solve the health problem if tripticase itself doesn't introduce any other problems. If, however, tripticase merely replaces one problem with another, as (E) has it, then the author's conclusion about its effectiveness as a solution is weakened.

(A) Okay, so tripticase is supereffective since it solves the giardia problem as well as others. This certainly doesn't weaken the author's argument that tripticase is an effective solution (even though other illnesses are technically outside the scope).

(B) The frequency and severity of giardia isn't the issue here. The author addresses the effectiveness of a solution for a particular health problem. The relative size of that problem has no impact on the effectiveness of the solution.

(C) Other illnesses are irrelevant to this consideration, as was mentioned above in (A).

(D) The author discusses water-induced cases of giardia, so cases that arise from other causes aren't within the argument's scope.

Remember:

- When you're asked to weaken or strengthen an argument, remember to evaluate the impact that each answer choice has on that argument without questioning the information you're given. Assume that the stimulus is true, and reconsider it in light of each answer choice. Does the new information make the conclusion more or less plausible? Don't question the information; just focus on its impact on the argument.

2 **(C)** This is a Point at Issue question that basically asks, "What are they fighting about?" Look to see where they disagree. The marketing analyst only disputes the manufacturer's conclusion; each person presents completely different evidence. They can only disagree about something that they both discuss, and the only thing that meets that criterion in this dialogue is the conclusion. Therefore they disagree about whether the company should switch to a less expensive brand of rubber, or (C).

(A) The manufacturer certainly assumes that other brands cost less, but the analyst in no way disputes this, or even directly mentions it. Both seem to agree that other brands would cost less.

(B) is not addressed by either person. The analyst mentions sales, but not sales *quotas*, and the manufacturer doesn't even get close to discussing sales.

(D) like (B), brings up an issue that neither person directly addresses. Even if you thought the analyst's comments might have some relevance to customer preferences, the analyst never addresses them directly and the manufacturer never gets near this subject.

(E) is addressed by the analyst, but not by the manufacturer, whose argument deals only with cost.

Remember:

- Notice that all of the wrong answer choices mention issues that would be more relevant to the analyst's comments than the manufacturer's. Don't neglect the first argument; the right answer will have to be something discussed, and discussed with different opinions, by both people.

3 **(A)** Before hunting for an answer choice that will strengthen this argument, look for assumptions in it. The salesman argues that the system will provide safety because it will keep predators out, but this argument assumes that predators are the only real threats to the flock's safety. Perhaps the system provides its own dangers; the electronic gate that would apparently toast any wayward predator certainly sounds capable of hurting the flock surrounded by it. By affirming the argument's assumption that the system itself cannot harm the animals, choice (A) strengthens the argument.

(B) So the system is being used for cattle. We don't know how effective it is, and in any case, this argument is about sheep, not cattle.

(C) picks up on and intensifies the potential drawback discussed in the last sentence. That sentence is tangential to the argument, which would nevertheless certainly not be strengthened by such information about how often this system errs.

(D) The argument concerns the efficacy of the contraption "when [the] flock is in danger of attack." The fact that some sheep predators are almost extinct does nothing to help the argument here; in fact, it makes the system seem, if anything, *less* necessary.

(E) is like (D) in that it would, if anything, weaken the argument. The system protects against predators, so if those predators don't provide a substantial threat, then it would be hard to sell this system as a splendid sheep protector. Again, the salesman might protest that he simply touts the system *in the event* of attacks, which is fair enough—but that would only make (D) and (E) irrelevant, and certainly not strengtheners.

Remember:

- Always try to identify the argument's assumption when dealing with Strengthen or Weaken questions. Making that assumption explicit is a surefire and common way to strengthen an argument.

4 **(D)** And now we get to that tangential sentence in the stimulus. What role does the cliché play? Well, the salesman mentions a potential drawback in the system and follows that with an important "but" which signals the shift in the second half of this sentence. While the system may not be perfect, the salesman clearly suggests through the well-known adage that the problem is not that serious. "Better safe than sorry" therefore functions in the argument to downplay an imperfection in the system.

(A) takes the shift too far. The salesman never suggests that the false alarms are actually a *good* part of the system; he merely suggests that they're not all that terrible.

(B) Again, the false alarms aren't one of the salesman's selling points. (What kind of sales pitch would *that* be? "And best of all, the darn thing often misfires!") He presents the false alarms as a flaw, but as a relatively unimportant one.

(C) does more to downplay the problem than the salesman does. The salesman only says that they happen, not that they happen rarely, and the statement in question can't play a role in the argument that *nothing* plays in the argument.

(E) entirely ignores the fact that "better safe than sorry" is said in relation to the false alarms flaw. It is uttered in reaction, not as *further* evidence for the need of such protection.

Remember:

- When you're dealing with a stimulus that has two questions, don't just rely on your memory when you get to the second question. A different question type means that you need to look for different things in the stimulus, so don't hesitate to do the necessary rereading before attacking the choices.

5 **(B)** Next up is an Assumption question. The administrator concludes that Sandra would not be an effective teacher. Why not? She has two flaws: she's too lenient to fail students and too critical to reward any with high marks. But are failing students and rewarding high grades the only criteria for teacher effectiveness? Why can't she be effective even if she does neither of these things? The author doesn't say, and that omission is the basis of her assumption. In making her argument, the administrator assumes that to be effective, a teacher must be able to do one of these two things. This assumption is laid out for us in choice (B).

(A) is a distortion of the administrator's assumption. She doesn't assume that effective teachers have only two options: failing students or rewarding them with high marks. Instead, she assumes they must be capable of doing at least one thing or the other in order to be effective.

(C) gets the cause and effect of the argument mixed up by telling us what teachers must do in order to fail or reward students. We're interested in what teachers must do in order to be effective, so nothing regarding the reverse need be assumed here.

(D) and (E) fail to address the key issue at hand, which again concerns what it takes to be an effective teacher. Neither need be assumed here.

Remember:

- Straightforward Assumption questions lend themselves well to prephrasing. To determine the assumption, first isolate the conclusion and the evidence. Then ask, "What unstated yet necessary premise does the author rely on to draw her conclusion? What premise must she accept in order for the conclusion to follow logically from the evidence?" The assumption must bridge the gap between the conclusion and the evidence given.

6 **(A)** Here we must choose an assumption upon which the argument in the stimulus depends. The conclusion is stated directly in the last sentence: In the coming years, Jenny will be less financially burdened by costs related to her job. The people most financially burdened by the costs associated with working are those making between $30,000 and $40,000 per year. Those who make less than $30,000 have lower job-related costs, so they generally are not as burdened—and folks who make more than $40,000 tend to make enough to compensate for their increased job costs, so they don't feel the burden as much either.

The author assumes that Jenny will move out of the $30,000–$40,000 income category in the coming years. Either she will start to make less than $30,000, or she will make more than $40,000 (for instance, if she receives a raise). If she stays in the same job, as the stimulus indicates, she's not likely to receive a pay cut, so the pay raise option is most feasible. Scanning the choices, we see that choice (A) captures this last possibility nicely. If Jenny is promoted, her salary will probably go up, and the burden of her job-related costs will decrease.

(B) Tempting, because it provides one avenue through which Jenny's job-related costs could be reduced. Yet it doesn't address the issue of salary that is central to the evidence. The evidence tells us that job costs are less burdensome if an individual's salary surpasses $40,000. If Jenny's salary doesn't increase, she may still feel the burden of her job-related costs even if they're lessened.

(C) provides irrelevant information. We might try the Denial Test to eliminate this one: Even if $40,000 was an entry-level salary for Jenny's job, the argument could still work as is.

(D) may also be eliminated with the Denial Test. If Jenny's co-workers *did* find their job costs as burdensome as she finds hers, how would this affect the argument? Not at all—therefore this choice cannot be a central assumption.

(E) Irrelevant. We are not interested in what Jenny made at her previous job; we are merely inter-

ested in her current salary, and how it and the financial burdens related to it are likely to change in the future.

Remember:

- Whenever possible, prephrase the answers to Assumption questions and scan quickly for your answer. If you can gain quick points through prephrasing here, you'll have more time to spend gaining points on more difficult questions later in the section.

7 **(C)** This stimulus doesn't offer an argument with a conclusion, but rather discusses two different qualities of physical beauty. Physical beauty can increase one's physical appeal, but the attention that physical beauty generates can also make someone arrogant and decrease that appeal. Since this is an Inference question and the stimulus is missing a conclusion, odds are pretty good that the right answer will be a conclusion supported by the stimulus as it stands. If you were to prephrase a conclusion, it would probably look something like, "Therefore, physical beauty can both increase and decrease one's personal appeal." (C) is entirely consistent with the information that the stimulus provides, and could easily serve as the conclusion towards which this author is moving.

(A) directly contradicts the stimulus, which creates two links between one's beauty and one's physical appeal.

(B) distorts the stimulus, which doesn't say whether beauty's impact on personal appeal is more positive than negative, or vice versa. The author merely mentions one positive effect and one negative; he doesn't rank them.

(D) Again, the author doesn't say whether the positive trait and the negative trait are of equal or of varying weights. We can't infer a statement that the author doesn't directly support.

(E) might be a nice cliché, but it's certainly not consistent with the stimulus. The stimulus discusses beauty as something that exists and has two contradictory impacts on appeal; the author doesn't discuss what determines beauty.

Remember:

• When looking for a choice that is "best illustrated" by the statements in a stimulus, the right answer must above all be consistent with the stimulus, and must also in some fundamental way reflect the essence of it. If a choice is inconsistent with the passage, kill it. If it's consistent but tangential, kill it. Something that is "best illustrated" by the stimulus must be better related to it than that.

8 **(A)** The educational consultant offers three reasons why school districts don't provide adequate educations: Teachers are inadequately trained, tight budgets limit opportunities for after-school academic programs, and parents aren't participating enough in the classroom. Those are the author's criteria for adequate education. The Prentice school district has experienced greater parental participation and is therefore "looking up" as a district. It is coming closer to meeting the third criterion, and is therefore coming closer to providing an adequate education, according to the terms of the argument. You're looking to identify a valid inference, and it's not always easy to prephrase inferences in cases like this, so you're probably best off evaluating the choices one by one without spending much time trying to prephrase an answer of your own. In evaluating each choice, the key is to not read too much or too little into the Prentice school district's accomplishment.

(A) Sound reasonable? Yup. This school district, because of its increased parental participation, displays at least one component of adequate education to a greater degree than it had. This inference is perfectly in line with the claims made about Prentice and about adequate education—and it doesn't overstep the bounds of the argument as do some of the other choices.

(B) This is far more than we can infer. All we know is that Prentice is making some improvements in one of the three criteria that define an adequate education. With such limited information, we can't infer that the district's education is adequate.

(C), (D), (E) We have no basis for comparing the Prentice school district to other districts, and all three remaining choices bite the dust on this account.

Remember:

• Often the key to answering Inference questions correctly is understanding the exact extent of the author's claims. Here, Prentice is improving in one particular category, but that allows us to infer nothing about its performance in terms of the other categories or about its educational system as a whole. Don't infer anything beyond what the argument specifically supports.

• Beware of common wrong answer choices, like (C) here, that offer to rank what the author never did.

9 **(E)** Again we're presented with two opposing views presented in a single argument. A survey showed that, as a group, action films were rated higher than romance films. Viewpoint number one comes from the survey organizers, who concluded from this that subject matter of popular movies must determine their appeal. Seems reasonable, but the author, making use of the contrast keyword "yet," states that this conclusion is probably wrong and offers an alternative explanation. She notes that the producers of the action films were more experienced in successful film production. Notice that the author doesn't disagree that actions films receive better ratings, but rather supports a different explanation for that superiority; the effect is the same in both viewpoints, but the causes differ. We're looking for an inference based on this argument, so once you have a firm grasp of the content, it's time to move to the answer choices.

(A) This answer choice confuses percentages and numbers. The survey is based on the percentage of films in each category to receive the highest rating, not on the actual number of films to receive the top rating. A lower percentage does not necessarily mean a lower number.

(B) *Au contraire:* The author *does* suggest a relationship between previous directorial successes and the popular appeal of the survey films.

(C) The argument is about independent feature films. Based on that argument, we cannot infer anything about what a survey of big-budget mainstream films would show.

(D) distorts the information in the stimulus. Sure, of the filmmakers whose work is represented in this particular survey, some have a hit film to their credit, while some have never even made a movie before. Does that allow us to conclude who's "more likely" to produce a hit? For all we

know, the folks with previous hits were new filmmakers themselves when they produced those hits.

(E)'s all that's left. The author suggests that having a previous hit film to the director's credit is more important than subject matter in determining ratings, so it logically follows that subject matter may not be a significant factor in the popular ratings of films made by directors with an equal number of previous hits. By positing another factor besides subject matter that accounts for the survey results, the author's argument certainly does allow for the possibility that subject matter *may* have no effect on the ratings.

Remember:

- Learn to recognize the kinds of wrong choices that appear again and again on the LSAT. Looking back over (A) through (E) here, you should notice some pretty common wrong answer types: confusing numbers and percentages (A); an "*au contraire*" choice that suggests the opposite of what's in the passage (B); a choice that strays outside the scope (C); and a classic distortion (D).

10 **(C)** The second question based on this stimulus asks us to locate the one answer choice that doesn't strengthen the author's argument. We therefore want to eliminate the four choices that strengthen the connection between the popular appeal of a director's film and that director's having a past hit film, as well as those that strengthen the connection between lack of a hit film and lesser popular appeal.

(A) If previous hits indicate talent, then the author's theory of the link between previous hit films and popular appeal of the survey films seems more plausible, and we're more likely to believe that the organizers *are* wrong, as the author maintains, about the effects of subject matter.

(B), (D), and (E) all strengthen the argument by tying past experience of success to present cinematic successes. (B) links previous experience to ratings directly. (D) takes it from another angle and explains that the films of first-timers do not often achieve the same popular appeal as that attained by previous hit-makers. (E) links prior experience of success to the ability to obtain the best actors, offering another benefit that accrues to experienced directors and makes them more likely to produce hit films.

(C) *Why* many first-time directors don't make action films has no impact on this argument. The fact remains that of the films in this particular survey, the action films were made by more experienced directors while the romances were made by novices, and the author uses this fact to counter a previous conclusion. (C) gives us one possible explanation for this fact, but has no effect on how this fact is *used* by the author, which, after all, constitutes the crux of her argument. This is the one choice that does not strengthen (or, for that matter, even affect) the author's argument.

Remember:

• Many question stems, like the one here, are not written in the clearest possible manner. Before proceeding to the answer choices, pause for a moment to consider what you're being asked

and what type of answer choice you're looking for, even when you can't specifically pre-phrase an answer. Here we want a choice that doesn't support the author's causal link between previous directorial success and the popular appeal of that director's other films.

11 **(E)** The question stem directs us to find a weakness in the manager's argument, and it lies in the survey. What if others who are skeptical about the candidate simply didn't respond to the survey? The fact that only 25 responded negatively does not necessarily mean that the other 975 are okay with the reports and have confidence in the candidate's ability to lead, although this is the interpretation the manager implies. (E) picks up on this problem in the manager's argument: If the skeptics were disinclined to respond to the survey, then the conclusion that the candidate need not worry may be unfounded, and the candidate's concern may be legit.

(A) is beyond the argument's temporal scope. The candidate and his manager only discuss the impact of the recent media coverage; the possible effects of future coverage don't play a relevant role in that discussion.

(B) identifies a possible use to which the candidate's opponent might put the media coverage, but that too is outside the scope. Maybe the opponent's survey won't show any residual concerns based on the survey, or maybe it will. By itself, (B) doesn't point out a weakness in the argument.

(C) There's no indication that the survey was intended to hide its main focus; presumably, those surveyed knew that the survey was intended to measure the fallout from the media coverage. So

(C) need not be something that the campaign manager's argument fails to acknowledge.

(D) deals with television interviews, which show up in the candidate's argument but not in his campaign manager's. Therefore, (D) doesn't identify a problem with the manager's argument.

Remember:

- Be suspicious of surveys in Logical Reasoning stimuli. Whenever you see one, ask yourself if there are any problems with it. Particularly, ask yourself whether the supposed results accurately represent the views of the whole group surveyed. Here, the campaign manager fails to specify how the majority of the participants in the survey responded, if they responded at all.

12 **(D)** We're asked to identify the role of the recommendation that shows up in the first sentence, and we can see that it constitutes the argument's conclusion based on the fact that the argument's evidence supports it. All of the information after sentence 1 answers the question "Why do you think Sarah's teacher should spend more time with her?" (If you were tempted to identify the last part of the last sentence as the conclusion, notice that it only pertains to that last sentence.) This confirms that the proposal in question is the conclusion, as choice (D) clearly states.

(A) is technically impossible since the recommendation is actually stated in the argument, and an assumption is never stated.

(B) would tempt those who saw the first sentence as setting the stage for the true conclusion in the last sentence. The fact that Sarah's teacher is not

displaying good judgment is still subordinate to the overall proposal that she needs to spend more quality time with her.

(C) Remember that a hypothesis is not a synonym for a conclusion on the LSAT. A hypothesis is a working theory that has yet to be adequately proven, which is not how the author presents her recommendation. Further, (C) totally misrepresents the argument, since the evidence in the argument *does* support the principal's proposal, whether or not we erroneously accept that proposal as a hypothesis.

(E) gets the pieces of the argument mixed up, putting "evidence" where "conclusion" should accurately be, and vice versa.

Remember:

- Identify conclusion and evidence only in the context of the argument as a whole. The first sentence above appears to be the conclusion at first glance, but you can only be sure of that by seeing how that sentence plays in to the rest of the argument. Withhold final judgment until all the information is in.

13 **(C)** Did you see the formal logic in this question? The author begins with the classic if-then formula: *if* there's too much pressure on the bottom shelf, *then* the bookcase will collapse. Since the stem directs you to find a weakness, you can anticipate that the logic will exhibit an error in the rest of the stimulus. A valid conclusion would be the contrapositive of this statement: If the bookshelf has not collapsed, then there is not too much pressure on the bottom shelf. This, however, is not what we get. Instead, the author concludes by flipping the original terms: If the bookcase has collapsed, then there must have been too much pressure on the bottom shelf. The correct choice is (C)—the author assumes that excessive pressure, because it's offered as one sure cause, is the *only possible* cause, even though there may be others.

(A) The evidence and the conclusion are both about the exact same issues, even though the conclusion misinterprets the evidence. The problem isn't that the evidence is irrelevant, but rather the way in which the conclusion distorts that evidence.

(B) The author never mentions or implies the concept of a "partial collapse." It's impossible, according to the author, for just the bottom shelf to collapse. The author talks about an "entire" collapse, and never deviates from this conception. There's no discontinuity in the meaning of collapse.

(D) The author has no obligation to consider the existence of single-shelf bookcases. This argument is specifically about Sherry's bookcase, which has at least a bottom shelf, which implies it has at least one more. We can't tell whether the author has overlooked the possibility mentioned in (D), but even if she has, that has no bearing on the validity of her argument.

(E) The conclusion is certainly too extreme, but since it just deals with Sherry's bookcase it would be hard to classify it as "broad." Also, the evidence doesn't contradict itself. As it stands, the evidence offers a perfectly valid formal logic statement; the problem comes in the conclusion drawn *from* this evidence.

Remember:

- This question offers a good example of the benefits of identifying the different parts of an argument. After isolating the evidence and the conclusion, look for the flaws. The evidence is fine, so (A) and (E) are out. That means that conclusion must be the problem, in and of itself or because it rests on a weak assumption. Of the remaining answer choices, only (C) deals with the conclusion specifically. Even if you aren't sure what the weakness is, you can go far by identifying where it must be.

14 **(D)** To parallel a dialogue accurately, we'll want to understand the structure of each part individually. The first speaker in the right answer choice will explain that everyone within a certain group receives one of two items. The second part of the right answer will describe how, no matter which item is originally chosen, everyone in the group receives the same item. On its most basic general level, then, the right answer choice will start off with two options and will then narrow down to one of those options that's common to both choices. We can't quite predict how this is going to look, so let's evaluate the answer choices.

(A) starts off fine, but the second speaker concludes that "most" of the bouquets included silver roses while the original argument concludes that "all" of kids have loans. "Most" will never parallel "all."

(B) proceeds from discussing a group to discussing an individual. The original argument makes a conclusion about the group, not one of its members.

(C) follows the pattern we've seen by starting off okay, but making its error in the second part. The psychiatrist discusses Ward A but the Nurse discusses an entirely different group residing in Ward B. The original argument deals with one and only one group.

(D) finally remains faithful throughout the second part of the argument. Margaret describes two options available to patients (corn or sprouts), and the cafeteria worker shows how the patients all share one of those options (sprouts) because anyone who choice one (corn) also chose the other (sprouts). Perfect.

(E) makes its error right away by describing the two choices as mutually exclusive. It can't parallel the original argument which combines the two options. You should have stopped reading this one at the phrase "but not both."

Remember:

- Be aware that many Parallel Reasoning questions can be cut down to size with strategic comparisons of the original to the choices. For example, (A)'s "most" and (E)'s "but not both" allowed us to chop through these choices rather quickly.
- When time's running out, you may wish to focus on paralleling only one part of the original argument (for example, its conclusion). That may help you at least improve your odds if you have to guess.

15 (C) Oddly, this stimulus presents us with nothing more than a list of different transportation vehicles and their definitions. With so much rather disconnected information, be prepared to refer back to the stimulus as you comb the answer choices for a proper inference. Choice (C) is the right answer, since any jeep meeting such criteria would also fulfill all of the criteria listed in the definition of a passenger vehicle. The author never says that a vehicle can't belong to more than one category.

(A) No, if the automobile in question were a passenger vehicle, then it *would be* fully enclosed with four wheels.

(B) knocks out three of the four vehicles described in the passage, and therefore chooses the fourth, but that's only valid if there aren't any other vehicle options. Perhaps there are; nowhere does the author say that these are the only four vehicles in existence.

(D) This makes an unsupported comparison among the vehicles. Even if the definitions of two of these vehicles are more similar, that doesn't suggest that the vehicles themselves are necessarily more *alike*. Too vague.

(E) may be true, but it may not. Since the stimulus doesn't discuss this possibility or provide any rules that would support it, we can't infer that the postal van and jeep categories overlap. It's possible that no postal vans are jeeps.

Remember:

- An inference is something that is well supported by the information and logically follows from it. Don't settle for choices that leave room for argument.

16 (E) In order to apply a principle, the first step is to have a very strong grasp of the principle as the author originally presented it. The

Superintendent provides a general rule and offers one definite exception to it. The argument also contains a justification of his hands-off policy: it hones student interaction skills. It's pretty much impossible to prephrase an answer to such a question, so once you have a solid grasp on the principle presented, proceed to the answer choices, looking for the one that best conforms.

(A) presents a hands-off gym teacher, but the teacher's noninvolvement contradicts the stimulus' principle by not intervening even though violence is involved. Since violence justifies intervention, the situation in (A) doesn't accord with the principle in the stimulus.

(B) presents a teacher intervening in a dispute that is not clearly defined as violent. We therefore can't tell whether it demonstrates the original principle or not.

(C) is outside of the author's scope, which specifically concerns *teachers'* intervention in student conflicts. Parents have no role in the principle as it is originally presented, so they can't be centrally present in a situation that applies that original principle.

(D) Generating debate in philosophy class seems like a fully justifiable teaching activity. This is not the type of student conflict toward which the principle is geared, especially when it is instigated by a teacher.

(E) While we may pity the student with the new 'do,' this is the right choice because it precisely follows the rules of the Superintendent's principle. The teacher does not intervene in a clearly nonviolent (teasing doesn't suggest violence) student conflict situation. Perfect.

Remember:

• When applying a principle, look for the answer choice that the author of the original statement would most likely agree with. In this sense, Principle questions are often similar to Inference questions—in both types, the right answers are strictly consistent with the information in the original argument.

17 **(D)** The first step in an Explanation question is to understand the situation described in the stimulus that needs explaining. Here, the author discusses two simultaneous trends that might seem to contradict one another. Tuition has increased at private universities, leading to a decrease in enrollment—so far that's logical. However, revenue at these universities has continued to increase despite the decreased enrollment. The correct answer must offer some source of revenue that more than compensates for the decrease in revenues created by the lower enrollment. That's where (D) fits in: If the tuition hikes have brought in more revenue than the loss of enrollment has taken away, then it's easy to see how both trends discussed in the stimulus can simultaneously coexist.

(A) The frequency with which private schools increase tuition doesn't begin to explain the revenue situation in the stimulus. The relevant fact is that tuitions are increasing, which triggers the rest of argument. In what specific manner they're increasing is irrelevant.

(B) offers an irrelevant distinction between vocational schools and private colleges that doesn't contribute any new information to the stimulus.

(C) tells us what happens to some students who can no longer afford private universities. Their fate, sorry to say, doesn't matter, and again it doesn't add any new information to the scenario. We already know that enrollment decreased; this choice just gives us a human-interest story when we really want to know how it's possible under these circumstances for revenues to actually increase.

(E) is similar to (B) in that it provides another irrelevant distinction. It compares the role of alumni contributions at public and private colleges, while the stimulus does not express any interest in public universities or in alumni contributions. Even if private colleges do get a larger percentage of money from alumni, decreasing enrollment shrinks the number of alumni and would, if anything, seem to decrease revenue even further, deepening the mystery but not explaining it.

Remember:

• In Explanation questions, the information provided in the stimulus remains true; your task is to reconcile, not to change, the presented facts. If you stay focused on that task, you'll see that only one answer choice will work. Understanding the seemingly unusual situation in the stimulus is key.

18 **(E)** The stimulus begins with an absolute statement and takes us directly into formal logic territory. Thus the first sentence can be restated: If children are guided by critical adults, then the children will not develop strong self-esteem. The question stem allows us to anticipate that the second sentence will offer an incorrect inference, as indeed it does. There, the author concludes that if children are NOT guided by critical adults, then they WILL develop strong self-esteem. Expressing the stem alge-

braically, we can rewrite the first sentence as: if A then B. The second sentence alters the equation to: if NOT A, then NOT B. That's an invalid inference, so we'll look through the answer choices for another argument that makes the same mistake.

(A) doesn't give us any formal logic statements, so it can't parallel the stimulus. The recommendation in (A) has no parallel in the original, either, so you may have axed (A) on that count as well.

(B) can be restated. If a solicitor has bad manners, then that solicitor won't sell any products (if A then B). The second sentence concludes that if a solicitor has low sales (which, you'll note, is different from NO sales), then that solicitor has bad manners (if C then A). That's a flaw, but it's not the one we're looking for.

(C) contains a description of an event, and a future prediction based on that event. Moreover, the first sentence contains no formal logic. Not parallel.

(D) restated, says that if a puppy is not well-socialized, then it won't interact well with a group of people (if A then B). The second sentence describes a proportional increase between socialization and comfortable interaction, which isn't a formal logic statement and which therefore can't complete the parallel.

(E) is all that's left, so it had better work. In fact, on test day, you shouldn't even spend time checking it if you're totally confident that the others are lousy. But for the record: If one takes calcium supplements, then one does NOT increase one's risk of heart disease (if A then B). In the next sentence, the author concludes that if one does NOT take calcium supplements, one

WILL increase one's risk of heart disease (if NOT A then NOT B). That's a perfect parallel of the flawed stimulus.

Remember:

- Always restate formal logic statements in an if-then format. That'll enable you to interpret them, form their contrapositives (by reversing and negating the terms), and, if necessary, compare them to one another accurately.
- The logical opposite of a negative statement is a positive statement! Here, the opposite of "NOT increasing a risk" is "increasing a risk."

19 **(D)** The author begins by describing the view of some sports historians, who subscribe to a basic formula: physical attributes + a coach's influence = a player's "unique" tennis style. After dismissing the relevance of modern players' greater strength and endurance, however, the author argues that current styles are really no different from previous styles, implying that the historians' claim of the existence of "unique" tennis styles is bogus. And this implication is stated outright in the last sentence, where the author posits the existence of a universally successful tennis style shared by all professionals. In other words, the author uses the fact that tennis styles haven't changed over the years to argue that there's simply one best way to play tennis; in contrast to the historians' theory of uniqueness, the author proposes the theory of universality. But the author ignores the role of the tennis coach: If, as (D) has it, the early coaches of today's players were the professionals of yesteryear, then it becomes plausible that the style that the author considers "universal" may simply be the style (one possible one among many) that was handed down from one generation to the next. Perhaps if the current crop of tennis stars don't go on to teach the next generation, whole new styles will develop. If the current style is learned, then it may not be universally inherent to the game. If (D) is true, the author's claim of "universality" is weakened.

(A) This answer choice emphasizes the truth of the first part of the sports historians' view regarding the individuality of physical attributes. Since the author doesn't explicitly disagree that players do vary in terms of some attributes, this choice doesn't weaken the argument. It just emphasizes a point on which the two views (historians and author) don't clearly disagree.

(B) if anything, strengthens the argument: If most current players don't know of the players of previous generations, yet their styles are for the most part similar to that of those players, then we'd be more likely to believe that the author is on to something with the claim that a universally efficient style exists in the world of professional tennis. (B) is somewhat the converse of correct choice (D) in that it lowers the probability that current players have simply copied the successful styles of previous players.

(C) This choice makes an irrelevant distinction between strength and endurance. Saying that one has a greater impact than the other has no effect on the argument which never even begins to rank those two factors.

(E) The factors that contribute to the greater strength and weight of today's players are beyond the scope of this argument.

Remember:

- When the author describes the view of some other people (in this case "some sports histori-

KAPLAN

ans"), be ready to encounter a contrasting view. The author often mentions such groups to contrast their views to his or her own. At the first sign of conflict in a Logical Reasoning argument or Reading Comprehension passage, ask yourself where the views differ. The answer choices often test your ability to recognize the distinction.

- One way to get through the more difficult questions is to pay extra attention to wrong answer choice elimination strategies. Even if choice (D) doesn't seem great to you, (A), (B), (C), and (E) all commit common errors. There's nothing wrong with eliminating four choices for good reasons and going with what remains.

20 **(D)** The author's conclusion is the companies' confidence that anemic children will be cured relatively simply with a new iron injection. The evidence presents itself in the first sentence: A new injection can apparently reverse children's anemia. Can you see any gaps between the conclusion and evidence? Notice that the evidence explains that something can be done and the conclusion states that something will be done. Just because the cure is possible doesn't mean it will automatically be administered. The author assumes that children will receive the injection based on the fact that it exists. (D) expresses this more concretely: the author assumes that children are aware of and willing to receive this injection.

(A) The argument focuses on the availability, not the production of this cure, so (A) is not necessary (or even relevant) to this argument.

(B) gives us irrelevant background information about causes. The author states that iron shots reverse children's anemia, regardless of the spe-

cific cause, so (B) may or may not be true without affecting the argument.

(C) basically states that a managed diet would not cure anemia. But the author doesn't state that the injection is the *only* cure for anemia, so the argument needn't assume that no other cure exists.

(E) The author only claims that the injection cures anemia "relatively simply." Safety never comes up as an issue—the injection could almost kill the kids and still not hurt the argument, which states only that the shot cures the condition, not that it does so safely.

Remember:

- Even though Logical Reasoning stimuli are shorter than Reading Comprehension passages, don't try to memorize the information in either situation.
- Push yourself beyond recognizing the conclusion to considering how it operates in the context of the argument. Instead of stopping once you've recognized that the author concludes that a drug will provide a cure, really think about how that relates to the evidence. That'll make it easier to see the gap between them.

21 **(E)** The author concludes that mission commanders should not choose pilots based on the candidates' performance on the isolation test. For evidence, the author says that a candidate who passes the test may have an antisocial personality disorder. Thus, the author argues against a current system of assessment by noting one particular instance in which the results might not indicate what they're meant to indicate. This is certainly not the strongest of arguments, offering as it does one apparently small disadvantage of the test and using it to condemn the test entirely, which is why we'll see four of its flaws among the answer choices. Notice that the question stem informs us that the four wrong answers will offer information that the author fails to consider; they will describe errors of omission.

(A) describes one way in which the isolation tests might work to accurately screen applicants. It describes a possible benefit offered by the test. The argument is flawed for failing to consider and rebuff this possibility.

(B) operates in much the same way as (A). Here we're told that mission commanders may select pilots more accurately if the tests they administer aren't limited. Since the author argues that such tests should be limited (arguing that there should be one fewer test), her argument is flawed since it fails to consider and, again, rebuff this opposing argument.

(C) and (D) again indicate two possible advantages of the isolation test. The author doesn't mention or contest these advantages, which means that she makes her conclusion without addressing the relevant issues that they describe. That's certainly a flaw in the argument.

(E) Rather than highlight a benefit of the test, (E) goes the other way by suggesting that the test itself may be flawed. The fact that a pilot may do well on the test and yet not do well under actual isolation conditions is, if anything, consistent with the author's conclusion that the test should be scrapped.

Remember:

- Be aware of the variations in the question stems throughout the exam. The stem here informs us

that the four wrong answer choices will describe things relevant to the argument that the author doesn't consider, which is a particular type of flaw. If you are aware of that, you can approach the choices knowing what to expect.

22 **(D)** The heart of the argument is the last sentence of the stimulus: Harry concludes that his brother's suggestion wouldn't help to organize his collection based on the evidence that no single special album could hold all his cards. Harry's argument depends on the assumption that the collection of cards cannot be organized if they're not in one singular album. (D) expresses the same idea: Harry's dismissal of his brother's suggestion makes sense only if the collection cannot be organized in more than one album.

(A) Harry needn't assume that the showcase albums from the olden days would have served his purposes. His argument isn't based on a comparison of what's available now compared to what used to be available, so (A) addresses a possibility that doesn't impact Harry's argument.

(B) isn't entirely relevant to this argument, since other albums types don't figure in to this argument. Moreover, we're concerned only with Harry's predicament.

(C) contradicts the stimulus, which explicitly states that no showcase album on the market is large enough to contain all of Harry's cards.

(E) The reason *why* Harry's collection is disorganized doesn't provide a link between the evidence and conclusion because neither part of the argument concerns this issue.

Remember:

- Even when you aren't able to prephrase an assumption, you can still go far with a knowledge of the issues involved in the argument. Here, those issues are organization and showcase albums. Only (B) and (D) actually mention both issues, and only (D) stays focused solely on them.

23 **(C)** We're asked for a situation that conforms to a principle, so your best bet is to understand the principle thoroughly, and then test the choices against this understanding. The author offers an absolute truth with two restrictions. First the rule: A free press always reports all information about a country's military operations. There are two cases, and only two cases, in which this might not be true. First, if such information would jeopardize the safety of the troops. Second, if such information would jeopardize the success of a mission. With such clear rules, we'll be looking for the answer choice that follows them faithfully.

(A) To make this answer choice work, you'd have to assume that such dissenting opinions would jeopardize the troops and/or the success of the mission. This choice supports no such assumption, so based on the information that it alone provides, it is not consistent with the stimulus' principle.

(B) and (D) discuss unfree presses, and therefore fall outside the scope of the argument. The rules pertain only to a free press, and we can't infer how an unfree press would behave in regard to these issues.

(C) This answer choice succeeds where (A) fails because, while it doesn't directly state that the publication of future military targets would jeopardize the success of a mission, the link between the two is far clearer and more logical. According to the principle, a free press *could* withhold information that endangers the troops or mission, and it's reasonable to say that the info discussed in (C) could fall into that category.

(E) The principle deals with *current* military operations, and therefore doesn't shed any light on what's appropriate behavior in regard to previous engagements. Clandestine past military operations are outside the scope.

Remember:

- No correct answer choice will require you to make a significant, unfounded assumption in order to make it work. The right answer choice will be correct on its own merit, without requiring you to introduce extra information.

24 **(C)** Lillian's goal is simple: to create cohesion in her drug addiction recovery group. In order to achieve this goal, she has encouraged members of the group to share their personal experiences openly. The problem: Some members have begun telling long and violent stories to shock the others, causing some members to quit and leaving inadequate time for others to share. The conclusion: Lillian should limit the time available for each member to speak. The stem alerts us that there's a flaw in this argument, and that flaw becomes apparent in the conclusion. The problem which the conclusion seeks to resolve stems from two causes: members telling long and violent stories. The conclusion as it stands might prevent the stories from being long, but it doesn't prevent them from being violent. Therefore, the argument is flawed because its conclusion would only remedy one of two factors which create the problem it seeks to resolve, which is what (C) states.

(A) Apparently, "two actions" refers to the telling of long scandalous stories and members dropping out. (A) is most immediately wrong because the author does not suggest that these incidents occur simultaneously. On the contrary, the author presents them sequentially: According to the argument, the stories "cause" other members to quit.

(B) is perplexing because there is no hypothesis in this argument. Also, there is no contradiction within the elements of this argument. The conclusion is flawed because it's incomplete, not because it runs counter to anything.

(D) The evidence is all perfectly relevant to the conclusion. They are, after all, both focused on the same issues.

(E), like (B), suggests that the elements of the argument contradict one another, but that is not true in this case. Lil's evidence is consistent with the conclusion—the problem is that the recommendation in the conclusion simply doesn't go far enough.

Remember:

- The answer choices for Logical Flaw questions are particularly formulaic and repetitive, leaving you with similar answer choices for different flaw questions. Thus, given a stimulus with a causality problem, (A) would be your choice or, if there were a scope shift, (D) would be attractive. The good news is that the flaws in the arguments are equally repetitive. The bad news is that the answer choices will likely sound famil-

iar, so it's important that you first prephrase the flaw in order that you not be lead astray.

25 **(B)** This Assumption question picks up on the confusion in the argument between groups and subgroups. The author's conclusion addresses all of the materials produced by American Synthetics Inc., but the evidence discusses only one particular material produced by the company: the kuva weave fabric. We're told that kuva weave, despite its impressive durability and strength, has an unfortunate tendency to burst into flames (a small drawback). Therefore, according to the author, manufacturers should eliminate ALL American Synthetics materials from their stocks. This would be a valid conclusion only if it were true that all of the materials produced by American Synthetics were equally likely to ignite. (B) states this assumption: If all of American Synthetics' materials contain kuva weave, then they're all flammable, and manufacturers should indeed get rid of their stocks. (B) makes the evidence about kuva weave relevant to the conclusion regarding all American Synthetics products—it connects the evidence to the conclusion, and thus qualifies as the assumption we seek.

(A) Sure, they didn't catch that flammability problem, but we're not concerned with the accuracy of the trials or when the problem showed up. We're solely concerned with the flammability of the material, and what that flammability means for the company's products as a whole.

(C) Plants that *don't* use the fabric may suffer from just as high or even a higher incidence of fires due to other reasons. In other words, the author need assume nothing about the type of comparison stated in (C) in order to make an argument about what should be done as a result of kuva weave's flammability. We can negate (C) and the argument does not fall apart, which confirms that (C) is not a statement that's needed here.

(D) Apparently they're not as durable as originally suspected if they're burning, but durability isn't the issue, flammability is. As we saw in (A), the early tests are irrelevant.

(E) The manufacturers' liability is far off scope. While (E) may offer an additional reason for manufacturers to expunge their stocks, we're not looking to strengthen this argument but to identify its assumption, and this answer choice doesn't link kuva weave to American Synthetics' products as a whole.

Remember:

- An assumption has a very specific definition on the LSAT; it is an unstated yet necessary link between the evidence and the conclusion. After identifying the evidence and conclusion, look to eliminate all of the answer choices that don't relate to both elements. Even when you can't prephrase the assumption, you can evaluate the answer choices with very specific criteria in mind and increase your chances of finding it correctly and quickly.

Section III: Logical Reasoning Explanations

1 **(B)** In order for the mother to conclude from her evidence that the sessions should end, she needs to assume that John is capable of accurately analyzing the sessions' usefulness. If he's not, then his feelings on the matter may not be an accurate indicator of the value of the sessions, and it may not be a good idea to base any decisions on them. Basically, John's mother assumes that John's is right in believing that the sessions aren't helping him, which is where answer choice (B) comes in. If she's assuming that John is right, then she must also assume that his judgment hasn't been impaired.

(A) is wrong because John's mother just discusses what should be done if John is unhappy with the sessions. Her conclusion does not depend on him being happy or unhappy.

(C) is far outside of the scope of the mother's argument. She never addresses the issue of the psychoanalyst's qualifications; she just discusses John's feelings and their indication of the sessions' value.

(D) Again, whether or not the analyst's methods are sound is not the issue for John's mother. For her, the central issue is John, and how his feelings determine the helpfulness of the sessions. Therefore, the validity of her conclusion does not rest on whether John's perceptions accurately indicate the soundness of the analyst's methods, but whether they indicate the value of the sessions in helping him to adjust to his parents' divorce.

(E) By stating that John should "act on *any* belief," choice (E) exceeds the argument's scope. The argument does not deal with anything so broad as whether John should always act on his beliefs. Rather, it addresses whether his beliefs should be acted upon in this particular situation.

Remember:

• You can often eliminate a number of choices right off the bat that are simply too broad in their scope to be necessary to the particular argument.

2 **(B)** Harriet's husband concludes that he will plan a trip to Sunshine Valley for he and Harriet. His evidence: Harriet wants to vacation in a culturally rich area, and her husband has discovered that Sunshine Valley is financially rich. His error: He responds to her desire for cultural richness with a city steeped in financial richness. He therefore mistakes her definition of richness. (B) captures this. To equivocate is to call two things the same even though they're not (*aequi* means equal and *vocare* means to call), which is precisely what Harriet's husband does when he equates cultural and financial wealth. Further, this richness certainly constitutes a key (even the key) factor in his decision.

(A) An argument is circular when its evidence and conclusion are basically the same (i.e., "I should go to the store because I should go to the store"). That's not the case here, where the conclusion and evidence are clearly different.

(C) All travel brochures are biased—they want to convince the reader to visit that area. Relying on such evidence to decide where to go isn't the basis of a logical flaw. Moreover, there's nothing here to indicate that the information in the brochure is unreliable. The problem here is how the husband *uses* the evidence to make his traveling decision.

(D) He certainly does this, but the fact that he doesn't consult Harriet doesn't constitute a flaw in the argumentation as it's presented. If anything, it's a subjective and personal, not a logical flaw, to make important decisions unilaterally.

(E), like (D), is certainly true, but why does he need to demonstrate the economic feasibility of his decision? We have no way of knowing whether they can afford the trip or not, but that's a separate issue. We're concerned only with the husband's decision as related to the evidence for it.

Remember:

- Flaw questions are distinct from Weaken questions in a few ways. A flaw is a logical error in the reasoning of the argument, or an objective mistake committed by the argument. You'll often encounter wrong answer choices for Flaw questions that would weaken the argument, but a flaw is an internal mistake in the argument, whereas anything that makes the conclusion less credible weakens the argument. You can sometimes weaken an argument by identifying its flaw, but remember that a choice that weakens an argument isn't its flaw unless it points out an internal, logical error in the argumentation as the stimulus presents it.

3 **(D)** This stimulus just tells us a story. Once you've grasped the basic contents of the stimulus, proceed to the answer choices.

(A) The stimulus tells us that *Theobroma cacao* is a tropical New World tree, but that doesn't allow us to infer that this tree *only* grows in the tropical New World. The tree might very possibly exist in other countries.

(B) contradicts the stimulus, which tells us that chocolate was introduced to Europe as a liquid.

(C) makes an unsupported comparison. We do know that more pounds of chocolate today are produced for eating than drinking, but we have no idea how the amount of drinkable chocolate in the 1800's compares to the amount of solid edible chocolate produced today.

(D) is valid: If the Swiss invented the first way to produce solid edible chocolate in the 1800's, then solid edible chocolate wasn't consumed anywhere in the 1500's.

(E) is entirely unsupported by the stimulus. Just because the Swiss made chocolate into a solid, that doesn't necessarily mean that nobody else would have done so if the Swiss hadn't. Take the Swiss out of the picture, and chocolate might very well be just as popular today.

Remember:

- Every once in a while you'll get a stimulus that isn't an argument (i.e., it doesn't have a conclusion and evidence, just a bunch of facts). The question that's attached to them will usually be Inference, since it's difficult to ask anything relating to how the evidence reaches the conclusion when there really is no conclusion to speak of.
- Make sure you stay within the scope when looking for the choice that must be true.

4 (A) The nuclear physicist argues that the *Times* should try harder to print the views of protesters in this particular controversy. She proceeds to state, three times and in three different ways, that such views are lacking. The engineer states that the protesters' views needn't be printed because the *Times'* coverage is fine. The engineer thus concedes that such views are not represented, but does not believe that they need to be. The engineer doesn't give us any concrete evidence to support this position, so the right answer will contradict this one idea given by the engineer. As you look through the answer choices, ask yourself which one shows that the engineer is somehow wrong to be satisfied with the absence of the protesters' views. (A) fits the bill because, if effective reporting needs to represent both sides of a controversy, then the Times' coverage is not adequate and the engineer's position is clearly contradicted.

(B) is consistent with the engineer's opinion that the *Times'* coverage is fine as it is, so it certainly wouldn't counter the engineer's claim.

(C) deals with the paper's readership, about which the engineer never offers an opinion. It doesn't justify why this issue is relevant to the engineer's position, so it can't counter that position.

(D), like (C), has no clear connection to the engineer's statements. This choice would only look tempting if you added more information to it.

(E) The engineer is totally comfortable with the imbalance in media coverage, so this information explaining an imbalance wouldn't counter his position.

Remember:

• When presented with more than one view, always make sure that you stay focused on the appropriate one when proceeding to the answer choices. Previewing the question stem will usually tell you where to focus your attention.

5 (E) The author of this rather skimpy argument only implies her conclusion: that the botanists were wrong. Evidence? The botanists believed that the Faura plants required a certain fertilizer composed of four specific elements, but adopting this approach actually hindered the growth of those plants. There's a lot of space available for information which would strengthen the author's conclusion, but since we can't predict anything concrete, let's go through them individually, crossing off anything that supports the conclusion.

(A), (B), and (D) all describe one negative effect of the botanists' belief. More specifically, each discusses the botanists' omission of one key ingredient which these plants need to grow. (A) explains in further detail that the botanists' advocacy of the fertilizer inhibited Faura species plant growth because it led to the omission of the valuable potash. (B) doesn't directly state that the omission of zinc caused the problems experienced by the Faura species plants, but it certainly implies it, calling zinc "essential" to the plants' growth and therefore suggesting that the lack of it harmed the plants. (D) directly states that the plants require a necessary ingredient which the botanists' fertilizer lacks. All three choices expand on the author's argument, more clearly defining *why* exactly the botanists' belief yielded such negative results. By adding to the evidence, all three choices strengthen the author's argument.

(C) doesn't identify a missing ingredient necessary for healthy plant growth but identifies a problem with the presentation of the list itself, as it fails to prioritize the most important elements. Despite this minor difference, (C) serves the same function as the aforementioned choices by explaining why the botanists' belief had negative results and thus strengthens the author's argument.

(E) is correct because it identifies one way in which the botanists' claim likely benefited the Faura species plants. The author is concerned with the negative effects of the belief, so this piece of information certainly doesn't strengthen her case.

Remember:

- Don't expect the right answer choice for these "all/except" questions to be 180 degrees different than the four others. The answer for this question doesn't need to weaken the argument; it only needs to NOT strengthen it. More often than not, the right answers for questions of this sort just have no real effect on the argument one way or the other.

6 **(E)** Ron and Crystal will open a restaurant when they can both put in the required hours. Accordingly, the argument offers this one condition that must be met before the two open the restaurant. The remainder of the stimulus focuses on Ron's realization that Crystal's year-long project won't give her enough time to focus on the restaurant. The author suggests as much when he writes that Ron thought she would have enough time, but was wrong. Therefore, the condition required for the opening of the restaurant has not been met and clearly will not be met in the current year. It is therefore reasonable to conclude that they will not open the restaurant this year, answer choice (E).

This could also be stated through formal logic: If the two open the restaurant, then that means they have enough time to dedicate to it. The contrapositive is that they don't have enough time (which the stimulus states), so therefore they won't open the restaurant (the implied conclusion).

(A) is stated in the stimulus, so it isn't what the argument "is structured to lead to." This is part of the evidence, not the conclusion.

(B) We can infer that Ron and Crystal would believe (B) to be true; hence, their pact that they would wait to open the restaurant until they were ready to devote their time and energy to it. However, this general statement, while certainly sounding consistent with the stimulus, is not the conclusion the argument is leading to. What about Ron? What about Crystal? What about their proposed restaurant? These things are the crux of the matter; the statement in (B) is too broad and general to be what the author is ultimately after here.

(C) might or might not be true; the stimulus certainly doesn't support or lead to this statement either way.

(D) might touch on some bigger problems in the relationship, but it doesn't get any support from the stimulus. Indeed, it contradicts the stimulus which defines only one barrier to the opening of the restaurant, and that barrier is time, not any secretive agenda of deception on Crystal's part.

Remember:

- Be on the lookout for this very common argument structure in which only one or two explicitly stated conditions determine whether a certain course of action will be followed. Only those conditions will impact the course of action in the argument and in any correct answer choice that is supposed to be faithful to it. You can also often rephrase such arguments through the aid of formal logic.

7 **(C)** This question asks us to determine what can be inferred from the statements in the passage. If the statistics cited by both of the speakers are true, which of the answer choices must also be true? A look at the statistics shows that over the past five years, the elderly care center has seen an increase in its applications from volunteers—the director says they've almost doubled. The nurse points out, however, that applications from patients' family members have actually decreased by 20 percent. If overall applications have increased, but family members' applications have gone down, what can we infer? (C) provides a logical deduction—that the center is receiving applications from volunteers who are not patients' family members. We can use the Kaplan Denial Test to check our accuracy here. If the clinic received no applications from persons who were not related to patients, then the statistics cited would not make sense.

(A) does not necessarily follow from the statistics in the passage. The statistics concern volunteer applications, not the size of the patient population. The data that we're given about the volunteer applications tells us nothing about the patient population one way or another.

(B) might be tempting, but does not provide us with the inference we need. Based on the statistics given, we cannot know whether patient care has improved or not. We're told that the number of volunteer applications has increased, but

we don't know whether the number of accepted volunteers has grown—and we certainly don't know whether the volunteers are providing better care to the patients.

(D) Again here, we cannot be sure that this statement is true, simply based on the passage. We merely know that more people are interested in volunteering. This doesn't necessarily mean that the extra volunteers are *needed*, and it tells us nothing about *why* they might be needed if they are.

(E) is again beyond the limits of what we can infer here. We are told that the number of applications has increased and that the number of applications from family members has decreased. But that's all that we're given. This is not enough information to tell us anything about the selection process for volunteers—for all we know, every person who applies may actually become a volunteer.

Remember:

- If you're not sure after scanning the answers on a "must be true" Inference question, you can use the Kaplan Denial Test to eliminate choices effectively and to confirm the choice that most appeals to you. It works the same way as it does in Assumption questions: If you deny an answer choice and the denied statement makes the passage appear illogical, you know you've found the correct answer.

8 **(D)** Next we're asked to find a statement that weakens the nurse's argument. Before we can choose a weakener, we must first isolate the nurse's conclusion and evidence. The nurse concludes that the director's interpretation is wrong, and that community members are less interested in working with their parents than they were five years ago. She bases this conclusion on one piece of evidence: Applications from patients' family members have decreased over this time period. To weaken the argument, we might find another explanation for why volunteer applications from family members are down. (D) provides just such an alternative: If family members are no longer required to fill out formal applications, their applications will obviously not be on file, which could easily explain the 20 percent decrease. But they may continue to volunteer just the same.

(A) Irrelevant. This doesn't affect the nurse's argument one way or the other, because it refers to "community members" in general. We do not know if these community members are volunteer applicants, or if they are related to the elderly at the center.

(B) touches on the issue of family activities, but it doesn't tell us anything about the center's volunteers.

(C) might be tempting, because it provides another reason, besides lack of interest, for why an individual might not volunteer. The problem with (C) is that it addresses individuals in general, and makes no distinction between family members and non-family members. Even if (C) is true, the fact remains that family member applications are down, and (C) does nothing to damage the conclusion that the nurse bases on that fact.

(E) If anything, this choice might serve to strengthen the nurse's argument. If the volunteer commitment is relatively not extensive, this might reinforce the notion that relatives don't volunteer because they lack interest. Whether we see it as a slight strengthener or not, (E) contains nothing that weakens the argument.

Remember:

• Make the most of "double" questions that rely on one stimulus. Read both question stems before approaching the stimulus. That way you know what you're looking for and can read for two questions at once.

9 (E) We know from the question stem that we're concerned with Theresa's method of argument, so when reading the dialogue between them look specifically at how Theresa responds to Angie. Angie argues that if Bernard allows Pepe to sleep at the foot of his bed, Pepe's disciplinary problems will worsen. Theresa disagrees and believes that the same course of action will have the opposite outcome. Her evidence is Julian's dog: When Julian allowed his dog to sleep at the foot of his bed, the dog's disciplinary problems lessened. (E) accurately characterizes this method of argument: She indeed makes a prediction about Bernard's dog based on a similar situation with Julian's dog.

(A) If you identify what exists as evidence in the two statements, this one won't be tempting. Angie doesn't really provide any evidence and Theresa's evidence about Julian is uniquely her own. There's no reinterpretation here.

(B) Theresa's recommendation is quite specific—let the dog sleep on the bed and he'll behave better.

(C) Angie might almost do this, but Theresa doesn't discuss the difficulties that might arise from a plan. She only discusses the benefits that would likely result given a certain course of action.

(D) Within Theresa's argument, the course of action (letting the dog sleep on the bed) remains the same. Her whole point is that the same course of action would likely have the same result, so (D) is wrong because it states that Theresa offered two different courses of action.

Remember:

- It's easiest to evaluate the difference between two statements in a dialogue stimulus by sticking to the basics: Identify each person's conclusion and evidence and you'll be able to see what the second person reacts to and how that person goes about it. The two views presented are always different, so be systematic in order to see where that difference lies.

10 **(E)** Let's start by looking for the author's assumption. The study shows that students remember a good deal of the specific material that they teach, and the principal concludes that the students should teach everything, but that conclusion is only valid if the students are actually capable of teaching every subject. Notice that the evidence only discusses students teaching some material, while the conclusion advocates that students should teach everything. The assumption needs to fill this gap by allowing that the small scale model will work on the large scale. This is an inadequately supported assumption and is thus a flaw in the argument. (E) expresses this flaw, noting that the assumption may not be true and that small scale student teaching may not work on the large scale.

(A) isn't a flaw since the principal doesn't suggest that teaching is the only way to learn and will be the students' only occupation.

(B) This assumption is not part of the principal's proposal, which makes no mention of written assignments or learning through hearing. Not even the study itself, which does mention these forms of learning, suggests that the two are equally valuable.

(C) Well, the argument certainly doesn't discuss this, but since the argument has nothing to do with test scores, this consideration wouldn't be relevant to the argument and thus its omission isn't a flaw.

(D) doesn't state that the survey is wrong, but that it's motivations might not be pure. Even if the survey were intensely self-interested, the principal is not concerned with its motivations but with its results. Her argument might be flawed if we knew she relied on results that were grossly inaccurate or results that she herself misinterpreted, but that's not what (D) says.

Remember:

- Flaw questions are so common and the different flaws they demonstrate are so varied that you should get a good sense of the possibilities before test day. The most common flaws are *unwarranted assumptions, ignored alternative possibilities,* and *scope shifts.* Use your practice to become familiar with each of these types of flaws.

11 **(D)** The author supports one explanation for why the hardly pitiable students at Carmine U. are overwhelmed by their elective course options. As the stimulus begins, he describes this scandalous problem and offers two possible

KAPLAN

explanations for it: improper categorization and overly extensive course descriptions. The author then concludes that, since each individual description isn't so long as to exceed the boundaries of what students can absorb (possibility #1), the problem must be with the categorization (possibility #2). Not so fast. Sure, each individual description isn't too long, but isn't it possible that all of the descriptions together are too long? (D) points out this missing step. If all the descriptions together are too much to absorb, then perhaps possibility #1 is the correct explanation after all.

(A) would certainly strengthen the argument, explaining as it does why students would be overwhelmed as a result of improper categorization, but it's not an assumption. The right answer choice needs to somehow address how the author selected his preferred explanation, and (A) does not.

(B) would weaken the argument, since it offers an alternative explanation that certainly could be true given the argument, but this is also not our task. An assumption doesn't undermine the argument's conclusion.

(C) suggests that perhaps the handbook is not properly categorized, which makes it somewhat similar to (A). (C), if anything, would only strengthen the argument; it doesn't begin to make reference to the argument's evidence.

(E) Our argument deals with course descriptions which are "far less lengthy" than that which students can absorb. This answer choice discusses "rather lengthy" descriptions, which aren't necessarily the same thing and which therefore aren't necessarily relevant to the argument.

Remember:

- While filling in an assumption is one surefire way of strengthening an argument, something that strengthens an argument is not necessarily an assumption. Don't be tempted by choices like (A) and (C) which support the author's conclusion, but don't support it by connecting it to the evidence, which any valid assumption must do.

12 **(B)** The organizers claim only that the participants in the rally will bond and will therefore be less inclined to display aberrant behavior. They do not claim that the entire student body will be less inclined to act up. If the pep rally really will help to remedy the student behavior problem in the way in which its organizers say it will, then the students with behavior problems must attend the rally. (B) states this assumption quite directly: Only if the students creating the problem go to the pep rally can they receive the positive effects of that rally and be discouraged from their unpalatable behavior.

(A) If this were true, then the whole argument would be unnecessary. The argument proceeds from the assumption that the pep rally *is* included among the extracurricular activities to be canceled, or else the coordinators wouldn't need to argue against its cancellation.

(C) is outside of the argument's scope. The pep rally organizers make no claims about the value of *other* extracurricular activities, and thus they don't need to assume anything about those activities in order for their conclusion to be valid.

(D) Too extreme. The organizers conclude that the pep rally will help, but (D) represents a much stronger version of that conclusion (i.e., that the pep rally will help *more than anything else*).

(E) again brings in the consideration of other events, and adds to that error by focusing on what the principal will do in the future. Nothing regarding what effect the rally will have on the principal's consideration of allowing *future* events is necessary for the argument to stand.

Remember:

- Choices that deviate from the specific scope of the argument in question in any major way cannot function as necessary assumptions for that argument. Neither the pep rally organizer's conclusion or evidence for that conclusion deal with any other canceled activities, so choices like (C) and (E) can be eliminated quickly.

13 **(A)** We start off with a statement of what "some individuals" believe, so be ready for the author to explicitly or implicitly disagree with their opinion. These individuals believe that the cooking schools in Southern France teach all that there is to know about French cooking. Nevertheless, one recent graduate of a cooking school in Southern France did not know how to make the ever-popular bechamel sauce. The keyword *yet* clearly suggests the author's belief that this piece of evidence undermines the first stated conclusion. The question stem directs us to look for an inference, and at this point in the argument we can see that the author doesn't actually make her own conclusion. She provides evidence that would weaken the first conclusion, thereby implying her own conclusion that cooking schools in Southern France do not necessarily teach a student all that there is to know about French cooking. Since the author doesn't directly state her conclusion and since this is an inference question, the right answer choice will likely state that implied conclusion, as (A) indeed does. Since the author provides an

exception to the first conclusion, then it must not always be true.

(B) Too extreme. All we know is that *one* graduate didn't know everything, so La Terrelle doesn't necessarily teach all that there is to know about French cooking. Still, some graduates could have learned everything.

(C) contradicts the stimulus which clearly states that all of La Terrelle's branches are in Southern France.

(D) Just because La Terrelle may not teach all that there is to know about French cooking to every student, it might still provide an effective education. Incomplete does not mean ineffective.

(E) Other schools outside the region lie beyond the scope of this argument.

Remember:

- If a question stem directs you to look for an inference, and you read the stimulus and see that the author doesn't actually state his or her conclusion, prephrase the conclusion and seek it among the answer choices. Whenever you can prephrase an answer, you're much more likely to find the correct choice quickly and correctly, so always look out for possibilities to use that tool.

14 **(A)** Four assumptions in the answer choices? Be prepared to see a pretty weak argument. The author concludes that, to achieve maximum healthiness, these bats should be fed certain nuts and veggies and a minimum amount of fruits and berries. The evidence comes in the second sentence: These bats, who are now fed mostly fruits and berries, develop endocrine imbalances.

There's clearly a causality problem here. The author provides no evidence that the fruits and berries cause this endocrine imbalance, but the author must assume that that is the case in order to have a valid conclusion. It's not worth the effort to try to prephrase all the assumptions you might find, but if a few ideas jumped out at you, great. At the very least, proceed to the answer choices with a clear understanding of the evidence and conclusion.

(A) The conclusion states that the bats will be fed a minimal amount of fruits and berries, while this choice says that they will eat none. Must that be a necessary part of this argument? No, it's too extreme: The author says straight away that eating some fruits and berries is okay, so it need not be assumed that the bats are denied these foods altogether.

(B) and (D) are valid assumptions. If the proposed diet will make the bats "healthiest," then the argument assumes that it will adequately nourish them (D) and that it won't malnourish them (B). Negate these choices via the Kaplan Denial Test and the argument falls apart, confirming that these are necessary assumptions here.

(C) is also valid. The author suggests that the bat's endocrine imbalance is a problem, and that a revised diet might fix that problem. Thus the argument does assume that bats should not be fed endocrine imbalance-producing foods.

(E) focuses again on the author's claim that the recommended diet will make the bats healthiest. If that is true, then the author must assume that it won't create any health problems that are more detrimental to the bats' health than the endocrine imbalances that inspired the proposed diet in the first place.

Remember:

• Read the answer choices carefully! Reading the stimulus carefully and strategically will certainly get you on the right path, but you still need to be able to notice minor inaccuracies in the answer choices, like the difference between "no" fruits and berries and "minimal" fruits and berries.

15 **(C)** The author clearly identifies the source of the confusion when he mentions what puzzles anthropologists. They're perplexed by two facts which seem inconsistent with each other. First, the advent of writing in certain Comaquogue clans seems to have caused the disappearance of the master storytellers within those tribes. Nevertheless, the second fact is that modern illiterate Comaquogue clans also lack master storytellers. The basic question is: Why do these modern illiterate clans lack storytellers when earlier clans lost their storytellers only after they learned how to read? Let's look to the answer choices and find one that specifically answers this question.

(A) does nothing to explain why the modern illiterate clans lack storytellers. Personality similarities don't have any clear relationship to literacy and storytellers.

(B) A comparison of the frequency of clan gatherings also does not in any way explain why the current illiterate tribes lack storytellers.

(C) would explain the discrepancy. If it were true, then the storytellers did disappear when the clans became literate, but they subsequently lost that literacy. Thus the modern tribes could both be illiterate and lack storytellers, as is the case in the stimulus, and they could have lost their storytellers during an earlier literate period.

(D) again touches on the issue of modern Comaquogue rituals without referring to literacy and storytelling, the central elements of the argument's paradox.

(E) Too broad. It might give you the room to start making assumptions, but it doesn't specifically address the issues of literacy and storytelling.

Remember:

- Don't read too much into a choice in order to try to make it work. A choice has to be right without any help from you.
- In Paradox questions, rephrase the paradox as a question and go through the answer choices trying to answer it. The temptation in these questions is to lose track of the paradox; hence we have answer choices like (A), (B), (D), and (E). If you stay focused on the seeming discrepancy, you can avoid this trap.

16 **(B)** The question stem tells us to focus on the dean's position, but the author gives us a good deal of background information before we hear about the dean. Apparently, Matthew's membership in a rock band has lowered his grades, which has hurt his chances of getting into a good business school. Matthew might be able to rock on, however, because extracurricular activities like his could compensate for the lower grades. Finally we get to the dean, who will not allow Matthew's musical hobby to better his chances of getting into Wentworth business school. Focusing on this last piece of information, let's look to the answer choices to find one that generalizes the dean's position.

(A) sounds extremely official and says relatively nothing that relates to this situation. What action does (A) refer to? If it's Matthew's rock

playing, then "consequences" probably would have to be his lower grades. If the action is the dean's refusal, the consequences for Matthew may be that he won't get in. Either way, there's no way to relate any of this to an evaluation of the action in light of "possible" consequences of an "opposing alternative action."

(B) is entirely consistent with the dean's position and would, if true, support its validity. We were told that participating in the band has hurt Matthew's chances for admission, so if something (like playing in a band) can't simultaneously hurt and help an applicant, then it makes sense that the dean sees no way for the rock band to increase Matthew's chances of getting into business school. (B) would therefore justify the dean's view that the band can have no positive effect. If you had trouble seeing this, match up the general terms in the choice with the specifics of the original: The "cause" is playing in the band; the "condition" is lower grades; the "consequence of that condition" is a lowered chance of admission. The dean simply refuses to allow Matthew's playing in the band to mitigate against the lower grades that resulted from his playing in the band.

(C) is inconsistent with the dean's position, since she is not stressing the positive value of Matthew's activities over their negative results. Rather, she sees no positive value in Matthew's musical activities.

(D) Irrelevant. Even if we argued that the dean's refusal is a decision that could affect Matthew's future, we have no idea how many factors go into admitting someone to business school, and whether this particular dean has considered them all or missed a few.

(E), like (D), is irrelevant, because the candidate is never eliminated from consideration. The dean won't give him credit for playing in the band, but that doesn't mean that she's tossed out his application.

Remember:

- For Principle questions, the answer will contain the elements of the relevant portion of the stimulus, rephrased and generalized, but otherwise not significantly altered. Stay away from choices that take you places that the stimulus never did.

17 **(B)** The two viruses clearly cause one problem: They mess up the file storage system, usually by putting the files in the wrong places. The author concludes that computer users who detect one or both of these viruses needn't worry about the destruction of their files, based on the evidence that there is no proof that either virus erases files entirely. Do you see the flaw? The author's evidence is basically that there is no evidence to support a causal relationship. Nevertheless, just because there's no proof that either virus destroys files, that doesn't mean that the viruses don't destroy files. The absence of proof doesn't mean that no proof is possible, so this argument is flawed because it doesn't adequately prove that the viruses don't cause the destruction of files. (B) expresses this flaw; according to the argument, it is still entirely possible that the viruses destroy files, even though there is "at present" no evidence that they do.

(A) is outside the scope. The issue is whether the viruses pose a threat to files, and not whether people believe that they do.

(C) The author certainly doesn't discuss this, but that doesn't constitute a flaw in the argument.

A discussion about the mechanism of file erasure wouldn't be relevant to the conclusion, so its omission is not a flaw.

(D) suggests that a keyword has more than one definition in the argument, which is not the case.

(E) describes a circular argument, which exists when the evidence and the conclusion are the same. In this argument the two are clearly different, and the extent of their difference is part of the real flaw.

Remember:

- The three most common types of flaws are unwarranted assumptions, unconsidered alternative possibilities, and scope shifts. This question gives us an example of the second type. Be on the lookout for all three when tackling Logical Flaw questions.

18 **(D)** This Parallel Reasoning question lends itself well to algebraic characterization. The question stem itself gives us some critical information: We're told that the argument in the stimulus is flawed and that we're looking for an answer choice that is flawed in a similar manner. If foods aren't stored properly, they can give people food poisoning (if X, then possibly Y). Since people at the Panhandler got food poisoning, the restaurant must have served food that wasn't properly stored (Y, therefore X). This argument makes the mistake of concluding that a "reverse cause and effect" relationship is operating: Because the consequence occurred, the cause must have been in effect also. We know from formal logic that we simply can't get from "if X then Y" to "if Y then X." So all we need to do is find the choice that commits the same error. There's of course no way to prephrase the specifics of the right choice, only its structure, so the best bet is to simply work through the choices:

(A) tells us that if a man over 65 has high blood pressure, he is at risk for heart disease (if X, then Y). That has the first part of the argument right. But the second sentence tells us that Tonare males over 65 do not have blood pressure, so they are not at risk for heart disease—which translates into not X, therefore not Y. This conclusion simply negates the terms without switching them as in the original.

(B) and (C) can both be eliminated because neither of them presents a "reverse cause and effect" argument; in fact, neither one contains anything that can be translated into a formal logic if-then statement. (B) contains a temporal flaw; for all we know, Magelli might have crafted the cabinet before he died. We would need information that the cabinet is less than fifteen years old before the conclusion would be valid. And (C)'s conclusion is certainly premature as well, but again does not contain the same formal logic structure as the original; there's nothing in there that can be translated into "if X, then Y."

(D) contains the kind of flaw we seek. This choice states that Relief-O! has been known to cause blurred vision in people who take it. We can translate that sentence as: "If people take Relief-O, they may experience blurred vision" (if X, then possibly Y). So far so good. The following sentences then tell us that Molly took a pain reliever and experienced blurred vision (Y), so she must have taken Relief-O! (therefore X). Perfect.

(E) This argument deals with cause and effect, but not in the same manner as in the stimulus. (E) lays out an initial cause: If tigermint grows out of control, it can kill other plants (if X, then Y). But its second sentence introduces a negative condition: Sally's plants did *not* get killed—in fact,

they look better than ever. Therefore, the tigermint must not be out of control. This reduces to not Y, therefore not X—and not parallel.

19 **(D)** When you see percents or ratios in a stimulus, you'll likely need to exercise your ability to distinguish between rates and numbers. This is an Inference question, as the stem makes clear, and you can prephrase an answer by considering what conclusion this evidence would support. If 57 percent equals the same number of paintings before the unveiling as 85 percent equals after the unveiling, then Déjère must have produced more paintings in the period before the unveiling—that's the only way that the numbers could work out. (D) states this from the other angle: Déjère must have painted fewer paintings after the unveiling.

(A) The author tells us that revenue from both periods is equal since Déjère sells the same number of paintings in both. Therefore, if she had charged more in the second period, she would have made more money than she had in the first, which would contradict the stimulus. Because this is inconsistent with the passage, it certainly can't be inferred from it.

(B) is outside of the scope since the author never mentions Déjère's motivations behind painting. Since there's no information about this, we can't reasonably concluding anything pertaining to it.

(C) If anything, this might suggest that Déjère sells more paintings in the second period, which the stimulus explicitly contradicts. Further, the stimulus provides no information about how art collectors might have responded to the review, giving us no basis to make a conclusion about those collectors.

(E) would also act to explain why her sales are higher in the second period, but the author says that the sales were not any greater. Also, marketing is never discussed.

Remember:

- Percentages show up often in Logical Reasoning sections; make sure you're comfortable analyzing such data. Sometimes the difference between percentages and raw numbers forms the basis of a logical flaw. Other times, as is the case here, you'll simply need to understand what the percentages represent in order to draw an inference from the data.

20 **(B)** Considering then the structure of the argument, the author states that something (the consumption of dairy products) doesn't usually create a certain result (stomachaches), and then concludes that something which might explain a causal relationship between the two (allergies) doesn't exist. In other words, if a causal relationship isn't usually present, then it isn't present. Looking for another choice which demonstrates the same structure, we can hold on to (B): There the author states that dog anxiety does not usually indicate coming earthquakes, and therefore argues against a necessary relationship between the two. It matches the original in all the major elements.

(A) is wrong because the conclusion argues *for* a correlation while the stimulus argues *against* a correlation between two occurrences.

(C) begins by saying that something sometimes doesn't create a certain result. Already it isn't parallel, since the evidence in the stimulus states that something doesn't *usually* create a certain result. "Many people" in (C) doesn't parallel the "most of the time" in the stimulus. Moreover, (C) argues about the efficacy of a program, whereas the original and correct choice (B) are concerned with the relation between two events.

(D) presents an entirely different argument, arguing that a claim isn't valid because there isn't enough evidence to support it. The original argument says that a claim isn't valid because two factors usually aren't related. The notion of "validity," like "efficacy" in (C), is one step removed from the gist of the terms in the original argument.

(E) argues against a causal relationship, but it doesn't parallel the original evidence because it mentions what "many" businesses do, not what "most" do. More centrally, the conclusion veers away from the evidence: The evidence suggests that decentralized operations often yield a profit, while the conclusion suggests that the two aren't directly related. In the original, both the evidence and conclusion argue against a causal relationship.

Remember:

- It's often difficult to remember several pieces of information in your head without getting them mixed up, especially while you're evaluating five new pieces of information. Don't hesitate to make notes if they'll help keep you on track.

21 **(D)** The argument begins by offering one route through which a student can gain a coveted membership to the Theta Delta Psi fraternity. For those aspirants who attended high school with a current member of the house and developed a strong social connection with that member before college, entrance into the fraternity is easy. People who didn't attend high school with a current member can't easily attain membership through this route, but we were never told that this was the only way to easily get into the fraternity. The author concludes that the unconnected individuals will have difficulty joining the fraternity, but that's only valid if the route the author describes is the only possible easy route. But the author never says that. (D) thus gets at the major point the author fails to consider in issuing her hasty conclusion: the possibility that there might be other ways to easily get into the frat.

(A) First of all, those who attended high school with fraternity members are not necessarily the same people who have forged strong social connections with them. So the "many" referred to here may not even be relevant to the argument. Secondly, even assuming these guys *are* good high school buddies of the members, the author argues only about what conditions make for easy entry into the frat, and need not consider the possibility that many high school classmates of the members would choose not to join.

(B) Associations with non-fraternity members are not relevant to the argument and fall outside of its scope. Additionally, this choice discusses the long-term benefits of such connections; we only care about entrance into the fraternity, not about lifelong happiness.

(C) The relative difficulty of building these connections has nothing to do with their necessity for membership. This choice also shares with (B) an interest in non-fraternity members, whom the author never mentions.

(E) is perfectly consistent with the author's argument, as it totally avoids the issue of the ease with which these "current members" got in. This choice falls outside of the author's scope, which is about the possibility of getting into the fraternity with ease, and we therefore can't fault the author for neglecting the possibility raised here.

Remember:

- Pay attention to author's topic and scope. Notice that answer choice (D) is the only one to address the difficulties of obtaining membership; most of the others fell outside of that scope.

22 **(C)** Again the stimulus begins with the author's conclusion, which basically opposes the continued enforcement of the new farm subsidy laws. The author stipulates the advantages of the laws, but nevertheless stresses their negative long-term results. The question stem directs you to determine the role of the second part of that second sentence, the part that discusses the negative effects of the laws. Before looking at the answer choices, it's possible to determine that this is evidence for the author's conclusion—it answers the question, "Why do you oppose the continuation of the laws?" Correct choice (C) goes one step further: It shows more specifically how the statement functions as evidence. The author discusses the negative effects in order to counter the positive effects, which enables him to support his conclusion that the laws should be ditched.

(A) Don't be thrown by the presence of the word "evidence" here. First, the author doesn't tell us that the positive effects of the laws have been used as evidence to support them. Secondly, the author doesn't use the negative effects to argue that the laws *haven't* enabled farmers to maintain their incomes or stabilized the market; he offers those as true, but stresses that the negative effects outweigh those benefits.

(B) commits the same error as (A). It distorts the passage by suggesting that the author contradicts and discredits the benefits of the laws, but he acknowledges that they have stabilized the agricultural market. The author doesn't disagree with that statement, but places it in the context of what he sees as the more serious negative effects.

(D) is way too strong: The author cannot "prove" that without the laws agricultural technology will remain a high priority, simply by stating that the laws discourage the need for competitive advancements. At most, the author suggests that in the absence of the laws, the opportunities for tech advances may improve, but that's far from "proving" anything.

(E) is half right and half wrong. It starts off on very strong footing by defining the statement as evidence, but it quickly takes a nosedive by making an irrelevant distinction between market stabilization and the development of competitive technology. The author does suggest that the negative effects of the laws outweigh the positive effects, and the author does mention these issues, but the author doesn't specifically rank one against the other. He shows that both of the negative effects outweigh both of the positive effects; he doesn't compare them piece by piece.

Remember:

- Be very careful when perusing the answer choices. Here, choices (A) and (E) use the word *evidence*, a sure temptation for those test takers who don't examine the answer choices careful-

ly. (C) doesn't use the term "evidence" but basically defines what evidence is in the context of the passage. Even when you have a prephrase, remember that you still need to look at the answer choices carefully and not jump at the first one containing a specific term you had in mind. The whole choice must pan out.

23 **(D)** Just because the organizers didn't give a complete list to everybody, it doesn't follow that they gave more complete lists to some people than others. You can use your formal logic skills on this one: We were originally told that if people are fully informed, then nobody has an advantage. It doesn't follow that if people are not fully informed, then somebody does have an advantage. That's a common formal logic error, and since the author commits it, the right answer choice will likely identify this as the flaw in the argument. (D) accomplishes this by stating what still could be true given the argument; everyone could have received the same incomplete list. In concluding categorically that some lucky participant has a leg up on the others, the author doesn't allow for the possibility stated in (D), and so (D) legitimately points to a flaw in the argument.

(A), (E) Probably the easiest way to eliminate (A) is to recognize that the author discusses who has the best *chance* of finding the diamond ring. The author never suggests that having a better chance of finding the ring means actually finding the ring. If the author had made such a suggestion, it would be a flaw, but since the author never did, it isn't. (E) takes this issue from another angle by suggesting that people with incomplete lists might still find the ring. The author never suggests otherwise, since again the author solely discusses who has the best chance of finding the ring, not who will therefore actually find it. So while (A) and (E) are indeed consistent with the stimulus, they don't point to a logical flaw in the argument.

(B) is close, but not fully there. Even if nobody receives a complete list (which is possible), there still exists the possibility that some people receive more complete lists than others, a situation that wouldn't by itself expose a flaw in the argument.

(C) just states one possible consequence of handing out different lists. The scenario in (C) is consistent with the facts in the stimulus, so it's okay on that count; but like (B), (C) still allows for the possibility that some person has a better chance than others, as the author maintains.

Remember:

• Reading critically means noticing small shifts in scope between the information in the passage and the focus of the choices. The author here is concerned with the participants' relative chances of finding the diamond. Choices like (A) and (E) that center around actually locating the ring are one step removed from this focus, so they aren't likely to point out a flaw in the logic.

24 **(E)** The stem tells us that the teacher will make some error in her response to the judges' decision, so we can read knowing that we'll see at least two arguments and that the teacher's will be flawed. The judges decided to disqualify Samuel's essay from the contest only because he broke one rule: He put his name on every page of the essay when the rules required that he put it only on the cover page. Samuel's teacher disagrees with the judges' conclusion, but in her argument she doesn't address the judges' reason for disqualifying

him. She completely ignores the judges' evidence, and introduces a new issue as her evidence: She believes that the personal problems in Samuel's life entitle him to have his essay considered in the contest. Her argument is flawed because she neglects to discuss the judges' actual reasoning and thus doesn't really address the judges' argument. While the emotional appeal may work on Oprah, in the world of argumentation it's a flaw to disagree with a conclusion without disputing the link between it and the evidence offered to justify it.

(A) The teacher *does* offer evidence when she explains that Samuel's essay deserves another chance because his parents got a divorce. Weak or irrelevant evidence is not the same as *no* evidence.

(B) The teacher doesn't make a causal argument. She thinks that personal considerations should override the judges' decision, but she isn't concerned with whether one thing causes another.

(C) is out because the teacher doesn't address *any part* of the judge's argument, which is the real flaw. She merely disputes their action on grounds entirely divorced (so to speak) from their argument in support of that action.

(D) again suggests that the teacher actually addresses the judges' evidence justifying their decision. She doesn't.

Remember:

• To see where two arguments differ, compare their conclusions and their evidence. Here, the conclusions were different and the evidence was different in the two arguments, so right off the bat you could eliminate (A), (C), and (D). The more structured you are in the way in

KAPLAN

which you compare two arguments, the easier it'll be to see where one differs or goes awry.

25 **(A)** The author begins by concluding that cross-training is more beneficial than single sport training for those who wish to improve their overall fitness. The author presents two pieces of evidence to support this opinion: First, cross-training develops a wider range of muscle groups. Second, cross-training increases phasic muscle fibers which burn more calories. Can you see any gaps, a.k.a., assumptions, between the conclusion and the evidence? The author assumes a link between developing a wide range of muscles/burning calories and overall fitness, so we can check to see if any answer choice strengthens the argument by asserting that assumption. We can stop at choice (A), since it establishes the connection between burning calories and overall fitness.

(B) The fact that athletic training *in general* is the best way to improve overall fitness doesn't strengthen an argument that one kind of athletic training (cross-training) is better for fitness than another (single-sport training).

(C) *Au contraire:* This would actually weaken the argument. Tonic muscle fibers are exercised by single sport training, so increasing their value would weaken the author's argument in support of cross-training.

(D) falls outside the scope: The author solely addresses which type of training works better to improve overall fitness in *healthy* individuals, so the danger of one type of training for those recovering from serious illness cannot have any bearing on the argument.

(E) On one hand, it would appear that (E) might actually weaken the argument. Single sport training targets slow-twitch muscle groups. If that exercise simultaneously exercises phasic muscle groups, then it provides one of the benefits of cross-training. Therefore, (E) would increase the value of single sport training in achieving overall fitness, which would run counter to the conclusion. But the fact that slow-twitch muscles contain many phasic muscle fibers doesn't necessarily mean that single-sport training would *increase* these fibers; that's still up in the air. So the best thing to say about (E) is that it is too ambiguous to have any effect on the argument at hand.

Remember:

• Whenever you see a central term in the conclusion that is unique to the conclusion, you're one step closer to prephrasing an author's assumption. Here, the conclusion contains a phrase—overall fitness—that shows up nowhere else in the argument. Since an assumption connects the evidence to the conclusion, it will make the evidence relevant to the dangling term in the conclusion. Specifically, developing a wide range of muscles and burning calories must lead to increased overall fitness if this argument is going to stand. Look out for terms unique to the conclusion as you search for assumptions that will help you to strengthen or weaken arguments.

Section IV: Reading Comp Explanations

PASSAGE 1—Frankenstein

Topic and Scope

Mary Shelley's novel *Frankenstein*; specifically, the great philosophical import of the book as compared to subsequent visual adaptations of it.

Purpose and Main Idea

The author's purpose in writing this passage is to demonstrate the complexities of Mary Shelley's *Frankenstein* and to argue for an appreciation of the novel on its own terms, apart from film adaptations of it. The main idea is that cinematic versions of the story of *Frankenstein* are actually based on a complex and compelling novel, the richness of which cannot be fully captured on film but nonetheless should not be overlooked.

Paragraph Structure

The first paragraph immediately contrasts the aura that the Frankenstein monster has taken on in popular culture with the thematic purpose known to serious readers of the book: to caution readers against the dangers of scientific hubris.

Paragraph 2 explains that the idea for the story came from a dream that Shelley had. The story is intended to refute the attacks of science on nature. It shows the negative consequences of not using our society's scientific capabilities responsibly.

In paragraph 3, we're told that the current appeal of the book is based on the many timeless themes that it contains, themes that have "only grown in importance" since its first publication. The full essence of the book cannot be captured by cinema, and the author hopes that film adaptations will not make people forget the book's richness.

The Big Picture

- As you read through each passage, focus on grasping the author's main idea. Once you've determined the main idea, whether it comes in the beginning or toward the end of the passage, lay out in your Roadmap how each paragraph works to support that main idea.
- Good critical readers pick up on particular phrases that provide clues to the author's attitude toward someone or something in the passage. Here, phrases like "one of the great philosophical and prophetic works," "timeless tale," and "genius of the original masterpiece" strongly suggest the author's great admiration for Shelley's novel, a notion that leads us directly toward the author's main idea.

The Questions

1 (D) This is a broad Inference question that asks us to choose the statement with which the author would most likely agree. Such an open-ended question is too difficult to prephrase, so the best approach is to evaluate the choices. Choice (D) fits well with paragraph 3: The author tells us that the enduring appeal of Shelley's book is attributable to the relevance of themes that she raises. The author would thus likely agree that a work's relevance in general increases when its elements resonate with its current audience.

(A) This choice is an exaggeration of the author's claim that visual adaptations have thus far not adequately captured the richness of Shelley's book. He believes this about film adaptations of *Frankenstein*, but doesn't apply his claim to every artistic work.

(B) This choice also misrepresents the author's argument. Shelley published her work anonymously because it was not acceptable at the time for women to write such "ghastly" stories. The author never suggests that *every* shocking work should be published anonymously.

(C), (E) Both of these choices distort elements of the passage. As for (C), the author never addresses works that receive no critical acclaim when they are written. We're not sure, in fact, how Shelley's work was originally received; all we know is that it was too risqué at first to attach her name to it. Further, the author never draws a relationship between the seriousness of a work and its ability to predict the future. Just because Shelley's work was both serious and prophetic doesn't allow us to infer the blanket statement in (E).

Remember:

• Wrong answer choices to Inference questions follow predictable patterns. Two of those patterns are represented in this question: extreme choices and distortions. Pay attention to the types of wrong answer choices that appear repeatedly and be prepared to avoid them on test day.

2 (E) This Explicit Text question is signaled by the words "according to the author," which lets us know that the answer will come straight from the text. A line reference is given to make our work easier. This question doesn't seem tricky, but it turns out that the science-nature clash is mentioned in another place after the notion is introduced in the second paragraph—namely, in paragraph 3. Here the author tells us that the science versus nature conflict increases the book's current relevance, an almost exact paraphrase of choice (E).

(A) This choice is half-right, half-wrong. The science-nature clash is one of the factors responsible for the current appeal of the book itself, not its film versions.

(B) This choice exaggerates the author's argument. The author merely suggests that movies are unable to portray the "science vs. nature" theme in all its "seriousness and complexity." He never argues that the movie versions don't portray this central theme at all.

(C) Here the issue of Shelley's anonymous publishing is again raised, but again, in an inappropriate context. We saw in choice (B) of the previous question that she published the book anonymously because society wasn't ready to accept women writing "ghastly" works. The science-nature clash itself doesn't seem to be the problem; the way in which that clash is *developed* (via the "ghastly" horror story device) is the reason she went underground for awhile.

(D) *Au contraire*: paragraph 3 tells us that the science-nature clash is one of the themes of the work that has "grown in importance" since Shelley's day.

Remember:

• Keep an open mind concerning line reference questions and avoid focusing too narrowly. The correct answer will likely involve reading beyond the referenced line and may often involve connecting the reference to other relevant parts of the text.

3 (B) If we read the portion of paragraph 3 that discusses the currently relevant themes of the work, we see that all of the choices are listed except for choice (B). If this *Frankenstein* example is any indica-

tion, we'd have to say that the author's complaint suggests the opposite of (B), namely that appreciation for artistic seriousness and complexity is waning.

(A) is covered by the phrase "technology as man's salvation."

(C) The theme in (C) comes up many times throughout the passage. Most relevant to this question is its appearance in the final paragraph as "science versus nature."

(D) is raised with "the role of visual appearance in society."

(E) is captured in the phrase "alienation of the outcast."

Remember:

- As always, watch the "EXCEPT" questions carefully. Be sure to choose the answer that is NOT implied or stated in the text. Sometimes the correct choice will simply be outside the scope. Other times, as is the case here, it may even go against the grain of the sentiments in the passage.

4 **(C)** This question addresses the author's attitude. To answer it, we should first determine whether the author's views on this issue are positive or negative. The wording of paragraph 1 gives us a clue: "endless Hollywood adaptations . . . campy TV shows . . ." Sounds like the author's not so hot on the visual adaptations, right? This is confirmed of course by the phrase in the final paragraph, "inability to capture in cinematic form the deep philosophical richness of the book." So this negativity kills (A) and (D) immediately. But just how negative are his views? Somewhat negative, although not drastic enough to say he displays "biting derision"

(B) or "unreserved condescension" (E). We're therefore left with the more moderate (C).

Remember:

- Use the Kaplan strategy to make "attitude/tone" questions easy to handle. Determine first whether the author's views are positive, negative, or neutral—and then eliminate all of the choices that don't conform to the general category you choose. If you determine the views are somewhat negative, as is the case here, then look to cross off any choices that contain any positivity. Then weed out any exaggerations or choices that are too weak and you should be left with the correct answer.

5 **(A)** This question tests whether you understand one part of the passage in the context of the overall argument. Why does the author mention Hollywood film adaptations early on in paragraph 1? As we see from paragraph 3, he will argue eventually that film versions can't capture the depth of Shelley's original work. Citing film versions in paragraph 1 is therefore a means of setting up what will be the main idea, or as (A) describes it, the "basis of the author's central concern." The author certainly does return to this concept when developing the main idea in paragraph 3, so that part of the choice is accurate. But does the whole choice work? Is the example of film adaptations provided as a "contrast" as choice (A) would have it? Yes—the "endless" Hollywood adaptations, along with the other pop culture manifestations, are meant to stand in contrast to the philosophical and prophetic cautionary tale that spawned them. This contrast will build in paragraph 3 when it indeed "resurfaces" as the basis of the author's concern that the visual forms may one day eclipse the genius of the original work.

(B) The author never raises a debate, much less try to settle one.

(C) The author does support Shelley's work, but doesn't deal with criticisms of it. No such criticisms appear in the passage.

(D) *Au contraire*. The author would not see film adaptations as an "inevitable successor" to literature. In fact, he believes that in this particular case, film cannot portray the literary work effectively.

(E) This choice is both too general and exaggerated. The author doesn't describe Hollywood adaptations as part of a larger "artistic movement." Neither does he make the sweeping claim that film can *never* capture literary works well. He just doesn't believe that film versions of *Frankenstein* do justice to the original book.

Remember:

• Reading with a critical eye toward purpose and structure will always pay off on the Reading Comp section. When you encounter new characters or material, ask yourself, "Why are they here? What function do they serve?" When you come to a question like this one, hopefully you can prephrase an answer or at least eliminate a handful of wrong choices based on your initial understanding of the purpose of each element of the passage.

6 **(A)** This question asks us for the author's purpose in writing the passage, so think back about what you've been focusing on all along. We've seen how the author's purpose is to lay out the complexities of Shelley's work and to argue that it should be appreciated on its own terms; that the

film versions should not overshadow the original story. The closest we get to this prephrase is found choice (A), which is a bit more general than our prephrase, but hits closest to the mark.

(B), (E) Too broad. The problem with (B) is that the author does not discuss "works of art" in general, but rather one work in particular. Similarly, with (E), the author does not pay tribute to the "art form" of literature in general—instead, he is praising one specific work of literature. Moreover, according to the author this work has not yet *been* overshadowed, but rather is *in danger* of being overshadowed by its visual adaptations.

(C) Too narrow. The author does discuss how Shelley's novel originated, but this is only a small part of what he does in the text.

(D) Be careful here: This is the argument that Shelley makes in her novel, not the argument made by the author in the passage as a whole.

Remember:

• Choices like (D) here reinforce why we must be careful to distinguish between the various views presented in a passage. Here we have an author of a passage presenting the views expressed by an author described in the passage. Make sure to keep the various views straight, and you won't be tricked up by a choice like (D) above.

• When answering Global LSAT Reading Comp questions, such as those pertaining to the author's purpose or Main Idea, be on the lookout for choices that are overly broad or too narrow. The correct answer to a Global question will match the author's scope in the passage and will reflect the point of the passage as a whole—not just one part of it.

PASSAGE 2—Weber and Objectivity

Topic and Scope
Max Weber's views on objectivity; specifically, the degree to which Weber upholds a strict concept of objectivity in his work.

Purpose and Main Idea
The author's purpose is to make an argument regarding how Weber views the concept of objectivity and employs it in his writing. The main idea is that Weber does not believe in strict objectivity across-the-board, and that his views on objectivity are therefore more complex than they are traditionally portrayed.

Paragraph Structure
The first paragraph of this passage presents the "traditional" or conventional explanation of Weber's views: Scholars normally see him as upholding a strict concept of objectivity in his work. Whenever we're presented with a traditional view in the opening paragraph, it's a good bet that the author will counter or refute that view in what's to follow. This paragraph is no exception—sure enough, the author quickly counters the traditional interpretation by asserting that Weber's views are "more complicated" than the traditional view would have it.

Given this starting point, we might expect the following paragraphs to show us how and why Weber's views are complicated. This is exactly what happens. Paragraph 2 concedes that in certain respects, Weber does believe in the possibility of strict objectivity: We see it in his views on the nature of reality. When it comes to questions of truth, Weber does believe that a value-neutral reality exists.

In paragraph 3, however, the complexities of Weber's views are introduced. Here the author shows that Weber doesn't think our knowledge of reality can be totally objective. This is because knowledge is rooted in the assumptions and perspectives of those who investigate reality—thus, some subjective bias enters in.

Paragraph 4 shows that Weber deviates most from strict objectivity on questions concerning ethics. When people use knowledge to decide how to behave, Weber thinks they should make their decisions subjectively, according to their own personal biases. So as the passage progresses, so does Weber's deviation from the strict concept of objectivity "traditionally" ascribed to him.

The Big Picture
- LSAT Reading Comp passages very often begin with an accepted view and then present an opposing view. When a passage starts out with a "traditional" perspective, be on the lookout for an opposing argument to come.
- If a passage starts out with a traditional view and provides an opposing argument, it is likely that the rest of the passage will develop that opposing argument. As you read through this type of argumentative passage, look for specific evidence that the author uses to support his or her counterview.

The Questions
7 **(D)** This question asks us for the main idea of the passage, and in this case the author presents an argument against a traditional view. Her opposing argument, or main idea, is laid out at the end of the first paragraph, where she tells us that Weber's views on objectivity are "more complicated than the traditional interpretation would have us believe." Choice (D) sums this up nicely.

(A) This choice goes beyond the scope of the passage. Nowhere are other theories of objectivity discussed—the passage focuses only on Weber's views.

(B) This choice contradicts what is stated in the passage. Paragraph 2 shows us that Weber upholds a strictly objective view concerning the nature of reality; he believes in the existence of absolute truth. It is in our attempt to *investigate* objective reality that Weber believes subjectivity creeps in.

(C), (E) Both of these choices are distortions of information in the passage. While the author argues that Weber's views on objectivity are complex, she never claims that these views are not clearly presented (C). Neither does she go so far as to claim that they are inconsistent (E).

Remember:

- If you focus on the author's purpose and main idea as you read, this type of question should be a snap. If you relate all of the content in the passage to the main idea as you read, you should be able to prephrase answers to questions like this one accurately.

8 **(A)** It's difficult to prephrase an answer to such an open-ended Inference question as this, so we must proceed to the choices to see which view can be most readily ascribed to Weber. Luckily, we don't have to look far: (A) presents a good summary of Weber's views on scientific knowledge as presented in paragraph 3. Here we learn that Weber believes that knowledge cannot be totally objective because it is influenced by the assumptions and perspectives of the particular scientific community involved in the investigation of reality.

(B) and (E) misrepresent Weber's use of "ideal types." Ideal types are presented in paragraph 2 as constructs that Weber believes can help scientists investigate reality, not their own biases regarding reality (B). And (E) goes way too far: Just because Weber believes that ideal types can be used to help the scientist investigate objective reality, that's far from saying that he believes this is "the *only* reliable method" possible.

(C) In paragraph 4 we're told that Weber believes that teachers should refrain from imposing their views on students *period*—regardless of how capable those students are.

(D) The fact that Weber believes that the *perception* of objective reality must be tinged by subjectivity doesn't mean that Weber finds the notion of objective reality itself "misleading"—on the contrary, paragraph 2 tells us that Weber *does* believe in the existence of strict objective reality.

Remember:

- Inference questions are usually not easy to prephrase, so the best approach to these questions is to quickly evaluate each answer choice. A good Roadmap can help you determine whether a given choice fits with the ideas in the passage.

9 **(B)** This question would have been a good one to prephrase, particularly if you looked for the author's purpose and main idea as you read the passage. Since this passage focuses only on Weber, the correct answer will indicate that one author's views are discussed. (B) throws in the key main idea word "complexities," describing the author's purpose succinctly.

(A), (C) It can be said that the author enters into a debate by countering the traditional view of

Weber's scholarship, but that's not the same as "resolving" a debate. If (A) were the intended right answer, two independent views would have to be presented, with the author choosing one over the other. Similarly, she does not "reconcile" opposing perspectives (C)—she merely develops her own position regarding Weber's views.

(D) The author does not argue against Weber's perspective but rather describes it for the reader.

(E) The author presents Weber's views, but does not *test* them. Furthermore, Weber's views represent his position on objectivity, but they do not take the form of a formal hypothesis.

Remember:

• Reading for topic, scope, and purpose has many benefits. Not only does it allow you to gain a better grasp of the passage overall—it can also lead to quick points if you're handed a straightforward Global question like this one.

10 **(C)** The phrase "according to the passage" here clues us in that this is an Explicit Text question; we can thus expect the answer to draw on a specific detail from the passage. Which paragraph discusses how individuals should use knowledge to guide their actions? Exactly—paragraph 4. A good Roadmap would have quickly led you to this part of the passage, and the phrase "free to choose how he or she acts upon the reality discovered by science" is the one that best captures the gist of Weber's position regarding the uses of scientific knowledge. Choice (C) stands out as the best paraphrase of this.

(A) distorts the author's meaning in the passage. Paragraph 4 tells us that teachers should help

students account for the meaning of their own conduct. It does not tell us that students should be restricted from making decisions if they cannot account for the meaning of their conduct.

(B) According to paragraph 4, Weber believes that individuals should use scientific knowledge in making decisions about action, not that they should distrust it.

(D) *Au contraire*. We are told that Weber believed that teachers should not guide their students' actions, but should allow students to make their own decisions.

(E) also goes against the grain of the passage. "Weber believes that individuals must make their own decisions. . ." suggests that teachers should *not* follow the lead of their students but should also act on knowledge independently when determining their own course of action.

Remember:

• Explicit Text questions can often be answered by referring back to the part of the passage that contains the detail in question. If you must quickly reread the relevant parts of the paragraph to make your selection, do so.

11 **(E)** Next up we're asked for the passage structure, and hopefully your work on the passage so far will help you prephrase an answer, or at least quickly eliminate choices that stray beyond your Roadmap. We know from our answer to question 9 that only one author's views (Weber's) are presented here, and our Roadmap tells us that different aspects of these views are described in each paragraph. This fits with the gist of choice (E): The "interpretation" expands on the traditional position regarding Weber's view of objectivity, and the author certainly does support this interpretation throughout the passage with specific references to Weber's views and teachings.

(A), (B) The author spends her time in this passage developing Weber's views. She does not reject his views as (A) indicates; nor does she first criticize these views as (B) states.

(C) *Au contraire.* As we saw with choice (A), the author does not negate Weber's views. Instead, she supports them.

(D) This choice tries the same trick we saw in question 9. We know that no hypothesis is presented here and that no testing is accomplished, so we can reject this choice.

Remember:

- The choices in "passage structure" questions are often phrased in general terms. The wrong answer choices will contain terms such as "reject" and "criticize" that violate the spirit of the passage, and others such as "hypothesis" and "empirical testing" that sound nice and official but don't apply to the passage at all. Put the choices through their paces before settling on the one you prefer.

12 **(A)** Our Roadmap can again come in handy here by helping us locate the assertion that "knowledge of reality cannot be totally objective." A quick review shows us that this point is raised in paragraph 3, where the author discusses scientific knowledge. This Explicit Text question asks for evidence specifically mentioned in the passage that supports the assertion in the stem, and again we return to the same idea that we've discussed previously: The interpretation of objective reality is biased by underlying assumptions.

(B) This choice reflects the opposite of what is stated in the passage. The author claims that Weber believes that methods of investigation can never be strictly objective, by their very nature.

(C), (D) These choices present ideas raised in the passage, but neither of these statements reflects evidence for the assertion in question. Ideal types are discussed in the passage, but only in paragraph 2. We're looking for evidence given in paragraph 3. The definition of "objective truth" is also raised in paragraph 2, but not as evidence for the point that knowledge can't be objective.

(E) once again plays off the distinction between objective reality and the *knowledge* of objective reality. Weber *does* believe in the concept of strict objectivity, so to say that objective reality is "illusory" goes against the grain of the passage, not to mention trying to posit it as evidence for something else in the passage.

Remember:

- When asked about specific details from the text, make sure to locate the part of the text from which the relevant details will be drawn. Then stick strictly to the author's argument. If you're asked for evidence, choose only the choice that provides support for the point or conclusion in question. Avoid choices taken from other parts of the text.

13 **(C)** Why would the author have given us the "traditional" interpretation of Weber's view? To let us know which view she was reacting against—to provide an introduction into her opposing interpretation of his views. Choice (C) describes this reason well.

(A) This choice is an exaggeration. Although the author rejects the traditional view, it would be going too far to say that she "dismiss[es] the relevance of all previous scholarship" on Weber.

(B) again distorts the author's purpose. She does not argue that objectivity has been historically misunderstood in general, but rather that Weber's views on objectivity have been misunderstood.

(D), (E) These choices state the opposite of the author's reason for presenting the traditional view. She does not use it to develop critics' views of Weber, but rather her own interpretation. Neither does she attempt to vindicate the traditional view; on the contrary, she refutes it.

Remember:

- Questions that end with the words "in order to" require you to look for how something functions to support the author's overall argument or purpose in the passage. When you're asked why an author includes something, think about the entire passage. What role is played by the part in question? How does it contribute to the passage? Some parts of the text may provide support or evidence; others may lay out the author's conclusions. Still others may serve as introductions or as background information. Focus on how the part in question fits within the whole.

PASSAGE 3—Murphy's Law

Topic and Scope
Morality; specifically, the pros and cons of Liam Murphy's views on morality.

Purpose and Main Idea
The purpose of the passage is to assess the value of Murphy's view. The main idea is that Murphy's argument may lack motivating force for those who don't have an inner sense of morality, but it also avoids having to justify the content of particular moral principles and is more practical than traditional views.

Paragraph Structure
Paragraph 1 introduces us to the "overdemandingness" problem in moral philosophy. If we define morality as requiring us to always act to produce the best circumstances, then morality may seem to ask too much of people. Paragraph 2 tells us that some people reject the idea that morality is overdemanding. The philosopher Liam Murphy, however, takes the "overdemandingness" problem seriously.

In paragraph 3, Murphy's philosophy is described. Murphy doesn't give people a set of firm beliefs or particular moral principles. Instead, he argues that each person should make moral decisions based first upon his or her own inner sense of right and wrong. If a person's inner sense of right and wrong is confused, the person can then use his or her reason to make the final decision.

Paragraph 4 lists the disadvantages of Murphy's view. The main disadvantage is that people who have no moral foundation aren't likely to get one through his approach. Paragraph 5 then gives the advantages of Murphy's perspective. Murphy's view starts with the individual's own inner sense of morality, so it doesn't have to go through the difficult task of justifying specific moral principles. This view ends up being more practical than traditional approaches.

The Big Picture
- Don't be intimidated by long, philosophical passages! They're best handled just like any

other passage. Invest your time in building a clear Roadmap and determining topic, scope, purpose, and main idea. Your time will pay off by increasing your grasp of the passage, thus producing more points.

- Remember that in certain Reading Comp passages, some questions can actually help you answer other questions on the passage. Sometimes you'll research an answer for one question that will give you information for a later question. In addition, some questions actually test your knowledge of the same concepts. Use this to your advantage on longer passages.

The Questions

14 **(E)** Here's a case where the first question of the set is a good question to answer first. This overall purpose question is a good one to prephrase based on your Roadmap. The author's purpose, which we determined earlier, is "to assess the value of Murphy's view." This answer is summed up well in choice (E), since the author is evaluating the merits of Murphy's model of ethical inquiry.

(A) Too narrow. The author does discuss the disadvantages of Murphy's view, but only in one paragraph of the passage. The answer to a primary purpose question must apply to the entire passage, not just one part.

(B), (C) Both of these choices are incorrect because they suggest that two views are addressed in the passage. Choice (B) suggests that two theories are discussed, while choice (C) suggests that two schools of thought are reviewed. In fact, only one view—Murphy's—is developed in the passage.

(D) The author does not pose a solution to an ethical problem.

Remember:

- Prephrasing is a good strategy for answering questions rapidly and correctly. If you can prephrase an answer, do so before looking at the answer choices. A quick scan of the choices will tell you whether your prephrase is on target.

15 **(B)** Here we're asked to draw an inference, as is denoted by the word "suggests." This Inference question is too broad to prephrase, so it's best to evaluate each answer choice, eliminating obviously incorrect choices. Each answer choice describes what might happen if Murphy's philosophy is applied to the situations of two different groups. Which outcome is more likely, based on the passage? We're told in paragraph 3 that Murphy's view starts with individuals' innate sense of right and wrong. We're also told in paragraph 4 that people's moral viewpoints might not converge. Thus, answer choice (B) is the most likely outcome: It's possible that the two groups could start with entirely different innate senses of right and wrong, and therefore come out with principles that radically differ. It's also possible that the groups could come out with principles that were relatively similar. This doesn't negate answer (B), however. Depending on how similar the groups' starting views are, their principles could either be alike or very different.

(A) If two groups were using the approach, it's possible that one group might come up with a resolution while the other did not—but there's no reason to believe that this necessarily would be the case.

(C) This choice misrepresents the author's argument. Murphy's view could be applied to two different groups regardless of what views those groups held. Its outcome in each case, however, would depend on the group's particular beliefs. It is true that the outcomes would be similar only if the groups held similar views. But the philosophy itself could be applied to any groups, regardless of whether they shared the same beliefs.

(D) This choice is beyond the scope of the author's argument. The author never discusses using Murphy's view to reconcile difference between groups. He merely describes how the view can be used to help individuals determine moral behavior.

(E) is a bit tricky. Again, as with choice (A) above, we must pay attention to the statement's wording. It's possible that Murphy's philosophy could be applied to two groups, and that neither group would use the philosophy effectively to determine a course of action for their group. This would be the case if both groups had no moral sense to begin with. This type of outcome is only possible, however—it's not certain.

Remember:

• When choosing an answer about potential outcomes, be careful to scrutinize the verbs in each answer choice. In LSAT Reading Comp, there is a significant difference between stating that something would happen and stating that something could happen. Pay attention to the difference as you choose your answer.

16 (D) This Inference question deals with the same issue as the previous question: What happens when you apply Murphy's philosophy to two different groups? We know from question 15 that Murphy's philosophy can be applied to differ-

ent groups, but that it would produce the same outcome for both only if both groups started with the same moral foundation. Another way of putting this is to say that two groups could apply Murphy's philosophy to their problems, but they would only come up with the same moral principles of action if they both started with the same beliefs. Therefore, a principle derived by one group would only apply to another group if the second group shared the same beliefs as the first.

(A) This choice is beyond the scope of the passage. Nowhere does the author discuss individuals sharing recommendations regarding Murphy's principles. The author tells us instead that principles are developed by first starting with individuals' own sense of right and wrong (as opposed to recommendations from others).

(B), (C), and (E) *Au contraire.* Each of these choices gives an answer that conflicts with the author's argument. If the moral viewpoints of the two groups did not converge, as (B) states, then the principle derived by one group might not apply to the other group at all. With (C), if the members of the second group had no firmly held beliefs, a principle developed using Murphy's view would be difficult to apply to them. Finally, if (E) were true, it would be difficult to even come up with the first group's principle—much less apply it to another group.

Remember:

• LSAT Reading Comp questions aren't always unique. Often one question will test the same concept as a another question in the set. When this occurs, use your previous work to help you answer the second question. This will save you time and increase your score.

17

(B) Here we are given a question that starts out with the words "according to the passage." That lets us know that we're being asked for specific detail from the passage—a good bet for a question to answer early on in the set. Where does the passage mention individuals who have no moral sense? In paragraph 4, where it tells us that individuals without moral beliefs would have no justification for using Murphy's system. This point describes one disadvantage of Murphy's approach, as we're told with answer (B).

(A) *Au contraire*. The existence of individuals without moral beliefs provides one reason for refuting Murphy's views. These individuals might not follow Murphy's views at all.

(C) This choice misrepresents the author's argument. The author does tell us that reason is necessary when people's beliefs conflict. But he tells us this in paragraph 3, as he's describing Murphy's approach. The issue of individuals without moral beliefs is not raised until the following paragraph, in the discussion of the philosophy's disadvantages.

(D) Again, this choice misrepresents the author's argument. The author does mention that traditional approaches might not be any more influential for some people than Murphy's approach would be. But he states this in paragraph 5, when discussing the advantages of Murphy's view. He doesn't raise the issue of people without moral beliefs to prove this point.

(E) This choice is beyond the scope of the argument. The author never discusses the consequences of the "overdemandingness" problem. He merely describes this problem for us.

Remember:

- Watch out for choices that slap together two separate parts of the passage, comparing them in a way that the author doesn't.
- Don't let the test dictate the order in which you'll do the questions. Scan the question set before you begin answering, and knock the easier questions out of the way first. This will help ensure that you score every point that you possibly can.

18

(B) This question asks us for an inference regarding Murphy's views (as distinct from the author's views). We can look back to the text to help us with the answer. Where is the issue of "reason" discussed? In paragraph 3, we're told that a person can use reason to determine moral principles if his or her fundamental beliefs are conflicting or confused. This would be a good prephrase to approach the answer choices with. As it turns out, choice (B) reflects the prephrase exactly.

(A), (C) The issue of some beliefs superseding others is not discussed in the passage. Neither is the issue of a belief system conflicting with an ethical principle.

(D) *Au contraire*. An individual who had no moral sense would not be able to apply Murphy's philosophy because he would lack an innate sense of right and wrong, which is Murphy's starting point.

(E) This answer choice explains the meaning of the overdemandingness problem, discussed in paragraphs 1 and 2. Murphy's philosophy responds to this problem in general—but the problem itself doesn't explain when reason should be used.

Remember:

- Prephrasing doesn't work with most Inference questions, but it can help with some. If an Inference question is phrased specifically and you can posit a reasonable prephrase, it's worth a scan of the answer choices to see if your prephrase shows up. If not, you can always rule out choices by elimination.

19 (A) This Application question requires us to take information from the passage and apply it to a situation not presented in the passage. We know from paragraph 3 that the use of Murphy's philosophy requires two steps: first, the person or group starts with innate beliefs about right or wrong and then uses reason if necessary to derive moral principles. The first step for the school board, then, is reflected in (A): Members would have to determine their fundamental beliefs regarding the dress code issue.

(B) and (D) are irrelevant to the application of Murphy's philosophy. The author never states that analysis of other situations or historical precedents is necessary for determining moral principles with Murphy's view.

(C) Since the school board members are deciding the policy, according to Murphy they would need to start with their own beliefs—not those of the students.

(E) This choice misrepresents the author's argument. In paragraph 3 the author is merely comparing Murphy to legal scholars who interpret the Constitution. He doesn't imply that people using Murphy's view must also consult the Constitution.

Remember:

- Application questions require you to apply ideas from the passage to alternative scenarios not raised in the passage. Make sure that the answer choice fits within the scope of the author's argument and can reasonably be deduced from the text.

20 (C) A good Roadmap can help us answer this efficiently. What does the author discuss in paragraph 5? We might prephrase here that he presents the pros of Murphy's view. A quick scan of the answer choices reveals the credited answer: (C) matches our prephrase almost exactly.

(A) This idea is not discussed in the passage. Murphy doesn't give us any means of determining the best interpretation of beliefs—at least not in what we're told here.

(B) The "overdemandingness" issue is discussed in paragraph 1.

(D) The author does not address two schools of thought. This point is raised in the explanations for question 14, answers (B) and (C).

(E) This idea is addressed in paragraph 3, where Murphy's views are summarized.

Remember:

- We can't emphasize section management too emphatically! This question again demonstrates why it's vital to choose your own order for answering the questions. Logic questions are good candidates for prephrasing, thanks to the power of the Roadmap. They should be tackled early to boost your score.

KAPLAN

21 **(D)** Which one of the answer choices would Murphy be likely to agree with? There's no way to form a prephrase here, so on to the choices:

(A) *Au contraire*. People who argue *from* firmly held beliefs would be following Murphy's approach, not a traditional approach.

(B) Again, *au contraire*. Paragraph 5 tells us that these sorts of works have value—they just aren't as practical as Murphy's approach.

(C) This choice exaggerates the author's argument. In paragraph 4, we're only told that people who lack moral sense won't be able to apply the particular approach developed by Murphy. However, they might still have contributions to make to ethical debates. We can't be sure from the passage that they would not contribute anything.

(D) is the winner. In the last paragraph of the passage, the author tells us that people who reject Murphy's premises aren't likely to accept traditional views either. What kind of people would reject Murphy's views? Moral skeptics, or those who have no moral sense at all, according to paragraph 3. So (D) provides the best answer choice here.

(E) We cannot determine whether the author himself believes that "overdemandingness" is a serious problem for traditional philosophy. We're only told that some scholars think it's not a serious problem, and that Murphy does take it seriously. The author's tone in the passage implies that he sides with Murphy—but we don't have enough information to be sure. So this statement is either definitely incorrect or too poorly supported to evaluate. Either way, it gets ruled out.

Remember:

- Know your strengths and weaknesses when answering Reading Comp questions. This will help you determine which questions to answer last in the set. If Inference questions are a weak point, you might have left this question until last or even skipped it altogether. Don't be afraid to skip questions that look like they'll take a long time. You're better off concentrating your efforts on the questions that are likely to gain you points.

Passage 4—Thermocline

Topic and Scope
Lake stratification; specifically, the process and effects of freshwater lake stratification.

Purpose and Main Idea
The author's purpose is to explore the cyclical process of lake stratification and its effects on lake ecology. The main idea is that seasonal temperature differences within lake water cause the cyclical formation of water layers of various temperatures separated by the thermocline, which prevents oxygen from reaching the colder, deeper lake waters and periodically causes redistribution of fish within the lake.

Paragraph Structure
Paragraph 1 introduces the thermocline phenomenon and describes its development using the example of freshwater lakes in the southern United States. The description of the cycle that the author will describe throughout the passage begins at the end of the paragraph with info about late winter, when lake water temperatures are uniform and fish species thrive at all depths of the lake.

Paragraph 2 describes the changes that occur in early spring: The water on the surface of the lake becomes warmer and lighter than the water below it. This warm water expands and forms a layer over the water below.

Paragraph 3 describes the development and results of the thermocline. In summer, the warm water on top of the lake becomes distinctly separated from the colder water below it by the thermocline, a temperature gradient that acts as a boundary between the two parts of the lake. The thermocline boundary prevents oxygen from reaching the lower depths of the lake, and this causes fish to swim up to the warmer surface of the lake to survive.

The final paragraph describes the reversal of the cycle. In fall, the water at the surface above the thermocline cools and becomes heavier than the water below the thermocline. This allows oxygen to plunge to the depths of the lake, and the lake reaches equilibrium again by early winter.

The Big Picture

- Science passages often present large amounts of detail that can bog down the unsavvy test taker. Skip this detail until you're asked a specific question on it. Instead, concentrate on the author's purpose and main idea, and on how the passage is structured. This will help you to know where to look in the passage should an Explicit Text question require you to do so.
- Don't spend time rereading the passage during your first run through. Focus on the most important points raised in each paragraph. This will help you create a good Roadmap, which will be your best tool for navigating through the question set.

The Questions

22 **(E)** This Inference question asks about the subject of dissolved oxygen, which is raised many times in the passage. It's not easy here to pinpoint exactly which part of the passage we should review to answer this question, so the best tactic is to evaluate the answer choices, returning to the passage for verification when necessary. We're told in paragraph 1 that wave action stirs oxygen into the water, making (E) the best inference in this set.

(A) We aren't given information relating water temperature to oxygen capacity. True, during certain months the thermocline prevents oxygen from reaching the cooler depths, but for all we know, cold water can hold just as much dissolved oxygen as warm water, given the chance.

(B) *Au contraire:* The passage tells us in paragraph 1 that during late winter, oxygen is found plentifully throughout all of a lake's water levels.

(C) The only thing we're told about ice formation is that ice melts in February and March, which is not nearly enough information to allow us to infer the statement in (C).

(D) This choice misrepresents the author's claim in paragraph 3. We're told that fish and zooplankton consume oxygen below the surface, but not that they're the *only* organisms that do so.

Remember:

- If you're not sure where to look back for information in the passage, move to the answer choices and allow them to guide you back to the relevant sections. If you can kill a choice on sight, fine, but it's usually worth quickly verifying that a choice is bogus, especially in such a detail-heavy passage like this one.

23 **(B)** Next up is a Global question concerned with the organization of the passage. Hopefully, in creating your mental Roadmap you took the time to focus on the passage's structure; if so, a prephrase was certainly in order. Even though the details may be a bit cumbersome, the overall structure isn't that complex, and (B) provides a good summary of this structure: A "remarkable property" (the unwillingness of different temperature water to mix) leads to a process (the formation of the thermocline) which has some effects (determining the supply of oxygen and forcing the species of lakes to behave in certain ways).

(A) and (D) can be ruled out quickly because the author describes a property and a related phenomenon, not a particular problem or solutions.

(C) sounds plausible at first, but fails in the end. The "benefits" of the thermocline aren't related here.

(E) Events from winter, spring, summer and fall are related in that order, so presumably it's okay to say that a "chronology is described," if only in the loose sense of the word. As in (C), the main problem comes at the end—no "predictions" are made. Describing results or effects of a process is not the same as making predictions.

Remember:

- Beware of half-right, half-wrong choices like (C)—and to a lesser extent, (E)—here. Some choices start off pretty well, but go awry towards the end. This reinforces the necessity to read and pay careful attention to the entire answer choice.

24 **(E)** This question ends with the words "in order to," which indicates a Logic question: How does the author's statement function in the context of the section in which it appears? In this case, why does the author mention that 50-degree water is lighter than 40-degree water? In general, he's attempting to explain the process of lake stratification—you might have prephrased this answer and scanned the choices for it. In fact, choice (E) comes pretty close: The author mentions the difference to help the reader better understand his explanation of a particular step in the lake stratification process—the step in which a layer of warmer water forms over a layer of cooler water.

If you weren't able to prephrase this answer, you needed to evaluate the answer choices to eliminate the ones that *don't* represent the purpose of this detail:

(A) can be ruled out quickly, because the author isn't attempting to refute any theories.

(B) *Au contraire*. The author explains in paragraph 2 why warmer water forms layers *on top of* colder water.

(C) is tricky because the author certainly does suggest that the number of fish dispersed through different layers of lakes is related to the thermocline, but showing this is not the reason the author included the bit about the 50-degree and 40-degree water. The comparison between these water temperatures doesn't prove anything, and besides, the information about the thermocline's effect on fish placement comes later.

(D) Zooplankton appear even later than the issue raised in (C), and is even further removed from the purpose of the author's comparison between 50-degree and 40-degree water.

Remember:

- In Logic questions, you're asked to determine the function of a specific detail in the context of a paragraph, or sometimes the function of an entire paragraph in the context of the passage as a whole. In the former case, pay strict attention to the lines surrounding the detail, and be wary of choices that bring up points that appear in much more distant sections of the passage.

25 **(A)** Here we have another Inference question, denoted by the word "suggests." What does the author suggest about the effects of temperature stratification? The most significant effect he discusses is how temperature stratification causes fishes to move to the top layer of lakes during the summer. This might be pertinent for fisheries, as choice (A) indicates.

(B) *Au contraire*, the passage shows that the effects of temperature stratification can be predicted to some degree, at least in terms of the general effect on lake ecology. It also shows that the general timing of these effects can be predicted as well. (Note that this doesn't conflict with the explanations above to question 23, choice (E), in which we say that the author doesn't make predictions. Suggesting that due to a stable process, results can be predicted is not the same as saying, from a passage structure point of view, that the author *himself* makes predictions.)

(C) and (E) exaggerate the author's claims in the passage. Paragraph 1 states that the thermocline plays an "important role" in lake ecology, but we don't know if it is the *most* important factor (C). It is also clear that temperature stratification affects southern U.S. lakes, but these effects aren't compared to those of other lakes,

so we can't determine the relative severity of the effects (E).

(D) is outside the scope of the argument. The age of lakes is never brought up in the author's discussion, nor is anything implied regarding the way lake age may affect the stratification process described.

Remember:

- Open-ended Inference questions like this one require that we evaluate the answer choices—there isn't enough information in the question stem to attempt a prephrase.
- Remember that deductions must be reasonably inferred from what the author has stated in the passage. The correct choice will stick closely to the scope of the author's argument and won't include exaggerated or extreme ideas.

26 **(C)** This Explicit Text question requires us to look for something that was NOT mentioned in the passage—a bit harder than the traditional detail question. Fortunately, the wrong answers are all stated in the passage fairly clearly. (C) is the only choice that's not mentioned; in fact, it even tends to contradict the passage: Paragraph 3 tells us that the depth of the thermocline fluctuates with temperature and winds, so we can't be sure when the depth is at its maximum.

All of the other answer choices repeat information from the passage. Paragraph 3 tells us that fish move above the thermocline in the summer, so this eliminates (A). We're told in paragraph 1 that water temperatures are uniform in late winter, eliminating (B). Paragraph 3 helps us eliminate (D), because it states that the thermocline shuts off the supply of oxygen to the lower depths. Finally, choice (E) can be eliminated by paragraph 4, which describes how the turnover brings oxygen to deeper, stagnant water.

Remember:

- Don't get caught off guard by questions containing the word NOT. Be careful to look for that which is NOT stated in the text—don't make the mistake of falling for an incorrect choice that IS stated in the text.

27 (D) This question is a basic Global question, albeit worded slightly differently than usual. The stem itself gives away the fact that the author's purpose is "to discuss" something, so there's no need to choose between various verbs (discuss, argue, refute, etcetera) —but what is he interested in discussing? The author's main concern should be firmly planted in your mind by now; he's simply interested in discussing the process and effects of lake stratification. Choice (D) comes very close to this prephrase, merely substituting "seasonal warming and cooling of water" for the process described.

(A) and (E) both reverse the direction of causality in the author's discussion. The author is interested in how the thermocline affects lake ecology, not vice versa, as in (A). Similarly, he shows how changing water temperatures, by means of the thermocline, affect oxygen levels—not the other way around, as (E) would have it.

(B) and (C) go beyond the argument's scope. The author mentions "stagnant" water in paragraph 4, but does not focus on water purity throughout the passage. And the phenomenon of overfishing, if it exists, is not discussed.

Remember:

- Sometimes, as is the case here, wrong answer choices use the right terminology but describe erroneous cause-and-effect relationships. If you're the least bit unsure about a relationship between two elements mentioned in the text, by all means take a quick look back. But never simply pick a choice because its terms are familiar.

PRACTICE TEST THREE

Remove or photocopy this answer sheet and use it to complete Practice Test Three.
See the answer key immediately following the test to correct your answers when you're finished.
Then use the score converter on pages 155 and 156 to calculate your score and percentile rank.

Start with number 1 for each new section. If a section has fewer questions than answer spaces, leave the extra spaces blank.

SECTION 1	SECTION 2	SECTION 3	SECTION 4
1 Ⓐ Ⓑ Ⓒ Ⓓ Ⓔ	1 Ⓐ Ⓑ Ⓒ Ⓓ Ⓔ	1 Ⓐ Ⓑ Ⓒ Ⓓ Ⓔ	1 Ⓐ Ⓑ Ⓒ Ⓓ Ⓔ
2 Ⓐ Ⓑ Ⓒ Ⓓ Ⓔ	2 Ⓐ Ⓑ Ⓒ Ⓓ Ⓔ	2 Ⓐ Ⓑ Ⓒ Ⓓ Ⓔ	2 Ⓐ Ⓑ Ⓒ Ⓓ Ⓔ
3 Ⓐ Ⓑ Ⓒ Ⓓ Ⓔ	3 Ⓐ Ⓑ Ⓒ Ⓓ Ⓔ	3 Ⓐ Ⓑ Ⓒ Ⓓ Ⓔ	3 Ⓐ Ⓑ Ⓒ Ⓓ Ⓔ
4 Ⓐ Ⓑ Ⓒ Ⓓ Ⓔ	4 Ⓐ Ⓑ Ⓒ Ⓓ Ⓔ	4 Ⓐ Ⓑ Ⓒ Ⓓ Ⓔ	4 Ⓐ Ⓑ Ⓒ Ⓓ Ⓔ
5 Ⓐ Ⓑ Ⓒ Ⓓ Ⓔ	5 Ⓐ Ⓑ Ⓒ Ⓓ Ⓔ	5 Ⓐ Ⓑ Ⓒ Ⓓ Ⓔ	5 Ⓐ Ⓑ Ⓒ Ⓓ Ⓔ
6 Ⓐ Ⓑ Ⓒ Ⓓ Ⓔ	6 Ⓐ Ⓑ Ⓒ Ⓓ Ⓔ	6 Ⓐ Ⓑ Ⓒ Ⓓ Ⓔ	6 Ⓐ Ⓑ Ⓒ Ⓓ Ⓔ
7 Ⓐ Ⓑ Ⓒ Ⓓ Ⓔ	7 Ⓐ Ⓑ Ⓒ Ⓓ Ⓔ	7 Ⓐ Ⓑ Ⓒ Ⓓ Ⓔ	7 Ⓐ Ⓑ Ⓒ Ⓓ Ⓔ
8 Ⓐ Ⓑ Ⓒ Ⓓ Ⓔ	8 Ⓐ Ⓑ Ⓒ Ⓓ Ⓔ	8 Ⓐ Ⓑ Ⓒ Ⓓ Ⓔ	8 Ⓐ Ⓑ Ⓒ Ⓓ Ⓔ
9 Ⓐ Ⓑ Ⓒ Ⓓ Ⓔ	9 Ⓐ Ⓑ Ⓒ Ⓓ Ⓔ	9 Ⓐ Ⓑ Ⓒ Ⓓ Ⓔ	9 Ⓐ Ⓑ Ⓒ Ⓓ Ⓔ
10 Ⓐ Ⓑ Ⓒ Ⓓ Ⓔ	10 Ⓐ Ⓑ Ⓒ Ⓓ Ⓔ	10 Ⓐ Ⓑ Ⓒ Ⓓ Ⓔ	10 Ⓐ Ⓑ Ⓒ Ⓓ Ⓔ
11 Ⓐ Ⓑ Ⓒ Ⓓ Ⓔ	11 Ⓐ Ⓑ Ⓒ Ⓓ Ⓔ	11 Ⓐ Ⓑ Ⓒ Ⓓ Ⓔ	11 Ⓐ Ⓑ Ⓒ Ⓓ Ⓔ
12 Ⓐ Ⓑ Ⓒ Ⓓ Ⓔ	12 Ⓐ Ⓑ Ⓒ Ⓓ Ⓔ	12 Ⓐ Ⓑ Ⓒ Ⓓ Ⓔ	12 Ⓐ Ⓑ Ⓒ Ⓓ Ⓔ
13 Ⓐ Ⓑ Ⓒ Ⓓ Ⓔ	13 Ⓐ Ⓑ Ⓒ Ⓓ Ⓔ	13 Ⓐ Ⓑ Ⓒ Ⓓ Ⓔ	13 Ⓐ Ⓑ Ⓒ Ⓓ Ⓔ
14 Ⓐ Ⓑ Ⓒ Ⓓ Ⓔ	14 Ⓐ Ⓑ Ⓒ Ⓓ Ⓔ	14 Ⓐ Ⓑ Ⓒ Ⓓ Ⓔ	14 Ⓐ Ⓑ Ⓒ Ⓓ Ⓔ
15 Ⓐ Ⓑ Ⓒ Ⓓ Ⓔ	15 Ⓐ Ⓑ Ⓒ Ⓓ Ⓔ	15 Ⓐ Ⓑ Ⓒ Ⓓ Ⓔ	15 Ⓐ Ⓑ Ⓒ Ⓓ Ⓔ
16 Ⓐ Ⓑ Ⓒ Ⓓ Ⓔ	16 Ⓐ Ⓑ Ⓒ Ⓓ Ⓔ	16 Ⓐ Ⓑ Ⓒ Ⓓ Ⓔ	16 Ⓐ Ⓑ Ⓒ Ⓓ Ⓔ
17 Ⓐ Ⓑ Ⓒ Ⓓ Ⓔ	17 Ⓐ Ⓑ Ⓒ Ⓓ Ⓔ	17 Ⓐ Ⓑ Ⓒ Ⓓ Ⓔ	17 Ⓐ Ⓑ Ⓒ Ⓓ Ⓔ
18 Ⓐ Ⓑ Ⓒ Ⓓ Ⓔ	18 Ⓐ Ⓑ Ⓒ Ⓓ Ⓔ	18 Ⓐ Ⓑ Ⓒ Ⓓ Ⓔ	18 Ⓐ Ⓑ Ⓒ Ⓓ Ⓔ
19 Ⓐ Ⓑ Ⓒ Ⓓ Ⓔ	19 Ⓐ Ⓑ Ⓒ Ⓓ Ⓔ	19 Ⓐ Ⓑ Ⓒ Ⓓ Ⓔ	19 Ⓐ Ⓑ Ⓒ Ⓓ Ⓔ
20 Ⓐ Ⓑ Ⓒ Ⓓ Ⓔ	20 Ⓐ Ⓑ Ⓒ Ⓓ Ⓔ	20 Ⓐ Ⓑ Ⓒ Ⓓ Ⓔ	20 Ⓐ Ⓑ Ⓒ Ⓓ Ⓔ
21 Ⓐ Ⓑ Ⓒ Ⓓ Ⓔ	21 Ⓐ Ⓑ Ⓒ Ⓓ Ⓔ	21 Ⓐ Ⓑ Ⓒ Ⓓ Ⓔ	21 Ⓐ Ⓑ Ⓒ Ⓓ Ⓔ
22 Ⓐ Ⓑ Ⓒ Ⓓ Ⓔ	22 Ⓐ Ⓑ Ⓒ Ⓓ Ⓔ	22 Ⓐ Ⓑ Ⓒ Ⓓ Ⓔ	22 Ⓐ Ⓑ Ⓒ Ⓓ Ⓔ
23 Ⓐ Ⓑ Ⓒ Ⓓ Ⓔ	23 Ⓐ Ⓑ Ⓒ Ⓓ Ⓔ	23 Ⓐ Ⓑ Ⓒ Ⓓ Ⓔ	23 Ⓐ Ⓑ Ⓒ Ⓓ Ⓔ
24 Ⓐ Ⓑ Ⓒ Ⓓ Ⓔ	24 Ⓐ Ⓑ Ⓒ Ⓓ Ⓔ	24 Ⓐ Ⓑ Ⓒ Ⓓ Ⓔ	24 Ⓐ Ⓑ Ⓒ Ⓓ Ⓔ
25 Ⓐ Ⓑ Ⓒ Ⓓ Ⓔ	25 Ⓐ Ⓑ Ⓒ Ⓓ Ⓔ	25 Ⓐ Ⓑ Ⓒ Ⓓ Ⓔ	25 Ⓐ Ⓑ Ⓒ Ⓓ Ⓔ
26 Ⓐ Ⓑ Ⓒ Ⓓ Ⓔ	26 Ⓐ Ⓑ Ⓒ Ⓓ Ⓔ	26 Ⓐ Ⓑ Ⓒ Ⓓ Ⓔ	26 Ⓐ Ⓑ Ⓒ Ⓓ Ⓔ
27 Ⓐ Ⓑ Ⓒ Ⓓ Ⓔ	27 Ⓐ Ⓑ Ⓒ Ⓓ Ⓔ	27 Ⓐ Ⓑ Ⓒ Ⓓ Ⓔ	27 Ⓐ Ⓑ Ⓒ Ⓓ Ⓔ
28 Ⓐ Ⓑ Ⓒ Ⓓ Ⓔ	28 Ⓐ Ⓑ Ⓒ Ⓓ Ⓔ	28 Ⓐ Ⓑ Ⓒ Ⓓ Ⓔ	28 Ⓐ Ⓑ Ⓒ Ⓓ Ⓔ
29 Ⓐ Ⓑ Ⓒ Ⓓ Ⓔ	29 Ⓐ Ⓑ Ⓒ Ⓓ Ⓔ	29 Ⓐ Ⓑ Ⓒ Ⓓ Ⓔ	29 Ⓐ Ⓑ Ⓒ Ⓓ Ⓔ
30 Ⓐ Ⓑ Ⓒ Ⓓ Ⓔ	30 Ⓐ Ⓑ Ⓒ Ⓓ Ⓔ	30 Ⓐ Ⓑ Ⓒ Ⓓ Ⓔ	30 Ⓐ Ⓑ Ⓒ Ⓓ Ⓔ

PRACTICE TEST THREE
SECTION I
Time—35 minutes
27 questions

<u>Directions</u>: Each selection in this test is followed by several questions. After reading the selection, choose the <u>best</u> response to each question and mark it on your answer sheet. Your replies are to be based on what is <u>stated</u> or <u>implied</u> in the selection.

Every day the mailboxes of America are filled with millions upon millions of solicitations provided by the direct marketing industry. Most often they are straightforward advertisements for goods and services, but they also include
(5) such things as fund-raising solicitations, sweepstakes entries, and free trial offers. America's response to this deluge has been strangely mixed. On the negative side, poorly executed direct marketing produces unwanted, annoying, and wasteful solicitations, also known as "junk mail." The deluge of these
(10) solicitations constitutes an imposition on each household, putting a condition on that household's use of the mail system. Even worse, aggressive direct marketing techniques represent a serious threat to informational privacy. Rapid increases in technology have allowed direct marketers to have
(15) access to the personal characteristics of virtually everyone. Further, sophisticated computer matching programs can produce intrusive personal profiles from information which, standing alone, does not threaten individual privacy. Direct mailers disseminate this personal information originally
(20) revealed with an expectation of privacy. This information is disclosed without the subject's consent, and the target is typically never notified of the transfer.

The 1991 Harris-Equifax Consumer Privacy Survey addressed popular attitudes towards direct mailing practices
(25) and their impact on informational privacy. When asked how they viewed direct mail offers in general, 46 percent said they were a "nuisance," 9 percent considered them to be "invasions of privacy," and only 6 percent said they were "useful." But if Americans have such a negative opinion of
(30) the direct marketing industry, they have a strange way of showing it. Direct marketing is an effective technique that has grown in influence. Direct mail advertising expenditures rose from $7.6 billion in 1980 to $23.4 billion in 1990. The laws of the market dictate that companies would not have
(35) made these efforts without prospects of success. Moreover, in the Equifax survey mentioned above, almost half of the citizens who considered direct mail offers to be "invasions of privacy" had themselves bought something in response to a direct mail ad in the past year. Why, then, did not more of
(40) them express more positive opinions of direct marketing offers?

Analysis of this seeming contradiction reveals the central problem of regulation in this industry: Everyone hates receiving "junk mail," and everyone ought to be concerned
(45) about informational privacy. Still, direct marketing offers real advantages over other means of shopping, and the industry as a whole probably offers something for everyone. Even those who believe that the direct mailing industry has a generally negative societal impact probably would prefer to
(50) remain on some mailing lists. We like shopping by mail, and we don't want to throw out the good with the bad.

1. Which one of the following best expresses the main idea of the passage?
   (A) Increases in technology have been the main catalyst for the direct marketing explosion during the 1980s.
   (B) Concerns over privacy issues as expressed in popular opinion polls have influenced the way direct marketers have targeted their audience.
   (C) The discrepancy between the public's stated views of unsolicited "junk mail" and individuals' actual reaction to direct marketing materials has fueled the recent boom in the direct marketing industry.
   (D) The mixed response of Americans toward direct marketing stems from aggressive marketing techniques that threaten individual privacy.
   (E) The success of the direct marketing industry in the face of apparent public opposition to its practices can be explained in the light of consumer tendencies.

2. Which one of the following, if true, would best strengthen the author's explanation of the "seeming contradiction" expressed in line 42?
   (A) Awareness of commercial infringements on the rights of citizens has never been higher.
   (B) The number of people on more than one mailing list has increased in direct proportion to the increase in direct marketing expenditures.
   (C) Consumers do not perceive a connection between their individual purchasing behavior and infringements on their personal rights.
   (D) Some people believe that the benefits associated with the recent success of the direct marketing industry will filter down to consumers over time.
   (E) Some opinion polls on other topics indicate a similar discrepancy between what people say about an issue and how they act in relation to that issue.

GO ON TO THE NEXT PAGE.

3. Which one of the following critiques most approximates the logic underlying the author's concern regarding the effects of the computer matching programs mentioned in lines 16–18?

(A) An ecologist who states that since each of three species individually would not damage an ecosystem, it is safe to introduce all three into the ecosystem overlooks the possibility that the dominance of one species may lead to the extinction of one or both of the other two species.

(B) An ecologist who states that since each of three species individually would not damage an ecosystem, it is safe to introduce all three into the ecosystem overlooks the possibility that the three species taken together may very well pose a serious threat to the ecosystem.

(C) An ecologist who states that since each of three species individually would not damage an ecosystem, it is safe to introduce all three into the ecosystem overlooks the possibility that the addition of the three species to the ecosystem may preclude the addition of any further species.

(D) An ecologist who states that since each of three species individually would not damage an ecosystem, it is safe to introduce all three into the ecosystem overlooks the possibility that the ecosystem may not be the optimal environment for the species in question.

(E) An ecologist who states that since each of three species individually would not damage an ecosystem, it is safe to introduce all three into the ecosystem overlooks the possibility that any one of the three species may have posed a risk to the previous ecosystem in which it lived.

4. Which one of the following can be inferred from the passage about direct mail advertising expenditures in the years between 1980 and 1990?

(A) The rise in expenditures during this period is suggestive of the expectations of companies engaged in direct marketing at the time.

(B) The profit derived from sales linked to these expenditures in 1990 was more than double the profit derived from such sales in 1980.

(C) The lowest yearly expenditure on direct mail advertising during this period occurred in 1980.

(D) Direct marketing companies expect the pattern of expenditures during this period to continue in the decades to come.

(E) The rise in expenditures during this period closely parallel the laws of the market.

5. According to the passage, the author believes that the American public's reaction to the direct mail phenomenon

(A) is in accordance with the true dangers posed by the enterprise

(B) demonstrates an unusual willingness of people to consistently act against their deeply held convictions

(C) stems primarily from its fear of the loss of privacy that results from direct mail practices

(D) is unusual at first glance but more understandable once the motivations of the public are considered

(E) signals that the direct mail industry will need to alter its practices to respect informational privacy

6. The opinions expressed in the Harris-Equifax Consumer Privacy Survey in lines 25–29 serve as

(A) a justification for the increase in direct mail advertising expenditures in the 1980s

(B) the basis for the solution to a seemingly paradoxical situation

(C) the primary evidence for the author's conclusion about computer matching programs

(D) a contrast to additional evidence derived from another part of the survey

(E) an indication that the boom in direct marketing is not likely to continue

7. The author would most likely agree with which one of the following statements?

(A) Despite its drawbacks, direct marketing has had an overall positive effect on American society.

(B) The attitudes revealed in opinion polls can provide insight into actual behavior.

(C) Regarding the effects of commercial enterprises, presenting a nuisance is a more serious offense to society than is invasion of privacy.

(D) Everyone who would prefer to remain on at least one mailing list thinks that direct marketing negatively affects society in some way.

(E) The growth in direct marketing would be even more significant in the future if the percentage of people who find direct mail offers to be a nuisance were to decrease.

GO ON TO THE NEXT PAGE.

KAPLAN

For at least 300 years prior to the beginning of the 20th Century, people had noticed that the bulge along the eastern edge of South America fits remarkably well into the bight of Africa. Indeed, Francis Bacon suggested in 1620 that the fit

(5) could not be accidental. Several 19th-century scientists offered explanations for the fit, but when Alfred Wegener first published the continental-drift hypothesis in 1912, his novel explanation for why the continents seem to fit together like pieces of a jigsaw puzzle drew explosive criticism from

(10) many geologists. Wegener used gravity measurements and observations of the Earth's surfaces to deduce that the continents are composed of lighter rock than the basalt that lies beneath the ocean floors. The continents, he suggested, float on the denser layer of basalt like icebergs on water.

(15) Wegener's early critics excoriated him for not proposing a mechanism for propelling the continental "icebergs" through solid basalt, although now there is some theoretical basis for thinking that convection might drive the process.

Wegener did not live long enough to find the clear and

(20) convincing evidence his hypothesis required, but since his death in 1930, geologists have learned much that supports his revolutionary idea. For example, belts of complementary rock formations found along the African and South American shorelines of the Atlantic Ocean make a strong

(25) argument for continental drift. In one experiment, geochronologists determined the age of a distinctive layer of crystalline basement rock in Ghana, Africa, and then predicted where the same rock layer would be found at the edge of South America if the two continents had indeed

(30) once been contiguous. By sampling and dating rocks in northeastern Brazil, the scientists demonstrated that the layer does occur in its predicted location. Another belt of two-billion-year-old rock that abruptly ends at the edge of the West African continental mass and begins again at the

(35) expected location along the coast of South America adds additional proof that the two continents once formed part of a larger land mass.

The fossil record contains additional evidence that Africa and South America were once connected. Large bodies of

(40) water act as barriers to the migration of many types of animals, yet the fossils of identical animal species are found on both sides of the southern Atlantic Ocean. For example, the remains of Mesosaurus, a small reptile of the Permian that lived in shallow, brackish swamps, are found in only

(45) two locations—in the Early Permian Dwyka Formation in South Africa and in the Irarare Formation in Brazil. The rock formations are the same age, are similar in composition, and lie directly across the ocean from each other, thus enhancing the plausibility of Wegener's theory of continental

(50) drift.

8. Which one of the following best expresses the main point of the passage?

(A) Several 19th-century scientists offered explanations for the apparent fit of the coastlines of South America and Africa, but none as intriguing as the hypothesis proposed by Wegener.

(B) Fossil evidence and the dating of certain rocks in South America and Africa has recently undermined the continental drift hypothesis.

(C) Scientists have uncovered a growing body of evidence for continental drift since the death of the theory's original proponent.

(D) The study of fossils and rock formations is an important aspect of geochronology.

(E) Scientists cannot conclusively prove the validity of Wegener's continental-drift hypothesis until the mechanism that causes it is understood.

9. The author's conclusion about the two-billion-year-old rock formations in West Africa and South America implies which one of the following?

(A) The rock formations would not be in their current locations if the continents had never been connected.

(B) Similar rock formations must be present in at least one other continent.

(C) The rock formations were formed by the same geological process that separated the continents.

(D) The rock formations must contain fossils common to both Africa and South America.

(E) Although much older, the rock formations resemble the crystalline basement rock found in Ghana.

GO ON TO THE NEXT PAGE.

10. According to the passage, Wegener's continental-drift hypothesis was originally

   (A) a modification of an earlier 19th-century hypothesis about the structure of continents
   (B) rejected by most geologists because it was inconsistent with Francis Bacon's suggestion regarding the apparent fit between Africa and South America
   (C) an attempt to explain why South America and Africa share common rock formations
   (D) formulated with the use of scientific observations but lacking in supporting evidence
   (E) used to explain why certain fossils are found on both sides of the South Atlantic

11. Which one of the following, if true, would most weaken Wegener's theory of continental drift?

   (A) Far more Mesosaurus reptile fossils were uncovered in the Early Permian Dwyka Formation in South Africa than in the Irarare Formation in Brazil.
   (B) A new mechanism has been discovered that could displace convection as the motive force behind continental drift.
   (C) Francis Bacon based his observation on the non-accidental nature of the structural fit between continents purely on speculation and not on scientific fact.
   (D) There are many rock formations around the world that are the same age but not of similar composition.
   (E) In many cases, continents that do not appear to have interlocking coastlines nonetheless share common rock formations and fossils of identical animal species.

12. It can be inferred that the author of the passage would most likely agree with which one of the following statements about fossil evidence?

   (A) Fossil evidence is less conclusive than rock formation evidence in substantiating Wegener's theory of continental drift.
   (B) Fossil evidence can contribute to the plausibility of a geological model.
   (C) No fossil evidence links the animal species of South America to those of Australia.
   (D) Fossil evidence proves that identical animal species once lived in widely separated locations.
   (E) Fossil evidence suggests that convection is the underlying mechanism responsible for continental drift.

13. The primary purpose of the passage is to

   (A) describe some of the evidence for a popular hypothesis
   (B) detail how belts of complimentary rock formations can be used to support geochronological hypotheses
   (C) argue that the continental-drift hypothesis has been conclusively proven
   (D) assess certain types of evidence relied upon by modern geochronologists
   (E) describe Wegener's evidence for continental drift

GO ON TO THE NEXT PAGE.

Sensing that government defined by the Articles of Confederation did not meet the needs of the newly born United States, the Congress of the Articles of Confederation authorized commissioners to "devise such further provisions

(5) as shall appear to them necessary to render the Constitution of the federal government adequate to the exigencies of the Union." These provisions were to be reported to Congress and confirmed by every state, and were to consist of alterations to the Articles of Confederation. Having given

(10) these instructions, Congress was quite surprised by the terms of the Constitution as submitted, and even claimed that the commissioners did not have the legal authority to submit such a revolutionary constitution.

In the Federalist Papers, James Madison defended the

(15) commissioners by returning to the terms of their mandate. Given the goals expressed by Congress, and the principle that conflicts ought to be resolved in favor of more important goals, Madison argued that the degree to which the Constitution departs from the Articles cannot make the

(20) Constitution illegal. Where the goal of amending the Articles conflicts with the goal of creating good government, the Articles must yield, since the goal of good government is an overriding consideration. This same argument, however, does not apply to the commissioners' decision to allow the

(25) Constitution to be ratified by only three-quarters of the states. Unanimous approval was a fundamental aspect of national government under the Articles. Requiring non-ratifying states to be bound by the new Constitution was thus a powerful diminishment of their sovereignty, as the

(30) Constitution changed the national government from a weak union of independent states to a strong union in which the interests of the many states could outweigh the protests of the few. Although history has validated the wisdom of the change, the question of whether the change was legal is

(35) another matter.

In authorizing the commissioners, the independent states requested a proposal for the alteration of the national government, but never intended to waive their veto power. So even if Madison is correct, and the commissioners could

(40) have proposed anything they deemed likely to fulfill the goal of good government, it does not follow that their proclamations should impinge upon the legal rights of the states. This does not, however, imply that the Constitution ratified by the states has no moral authority. No government

(45) ought to have the power to entrench itself against amendment, and so the fact that the government under the Articles of Confederation did not consent to the alteration of the ratification process does not establish the moral illegitimacy of the Constitution. The case for rebelling

(50) against the government under the Articles is further strengthened by the fact that the government itself admitted its unfitness for the exigencies of the Union.

14. It can be inferred that Congress's surprise over the radical nature of the Constitution submitted by the commissioners could be attributed in part to the fact that its members did not foresee

(A) the inevitability that the Constitution it requested would be adopted without the unanimous ratification of the states

(B) the possibility that the Constitution it requested would contain provisions that jeopardized the government's moral authority

(C) a conflict between the modification of the Articles of Confederation and the creation of a Constitution adequate to the needs of the nation

(D) the possibility that the Constitution it requested would differ from the Articles of Confederation

(E) the likelihood that one such as Madison would invoke a principle as part of an argument attempting to justify the legality of the Constitution submitted

15. Which one of the following views can be attributed to Madison?

(A) In the case of conflicting interests, priority should be given to the course of action that best promotes peace in the nation.

(B) Applications of conflict resolution principles can be used to determine the legality of an action.

(C) Unanimous approval is the most important objective in drafting a new Constitution.

(D) The Constitution drafted by the commissioners corresponded precisely to the expectations of the Congress of the Articles of Confederation.

(E) In drafting the new Constitution, the commissioners had a moral obligation to forge a strong nation out of the weak union of independent states.

GO ON TO THE NEXT PAGE.

16. If a government decrees that it is illegal to make any changes to the structure or practices of the state, the author would most likely view a group within the state that attempts to violate the decree

   (A) with skepticism regarding its motivations
   (B) with admiration, since any law passed by such a government has no moral authority
   (C) with concern regarding the government's reaction to the group's act of dissent
   (D) with disdain for its violation of the orders of the state
   (E) with approval regarding its moral right to disobey the decree

17. Which one of the following, if true, would most seriously weaken the argument put forth in defense of the legality of the Constitution submitted by the commissioners?

   (A) Nonunanimous ratification of such a new Constitution is incompatible with the goal of creating a good government.
   (B) Extensive debate among statesmen is necessary in order to create a fair and legal Constitution.
   (C) It is nearly impossible to create an effective Constitution out of the pieces of a previous Constitution.
   (D) No legal Constitution can include provisions to safeguard the power of the ruling elite that commissioned the document.
   (E) In regard to heated political issues, arguments presented orally are generally more persuasive than arguments presented in written form.

18. According to the passage, which one of the following provided justification for the revolutionary nature of the new Constitution?

   (A) the current government's admission of its inadequacy in national affairs
   (B) the right of any given state to refuse to ratify the new Constitution
   (C) the moral right of a new government to entrench itself against amendment
   (D) the recommendation that the new Constitution be created from alterations of the current Articles of Confederation
   (E) the analysis presented by Madison that showed that the new Constitution did not differ from the Articles of Confederation to the extent asserted by Congress

19. Which one of the following relationships between legal and moral authority is implied by the author?

   (A) The morality of a constitution is the primary determinant of its legality.
   (B) A principle lacking moral authority can still be legally binding.
   (C) The morality of an action can never be determined irrespective of the legality of that action.
   (D) A document lacking legal authority can still carry moral weight.
   (E) The moral justification for an action can be used by a court to override the illegality of that action.

20. The primary purpose of the passage is to

   (A) reconcile two opposing viewpoints
   (B) illustrate the argumentative power of a principle
   (C) argue for the reconsideration of an established doctrine
   (D) support the establishment of one form of government over another
   (E) assess the authority of a political event on two grounds

GO ON TO THE NEXT PAGE.

Both Alexander Gerschenkron and Jerry Hough view the former Soviet Union as an "anomalous" nation in certain fundamental respects. Gerschenkron focuses on the degree to which the Soviet Union deviated from the expected
(5) European pattern of industrialization, while Hough emphasizes how the Soviet Union differed from the standard type of bureaucratic organization. Despite this difference in orientation, both authors share a similar theoretical approach.
(10) First, both authors react in their works to specific explanations already existing in their fields. Gerschenkron responds to the prevailing belief that all countries pass through similar stages of industrialization that can be modeled after England's industrial growth. He also reacts to
(15) the accepted notion that states must possess certain specific prerequisites before they can industrialize. Hough as well develops his argument in reaction to an existing view, the notion that the only type of bureaucracy that can operate efficiently is one that embodies the conventional American
(20) image of the ideal organization. This American image, known as monism, sees efficiency as maximized when bureaucrats perform only those duties passed down to them from a central authority.
Second, both Gerschenkron and Hough also clearly
(25) attempt to use their work to supplement the existing explanations prevailing in their fields. Gerschenkron expands W.W. Rostow's industrialization model by defining a causal factor that he calls the "degree of economic backwardness." Specifically, he argues that backwardness impacts the speed,
(30) organizational structure, institutional instruments, and ideology of a country's industrialization. In a similar vein, Hough broadens the conventional explanation in his field, concluding from his findings that the centralized, monistic model of organization must be expanded if it is to enable
(35) efficient administration. He uses the Soviet experience to show that overlapping bureaucratic duties can actually promote organizational efficiency in certain cases.
While Gerschenkron and Hough differ sharply regarding the focus of their research in their works, both authors
(40) portray the Soviet Union as anomalous with respect to the phenomena of industrialization and bureaucratic organization that they study. Both authors also attempt to use the anomalies that they discover to enhance the explanatory value of the theories already existing in their
(45) fields. Ultimately, Gerschenkron and Hough succeed at their similar tasks, because they develop explanations for their anomalous cases that enable the existing theories to more accurately explain the issues under investigation. Not only do both authors provide enough evidence to document the
(50) anomalous nature of the cases they investigate, but they use their anomalous cases to increase the explanatory range of the existing theories without altering those theories beyond recognition.

21. The author's main point in the passage is reflected most accurately in which one of the following statements?
   (A) Gerschenkron and Hough share a similar theoretical enterprise in their works, and both manage this enterprise successfully.
   (B) In their research, both Gerschenkron and Hough react to prevailing theories within their fields.
   (C) Gerschenkron and Hough both use evidence from the Soviet case to highlight the anomalous features of the former Soviet experience.
   (D) The works of Gerschenkron and Hough are expansive because both authors attempt to refute existing theories within their fields and to replace these theories with better explanations.
   (E) The works of Gerschenkron and Hough are similar with respect to the specific central tenets of their research.

22. According to the author, the works of Gerschenkron and Hough are similar in that they both
   (A) provide evidence to show how the experiences of the former Soviet Union invalidate prevailing theories in their fields
   (B) adhere to the standard interpretations of prevailing theories in their fields
   (C) develop the explanatory power of existing theories through the investigation of anomalous cases
   (D) address anomalies in the stages of industrialization experienced by the former Soviet Union
   (E) portray the development of the former Soviet Union in a generally critical light

23. The passage states which one of the following about Hough's portrayal of the former Soviet bureaucratic system?
   (A) The former Soviet bureaucratic system mirrors the monistic model of bureaucratic organization exemplified in the American bureaucratic system.
   (B) The experiences of the former Soviet bureaucratic system support the notion that bureaucracies must be organized according to the monistic model if they are to run efficiently.
   (C) Throughout its development, the former Soviet bureaucratic system underwent growth stages similar to that experienced by England during its industrial growth.
   (D) The development of the former Soviet bureaucratic system was impeded by the system's degree of economic backwardness.
   (E) The experiences of the former Soviet bureaucratic system demonstrate that bureaucratic efficiency can be enhanced through the overlapping of organizational functions.

GO ON TO THE NEXT PAGE.

24. Which one of the following best describes the function of the third paragraph in the context of the passage as a whole?

    (A) It demonstrates that despite similarities in their approaches, the two authors cited study fundamentally different subjects.

    (B) It suggests that the most effective method for comparing the works of Gerschenkron and Hough is to focus on their research concerning the former Soviet Union.

    (C) It illustrates the role of W.W. Rostow's industrialization model in influencing Gerschenkron's analysis of the former Soviet Union.

    (D) It provides additional support for the notion that Gerschenkron and Hough share similar theoretical goals in developing their works.

    (E) It serves to refute the contention that the works of Gerschenkron and Hough exhibit any fundamental similarity.

25. The passage suggests that both Gerschenkron and Hough would be most likely to agree with which one of the following statements?

    (A) Scientific studies of the former Soviet Union should be limited to an emphasis on industrialization patterns or methods of bureaucratic organization.

    (B) W.W. Rostow's industrialization model can be expanded by incorporating the variable of economic backwardness.

    (C) All countries pass through stages of industrialization similar to those experienced by England during its early growth.

    (D) Empirical research into anomalous cases can broaden the explanatory range of current theories.

    (E) Empirical research should focus on attempting to falsify theories through emphasis on disconfirming cases.

26. Which one of the following is explicitly cited as evidence to demonstrate a specific use to which Gerschenkron put his work?

    (A) Gerschenkron reacted to the accepted notion that industrialization does not require states to possess any prerequisite characteristics.

    (B) Gerschenkron and Hough differed regarding the specific orientation of their respective works.

    (C) Gerschenkron described the monistic image of bureaucratic organization in order to show how centralized authority helps to promote bureaucratic efficiency.

    (D) Gerschenkron demonstrated that the speed of a country's industrialization affects the country's degree of economic backwardness.

    (E) Gerschenkron incorporated a new factor into the model of industrialization put forth by a previous theorist.

27. The author refers to the concept of monism in the second paragraph in order to

    (A) support the claim that the former Soviet Union deviated in its development from the normal European pattern of industrialization

    (B) refute the notion that Hough provides an alternative conception of bureaucratic efficiency

    (C) demonstrate that Hough's work takes issue with the conventional view that efficient bureaucratic organization must conform to the American idealized image

    (D) support the claim that Hough portrays the former Soviet Union as similar to most industrialized nations in its bureaucratic structure

    (E) provide evidence for the conclusion that the former Soviet case displayed many elements of the idealized American model of bureaucratic organization

S T O P
**IF YOU FINISH BEFORE TIME IS CALLED, YOU MAY CHECK YOUR WORK ON THIS SECTION ONLY.
DO NOT WORK ON ANY OTHER SECTION IN THE TEST.**

SECTION II
Time—35 minutes
25 questions

<u>Directions</u>: This test is composed of questions that ask you to analyze the logic of statements or short paragraphs. You are to choose as the answer to each question the one choice you consider <u>best</u> on the basis of your common-sense evaluation of the statement and its assumptions. Although a question may seem to have more than one acceptable answer, there is only one <u>best</u> answer, and it is the one that does not entail making any illogical, extraneous, or conflicting assumptions about the question. These questions do not presuppose any knowledge of formal logic on your part.

1. Cross-species studies of animal groups indicate that offspring who are separated from their mothers during the first months of life frequently develop aggression disorders. During group feedings, for example, separated offspring exert excessive force in the struggle over food, continuing to strike at other offspring long after the others have submitted. The best explanation for this observed behavior is the hypothesis that aggression disorders are caused by lack of proper parent-led socialization during the first stage of an offspring's development.

   Which one of the following, if true, provides the most support for the hypothesis above?

   (A) Some wildebeests who are not separated from their mothers during infancy display excessive aggression in conflicts that establish their place in the dominance hierarchy.

   (B) Human babies adopted in the first three months of life often display aggressive behavior disorders during early childhood.

   (C) Chimps raised in captivity in environments simulating traditional parent-led socialization display far less aggression in mating-related conflicts than do chimps raised without such social interaction.

   (D) Many polar bears display more aggression in conflicts over food and social dominance than they do in mating-related conflicts.

   (E) Elephants who are separated from their mothers during the first months of life do not display excessive aggression in food or social dominance struggles.

2. Sarrin monks practice the Pran meditation technique only when extremely damaging weather conditions confront the farming villages surrounding Sarrin monasteries. Pran meditation is a more highly disciplined form of the ritual meditation that the monks practice daily, and involves unique practices such as isolation and fasting.

   Which one of the statements below does NOT follow logically from the passage above?

   (A) Some meditation practices are less disciplined than Pran meditation.

   (B) Pran meditation among Sarrin monks does not take place according to a precisely regulated schedule.

   (C) The ritual meditation that a typical Sarrin monk practices daily does not take place in an atmosphere of isolation.

   (D) Monks practice some types of meditation in response to threats faced by the local population.

   (E) The ritual meditation that Sarrin monks practice daily is largely undisciplined.

GO ON TO THE NEXT PAGE.

3. Movie pirating, the illegal videotaping of a new theater release and subsequent selling of the tape on the black market, is a major concern to the film studios that produce today's mainstream movies. When pirating sales are high, individual studios whose movies are being taped and sold illegally lose a large amount of revenue from black market viewers who would otherwise pay the full theater price. A low level of pirating sales during a specific period, however, is a fairly reliable indicator of an economic downturn in the movie industry as a whole during that period.

Which one of the following, if true, most helps to reconcile the discrepancy noted above?

(A) The film studios that produce today's mainstream movies occasionally serve as distribution outlets for smaller budget independent films that are also susceptible to pirating.

(B) Movie piraters exclusively target blockbuster hits, the existence of which is inextricably tied to the financial success of the movie industry during any given period.

(C) Most movie piraters use small, hand-held video cameras that are specially designed to record images in the darkened environment of a movie theater.

(D) The five largest film studios take in a disproportionate amount of movie revenue compared to hundreds of smaller and independent film studios, regardless of whether pirating activity during a specific period is high or low.

(E) A movie pirater who is highly active in selling movies on the black market can sometimes make a full living doing so, while a less active pirater will usually have to supplement the income generated from pirated movies.

4. Six months ago, a blight destroyed the cattle population in the town of Cebra, eradicating the town's beef supply. As a result, since that time the only meat available for consumption in Cebra has been poultry, lamb, and other non-beef meats.

If the above statements are true, which one of the following must also be true on the basis of them?

(A) Villagers in the town of Cebra consume only beef raised by Cebra farmers.

(B) Cebra villagers prefer lamb and poultry to beef.

(C) The town of Cebra has not imported beef for consumption during the last six months.

(D) Most of the residents of Cebra are meat eaters.

(E) Before the blight occurred, Cebra villagers ate more beef than any other type of meat.

5. The food critic who writes for the magazine Dining Today was misguided in his review of Fabri's Restaurant. He criticized the cold strawberry soup because it contained cilantro and sun-dried tomatoes. But Fabri's roasted chicken dish contains cilantro and sun-dried tomatoes, and the same critic awarded that dish the highest rating possible. Clearly, such blatant inconsistency proves that the critic is unqualified.

The argument above is based upon which one of the following assumptions?

(A) Fabri's roasted chicken dish is disliked by some of Fabri's customers.

(B) The evaluation of Fabri's cold strawberry soup should not suffer on account of its inclusion of a few ingredients that the critic happens to dislike.

(C) As enhancing ingredients, cilantro and sun-dried tomatoes are less appropriate for appetizers than for main dishes.

(D) Cilantro and sun-dried tomatoes enhance roasted chicken and cold strawberry soup dishes in a comparable manner.

(E) Cilantro and sun-dried tomatoes are best used in chicken dishes that are not roasted.

GO ON TO THE NEXT PAGE.

KAPLAN

6. Peter Dovak has stated that his soon-to-be-released new novel *From Bad to Worse* will exhibit the same literary form as his previous six novels. Each of these previous books was a "philosophy novel," also known as a "novel of ideas," in which characters and events represent various expressions of the author's deeply-held philosophical convictions. Therefore, while the plot will surely be different from those of his previous books, any astute literary critic will know in advance what underlying issues will dominate Dovak's forthcoming book.

The argument above assumes which one of the following?

(A) Dovak is consistent in the philosophical convictions that he expresses through the characters and events of his books.

(B) The plot of *From Bad to Worse* will have nothing in common with the plots from any of Dovak's previous six books.

(C) Nothing written by Dovak prior to the publication of his previous six books took the form of the philosophy novel.

(D) One of the functions of literary critics is to predict what will be in an author's forthcoming book.

(E) The plot of *From Bad to Worse* is less important than the underlying philosophical convictions expressed through its characters and events.

7. Despite the threat of legal prosecution, many agencies gather personal data from phony telephone solicitations, often luring details from the respondent through the promise of non-existent prizes. Such solicitors sell this data to individuals and agencies that are willing to pay for information on people's personal lives, buying habits, and political views. Politicians, however, have relied less on phony solicitors thanks to recent advances in public opinion polling, which generally supplies them with reliable information regarding voter attitudes on major issues. It is therefore likely that the phony solicitation industry will dwindle significantly in the years to come.

Which one of the following, if true, most seriously undermines the conclusion above?

(A) Public opinion polling is not only effective at discerning the political attitudes of individuals, but also at revealing their buying habits and details of their personal lives.

(B) Most people are unwilling to share personal information on their preferences and attitudes with strangers over the telephone.

(C) Large retailers are by far the largest consumers of pirated personal information, and do not benefit from the information gathered in public opinion polls.

(D) Those politicians who rely on legal public opinion polls for information on voter attitudes are nonetheless hesitant to encourage the prosecution of the illegal data-gathering agencies.

(E) Due to the recent success of public opinion polling, the phony solicitors have begun to co-opt the public opinion agencies' techniques for getting people to disclose information on their personal lives.

GO ON TO THE NEXT PAGE.

Questions 8–9

Albert: The CEO's proposal to conduct free career seminars for high school students does not make business sense. Teenagers do not use our products, since they do not have the disposable income to purchase luxury items.

Bill: I disagree. Any activities that improve the company's image can enhance our profit margins in the long run. The positive publicity received from the seminars will boost the company's image in the public's eye. Image enhancement, it has been proven, increases sales significantly.

8. A point at issue between Albert and Bill concerns whether

(A) the business has suffered from recent problems with its image

(B) the CEO's plan to offer career seminars makes financial sense for the company

(C) the publicity received from the seminars is likely to be highly positive

(D) the advice given in the free career seminars would enable high school students to buy the company's products

(E) teenagers would be more likely to buy the company's products if the company maintained a stronger public image

9. Bill responds to Albert by

(A) broadening the scope for the determination of whether offering the career seminars will be financially beneficial for the company

(B) comparing the values of short-term versus long-term business gains

(C) providing examples that demonstrate that image is more important to a company's financial health than its profit margins

(D) showing that Albert's argument relies on the erroneous presupposition that increased product sales are not the only route to financial growth

(E) presenting evidence that clarifies the issue of whether teenagers have enough disposable income to purchase the company's products

10. Veterinary technician: I disagree with Dr. Markey's analysis concerning the medical problems of Wisecrack, the Smiths' horse. Dr. Markey recommends that Wisecrack undergo hoof surgery because his hoof problems are causing him great pain. But the Smiths cannot afford to pay for this procedure, much less the cost of Wisecrack's hospital stay.

The argument above is logically suspect because it

(A) supports its conclusion on the basis of evidence that fails to take into account the emotional or financial costs of not treating Wisecrack's condition

(B) fails to draw a conclusion that is in the best interest of the owners of the horse

(C) resorts to attacking the personality of an individual involved in order to direct attention away from the relevant issue

(D) uses evidence regarding the feasibility of acting on a recommendation as grounds for questioning the validity of the analysis supporting that recommendation

(E) supports its main point with evidence that is derived from sources that cannot be independently verified

GO ON TO THE NEXT PAGE.

11. Pharmaceutical scientist: Any bone marrow taken from lab rats after their primary growth phase is degenerative and will not function properly in transplants. All marrow in this shipment was extracted from laboratory rats provided by Chronin Labs. Chronin Labs has a policy of supplying only rats that are four months of age or older. Therefore, the marrow in this shipment is degenerative and should not be used.

Which one of the following, if true, most helps to justify the subsidiary conclusion that leads to the pharmaceutical scientist's recommendation?

(A) The degenerative quality of a particular bone marrow supply is not a valid reason for definitively ruling out its use in transplants.

(B) All rat bone marrow that displays degenerative properties comes from rats that are more than four months old.

(C) Some bone marrow extracted from laboratory rats during the rats' primary growth phase is degenerative.

(D) Laboratory rats go through their primary growth phase between birth and four months of age.

(E) In rare instances, Chronin Labs agrees to supply rats under four months of age to certain experiment sites containing appropriate environmental conditions.

12. Many Maids, a well-known commercial cleaning franchise, has always relied heavily on income from its major clients and would have been forced to close down this year if any of its major clients had closed their accounts. However, Many Maids has not only been able to continue its operation throughout the year, but it has also announced the grand opening of its second office.

The above statements, if true, support which one of the following conclusions?

(A) During this year Many Maids' clients have placed a larger than usual number of special cleaning orders.

(B) Over the past few months, Many Maids developed many new small client accounts, which made the company less dependent on its major clients for income.

(C) None of Many Maids' major clients closed its account with the company this year.

(D) Corporate use of cleaning services like Many Maids has recently increased.

(E) Major clients were the source of more than half of Many Maids' income for the current year.

13. The Fines Museum has a totem pole that was too tall to be stored in the museum's temperature-controlled storage vault. Fortunately, the totem pole can now be stored in the temperature-controlled vault, thanks to the efforts of restoration artists who have discovered a way to separate the pole into two parts for storage purposes while allowing it to be reassembled later without any noticeable change in the appearance of the artifact.

The argument above depends on which one of the following assumptions?

(A) Neither of the separated parts of the totem pole is too tall to fit into the vault.

(B) The totem pole can be separated into two equal-sized parts.

(C) The procedure for separating the parts of the totem pole will not cost more than it would cost to replace the totem pole if it deteriorated.

(D) Placing the two parts of the totem pole into the vault would not require removing other key artifacts from the vault.

(E) The optimal temperature required to preserve the totem pole can be attained in the temperature-controlled vault.

GO ON TO THE NEXT PAGE.

14. Psychologists who wish to have one of their book reviews nominated for the prestigious *Boatwright Psychology Review* award should not submit book review articles that review more than three books at a time. This is because editors for the *Boatwright Psychology Review* will not publish a book review article if it is too lengthy and cumbersome to read. In their submission guidelines, the editors explicitly state that review articles that cover more than three books at a time are considered too lengthy and cumbersome to read.

Which one of the following statements represents an assumption upon which the argument above depends?

(A) The books review article that covers the most books must be the lengthiest and most cumbersome article to read.

(B) If a book review article is published in the *Boatwright Psychology Review*, that article will receive the prestigious *Boatwright Psychology Review* award.

(C) All articles published in the *Boatwright Psychology Review* must be limited to a certain length specified by the editors.

(D) The *Boatwright Psychology Review* editors generally prefer book review articles that cover one book rather than two books.

(E) To be nominated for the *Boatwright Psychology Review* award, a psychologist's book review article must be published in the *Boatwright Psychology Review*.

15. The best-tasting premium ice cream requires milk from organically raised cows. When milk supplies are obtained from non-organic sources, ice cream manufacturers are unable to ensure that their products are free of pesticide residues, and taste tests have shown that only those products that are free of pesticide residues meet the highest quality standards for taste.

Which one of the following roles is played in the argument by the claim that ice cream products can meet the highest quality taste standards only if they are free of pesticide residues?

(A) It serves as support for the argument's conclusion.

(B) It represents a logical consequence of the argument.

(C) It is an assumption upon which the argument depends.

(D) It is a statement that must be proven false in order to weaken an opposing viewpoint.

(E) It functions as the argument's conclusion.

Questions 16–17

The proliferation of colloquialisms is degrading the English language. A phrase such as "she was like, 'No way!', you know?," a meaningless collection of English words just a few decades ago, is commonly understood by most today to mean "she was doubtful." No language can admit imprecise word usage on a large scale without a corresponding decrease in quality.

16. The argument relies on which one of the following assumptions?

(A) Colloquialisms always evolve out of a meaningless collection of words.

(B) The colloquialisms appearing in the English language introduce imprecision into the language on what would be considered a large scale.

(C) The Russian, French, and German languages cannot admit imprecise word usage on a large scale without an inevitable decrease in the quality of those languages.

(D) The English language would not be degraded if there did not exist an alternative informal way to express the sentiment "she was doubtful."

(E) The widespread use of colloquialisms represents the most serious form of language degradation.

17. Which one of the following, if true, most weakens the argument above?

(A) Linguists have shown that the use of imprecise language on a small scale does not generally impair understanding.

(B) Many colloquialisms that appeared in earlier forms of the English language disappeared over time as the people who used those particular phrasings were assimilated into larger groups with different language patterns.

(C) Dissemination of a new word or phrase by the mass media is an important factor in whether or not the new word or phrase will become a colloquialism.

(D) Colloquialisms are more likely to be coined by the youth in a culture than by any other segment of the population.

(E) Languages of the highest quality often evolve over time out of a collection of colloquial usages woven into the formal dialect of a given people.

GO ON TO THE NEXT PAGE.

18. In order to teach in the writing program at Brenton University, graduate student instructors must complete the writing program themselves. The course directors justify this policy by invoking the principle that those who teach must thoroughly understand the subject matter, and point out that the best means of learning the course material is to take the course as a student. Without taking the course, potential instructors might under-emphasize certain key concepts in their preparation.

The principle relied upon in the argument above is most applicable to which one of the following situations?

(A) Dog trainers should be required to obtain kennel licenses before they open their practices, since most dog trainers end up boarding their clients' dogs for a period of time during the dogs' schooling.

(B) Youth probation officers should be required to take a psychological development class as part of their on-the-job training, because it is difficult to document which officers previously completed such a class before they applied for their jobs.

(C) Paramedic trainers should be required to ride as patients in ambulances before they become certified trainers, since only by experiencing the plight of the patient first-hand can the paramedic trainer truly convey the patients' needs to paramedic students.

(D) Vocal coaches should train their students extensively before allowing their students to compete in singing competitions, because untrained singers often waste a good deal of judges' time in these competitions.

(E) Zookeepers should be required to have in-depth training in the botanical sciences, because serious illnesses can occur if animals are placed in environments containing plants that are poisonous to the animals' species.

19. Without a fundraising specialist, foundations have trouble meeting their fundraising targets. Research shows that fundraising specialists help foundations raise the majority of their yearly funds. Financial planners serve a key organizing and advisory role, but financial planners raise only a small percentage of foundation funds, if they raise any funds at all. Therefore, _____

The argument above can be best completed by which one of the following?

(A) a foundation interested in raising funds should entrust its fundraising activities to fundraising specialists rather than financial planners

(B) no foundation that does not employ fundraising specialists can raise the same amount of funds as a foundation that employs financial planners

(C) fundraising specialists lacking financial planning knowledge will provide less help to foundations than will financial planners with no fundraising knowledge

(D) foundations that employ fundraising specialists meet their annual fundraising targets

(E) foundations should not routinely engage the services of financial planners

GO ON TO THE NEXT PAGE.

20. It would be futile to ask any of the runners to move that boulder on the path. None of the runners individually could move the bolder, so it will not be possible for the runners to move the boulder as a group.

Which one of the following arguments contains reasoning that is flawed in a manner most similar to that in the argument above?

(A) Charlotte should not be appointed for the new position. She has not succeeded in her previous position, so there is no reason to think that she would perform well in the new position.

(B) Our Board of Trustees is incorrect in suggesting that a committee should be appointed to oversee Treasury matters. We would not trust any individual member with the responsibility of overseeing these matters, so we should have no more trust in a committee, which after all is merely a conglomerate of individuals.

(C) This code will remain unbroken. Detective Tally cannot break the code, so none of the other detectives will be able to break it either.

(D) Wearing fashionable clothing will not ensure that a person is considered stylish. Many styles go quickly in and out of fashion, so clothing that is considered stylish by one group may not be seen as stylish by all.

(E) It is useless to argue with Arthur. No one but Margaret can win an argument with him, so it will not be possible to win no matter how hard we try.

21. Leroy could not possibly have given the flu to his co-worker on Monday. In fact, Leroy's records lead to only one conclusion: that Leroy did not have the flu himself on Monday. It is true that Leroy spent the day on Sunday visiting a friend who had the flu, but there is no evidence to show that Leroy had the flu on Monday. His records show only that Leroy had the flu on Tuesday, the day he went to see his doctor.

The reasoning in the argument is flawed because the argument does which one of the following?

(A) It concludes that there is a lack of evidence for Leroy having the flu, based on evidence suggesting that Leroy did not have the flu.

(B) It fails to consider that Leroy's co-worker might have caught the flu from exposure to someone other than Leroy.

(C) It overlooks the possibility that Leroy's flu diagnosis on Tuesday serves as an indicator that Leroy had the flu on Monday.

(D) It assumes that an individual's association with an ill person is relevant to the question of whether he or she contracted an illness from that person.

(E) It raises the question of Leroy's professional ethics without providing evidence to document the relevance of his ethics to the issue at hand.

GO ON TO THE NEXT PAGE.

22. Until 1990, the results of the Reading Level Assessment Test given in junior high schools of school districts X and Y indicated that the reading ability of students in the two districts was nearly identical. Since 1990, however, the average score on the test has been markedly higher in district Y than in district X. The Superintendent of district Y theorizes that the difference is due to the reinstatement of the minimum reading level requirement in all junior high schools in his district, which mandates students reading below grade level to attend after-school reading workshops one day a week.

If the statements above are true, which one of the following must also be true?

(A) The average score on the Reading Level Assessment Test in district Y has risen dramatically since the reinstatement of the minimum reading level requirement.

(B) There was a minimum reading level requirement in the junior high schools of district X at some point before 1990.

(C) There was no minimum reading level requirement in the junior high schools of district Y at some point before 1990.

(D) There was no minimum reading level requirement in the junior high schools of district X at some point after 1990.

(E) Since 1990, the Reading Level Assessment Test score of every student in district Y has been higher than the Reading Level Assessment Test score of every student in district X.

23. An economic or political crisis in a poor country can lead to a lack of faith in the country's leaders, which is often followed by violent behavior, dissent, and even revolt among specific segments of the population. In many cases, propaganda is immediately issued from media outlets that quells such reactions by downplaying the extent of the recent crisis, thereby helping to restore belief in the efficacy of the government. However, the habitual violence exhibited by certain groups of disaffected youths in such countries generally has nothing to do with a lack of faith in their leaders, but rather is the consequence of an endemic boredom and lack of any vision of a positive future for themselves.

Which one of the following statements follows most logically from the statements in the passage above?

(A) It is easier to quell periodic revolts in poor countries than it is to solve the habitual problem of youth violence.

(B) In all poor countries, propaganda alone cannot entirely diffuse dissent stemming from an economic or political crisis.

(C) Economic and political crises do not lead to any instances of youth violence in poor countries.

(D) The effect that propaganda has in putting down revolts in poor countries is primarily related to its ability to alter people's fundamental beliefs.

(E) To the extent that propaganda may help to decrease youth violence in a poor country, it is probably not the result of restoring the youths' faith in their country's leadership.

GO ON TO THE NEXT PAGE.

24. Derek won this year's school science fair, and is a star on both the school's football and basketball teams. Outside of school, he runs his own successful business and is an accomplished musician. Obviously Derek is good at everything he does, and thus will undoubtedly make an excellent Student Government President if elected.

The argument above is suspect because it overlooks the possibility that

(A) Derek participates in only those activities at which he knows he will excel

(B) presiding over the Student Government requires different skills than those necessary to becoming an accomplished musician

(C) school, athletics, music and business are the only activities in which Derek is engaged

(D) there may be other students as qualified as Derek to preside over the Student Government

(E) Derek has no time in his schedule to devote to the Student Government

25. Pediatric nurses in Downs Valley have typically been willing to accept overtime emergency home-care cases on short notice, despite the fact that this work is stressful, difficult, and not well compensated relative to the demands related to home-based pediatric care. Many accepted these voluntary assignments because of the professional and personal satisfaction that comes from personally helping a child and the child's family through a true time of need, especially after a relationship with the patient had been forged. Over the past six months, however, the cynicism pervading the Downs Valley medical establishment has clearly taken root among the pediatric nurses. They are now less willing to sacrifice for the well-being of their patients, as evidenced by the steep decline during this period in nursing assignments to home-care cases, despite an overall increase in available pediatric nurses.

Which one of the following, if true, best strengthens the argument above?

(A) Over the past six months, the total number of medical cases in Downs Valley requiring a nurse's care in a hospital setting has greatly increased.

(B) Despite certain advances in the treatment of childhood diseases, there has been no decrease in the last six months in the number of illnesses in Downs Valley requiring the service of an at-home pediatric nurse.

(C) Over the past six months, an increase in the paperwork required by insurance companies has obligated pediatric nurses to spend more time producing reports and less time with patients and their families.

(D) The financial compensation for home-care nursing assignments in Downs Valley is far greater than that in communities of neighboring states due to differences in state funding of pediatric home-care treatment.

(E) The cynicism pervading the Downs Valley medical establishment stems from disgruntled doctors who are furious over recent substantial increases in the cost of malpractice insurance.

STOP
IF YOU FINISH BEFORE TIME IS CALLED, YOU MAY CHECK YOUR WORK ON THIS SECTION ONLY. DO NOT WORK ON ANY OTHER SECTION IN THE TEST.

SECTION III
Time—35 minutes

24 questions

<u>Directions</u>: Each group of questions is based on a set of conditions. You may wish to draw a rough sketch to help you answer some of the questions. Choose the <u>best</u> answer for each question and fill in the corresponding space on your answer sheet.

<u>Questions 1–6</u>

A stadium has two walls available for advertisements, one circling its upper deck and one circling its lower deck. Each of six companies places exactly one ad on one of the two walls. Three of the companies—F, G, and H—sell beverages, and the other three companies—M, N, and—sell clothing. No other companies will advertise at the stadium. The ads will be placed according to the following conditions:

Each wall must contain at least one beverage ad and at least one clothing ad.

M will advertise on the lower wall only if the upper wall contains exactly four ads.

Neither F nor N will advertise on a wall containing exactly two ads.

1. If the upper wall contains exactly four ads, which one of the following companies must advertise on the upper wall?

(A) G
(B) H
(C) M
(D) N
(E) P

2. If G is one of exactly two companies that advertise on the upper wall, all of the following companies must advertise on the lower wall EXCEPT:

(A) F
(B) H
(C) M
(D) N
(E) P

3. Which one of the following could be a complete and accurate list of companies that advertise on the upper wall?

(A) F, G, M
(B) G, H, N, P
(C) G, N
(D) H, N, P
(E) M, P

4. If N and P advertise on the upper wall, which one of the following must be true?

(A) F advertises on the upper wall.
(B) G advertises on the upper wall.
(C) H advertises on the lower wall.
(D) H advertises on the same wall as M.
(E) P advertises on a wall containing exactly three advertisements.

5. F cannot be the only beverage company to advertise on the lower wall UNLESS:

(A) G advertises on the same wall as N.
(B) H advertises on the lower wall.
(C) M advertises on the lower wall.
(D) M advertises on the same wall as P.
(E) N advertises on the lower wall.

6. If one wall contains exactly two beverage ads and exactly two clothing ads, then which one of the following must be true?

(A) F and H cannot advertise on the same wall.
(B) G and H advertise on the same wall.
(C) G and N advertise on the same wall.
(D) M and N cannot advertise on the same wall.
(E) M and P cannot advertise on the same wall.

GO ON TO THE NEXT PAGE.

Questions 7–12

Three divers—Xavier, Yulissa, and Zeke—perform exactly six dives, numbered one through six from first to last, as part of a theme park exhibition. Exactly one diver performs each dive. The following additional restrictions apply:

Xavier performs exactly three dives, but none consecutively.

Yulissa performs exactly two dives, at least one of which must be the first dive or the second dive.

Zeke does not perform a dive immediately before or immediately after Yulissa performs a dive.

7. Which one of the following could be an acceptable ordering, from first to sixth, of divers performing in the exhibition?
   (A) Xavier, Yulissa, Xavier, Zeke, Yulissa, Xavier
   (B) Yulissa, Xavier, Xavier, Zeke, Xavier, Yulissa
   (C) Yulissa, Xavier, Yulissa, Xavier, Zeke, Xavier
   (D) Yulissa, Xavier, Zeke, Xavier, Xavier, Yulissa
   (E) Zeke, Xavier, Yulissa, Xavier, Yulissa, Xavier

8. If Zeke performs the fifth dive, which one of the following must be true?
   (A) Xavier performs the first dive.
   (B) Xavier performs the second dive.
   (C) Xavier performs the third dive.
   (D) Yulissa performs the first dive.
   (E) Yulissa performs the third dive.

9. Which one of the following cannot be true?
   (A) Xavier performs the first dive.
   (B) Yulissa performs the fourth dive.
   (C) Yulissa performs the sixth dive.
   (D) Zeke performs the first dive.
   (E) Zeke performs the sixth dive.

10. If Xavier performs the third dive, which one of the following must be false?
    (A) Xavier performs the first dive.
    (B) Xavier performs the sixth dive.
    (C) Yulissa performs the second dive.
    (D) Yulissa performs the fourth dive.
    (E) Zeke performs the fourth dive.

11. If Yulissa performs two consecutive dives, then each of the following must be true EXCEPT:
    (A) Xavier performs the first dive.
    (B) Xavier performs the sixth dive.
    (C) Yulissa performs the second dive.
    (D) Yulissa performs the third dive.
    (E) Zeke performs the fourth dive.

12. If the restriction that Xavier's performances must not be consecutive is changed to the requirement that Xavier's performances must be consecutive, but all other conditions remain the same, then the number of possible orderings of divers performing the six dives is
    (A) 1
    (B) 2
    (C) 3
    (D) 4
    (E) 5

GO ON TO THE NEXT PAGE.

KAPLAN

Questions 13–18

Seven instructors—J, K, L, M, N, P, and Q—teach adult education courses at a community college. Each instructor teaches during exactly one semester: the fall semester, the spring semester, or the winter semester. The following conditions apply:

K teaches during the winter semester.
L and M teach during the same semester.
Q teaches during either the fall semester or the spring semester.
Exactly twice as many instructors teach during the winter semester as teach during the fall semester.
N and Q teach during different semesters.
J and P teach during different semesters.

13. Which one of the following could be an accurate matching of instructors to semesters?

(A) M: the fall semester; P: the spring semester; Q: the fall semester
(B) J: the winter semester; L: the winter semester; P: the winter semester
(C) L: the fall semester; N: the spring semester; P: the winter semester
(D) J: the fall semester; M: the winter semester; N: the spring semester
(E) K: the spring semester; L: the winter semester; P: the winter semester

14. Which one of the following cannot be true?

(A) L teaches during the fall semester.
(B) M teaches during the spring semester.
(C) M teaches during the winter semester.
(D) N teaches during the spring semester.
(E) P teaches during the fall semester.

15. If exactly one instructor teaches during the spring semester, which one of the following must be true?

(A) J teaches during the winter semester.
(B) L teaches during the fall semester.
(C) M teaches during the winter semester.
(D) P teaches during the spring semester.
(E) Q teaches during the fall semester.

16. Each of the following contains a list of instructors who can all teach during the same semester EXCEPT:

(A) J, K, M
(B) J, L, M
(C) K, L, P
(D) K, P, Q
(E) L, M, P

17. Which one of the following could be a complete and accurate list of instructors who do not teach during the winter semester?

(A) J, L, Q
(B) J, Q
(C) L, M, Q
(D) N, P, Q
(E) N, Q

18. If more instructors teach during the spring semester than teach during the fall semester, then which one of the following instructors must teach during the spring semester?

(A) J
(B) M
(C) N
(D) P
(E) Q

GO ON TO THE NEXT PAGE.

Questions 19–24

Exactly six passengers occupy four adjacent rows on a landing commuter plane. The rows are numbered 1 through 4 from front to back. Three of the passengers are businesspeople, and three are tourists. Two of the passengers are connecting to another flight, and four are arriving home. The rows are occupied by passengers in accordance with the following conditions:

> If a row is occupied by a tourist, it is not also occupied by a businessperson.
> No arriving tourist occupies a row immediately adjacent to a row occupied by a connecting businessperson.
> Each row is occupied by fewer than three passengers.

19. Which one of the following is an acceptable assignment of passengers to rows?

(A) row 1: one arriving tourist, one connecting tourist; row 2: empty; row 3: three arriving businesspeople; row 4: one connecting tourist

(B) row 1: one arriving businessperson; row 2: one arriving tourist; row 3: one arriving tourist, one connecting tourist; row 4: one arriving businessperson, one connecting businessperson

(C) row 1: one arriving businessperson, one connecting businessperson; row 2: one connecting tourist; row 3: two arriving tourists; row 4: one arriving businessperson

(D) row 1: one connecting tourist; row 2: two arriving businesspeople; row 3: one connecting tourist, one arriving businessperson; row 4: one arriving tourist

(E) row 1: two connecting businesspeople; row 2: one arriving tourist; row 3: two arriving tourists; row 4: one arriving businessperson

20. Which one of the following must be true?

(A) No row is occupied by exactly one passenger.
(B) No row is occupied by exactly two passengers.
(C) No row is empty.
(D) Row 1 is occupied by the same number of passengers as is row 3.
(E) Row 4 is occupied by twice as many passengers as is row 2.

21. If a tourist is seated alone in row 4, and no two adjacent rows are occupied by businesspeople, then which one of the following must be true?

(A) Row 1 is occupied by exactly one businessperson.
(B) Row 2 is occupied by exactly two tourists.
(C) Row 3 is occupied by exactly two businesspeople.
(D) Row 1 is occupied by a connecting passenger.
(E) Row 4 is occupied by an arriving passenger.

22. If a connecting businessperson occupies row 3, and exactly two of the six passengers are arriving businesspeople, then which one of the following must be true?

(A) An arriving tourist sits alone in one of the rows.
(B) Two arriving businesspeople sit together in one of the rows.
(C) A connecting businessperson sits alone in one of the rows.
(D) An arriving businessperson and a connecting businessperson sit together in one of the rows.
(E) A connecting tourist sits alone in one of the rows.

23. Each of the following could be a complete and accurate list of the passengers in row 2 EXCEPT:

(A) one arriving businessperson
(B) two connecting businesspeople
(C) one arriving businessperson, one connecting businessperson
(D) one connecting tourist
(E) two arriving businesspeople

24. If all of the businesspeople are arriving home, which one of the following is impossible?

(A) Both connecting passengers are seated alone in different rows.
(B) Exactly one arriving passenger is seated alone in a row.
(C) Exactly two of the arriving passengers are seated alone in different rows.
(D) Both connecting passengers are seated together in a row.
(E) Exactly two of the arriving passengers are seated together in a row.

STOP

IF YOU FINISH BEFORE TIME IS CALLED, YOU MAY CHECK YOUR WORK ON THIS SECTION ONLY. DO NOT WORK ON ANY OTHER SECTION IN THE TEST.

SECTION IV
Time—35 minutes
25 questions

<u>Directions</u>: This test is composed of questions that ask you to analyze the logic of statements or short paragraphs. You are to choose as the answer to each question the one choice you consider <u>best</u> on the basis of your common-sense evaluation of the statement and its assumptions. Although a question may seem to have more than one acceptable answer, there is only one <u>best</u> answer, and it is the one that does not entail making any illogical, extraneous, or conflicting assumptions about the question. These questions do not presuppose any knowledge of formal logic on your part.

1. Attention Deficit Disorder (ADD) is a condition characterized by an inability to focus on any topic for a prolonged period of time, and is especially common among children five to ten years old. A recent study has shown that 85 percent of seven-year-old children with ADD watch, on average, more than five hours of television a day. It is therefore very likely that Ed, age seven, has ADD, since he watches roughly six hours of television a day.

   The argument above is flawed because it

   (A) cites as a direct causal mechanism a factor that may only be a partial cause of the condition in question

   (B) fails to indicate the chances of having ADD among seven-year-old children who watch more than five hours of television a day

   (C) limits the description of the symptoms of ADD to an inability to focus for a prolonged period of time

   (D) fails to consider the possibility that Ed may be among the 15 percent of children who do not watch more than five hours of television a day

   (E) does not allow for other causes of ADD besides television watching

2. Industry analyst: Individuals typically buy Internet access accounts from American providers for about $19.95 a month, which includes e-mail but no other services. Recently, however, foreign Internet providers have begun offering web site design and management in addition to Internet access and e-mail, for the same fee of $19.95. Representatives of these foreign Internet providers have boldly predicted that their services will put the American providers out of the Internet access business in the next few years. But they have yet to demonstrate that their companies will provide quality, reliable customer service that is as good as or better than that currently offered by American Internet providers.

   In the argument above, the industry analyst

   (A) demonstrates that any concern on the part of certain companies regarding the threat of foreign competition is entirely unfounded

   (B) suggests that the proponents of a view are basing their conclusion on erroneous information

   (C) reconciles a prediction with analogous facts from a previous situation

   (D) casts doubt on a contention by introducing an additional consideration

   (E) proposes a way for one group of companies to ward off competition from another group of companies

GO ON TO THE NEXT PAGE.

Questions 3–4

The incidence of suicide in the country of Travonia has increased dramatically in recent years, as evidenced by the fact that since the introduction of several non-prescription brands of sleeping pills, the number of deaths from overdoses alone has nearly doubled. However, certain types of suicides have not increased in number during this period. It is true that elderly suicides have seen a greater than 70 percent increase, but teen suicides now account for only 30 percent of all suicides in the country. This is a significant decrease over 1985, when teen cases represented 65 percent of all country-wide suicides.

3. The argument above is most vulnerable to criticism on the grounds that it does which one of the following?

(A) It discounts the possibility of suicides occurring in groups other than the elderly and teenagers.

(B) It takes for granted that the introduction of non-prescription sleeping pills has had the same effect on two different demographic groups.

(C) It assumes that a decrease in the percentage of teen suicides necessarily signifies a decrease in the number of teen suicides.

(D) It overlooks the possibility that the total number of deaths in Travonia has increased since 1985.

(E) It relies on evidence that contradicts its conclusion.

4. The assertion that suicides are increasing in Travonia is most justified if which one of the following is assumed?

(A) The elderly suffered the greatest number of overdoses from the non-prescription sleeping pills.

(B) Overdosing on sleeping pills was not the most pervasive method of suicide in Travonia ten years ago.

(C) The number of deaths from natural causes in Travonia has decreased in recent years.

(D) The majority of deaths resulting from overdosing on non-prescription sleeping pills were not accidental.

(E) Travonia's suicide rate is higher than the world-wide average suicide rate.

5. The overall rate of emphysema has declined 15 percent over the last 15 years in region A. During that period, the total cost of care for emphysema sufferers in region A, after accounting for inflation, declined by two percent per year until eight years ago, at which time it began increasing by approximately two percent per year, so that now the total health care cost for treating emphysema is approximately equal to what it was 15 years ago.

Which one of the following best resolves the apparent discrepancy between the incidence of emphysema in region A and the cost of caring for emphysema sufferers?

(A) The overall cost of health care in region A has increased by seven percent in the last 15 years, after accounting for inflation.

(B) Improvements in technology have significantly increased both the cost per patient and the success rate of emphysema care in the past 15 years.

(C) About seven years ago, the widespread switch to health maintenance organizations halted overall increases in health care costs in region A, after accounting for inflation.

(D) The money made available for research into the causes and cures of emphysema had been declining for many years until approximately eight years ago, since which time it has shown a modest increase.

(E) Beginning about nine years ago, the most expensive-to-treat advanced cases of emphysema have been decreasing in region A at a rate of about five percent per year.

GO ON TO THE NEXT PAGE.

6. City planner: The businesses along Maple Street are struggling, while the shops along the much broader Walnut and Crescent Streets have been prospering recently. Therefore, I propose to widen much of Maple Street, which will benefit the stores along the widened portion of the road by increasing vehicle traffic and bringing more shoppers to the stores.

    Which one of the following, if true, best supports the city planner's recommendation?

    (A) Widening Maple Street will make the sidewalks narrower, making it less appealing to pedestrian shoppers.
    (B) The increased traffic on Maple Street will consist almost entirely of drivers using the widened street to get to distant destinations more quickly.
    (C) Maple Street is farther from the densely populated city center than is Walnut Street, while Crescent Street is farther from the city center than is Maple Street.
    (D) Walnut Street was once a thoroughfare and is now a pedestrian mall.
    (E) Widening Maple Street will create room for many more parking spaces near the shops on the street.

7. In theory, establishing the democratic principle of respecting the basic rights of individuals is unambiguous, but in actual practice, may involve some rather interesting scenarios. For example, recently in country Q major reforms of the legal system were enacted to prevent the violation of the basic rights of its minorities. However, these reforms were only possible because country Q is led by a non-elected dictator who may act directly contrary to the popular will without fear of being voted out of office.

    The argument relies on which one of the following assumptions?

    (A) In a democracy, when a political figure acts directly contrary to the popular will, that figure will be voted out of office.
    (B) Non-elected dictators who act directly contrary to the popular will have no reason to fear being removed from office.
    (C) The principles of democratic government and of respect for basic individual rights are inconsistent.
    (D) The popular will in country Q does not support the protection of the basic rights of minorities in the country.
    (E) The rights of minorities in dictator-led countries such as country Q are more restricted than they are in democratic countries.

8. The city is required by federal environmental regulations to build a new water treatment plant. If this plant is built inside the city limits it will disrupt the lives of many more citizens than if it is built on vacant land near the city. However, despite the availability of the vacant land, the plant should be built inside city limits because of the increased economic benefits its construction would provide to the city in the form of jobs.

    Which one of the following, if true, most weakens the argument above?

    (A) The available land outside of the city is privately owned, whereas there is an adequate site within the city that is city-owned.
    (B) Regardless of the site location, most of the jobs created by the plant's construction will go to residents of the city.
    (C) A municipal plant like the water treatment plant will pay no taxes to city government regardless of its location.
    (D) Most citizens of the city will tolerate brief disruptions in their daily lives if such disruptions will secure better water quality in the future.
    (E) The amount of taxes paid by workers depends both on where they work and where they live.

GO ON TO THE NEXT PAGE.

9. School Chancellor: Just one school in this school district has failed to meet newly enacted minimum achievement standards for the three years the standards have been in existence. An investigation has shown that at this school counterproductive work habits have become entrenched among most of the teachers and administrators, so that simply firing a few "bad apples" will not solve the problem. Therefore, the best solution is to close the school and send the students to neighboring schools in order to improve the overall educational performance in the district as a whole.

Each of the following, if true, weakens the argument above EXCEPT:

(A) Nearby schools in the district do not have the resources to adequately accommodate the children from the closed school.

(B) The school had failed to meet the recently imposed minimum standards for over 10 years, but has recently shown significant improvement.

(C) In other districts, a thorough retraining program has been successful in improving the work habits of most sub-par teachers and administrators.

(D) Earlier in her career, the principal at the school had proven herself to be a competent administrator outside the district.

(E) The children from the school are academically so far behind the children from the other schools in the district that teachers in neighboring schools will be forced to slow down and teach at the level of the new students, thus disadvantaging the current students.

10. If ad pages in *Fission* magazine have increased in December, then either ad rates have decreased or circulation has increased for the month, but not both. If circulation has increased in December, then the editors will receive year-end bonuses. If ad pages have not increased in December, then the editors will not receive year-end bonuses.

If all of the above statements are true, which one of the following can be concluded from the fact that the editors of *Fission* will not receive year-end bonuses?

(A) Ad rates have not increased in December.
(B) Ad pages have increased in December.
(C) Ad pages have not increased in December.
(D) Circulation has increased in December.
(E) Circulation has not increased in December.

11. Historian #1: The *metis* were a distinct people within Canadian society, the offspring of Native Americans and Europeans. Rejected by both groups, they sought to forge an identity for themselves and made claims for land and political autonomy much like the Native Americans. Tragically, these requests were not granted, with the result that the *metis* have gradually lost a distinct identity to the great detriment of Canada's cultural diversity.

Historian #2: I disagree that this denial of the *metis'* demands was tragic. The *metis* were an artificial creation who lacked long-standing cultural traditions of their own. They were not so much a separate cultural group as a name given to all those who were neither fully European nor fully Native American—a wide range forming a necessary continuum connecting the two cultural poles.

A point of disagreement between the two historians is whether

(A) the denial of a people's request for identity can be considered tragic

(B) the *metis* were a distinct cultural entity within Canadian society

(C) the *metis* were offspring of Native Americans and Europeans

(D) the denial of a people's request for identity can diminish a country's cultural diversity

(E) the *metis'* claims for land and autonomy resembled the claims of the Native Americans

GO ON TO THE NEXT PAGE.

12. Before it closed last year, Betty's Beauty Parlor had been in the same location for 25 years. Two years ago, Felix's Hair Salon opened one block away offering similar services. The opening of Felix's Hair Salon directly caused the demise of Betty's Beauty Parlor. This provides yet another example of the effects of competition in a free marketplace.

Which one of the following can be inferred from the statements in the passage above?

(A) Competition is ultimately destructive in a free marketplace.

(B) Betty's Beauty Parlor did not face competitive pressures other than from Felix's Hair Salon.

(C) Felix's Hair Salon served some of the same customers who would have gone to Betty's Beauty Parlor.

(D) Betty's Beauty Parlor would be open today if Felix's Hair Salon had not opened nearby.

(E) Two businesses that offer the same services cannot both survive for long in close proximity.

13. General: The commander of the Air Force has recommended that we deploy the G28 aircraft in the reconnaissance mission, because the G28 can fly lower to the ground without being detected and could therefore retrieve the necessary information more efficiently than the currently stationed D12. But the D12 is already in the area and poised for takeoff, and would have just enough time to accomplish the mission if deployed immediately, while the G28 would require four days just to arrive in the area and get outfitted for the mission. Since the mission's deadline is immovable, I am forced to overrule the commander's recommendation and order the deployment of the D12.

Which one of the following is assumed in the general's argument?

(A) The quality of information retrieved from the mission would be higher if the D12 were deployed than if the G28 were deployed.

(B) By the time the G28 arrived in the area and was outfitted for the mission, the D12 would have already completed the mission if deployed immediately.

(C) The ability of an aircraft to fly low to the ground is not a significant consideration when choosing aircraft for a reconnaissance mission.

(D) It would take longer for any aircraft not currently in the area besides the G28 to arrive in the area and get outfitted for the mission.

(E) Any time saved during the mission due to the operation of the more efficient G28 would not offset the additional time required to deploy the G28.

GO ON TO THE NEXT PAGE.

14. For exactly ten years, it has not been legal to bungee-jump in state A. All of the members of the Rubberband Club must live in state A and have bungee-jumped at least once in the last two years. The Rubberband Club is currently taking applications for new members.

Which one of the following necessarily follows from the information provided above?

(A) Every current member of the Rubberband Club has bungee-jumped outside of state A.

(B) No current applicant to the Rubberband Club has legally bungee-jumped in state A.

(C) The current members of the Rubberband Club have bungee-jumped illegally at least once.

(D) Current members of the Rubberband Club who have never bungee-jumped outside of state A have broken the law in state A.

(E) The Rubberband Club does not include members who have bungee-jumped legally in state A.

15. The influence of McTell's work on Waters' formulation of psychosocial theory has long been recognized in the academic community. McTell was Waters' mentor and main confidant during the 1950's, the time just before Waters published his revolutionary findings. There is ample evidence of communication during this time between the two regarding the core issues that would eventually coalesce in Waters' theory. However, a recently discovered letter dated 1947—years before Waters met McTell—indicates that Waters had already formulated the basic conceptions of his psychosocial theory. While McTell may certainly have helped Waters develop his theories, it is not possible that McTell influenced the formulation of Waters' scholarship in the manner originally believed.

The author of the argument above assumes that Waters

(A) did not know of and read McTell's work before he met him

(B) did not model his theory on the work of some scholar other than McTell

(C) did not have a mentor and confidant during the 1940's

(D) did not allow McTell to influence any aspect of his psychosocial theory

(E) did not benefit in any way from his association with McTell in the 1950's

16. Fewer geniuses have emerged from the present era than had emerged in previous eras. In the seventeenth century, there were only about one one-hundredth as many people as today, and yet in Europe alone geniuses like Galileo, Descartes, Newton, and Shakespeare flourished. In the twentieth century, Einstein is the only accepted genius of that stature.

Which one of the following, if true, provides the most support to the argument above?

(A) Geniuses are widely recognized during their lives or soon after their deaths.

(B) There are many different kinds of geniuses, some of which are not easily comparable.

(C) The very idea of genius has been questioned and seriously criticized.

(D) The twentieth century has seen the spread of education to a much greater proportion of the population, reducing the extremes in educational attainment present in previous centuries.

(E) Scientific knowledge has been expanding at an ever-increasing rate for hundreds of years.

GO ON TO THE NEXT PAGE.

17. Sylvia: The public has a false perception that Banner clothes dryers are dangerous machines that frequently catch on fire. In fact, the number of Banner dryers that have actually caught on fire is quite small. Moreover, that number is minuscule compared to the number of major manufacturers' dryers that have caught on fire.

Alice: It is possible, however, that the percentage of Banner dryers that catch on fire is larger than the percentage of dryers from major manufacturers that do so. After all, the total number of dryers manufactured by the Banner company is relatively small compared to the extremely large numbers of dryers that major dryer companies have produced.

In responding to Sylvia's argument, Alice does which one of the following?

(A) She accepts Sylvia's conclusion but shows that different evidence may be used to reach that conclusion.
(B) She disproves Sylvia's conclusion by bringing up evidence that contradicts the evidence used by Sylvia to support her conclusion.
(C) She proves the irrelevance of Sylvia's evidence by pointing out that Sylvia is comparing two groups of items that cannot be compared.
(D) She refutes the evidence that Sylvia uses to support her conclusion.
(E) She demonstrates that Sylvia's conclusion is suspect because it is based on a faulty comparison involving total numbers instead of percentages.

18. A building that does not have adequate ventilation and natural light cannot be well-designed. A building with many windows will have adequate natural light, and so the presence of many windows in a building ensures that it is well-designed.

A reasoning error in the argument is that the argument fails to establish that

(A) adequate ventilation is only possible with many windows
(B) natural light ensures the presence of many windows
(C) the presence of many windows suffices to provide adequate ventilation
(D) some buildings without many windows are well-designed
(E) some buildings that have adequate ventilation and natural light may not be well-designed

19. It is not illegal to use hairspray, air conditioners, or vacuum-pressurized aerosol food containers, but it is well known that the use of such products damages the ozone layer, which may in turn have serious negative ecological consequences for future generations. It is therefore incumbent upon us to stop using these products so as to preserve the environment as best we can, even though we believe these products may enrich our lives and there are no legal sanctions against them.

Which one of the following principles is most consistent with the line of reasoning presented above?

(A) The legality of one's self-interested actions should be determined in light of the moral quality of that action.
(B) The morality of one's self-interested actions should be judged in light of the legal ramifications of performing those actions.
(C) The legality of one's self-interested actions should be determined based on the consequences such actions had on previous generations.
(D) The morality of one's self-interested actions should be judged in light of the consequences those actions may have for others.
(E) The severity of punishment for an illegal action should be determined based on the moral quality of that action.

GO ON TO THE NEXT PAGE.

20. Public service announcements attempt to persuade teenagers to follow useful advice, but cause them to resent being preached to. Teenagers will follow advice only if they do not resent being preached to. Therefore, public service announcements are ineffective, and should be discontinued.

Which one of the following exhibits reasoning most similar to the reasoning displayed in the argument above?

(A) Mandatory seat belt laws are directed at those who do not like to feel constricted when they drive. Freedom from unnecessary restrictions is one of the fundamental principles of this country. Thus, mandatory seat belt laws damage one of the fundamental principles of this country, and should be repealed.

(B) Zoning restrictions prevent the development of neighborhoods that include both industrial and residential buildings. Including both industrial and residential buildings in the same neighborhood is dangerous and very harmful to residential property values. Therefore, including both of these types of buildings in the same neighborhood should be prevented.

(C) The estate tax applies to those who possess large estates when they die, but encourages them to reduce their savings. Savings are needed to stimulate growth in the economy. Thus, the estate tax causes more economic harm than good, and should be repealed.

(D) Conservation laws are intended to protect endangered wildlife, which induces their expansion into land presently occupied by people. People will not support conservation laws when their land is occupied by the animals under protection. Thus, the conservation laws are self-undermining, and should be abandoned.

(E) The use of twelve-hour shifts at a company is intended to maximize production by employees, but encourages them to work inefficiently. Employees must work efficiently in order for a company to maximize production. Therefore, the use of twelve-hour shifts fails to further the company's objective, and should be abolished.

Questions 21–22

In addressing the region-wide recession, the comptroller of County X has asserted that the depressed economy of County X is indicative of the inevitable consequences of the recession for all counties in the region. But that must be false, considering that the economy of neighboring County Y is as robust as ever, despite the overall current financial difficulties of the region.

21. Which one of the following, if true, most helps to explain the fact that the economy of County X is suffering while the economy of County Y is not?

(A) The level of economic recession in the region is less severe than that of its neighboring regions.

(B) In overall revenue generated, the economy of County X surpasses that of County Y, even during recessionary periods.

(C) Unlike County Y, County X's economy relies almost entirely on tourism, which has been crippled by the region's recession.

(D) County Y relies on imports for most of its non-essential consumer items, most of which come from County X.

(E) When the recession struck, a few retail businesses relocated from County X to County Y.

22. The argument above does which one of the following?

(A) It counters a claim by providing evidence that directly conflicts with that claim.

(B) It contests the relevance of one piece of evidence on the grounds that it is categorically dissimilar from an opposing piece of evidence.

(C) It counters a claim by asserting the impossibility under the current circumstances of that which is claimed.

(D) It supports its conclusion by appealing to an authority.

(E) It provides evidence in the form of a generalization that counters the claim being opposed.

GO ON TO THE NEXT PAGE.

23. Researchers, perplexed by the development of measles immunity in children who were not given the measles vaccination, believe that they now understand this phenomenon. The children in question were all raised from birth on a baby formula produced by the manufacturer Dihydro. The Dihydro formula contains a synthetic chemical known as dihydron-X, which has been shown in lab tests to rapidly destroy cells infected with measles. Researchers have concluded that those children who ingest the Dihydro formula maintain dihydron-X in their bloodstreams indefinitely. When measles-infected cells proliferate in the child's body, the dihydron-X responds to the invasion by quickly killing off all infected cells, thus arresting the progress of the disease so rapidly that the child is perceived to have a measles immunity.

Which one of the following most accurately characterizes the role played in the passage by the unstated assumption that some children who receive measles vaccinations develop an immunity to measles?

(A) It is a point that, taken together with the fact that some children who do not receive the measles vaccine develop an immunity to measles, generates the problem that motivated the research described in the passage.

(B) It is a generalization assumed by the researchers to prove that the explanation of their puzzling case must involve a reference to the chemical composition of measles-resistant cells.

(C) It is a generalization that, if true, makes impossible the notion that some children who do not receive a measles vaccine develop an immunity to measles.

(D) It is a hypothesis that the researchers take to be proven conclusively by the findings put forth in the passage.

(E) It is a conclusion that is overturned by the researchers' discovery that some children who do not receive vaccines nonetheless develop a measles immunity.

24. The Chief of Personnel declared yesterday that no human resource employees were fired in the embezzlement scandal. However, the records show that some human resource employees were fired in March, and they also show that some of the employees who were fired in March were fired in the embezzlement scandal. It thus stands to reason that the Chief of Personnel made a false declaration.

Which one of the following arguments contains reasoning that is flawed in a manner most similar to the reasoning in the argument above?

(A) Candy must have extremely good manners. She is a member of the hospitality team at the summer lodge, and all hospitality team members at the lodge have extremely good manners.

(B) Some of the summer theater actors who starred in *Icarus* also starred in *Mrs. Jones*, and some of the actors who starred in *Mrs. Jones* were schooled at the Zeller Drama School. Therefore, some of the summer theater actors who starred in *Icarus* were schooled at the Zeller Drama School.

(C) Many of the Parkers' neighbors have young children. People with young children tend to stay home on weekend nights. So at least some of the Parkers' neighbors probably stay home on weekend nights.

(D) Some artificial Christmas trees have white branches. Other types of artificial Christmas trees have blue branches. Therefore, some artificial Christmas trees have both white and blue branches.

(E) This is Bradley's third year on the delivery crew for Arlene's Grocery. Arlene's Grocery is famous for its efficient delivery service, so Bradley must be a fast worker.

GO ON TO THE NEXT PAGE.

25. Principal: Excellence Learning Services offers reading and math programs for elementary school children. In its promotional literature distributed last year, the company argued that the deficiencies in the current educational system put children at risk of failing statewide math and reading tests. The literature further claimed that the company's programs will remedy these problems. Our school responded to this message by enrolling our children in Excellence Learning Services' programs. However, this year the percentage of our students that passed the statewide math and reading tests is the same as it was twenty years ago. Therefore, the claims in Excellence Learning Services' promotional literature were misleading.

The principal's reasoning is most vulnerable to criticism on which one of the following grounds?

(A) It merely criticizes the math and reading programs without offering an alternative method of addressing the problems of the current educational system.

(B) It assumes that the parents of the enrolled children were not capable of critically evaluating Excellence Learning Services' promotional literature.

(C) It uses emotionally-charged terms as a substitute for relevant evidence.

(D) It does not demonstrate that the programs did not provide benefits in areas other than math and reading skills.

(E) It fails to consider the possibility that the programs were effective in improving math and reading scores.

STOP
**IF YOU FINISH BEFORE TIME IS CALLED, YOU MAY CHECK YOUR WORK ON THIS SECTION ONLY.
DO NOT WORK ON ANY OTHER SECTION IN THE TEST.**

PRACTICE TEST THREE ANSWER KEY

Section I Reading Comprehension	Section II Logical Reasoning	Section III Logic Games	Section IV Logical Reasoning
1. E	1. C	1. D	1. B
2. C	2. E	2. C	2. D
3. B	3. B	3. A	3. C
4. A	4. C	4. A	4. D
5. D	5. D	5. E	5. B
6. D	6. A	6. E	6. E
7. B	7. C	7. C	7. D
8. C	8. B	8. E	8. B
9. A	9. A	9. D	9. D
10. D	10. D	10. B	10. E
11. E	11. D	11. E	11. B
12. B	12. C	12. A	12. C
13. A	13. A	13. D	13. E
14. C	14. E	14. A	14. D
15. B	15. A	15. C	15. A
16. E	16. B	16. D	16. A
17. A	17. E	17. D	17. E
18. A	18. C	18. B	18. C
19. D	19. A	19. C	19. D
20. E	20. B	20. C	20. E
21. A	21. C	21. B	21. C
22. C	22. C	22. E	22. A
23. E	23. E	23. B	23. A
24. D	24. A	24. A	24. B
25. D	25. B		25. E
26. E			
27. C			

PRACTICE TEST THREE EXPLANATIONS

Section I: Reading Comp Explanations

PASSAGE 1—Direct Marketing

Topic and Scope
Direct mail marketing; specifically, the discrepancy between Americans' attitudes towards direct mail and their behavior in response to it.

Purpose and Main Idea
The author's purpose is to explain why direct mail marketing has been so successful despite Americans' seemingly negative attitudes towards direct mail techniques. The main idea is that even though Americans dislike receiving "junk mail," they value the advantages of shopping by mail and continue to respond positively to direct mail marketing, increasing the industry's success.

Paragraph Structure
Paragraph 1 introduces us to the notion that Americans' response to direct mail marketing has been "strangely mixed." We get the "negative side" of the American response in the first paragraph, as the author explains why Americans view direct mail marketing as annoying and invasive.

Paragraph 2 then helps us to see why the American response can be considered "mixed." It starts out by providing evidence from an opinion survey that supports the author's claim that Americans view direct mail negatively. It then shows that despite their atti-tudes, Americans' behaviors in response to direct mail have been positive: Direct mail has become a highly successful marketing industry. Evidence from the same opinion survey cited earlier is given to show that Americans buy items through direct mail even though they dislike its techniques.

This "seeming contradiction" is explained in paragraph 3, where the author tells us that Americans shop by direct mail even though they dislike it because it is convenient and offers distinct advantages over other types of shopping. In essence, Americans like shopping by mail—so they put up with the drawbacks of direct mail techniques.

The Big Picture
- As you read through the first paragraph of an LSAT passage, be on the lookout for the main idea or at least a guiding framework for what is to come. In this passage, the statement that "America's response . . . has been strangely mixed" strongly suggests that the passage will discuss both sides of the issue. Stay alert as you read to make sure that that indeed is what is discussed.
- Often LSAT passages will not present the entire main idea in the first paragraph of the passage. We may have a sense of what will be presented, as with this passage, but by the end of the first paragraph we may only get part of the story. If

you don't think you have the main idea by the end of the first paragraph, keep reading and focus especially on the final paragraph. There's a good chance that the main idea will be summed up there.

The Questions

1 **(E)** First off is a standard Global question looking for the main idea of the passage. If you've properly developed your Roadmap and put some thought into the author's purpose and main idea up front, this question should be a good one to prephrase. The author argues that direct mail has been successful, despite negative attitudes about it, because people like the advantages of shopping by mail. This point is nicely summarized in choice (E).

(A) distorts the technology issue presented in the passage. Increases in technology are seen as responsible for the fact that direct mail marketers now have access to individuals' private information, but technology is not cited as a reason for the success of direct marketing.

(B) We are never told that concerns over privacy issues have affected the targeting of direct mail audiences. In fact, the opposite may be true—direct marketers seem to ignore individuals' concerns over privacy.

(C) misrepresents the author's argument. The boom in direct mail marketing appears to be the result of individuals' actual reaction to the technique, not a result of the discrepancy between attitude and reaction.

(D) Too narrow. Part of America's "mixed response" does stem from the perceived threat to privacy caused by aggressive marketing techniques—but what about the other reasons for this mixed response, especially the positive reasons?

Remember:

• When choosing the answers to Global questions, be careful to avoid choices that are either too narrow or too broad. Choices that are too narrow focus only on part of the passage, while overly broad choices go beyond the passage's scope. The correct answer will cover the main gist of the entire passage while accurately reflecting the passage's scope.

2 **(C)** This Strengthen question requires that we first understand how the author explains the "seeming contradiction" in paragraph 3. He argues that Americans respond to direct marketing because of its conveniences, even though Americans don't like the annoyance or the invasion of privacy. This evidence assumes that Americans are willing to maintain certain shopping habits despite the drawbacks associated with them. Choice (C) bolsters this assumption and therefore strengthens the argument.

(A), (B) These choices focus on one portion of the author's argument but do not help strengthen it as a whole. In (A), the fact that awareness of infringement is high would strengthen only one part of the author's claim—that people don't like direct mail. It doesn't bolster the full argument that direct mail marketing is successful *despite* these infringements due to the fact that Americans like to shop by mail. Similarly, with (B), the increased number of people on multiple mailing lists does not necessarily strengthen the argument that people use direct mail despite its drawbacks because they like its conveniences. These individuals may be on multiple lists simply because their names were sold to direct mail companies.

KAPLAN

(D) contradicts the author's explanation of why direct mail marketing is successful. (D) states that direct marketing may eventually benefit consumers—its success will filter down to consumers over time. But the author tells us that people respond to direct mail marketing because they like its advantages—in other words, they benefit from it now, as they are using it. That's why they put up with its annoyance and invasion of privacy. If (D) is true, perhaps there's more to the story than the author perceives.

(E) The only thing that (E) may strengthen (and it's tenuous at best) is the notion that the "seeming contradiction" that the author describes exists.

Remember:

- The answer to any Strengthen/Weaken question will always be linked to the author's argument concerning the issue at hand in the question. To find a strengthener, first determine the components of the author's argument in that portion of the passage. Once you've isolated the evidence and conclusion, you'll be in a better position to look for the author's assumptions. As in the Logical Reasoning sections of the LSAT, strengtheners and weakeners in Reading Comp often work by bolstering or damaging the assumptions in an author's argument.

3 (B) This question asks us to identify the criticism that most closely approximates the logic of the author's concern over the use of computer matching programs. Well, why is the author concerned about these? The line reference brings us right to the crux of the matter: "Further, sophisticated computer matching programs can produce intrusive personal profiles from information which, standing alone, does not threaten individual privacy." Extracting the general logical structure of this, we have a situation in which harmless individual elements, when combined, become harmful in some way. That's the situation we need to find among the choices, and (B) best approximates this situation: the species alone aren't dangerous to the ecosystem, but put them together and look out!

It's helpful to restate exactly what we're looking for in order to eliminate the wrong choices: The logic of the original example in the passage states that things (bits of information) that individually don't have a certain effect (i.e., threaten privacy) DO have that effect when put together.

(A) Here, we have species that individually don't harm the ecosystem (so far so good), but when put together may harm *each other*. Not the same thing.

(C), like all of the wrong choices, starts out okay with individual species that by themselves don't harm the ecosystem, so we have to look to the end of the choice to see where it goes awry. In this case, the ecologist is chastised for asserting the safety of throwing the three species together into the ecosystem on the grounds that they may not allow other species to join later. Boo hoo. This result would not necessarily cause damage to the ecosystem.

(D) This time the ecologists' assertion is bashed on the grounds that the species in question may be happier somewhere else. Again, the "overlooked possibility" is not one that necessarily causes harm: The ecosystem might not be an optimal environment for the species, but that doesn't necessarily mean that the ecosystem itself will be damaged.

(E) Their *previous* ecosystems? What does that have to do with putting them together here in the ecosystem in question? This is far from the logic underlying the example in the passage.

Remember:

- Application questions ask you to "apply" something you've learned in the passage to another issue in a different context. If the question seems difficult, and you're having trouble making the connection, it might be a good one to save until the end of the passage—or to skip altogether.
- Questions with long answer choices may not be as difficult as they seem. Notice that every choice in this question starts with the same 29 words. Once you picked up on that, you should have had an easier time—in truth, you really only needed to read the last part of each choice to see how it differed from the others.

4 **(A)** The mention of "expenditures from 1980–1990 brings us squarely to paragraph 2, where the author informs us that expenditures rose significantly during that stretch, and that "companies would not have made these efforts without prospects of success." Inference questions are not great candidates for prephrasing, so you probably moved on to the choices at this point. Hopefully you saw that (A) is a reasonable inference based on this information. It stands to reason that companies spent more money on advertising because they expected to benefit from it (in accordance with the "laws of the market"). Therefore, the rise in direct marketing expenditures can be reasonably said to reflect their expectations regarding success.

(B), (C), and (D) The passage implies that companies benefited from direct marketing—mean-ing, they made greater profits—but we have no idea how much they benefited. Thus, a specific claim like (B)'s assertion that they made "more than double" the profit at the end than at the beginning of the period is not warranted. Similarly, we are told that expenditures rose from 1980 to 1990, but we don't know how much they rose in any given year. In fact, we can't be sure that expenditures rose every single year—we're only told that the 1990 figure was greater than the 1980 figure. So we don't have enough information to infer choice (C). The same is true of choice (D). We're only told that expenditures rose from 1980–90. We cannot infer anything about what companies might expect expenditures to be in the future.

(E) distorts information in the passage. The author tells us that "the laws of the market dictate" that companies would not have invested in direct marketing unless they expected it to be success-ful. But to say that the rise in expenditures "par-allels" the laws of the market is a distortion of this concept. The rise in expenditures may be explained with reference to the laws of the eco-nomic market, but that's about it. (E)'s manner of combining these two elements of the passage is unwarranted.

Remember:

- Inference questions often refer to only a small part of the passage. Zero in on the relevant sec-tion using the specific words of the stem as your guide. Here, "expenditures" and "between 1980 and 1990" should lead you quickly to paragraph 2, and a quick rereading of the author's points regarding these matters should put you in an excellent position to evaluate the choices with confidence.

5 **(D)** The words "according to the passage" clue us in that this is an Explicit Text question. The answer to a detail question like this will most likely not restate the passage's information directly, but will often be recognizable, nonetheless, as a close paraphrase. Since a number of parts of this passage deal with Americans' reaction to direct mail, perhaps the best method is to move right to the choices, seeing if any jump out. (D) is, in fact, a very close paraphrase of the author's main idea that emerges along the way and is summarized rather explicitly in the final paragraph.

(A) goes beyond the scope of the passage. The author does not discuss the "true dangers" of the enterprise (whatever these may be).

(B) This choice exaggerates material from the passage. The author states in paragraph 3 that Americans are willing to put up with the drawbacks of direct mail because they like its conveniences. We might interpret this as meaning that people are willing to overlook some problems in order to receive certain benefits. To say that people "consistently act against their deeply held convictions," however, is going too far. Besides, the dislike of direct mail probably doesn't qualify as a deeply held conviction in most people's books.

(C) This choice only gives us part of the author's view, and is a distortion to boot. The author distinctly tells us that the public's reaction is mixed—it's not just negative, as this answer choice portrays it. In addition, the negative attitude of the American public revolves around both the privacy issue and the "annoyance" factor. It's a distortion to say that privacy is the primary issue.

(E) *Au contraire*. The author tells us that the industry has been very *successful* despite the public's negative attitudes. There is no indication that the industry will need to alter its practices.

Remember:

- The answers to Explicit Text questions will be drawn directly from material given in the passage. Rule out any answer choices that stray too far from the details in the passage and look for those that convey what the author has already stated.

6 **(D)** This Logic question asks us to determine what function is served by the opinions expressed in the survey mentioned in the beginning of paragraph 2. These opinions are provided as evidence for the public's negative view of direct mail. But, later in paragraph 2, these opinions seem to contradict further findings of the same survey, which show that people who don't like direct mail buy from direct mail ads anyway! This function is captured in choice (D)—these opinions are brought up to form a contrast to the behavior of consumers described later in the paragraph, which in turn forms the basis of the author's main concern.

(A) goes beyond the scope of the passage. The negative attitudes revealed in this part of the survey would make it rather unlikely that the opinions were used by the author to justify increased direct mail spending.

(B) The author does not provide a "solution" to a paradoxical situation but rather an explanation for a seemingly contradictory phenomenon. If anything, the opinions cited contribute to a contradictory phenomenon, not to its explanation.

(C) The information about computer matching programs is presented in paragraph 1 and is unrelated to the author's discussion of the survey. The author develops his conclusion about the problem of the matching program without resorting to any opinion data.

(E) The opinions expressed in the survey *could* reasonably be used to argue that the direct marketing industry will fall on hard times; after all, the opinions expressed are quite negative. But that would be a different passage altogether—here, the author goes on to say that the industry seems to be booming *in spite of* these opinions.

Remember:

- A good Roadmap can help you answer Logic questions more quickly by providing an outline of the entire argument and the author's main idea. Once you know the full argument and how each paragraph fits within it, you're in a better position to determine how any given part of the passage serves the whole.

7 **(B)** This Inference question requires us to determine which statement could most likely be attributed to the author, based on the information presented in the passage. Again, our grasp of the author's purpose in writing the passage comes into play. This passage looks at the difference between Americans' attitudes about direct mail and their behaviors in response to it. Evidence for the public's attitudes is provided through opinion surveys, which suggests that the author believes that the attitudes revealed in surveys can help us understand public behavior, choice (B). Think of it this way: If the author didn't agree with (B), then there would be no contradiction to resolve, because the data from the opinion polls would be meaningless. The

passage as is can exists only if the author believes that polls can provide insight as stated in choice (B).

(A) This choice exaggerates the author's conclusion. We are told that Americans respond to direct mail because they perceive its benefits, but it would be going too far to conclude from this that the author believes that direct mail has "an overall positive effect on American society."

(C) presents an unwarranted comparison that in no way can be attributed to the author. Nuisance and privacy invasion are two categories of responses from the poll of paragraph 2, with the former outranking the latter in the public's mind, but we can't infer from this that the author believes that presenting a nuisance is a greater offense than invading privacy when it comes to direct marketing, no less in the context of "commercial enterprises" as a whole.

(D) switches the terms of the second-to-last sentence of the passage. It also fails to take into account the qualified nature of the author's assertion indicated by the word "probably."

(E) Again, we are not given enough information to draw this inference. The author does not discuss the future growth of direct marketing, so it's too much of a stretch to infer how the author thinks the industry might increase or decrease. In addition, the passage states that the direct marketing industry has grown *despite* people's negative attitudes about it. Growth in the industry does not therefore seem directly proportional to negative attitudes, which is another reason why it is unwarranted to ascribe the belief in (E) to the author.

Remember:

- Watch out for answer choices to Inference questions that exaggerate the author's points or go beyond the scope of the passage. If a choice contains information about a subject that the author doesn't discuss, be wary of it. The correct answer to an Inference question will stick closely to the topic and scope of the passage.

PASSAGE 2—Continental Drift

Topic and Scope
Continental-drift theory; specifically, support for Wegener's continental-drift theory.

Purpose and Main Idea
The author's purpose is to demonstrate support for the theory of continental drift, first posed by Alfred Wegener. The main idea is that since Wegener's death, geologists have learned much that supports Wegener's revolutionary continental-drift hypothesis.

Paragraph Structure
Paragraph 1 introduces continental-drift theory. This theory was first posed by Alfred Wegener in 1912 as a way of explaining why the edges of South America and Africa seemed to "fit" with one another. There follows some technical description of the theory, but for our purposes, it's best to simply note at this point that Wegener's theory was at first rejected by scientists on the grounds that no causal mechanism had yet been discovered to explain how continents could "float" like icebergs on top of the denser basalt lying beneath them.

Things look up for Wegener in paragraph 2—or at least for his theory, since he didn't live to see its acceptance. The second clause of the paragraph's first sentence essentially outlines the direction of the remainder of the passage: The author states that "since his death in 1930, geologists have learned much that supports [Wegener's] revolutionary idea." Well, what have they learned? That alone is the subject of paragraphs 2 and 3. The support described in paragraph 2 concerns rock formations on the edges of South America and Africa. Scientists used continental-drift theory to trace rock formations on the African continent and predict the location of similar rock formations in South America. Empirical findings upheld the theory's predictions.

Paragraph 3, not surprisingly, provides further evidence for continental drift, this time in the form of fossils. Both Africa and South America contain fossils of identical animal species, despite the fact that these continents are separated by an ocean that today would prevent animals from migrating from one continent to the other. The final sentence returns to rock formation evidence that further enhances the plausibility of Wegener's theory.

The Big Picture
- Don't shy away from a passage just because it contains what appears to be technical scientific jargon! First check out the organizational structure of the passage to determine how difficult the passage might be. Some science passages, like this one, are well-organized and contain clear main idea statements. Their clarity makes them as good candidates as any to handle early in the section.
- Clear, well-organized passages like this one are easy to Roadmap, which suggests that several question types (Global, Logic) may be very manageable—even easier than you might expect for a technical science passage.

• Think ahead as you read; anticipate where the author is likely to go. When an author states that support has been found for a theory, expect to find out what it is. The details may be technical, even cumbersome (although these weren't so bad), but you're one step ahead of the game when you know what purpose such details are meant to serve.

The Questions

8 **(C)** This Global question is a great one to get you off to a quick start. It lends itself well to prephrasing if you picked up on the huge importance of the first sentence of paragraph 2, as discussed above. The main idea of the passage appears in that sentence, namely that geologists have discovered support for Wegener's theory since his death. We know this is the main idea because everything in paragraph 1 serves as background for this notion, and everything in the rest of the passage serves to demonstrate it. Choice (C) captures this main point perfectly.

(A) Nowhere is it stated that Wegener's hypothesis is "more intriguing" than other theories, but even if this were implied, it still wouldn't constitute the passage's main point. What about all the *support* for Wegener's theory that makes up the bulk of the passage?

(B) *Au contraire*—the evidence discussed concerning fossils and rock dating clearly supports the continental-drift hypothesis.

(D) Too broad. The author is concerned specifically with continental-drift theory, not simply "geochronology."

(E) This may have been the main idea of Wegener's early critics, but even then it's possibly shot down by the end of the first paragraph by the mention of "convection," a factor that may bypass their objection. In any case, the author doesn't discuss "conclusive proof" of Wegener's theory, but rather evidence that makes that theory more likely to be valid.

Remember:

• Always strive to determine the purpose, main idea, and structure of each passage. If you do, you'll have an excellent shot at prephrasing an answer to Global questions that address these three issues.

9 **(A)** This Inference question asks us about an issue that is developed in paragraph 2. The two-billion-year-old rock formations are mentioned as evidence to lend support to the continental-drift theory. The author tells us that this example lends proof to the idea that Africa and South America were once connected. If this is correct, the author must believe the statement in choice (A): The rocks would not be located where they are if the continents had not been connected.

(B) Nothing is suggested by the passage regarding rock formations on other continents; for all we know, the rock formations on Africa and South America that are mentioned in the passage are unlike any formations anywhere else in the world.

(C) takes a rather large leap: We're never told how the rock formations were formed—what would make us believe that they were formed by the same force that drove them apart? We're merely told that scientists can use rock formations to accurately predict the location of similar rock formations.

(D) Fossil evidence doesn't come into the picture until paragraph 3, where the author maintains that in some places fossils of identical species are found on both sides of the Atlantic. The example given concerns formations in South Africa and Brazil. But the rock formations that are the focus of this question need not have any fossils in common, or even if they do, nothing says these formations need to contain fossils that are common to both continents.

(E) There is simply no evidence given to indicate that the two-billion-year-old rock formations resemble the basement rock in Ghana.

Remember:

- In Inference questions, beware of choices that attempt to link elements of the passage that have no logical connection. Sometimes, as in (D) here, facts from two different paragraphs are erroneously linked. Other times, facts from the same paragraph are tied together in a bogus way, such as (E)'s attempt to relate the two-billion-year-old rock formations to the basement rock of Ghana. Does the author even imply that these "resemble" each other? No. If the author doesn't explicitly make a connection, then neither should we.

10 (D) The word *originally* in the stem of this Explicit Text question is a good indication of where this answer is likely to be found: Your mental Roadmap should point you right to paragraph 1 where Wegener's theory and the original reception to it are introduced. Paragraph 1 tells us that the theory was developed through gravity measurements and observations, and was originally rejected for lack of a propelling mechanism. We're then told in the first sentence of paragraph 2 that Wegener never found clear and convincing evidence for his theory while he was alive. It is certainly fair to say based on these pieces of evidence

that Wegener's work was developed through observation but was not fully supported with evidence, choice (D).

(A) *Au contraire*. Wegener's theory didn't modify an early hypothesis; it was a "novel" approach to the problem it addressed.

(B) *Au contraire* again: The theory wasn't originally rejected because it was inconsistent with Bacon, but rather because it provided insufficient evidence for its physical plausibility. Contrary to (B), Wegener's theory seems to have supported Bacon's suggestion that the "fit" between the continents was not merely a coincidence.

(C) and (E) distort the author's meaning in the passage. Wegener's theory attempted to explain why the edges of the two continents seemed to "fit together." Analysis of shared rock formations was one means of supporting Wegener's hypothesis; so was the evidence given regarding fossils on both sides of the South Atlantic. Wegener's theory wasn't used to explain these things—it was rather supported by them.

Remember:

- Beware of wrong answer choices that reverse the relationship between evidence and conclusion. In this case, rock formations and fossils are discussed as support for the continental-drift hypothesis, not the other way around.

11 (E) To answer this Weaken question, we must first understand Wegener's theory and the support provided for it. The author describes two pieces of evidence that uphold Wegener's claims about continental drift: (1) Studying rock formations in Africa successfully helps predict the location of rock formations in South America; and (2) Fossils found on both continents suggest that the continents were once contiguous. These details are given as evidence that the continents were once locked together, but (E) weakens this argument significantly. If common rock formations and fossils exist on continents *without* interlocking coastlines, there is much less reason to believe that the existence of common rock formations and fossils points to a previous history of interlocked coastlines.

(A) Regardless of whether or not more fossils were uncovered in South Africa, the fact still remains that identical fossils were found on continents now separated by an ocean, so this statement does not weaken the argument at all.

(B) If a new explanation for the cause of continental drift were discovered, this could only strengthen Wegener's theory, not weaken it.

(C), (D) Both of these choices are irrelevant to Wegener's argument. Even if Bacon's argument was based on speculation, this does not affect Wegener's views. Further, the relationship between age and composition of rock formations in general does nothing to cast doubt on evidence regarding the age, composition, and structure of rock formations in Africa and South America, or what these factors portend for the validity of Wegener's theory.

Remember:

- To answer a Weaken question effectively, you must first have a good grasp on the argument to be weakened. Before answering, think about the conclusion and evidence of the argument or view in question. Then look for the choice that detracts from the author's reasoning by attacking the evidence, conclusion, or assumptions underlying the argument.

12 (B) This Inference question relates to fossil evidence, an issue discussed only in paragraph 3. We're told that fossil evidence supports Wegener's theory of continental drift. In general, therefore, the author would be likely to believe (B)—that fossil evidence can contribute to the plausibility of a geological model. If the author didn't believe this, it would be hard to understand why he introduces the fossil evidence at all.

(A) offers a classic unwarranted comparison. The author presents rock formation evidence, and fossil evidence, but never compares the relative merits of one versus the other. We have no way of knowing which kind of evidence the author thinks is stronger.

(C) Australia is not mentioned or alluded to in the passage, nor does the author suggest that the fossil similarity described is unique to South America and Africa, so we have no way of knowing what the author would think about possible fossil links between South America and other continents.

(D) *Au contraire:* According to paragraph 3, fossil evidence suggests that certain species now greatly separated once lived in the same location. It is only *now* that those locations are separated because, according to the theory, the continents drifted apart. If you need another reason to reject (D), consider that the word "proves" is way too strong here—fossil evidence is used to merely support a hypothesis.

(E) Fossil evidence appears in the last paragraph, convention in the first. Nothing in between even remotely suggests any link between them, so (E) should have been a quick kill.

Remember:

- Be on the lookout for inferences that move from the specific to the general while still staying within the argument's scope. If an author uses a particular piece of evidence (fossils in Africa and South America) to uphold a claim (continental-drift theory), he or she is likely to believe that this category of evidence (fossils in general) is valid for supporting this sort of claim (geochronological hypotheses).

13 **(A)** This straightforward Global question is found at the end of the question set, but good section management would recommend that you answer the question earlier rather than later. This might have been a great question to tackle second, after the first question on the author's main idea; after all, the answers to these two must be related. We've seen early on how the author's purpose here is to demonstrate support for continental-drift theory. Here we find this paraphrased in answer choice (A), which gives a more general depiction of the author's purpose.

(B) Too narrow. The author does discuss rock formations, but only in one part of the passage. (B) is part of the author's support for the main idea, but does not represent the author's full intention.

(C) Too extreme. This harks back to choice (D) of the previous question, where we discussed how the concept of "proof" is too strong for this passage. Here, the author doesn't set out to convince us that continental drift is beyond question, merely that it has strong support.

(D) The author doesn't *assess* evidence in this passage; rather, he *presents* evidence to support a theory.

(E) This tricky choice tests your eye for detail. The author *does* describe evidence for continental drift, but it's not *Wegener's* evidence. He tells us in paragraph 2 that this evidence wasn't discovered until after Wegener's death.

Remember:

- Read critically! Take out the creator of the theory in choice (E) and we're pretty much back to correct choice (A). If you blew past Wegener in (E), you'd surely have the darndest time choosing between the two.
- Not all questions in a Reading Comp set deal with strictly separate issues. If a question set contains both a Primary Purpose and a Main Idea question on a well-organized passage such as this one, you're in luck: The same concept is basically being tested twice. You may even wish to answer them consecutively, no matter where in the set they appear.

PASSAGE 3—Illegal Constitution

Topic and Scope
The Constitution; specifically, the legality and moral legitimacy of the Constitution.

Purpose and Main Idea
The author's purpose is to evaluate whether the Constitution is legal and morally legitimate. The main idea is that while the Constitution may not be legal (because its adoption by three-quarters ratification violated the sovereignty of nonratifying states), it nonetheless carries moral weight.

Paragraph Structure
The first paragraph tells us that although Congress authorized a group of commissioners to create the U.S. Constitution by revising the Articles of

Confederation, Congress was surprised by the revolutionary nature of the Constitution that the commissioners submitted.

Paragraph 2 starts by explaining James Madison's argument that the commissioners were justified in submitting a revolutionary Constitution because the document served the goal of creating good government, a goal that was more important than adhering strictly to the Articles. Despite Madison's argument, the author questions the legality of the Constitution because it was ratified by only three-quarters of the states.

In the final paragraph, the author expands her argument from paragraph 2 by showing that the "three-quarters ratification" provision violated the rights of non-ratifying states. At the same time, however, she claims that the Constitution's questionable legality does not cast doubt on its moral legitimacy, and gives two reasons why this is so.

The Big Picture
- In some passages, the main idea will not be readily apparent early on. Here, paragraph 1 serves as background, but for what? The passage could go in many different directions, and you have to constantly ask the question, "Why was this thing written?" until you're satisfied that you've located the main idea. You may not get a full grasp of the main idea until the end of the passage.
- Taking note of contrast keywords help you to follow an author's twists and turns. One of the most popular and powerful contrast keywords is "however," a word that is used by authors to signal a change in direction. Note the strategically placed "howevers" in the middle of paragraphs 2 and 3; both are fundamentally related to the author's main idea. The first prefaces the notion that despite Madison's justifications, the new

Constitution may not be legal, while the second sets up the idea that despite its possible illegality, it nonetheless may carry moral weight.

The Questions

14 **(C)** This Inference question asks us for a reason why Congress may have been surprised by how much the Constitution differed from the Articles of Confederation. What possibility might the Congress have overlooked? This topic is discussed in the very beginning of the passage, where we see that Congress authorized the commissioners to revise the Articles to create an "adequate" federal government. They asked for some alterations, and got back something they deemed to be an illegal revolutionary document. To carry out Congress's wish, the commissioners felt they had to radically depart from the Articles, not just modify them. We can infer from its reaction that Congress did not foresee that mere modification of the Articles would not suffice to carry out its charge, choice (C).

(A) distorts information from the text. While the Constitution was adopted without unanimous ratification, this fact is not described by the author as an "inevitability," or as something that was bound to occur. Any lack of foresight on this issue cannot be blamed for Congress's surprise.

(B) Moral authority appears later in the passage, and has no recognizable connection to Congress's surprise over the revolutionary Constitution. Congress certainly felt that the document submitted lacked legal authority, but the issue of moral authority is not raised at this point.

(D) *Au contraire:* Congress was presumably aware that the Constitution would differ from the Articles, because it specifically commissioned a revision of the Articles. What the Congress did not anticipate was the *extent* of this difference.

(E) The reaction of an individual such as Madison is irrelevant to Congress's surprise. The question concerns why Congress was surprised about the content of the Constitution, not how or why someone would later justify this content.

Remember:

- Since Inference questions are often not suited for prephrasing, the best tactic on such questions is to evaluate each answer choice and eliminate wisely. If you're having trouble spotting an attractive choice, ruling out two or three answer choices will still greatly improve your odds.

15 **(B)** Next up is a question that asks us to draw an inference based upon Madison's views. In other words, given the discussion of Madison's perspective, which statement could he be expected to uphold? Since Madison's views are primarily discussed in paragraph 2, we can look to that paragraph to determine an answer. Madison based his argument about the legality of the Constitution on the principle that conflicts ought to be resolved in favor of more important goals, so choice (B) represents a statement he would be likely to agree with.

(A) Madison used the principle that conflicts should be resolved in favor of more important goals, but the author never stated or implied that Madison viewed "peace in the nation" to be an overriding national goal that should be used to resolve conflicts of interest.

(C) misrepresents the author's meaning in the passage. The author never specifies that unanimous approval is the most important objective in drafting a new constitution, nor does he imply that Madison believed this. The issue of unanimous approval comes up later in a different context.

(D) *Au contraire.* The reason Madison raised his voice to justify the new Constitution in the first place was because it did *not* meet Congress's expectations.

(E), like (C), appeals to an issue that comes up later in the passage: moral obligation. The author states that the result of the Constitution was to forge a strong union of the states, but he does not indicate that Madison believed that the commissioners were *morally obligated* to create a Constitution that did so.

Remember:

- Some Inference questions can be answered by reference to one specific part of a passage. When this is the case, take advantage of it— keep your review limited to just the relevant portion, and dismiss choices like (C) and (E) here that attempt to bring irrelevant elements of the passage.

16 **(E)** With this third Inference question, we are asked for a deduction based on the author's views. Where are we given the author's views about the legality of making changes to government? In paragraph 3, the author states flat out that "no government ought to have the power to entrench itself against amendment." So the author would be likely to support a group that rebelled against a state's decision to protect itself from changes.

(A) and (D) are *au contraire* choices that violate the spirit of the author's view on this matter. These choices can be eliminated at first glance, because we're looking for a positive or supportive attitude.

(B) Too extreme. First of all, it can be argued that "admiration" is too strongly positive; the author's views are more moderate than that, and "approval" matches her tone a little better. Secondly, the author would certainly believe that opposition to the law in question would carry moral weight, but would she believe that "*any law* passed by such a government has no moral authority"? We can't tell—that's a different issue. We can speculate, but this is too extreme to be fully inferable here.

(C) The most we can infer here is how the author would react to the legitimacy of such an act of dissent. How she would feel about the reaction *to* the reaction against such a law is one step beyond the scope. While we can infer that she would support such dissent on moral grounds, there's no way to tell if she would be concerned about government reprisals or not.

Remember:

- Questions about author's attitudes lend themselves well to quick scanning of the main verb in each answer choice. Once you've determined whether the author's attitude is likely to be positive or negative, scan the choices looking for appropriate verbs. Here, you could have skipped over any negative verbs and focused on only the choices with positive verbs.

17 **(A)** In order to choose the best weakener, we must first understand which argument the question is referring to. We are asked to determine

which statement would best weaken the argument put forth in defense of the legality of the Constitution. Where is this argument made, and by whom? A quick reference to your Roadmap should reveal that Madison argued in defense of the Constitution's legality, and this argument is presented at the beginning of paragraph 2. Here Madison claims that the Constitution is justified despite its radical nature because it upholds the overarching goal of creating a good government. Choice (A) serves as a good weakener: If one of the Constitution's provisions (non-unanimous ratification) prevented it from creating a good government, then Madison's argument would be far less convincing.

(B), (D), (E)   These choices are irrelevant to Madison's argument. The issue of "extensive debate" is not addressed in his justification. Neither are the issues of safeguarding the power of the ruling elite or the relative merits of oral versus written arguments. Since an argument can only be weakened on its own terms, these answer choices do not accomplish the task at hand.

(C) If anything, (C) supports the necessity for the radical nature of the Constitution handed in by the commissioners. However, it does not relate to Madison's specific reason for why he believed the Constitution to be legal. He viewed it as justified because it upheld the overriding goal of good government. If anything, (C) might strengthen Madison's *cause* (defending the Constitution), but since it does not address Madison's reasoning, we can say that it has no real effect on his particular argument.

Remember:

- LSAT Reading Comp arguments can only be weakened on their own terms. To choose a weakener, therefore, you must first understand the argument at stake. When a specific argument is referenced in a question stem, read back in the passage to make sure you understand the evidence and conclusion of that particular argument, and make sure the choice you select is directly relevant to them.

18

(A) "According to the passage" lets us know that we're being asked for something that is found directly in the text. We need to find something that provided justification for the revolutionary nature of the new Constitution. Justification is given in two places: Madison justifies the Constitution's legality, and the author justifies the Constitution's moral authority. Choice (A) relates to the final sentence of the passage in which the author justifies rebelling against the government under the Articles on the grounds that that government itself admitted it wasn't up to the task of dealing with the "exigencies"—that is, pressing needs—of the nation.

(B) The author uses this reason to argue against Madison's justification of the Constitution's legality.

(C) *Au contraire.* In paragraph 3, the author states that no government has the right to entrench itself against amendment.

(D) also presents the opposite of what we're looking for: If the commission followed Congress's recommendation, it would not have submitted such a radical document. Far from justifying the revolutionary Constitution, (D) describes a factor that would presumably guard against the creation of such a document.

(E) Madison does no such thing: His analysis attempted to justify the differences between the Articles and the Constitution. Nowhere does the author state that Madison questioned the extent of these differences.

Remember:

- In Explicit Text questions, be on the lookout for choices that describe the opposite of that which is stated in the passage.

19

(D) Nowhere does the author directly relate legality to morality, but since we know about the author's attitude toward each independently, we must be able to infer a connection—otherwise, this question wouldn't exist. Briefly review what we learned about each: The author believes that the legality of the Constitution is questionable, but that its moral authority is not. It's a simple matter of putting these facts together: Inferably, the author believes that moral authority can exist without legality, choice (D).

The remaining choices are difficult insofar as they include all of the same terms as the correct choice, but each choice somehow fouls up the relationship between morality and legality:

(A) *Au contraire:* In stating that a document with questionable legal validity can nonetheless carry moral weight, the author evidently sees moral authority and legality as two separate issues.

(B) First of all, the author is concerned with the morality and legality of a written document, not a principle. But even if we overlook that fact, (B) reverses the situation in the passage, where there's something that could be illegal yet moral. Would the author think that something lacking morality can be legal? It's doubtful, since morality seems to carry lots of weight with this author. But still, there's no real way to tell.

(C), like (B), switches the scope from documents to "action." Still, had you overlooked that, you should still have recognized that (C) runs counter to the author's beliefs: *Despite* its possible illegality, in the author's mind the new Constitution can still have moral authority.

(E) goes beyond the scope of the passage. The author's argument does not address court decisions, but rather the country's governing documents.

Remember:

- In Inference questions, beware of choices that shift the scope from the focus of the passage.

20 **(E)** The last question of this set is a straightforward Global question, showing that it pays to scan the question set before answering the questions! Your Roadmap should have helped you to determine the author's purpose in writing the passage: to evaluate the legality and moral legitimacy of the Constitution. Answer choice (E) expresses this purpose in a more general manner to "assess the authority of a political event [i.e., the Constitution] on two grounds [i.e., legal and moral]."

(A) What two viewpoints are *reconciled*? The author argues against Madison's view, but that's about as close as we come in this passage to opposing viewpoints.

(B) The author does make an argument, but she isn't interested in illustrating the "argumentative power" of anything (except perhaps the evidence she provides).

(C) This choice misrepresents the author's purpose. She doesn't argue for a *re*consideration of the Constitution (after all, she states that "history

has validated the wisdom of the change"), but apparently for an *initial* consideration of it. And besides, the Constitution can be considered a governing document, not a "doctrine" *per se*.

(D) The author's argument does not support the establishment of the Constitution over the Articles as much as it reviews some legal and moral considerations of the Constitution itself.

Remember:

- Because they lend themselves so well to prephrasing, Global questions are usually among the easier questions to answer in any RC question set. Don't let their positions in a question set lead you to answer them last! You can maximize your points on test day by scanning a passage's questions and answering the easiest ones first, no matter where they're located in the set. This strategy will allow you to accumulate points quickly at the outset of the passage, raising your confidence and giving you extra time to spend on the harder questions.

PASSAGE 4—Gerschenkron & Hough

Topic and Scope
The views of authors Gerschenkron and Hough; specifically, a comparison of these two authors' work on the former Soviet Union.

Purpose and Main Idea
The author's purpose is to compare how Gerschenkron and Hough approach the case of the former Soviet Union in their scholarly works. The main idea is that both authors share a similar theoretical approach in their works, and both are successful in their theoretical endeavors.

Paragraph Structure

Paragraph 1 introduces the passage by noting that both Gerschenkron and Hough view the former Soviet Union as an anomalous nation. Although they focus on different aspects of the former Soviet anomaly, they nonetheless share a similar approach in their research.

Paragraph 2 explains one aspect of similarity between the authors' approaches: Both develop ideas in reaction to existing theories in their fields. We are told first what Gerschenkron reacts to and then what Hough reacts to in his work.

Paragraph 3 provides a second aspect of similarity between the authors' approaches: Both attempt to supplement existing theories in their fields. Again, we are given a description of Gerschenkron's attempt, and then a description of Hough's.

The final paragraph summarizes the points made in paragraphs 2 and 3. It also draws a final conclusion: Not only are the authors' tasks similar, but they both succeed in these tasks.

The Big Picture

- A good Roadmap doesn't include every detail of a passage. In a complex passage such as this one, your Roadmap should recap the points of each paragraph and remind you where the evidence is to support these points. If you're asked a question regarding a specific detail from a paragraph, you can always go back to it.

- As you read, focus on isolating the author's purpose and main idea, along with significant pieces of evidence the author gives to uphold his or her conclusion. If you have a good grasp of the overall argument, you'll be able to answer several questions accurately and quickly—giving you more time to research detail questions if necessary.

The Questions

21 **(A)** This question asks for the author's main point, or the main idea of the passage. This question would be a good one to prephrase, since a careful focus on purpose and structure should make the main idea clear. In this case, the main idea has two parts and is summed up in paragraph 4: The theorists share similar tasks, and they succeed at these tasks as well. This is well stated in choice (A).

(B), (C) These choices describe only parts of the author's claim; they are not broad enough to reflect the main idea. Choice (B) summarizes the point of paragraph 2, while choice (C) discusses a point raised in paragraph 1 about the anomalies of the former Soviet case.

(D) *Au contraire:* This choice contradicts the author's argument as laid out in paragraph 4. The author specifically states that the theorists use their anomalous cases to "enable the existing theories to more accurately explain the issues under investigation." In other words, their works supplement the existing theories. This is a far cry from replacing the theories, as choice (D) suggests.

(E) Again, *au contraire.* The author tells us in paragraph 1 that Gerschenkron and Hough focus on different aspects of the Soviet experience—Gerschenkron on industrialization and Hough on bureaucratic organization. Their specific central tenets differ, but their overall theoretical *approach* is the same.

Remember:

- Be careful of answer choices that state the opposite of the author's claims in the passage or that focus on only part of the author's argument. The correct answer to a Main Idea question will reflect the author's argument accurately and will summarize the entire argument, not just one part.

22 **(C)** This question begins with the words "according to the author," so we know that we're being asked for a detail from the text. How are the works of the two theorists similar? Maybe you were able to prephrase an answer here—after all, the first sentence tells us that both theorists view the Soviet Union as an anomalous case, and perhaps that stuck in your head. Or the fact that despite differences in their specific concerns, they share a similar overall theoretical approach. Either of these ideas would work. Unfortunately, however, the testmakers decided to cull the answer to this one from paragraph 4, where it's stated that "Both authors also attempt to use the anomalies that they discover to enhance the explanatory value of the theories already existing in their fields." Choice (C) is a very close paraphrase of this.

(A) This answer choice contradicts the author's argument and is similar to incorrect answer choice (C) from the previous question. The author specifically tells us in paragraph 4 that the works of Gerschenkron and Hough enhance the explanatory power of existing theories—they do not invalidate these theories.

(B) Again, this goes against the grain: In paragraph 2 we're told that Gerschenkron and Hough react to existing theories in their fields, and later that they expand upon them. Thus it cannot be said that they adhere to these interpretations.

(D) Gerschenkron addresses industrialization, but Hough investigates bureaucratic organization. This is not a similarity in their works.

(E) misrepresents the author's meaning in the passage. She says that Gerschenkron and Hough use the former Soviet experience to draw attention to factors that expand existing theories. Nowhere are we told that their portrayals of the Soviet case are critical.

Remember:

- Don't be discouraged if you form a valid prephrase that's not reflected in a correct choice—it still may help you to eliminate wrong choices, and your attempt to prephrase answers is bound to pay off in the long run.

23 **(E)** Here we're presented with another Explicit Text question, this time about Hough's work. Hough's work is discussed in detail in two places—paragraphs 2 and 3—so now is a good time to return to the passage and examine those in detail. The author states at the end paragraph 3 that Hough believes that the Soviet experience shows that overlapping bureaucratic duties can promote organizational efficiency—a point reflected in choice (E).

(A), (B) *Au contraire*. The author states in paragraph 3 that the former Soviet Union has an overlapping model of bureaucratic function that differs from the American monistic model. As we saw with correct choice (E), he also states here that the Soviet overlapping model may promote efficiency in certain cases.

(C) and (D) confuse Hough's work with that of Gerschenkron. England's industrial growth is part of Gerschenkron's work, and nowhere is this compared to the growth of Soviet bureaucracy (C). Similarly, the degree of economic backwardness is another element of the Gerschenkron discussion of paragraph 3, and nothing is stated about its effect on Soviet bureaucracy. Gerschenkron deals with industrialization, while Hough deals with bureaucratic organization. Choices (C) and (D) try to combine them, and thus must be tossed.

Remember:

- Beware of choices that combine elements of the passage in ways that are unwarranted. This is an especially common ploy in passages that deal with more than one view or theory. Keep the theories straight, and you won't fall for choices that attempt to mix them together like (C) and (D) here.

24 **(D)** This Logic question asks you to determine the role played by one part of the passage in upholding the author's main idea. The paragraph focuses mainly on the way both theorists attempt to supplement existing theories in their fields. That's the specific gist of paragraph 3, but we're asked what this has to do with the passage as a whole. The best clue is the first word of the paragraph: "Secondly." This structural signal tells us that what's about to follow harks back to the earlier claim, back in paragraph 1, that their overall theoretical approaches were similar. Paragraph 2 presented the first similarity, and now in paragraph 3 we get the second. So this paragraph simply serves as additional support for the author's claim in the last sentence of paragraph 1, and (D) captures the gist of this nicely.

(A) It is true that Gerschenkron and Hough study different aspects of Soviet development. This point is raised in paragraph 1 and may even be reinforced in paragraph 3, where again we see how Gerschenkron is concerned with industrialization while Hough is into bureaucratic structures. However, this is not related to the

function of paragraph 3. These illustrations merely support the larger point that their overall goals are similar despite the fact that their specific subject matter differs.

(B) This answer choice distorts the author's argument. Nowhere does she state that Gerschenkron and Hough's works can most effectively be compared by reviewing their research on the former Soviet Union.

(C) This choice captures part of what occurs in paragraph 3, but it does not describe the function of paragraph 3 in the entire argument. It merely describes one idea that is developed in that paragraph.

(E) *Au contraire*—the third paragraph supports the notion that Gerschenkron and Hough have similar approaches by showing that both theorists attempt to supplement existing theories in their fields. That's the overall point of the paragraph, differences in their specific topics notwithstanding.

Remember:

- A correct answer choice may not match your prephrase exactly. It may be more general, or more specific, than the prephrased answer you come up with. Still, a good prephrase will help you anticipate the correct answer and will help you recognize a broader or narrower variation when you see it.

25 **(D)** This question begins with the words "the passage suggests," which lets us know that it is an Inference question. We are asked to choose a statement about which both Gerschenkron and Hough would likely agree. Rather than attempt to prephrase the answer (the possibilities could be very broad), we should scan the choices to determine the correct one. (D) provides the best summary of a statement that would align with both theorists' views, since paragraph 4 tells us that both men use research into anomalous cases to broaden the explanatory value of existing theories. Presumably, since both theorists use such cases to broaden such explanations, they would agree that using such research in this way is possible.

(A) The author doesn't suggest that studies of the former Soviet Union should be limited to any subjects, and neither does she imply that Gerschenkron and Hough believe this. All we know is that industrialization and bureaucracy are their respective areas of concern. We can't infer that they think that Soviet studies should be limited to their subjects.

(B) Gerschenkron would agree with this, but the passage does not indicate Hough's views on Rostow's model.

(C) Not even Gerschenkron would buy this one—the author states in paragraph 2 that Gerschenkron reacts against this notion. And of course, we don't know what Hough's views would be on the subject.

(E) *Au contraire*. Gerschenkron and Hough do not attempt to falsify the existing theories they deal with—they attempt to supplement them. They would therefore, if anything, probably *disagree* with the notion that empirical research should focus on falsification.

Remember:

- Inference questions often ask for the likely opinions of the characters, not the actual author, of the passage. When you answer a question pertaining to the views of two authors or theorists discussed in a passage, be sure to avoid choices that only relate to one author's views, such as (C) here.

26 **(E)** This question asks again for a detail from the passage. We know this because we're asked for a statement that is "explicitly cited" in the text. Can't get much clearer than that! (E) generalizes the author's point in paragraph 3 regarding Gerschenkron, the references being to the discussion of Gerschenkron's incorporation of the "economic backwardness" factor into Rostow's industrialization model.

(A) *Au contraire*. Paragraph 2 tells us that Gerschenkron reacted to the notion that states *must* possess specific characteristics in order to industrialize.

(B) True, Gerschenkron may differ from Hough in the specific orientation of his work, but this statement is not explicitly cited as evidence of how Gerschenkron put his work to use.

(C) This description applies to neither Gerschenkron nor Hough's work. Gerschenkron addressed industrialization, not bureaucratic organization, and Hough's work showed that monism is not the only efficient method of bureaucratic organization.

(D) reverses the evidence in the text. Paragraph 3 tells us that Gerschenkron showed that economic backwardness affects the speed of industrialization, not vice versa.

Remember:

- The wrong answer choices to Explicit Text questions will attempt to throw you off course in many ways: by providing statements that contradict the text, by providing statements that reverse or confuse an idea given in the text, or by providing statements that were not explicitly laid out in the text at all, to name a few. If you are aware of these typical wrong answer pitfalls, you're more likely to avoid them on test day.

27 **(C)** This Logic question asks us to determine what function is served by the introduction of the concept of monism in paragraph 2. Paragraph 2 demonstrates that both authors react in their works to existing theories. Without looking at the answer choices, we can prephrase that "monism is introduced to show that Hough's work reacted to an existing theory." Do we find such an answer with a scan of the choices? In fact, (C) conveys just this idea—albeit a bit more specifically than our prephrase.

(A) This choice refers to the subject discussed by Gerschenkron, not Hough.

(B), (D) *Au contraire*. Hough reacts against the American system known as monism, and according to paragraph 3, Hough's examination of the former Soviet case results in an alternative conception of bureaucratic efficiency. In addition, the author tells us in paragraph 1 that Hough portrayed the former Soviet Union as anomalous, or different, in its bureaucratic

structure. The mention of monism in paragraph 2 is in no way included to show otherwise.

(E) Again, the author states that Hough portrayed the former Soviet Union as *different* from the American monistic model.

Remember:

- *Au contraire* choices are ones that reflect the opposite of what the passage, author, or characters in the passage believe or suggest. They are quite common in passages that include a number of theorists and theories. The test makers are simply testing whether or not you're able to keep the various elements of the passage straight.
- If you find yourself frequently choosing *au contraire* choices, you may be prone to reversing the information in the passage, and you need to take better care in your initial reading of the passage to distinguish between the various characters and the views they espouse.

Section II: Logical Reasoning Explanations

1 **(C)** The author explains that animals who get separated from their mothers early in life don't play and live well with the other animals. Specifically, they acquire aggression disorders, possibly leading to food fights and other unattractive behavior. The author's conclusion: These animals acquire aggressive disorders because they lack early, proper, parent-led socialization training. We're looking to strengthen this argument, which means that we want to reinforce the causal relationship between the lack of parent-led socialization training and aggressive disorders. (C) gets at this issue, and the fact that it approaches the issue from the other angle, saying that simulated parent-led socialization leads to less aggression, doesn't make it any less right. This choice strengthens the link between the two terms of the conclusion, and therefore strengthens the argument by making us more likely to believe that the causal mechanism cited by the author is valid.

(A), if anything, weakens the hypothesis by linking aggressive disorders with animals *not* separated from their mothers. If separation and the resulting lack of parent-led socialization is the cause of aggression disorders, how would the hypothesis explain the excessive aggression of these non-separated wildebeests?

(B) In order to make this answer choice work, you'd have to assume that a child who is put up for adoption inherently lacks access to parent-led socialization. If that were the case, then this would help support the hypothesis. But the assumption is unsupported; for all we know, adopted human babies receive plenty of parent-led socialization. (B) thus has no direct bearing on the argument.

(D) Since we don't know whether these polar bears did or did not have early parent-led socialization, their aggressiveness does not strengthen (or weaken, or do anything to) this argument. The argument discusses aggressive behavior in terms of socialization, so any information about aggression outside of that context doesn't affect the argument.

(E) This is the exact opposite of what we're looking for. The proposers of the hypothesis would feel better about their idea if these elephants were rude, ornery, stampeding aggressive beasts.

Remember:

- Always be prepared to see and eliminate an answer choice that would weaken an argument in a strengthen question, and one that would strengthen an argument in a weaken question. They're often present to tempt less-focused test takers.

2 **(E)** Since you'll need to find the one choice which isn't an inference, be prepared to keep track of the boundaries around the argument. That way you'll be better prepared to spot what isn't there. The author begins by noting that the Sarrin monks use Pran meditation only in cases of severe weather. The author then explains the differences between Pran meditation and ritual meditation. Understanding the difference will likely be key to getting this question right. Pran meditation is different than ritual meditation because it's more highly disciplined and uniquely involves isolation and fasting. Thus there are three ways in which Pran meditation is different than ritual meditation. Let's go to the choices.

(A) The author states that Pran meditation is more disciplined than ritual meditation, so (A) must be true. Remember that "some" in the LSAT means "one or more." We have one example of less disciplined meditation and that means that some practices are less disciplined. This is a valid inference, so it's not the answer.

(B) The monks only practice Pran meditation when there's severe weather and, since weather isn't precisely scheduled, then Pran meditation must not be precisely scheduled either. Sure, that's an inference.

(C) If Pran meditation involves the *unique* practice of isolation, then no other meditation, including ritual meditation, involves isolation.

(D) Again, "some" means "one or more," so since the monks practice Pran meditation in response to local weather threats, then some types of meditation do in fact exist as a response to local threats.

(E) is correct because, even though the author implies that ritual meditation is *less* disciplined than Pran, that doesn't mean that it's *un*disciplined. (E) takes us beyond what the passage supports, so it's not a valid inference and is the correct answer here.

Remember:

- Get comfortable with the specifics of LSAT vocabulary well before test day, so that you don't have to take time to think about what words like "some" or "unique" mean when you're taking the exam.

3 **(B)** Following the lead of the question stem, our first task is to understand the discrepancy. The author tells us that a high volume of pirating sales causes studios to lose a great deal of money. However (a keyword that signals the discrepancy in the stimulus), a low volume of pirating sales generally indicates a period of economic weakness in the movie industry. Why does a low level of pirating sales, which would seem to benefit the industry, actually signal a period of economic weakness in the industry? This is the question that we need to answer, so let's proceed to the answer choices.

(A) doesn't address the issues involved in the discrepancy, focusing as it does on whether these studios distribute smaller films.

(B) is correct because it creates a direct connection between pirating and the financial success of the entire industry. If pirating is related exclusively to big hits, then a low level of pirating signals a lack of blockbuster hits, in which case it's more understandable how a low level of pirating would correspond to periods of economic downturns in the industry.

(C) is off base, focusing as it does on the methods of pirated tape production and not on the connection between pirating and the economic health of the movie industry.

(D) is similarly off base, since it offers a comparative analysis between the largest and not so large studios, which isn't a comparison relevant to the original discrepancy.

(E) gives us information about the profitability of selling pirated movies, which may be interesting but doesn't explain why low pirating sales would signal an economic low point in the entire movie industry.

Remember:

- When dealing with complex discrepancy questions like this one, make sure to identify the primary issues involved, and then search for a choice that addresses those issues. Here, note how only (B) actually keeps focused on the issues at hand.

4 **(C)** The author concludes that no beef has been available in Cebra for the past six months. The evidence is the first sentence: A blight wiped out all of the town's beef supply six months ago. With such a skimpy argument, we can anticipate that the correct inference will require us to have read it carefully. Since Inference questions are often tough to prephrase, there's not much else to do but to go to the answer choices.

(A) If we interpret this choice to mean that Cebra folks consume nothing but Cebra beef (i.e., no fruits, veggies, etcetera), then (A) is easy to dismiss—there's been no Cebra beef for six months, and these people must eat something. The more plausible reading of (A) is that the only type of beef Cebra residents consume is that raised by Cebra farmers. Still, this is going too far: Although for the past six months no non-Cebra beef has been brought into town (which is, incidentally, correct choice (C)), for all we know there was plenty of outside beef consumed in Cebra prior to the blight.

(B) makes an unsupported distinction between the categories of meat, and discusses the issue of preferences. According to the author, lamb and poultry are available for consumption while

beef is not. What's available is clear; what's *preferred* is not.

(C) must indeed be true if the conclusion and evidence are true. If the elimination of the town's beef supply means that no beef is available, then the town must have no external beef provider during the last six months.

(D) Technically, we don't even have enough information to infer that one resident is a meat eater, although since they do have meat available for consumption, it's likely that someone's eating it—otherwise, why would they have various kinds of meat available? However, we certainly can't infer that *most* people eat the stuff—that's just going too far.

(E) pushes us out of the stimulus' time frame. It provides no information about consumption patterns before the blight, or even after. The argument concerns meat availability, not its consumption, so the comparison stated in (E) has no support in the passage.

Remember:

- What's the difference between an inference and an assumption? Both are unstated and must be true if the statements in the argument are true, but an assumption is central to the argument, connecting its evidence to its conclusion, while an inference can come from any part of the argument.

5 **(D)** The author concludes that the food critic's review is flawed based on the following evidence: The critic criticized the soup for containing cilantro and sun-dried tomatoes, but praised a chicken dish with those same ingredients. The

author calls this an inconsistency which shows the critic to be unqualified. Thus the critic's review is misguided because the critic is inconsistent. In order for the author's conclusion to be valid, one must assume that the two pieces of the comparison in the evidence are fully relevant to one another. Only if the two dishes are comparable can the critic's difference of opinion about the two be construed as an inconsistency. Therefore, the author must assume that cilantro and sun-dried tomatoes have the same culinary impact on strawberry soup and roasted chicken, which is what (D) says.

(A) is irrelevant because the author is concerned with the critic's inconsistent reviews, not with some customers' preferences.

(B) contradicts the argument. The critic clearly does like cilantro and sun-dried tomatoes in the chicken dish, so it's not the ingredients that he dislikes.

(C) would weaken the argument, showing how these particular ingredients are more appropriate to some dishes than others. If (C) were true, we'd be more likely to see the critic's supposed "inconsistency" as warranted, and the author's criticism of the critic as off base. Nothing that would weaken an argument need be assumed by that argument.

(E) is entirely irrelevant to the argument, since the author never discusses non-roasted chicken. Information about that dish has no relationship to the author's conclusion.

Remember:

- Whenever an author uses one fact to prove the truth of another, make sure that the two objects of comparison really are fully comparable. If

that comparability isn't demonstrated, then the author must assume it.

6 **(A)** The author concludes that any astute literary critic will be able to correctly anticipate which underlying issues are addressed in Dovak's new book. The evidence comes earlier in the stimulus: Dovak's new novel will have the same form as his six previous works, all of which were philosophy novels in which the plot and characters demonstrated the author's own philosophical convictions. Thus it seems clear that Dovak's new book will also demonstrate his philosophical convictions, but that will only yield the same underlying issues if the author assumes that Dovak's philosophical convictions have remained constant. The author's evidence provides information about the Dovak's motivations in writing, but they only support the conclusion's prediction about the content of Dovak's new book if those motivations, i.e., his philosophical convictions, have remained constant. (A) clearly states this assumption.

(B) The author says that the plot will "surely be different," but (B) makes that assertion even stronger by claiming that the plots have absolutely not one thing in common. (B) is wrong both because an assumption doesn't make the author's assertions more extreme, and because the plot of the text, unlike its underlying issues, is not the central concern in this argument.

(C) journeys outside of our scope as soon as it mentions the novels that Dovak wrote *before* the seven in which we're interested.

(D) The stimulus states that competent critics *can* make such predictions, but doesn't suggest that their jobs involve such predictions on a regular basis. Also, the critics are less central to the conclusion than the underlying content of Dovak's new book, and that's what the correct assumption must address.

(E) ranks two elements in the stimulus—plot and underlying convictions—that aren't ranked by the author and that needn't be ranked for the author's conclusion to stand.

Remember:

- Be suspicious of comparisons and rankings that appear in the answer choices. The first thing you must ask yourself about such comparisons is, "Is this relevant?" The "irrelevant comparison" is a common wrong answer choice in Inference, Assumption, and Strengthen/Weaken questions.

7 (C) We get a lot of information before the author finally gets to the point, which is that the phony solicitation industry will likely "dwindle significantly" in the years to come. To support this opinion, the author explains that politicians are using phony solicitors less often, and that's basically the extent of the evidence. In order for the loss of some politicians' business to so dramatically affect the phony solicitation industry, the author must assume that politicians represent a significant portion of that industry's clientele. Since this is a Weaken the Argument question, we can scan the answer choices to see if one might deny this central assumption. (C) fits the bill—it basically tells us that politicians are not the industry's major clients, and suggests that the really major clients, the large retailers, are not following the politicians out the door. This weakens the argument because it downplays the importance of the politicians in this industry's survival; that is, it undercuts the author's central assumption.

(A) We already know that some politicians find public opinion polling useful enough to make them stop using the solicitors. Anything that further suggests the efficacy of public opinion polling could only strengthen the argument by suggesting that more than just politicians may begin to take advantage of it to the detriment of the phony solicitors.

(B), if true, wouldn't hurt or help the argument. The stimulus tells us that some people do share such information; whether or not *most* people share personal information isn't important in terms of this argument.

(D) Prosecution itself is not an issue central to the argument's conclusion or evidence, so (D) is just largely irrelevant.

(E) deals with the solicitors' techniques, when all we really care about in terms of the argument is whether the solicitors are going to go out of business due to the withdrawal of some politicians' business.

Remember:

- When evaluating the answer choices for Strengthen/Weaken questions, it's crucial that you be able to distinguish between choices that provide useless background information and those that really have some impact on the argument. The easiest way to make this distinction is to evaluate each answer choice in terms of the author's conclusion and evidence. If a choice doesn't directly affect the way in which the evidence leads to the conclusion, then it cannot strengthen or weaken the argument.

8 **(B)** This dialogue stimulus begins with Albert arguing that the CEO's proposal doesn't make business sense. His evidence: Teenagers can't afford luxury products. Bill disputes Albert's conclusion with the evidence that image enhancement boosts sales in the long run. The point at issue between them will be something that both men address, and on which both men offer differing opinions. They use different evidence, so that's not the point of contention. They only explicitly disagree about whether the CEO's proposal will create sales. (B) captures that perfectly. Bill's would vote "yea" on (B), believing as he does that the CEO's proposal will financially benefit the company (albeit down the road), while that opinion is certainly one with which Albert, who's focusing only on immediate sales, disagrees.

(A) and (D) present views that neither person supports. Looking at (A), since neither man addresses any recent image problems, they certainly aren't disagreeing about that. Albert never discusses image at all, and Bill merely states a correlation between image enhancement and sales, which is not nearly strong enough to say that he feels the company's image is suffering. Sure, positive publicity can help image, but that doesn't mean that the company's image is bad as is. (D) directly contradicts Albert's evidence that teenagers would *not* be able to purchase the products, and it's an issue that Bill does not address.

(C) presents a view with which only one person, specifically Bill, would agree. This is a fundamental assumption in Bill's argument, but Albert never addresses the issue of publicity.

(E) distorts Bill's statement. He discusses the long term financial benefits of a good public image, but doesn't suggest that teenagers could buy the products. Furthermore, Albert never addresses the issue of publicity.

Remember:

- Dialogue stimuli are very similar to single stimuli which present different views: The second person in a dialogue never says "Yeah, you're 100 percent right! I have nothing to add." In both cases, you need to recognize what distinguishes the two views, as well as the scope of each view presented.
- The answer to a Point-at-Issue question has to revolve around an issue that's addressed by both people. If one of the parties has nothing to say regarding the subject of a particular choice, that choice must be wrong.

9 **(A)** Next up is a Method of Argument question based on this same conversation between Albert and Bill, so you'll need to characterize the way in which Bill responds to Albert's argument. We already know that Bill disagrees with Albert's conclusion and that Bill offers supporting evidence for his claim. More specifically, Bill introduces the new issue of publicity and uses it to dispute Albert's conclusion. By adding a consideration of the long term benefits of image enhancement, Bill certainly does "broaden the scope" of the argument in order to argue for the financial benefits of the CEO's proposal, as stated in (A).

(B) is tempting insofar as it mentions long-term gains. However, this answer choice is far too broad. Bill does not offer a general assessment of the values of short versus long-term gains, but merely discusses one instance in which long-term considerations might benefit the company.

(C) First of all, Bill doesn't offer examples, or even one singular example. Secondly, he doesn't rank the issues of image and profit margins as competing factors in financial health; he suggests that a good image leads to higher sales which leads to enhanced profit margins (returning to his first sentence).

(D) *Au contraire.* Bill does not argue that product sales do *not* lead to financial growth, but quite the opposite. Bill argues that a positive image leads to sales which leads to financial growth. He introduces a new variable, but maintains the direct relationship between sales and financial growth.

(E) Bill does not address Albert's concern with teenagers' disposable income. Bill immediately embarks on a different approach (the image enhancement theory of financial well-being), and neither argues against or supports Albert's contention that teenagers can't afford the company's products.

Remember:

- Method of Argument answer choices are sometimes difficult since they often depend on general terms like "presupposition," "scope," and "evidence." It's particularly easy to get lost in them if you aren't clear about what you're seeking. Tie the general terms back into the argument. In (A), for instance, consider what the scope really is, and then ask yourself if Bill has broadened it. Relate the general terms of the answer choices to the specific elements of the stimulus in order to assess them, and throw out any choice that deviates from the stimulus in even one respect.

10 **(D)** The veterinary technician does not discuss the medical merits or weaknesses of Dr. Markey's recommendation, but solely discusses Wisecrack's owner's financial situation. Because the Smiths cannot afford the procedure, the technician disagrees with the doctor's analysis concerning the horse's medical problem. The technician's flaw is her shift in the discussion—did you spot the scope shift? Just because the Smiths can't afford the surgery is no reason to disagree with the doctor's analysis; the fact that they can't pay for the surgery doesn't allow one to conclude that therefore the doctor was wrong in his diagnosis and subsequent recommendation. In other words, just because the Smiths can't act on Markey's recommendation doesn't mean that the analysis that prompted the recommendation is suspect. What's suspect here, as the stem puts it, is this form of logic—and (D) captures the technician's flaw perfectly.

(A) Indeed the technician is not quite the animal advocate that we might want our veterinary technician to be, but (A) doesn't characterize how her argument is flawed in this particular context. Her evidence is concerned only with the costs of treatment; she has no real obligation to take the costs of *not* treating Wisecrack into consideration.

(B) Who's to say what's in the "best interest" of the owners? As uncaring as it may sound, perhaps not spending money they can't afford is a higher priority for them than is treating the suffering horse. "Best interest" is too ambiguous here for (B) to be the flaw in this argument. And once again, one is obligated only to draw a logical conclusion—not one that's in the best interest of some party or another.

(C) Just in case this comes up in your own life, a disagreement is not necessarily a personal attack!

The technician disagrees with the doctor's analysis, but she doesn't attack him personally.

(E) The technician's evidence concerns the inability of the Smiths to pay for the procedure. Certainly this can be independently verified.

Remember:

- Often among the wrong answer choices for an LR question, you'll see an answer choice that confuses what can be done for what should be done. For instance, if an argument argues for a certain course of action, it doesn't strengthen the argument to say that the course of action is actually achievable. By the same logic, it doesn't weaken an argument to assert that a course of action cannot be achieved. An argument that discusses what should happen is not weakened by a consideration of what can happen—they are entirely different arguments.

11 **(D)** First things first: The recommendation is that the marrow in the shipment should not be used. What is the subsidiary conclusion justifying this recommendation? It's the conclusion that the marrow shipped is degenerative. The author presents two key pieces of evidence to support this: (1) The shipment comes from rats supplied by Cronin Labs which has a policy to supply rats that are four months old or older. Somewhat separated from this is key evidence number (2): Degenerative marrow comes from rats who are beyond their primary growth phase. If the rats provided by Cronin Labs do in fact provide degenerative marrow, then the author must assume a connection between the two pieces of evidence. Specifically, she must assume that rats four months old or older are past their primary growth phase. Since we're looking to strengthen this argument, we

should look to see if any choice states this assumption. (D) is perfect since it informs us that four-month-old rats are indeed past their primary growth phase.

(A) contradicts part of the evidence, so it certainly doesn't strengthen the argument.

(B) doesn't help to justify the author's conclusion, which concerns a particular shipment of marrow derived from rats four months old *or* older. (B) just gives information on rats *more* than four months old. Assuming (B) were true, the shipment still could have come from rats exactly four months old, and we aren't given any information about whether their marrow is degenerative. Therefore this doesn't support the argument because it only discusses part of the group of rats involved in it.

(C) wouldn't justify why this particular batch of marrow is degenerative because it doesn't link its information to the rats in the stimulus. Were those rats in their primary growth phase? Were they the ones with degenerative marrow? We don't know, so this information needn't underlie the argument.

(E) Even if you assume that the argument constitutes one of these rare instances, (E) would seem to weaken the argument, suggesting that the marrow may not have been degenerative because it might have come from younger rats in their primary growth phases.

Remember:

- When you have two pieces of disconnected evidence, often an assumption is necessary to tie them together, enabling them to lead to the conclusion as the author intended. Remain on the lookout for gaps in the argument, and don't neglect to prephrase assumptions in Strengthen/Weaken questions when possible. Questions like this one reward you for that effort.

12 **(C)** You can view this Inference/Conclusion question from a formal logic angle: If a client had pulled out, the company would have closed. The company didn't close, so you can continue along with the contrapositive to infer that no major client closed his or her account. You could pause at this point to scan the answer choices, and indeed you would see that (C) takes you exactly where you want to go. After all, the author tells us that a certain action would inevitably result in the company's closure. Since the company expanded, the death blow wasn't dealt—it must be the case that no major client pulled out.

(A) There's no information in the stimulus which would support this specific possibility. It could be true, but it might not be, so we really can't infer it.

(B) and (D) basically suggest ways in which Many Maids' business might have increased in the past year. But nothing in the stimulus suggests that business *must* have increased in these particular ways. (In fact, (B) mildly runs counter to the argument which states that Many Maids absolutely depends on the major clients to stay in business. Sure, it's possible that this dependence has been lessened by the acquisition of small accounts, but the fact remains that if one biggie pulls out, it's bye-bye cleaning company. So we can quibble over whether (B) is possible, possible but not probable, or what have you—but we can definitely say that it is not inferable.)

(E) Again, this might be true, and it seems reasonable that major clients provide this company with much of its revenue, but we have no information that would enable us to make such a precise statement as (E) offers.

Remember:

• When you see formal logic in the stimulus of an Inference question, you'll often see the statement's contrapositive among the answer choices as your correct answer. Consider that your reward for recognizing the formal logic and knowing how contrapositives work.

13 **(A)** The author here begins by explaining a certain problem that the Fines Museum had: Its totem pole was too tall to fit into the storage vault. The author then concludes that the problem has been solved and the totem pole can now be stored in that vault. The author's evidence is the ensuing explanation: The pole can now be separated into two pieces and then later reassembled without damaging the artifact. If you don't see the assumption, scan the answer choices while keeping the central issues of the conclusion and evidence in mind, which are size and storage. In order to work on a prephrase, consider the relationship between the pieces of the argument. The author argues that dividing the totem pole into two pieces will enable its storage in the vault, thereby overcoming the initial problem concerning the height of the pole. Size offered the only barrier to putting the pole in the vault, so if the pole can presently fit into the vault, it must have overcome the size problem. Accordingly, the author assumes that each piece of the separated pole can fit into the storage vault, as (A) states.

(B) is more precise than we need it to be. In order for the divided totem pole to fit into the storage vault, it just needs to be short enough to fit. That may not require that it be divided into equal pieces.

(C) focuses on the issue of expense, which the author never addresses as a relevant factor. The argument's only real issues are size and storage, so the correct assumption needs to maintain that focus.

(D) Again, this answer choice strays from the central issues of size and storage. The author really only cares about this particular totem pole. How its storage would affect the *other* pieces doesn't matter, so nothing about this need be assumed.

(E) While the vault is temperature-controlled, the actual temperature of the vault isn't a crucial issue in the author's argument. We can't even presume that temperature is a motivation for putting the pole in the vault—it seems likely, sure, but we're not told one way or the other.

Remember:

- Prephrasing doesn't necessarily mean that you should have a full sentence in your head which you seek to more or less match with an answer choice. It means that you recognize the key issues that the right answer choice will likely address and understand the ways in which the choice should address them. If you identify the conclusion and evidence in this argument and recognize that the divided totem pole has to be short enough to fit into the vault, only (A) and (B) will have any appeal, and only (A) will survive a closer analysis.

14 (E) The author concludes that psychologists who want their work to be nominated for the *Boatwright Psychology Review* award should

only submit articles containing reviews on three or fewer books. The evidence: *Boatwright Psychology Review* basically will not publish any book review article that reviews more than three books. Look back over the conclusion and evidence, and you'll realize that they aren't really talking about the same thing. The conclusion is about what one should do in order to get his work nominated for the award, and the evidence is about what one should do in order to get his work published. That's a classic scope shift. The only way to make these two different subjects relate to one another is to assume that one must have a review article published in *Boatwright* in order to be eligible for the award. Otherwise the evidence about publication requirements would have no relevance to the conclusion about nomination requirements. (E) expresses this central assumption faithfully, tying the evidence concerning publishing to the conclusion concerning nominations.

(A) While the stimulus suggests that articles covering more books are longer, it nowhere suggests that this proportional relationship carries out to the extremes. What makes for the longest articles isn't central to the evidence and conclusion, and hence need not be assumed in order for this argument to work.

(B) overstates the link between the two subjects. The argument in the stimulus assumes that publication is necessary for a book to be *nominated*, while (B) says that publication guarantees that a book will *win* the award.

(C) Too broad. The argument concerns book review articles, which do come with certain length restrictions. But (C) deals with *all* articles, and we don't know nor do we really care anything about articles besides book reviews that *Boatwright* may contain.

(D) makes an irrelevant distinction that doesn't directly pertain to the central issue: what must be done with an article before it can be nominated for the prestigious award. One book and two books are both on the acceptable side of the length restriction—no distinction between them need be assumed here.

Remember:

- A scope shift occurs when the nature of the evidence differs in some fundamental way from the nature of the conclusion, but the author treats them as if they were the same. The gap that results from this is often bridged by an assumption. In other cases, you'll be asked to recognize the discrepancy as a flaw in the logic.

15 **(A)** The question asks you to determine the role played by a specific piece of information in the argument, so it stands to reason that we should begin by identifying the basic pieces of the argument. The author concludes that milk from organically raised cows is a necessary ingredient for the best-tasting ice cream. The evidence focuses on one factor: pesticides. Pesticide residues can make their way into the milk of non-organically raised cows and lower the quality of taste for ice cream made from that milk. Since you are asked to consider how the statement about taste and pesticides fits into the argument, you can see before you reach the answer choices that the statement is part of the author's evidence: It supports the author's conclusion that the best tasting ice cream must come from organically raised cows—answer choice (A).

(B) A logical consequence is something that follows from the author's conclusion, or takes the author's conclusion one step further. The statement we're told to look at doesn't extend beyond the author's conclusion but rather serves to support that very conclusion as it is.

(C) The claim about taste and pesticides is stated in the argument, so by definition it cannot be an assumption, which, remember, is an *unstated* yet necessary component of the argument.

(D) This is a confusing answer choice, and the logic is a bit circuitous, but if you pick it apart you'll see why it's wrong: To the extent that the statement in question supports the author's argument, proving it false would, if anything, *strengthen* a viewpoint that opposes the one set forth by our author. To weaken an opposing viewpoint, we'd want to shore up, not falsify, the statement in the stem.

(E) The statement we're looking at explains the results of a taste test, and thus present facts that contribute to the author's larger point, which is the conclusion in the first sentence.

Remember:

- To help identify the evidence and the conclusion in an argument, distinguish the facts from the opinions. Since an LSAT conclusion has evidence that supports it, that conclusion cannot be self-evident by itself; it cannot be presented as an uncontested fact or else it wouldn't need support. Surveys, statistics, and other facts usually support the opinion (a.k.a., the conclusion), and thus take the form of evidence.

16 **(B)** The author begins with his conclusion that the increase in colloquialisms degrades the English language. For evidence, he then gives us an example of a colloquialism and states that imprecise word usage present on a large scale basically decreases the quality of the language; hence, the tie-in with the conclusion in the first sentence. The assumption resides in the gaps between these pieces of information; we were never told that these colloquialisms were rampant or imprecise. Indeed, the author states that imprecise words admitted on a large scale decrease a language's quality, without showing that colloquialisms really fall into either category. For the author's conclusion to be valid based on this evidence, he must assume that the evidence is relevant to the conclusion, and that colloquialisms are both imprecise and prevalent in English. The right answer choice, (B) picks up on both: Colloquialisms are both imprecise and appear on a large scale. Without this, the evidence simply doesn't lead all the way to the conclusion.

(A) focuses on the source of colloquialisms, which the author addresses but which plays a central role in neither the evidence nor the conclusion. This could or could not be true without impacting the conclusion.

(C) basically restates the evidence. If "no language" can permit such laxity, then these three languages would logically follow along, but since the stimulus already tells us this much, (C) is not a necessary assumption here.

(D), if anything, presents us with a flawed inference, which would only be accurate if the author assumed that the stated colloquialism were the *only* colloquialism in English, and that *only* colloquialisms degrade the English language. He assumes neither, so if this were an Inference question, (D) would be wrong on these counts. As far as being assumed—that is, being something that's *required* by the argument—(D) is even further off base.

(E) is too extreme. The author identifies one cause (proliferating colloquialisms) which leads to one effect (like, um, degraded English). To make this argument, he does not need to assume that this cause is more or less serious than any other; even if colloquialisms were a minor part of this problem, the author's conclusion could still be valid.

Remember:

• When in doubt on an Assumption question, use the Kaplan Denial Test. If you denied, for example, (A) or (E), the conclusion might still be true. However, if (B) were false, then the conclusion would no longer be supported by the given evidence and the argument would fall apart. Thus, (B) is necessary if the conclusion is to be true, which is why it's the assumption we seek.

17 (E) Now we're asked to weaken the same argument. The right answer probably won't involve denying the argument's assumption, since the first question for this stimulus already focused on that element. Therefore, we can go through the choices one by one, looking for a choice that will decrease the viability of the conclusion.

(A) discusses imprecise language "on a small scale" while the stimulus focuses on such language "on a large scale." Therefore, (A) is outside of the argument's scope.

(B) Since the author's argument relates colloquialisms to the quality of a language, information about their historical longevity does not impact the argument one way or the other. The real issue is the damage they do to the language while they're around.

(C) explains the media's role in determining the fate of a potential colloquialism and, since the argument itself does not concern itself with the media or with the mechanisms by which a colloquialism becomes a colloquialism, (C) has no effect on this argument.

(D) Like (C), (D) brings up the issue of the source of colloquialisms. The argument focuses on the *effect* of colloquialisms; their source plays no role in that focus.

(E) breaks apart the author's causal argument. The author asserts that colloquialisms lower the quality of a language, while (E) explains that they actually often contribute to the "highest quality" languages in the long run. (E) thus addresses a possibility that the author doesn't consider and that would weaken the author's argument.

Remember:

- The two most common ways of weakening an argument are by breaking down the argument's assumption, and by locating alternative possibilities relevant to the argument. If you have a sense of what types of answers you might be looking for (even just knowing the common categories that they fall into), they'll be easier to find.

18 **(C)** The author kindly identifies the relevant principle in the second sentence of the stimulus. Basically the principle is that a teacher should learn his or her subject matter as a student, since that will enable the teacher to understand the subject matter well enough to then teach it. In other words, one should be on the receiving end of instruction before proceeding to train others in that same skill. The other parts of the stimulus provide additional information, but since the question instructs us to apply this specific principle to another situation, the principle is what we should focus on as we evaluate the answer choices.

(A) is off track because it emphasizes that dog trainers need to be licensed, not trained. Education and instruction are the key elements of the stimulus' principle, and this answer choice focuses on neither.

(B) starts off well, but falls apart because the officers aren't going to use their psychological training to teach others about the same subject; they simply need to make sure they take the class. According to the stimulus, a group needs to learn a skill in order to then proceed to teach it to others.

(C) is entirely consistent with the original principle, as it explains that one must be taught how to treat a patient from the patient's perspective, before teaching others the same skill. One must then receive another's instruction before instructing others to perform that same skill. This is therefore the situation that relates best to the principle in the passage.

(D) discusses the importance of training, but is wrong because these students aren't using their training to teach others the same skill, but rather to prepare themselves to perform in competitions.

(E) again tells us why training is necessary to perform a job well, but misses the element central to the stimulus where the trained individual then proceeds to train others.

Remember:

- When applying a principle to a new situation, bear in mind that the new situation must contain every important part of the original situation. Incomplete applications, like those in answer choices (D) and (E), are never correct, so develop a clear sense of the precise elements that need to be applied before looking through the answer choices.

19 **(A)** The argument begins by explaining that fundraising specialists help foundations to raise much of their money, unlike financial planners who raise much less money but serve an important function as organizers. Before the blank, we see the ever-important keyword "therefore." That means that the right answer choice will provide a conclusion based on the information thus far provided. Remember that this is still an Inference question, so the right answer will need to be perfectly consistent with and supported by the information already provided in the stimulus. (A) is perfectly consistent with the argument and represents a logical conclusion for it. If fundraising specialists raise more funds, then it is certainly logical that a foundation seeking to raise funds should entrust such activities to those specialists.

(B) is too extreme. The stimulus discusses general trends, but never states or supports the notion that companies lacking fundraising specialists can't still raise lots of money. It's not difficult to imagine how a huge company lacking financial planners may still raise as much if not more money than a tiny company with financial planners.

(C) ranks fundraising specialists based on what knowledge they do or don't possess. The author never breaks the specialists into these groups, or provides information about the specialists in terms of their knowledge of financial planning, so the stimulus as it stands provides no direct support for this conclusion.

(D) again takes us far beyond what we can reasonably infer from the stimulus. Financial specialists generally raise more money than financial planners, but whether or not that enables foundations who use specialists to meet their goals is more than we have the information to determine.

(E) isn't consistent with the passage, which states that financial planners serve a "key" role as organizers and advisors. Maybe they shouldn't be in charge of fundraising, but the stimulus does explain that financial planners serve important and useful functions for foundations. It doesn't follow that they therefore shouldn't be hired.

Remember:

- Fill-in-the-blank questions are always Inference questions, so they always follow the rules of Inference questions. This means that the right answer will make statements entirely consistent with the argument without unsupported innovation, and that it won't stray beyond the scope of the argument.

20 **(B)** In order to parallel the flaw, let's figure out what exactly that flaw is. The author argues that, since every individual in a group is unable to accomplish a certain task, the individuals working together must also be unable to accomplish that task. In general terms: An individual's deficiency must also imply a communal deficiency. Let's look for that in the choices:

(A) discusses only one individual without tying that individual to a group. Further, this choice argues for a certain course of action, while the stimulus applies to a group what is true of its individual members.

(B) Yes. Because something is true of individuals, it is therefore true of a group comprising those individuals. Flawed, parallel, and the correct choice here.

(C) says that if one person can't do something, then none of the others can either, but it doesn't mention whether they could do it working together. That's what we're after.

(D), like (A), has the wrong method of argument. (D)'s is a causal argument, arguing that one thing won't create a certain effect. The original argument doesn't argue against causation but makes a conclusion about a group based on the individual qualities of its members.

(E) mentions one person who *can* do something and others who cannot. In the stimulus, all individuals are equally incapable, by themselves and as part of the group.

Remember:

- The key to Parallel Reasoning questions is characterizing the stimulus in such a way that you recognize the key elements that the right answer must contain while recognizing which elements are changeable. For instance, the order of the evidence and conclusion can change, but the relationship between them cannot. The subject matter can (and almost always will) change, but the method of argument cannot. Focus on what must remain the same, and quickly axe any choice that deviates in any fundamental way.

21 (C) The author concludes that Leroy absolutely did not have the flu on Monday. His evidence is that Leroy had the flu on Tuesday and visited a friend with the flu on Sunday, and that "there is no evidence that Leroy had the flu on Monday." Just because there's no evidence that Leroy had the flu on Monday doesn't mean that he definitely did not have it—we all know it's certainly possible to be sick the day before seeing a doctor and receiving official proof of the illness. Lack of evidence to prove an event doesn't mean that the event itself didn't exist. (C) expresses this argument's error by pointing out that it is indeed possible that the diagnosis on Tuesday suggests that Leroy had the flu on Monday.

(A) gets the conclusion and evidence mixed up. Actually, the argument concludes that Leroy *didn't* have the flu based on the fact that there is no evidence to prove that he *did* have the flu.

(B) The author nowhere discusses how Leroy's co-worker got the flu, and there's no flaw in something that isn't part of the argument.

(D) isn't consistent with the argument, which suggests that Leroy's association with an ill person *isn't* entirely relevant to his own health status.

(E) is just strange. Leroy's professional ethics aren't discussed at all in the argument, and certainly aren't central to the argument, as (E) suggests.

Remember:

- In every section of the LSAT, it is absolutely crucial that you maintain a structured approach. By breaking arguments like this one into conclusion and evidence, you can more easily ascertain whether the flaw comes up in one, the other, or both, and then proceed to define what that flaw is. If you don't take the time to understand the argument, you have terrible odds of getting the question right.

22 **(C)** The author tells us that two school districts were running neck and neck until about 1990 as far as their junior high school students' reading scores were concerned. After 1990, district Y consistently took the lead, with its students demonstrating much higher average scores on the reading test. The superintendent of district Y proposes an explanation for this occurrence, attributing it to her district's reinstatement of a minimum reading requirement in the junior high schools. This is an Inference question, so once we have a good grasp of the stimulus, we should move on to the answer choices.

(A) is more than we know, since it deals with a non-relative increase in the average scores themselves. All we know is that district Y's average score is higher than district X's, but we were given no information to suggest that the actual average score in district Y has been increasing.

(B) deals with minimum reading requirements in district X before 1990, which isn't a subject that the stimulus even addresses.

(C) is inferable. The superintendent attributes her district's successes to the reinstated reading requirement, and these successes began in 1990. This strongly suggests that the program must have been reinstated sometime around when the change in relative average scores occurred. Otherwise, it couldn't account for the district's post-1990 achievements. This leads to (C): If the requirement was reinstated around 1990 when district Y began to outpace district X, then it must be true that the requirement

was not in effect at some point in district Y before 1990.

(D) is exactly the same as (B) except that it discusses the possibility that there was no reading requirement in district X at some point in time. But it's wrong for the same reason as (B): We know nothing about district X's history with the reading requirement, so we can't infer either answer choice.

(E) confuses averages with individual students. The stimulus states that the average score has increased in district Y relative to district X, but that certainly doesn't mean that each and every student in district Y is beating each and every student in district X.

Remember:

- Choices like (B) and (D) exist for those students who don't read answer choices carefully enough and miss the fact that both choices discuss district X. Don't put your critical reading skills aside once you get to the answer choices; they need to be read at least as carefully as the stimulus.

23 **(E)** This argument begins with a chain of causality: A crisis (step 1) can lead to a decrease in people's faith in their country's leaders (step 2), which can in turn lead to violence in unspecified segments of the population (step 3). Propaganda limits the perception of the crisis, thereby keeping the first domino from falling, and therefore favorably impacting at least the second step in the chain. This is the author's first explanation for violence, and the propaganda solution refers only to it. The author then gives an entirely different explanation for violence, this time more specifically explaining youth violence: Youth violence is caused by boredom and lack of vision regarding a promising future. We have two paths explaining violence, and the answer to this Inference question will certainly test our ability to distinguish between them. Let's evaluate the answer choices, keeping the distinctions in mind.

(A) While the author offers us one potential antidote to the first type of violence without making any such reference in regards to the second, that doesn't mean that there is no solution for the second type. Because something isn't mentioned, that doesn't mean it doesn't exist, so we have no way of inferring which type of violence is easier to quell.

(B) For all we know, propaganda alone may be enough to entirely diffuse dissent in some poor countries, possibly those without disaffected youth, or even those with disaffected youth who are not driven to dissent by such crises.

(C) is too extreme and distorts the argument. The author writes that economic and political crises lead to violence among "specific segments of the population," which may include youth; the author certainly doesn't rule out that possibility. Further, because boredom and lack of vision lead to habitual youth violence, that doesn't mean that *only* boredom and lack of vision lead to youth violence. The two explanations aren't mutually exclusive.

(D) also goes too far out on a limb. The author mentions two effects of the propaganda—it downplays the extent of the crisis and restores faith in the government. However, we don't know that an alteration in people's "fundamental beliefs" is inherent in either one of these cases; we simply know that the propaganda has an effect on their immediate actions at the time of the crisis.

(E) Yep. Since the author does not directly link habitual youth violence to economic or political crises, or to the decrease in faith which such crises create, propaganda probably doesn't decrease that violence by restoring faith in the country's leaders. The author says that habitual youth violence is not caused by a loss of such faith, so restoring the faith probably wouldn't help matters any. If propaganda helps to quell habitual youth violence, then it probably does it in some other way.

Remember:

- Beware of extreme answer choices in Inference questions. Notice all of the overly eager claims in answer choices (A) through (D): (A) mentions which revolt is "easier" to quell; (B) discusses the powers of "propaganda alone"; (C) affirms that crises don't lead to "any" instance of youth violence; (D) discusses the "primary" effect of propaganda. All of these choices go farther than our author, who doesn't make such assertive claims. The right choice won't intensify the argument but, like choice (E), will more often discuss the possibilities that the argument leaves open.

24 (A) The question stem directs us to locate a particular type of flaw in the stimulus; specifically, we're looking to find what the stimulus is wrong to neglect. The author states that Derek is good at everything he does, and then predicts that Derek will be a good student president. We can immediately be suspicious of the word "everything" since the author's evidence shows that Derek is good at science, two sports, capitalistic ventures, and music. Is this a representative sample? Because Derek is good at these four things, does that mean that he'll be good at anything one asks him to do? We don't really know if being a good president necessarily follows from the fact that he's good at the activities mentioned—perhaps he's particularly interested in and suited for those things and that's why he does them in the first place. This argument's flaw of omission is its failure to mention whether or not the four successes described accurately indicate that Derek will be good at anything he does. (A) captures the flaw: The author fails to consider that the causal mechanism may be the other way around; that is, Derek may only do those things he knows he's good at. If that's the case, the prediction of his presidential prowess may be a miscalculation.

(B) The author doesn't necessarily overlook this possibility. In painting Derek as a "Renaissance man" and making the bold prediction, the author evidently believes that any skill is within his grasp. His flaw lies there, not in overlooking the fact that the president's job will call on skills other than his musicianship.

(C) comes close, since it would be a viable answer choice if those four skills weren't Derek's only skills. The author assumes that they are, so this answer choice states an assumption rather than identifying a flaw.

(D) is irrelevant, since the conclusion only asserts that Derek would be a good president, not that nobody else would do the job as well. The argument is only about Derek, so the author's failure to mention other people isn't a flaw.

(E) isn't a flaw because the author isn't arguing that Derek can do the job; he's arguing that Derek would be good at it if he did.

Remember:

- When you have a question stem that's an incomplete sentence, like the one in the question above, make sure that you read each answer choice as an extension of that sentence, meaning you may want to reread the stem with each answer choice.

25 **(B)** The first two sentences of this argument provide background information explaining why pediatric nurses were willing to take the difficult home-care assignments. The heart of the argument is the last two sentences. The author concludes that the nurses have clearly become cynical, and supports that conclusion by citing an increase in the number of nurses but a decrease in the number of home-care nursing assignments. The author argues that nurses have consciously rejected these home-care cases, and assumes that no other factor might be responsible for this situation. Since we are asked to strengthen this argument, we'll look to support the author's argument that the decline in home-care nursing assignments truly is the result of growing cynicism among the nurses and not the result of other factors. (B) strengthens the argument precisely because it eliminates a possible alternative explanation. If there were simply fewer cases requiring at home pediatric nurses, we'd be able to argue that cynicism is not really the reason for the decrease in such assignments. The author assumes this very plausible alternative (less demand) is not the case. (B), by explicitly shoring up this assumption, strengthens the argument: If the demand for home-care pediatric nurses has remained constant, the author's explanation for the decline in accepted cases seems more reasonable.

(A) On the face of it, cases in a hospital setting may seem to fall outside the scope. The author is concerned with home-care cases, so our correct answer choice will most likely maintain that specific focus. On another reading, however, (A) may be seen to weaken the argument: If demand for hospital nurses in this area is way up, that could explain the steep decline in home care assignments—it may simply be a matter of prioritizing finite resources. If that were the case, then the author's cynicism theory would take one on the chin.

(C) This choice would provide a different reason for the nurses to take fewer home-assignments. Like (A), if anything, it would weaken the argument by providing an alternative explanation for the decline in accepted nursing home-care assignments.

(D) This comparison of compensation rates across communities doesn't strengthen this argument because it doesn't add anything new. The author states that the assignments pay poorly; the relative degree to which they pay poorly doesn't change the stated fact that money is not a strong incentive to take such cases. Since the information has no real impact, it doesn't strengthen the argument.

(E) The reason *why* the cynicism exists is irrelevant to this argument. We only care whether it's the cause of the decrease in nursing assignments to home-care cases.

Remember:

• In a Strengthen the Argument question in which an author constructs a causal relationship offering one way to explain a certain situation, you'll want to strengthen that link. The right answer choice will often do that directly. However, it may strengthen the argument indirectly by ruling out another possible cause, as (B) does here.

Section III: Logical Games Explanations

GAME 1—Stadium Ads

The Action

Six companies each advertise in one of two places—either the upper wall or the lower wall. So this is another Grouping game of distribution, but we'll also have to keep track of beverage and clothing companies. The *Key Issues* are:

- Which beverage companies can, must, and cannot be advertised on each wall?
- Which clothing companies can, must, and cannot be advertised on each wall?
- Which companies can, must, and cannot be advertised with which other companies?

The Initial Setup

A list of entities with two rows—one for the upper wall and one for the lower wall—will do just fine. We can distinguish beverage companies from clothing companies by writing the former in ALL CAPS:

```
F G H m n p

upper   |
lower   |
```

The Rules

1) Now we see how the beverage/clothing distinction will play itself out. Each wall will have at least one of FGH and at least one of mnp. We can build this in directly by placing a "1+ in each" below the clothing ads and the beverage ads.

2) This one requires some translation. Remember, when an "only if" statement is translated into a standard if-then, the statement that follows the "only if" will follow the "then." So Rule 2 means that if M is on the lower wall, then the upper wall must have four ads, which in turn means that the lower wall must have two ads. "M (lower) —> 4/2 upper/lower" is one way to capture this. Taking the contrapositive, we can deduce that if we don't have a 4/2 upper/lower distribution, then M cannot be on the lower wall, which in turn means that M must be on the upper wall.

3) This also requires some translation. Neither F nor N can be on a wall with exactly two ads. What does this mean in the context of this game? Let's turn to the *Key Deductions*.

Key Deductions

When you get a Grouping game, always pay attention to the numbers governing the game. Here, each deck gets at least one ad from each of two groups. In that case, the minimum number of ads on each wall is two, and the maximum number of ads on each wall is four. We can also expand on Rule 3. Since the minimum number of ads on a wall is two, and since neither F nor N will advertise on a wall containing exactly two ads, any wall with either F or N will have at least three ads.

The Final Visualization

```
F G H                    m n p
1+ in each               1+ in each

         upper   |
         lower   |
```

M (lower) → 4/2 upper/lower
no 4/2 upper/lower → M (upper)
F or N on a wall → 3+ on that wall

The Big Picture

- This wasn't a bad place to start your Logic Games section. As it happens, the next game is probably easier, but a straightforward Grouping game is a good place to build some points and confidence.
- When you see a Grouping game, examine the numbers, looking for minimums and maximums. When you do, you'll probably discover that the game isn't as wide-open as it seemed initially.
- Treat "only if" statements with care! "X only if Y" means "If X then Y."
- Keep driving the abstract to the concrete, especially when forming contrapositives. Here, if M isn't on the lower wall, M must be on the upper wall, since those are the only two possibilities.

The Questions

1 **(D)** First up is a straightforward hypothetical. If the upper wall has four ads, then the lower wall contains exactly two. In that case, neither F nor N can be on the lower wall (rule 3) and so they must both be on the upper wall. F isn't among the choices, but N is choice (D). The other choices are possible only.

Remember:

- When you get a hypothetical, build in the new information, and see where it takes you. Don't look at the choices without looking for some deductions.

2 **(C)** If G is one of only two companies that advertise on the upper wall, then rule 2 comes into play. We don't have 4 companies on the upper wall, so M can't be on the lower wall, and therefore M is on the upper wall. That's (C).

Remember:

- You could have found this answer by deducing that the other companies must advertise on the lower wall; it just would have taken a little longer. That's OK, though. You can always find the correct answer by eliminating the other choices.

3 **(A)** Here's a partial Acceptability question. We get only part of the setup, which means that some of the choices will likely be wrong because of their implications for the other deck. We can eliminate (C) and (E) fairly easily, since they contain pretty straightforward violations of Rules 3 and 1, respectively. Getting rid of (B) and (D) is a little harder. Rule 2 gets rid of (D), since (D) places M on the lower wall but places only three companies on the upper wall. Rule 3 gets rid of (B), which places only F and M on the lower wall, and we know that any wall with F must contain at least three ads. So (A) is correct.

Remember:

- When you get an Acceptability question that only gives you part of the arrangement, expect that you'll have to make deductions concerning the entities that aren't mentioned.

4 **(A)** With N and P on the upper wall, M will have to go to the lower wall since M is the only clothing company left. That brings rule 2 into play. Since M is on the lower wall, the upper wall will have four ads. Now rule 3 comes into play. Since the lower wall has two ads, F must be on the upper wall. We can place every ad definitively except G and H. One of these two goes on each wall, but we can't tell which. So (A) must be true and is correct.

(B), (C), and (D) are possible only, since we don't know where G and H are.

(E) is impossible. P is on the upper wall, which has four ads.

Remember:

- To find deductions, look for the most relevant rule. Placing N and P on the upper wall should direct you to rule 1. Once M is placed on the lower wall, rule 2 comes into play, etcetera. Sometimes success in Logic Games is just a matter of knowing where to look.

5 **(E)** In a different way, this question is asking what must be true if F is the only beverage company on the lower wall. In that case, G and H must be on the upper wall, and according to rule 1, they must be joined by at least one clothing company. Now rule 3 comes in. Since F is on the lower wall, the lower wall needs at least three ads. So the ads are split 3/3, which in turn means that M is on the upper wall (contrapositive of rule 2). So N and P, the only ads left, must go on the lower wall. Here's what we've just deduced:

upper	G H m
lower	F n p

All the choices must be false except (E). N must be on the lower wall.

Remember:

- "X cannot be true unless Y" means "If X then Y."

6 **(E)** This question is a little tougher since we don't know which wall has two of each ad type.

So let's start by seeing what happens when the upper wall has two of each type. We know that F and N will have to be on the upper wall, since they can't be on a wall with only two ads. Beyond that, there isn't much to deduce. Each wall will have one of G and H, and each wall will have one of M and P.

upper	F n G/H m/p
lower	G/H m/p

From here, we can eliminate all the wrong choices. This scenario demonstrates that F and H could be together, (A); G and H could be apart, (B); G and N could be apart, (C); and M and N could be together, (D). So (E) must be true.

At this point, you don't have to explore what happens when the lower wall has two of each ad type, but if you did, here's what you might have found: F and N still have to be on the wall with four ads, and they still have to be joined by exactly one of G and H. However, we can make one extra deduction: Since the upper wall doesn't have four ads, M cannot be on the lower wall (contrapositive of rule 2). So M is on the upper wall, which means P must be on the lower wall. Here's what we've deduced:

upper	G/H m
lower	F n G/H p

In either scenario, M and P are on separate walls, so again, (E) must be true.

Remember:

- If a question breaks down into two distinct scenarios, work them both out. Then you'll know what must, could, and cannot be true.

GAME 2—Six Dives

The Action

Six dives are performed, one after the other in a row, so we're dealing with another Sequencing game. This one is a little different in that some divers will dive more than once, but otherwise this is business as usual. The *Key Issues* are:

- Which dives can, must, or cannot be performed by which people?
- Which dives can, must, or cannot be performed by the same person as which other dives?

The Initial Setup

Nothing fancy is required here. A list of the entities (X, Y, Z) and six slots will do just fine.

X Y Z

$$\frac{\quad}{1} \quad \frac{\quad}{2} \quad \frac{\quad}{3} \quad \frac{\quad}{4} \quad \frac{\quad}{5} \quad \frac{\quad}{6}$$

The Rules

1) So X performs three dives, and none in a row. At this point, you should be asking: how many different ways are there for this to happen? There aren't too many, and that leads to the *Key Deduction* below.

2) Y gets two dives, and we know we'll need to place at least one Y in one of the first two slots.

3) The meaning of this is clear enough: We can't have YZ.

Key Deductions

X gets three dives, but none consecutively. With only six slots, there aren't many ways to fit this in. So let's explore them. If X is first, then Y must be

second (rule 2). Now, if another X is third, where can the last X be? It can't be fourth or sixth, since that would leave YZ together. So the last X would have to be fifth. Y and Z will split the fourth and sixth slots, in either order. Let's call this Option I.

Option I

X	Y	X	Y/Z	X	Y/Z
1	2	3	4	5	6

If X dives first and fourth, then X's third dive must be sixth. Now we have to split up YZ. The two Y's go second and third, and Z goes fifth. Let's call this Option II.

Option II

X	Y	Y	X	Z	X
1	2	3	4	5	6

Finally, if X dives second, then X's other dives must be fourth and sixth. Y then dives first (rule 2), and Y and Z split the third and fifth slots. Let's call this Option III.

Option III

Y	X	Y/Z	X	Y/Z	X
1	2	3	4	5	6

That's it! There's no other way to spread out the three X's. So the entire game breaks down into three options. It takes a little time to find them, but once you do, the questions will drop like flies.

The Final Visualization

Option I

X	Y	X	Y/Z	X	Y/Z
1	2	3	4	5	6

Option II

X	Y	Y	X	Z	X
1	2	3	4	5	6

Option III

Y	X	Y/Z	X	Y/Z	X
1	2	3	4	5	6

The Big Picture

- Knowing when to stop looking for deductions is an acquired skill. Early on, expect to stop looking too early in some instances and too late in others. That's OK, it's part of the learning process. In time, though, develop a sense for the "likely suspects," but move on when they aren't there.
- One of those "likely suspects" is Limited Options. If a game breaks down into only two or three scenarios, work out those scenarios. You'll fly through the questions.

The Questions

7 **(C)** First up is a standard Acceptability question. Again, the Kaplan Method of using the rules to eliminate choices yields a quick point. Rule 1 kills (B) and (D). Rule 2 kills (E). Rule 3 kills (A). (C) remains and is correct.

Remember:

- When you get an acceptability question, use the rules to eliminate four choices, then pick the one that remains without checking it.

8 **(E)** If Z is fifth, then we're either in Option II or Option III. In Option III, X dives neither first nor third, so (A) and (C) are wrong. In Option II, X doesn't dive second and Y doesn't dive first, so (B) and (D) are wrong. So (E) must be true. You don't have to check it, but Y is always third in Option

II, and Y must be third in Option III whenever Z is fifth, since Y and Z split the third and fifth positions.

Remember:

- When you have set out a game's options, use the stem to tell you which scenarios are in effect.

9 **(D)** This one is a quick battle once you have the options. In Option I, X is first, Y can be fourth, Y can be sixth, and Z can be sixth. So (A), (B), (C), and (E) are all wrong. So (D) must be correct, and yes, Z can never be first.

Remember:

- When you're worked out all the possibilities up front, you always know what could, must, and cannot be true.

10 **(B)** If X is third, then we're in Option I. (A) and (C) must be true. (D) and (E) could be true, but (B) must be false and is therefore correct. X can't be sixth since that wouldn't allow us to break up Y and Z.

Remember:

- If things are going well, don't second-guess yourself. Move swiftly and save time for harder games.

11 **(E)** If Y performs two dives consecutively, then we're in Option II:

Option II

X	Y	Y	X	Z	X
1	2	3	4	5	6

All the choices must be true except (E). Boom.

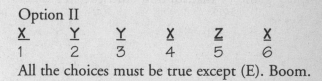

Remember:

- Always read the question stem carefully! It can be easy to miss a word like "EXCEPT," even when it's in ALL CAPS.

12 **(A)** Now the test makers have switched things around on us. Now X's dives must be consecutive. So how many ways can they be placed? X's dives cannot be first through third, since we need a Y in the first two. If X's dives are second through fourth, then we can place Y first, but now we have YZ in fifth and sixth in violation of rule 3. So can X's dives be third through fifth? Sure. Y's dives will be first and second, and Z will be sixth. That's one combination so far. Now can X's dives be fourth through sixth? No, since we wouldn't be able to split up Y and Z. So (A), one combination, is correct.

Remember:

- If a question involves a rule change, don't panic. You may have to rethink part of your understanding of the initial setup, but your experience working with the other rules will see you through.

GAME 3—Seven Instructors, Three Semesters

The Action

Seven instructors—J, K, L, M, N, P, and Q—each teach during exactly one of three semesters. In other words, we have to *distribute* the seven instructors among the three semesters. So this is another Grouping game of distribution, and the *Key Issues* will be:

- Which instructors can, must, or cannot teach during which semesters?
- Which instructors can, must, or cannot teach during the same semester as which other instructors?
- How many instructors teach during each semester?

The Initial Setup

A list of the entities and three columns (one for each of the semesters) will allow us to keep track of the action here.

J   K   L   M   N   P   Q

| Fall | Spring | Winter |

The Rules

1) Here's a concrete rule: We can place K in the winter column permanently.

2) Rule 2 is a familiar enough Grouping rule. L and M are always together. "Always LM" captures this.

3) Rule 3 can be built in directly, with arrows pointing to the fall and spring semesters.

4) So the winter semester gets twice as many as the fall semester. OK, what does that mean in the context of this game? With seven instructors, there really aren't that many ways to split them up so that exactly twice as many wind up in the Winter semester. So how many combinations are there? If one instructor taught in the fall, then we'd need two in the winter, and the remaining four would teach during the spring semester. Or, we could have two in the fall, four in the winter, and one in the spring. That's it.

It's either 1/4/2 or 2/1/4. We can't have three or more in the fall, since that would force us to have six or more in the winter, and that's no good because there are only seven instructors.

5) and 6) are familiar enough Grouping rules. We cannot have an NQ, and we cannot have a JP.

Key Deductions

The Big Deduction here was the 1/4/2 or 2/1/4 breakdown of the instructors. This essentially comes straight out of Rule 4, but if you noticed it at this point, that's ok, too. From here, you could have explored different scenarios, seeing if they set off any chains of inferences, but there wasn't anything else that qualifies as a major deduction. On to the questions!

The Final Visualization

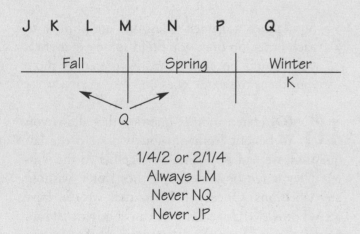

J K L M N P Q

Fall	Spring	Winter
		K

Q

1/4/2 or 2/1/4
Always LM
Never NQ
Never JP

The Big Picture

- This wasn't an easy game, but it was less complicated than Game 4. This game was probably best handled third, after Games 1 and 2.
- Get to know the usual suspects that appear in Logic Games. Grouping games are very com-

mon, and so you should get a feel for their mechanics. This will help should you encounter a similar game on test day.

- Always investigate the numbers behind Grouping games, and always turn abstract rules into concrete rules. Here, the game was pretty tough if you didn't make the numbers deduction early. But don't get down if you didn't make it. Instead, focus on the clues that will lead to similar deductions on test day.
- When a rule is abstract, think of concrete scenarios that would violate it, and see if there are a limited number of scenarios that don't violate it. Rule 4 is tough to deal with without paraphrasing, but once you see how it applies in context, you have the key to the game.

The Questions

13 **(D)** This is a harder Acceptability question than most, since we're only given part of the lineup. So you may have been forced to work out scenarios for each choice. Only (B) and (E) contain a straightforward violation of a rule. (According to rule 6, we can't have J and P together, and according to rule 1, K teaches during the winter). The rest of the choices require some work:

(A) With Q and M in the fall, we need L there as well (rule 2). That's three in the fall, which is no good, since it would force us to place six in the winter.

(C) If L is in the fall, then so is M. Since the fall can hold no more, Q must go in the spring (rule 3). That leaves K, J, P, and N for the winter. But we can't have J and P together, so (C) doesn't work. So (D) is correct by the process of elimination.

(D) For the record: Placing J, M, and N as the stem dictates means we must also place L in the winter. Since the winter now has three instructors, it will need a fourth to satisfy the 2/1/4 distribution. We also need to split up J and P. So we can place Q in the fall and P in the winter, and we have an acceptable arrangement.

Fall	Spring	Winter
J	N	K
Q		M
		L
		P

Remember:

- Acceptability questions are usually quick points, but they can be harder when you only see part of the arrangement. Often, the wrong choices in these questions don't contain obvious violations of the rules. Rather, they violate the rules by virtue of their implications for the other entities.

14 **(A)** This one was quick if you worked out the scenario in (C) from the previous question. In that choice, we saw what happens when we put L in the fall: We need to put M there are well, and we're forced to place J and P together in the winter. So we can never put L (or M, for that matter) in the fall, and choice (A) is correct.

If you didn't see this, you still could have attacked this question strategically by postponing working on it until after you've built some acceptable scenarios from the other questions. (B) must be true in question 18, (E) could be true in question 18, and both (C) and (D) are true in the correct answer to the Acceptability question.

Remember:

- Postpone working on questions when your work in the other questions will eliminate some choices.
- Don't forget about the correct answer to the Acceptability question. It often eliminates a few wrong choices elsewhere.

15 **(C)** If only one instructor teaches in the spring, then we have a 2/1/4 setup. As we've seen we can't place L and M in the fall, since that would force J and P together in the winter. So L and M teach in the winter, and (C) is correct.

(A), (D), and (E) are all possible only.

(B) is impossible. L teaches in the winter.

Remember:

- Sometimes a game's questions are similar to each other. So once you build some experience, you should be able to make inferences more quickly as the game goes on.

16 **(D)** Here's another question that allows you to benefit from previous work. In the last question, we had K, L, and M together in the winter. They could be joined by either J or P without any violations. Once you know that we can have KLMJ or KLMP together, you can eliminate all four wrong choices, since they all contain a subset of one of those groups. You also might have spotted correct choice (D) directly: K must be in the winter, and Q can never be in the winter. So (D) is correct.

Remember:

• Use your previous work whenever possible. It saves time.

17 **(D)** Who doesn't teach in the winter semester? Since the winter semester has either 2 or 4 instructors, either three or five instructors don't teach during the winter semester. So (B) and (E) are wrong. Eliminating the other wrong choices was a little harder:

(A) splits up L and M, in violation of rule 2.

(C) places J and P in the winter and thus violates rule 6. So (D) is correct.

(D) For the record, we could place Q and P in the fall, N in the spring, and K, L, M, and J in the winter.

Remember:

• Numbers deductions are key in Grouping games. Always look for minimums and maximums, and then use that information to cut down on your work later on.

18 **(B)** If more instructors teach during the spring semester, then we're dealing with the 1/4/2 setup. So where could L and M go? They can never go in the fall, and they can't go in the winter, since there are only two winter instructors and K is always there. So they must go in the spring. So (B) is correct. The wrong choices are possible only.

Remember:

• The challenge with this game was timing. Lots of people could find the right answers given unlim-

ited time, but the real challenge is to find the right answers as quickly as possible. Take a second look at your work on these questions, and ask yourself how you could have used good test-taking strategies to save time. Then practice these strategies until you apply them automatically.

GAME 4—Businesspeople and Tourists

The Action
There's quite a bit going on here. The first sentence in the opening paragraph indicates that the four rows are adjacent, implying that this game has a Sequencing element. Also, there are six passengers for only four rows, which means that some of the rows will have more than one passenger. In other words, there must be a Grouping element at work here as well. Finally, we have a Matching element to consider: Passengers are either businesspeople or tourists, and either arriving home or connecting. The *Key Issues* (and there are a lot of them) are:

• How many passengers are in each row?
• Which passengers are tourists, and which are businesspeople?
• Which passengers are connecting, and which are arriving home?
• Which passengers could, must, or cannot be next to which other passengers?

The Initial Setup
When in doubt, start with the most familiar element. A simple row of four will help us keep track of the four rows, and the entities listed above the sketch will remind us what we need to fill into those rows. The fact that each traveler has two characteristics makes for the matching element of the game. Our task is to match up these elements to fill different types of travelers into the rows where appropriate, given the grouping and sequencing restrictions noted in the rules.

B B B T T T
cn cn ar ar ar ar

1	2	3	4

2 MAX per row
No B/T
No cnB next to arT
At least 1 arT
At least 1 arB

The Rules

1) We can't have businesspeople and tourists together. "No B/T" will do.

2) Here's where the sequencing element comes into play. We can't have an arriving tourist *next to* a connecting businessperson. From the previous rule, we know these two types can't be in the same row, but Rule 2 takes it one step further.

3) If the maximum number of passengers in any given row is two, how could we split up our six passengers? This brings us to our Key Deduction.

Key Deductions

Since we can't mix businesspeople and tourists, and we can have no more than two passengers per row, one row will have two tourists, and one row will have one. Similarly, one row will have two businesspeople, and one row will have one. There's one more deduction worth making: Since four passengers are arriving home, at least one businessperson and at least on tourist is arriving home.

The Final Visualization

B B B T T T
cn cn ar ar ar ar

1	2	3	4

The Big Picture

- Sometimes the hardest game appears last, but not always. On some recent tests, the games were more or less given in order of difficulty, but you can't count on that on your LSAT.

- Read the opening paragraph carefully. It often contains information that's just as important as the indented rules. Here, we get the exact numbers of businesspeople, tourists, etcetera, without which this game is impossible.

- If you have a hard time visualizing a game, start with the element that's most familiar, then add the other pieces. Focus on the entities and the action: Who are the characters, and what do you have to know about them? If you can answer those questions, you always have a fighting chance.

- When you get a monster of a game, don't get greedy. Be content (and confident) getting some quick points and then making some educated guesses. You always feel a little bit of regret when you don't have time for all the questions, but you can't let that get you down. Actively make the choices that will maximize your score, and you'll keep your confidence even in the face of adversity.

The Questions

19 (C) We start with an always-welcome Acceptability question, so we'll apply the familiar method of using the rules to knock off choices. Rule 1 kills (D), which mixes tourists and businesspeople. Rule 2 kills (B) and (E), which have arriving tourists next to connecting businesspeople.

Rule 3 kills (A), which has three people in one of the rows, and we're done. (C) remains.

Remember:

- Even hard games have easy questions. Even if this game as a whole gave you trouble, you could have salvaged this one.

20 **(C)** This flows from the Key Deduction. No row could be empty, since that would place six people in the remaining three rows, and we can't do that without mixing businesspeople and tourists. So (C) is correct.

(A) and (B) are impossible. We always need two singles and two doubles, so it can't be true that no row is occupied by exactly one passenger, (A), or that no row is occupied by exactly two passengers, (B).

(D) and (E) are possible only.

Remember:

- When you see a non-"if . . . must be true" question, you may be able to answer it directly if the game contains a Big Deduction.

21 **(B)** If a tourist is alone in 4 and the businesspeople rows aren't adjacent, then the businesspeople must be in rows 1 and 3. So the other two tourists go in 2. That's (B).

(A) and (C) both could be true, but we could have two passengers in 1 and only one passenger in 3.

(D) is impossible. If one of the businesspeople in 1 were connecting, then they'd be next to two tourists in 2, at least one of whom would have to be arriving.

(E) is possible only.

Remember:

- Work with the question stem as far as possible before you hit the choices. With hypotheticals, it's usually easier to find the correct answer than it is to eliminate the wrong choices.

22 **(E)** The stem tells us that one businessperson is connecting and two businesspeople are arriving. That means that one tourist is connecting and two tourists are arriving. The arriving tourists can't be adjacent to the connecting businessperson in 3, so those two arriving tourists are in 1. The other tourist, the connecting one, will be alone in either row 2 or row 4. So (E) is correct.

(A) is impossible. The arriving tourists are together in row 1.

(B), (C), and (D): Careful! The stem says that a connecting businessperson occupies row 3, but it doesn't say that *only* a connecting businessperson occupies row 3. We don't know how the two arriving businesspeople are distributed. They could go together, or one of them could join the connecting businessperson in row 3. So these choices are possible only.

Remember:

- When you get a tough hypothetical, consider how the information given affects the other entities. Here, the key was understanding the implications for the tourists, even though the tourists aren't mentioned in the stem.

23 **(B)** From here, you could have tested each choice one by one, tried to apply your previous work, or skipped the question altogether. As it happens, (A), (D), and (E) could have been true in the previous question, and (C) is OK if we place an arriving businessperson in 1, a connecting tourist in 3, and two arriving tourists in 4. (B), however, is impossible. If we have two connecting businesspeople in 2, then all the tourists must be arriving, and no matter how we arrange them we'll always have at least one adjacent to row 2. So (B) is correct.

Remember:

• Take control of the test! You choose the order in which you handle the games as well as the order of the questions within those games. Get in the habit of postponing work on questions that just aren't worth it. Remember, every question is worth just one point.

24 **(A)** If all the businesspeople are arriving home, then we don't have to worry about connecting businesspeople sitting next to arriving tourists. So rule 2 is off the table for this one. Who's left? The three tourists, and we know which ones they are: two connecting, and one arriving. Of the three arriving businesspeople, two must be together in a row while the other sits alone. As for the tourists, there are two ways to break them up: Either the arriving tourist sits alone with the connecting tourists paired up, or the arriving tourist sits with one of the connecting tourists while the other connecting tourist sits alone. Notice that while we don't know what rows these pairs and solo folks occupy, it doesn't matter—the choices don't mention specific row numbers, so we needn't worry about that. On to the choices:

(A) We don't have to look far for our violator: As we saw, either the two connecting tourists sit together, or one sits alone while the other hangs with the arriving tourist. There's no way for both connecting passengers (tourists in this case) to fly solo. For the record:

(B) could be true: If we pair the arriving tourist with one of the connecting tourists, then the arriving businessperson sitting alone is the only arriving passenger sitting alone.

(C) However, (C) could be true also: If we place the arriving tourist in her own row, then exactly two arriving passengers (that one and the solo arriving businessperson) would be alone in a row. That, of course, would require the two connecting tourists to share a row, so this scenario also eliminates (D).

(E) must be true: Our arriving tourist is either by herself, or paired with a connecting tourist. Either way, we're still left with the pair of arriving businesspeople mentioned above who must share a row while the other arriving businessperson flies solo.

Remember:

• This wasn't easy, but rest assured: If you get a super-tough game on your LSAT, you'll still get the lion's share of the points if you follow the Kaplan strategies. Find the easy points, make educated guesses, use your previous work, and don't be afraid to move on.

Section IV: Logical Reasoning Explanations

1 **(B)** The author's conclusion pops up at the end, where she states that Ed is likely to have ADD because he watches television a lot and is seven. The key piece of evidence is a recent study that the author cites which states that 85 percent of seven-year-olds with ADD watch more than five hours of television per day. The study thus only discusses the television-watching habits of seven-year-olds *who have ADD*. The author's conclusion is flawed because it makes a conclusion about a seven-year-old television watcher based on a study about seven-year-old television watchers *with ADD*. In other words, there's a scope shift between the evidence and the conclusion. The author errs in accepting the survey as relevant to Ed. (B) expresses this flaw most clearly: In order to make conclusions about Ed and whether he might have ADD, the author must come up with evidence that pertains to Ed, since the original evidence does not. She needs a statistic that states the likelihood that a seven-year-old who watches more than five hours of TV a day would have ADD. The evidence provided sounds like that, but isn't, and (B) captures the gist of the author's mistake.

(A) is confusing, but the argument above isn't really about degrees of causation. The author doesn't suggest that age and television watching *cause* a child to contract ADD, but that those factors generally appear with the disorder. (A) distorts the author's conclusion by suggesting that it says that Ed's television watching has caused him to contract ADD, but the author never suggests this.

(C) Yes it does, but that's not a problem. Perhaps some doctors might disagree with the author's definition, but its validity is not the issue at the heart of this argument. Rather, the argument's concerned with Ed's chances of having ADD based on a particular study.

(D) is easiest to remove for the fact that it contradicts the stimulus, where we learn that Ed *does* actually watch more than five hours of television per day. (You may have also noticed that the 15 percent figure is bogus—it's derived from the 85 percent figure in the stimulus, but that figure refers to the percentage of children with ADD who watch more than five hours of TV a day. Inferably, we can therefore say that 15 percent of children with ADD do not watch more than five hours of TV a day, but we can't turn this into 15 percent of children *in general* who don't watch more than five hours, as (D) attempts to do.)

(E) again distorts the argument, which never suggests that television watching causes ADD. Since no causality is mentioned, we can only assume that the data represents a correlation.

Remember:

- Scope shifts are often hard to spot, but the rewards are great when you find them. They often involve subtle distinctions between the evidence and the conclusion, so look carefully at the terms of each, especially in Logical Flaw questions, to determine whether the author shifts gears en route.

2 **(D)** Even though the stem is skimpy, it does indicate that this is a Method of Argument question, so track the argument carefully. Basically, American and foreign Internet providers charge the same monthly fee, but foreign providers offer more services. Representatives for these foreign providers predict that their services will put the American providers out of business. The industry analyst clearly disagrees with this assertion in the sentence that begins with the contrast keyword "but." In that sentence, the analyst mentions two services offered by American providers that foreign providers may not be able to match. The analyst therefore disagrees with the representatives' conclusion, and does so by introducing new factors into the equation. (D) perfectly captures this: The analyst's additional consideration (quality and customer service) does weaken the initial contention (that foreign providers will drive American providers out of the Internet industry).

(A) Too extreme. The analyst does suggest that foreign takeover may not be imminent, but he never suggests that American companies needn't have any fear of foreign competition.

(B) The analyst does not dispute the representatives' evidence that foreign providers offer two perks which most American providers do not. The analyst offers additional elements to consider but does not disagree with those that have been mentioned previously.

(C) starts off badly with the verb "reconciles" and doesn't get any better. The analyst disagrees with the representatives' prediction, neither offering his own nor harmonizing his view with that of the representatives. Also, the analyst doesn't refer to a "previous situation," so this choice is zero for three.

(E) Again, the analyst doesn't really make any proposals so we can be suspicious right off the bat. The analyst doesn't offer a plan by which American companies might ward off foreign competitors; he merely mentions an additional

consideration that might make the representatives rethink their "bold" prediction.

Remember:

- Always be attuned to the presence of different views. This is more or less a dialogue stimulus without the dialogue formatting, since it begins with the explanation of one view and offers a second opinion in response to the first. Therefore, the analyst's method of argument is tied to the way in which he responds to the representatives' argument.

3 **(C)** The author states that Travonia's suicide rate has increased, citing an increase in the number of overdoses following the recent release of certain brands of sleeping pills. Getting to the heart of the argument, the author then asserts that certain types of suicides have not increased in number, conceding that the percentage of elderly suicides has increased but noting that the percentage of teen suicides has decreased. The flaw is the author's blurred distinction between numbers and percents. Just because the percentage represented by teen suicides has decreased, that doesn't mean that fewer teens are committing suicide. A decreased percentage needn't signify a decreased number of suicides, and the author's flaw comes in failing to recognize this, as (C) expresses.

(A) The argument doesn't explicitly discuss other groups (we don't really know where the sleeping pill poppers fall), but it certainly doesn't discount the possibility that other groups might exist.

(B) Not really, since the author doesn't link the sleeping pill takers to either demographic group, as mentioned in the explanation for (A).

(D) The total number of deaths in general is outside the scope of the argument, which deals exclusively with deaths from suicides and overdoses. The author need not consider the overall death figures in Travonia in order to make this argument.

(E) Too vague. The evidence about percentages doesn't contradict the author's conclusion, it just doesn't necessarily support it.

Remember:

- Whenever you see numbers and percentages discussed in a stimulus, look to see if the author is maintaining the distinction between them. You'll be rewarded for your effort in questions like this.

4 **(D)** Re-evaluating the argument, we can see that the author presents one piece of evidence to support this assertion: Deaths resulting from sleeping pill overdoses have almost doubled since new non-prescription sleeping pills have been released. In order to use these overdoses to support the assertion that suicides have increased dramatically, the author must assume that the overdoses were indeed deliberate and hence qualify as suicides.

(A) brings up the same problem that we saw in the previous question's answer choices: the author makes no links between the people overdosing on the sleeping pills and the teens and elderly folk discussed later in the stimulus. The author needn't assume such a connection in order to assert that suicides have increased dramatically.

(B) Knowing what was the most pervasive suicide method ten years ago doesn't have any real bearing on the claim in the first sentence of the passage.

(C) is far outside the scope. Deaths from natural causes have no necessary relation to this argument about suicide.

(E)'s relative comparison of Travonia's suicide rate to the world's is not relevant to the assertion in question. The author only asserts that suicides in Travonia have increased; there is no mention of their relative increase or of the suicide rate in other countries.

Remember:

- Assumptions play a key role not just in Assumption questions, but in many other question types as well. You may have picked up on the central assumption that's tested in this question as soon as the author cited the evidence about the doubling of overdose deaths. Thinking ahead, you may have asked yourself right then and there, "But are these overdoses necessarily suicides?" Such proactive thinking is what allows you to prephrase answers and select choices with greater confidence.

5 **(B)** Here's the paradox: Despite the fact that the rate of emphysema has declined 15 percent within the past 15 years in region A, the cost of caring for emphysema sufferers in the region is now roughly equal to what it was 15 years ago. In other words, the decline in the percentage of emphysema sufferers has not been accompanied by a corresponding decrease in the cost of treating such sufferers. Without trying to predict what might resolve this discrepancy, let's look to the answer choices for some sort of explanation:

(A) deals with the overall cost of health care in the region, which goes beyond our concern with one particular category of costs: the money spent on emphysema sufferers. Thus, knowing that the region's overall health care costs have increased doesn't help to explain what's going on with the cost of emphysema care in particular.

(B) addresses both parts of the paradox and does help to explain it. If improved technology has increased the cost of caring for emphysema sufferers, then a decline in sufferers wouldn't necessarily yield a decrease in costs, since the cost per patient would increase. Also, if the technology worked, then there would be fewer sufferers. This technology would thus decrease the overall incidence of emphysema without necessarily decreasing the costs attending such care. Perfect.

(C) tells us that the region's overall health care costs haven't really increased in the past seven years which, if anything, would only heighten the paradox. After all, the stimulus informs us that the costs of emphysema care *have* increased in the past eight years. After reading this choice, we still don't know what might account for that.

(D) doesn't connect the dots enough to really help. It only contributes to explaining the paradox if we assume that the research funds which have recently increased have actually been used, and then assume that the "modest increase" in such funds would counteract the savings offered by the decline in the rate of emphysema sufferers. (D) doesn't tell us this much.

(E), like (C), would if anything only deepen the mystery: If the most expensive cases are becoming more rare, why hasn't the cost of caring for emphysema sufferers declined?

Remember:

- There are so many different ways to resolve any paradox that prephrasing one possible explanation usually won't help— you'll usually end up evaluating all of the choices anyway. Therefore, be careful not to fall into the common test-taker trap of losing track of the question by the time you get to choices (D) and (E); stay focused on what you're looking for.

6 **(E)** The planner wants to broaden Maple Street, an action that he thinks will help the shops on that street. He supports this recommendation by noting that the shops on Maple Street aren't doing well, but the shops on two wider streets are doing quite well. This argument demonstrates a classic causal flaw. The author assumes that, since the shops on Walnut and Crescent Streets are doing well and since the streets are wide, the width of the streets in some way *causes* the success of the shops. We're looking to strengthen this argument, and a good candidate would be one that supported this assumption and showed how wide streets really do help the businesses that reside on them. (E) works because it shows how wide streets will make it easier for people to shop, strengthening the connection between the two key elements of the argument.

(A) weakens the argument by explaining how wider streets *deter* shoppers. Wrong way.

(B) also heads in the other direction, explaining that the planner's recommendation will not bring more shoppers to the stores, only more congestion from drivers looking to get somewhere else.

(C) The comparison between the locations of Maple and Walnut seems relevant; if Maple is in a less populated area, perhaps widening the street won't help to attract business. In that case, this info would seem, if anything, to weaken the argument. But then we learn that Maple is *closer* to the city center than is Crescent, yet Crescent is prospering recently just like Walnut. All we can conclude, then, is that these relative distances from the city center have no apparent effect on the argument regarding the proposal to widen Maple.

(D) Oh good, street history. If anything, (D) might suggest why Walnut does so well, but it doesn't suggest that Maple would achieve the same success. Indeed, it doesn't draw any connection between or even discuss wide streets and shopping.

Remember:

- If you notice a logical flaw in the argument, it's tempting to weaken the argument by noting that flaw, which perhaps explains why many of the wrong choices here would, if anything, weaken the argument. Even if an argument is deeply flawed, if your task is to strengthen it then you don't get to criticize it. Resist the temptation, and look instead for something that will bolster one of the argument's major assumptions.

7 **(D)** The author concludes (though not explicitly) that the democratic principle of respecting basic individual rights can be ambiguous. As evidence, he discusses country Q, where minorities' basic rights were protected through the laws enacted by a non-elected dictator. According to the author, the dictator was able to enact such laws only because he didn't have to fear being ousted from office and could thus act contrary to public will. If country Q really does provide an accurate example of a situation where the principle of respecting individual rights is ambiguous (which it must for the author's argument to hold), then there needs to be some sort of confusion around the issue of individual rights in that country. The author says that the dictator "may" act against the public will in order to actually protect certain individuals' rights. The situation in country Q is only ambiguous if the dictator actually does act against the public will in order to bring about this particular democratic principle—otherwise he wouldn't need to be a dictator in order to enact his reforms. (D) states this assumption: The author's conclusion is only valid if it is assumed that the public would not have supported such reforms. Try the Denial Test: If popular will did support the protection of minorities' rights, then this example would not serve as an illustration of how establishing democratic principles leads to some "interesting scenarios." Everything would be harmonious—there would be no ambiguity, and no argument, for that matter.

(A) is outside of the argument's scope since it focuses on situations in democracies. Since the author never discusses democracies, we have no way to accurately relate this information back to the stimulus. In any case, (A) certainly isn't necessary for the validity of the author's conclusion.

(B) If non-elected dictators can be ejected from office, then the dictator of country Q might have been taking a chance, if he was acting against the popular will. But even so, it's still possible that the dictator's immunity to being voted out was the key factor. So (B) fails the Denial Test.

(C) The author never discusses democratic government. He only discusses one democratic principle, and even in that case he doesn't suggest that it's incompatible with individual rights but that situations involving individual rights can sometimes become ambiguous.

(E) makes an irrelevant comparison regarding minority rights in dictator and non-dictator-led countries. (E) doesn't seem particularly consistent with the argument as regards country Q, and its comparison clearly does not link the author's evidence to his conclusion.

Remember:

- This stimulus offers a clear example of a quite common argument structure, where the author will make a claim in his conclusion and will support it with an example in his evidence. The validity of such arguments rests on whether the example illustrates the claim(s) made in the conclusion. When answering Assumption questions for such arguments, look to fill any gaps between the example and the conclusion. The right answer will be the one that allows the example to actually illustrate the author's primary point.

8 (B) The author's conclusion comes toward the end, when she says that the plant should be built inside the city limits. Despite her acknowledgment that a plant built inside the city limits will disrupt more lives, she advocates this option because it will create jobs for the city residents and therefore offer economic benefits to the city. She's therefore deciding between two options. She concludes that one option is better than the other because it promises a certain benefit to the inhabitants of the city. In order for that conclusion to be valid, she must assume that the other option does not promise such a benefit. Thus she must assume that only the inside city limits option would create jobs for the city's residents. (B) weakens the argument by denying this assumption, stating that either alternative will create jobs for the residents of the city.

(A) doesn't do a whole lot unless you assume more than the answer choice tells you (a sin for any LSAT test taker). Perhaps private-owned land is more expensive, in which case this choice would strengthen the argument, or perhaps it isn't. As it stands, there's no clear link between (A) and the central issues of the argument.

(C) shows how the location of the plant doesn't matter in terms of taxation. It's wrong because taxation isn't one of the criteria determining which option the author prefers. Choice (B) also notes a similarity between the options, but it's right because the similarity there pertains to job creation, which *is* central to the argument and which determines the option the author prefers.

(D) would, if anything, strengthen the argument by suggesting that the possible defect of the author's choice, disruption, isn't so bad.

(E) brings up taxes again, though this time the choice is about the workers' taxes and not the plant's. Still, the issue of taxation isn't even mentioned by the stimulus, and neither (C) nor (E) makes it relevant to the issues discussed in the argument.

Remember:

- When more than one choice addresses an issue that you don't remember encountering in the stimulus, it's tempting to reread the stimulus to see if you missed something. Resist that. If you've read carefully, you'll know what's important in the stimulus, and you can stay on track even when the answer choices might tempt you to question your understanding of the passage.

9 **(D)** Four choices are going to weaken the argument? The argument's probably going to be pretty bad. The chancellor concludes that the lackluster school should be closed and the students redistributed so as to improve the performance of the whole district. His evidence is that firing a few people at that school won't help, and that the school isn't meeting minimum achievement standards. There are lots of questionable assumptions tied into this argument, but it's not a good use of time to try to prephrase all four. Instead, evaluate the choices keeping the terms of the argument in mind, keeping in mind that the choice we seek will most likely be irrelevant to the argument.

(A) would indeed weaken the argument, since it suggests that redistributing the students will not strengthen the overall educational performance of the entire district.

(B) would also weaken the argument by suggesting that the school may not need to close since it's actually improving.

(C) weakens the author's evidence where he indicates that the school employees' poor work habits are untreatable. (C) suggests otherwise.

(D) is entirely irrelevant to the argument, since the school principal's previous successes don't have a clear relationship to the current problems at the school or the chancellor's "solution." Even if she's a "competent administrator" now (which we can't even be sure of), the fact remains that most of her teachers and administrators stink, so nothing's really changed. (D) is correct because it has no impact on the argument.

(E), like (A), weakens the argument by indicating that the students' redistribution won't improve the educational performance of the entire district. In fact, both choices strongly suggest that if the plan is carried out, the neighboring schools will suffer.

Remember:

- In these sorts of questions, don't expect to find a choice that would strengthen the argument. It's possible, sure, but usually the right answer to a "weaken EXCEPT" or "strengthen EXCEPT" question will be the choice that just has no impact on the argument one way or the other.

10 **(E)** That's a pretty user-friendly question stem, since it tells us which part of the argument the inference will address. And with so many formal logic statements to choose from, it's a good thing we know where to start. The question stem gives us the first half of an if-then statement; the correct answer will likely be the second half. So, if the editors don't receive year-end bonuses, then what do we know? Scoping out the part of the stimulus that deals with bonuses, we come to sentences 2 and 3. Let's see if sentence 2 helps: If circulation has increased, then editors get their bonuses. We form the contrapositive of an if–then statement by reversing and negating the terms, so the contrapositive of sentence 2 will read "if editors DO NOT get bonuses, then circulation has NOT increased." We're given the first part, the "if" clause in the stem; the second part, the "then" clause that must follow is found in correct choice (E).

(A) deals with ad rates, about which we can make no inferences based on what we're told about bonuses.

(B) and (C) offer the two options regarding ad pages, but neither is right because, according to what we know, ad pages might have increased or not. There's no accurate inference that we can draw on this subject based on the information we're given.

(D) *Au contraire.* As we saw above, forming the contrapositive allowed us to deduce that circulation has not increased. Be careful when constructing contrapositives to flip the statement and negate each part.

Remember:

- In detailed formal logic questions like this one, use the information in the question stem whenever possible to provide you with a starting point. Find the relevant statement in the stimulus and work backwards from there, employing the contrapositive whenever you can.

11 **(B)** The two historians here offer two different views on the *metis,* a Canadian group derived from Native American and European heritage. The first historian thinks that the rejection of the *metis'* request for some autonomy was tragic since it led to their loss of a distinct identity and weakened Canada's cultural diversity. The second historian clearly expresses where she disagrees: She doesn't think that the rejection of the *metis'* request was tragic basically because the *metis* never constituted a culturally distinct group. They therefore disagree about whether the rejection of the *metis'* request was tragic and about whether the *metis* comprised a culturally distinct group. (B) picks up on that second difference: The first historian clearly believes that the *metis* were a distinct cultural group while the second historian clearly believes they weren't.

(A) is off track because it focuses on the denial of a "people's" request and not on the *metis* in particular. Both historians only express views on that one particular group without making generalizations from it. The fact that historian #2 believes that the denial of the *metis'* requests was not tragic doesn't mean that she necessarily believes that such a denial can *never* be considered tragic.

(C) is stated by the first historian and uncontested by the second. In fact, the second historian's argument suggests that she also believes the *metis* were a mixture of both cultures.

(D) The first historian certainly believes that the denial of a people's request for identity can be detrimental to a country's cultural diversity—he says this is the case with the *metis* and Canada. The second historian, however, doesn't venture an opinion on this issue of the *effect* of denying identity; she merely argues that the denial in this specific case was the right thing to do.

(E) is again something suggested by the first historian, but that's not discussed, much less disputed, by the second historian.

Remember:

- The correct answer to a Point-at-Issue question must relate to an issue taken up by both participants of the dialogue. It's common for wrong choices to focus on an issue that's addressed by only one speaker, so make sure when you evaluate a choice to check to see that both care about the issue it contains.

12 **(C)** The author tells us that Betty's bad fortune was directly caused by Felix's salon, and then proceeds to hold forth on the subject of competition in a free-market economy. Taking all of this to be true (accepting, for example, that Felix's store really did drive Betty's out of business), let's proceed to the answer choices to find a logical inference based on this information:

(A) might seem consistent with the author's attitude, but even then it's a little too strong to be a view we can attribute to the author. Of course, that's not what we're looking for anyway—we simply want a statement that must be true based on the facts of the passage.

(B) might or might not be true. Since the author gives us no information about other salons, we can't make inferences on that topic.

(C) is valid. If Felix's store drove Betty's out of business, then he must have taken some customers from Betty. It's hard to imagine any other way that the appearance of Felix on the scene could "directly" cause Betty's store's demise.

(D) is too extreme. The author says that Felix's store caused the closure of Betty's store, but that's doesn't necessarily mean that Betty's store would still be open were it not for Felix's. Perhaps someone or something else would have had the same effect; the author identifies one cause but doesn't suggest that it's the only possible cause.

(E) makes a generalization that would be more appropriate to a principle question. We're given information only about two specific stores; we don't know if their freemarket experience is representative of all businesses everywhere.

Remember:

- One of the reasons why it's so important to start off with the question stem is that different question types have different sets of rules. If you were supposed to find a flaw in this question, you wouldn't want to assume that the conclusion were true, but since it's an Inference question, you do. The difference is entirely a result of the different question types, so it's a good idea to become very familiar with them and with what's expected of you in each.

13 **(E)** A stimulus where logical reasoning meets Top Gun. In this argument, the general determines which of two types of aircraft would better the needs of the Air Force for an upcoming mission. While the commander of the Air Force prefers the G28 because it could perform the necessary task more efficiently, the general orders that the D12 be used instead. He provides one piece of evidence to support this decision: Only the D12 can perform the task in time to meet the mission's deadline. We've seen this type of argument before. When an author argues for one option over another, the author must assume that the benefit provided by the preferred option can only be found in that option. In other words, the author must assume that the G28 would not fulfill the mission in the allotted period of time. The general says that it would take four days for the G28 to be ready for the mission, but he doesn't say that the G28 couldn't meet the deadline. Perhaps the plane's greater efficiency would enable it to still complete the mission in the allotted period of time. (E) expresses this assumption because, in order for the general's conclusion to be valid, he must assume that the G28 could not perform the mission by the immovable deadline. Thus he assumes that the G28's efficiency would not save the time that it would take for the G28 to begin the mission.

(A) is unnecessary to the argument. The stimulus doesn't state that one aircraft retrieves higher quality information than the other.

(B) goes too far. The author never states how long the mission would take, so there's no basis for stating that the D12 would be done before the G28 arrived. All the author needs to assume is that only the D12 could meet the mission's deadline, not that it would do so in the next four days.

(C) contradicts the stimulus, in which such an ability is a significant consideration to the commander. The general never contests the importance of the consideration; he just overrides it by making the deadline a *more* significant consideration.

(D) focuses on aircraft other than the G28. Aren't two enough to deal with? The author seems to think so, because he only discusses two types of aircraft between which he has to choose. Any others aren't relevant.

Remember:

• This assumption might be difficult to prephrase since the author comes quite close to saying that the G28 couldn't meet the mission's deadline. Don't worry if you can't prephrase; just stay focused on the author's evidence and conclusion and you'll find only one choice that links the two.

14 **(D)** This Inference question is an exercise in keeping track of the many little pieces of information given to us through the stimulus. Everyone in the Rubberband Club lives in state A. Everyone in the Rubberband Club has bungee-jumped at least once in the past two years. The club's still chugging along, despite the fact that it's been illegal to bungee-jump in state A for the past ten years. Even though it may seem like there's a possible contradiction in the stimulus, don't seek to resolve the seeming discrepancy; rather, remain faithful to the four primary pieces of information while searching for a proper inference.

(A) Too extreme. The stimulus doesn't tell us that they *can't* bungee-jump in state A, but that it's illegal to do so. While each current member must have jumped in the last two years, some of them may have broken the law and jumped away in state A anyway.

(B) and (E) take us too far also: It's quite possible that one or more of the current applicants or current members took the plunge legally in the state A ten or more years ago, before the ban was enacted.

(C) Too extreme. As mentioned above, while each must have jumped at least once in the last two years, they needn't have jumped in state A; perhaps they're getting all of their kicks in another state where jumping is legal.

(D) is perfect. If they didn't jump outside of state A, then they must have jumped within state A sometime in the last two years to fulfill the club's requirements. And if they did that, then they must have bungee-jumped illegally. There are no unsupported steps in this chain of reasoning, so it's a logical inference.

Remember:

- Sometimes Inference questions put you in the position of Goldilocks, looking for a choice that's not too narrow, not too broad, but just right. (D) is the best bowl of porridge here because, by explaining a possibility, it doesn't commit the flaw of the other four choices, i.e., making overly generalized claims.

15 **(A)** The author concludes that Waters was not influenced by McTell in his formulation of the key elements of his psychosocial theory (although McTell may have aided in the theories' subsequent development). As evidence she notes that Waters had already determined the basic components of his theory by 1947, years before Waters ever met McTell. The author gives you lots of other information about the two theorists and their relationship in the 1950s, but that's just extra information; the author's argument basically consists of the final two sentences. In order for the author's conclusion to be valid, she must assume that McTell could only influence Waters in person. Note that the author says that the two theorists had never "met" before the 1950s; she doesn't say that they had never communicated or that Waters knew nothing of McTell's ideas. Therefore, if she's correct in arguing that McTell didn't influence the formulation of Waters theory at all, she must assume that Waters was not influenced by McTell in any way before they met. (A) gives a more concrete expression of this assumption: The author assumes that Waters hadn't read anything by McTell prior to their meeting, and thus that Waters wasn't influenced by McTell in 1947. The Denial Test confirms this: What if Waters did know of and read McTell's work before he officially met him? Could the author then be so sure that the formulation in 1947 of Waters' theory was not influenced by the ideas of McTell? No, she couldn't, so (A) is necessary for this argument to work.

(B) Outside the scope. The author only discusses whether Waters got his ideas from one particular scholar, McTell. Waters could have completely plagiarized from someone else and the conclusion might still be valid.

(C) Outside the scope. The author's claim isn't that Waters' ideas were completely original, in which case (B) and (C) would be relevant, but that he didn't get them from McTell. Other scholars, confidantes, mentors, etcetera just aren't relevant.

(D) goes against the grain—the author strongly suggests that McTell did influence Waters' ideas in the 1950s, and helped him develop his theory. The only part the author feels McTell did not influence was the initial formulation.

(E) would be sad for McTell, but it's wrong because it deals with the 1950s. Technically, whether or not Waters benefited from his association with McTell in the 1950s has no impact on whether Waters' 1947 ideas were influenced by McTell. However, like (D), (E) seems to contradict the passage, which suggests that Waters *did* in fact benefit from his association with McTell in the 1950s.

Remember:

- Read proactively! Often, when we hear that something has "long been recognized . . . ," it will be followed up by opposition of some sort to the long-held theory. This is common in both Logical Reasoning and Reading Comp passages. Be on the lookout for this shift in sentiment. Here, the classic contrast keyword "however" in the second to last sentence signals the onset of the author's major point, which, not surprisingly is a reworking of the academic community's long-held belief.

16 **(A)** Too bad we don't get to weaken this one. The author states that there are fewer geniuses nowadays than there were, oddly, in the seventeenth century. The argument is pretty flimsy, based primarily on assumption that it's legitimate to compare the two periods. To strengthen this argument, we'll want a choice to demonstrate that this comparison is more likely to be valid. This is where (A) comes in, stating a more specific element of this assumption. If people are indeed able to recognize geniuses while they're alive or soon after they die, then it's more valid to compare modern genius production to seventeenth century genius production. After all, in order to make a valid comparison about the number of geniuses by period, the author must assume that we can count them accurately, and if it took, say, a hundred years or more to recognize genius stature, then the comparison wouldn't allow the author to form the categorical conclusion in the first sentence; we'd just have to wait and see. Maybe in the year A.D. 2100, notables such as James Joyce and Howard Stern will grace the genius list, too.

(B) doesn't help the argument since the author concerns himself only with the geniuses of one certain (though undefined) stature. If anything, (B) might weaken the argument by suggesting the author's comparison is not valid. Maybe there's only one twentieth century genius (Einstein) who's in the same category as the seventeenth century geniuses listed, but if there are other types of geniuses besides scientists and writers to consider, the author's conclusion may be a bit hasty.

(C) also does nothing to help the author's case, since the author relies on a stable definition of the term genius in his argument. Throwing that definition into question would only weaken his argument.

(D) would only be relevant if it could be shown that extremes in educational attainment were somehow related to the development of geniuses. We have no support to make such a leap, so (D) can't assist our author here.

(E) At first glance, (E) would seem inconsistent with the author's argument: If scientific knowledge is increasing at an ever-greater pace, then why do we have so few geniuses? Still, this is all too vague. We can't be sure of the relationship between the expansion of scientific knowledge in general and the production of geniuses; maybe geniuses create themselves through the process of being forced to discover stuff on their own without simply looking it up on the Internet, for example. Besides, (E) is also too specific, focusing as it does only on science; Shakespeare was no scientist. All in all, no help here.

Remember:

- Arguments that rely on a central comparison are so common that it's useful to recognize them as a type. When they show up for Weaken questions, you can usually weaken the argument by undermining the comparison, and for Strengthen questions you can look for a choice that somehow validates the comparison. Be on the lookout for specific information which could serve those purposes.

17 **(E)** According to Sylvia, the public's belief that Banner clothes dryers are particularly fire-prone is false, since the number of such dryers that actually erupt into flames is small. She also compares this number to that of major manufacturers' dryers that catch on fire, stating that the number of Banner dryers fires (a rhyme which must plague their marketing department) is smaller. Alice does not offer an alternative argument but merely notes a flaw in Sylvia's evidence. Like a good LSAT student, Alice recognizes that Sylvia compares the number of Banner dryers and the number of major manufacturers' dryers that catch on fire rather than their rates of occurrence. Looking through the answer choices, we find (E): Alice does indeed note a flaw in Sylvia's argument and that flaw does involve a distorted use of numbers where percents would be more appropriate.

(A) Alice neither accepts nor rejects Sylvia's conclusion; rather, she identifies a problem in Sylvia's evidence. She certainly doesn't offer another path toward proving that the public is wrong to distrust Banner clothes dryers.

(B) is partially right, since Alice does present new evidence, but that evidence doesn't contradict Sylvia's nor does it show how Sylvia's conclusion is wrong. Alice only criticizes the appropriateness of Sylvia's evidence in getting to where she's trying to go. She suggests that Sylvia's conclusion may be hasty, but she certainly doesn't "disprove" it.

(C) can be axed because Alice herself compares the same two groups of items (she simply compares them in a different and what she believes to be a more appropriate way).

(D) Too extreme, since Alice doesn't refute Sylvia's evidence but merely demonstrates a flaw in using it to get to her conclusion. She never says or suggests that Sylvia's evidence (that Banner has fewer dryer fires than the major manufacturers) is incorrect.

Remember:

- Notice how frequently Method of Argument answer choices mention the conclusion and evidence of the initial argument. The prominence of those terms just underscores how important it is to identify the conclusion and evidence in the initial argument and to determine what precisely the respondent says in terms of them.

18 **(C)** The first step in this stimulus is to recognize these assertions as formal logic statements, and to translate them into if–then statements. The author first states that IF a building lacks sufficient ventilation and natural light, THEN it is not well designed (if A and B then C). You can also form that statement's contrapositive: IF a building is well designed, THEN it has sufficient ventilation and natural light. Next: IF a building has many windows, THEN it has natural light (if D then B). Finally, the author's conclusion is: IF a building has many windows, THEN it is well designed (if D then C). Do you see the problem? The author first identifies two qualities necessary for a building to be considered well designed. The author then proceeds to discuss only one of those elements, completely neglecting to mention whether the building has sufficient ventilation. Instead of maintaining that a well designed building needs good ventilation and natural light, the author concludes that natural light itself (coming from many windows) can determine whether a building is well designed. The author fails to consider whether the building is also well ventilated, which is what (C) states. (You may have noticed that there's another major flaw here: Even if it were ascertained that a building had good ventilation and natural light, that would still not "ensure" that it is well designed; those factors are necessary, but not necessarily sufficient for well designed build-

ings. The stem asks for "a" flaw in the argument, most likely because here, there are two big ones.)

(A) is too extreme. The author needn't show that ventilation is *only* possible through windows, but that windows provide adequate ventilation.

(B) is not established by the argument, but that's not a flaw. The author shows that windows provide natural light, which is sufficient for the author's conclusion in terms of the natural light issue. The author has no obligation here to switch the first clause of sentence 2 around.

(D) could be true, but it isn't really relevant to this argument which concerns a building which does have many windows. Remember, windows are not part of the original rule, but come in later as one possible factor that ensures the presence of one of the elements (natural light) of the main rule. That's why the author need establish nothing about buildings *without* windows.

(E) points out a possibility that conflicts with the stimulus; failing to consider the impossible isn't a logical problem.

Remember:

- Since you will definitely see some Logical Reasoning questions involving formal logic on your exam, try to get comfortable with spotting formal logic statements, translating them, finding their contrapositives, and differentiating between necessity and sufficiency.

19 **(D)** The author concludes that we should stop using certain products which harm the ozone layer despite the fact that their use is both legal and enjoyable. Rather, we should focus on our obligation to act in the best interests of future gen-

erations. Let's rephrase to make this sound more like a principle. The author argues against a course of action by stressing our obligation to consider the consequences of those actions on future generations. Thus we shouldn't do something now because it'll hurt people later on. According to (D), the morality, or rightness, of an action depends on its future consequences, which is entirely in line with the logic underlying the author's argument.

(A), (C) The author doesn't suggest what should determine the legality of one's actions. According to the stimulus, it's legal to use the mentioned products, so what determines legality isn't the issue.

(B) goes against the grain of the argument. It's legal to use the products but the author argues that they still shouldn't be used, therefore arguing that the legality of an action does *not* necessarily determine its morality.

(E) discusses appropriate punishment, which the author never addresses. Also, the author never discusses any "illegal action." Out on two counts.

Remember:

- Try to generalize the stimulus before you get to the answer choice when dealing with Principle questions. The answer choices often sound so abstract, and sometimes even so similar to each other, that you can get lost in them without some sort of guide. Prephrase an answer by abstracting from the stimulus and putting the specifics of the situation into more general terms.

20 **(E)** A Parallel Reasoning question with some formal logic thrown in—proceed carefully. The stimulus starts off by telling us that public service announcements try to advise teens but really just annoy them. Then comes the formal logic "only if" statement, which, when properly translated, means that IF teenagers follow advice, THEN they do not resent the delivery of that advice. (If you have any trouble translating "only if" statements into standard "if–then" statements, stop and work through this translation again until you see it.) The author then concludes that the announcements should be discontinued. Since this is a Parallel Reasoning question, we should get a better sense of the general structure of the passage. The author shows that a certain program has a goal and an unintended negative side effect. The author then explains that the goal can't be met if the side effect exists (which we know it does), and concludes therefore that the program doesn't work and should be scrapped. It's a pretty solid argument, and we can proceed to look for the same elements in the answer choices.

(A) identifies the goal of a certain program but never identifies an unintended negative side effect. You can stop there, without having to delve too deeply into the touching patriotism in the remainder of the choice.

(B) never discusses the goal of zoning restrictions, and so never survives past consideration of the very first element of the stimulus.

(C) again never explains the goal of the estate tax. Don't be fooled by the fact that it does include what could be called a side effect and a negative consequence of it—if every element is not present, then you have to move on.

(D) identifies the goal of a certain program and explains a negative side effect. But the second sentence the issue shifts away from the success

of the conservation laws to their ability to get support. The original argument stays focused only on the program's potential for success.

(E) is correct because it outlines the goal of a program, discusses an unintended negative side effect, shows that the program can't succeed in the presence of that side effect, and concludes that the program should be eliminated. All the necessary elements are present.

Remember:

- Make a mental (or written) checklist for yourself when dealing with Parallel Reasoning. The absence of one key element invalidates any choice.

21 **(C)** This argument discusses the effects of a region-wide recession on two counties (X and Y). The comptroller of County X has stated that County X's depressed economy represents what will happen to all counties in the financially struggling region (the "inevitable" consequences). However, County Y is not currently suffering any financial difficulties, so the author concludes that County X's comptroller must be wrong. Our task is not to determine whether or not this conclusion is correct, but to explain the apparent contradiction presented in the stimulus. More specifically, we want an answer choice that will show how County X could be adversely affected by the recession while County Y is not. Keeping that in mind, let's look through the choices.

(A) doesn't explain the situation within the region, which is all the stimulus addresses. Comparing this region to any other doesn't shed light on the different situations occurring in Counties X and Y.

(B) compares the overall revenue generated by the two counties, which has no relationship to the issue at hand. Maybe X is ten times bigger than Y, accounting for the greater revenue. That wouldn't alter the fact that X is suffering compared to its usual economic state, and that Y is robust.

(C) explains one important way in which County X is different than County Y, which certainly does help to explain the counties' different financial situations. If the region's recession decreased tourism, and County X depends on tourism for revenue more than County Y, then it makes sense for County X to be more affected by the recession than County Y.

(D) doesn't make this information relevant to the recession and its different impact on the two counties. Both (C) and (D) discuss one factor contributing to one county's revenue, but (D) is wrong because, unlike (C), it doesn't show how the issue relates to the recession's impact.

(E) doesn't do quite enough to explain the initial situation. Would the relocation of "a few retail businesses" hurt County X and stabilize County Y? We don't know; we can't even be sure that the businesses that relocated were successful. In (C), we were told that County X relied "almost entirely" on tourism which was "crippled" by the recession; the terms in that choice are far stronger. In contrast, (E)'s discussion of the relocation of a few businesses doesn't help to explain the larger differences in the financial situations of the two counties.

Remember:

• It's pretty common to see an argument in which an author discusses a difference existing between two apparently similar people or groups. The trap is to assume that, since two groups are similar in one way, they're similar in all ways. That's seldom the case and, as we see in this question, it's often important that you allow that dissimilarities might account for the differences between the groups.

22 **(A)** For our second question relating to this stimulus, we're asked about the author's method of argument. Looking at the structure of the stimulus, we can see that the author begins by expressing the views of County X's comptroller, who makes a generalization about all of the counties in the state. The author then notes an exception to the comptroller's generalization, and uses it to show that the comptroller must be wrong. Therefore, to make his argument, the author provides evidence that disproves a generalization. (A) best expresses this: The author counters the comptroller's claim with evidence about County Y that directly contradicts the comptroller's assertion that a depressed economy is the inevitable consequence for all counties in the region.

(B) The author doesn't dismiss any part of the comptroller's statement as irrelevant; he just says that the statement is wrong. Further, the comptroller doesn't provide any real evidence for his claim, so there's no evidence for the author to contest.

(C) starts off well, but goes awry in the second half. The author clearly believes that the comptroller is wrong, but (C) misrepresents the way in which the author expresses his opinion. The author doesn't dispute the comptroller's statement by saying that it's *impossible* in this situation for all of the region's counties to be economically depressed. Rather, he provides opposing evidence (the booming economy of County Y) that proves that this is simply not the case.

(D) Who would be the authority appealed to in this scenario? There is no one in the stimulus who would fit this description, so (D)'s out.

(E) gets the argument all muddled up. The author doesn't make the generalization, the comptroller does. The author gives a specific example, and while it does counter the claim he opposes, a specific example is not a generalization.

Remember:

• In Method of Argument questions, test the general terms of the choices against the specifics of the stimulus. Here, ask yourself: "Is there an impossibility asserted? Is there an authority here?" Every aspect of the right choice must pan out.

23 **(A)** Were you feeling unchallenged? Actually, this question type is one that you've seen many times before, but it has a little twist since you're directed not to determine the role played by just any piece of information, but by a certain assumption. The first task is therefore to see where the given assumption exists in the argument. The author begins by explaining a paradox: Kids who weren't vaccinated seemed to be immune to measles. This is the only place in the stimulus where the author discusses vaccination, so it must be where the stem's assumption comes in. Indeed, in this first sentence the author does assume that vaccinations give kids immunity, or else the researchers wouldn't have been so surprised by this non-vaccination based immunity. How does this function in the argument? Well, it helps to set up the strange situation which the rest of the stimulus will strive to explain or, in

other words, the problem which requires a solution provided in the argument. (A) captures this by noting that the first sentence (statement plus assumption) creates the confusion which the researchers then worked to explain.

(B) would tie the assumption into the evidence regarding dihydron-X, but this assumption doesn't come from that part of the passage.

(C) contradicts the passage, which explains how the kids were able to achieve such an immunity. Therefore, such immunity is not impossible.

(D) This assumption is not what the researchers seek to prove; they seek to prove how the kids who *don't* receive the vaccination could get such immunity.

(E) Just because the kids became immune through their formulas, that doesn't overturn the assumption that vaccinations also create immunity. The researchers' conclusion does not contradict or undermine this particular assumption.

Remember:

• This isn't the way in which assumptions are normally tested on the LSAT, but that's foreseeable since, if this were a regular assumption, you would already know what role it played in the argument without reading it. If you see something a little different on test day, just do what you would normally do with that question type. The first step on these "role in the passage" questions is to locate the information, and then to identify its function.

24 **(B)** Next up is a "parallel the flaw" type of Parallel Reasoning question, so let's first find the flaw. This one is particularly amenable to an algebraic treatment. The author tells us that the Chief of Personnel claimed that no human resource employee was fired in the embezzlement scandal, but ends up asserting that this claim must be false. So the author actually concludes that some human resource employees were fired in the embezzlement scandal. Let's find the evidence for this, and begin our algebraic representation there (it's easier in a case like this to build the argument in order from evidence to conclusion). "Some human resource employees were fired in March" can be represented as "some X are Y." And "Some employees fired in March were fired in the embezzlement scandal" breaks down to "some Y are Z." The conclusion mentioned above would then be "some X are Z"—which we know is not necessarily true, because the group of human resource folks canned in March and the group of embezzlers who were tossed can be totally distinct groups. Searching the choices, we find that (B)'s logic is botched in the same way as the original: Some stars of *Icarus* starred in *Mrs. Jones* (some X are Y). Some *Mrs. Jones* folks went to Zeller (some Y are Z). Therefore, some *Icarus* actors went to Zeller (some X are Z). Same structure, and the same flaw: The stars of *Icarus* who were also in *Mrs. Jones* may not have been the same *Mrs. Jones* folks who attended Zeller.

(A) is out immediately because it doesn't commit any flaw. All members have good manners and Candy is a member so she must have good manners. That's fine, at least in terms of logic. No flaw, no good.

(C), like (A), commits no logical error. If the neighbors have young kids, and many people with kids stay home on weekend nights, then it's certainly reasonable to conclude that some of the neighbors *probably* stay home on weekend nights. The qualified nature of this argument—

that is, the use of the word "probably"—makes this a very reasonable conclusion, and differentiates it from the original argument in which the author claims that the Chief was wrong and that some human resource employee definitively *was* fired.

(D) Some X are Y. Some X are Z. Therefore, some X are both Y and Z. Flawed, but not parallel.

(E) contains no "some" terms to play with, so it's impossible for this choice to mimic the original. Kill it for that reason alone.

Remember:

• Algebraic representation is valuable in Parallel Reasoning questions made up of (or that can be translated into) formal logic terms. When you see words like *some*, *all*, *no*, *none*, *if*, and *then*, think of breaking down the terms in the original and in the choices into letters in order to find the one that matches.

25 **(E)** The principal concludes that the Excellence Learning Services' promotional materials were "misleading" and supports this conclusion by discussing his own school's experience with the Service. Even though the school used the Excellence program to improve its students' reading and math scores, the students' performance on the tests was the same as it was twenty years ago. The principal uses this information to demonstrate that the Excellence program does not improve test scores, but there's an unwarranted assumption involved in his argument—did you spot it? Just because the students' scores equal those of the students twenty years ago, that doesn't necessarily mean that the Excellence program was wholly ineffective. Perhaps the students' scores would have been lower than those of the students twenty years earlier without the program. Perhaps equaling the scores of twenty years ago is a marked improvement over the score levels of recent years. The principal assumes that the Excellence program did not improve the students' scores, but that assumption is unwarranted because it's unsupported by the argument's evidence. (E) picks up on this flaw, noting that the principal does not demonstrate that the Excellence program did not improve student test scores.

(A) Since the author's conclusion solely concerns the accuracy of the Excellence program's advertisements, and thus solely intends to criticize the program, it needn't offer alternative solutions for support.

(B) is wholly irrelevant, since the author never directly or indirectly discusses parents and their capacities. Parents are outside the scope here.

(C) criticizes the author's language, but it's hard to identify any language that might be called "emotionally charged" in the argument. "Misleading" certainly doesn't qualify and that's the author's strongest term, so (C) identifies a flaw that the argument doesn't commit.

(D) is not directly relevant, since the author's argument only concerns the program's claims to help students improve their math and reading scores. Other possible benefits aren't discussed or pertinent to the program's ability to specifically raise these test scores.

Remember:

- Many answer choices for Logical Flaw questions discuss issues that the author never addresses. Those choices only constitute correct flaws if the issues they introduce are directly relevant to the argument. Alternative solutions in choice (A), parents' capabilities in (B), and benefits in other areas in (D) do not fit this requirement.

GETTING INTO LAW SCHOOL

BY PAT HARRIS

CHAPTER 8

INTRODUCTION TO LAW SCHOOL ADMISSIONS

I can still remember the day I received my LSAT score report in the mail. I was jubilant about my score, which put me in the top two percent of all test takers. This kind of LSAT performance, I thought—combined with my high college GPA—would surely get me into any law school I desired; all I had to do was decide which one I would deign to attend. I proceeded to apply to ten top law schools, fully confident that I would be accepted by all ten.

Well, it didn't turn out quite that way. By the following April, I had received a meager two acceptance letters, one wait-list letter, and an appalling seven rejection letters, including ones from Harvard and Stanford. As the rejection letters rolled in, one after the other, my original hubris slowly and painfully gave way to humility.

Two weeks after the last rejection, still reeling from the shock, I had the good fortune to bump into an admissions officer from a local law school at a party. I cornered her and began peppering her with questions about what could possibly have gone wrong. She mentioned several potential problems and suggested that I call a friend of hers at one of the law schools I had applied to and ask her to critique my application. What I found out was eye-opening: my application could not have been more inept. In fact, just about everything I'd done had contributed to preventing my admission to law school, including carelessly misspelling my name on the application (fortunately, the University of Michigan Law School saw fit to let me attend despite these blunders).

Today, after years of conversations with other lawyers, law students, and members of my Kaplan LSAT classes, I realize that my experience was hardly unique. An astonishing number of people apply to law school without a clue about the admissions process. That's why I've made something of a career out of ensuring that others don't make the same mistakes I did. In the last several years, I've spoken to admissions officers at more than sixty-five schools in all regions of the country, gleaning as much information from them as I could. And I've gathered together their combined wisdom in this book.

One cautionary note—admission officers are human beings; they don't all think alike. Attitudes and priorities vary from law school to law school. However, the suggestions that follow are the ones I've heard over and over again, straight from the most important source—the admissions officers themselves. Stick closely to these suggestions and you'll increase your chances of getting in the law school you want to attend.

CHAPTER 9

WHERE TO APPLY

The question of where you should apply is usually a two-part question. What schools should you consider, regardless of your chances, and which of these schools can you actually get into? Let's begin with the first question.

What Schools Should You Consider?

In a recent article about law school education, I came across a remarkable statistic. Upon graduation, according to one study, 58 percent of all law students end up living and working within a one-hour drive of where they went to law school. That's nearly six out of every ten students!

There are many reasons for this surprising statistic. Obviously, a lot of people attend the local law school in the town where they have always lived and want to continue living. Also, since employers tend to interview and hire from nearby law schools, many recent grads stay put. Some students find that they just like the area and don't want to leave. Still others meet and marry a local person during their three years. Whatever the explanation, a majority of all law students end up spending more than just the required three years in the city or region where they attend law school.

Despite the importance of law school selection, however, it's frightening how lightly many applicants treat the whole process, even students who spend a great deal of time studying for the LSAT or working on their applications. Horror stories abound—of distant relatives convincing a cousin to attend State University Law School just because they themselves did forty years ago, or of a student who decides not to apply to a school because his girlfriend's cousin heard that the social life was not so hot.

I cannot emphasize this point enough. *Choosing a law school is a major decision in your life and should be treated as such.* There are several factors to consider when choosing where to apply, including reputation, location, and cost.

DON'T TAKE IT LIGHTLY

Deciding which law schools to apply to is an important decision. Treat it with the appropriate seriousness, which doesn't mean that you can't have a fun time researching schools.

Reputation

How much does a law school's reputation matter? The short answer is that it matters very much in your first few years out of law school, when you're looking for your first job or two. Most employers evaluating you at this time will have little else to go on, and so will tend to place a lot of weight on school reputation. After a few years, when you've established a reputation and a record of your own, the importance of your alma mater's rep will diminish.

The long answer to the question of academic reputation, however, is a little more complex. Each applicant must look at his or her situation and ask several questions:

- **Am I looking to work for a law firm or to do public-service work?** Law firms tend to put more emphasis on the reputation of the school.
- **Do I want to stay in the area or have more mobility nationwide?** Some schools enjoy strong local reputations as well as strong alumni bases, whereas other schools have a nationwide appeal.
- **How competitive do I want my law school experience to be?** Although there are exceptions, as a general rule the schools with better reputations tend to be very competitive.
- **Do I want to consider teaching as an option?** Virtually all law school professors come from a handful of top-notch law schools. The same also applies for the most prestigious judicial clerkships.
- **To what extent am I willing to go into debt?** The schools with the big reputations also tend to have the biggest price tags.

How to Research Reputation

What's the best way to research reputation? Many publications rank law schools. How accurate these rankings are is anybody's guess, but they tend to become self-fulfilling. Once published, they're discussed over and over by students, lawyers, and faculty until they become fact. Although the methodology behind these rankings is often suspect, the results are frequently heeded by employers. Studies rank the top fifty schools, the top fifteen schools, or categorize all schools into four or five levels. (Most of these books can be found in the reference section of your local bookstore.) Many law firms rely heavily on such rankings in making their hiring decisions.

SO YOU WANT A BIG-NAME SCHOOL?

It's worth thinking about now: how important is it to you to get into a high-prestige school? Will you need the fancy credential for the kind of law you want to pursue?

But there are other methods to determine a school's reputation. Speak to friends who are lawyers or law students. Lawyers have a habit of noting who their most formidable opponents are and where they went to law school. Look through law school catalogs and see what schools the professors attended. Finally, ask the placement offices how many firms interview on campus each year, and compare the numbers. Their answers can give you a strong indication of what the law-firm community thinks of a school.

Location

Location is of prime importance because of the distinct possibility that you'll end up spending a significant part of your life near your law school—three years at the very least. Even under the best of conditions, law school will be a difficult period in your life. You owe it to yourself to find a place where you'll be comfortable. Pick cities or areas you already know you like or would like to live. Pay particular attention to climate problems. Think about rural areas as opposed to urban centers.

How to Research Location

Visit as many law schools as possible, your top two or three choices at the very least. You may be surprised at what you find. For example, a recent student was telling me that his dream was to get into the law school of one particular university because he'd visited its campus several years ago and loved it. I quickly had to crush his dream by explaining that the university's law school is not on the campus, but rather thirty minutes away in an area closer to downtown. Spend some time researching location by visiting *when school is in session*, which is when you'll get the most accurate picture. You should also:

- Buy a local newspaper and scan the real estate ads for prices near campus; check out campus housing to determine whether it's livable.
- Check out transportation options at the law school.
- Take the school's tour so you can hear about the area's good points.
- Look at bulletin boards for evidence of activities.

Finally, don't be afraid to wander into the student lounge and just ask several law students what they think. Most are more than willing to provide an honest appraisal, but be sure to get more than one opinion.

LOCATION, LOCATION, LOCATION

Statistics show that you'll probably end up spending at least part of your working life in the area where you went to law school. So be sure to pick one in a location you can live with (and in).

Costs

Cost ranks at the bottom of many law students' list of criteria to consider, because law school financial aid works in much the same manner as a credit card—you get it now and pay for it later. Each year a number of students enter law school with the goal of doing some type of public-service work, but then are forced to take higher-paying firm jobs in order to meet their loan payments. This is certainly understandable when you realize that many law students rack up debts of $50,000 to $100,000 over the course of three years.

Among the cost issues to consider are:

- **Low-Cost State Schools**
  State schools tend to have lower tuition, particularly for in-state residents.
- **Urban versus Rural Living Costs**
  Schools in large urban areas will almost invariably have higher living costs than those in rural areas (although the larger cities also tend to have more part-time jobs for second- and third-year students, which can offset the extra cost).
- **Special Loan Programs**
  Many schools now offer special loan repayment or loan forgiveness programs for students who take low-paying public service jobs.
- **Special Scholarship Programs**
  Many law schools offer special scholarship programs that range from small grants to full three-year rides.

THE COSTS OF EXPENSIVE SCHOOLS AREN'T ALWAYS FINANCIAL

Cost should be a factor in your choice of law school, even if you're convinced that you can get enough loans to cover tuition. Loans have to be paid back, after all, and a high burden of debt might ultimately force you to make a less-than-desirable career choice.

How to Research Cost

The law school application will tell you what the annual tuition was for the previous year. Many applications will even give you an estimate of living expenses. If you want to dig deeper, call the financial aid office and ask them to send you the breakdown of living expenses of the average law student. Also ask them to send information about any loan forgiveness programs and about scholarships offered by the law school.

Job Placement

With the legal job market shrinking, the proficiency of a law school's placement office is now a major factor to be considered. If my interviews with law students can be believed, the competency of placement officers varies widely. Some see their job as simply setting up on-campus interviews and making sure they run smoothly. Others call and write letters on behalf of students and are constantly selling the school to employers. Some schools direct almost all of their efforts into placing students into private law firms. Other schools provide information on an entire range of opportunities. At some schools students are lucky if the placement office even provides them with a list of alumni in cities in which they'd like to live. At other schools the office calls alumni to hunt for leads.

How to Research the Job Placement Office

Ask the placement office for the percentage of graduates in the most recent class who had jobs upon graduation. Don't be fooled by statistics that show 98 percent of all graduates employed. Almost all law students are eventually employed, even if they drive taxis. The key is to determine how many are placed in law jobs *before* they leave law school.

Second, stop by the placement office on your visit and look around. Ask to see the placement library and check whether it's well organized and up-to-date. Note whether it carries materials on public-interest or teaching jobs and how large this section is. Also ask whether a newsletter is published to keep alumni informed of any recent job openings.

Again, talk with law students. Most have very strong opinions about the performance of their placement office. Most students recognize and appreciate when the placement office is making an extra effort.

Course Selection

One of the nicest things about law schools in the 1990s is their growing number of course selections and the new areas of law that are opening up. International trade, employment discrimination, sports and entertainment, and environmental law are all areas in which schools are providing more offerings. Many law students nowadays are becoming specialists, because of both personal preference and better marketability. If you're one of the many students who enter law school without a clue about what kind of law they want to practice, look for schools that offer a lot of different areas of study.

How to Research Course Selection

As a rule, schools with larger student populations offer not only more classes but also a greater variety. They need more professors to handle the standard course load, and most professors also like to teach and explore new areas of law as well.

Schools list the courses most recently taught in their recruiting brochure, which they will gladly send you. One note of caution: just because a class has been taught in the past and is listed in the brochure doesn't mean that it's taught every year or will be taught in the future. If

DON'T PUT YOUR CAREER IN THE HANDS OF SLACKERS

Some placement offices are far better than others. It's a good idea to find out how effective the offices are at the schools you're considering.

CAN'T LIVE WITHOUT THAT COURSE ON MEDIEVAL TORTS?

Some courses, particularly unusual ones, may not be taught regularly. If a particular course offering is important enough to you to affect your school selection, just make sure that the course will indeed be available should you go to that school.

you're interested in a particular class, call the registrar's department and find out how often the class has been taught in the past and whether it will be offered again in the future. Ask to speak with the professor who has taught the course in the past.

Social Life

Although it's an important part of the law school experience, social life should rank near the bottom of the list of factors to consider when choosing a law school. Why? Because your social life at any law school is what you make of it. Almost all law schools have monthly parties or weekly Thursday night get-togethers at local bars. And if you choose to expand that schedule, you can always find a willing accomplice. Furthermore, most schools now have a comparably full range of social organizations that cover race, religion, political affiliation, and gender.

How to Research Social Life

Examine the area surrounding the law school. During your first year, locale probably won't matter much. But as you get into your second and third years, you'll likely find that you do have some free time, particularly on weekends. Think about whether you want a quiet rural area where canoeing or skiing are readily available, or whether you'd prefer a larger city with a vibrant restaurant and nightlife scene.

Additional Considerations

There are a few other factors that you may want to toss into the equation when deciding which law school is right for you.

Class Size

This factor is not as important as it is when choosing a college because, despite what you may read in a catalogue, virtually all first-year classes will be large. Nevertheless, there are some differences between a school such as Georgetown, with more than 2,000 students, and a school such as Stanford, with fewer than 800. In the second and third years, the larger schools tend to have more course offerings, whereas the smaller schools focus on smaller class size and more contact between professors and students. Smaller schools also tend to encourage a greater sense of camaraderie and less competition. Larger schools, on the other hand, produce more alumni and thus more contacts when it comes time for your job search.

Attrition Rates

Law schools generally try to keep their attrition rate below 10 percent. There are exceptions, however, and if the school you're interested in has an attrition rate above 10 percent, you should ask an admissions officer why. There may be a reasonable explanation, but you should probably approach the school with some caution.

Joint-Degree Programs

Joint-degree programs are designed to help students pursue two degrees jointly in less time than it would take to earn them separately. The most common examples are the Master of Public Policy (MPP) or the Master of Business Administration (MBA) combined with the law degree. These programs generally take four to five years to complete. Most schools are becoming more daring in this field—indeed, some are now encouraging students to create their own joint-degree program in any area that they choose, as long as it meets both departments' approval. It's not uncommon now to see joint degrees in law and foreign languages, music, or sociology. Check with the schools to see what joint-degree programs are routinely offered, but don't be limited by them. If you have a specialized program in mind, call the registrar's office and see how flexible they are.

Clinical Programs

Every law school in the country now offers one or more clinical programs. A clinic is a unique, hands-on opportunity that allows law students to see how the legal system works by handling actual civil cases for people who can't afford an attorney (and getting credit for it at the same time). Not only are these clinics a tremendous learning tool, but they are also the highlight of many law students' three years of study.

Usually the workload is heavy on landlord/tenant disputes or other debt-collection cases. However, many schools are branching out and offering specialized clinics in such areas as child abuse, domestic violence, and immigration. One word of caution: Clinics tend to be popular with students. In many cases, it's very difficult to get a spot in the class, and admission usually depends on the luck of the draw. As a general rule, the schools in large cities have bigger and more clinics because they tend to have more clients.

Internships

Like clinical programs, internships are becoming more popular and varied. Internship programs vary widely from school to school, and may include

---

WHAT COLOR IS YOUR PARACHUTE?

At many colleges, you can create your own joint-degree program, combining a law degree with just about anything imaginable. If that kind of flexibility is important to you, make sure you choose schools that are willing to accommodate you.

CLINIC AVAILABILITY

If clinical work is important to you, find out now how many clinics are offered by the schools you're considering—and how hard it is to get into these clinics.

anything from working for an international trade organization in Europe for an entire year to getting three hours credit for part-time work at the local prosecutor's office. Internships are often overlooked by students who are afraid to veer from the traditional path. Yet they can be a welcome break from regular law studies and may also help in the later job search.

Computer Facilities and Law Library

Legal research is a big part of your three years in law school. Nothing will frustrate you more than to have a brief due the next day only to find that your library lacks essential volumes on the subject, or that the few computers they have are either occupied or not working. If you make a visit to the law schools, check out their facilities. Again, don't be afraid to ask students for their opinions.

Where Can You Get In?

Let's turn to the second major question in the selection process: "Where do you have a chance of being accepted?"

Anyone who tells you that he can predict where you'll be accepted is fooling himself and, worse, fooling you. Stories of students accepted by a Harvard, Stanford, or Michigan only to be turned down by schools with far less glamorous reputations are common. Yet what is often overlooked is how well the process does work, considering the volume of applications and the amount of discretion exercised by admissions officers.

One reason the admissions process runs smoothly is that all law schools use the combined LSAT score and GPA as the most important determinant in making the decision. This provides a degree of consistency to the admissions process and gives the applicants some direction in deciding where to apply.

Those Legendary Law School Grids

Each year, Law Services publishes the *Official Guide to U.S. Law Schools* (the LSAT application booklet tells you how to order it). This guide includes a wealth of information on all the accredited law schools in the United States. The schools themselves provide most of the information for the book, including the LSAT scores and GPAs of the most recently admitted class. These are generally presented in grid form and are the single most valuable tool in determining your chances of being accepted at any particular law school. The grid shown here is a hypothetical grid, similar to the ones found in the *Guide*.

STATE UNIVERSITY LAW SCHOOL

LSAT Percentile Rank

GPA	< 40%	41–50%	51–60%	61–70%	71–80%	81–90%	91–99%
4–3.75	11/1	21/3	29/5	41/12	62/33	68/55	48/47
3.74–3.5	16/0	14/0	8/2	38/16	84/38	115/64	102/81
3.49–3.25	18/0	9/1	12/0	24/8	73/28	96/38	76/48
3.24–3.0	13/0	13/0	22/2	25/6	55/15	71/28	53/27
2.99–2.75	3/0	5/0	8/0	19/2	38/6	49/10	31/9
2.74–2.5	1/0	0/0	3/1	18/3	41/2	32/4	11/5
<2.5	1/0	1/0	3/0	9/1	9/0	6/2	3/1

Take a close look at the hypothetical grid above. Note that GPAs are divided into categories that drop .25 every line. Also note that LSAT scores are listed by percentile rank rather than by score. This is done because the scoring system for the LSAT was changed in 1991, and law schools still receive applications from students with scores under the old system. In order to use the grid, first find the line where your GPA fits in. Then read across until you find the percentage category of your existing or anticipated LSAT score. There you'll find two numbers, divided by a slash. The first number indicates the number of people in that range of LSAT scores and GPAs who applied to that school. The second number is the number accepted.

Most students apply to too few schools. According to Law Services, the average applicant applies to only about five schools. Admittedly, the cost of applications is rising, and sending out ten or more applications can result in an outlay of $500 or more. But keep in mind that if the cost of application presents a real hardship, most schools will waive the application fee—provided you give them a good, credible reason.

DON'T CHEAT YOURSELF

Don't skimp on the number of applications you make. Yes, it's expensive, but this is one of the most important decisions you're likely to make in life. It pays to give yourself as much of a choice as possible.

**MAKE A
LITTLE LIST**

Draw up a list of
schools to which
you intend to apply.
Include at least:

- Two or three
  preferred schools
- Four to seven
  competitive schools
- Two or three
  safe schools

Assembling a List of Schools

Using the grid numbers as a guide for determining your chances of acceptance, you should create a list of schools to apply to, dividing the list into three categories: preferred schools, competitive, and safe schools.

Preferred Schools

These are schools you'd *love* to attend, but your numbers indicate a less than 40 percent chance of admission. Apply to two or three schools in this group. Long-shots rarely pay off, but daydreaming about them is always nice.

Competitive Schools

Competitive (or "good fit") schools are those where your grid numbers are in the ballpark and where, depending on the rest of your application, you have a decent chance of getting admitted. These are schools where your numbers give you a 40–80 percent chance of admission. These are the schools on which you should focus most of your attention. Applying to four to seven schools in this group is reasonable, and increases your odds of getting into at least one school where you are competitive.

"Safe" Schools

These schools are not high on your preference list, but your odds of admission are excellent there. Look at the grids and determine two or three schools where your chances of getting in appear to be 80 percent or better. One suggestion for this list would be to pick schools in locations that you particularly like.

Note: Students with low numbers may need to be a little more flexible and work a little harder. Be willing to travel a little farther to go to school. Also, look at schools in areas that aren't quite as popular or that tend to draw mostly local students. Sometimes the more expensive schools are applied to by fewer applicants and can be easier to get into.

Drawbacks to Using the Law School Grids

Although the grid system is very helpful, it does have its problems. Remember that the law schools provide the grids. Some schools take the opportunity to enhance their reputation by making their numbers seem higher than they really are. This is not done by lying, but rather by the schools' selectively using pertinent information to artificially enhance the numbers. If a school's numbers don't jibe with its reputation, be skeptical.

Second, because each category in a grid covers a fairly wide range of numbers (i.e., 10 LSAT percentile points or .25 GPA points), don't be fooled into thinking that your 3.51 and 71 percent put you on the same level as the student with the 3.74 and 79 percent, even though you fall in the same place on the grids. There are wide gaps in every category.

Third, many law schools—including some of the very best—do not provide Law Services with grids. However, these schools generally will tell you the average GPA and LSAT score for the previous year's entering class. If you want to get a picture of your chances at these schools, try determining which schools are similar in reputation. You can do so using the published ranking lists discussed earlier. Then determine which one of these schools comes closest in number of applications and size of the entering class to the school in question and use that grid.

Use the application list on the following page to plot out your law school application campaign.

APPLICATION LIST

Note: You should apply to at least eight schools.

Preferred Schools
Chances of admission 40 percent or less. Choose two or three.

1. _____

2. _____

3. _____

Competitive Schools
Chances of admission 40–80 percent. Choose four to seven.

1. _____

2. _____

3. _____

4. _____

5. _____

6. _____

7. _____

"Safe" Schools
Chances of admission 80 percent or greater. Choose two or three.

1. _____

2. _____

3. _____

CHAPTER 10

WHEN TO APPLY

With the explosion in the number of law school applications in the 1980s, law schools have had to make a number of adjustments. Foremost among them has been the lengthening of the application season and the move toward rolling admissions. Now let's see how these changes affect you.

Admission Schedules

Prior to the 1980s, the typical law school application season began in October or November with the mailing of the brochures and application forms. The schools would begin accepting applications in December or January and set a deadline for all applications to be completed by around March. Once all applications were received, the schools would begin the decision-making process, usually sending out acceptances or rejections in April, May, or June.

Today, the scenario is quite different. Schools send out application forms in August and September, begin accepting applications in October, and start sending out acceptance letters by November. (As proof that they have a heart, most law schools will not begin sending out rejection letters until after the holiday season.) Application deadlines may still be in February or March, but because the schools have begun filling their classes in the fall, it is not unusual for more than 75 percent of the anticipated acceptance letters to have been sent by the spring deadline date. This is what's known as rolling admissions, which creates the scenario of unaware applicants who proudly deliver their applications on the deadline date only to find that they have put themselves at a distinct disadvantage.

GET THE WORM

Does it really pay to go to a lot of trouble to apply early? Yes, particularly in this era of rolling admissions. Start your campaign eighteen months before you intend to step into your first law class.

The Advantages of Early Application

Does applying early really provide you with an advantage? The answer is a definitive yes! Here are the major reasons why.

Rising Index Numbers

The first reason has to do with index numbers. Your index number is based on the combination of your LSAT score and your GPA. At the beginning of the application process, most schools set an automatic admittance index number. Applicants whose index numbers surpass that figure are admitted quickly with only a cursory look at their application to confirm that they are not serial killers. At the beginning of the process, law schools are always afraid that they'll have too few applicants accepting their offers, which would mean less tuition money and almost certainly some complaints from the school's administrative office. Thus, they usually begin the application process by setting the automatic admittance index number on the low side. Then they gradually increase it as the admission season wears on and they discover that, their fears are unfounded.

Fewer Available Places

Because schools have a tendency to be a little more lenient early in the process, they begin reaching their admission goals fairly quickly. By February, the school may well have sent out more than 75 percent or more of all the acceptance letters it plans to send. Yet, at this point, all of the earlier applicants haven't been rejected. Instead many people are left hanging, just in case better applicants don't start coming through the system. This means that if you apply in March, you're now shooting for fewer possible positions, yet you're still competing against a fairly substantial pool of applicants.

The "Jading" Effect

If they are candid, admissions officers will admit that by the time they get to the two thousandth essay on "Why I want to go to law school," they're burned out, and more than a little jaded. Essays or applications that might have seemed noteworthy in the beginning now strike the reader as routine.

The Nay-Sayers

A handful of prelaw advisors and admissions officers dispute the importance of early applications, and at a few schools, there may indeed be no special advantage. Law schools are almost always open to exceptional applicants, and will sometimes admit someone well after the deadline if the student can give a good reason for the late application. Furthermore, a few schools routinely accept applications up until a week or two before classes start.

But these are exceptions. I became convinced of the importance of early applications while working with a student a few years ago. She hadn't taken the LSAT until December and was running late on her applications, barely making the deadline at the eight law schools to which she applied. Eventually she was rejected by seven of the schools and accepted by one. She decided to sit out a year and try again. The next time, she applied in November to the same eight schools, changed almost nothing on her application, and was accepted at five of the schools and wait-listed at two others. The only logical explanation was the timing of the application.

How Early Is Early?

For the most part, a pre-Halloween application is overdoing it. When schools are just gearing up, you run the risk of documents being misplaced. Pre-Thanksgiving is the preferable choice and assures that you'll be among the early entries. Shortly before Christmas is not as desirable, but should still hold you in good stead. After Christmas and the holidays, however, you're on the downside and may well find yourself among the last 30 percent of all applications received. And if you go with a post-Valentine's Day application—well, you'd better have strong numbers.

Remember that this discussion applies to the date on which your application is *complete*, not just the date on which the school receives your application forms. Applications are not considered complete until the LSAT score, LSDAS (Law School Data Assembly Service) reports, transcripts, and all recommendations have been received. Even though other people are sending these pieces, it's your responsibility to see that they arrive at the law school promptly. This does *not* mean calling the law school three times a week to see if they've arrived. It means prodding your recommenders or your college to send in the necessary documentation. Explain to them the importance of early applications.

When to Start

If you want to have a complete application at the law schools by, say, late November, you can't start planning just a few weeks in advance. Your

LSDAS AT A GLANCE

LSDAS organizes, analyzes, and summarizes biographical and academic information about school applicants, to provide a single, standard format for schools to compare candidates directly to one another. LSDAS provides member law schools with a single standard report with LSAT scores (including average), a normalized GPA, copies of college transcripts, and LSAT writing sample. The LSDAS service is mandatory.

- Cost (at press time): $93 for a twelve-month subscription to LSDAS.
- You sign up for LSDAS at the same time that you register for the LSAT. You will need to have your college transcripts forwarded to LSDAS.
- LSDAS sends your application, scores, transcripts, and writing sample to each school you apply to. You do not have to specify the number of schools you will be applying to when you sign up for the LSDAS, but if you do you will save some money.
- Check your college transcripts and your LSDAS files for accuracy.
- LSDAS sends you monthly updates on which schools have received your records.

MAKE A MASTER SCHEDULE

Use the application schedule/checklist we give you at the end of this chapter to keep yourself on track. Check it often to make sure you're not letting an important deadline pass.

campaign for admission should begin five or six months before that deadline—i.e., eighteen months before your first day as a law student. We've included, at the end of this section, a schedule that you can use to organize your campaign. As you'll see, you should plan to devote plenty of time to your applications the summer before they're due.

Here are some of the important things to do each season. For convenience, let's assume that you want to go to law school the fall after you graduate from college.

Spring of Junior Year

Your first step should be to register for the June LSAT. You won't need your LSAT score for a while yet, but if you take the June test and bomb out, you'll be able to retake the test in October. Get a copy of the LSAT/LSDAS Registration and Information Book at any local college or law school admissions office or at any Kaplan Center. The registration booklet will tell you not only about the LSAT but also about the LSDAS. The LSDAS is the organization that will be sending your LSAT scores and transcripts to the law schools you apply to. You'll want LSDAS to open a file on you as early as possible. The book will explain exactly how to do this and how much it will cost (yes, they charge for their mandatory services).

It's a good idea to buy the *Official Guide to U.S. Law Schools*, which contains those grids we talked about, as well as other information about American law schools. If you can't find it in your local bookstore, you can order it from LSDAS.

The Summer Before Senior Year

Start thinking about a "theme" for your application, which can serve as a way to stand out from the crowd and as an organizing principle for personal statements, recommendations, and everything else in your file. Think about how you'd like to be identified. As the environmentalist who plays oboe recitals for the local recycling center? Of course, you don't *have* to have a theme, but any kind of "high concept" will help your application stick in the minds of admissions officers. You should also be assembling your list of schools at this point. Visit as many of them as you can. Send for their catalogues and applications.

Early Fall of Senior Year

This is when the action really starts. Applications will start arriving. (In filling them out, follow the procedures outlined in the How to Apply section.) Line up your recommenders. Make sure they have everything they need to write you a great letter. (More on how to do so in the How to Apply section.) Take the October LSAT, if you've decided to do so. Revise your personal statement. Revise it again. And again.

Late Fall of Senior Year

Complete and submit your applications. Mail your matching forms to LSDAS, so that they know where to send your scores and transcripts. Prod recommenders so that your applications are complete before Thanksgiving.

Applying to law school is a time-consuming process that tests your organizational skills and your attention to detail. Students who believe that they can simply plot out four hours on a weekend to complete this ordeal are kidding themselves. Plan to set aside some big blocks of time well in advance to work intensively on this important step in achieving your admission goals.

An Ideal Law School Application Schedule

Your campaign for law school admission should start up to eighteen months before you step into your first law classroom. Here's a schedule of what you should be doing when:

Spring of Junior Year
❏ Get the *Official Guide to U.S. Law Schools*.
❏ Register for the June LSAT (you can retake it in October if you blow it).
❏ Prepare for the LSAT.
❏ Subscribe to LSDAS (they take care of sending your transcript and LSAT scores to each school you apply to).

Summer Before Senior Year
❏ Take the June LSAT.
❏ Start drafting your personal statement.
❏ Think about whom you'll be asking for recommendations.
❏ Make a list of schools you'll be applying to, using the grids from the *Official Guide* as an aid.
❏ Send away for applications, and start visiting as many schools as you can.
❏ Register for the October LSAT if you're not satisfied with your June score.

TEST EARLY

Register for the June LSAT. Yes, it's early—you won't need your score until late fall—but taking the June test gives you the opportunity to take the test again in October if you're not satisfied with your score.

Early Fall of Senior Year

❏ Familiarize yourself with the applications as they roll in.

❏ Make a checklist and schedule for each application, and photocopy all forms.

❏ Send transcript request forms to all undergraduate and graduate schools you've attended.

❏ Line up your recommendation writers. Give them the specific info they need to write an outstanding recommendation of you.

❏ Revise your personal statement. Tailor it to specific essay topics, if any, on individual applications.

Midfall of Senior Year

❏ Finalize your personal statements.

❏ Transfer application information from the photocopies to the actual application forms.

❏ Make sure your recommendation writers are on board.

❏ Take the October LSAT (if necessary).

❏ Send in your applications. (Make sure you don't mix up the mailings!)

Late Fall of Senior Year

❏ Remind your recommendation writers to send in recommendations ASAP.

❏ Get Master Law School Report from LSDAS, summarizing transcripts, etcetera.

Winter and Spring/Summer after Senior Year

❏ Receive monthly updates from LSDAS, telling you which schools your records have been sent to.

❏ Cross your fingers while you wait for the acceptances to roll in.

❏ Decide which offer to accept.

❏ Send in acceptance.

❏ Apply for financial aid.

Fall after Graduation

❏ Start your first semester at the law school of your choice.

LSDAS CHECKLIST

❑ Get the *LSAT/LSDAS Registration and Information Book.*
To order a free copy, call LSAC at (215) 968-1001, or e-mail your request to
lsacinfo@lsac.org.
The book is also available at law school admission offices and prelaw advisor offices.

❑ Subscribe to LSDAS by completing the registration form in the *Registration and Information Booklet.*
Parts A, C, and D apply to LSDAS.
You can subscribe to LSDAS on the same form you use to register for the LSAT.
Again, don't forget to sign the form and send payment!

❑ Use transcript request forms (they're in the *Information Book*) to request transcripts from all undergraduate and graduate institutions you've attended.
They will send transcripts directly to LSDAS.

❑ Receive LSDAS Subscription Confirmation.

❑ Receive Master Law School Report—summarizing your academic information.
They get sent shortly after LSDAS receives your transcripts.
Check it carefully; report any inaccuracies to Law Services.

❑ Include an Application Matching Form (they're also in the *Information Book*) with each law school application you make.

❑ If you've decided to apply to more schools than you originally planned to, order extra reports from LSDAS and pay an additional fee.

❑ Receive monthly reports from LSDAS.
Check them for accuracy or discrepancies.

❑ If necessary, renew your LSDAS subscription after twelve months.

CHAPTER 11

HOW TO APPLY

After you've made the decision to apply to law school and have decided where and when to apply, you need to order the application forms from the various schools you've chosen. This can be done by mail, but the quickest way is just to call the admissions offices around July and get put on their mailing lists. Once the applications begin arriving (usually around Labor Day) you'll notice one thing quickly: *no two applications are exactly alike.* Some require one recommendation, others two or three. Some ask you to write one essay or personal statement, while others may ask for two or even three. Some have very detailed forms requiring extensive background information; others are satisfied with your name and address and very little else.

Despite these differences, most applications follow a general pattern with variations on the same kinds of questions. So although not all of this section is relevant to all parts of every application, these guidelines will be valuable for just about any law school application you'll encounter.

The Application as Marketing Tool

The most important thing to keep in mind about your law school application is that it is, above all else, a sales pitch. The application is your single best opportunity to sell yourself. Remember, every person who applies will have strengths and weaknesses. It's how you *present* those strengths and weaknesses that counts. *You* are in control of what that admissions committee sees on your application and how they see it.

So what's the best way to sell yourself? We all know that some people are natural-born sellers in person, but the application process is written, not spoken. The key here is not natural talent but rather organization—carefully planning a coherent presentation from beginning to end and paying attention to every detail in between. But be careful not to focus

LIKE SNOWFLAKES

No two law school applications are exactly alike, but most ask for the same kind of information and look for the same qualities in the applicant. You won't be writing ten different applications so much as ten variations on a single application.

DEVELOP A THEME

Start thinking early about what theme you want your application to convey. Decide what your real purpose is in applying to law school, and make sure that this sense of purpose comes through in all aspects of your application.

For instance, is it your goal to pursue environmental law? If so, give your entire application an environmental theme. Do some volunteer work for a local recycling organization (and make sure to list that activity on your application form); ask the head of the same organization to write a recommendation for you; use the personal statement to discuss your involvement in the organization's various causes. All of these efforts will give your application coherence and a sense of purpose—and help it stick in the minds of the admissions officers.

TAKE CONTROL

You control how you are perceived by the admissions committee—through your application. You can't afford to miss a single opportunity in the application process to make yourself seem desirable as a law student. And the first step is *getting organized*.

so much on the overall theme that you neglect the details. That can be disastrous.

Getting Organized

You must first put together a checklist of the forms that each of your chosen schools requires, double-checking to make sure you don't overlook anything. Some schools may require you to fill out residency forms or financial aid forms in addition to the regular application forms. Don't ignore these and put them off until last. Schools may require proof of residency or income verifications that you might not have readily available.

Next, make photocopies of all forms before you complete them. Changes and corrections will have to be made no matter how careful you are. These changes should not be made on the original form, which will go to the school. Almost every admissions officer I have spoken with explicitly prizes neatness. The feeling is that if the application is sloppily prepared, the student is not very serious about attending that law school. Work on your photocopied rough draft until you are sure you are ready to transfer to the original application.

The Application Form

For the most part, filling out the application form requires simply putting down factual information. But even in something so apparently mindless, you can still make sure you present yourself as a thorough, organized person who can follow directions.

The key to filling out the application form can be summed up in a single sentence: *Don't make the admissions officers do more work than they have to.* Make sure that they have all of the information they need at their fingertips. If they have to hunt up your statistics, if your application is full of unexplained blanks, if they can't read what you've written—all of these things will just serve to annoy the very people you want to impress.

One key to not annoying the admissions people is to make sure you answer *all* of the questions asked on the application form. If some questions don't seem to apply to you, type in "not applicable"; leave nothing blank. If the admissions officers see blank spaces, they don't know whether you found the question not applicable, just didn't want to answer it, or overlooked it. Many schools will return the application if even a single question

KAPLAN

is left blank. This can be a real problem, because it may be a month or more before the application is looked at and returned and then filled in and looked at again. That kind of delay can easily turn an early application into a late one.

Along these same lines, don't answer questions by saying *see above* or *see line 22*. Most applications will ask you for things like your address or phone number more than once. Go ahead and fill them in again. Remember that law schools are flooded with documentation and may separate parts of the application. They don't appreciate having to find what you wrote back on line 22 if they've asked you for that information again on line 55.

As long as we're talking about practices that annoy the decision makers, another is the failure to follow directions on the forms. If the form says, "Don't write below this line," then don't write below the line. You are not an exception to this rule. If they ask for an explanation in 150 words or less, then don't give them 300 words. One admissions officer told me that the comment, "He couldn't even follow directions," is heard several times a year in committee meetings.

Addendums

An important part of the application form will not be in the package sent from the law school. These are your addendums. Addendums (or *addenda*, if you want to be fancy) are the additional page or pages that you staple onto the forms when the space they give you to answer a question is too small.

This is where an addendum comes in. Simply write "continued on addendum" on the application form after you've used their space up, and then clearly mark what you are listing at the top of the addendum. Staple this addendum at the back, and you've solved a tricky problem. Law schools appreciate addendums because they're much neater than attempts to cram things into a limited space—*and* they show careful organization. But don't overdo it. One or two addendums should be sufficient for any application.

Addendums can be used to preserve neatness when the application blanks are of insufficient length. But they can also be helpful if an answer requires further explanation. For example, if you won the Grant R. Humphrey Science award, it's not enough just to list it. You need to explain what it is, what it's given for, and possibly how many others were competing for it or how prestigious it is.

Honesty

One final topic about the application form that needs to be discussed is honesty. If you think you can get by with a lie or two on your application—well, you may be right. Law schools as a rule don't have the resources to verify all aspects of every application. But before you go overboard and decide to put down that you were once the Prince of Wales, you should realize that you're taking a big chance.

First of all, many schools are beginning to devote more time to checking up on applicants' claims. Last year I spoke to the president of an undergraduate prelaw society who told me that she regularly gets calls from law schools verifying membership of applicants. Secondly, there's always the chance that, if you lie, some other part of your application will contradict the lie and get you booted.

Finally, even if you fool the law school, get in, and graduate with honors, you'll find that any state in which you apply to take the bar exam will do a much more extensive background check than that done by the law school. This check very well might include looking for contradictions in your law school application. Lying on your law school application, in fact, is considered grounds for refusing admittance to a state bar.

Additional Points
Here are a few more things to take note of when filling out the application form:

Be sure to type the application from start to finish. A surprising number of applicants still hand-write the application—something that, according to admissions officers, costs you dearly.

Don't use application forms from previous years. Most applications change from year to year, often substantially. Also, don't use other school's forms because you lost the form of the school you're applying to (yes, people have done that, believe it or not).

Staple extra sheets to the forms. Don't use paper clips unless told to do so. Paper clips—and the pages they attach—tend to get lost.

Always double- and triple-check your application for spelling errors. You lose a certain amount of credibility if you write that you were a "Roads Scholar."

Check for accidental contradictions. Make sure that your application doesn't say you worked for a law firm in 1997 when your financial aid forms say you were driving a cab that year.

Prioritize all lists. When a question asks you to list your honors or awards, don't begin with fraternity social chairman and end with Phi Beta Kappa. Let the admissions committee know that you realize what's important—that is, always list significant scholastic accomplishments first.

Craft your list of extracurricular activities. Don't list every event or every activity you ever participated in. Select the most significant and, if necessary, explain them.

Don't mention high school activities or honors. Unless there's something very unusual or spectacular about your high school background, don't mention it, even if it means you don't take note of the fact that you were senior class president.

Clear up any ambiguities. On questions concerning employment, for instance, make sure to specify whether you held a job during the school year or only during the summer. Many applications ask about this, and it may be an important point to the admissions officer.

The Personal Statement

There are about as many theories on what constitutes a winning personal statement as there are theories on the Kennedy assassination—and, unfortunately, many of them have about the same validity. To begin with, how can you tell 85,000 annual applicants with 85,000 different personalities and backgrounds that there is one correct way to write a personal statement? Furthermore, if even a small percentage of those applicants read and come to believe that a certain way is the correct way, it automatically becomes incorrect, because law schools despise getting personal statements that are familiar—that are, in other words, *im*personal.

For that reason, I've broken down the section on personal statements into two parts. First, we'll look at the procedure of putting together a personal statement. Then we'll look at a list of DOs and DON'Ts that admission officers most frequently mention.

Putting Together an Outstanding Personal Statement

Next to your LSAT score and GPA, the personal statement is probably the most important part of your application. If your numbers are excellent or very poor, the essay may get only a cursory glance. But if your numbers place you on the borderline at a school, then it may very well make the difference between acceptance and rejection.

What Kind of Essay to Write

The personal statement is exactly what its name implies—a statement by you that is meant to show something about your personality and character. But that doesn't mean you are to create a lengthy essay detailing every aspect of your life since birth. Nor is the personal statement intended to be a psychological profile describing all of your character attributes and flaws. Several admissions officers have told me that the best essays are often only remotely related to the applicant. The point is that you need not write an in-depth personality profile baring your innermost soul. Admissions officers are adept at learning what they want to know about you from your essay, even if it doesn't contain the words *me, myself,* and *I* in every sentence.

One exception, however, should be noted. Although most schools still provide wide latitude in their directions about what the personal statement should be about, some schools are becoming more specific. The problem with specific requirements like these is that you may well have to write a separate essay for that school alone. Be sure to check the instructions carefully and follow them closely. If a law school asks for a specific type of essay and you provide them with a more general one, they'll likely feel that you're not very interested in attending that particular school.

But take heart. Most schools provide few restrictions on what you can write about, so unless you're very unlucky, you should be able to limit the number of essays you must write to two or three.

How Long an Essay to Write

How long should the personal statement be? Some schools place a word-limit on the essay; others specify one or two typed pages. Always follow the specific directions, but you should be in good shape with virtually all schools if your essay is one and a half to two pages in length.

Writing the Essay

The personal statement shouldn't be done overnight. A strong personal statement may take shape over the course of months and require several different drafts. One practice that many have found particularly effective is to write a draft and then let it sit for four to six weeks. If you leave it alone for a significant period of time, you may find that your first instincts were good ones. On the other hand, you may shudder at how you could

DON'T DRONE ON

Your reader might not find your life quite as fascinating as you do, so be careful not to go on at length. A boring personal statement is a good excuse to toss an application onto the "No" pile.

TIME LENDS PERSPECTIVE

Start drafting your personal statement now, so that you'll be able to put it aside for a few weeks or even months. You'll be amazed at how different it will look when you go back to it.

ever have considered submitting such a piece of garbage. Either way, time lends a valuable perspective.

Try to start the essay sometime during the summer before you apply. Allow at least three months to write it, and don't be afraid to take it through numerous drafts or overhaul it completely if you're not satisfied. Get several different perspectives. Ask close friends or relatives to scrutinize it to see if it really captures what you want to convey. Be sure to ask them about their initial reaction as well as their feelings after studying it more carefully. Once you've achieved a draft that you feel comfortable with, try to have it read by some people who barely know you or who don't know you at all. If certain criticisms are consistently made, then they're probably legitimate. But don't be carried away by every suggestion every reader makes. Stick to your basic instincts because, after all, this is *your* personal statement, no one else's.

Proofreading is of critical importance. Again, don't be afraid to enlist the aid of others. If possible, let an English teacher review the essay solely for spelling and grammar mistakes.

Essay Content

As stated earlier, there's no one correct way to write an essay, but admissions officers do provide some helpful tips about what they like and don't like to see in a personal statement. Let's begin with a list of the things that officers most often mentioned they disliked seeing.

Personal Statement DON'Ts

Don't turn your personal statement into a résumé. This is the personal statement that begins at birth and simply recites every major (and sometimes minor) event of the person's life. Most of this information is repetitive since it's included on other parts of the application. But worse than that, it's just a boring format.

Avoid the "why I want to go to law school" essay. Although this can be a *part* of any law school essay, too many people make it the entire focus of their statement. The problem is that there are not many new variations on this theme, and the admissions officers have likely heard them all before, probably many times.

LINE UP YOUR READERS

Try to let as many people as possible read and comment on your personal statement. But don't be swayed by everything that every person says. Listen to all comments, but only take them to heart if you really think they're valid.

OH NO, NOT ANOTHER ALBERT SCHWEITZER!

Admissions officers read about a lot of noble intentions in personal statements. Naturally, they're skeptical of such claims, especially if the rest of your application demonstrates no such selfless impulse. So be careful with protestations of high ideals. If you can't back them up with hard evidence, they're bound to come off sounding empty and insincere.

AVOID LEXICAL PROLIXITY

Don't try to impress your reader with many difficult words. It won't work. Take our word for it.

NO AMBULANCE-CHASER JOKES, PLEASE

You may think it'll come across as refreshing when you put down lawyers and the law profession in your personal statement. It won't. Your reader won't be amused.

Avoid talking about your negatives. The personal statement is not the place to call attention to your flaws. Don't forget that you're selling yourself, and the personal statement is your most prominent sales tool.

Don't be too personal. Stories of abuse or trauma are often very moving and can be particularly effective if tied into a person's reason for wanting to practice law. Several admissions officers, however, have noted a trend toward describing such problems in graphic detail in personal statements. This kind of confessional essay can easily cross the line and become too personal.

Don't discuss legal concepts. Along those same lines, don't try to impress the reader with much you already know about the law. The school assumes that they can teach you what you need to know, regardless of the level at which you start. By discussing a legal concept, you also run the risk of showing a certain amount of ignorance about the subject, while at the same time appearing arrogant enough to have tried to discuss it.

Don't put down lawyers or the legal profession. Although it may seem that spewing cynicism about the legal profession is a clever device, trust me when I tell you that it isn't. Once you become a member of the legal profession, you can make as many lawyer jokes as you want. Until then, watch your step.

Don't try to cover too many subjects. Focus on one or two areas you really want to talk about. One of the worst mistakes applicants make is writing essays that ramble from one subject to another and back again. Fight the desire to talk about every highlight of your life.

Now that you've got a sense of what not to do in your personal statement, let's turn to a list of suggestions for things that you *should* do.

Personal Statement DOs

Tell stories. Readers respond much better to a concrete story or illustrative anecdote than to an abstract list of your attributes. Instead of just writing how determined you are, for instance, tell a story that demonstrates it. Stories stick in people's memories. The same holds true when you're trying to make sure the admissions officers remember you.

Be funny—if you can pull it off. Humor, particularly self-deprecating humor, is a very effective device. Admissions officers appreciate occasional flashes of irony. However, be careful in your use of humor. Don't overdo it—a couple of funny lines or a funny story can be great, but include too many jokes and you start to sound flippant. Finally, think about using *self-deprecating* humor. Law schools often complain about the lack of humility among students and appreciate those who show some.

Be unique. The term *unique* has been overused. Even some applications now ask you to describe what is unique about you. Applicants rack their brains trying to figure out how they're different from the other 5,000 people applying to that law school. Or worse, some interpret *unique* to mean disadvantaged, and rack their brains trying to think how they have suffered more than others. But what the admissions officers want to know is what qualities or experiences in your life would make you a particularly valuable member of a law school class.

Start strongly. In private moments, admissions officers will often admit that they don't read every essay carefully. They may just glance at an essay to get a general impression. That's why it's important to grab them from the beginning. Tell the ending of a story first and make them want to read on, to see how it all started, for example.

The above points, I feel, are as much general advice as one can responsibly give about the personal statement in a book such as this. I hope that they'll provide you with some ideas or keep you from making some costly mistakes. In the end, however, it *is* a personal statement, and it must come from you.

Recommendations

During the last ten years, as law school applications have increased dramatically and the odds against being accepted at any particular school have risen, applicants have taken various approaches to stand out from the crowd. Too often overlooked in this mad pursuit, however, is one of the very best ways for an applicant to stand out—that is, by getting terrific, vividly written recommendations.

Because so many recommendations tend to be blasé, an outstanding recommendation that goes beyond the standard language can really make

SHE'S SO UNUSUAL

Admissions officers try to assemble a law school class that includes a rich variety of perspectives. Let them know what you could contribute to the diverse intellectual atmosphere they're trying to achieve.

THE IMPORTANCE OF RECOMMENDATIONS

To be honest, your recommendations probably won't matter all that much in the admissions decision—unless, of course, your recommendations are outstanding.

an applicant stand out. Not only does such a recommendation serve the purpose of pointing out an applicant's strengths, it also shows that the recommender thought enough of the person to put time and effort into carefully writing it.

What Makes a Recommendation Outstanding?

Outstanding recommendations can vary in format, but there are several qualities they all tend to have in common.

An Outstanding Recommendation Must Be Personal

By far the most common mistake made by applicants is believing that the prestige or position of the recommender is more important than what that person writes. Admissions officers tend to treat recommendations from senators, governors, and chief executive officers of major corporations with a great deal of skepticism, because very few applicants have a truly personal relationship with such people. To make matters worse, these officials tend to respond with very standard recommendations that rarely offer any real insight into the applicant's character; in a worst-case scenario, they may even be computer-generated.

Find people who truly know you and are able to make an honest assessment of your capabilities. This means that it may be better to have the teaching assistant with whom you had daily contact write the recommendation, rather than the prestigious professor you spoke to once during the year.

An Outstanding Recommendation Compares You to Others

When an admissions officer reads a recommendation, he or she often has to put into perspective the meaning of overused phrases—such as *hardworking* and *quick mind*—as they relate to the applicant. A much better format, and one that admissions officers appreciate, is the comparison recommendation, one that compares the applicant to other people that the recommendation writer previously knew in the same position, or (in a best-case scenario) to people he or she has known who are alumnae of that particular law school.

An Outstanding Recommendation Tells Stories

A concrete and specific recommendation stands out. Rather than merely listing attributes, a good recommendation engages the reader by telling an insightful story about the applicant. Recently, a professor of political science chose not to submit the standard phrase about what a quick study a

---

I CAN WHOLEHEARTEDLY RECOMMEND . . . UH, WHAT WAS YOUR NAME AGAIN?

Beware the impersonal recommendation. It's a definite red flag to the admissions officer. Better to have a recommendation written by a lab assistant who knows you well rather than the Nobel-winning professor who doesn't remember your name.

student was. Instead, he related a story about the student in class. It seems the professor introduced a new and difficult concept in class that the student discussed intelligently and actually took further than the professor was prepared to do. That kind of story sticks in a reader's mind.

An Outstanding Recommendation Focuses on Scholastic Abilities

Although recommendations often cover a lot of ground, from the applicant's attitudes about school to his or her personality traits, admissions officers focus on comments about a person's scholastic ability. Obviously, this means that a strong recommendation from a professor carries a great deal of weight. However, a lot of people are in a position to observe a person's intellectual aptitude. Employers, friends, clergy, and workers at volunteer agencies are all usually able to discuss an applicant's scholastic abilities—and should.

An Outstanding Recommendation Will Contain Some Negative Comments

In many ways, this is the trickiest area of writing a recommendation, yet it can also prove to be a vital component. A recommendation that is only laudatory, failing to mention a single negative thing about an applicant, may lose credibility. By pointing out a small character flaw or a potential weakness, the recommender gains credibility with the admissions officers and tends to make them less skeptical about the preceding positive comments.

One word of caution, though: Admissions officers universally hate "fake" negatives—for example, "If Suzy has one fault, it is that she works just too darn hard." Much more appreciated are such comments as, "Joe can afford to improve his attention to detail." Combined with effusive praise for the applicant's strong points, this sort of comment impresses admissions officers as being straightforward and helpful.

How to Ensure You Receive Outstanding Recommendations

Now that you know what makes for an outstanding recommendation, all you have to do is ensure that each of your recommenders produces one. While you can't actually write the recommendations yourself, you *can* have a great deal of influence over how accurate and persuasive they are.

Choose the Right People to Recommend You

What are the qualities of a good recommender? Obviously, you should choose someone who likes you, and who thinks you're good at what you do. This doesn't mean that you have to be intimate pals, but sworn

HE SAID, SHE SAID

Discrepancies between your personal statement and a recommendation can undermine the credibility of your entire application. Make sure your recommendation writers know who you are and what you're about.

JUST SAY NO

When asked whether you want to see what your recommendation writers have written about you, *say no!* If admissions officers know that you'll be seeing your recommendations, they'll discount much of what is said in them.

LET'S DO LUNCH

Try to set up an appointment with each of your recommenders—to make sure they're up to speed on who you are and what you're all about.

DON'T BE (OBVIOUSLY) MANIPULATIVE

Be diplomatic. Make sure you let your recommendation writers know what *kind* of things you'd love their recommendations to contain. But be careful not to create the impression that you're manipulating them. It could easily backfire.

enemies don't often write good recommendations. It helps if the person is a good writer, so that he or she can clearly express an opinion about you.

Most, if not all, of your recommendations for academic programs should come from professors or other academic faculty. If you've been out of school for a few years and haven't kept in touch with your professors, call or write the admissions offices of the schools to which you're applying. Don't assume that it's okay to send fewer letters than required or to substitute other kinds of information for recommendation letters. Most likely, schools will allow you to submit recommendations from employers or from other nonacademic people with knowledge about your background, skills, and goals.

Balance Your List of Recommendation Writers

Three professors from your undergrad major department probably will have similar things to say about you, so why not include someone from another field who can speak to your thinking and writing skills?

Be Considerate of Your Recommendation Writers

As soon as you decide to go to law school you should start sizing up potential recommenders and letting them know that you may ask them for a letter. This will give each plenty of time to get to know you better, and to think about what to say in the letter. Once they've agreed, let them know about deadlines with plenty of lead time to avoid potential scheduling conflicts. The more time they have, the better the job they'll do recommending you.

Make Sure Your Recommendation Writers Know What They Need to Know

Once someone has agreed to consider writing a letter for you, you should arrange an appointment to discuss your background and goals for your future. If you live thousands of miles away from your recommender, arrange a telephone appointment.

Bring to the appointment copies of appropriate documentation such as your transcript, papers you've written, your résumé or curriculum vitae, your personal statement, and a sheet of bullet points that you plan to feature in your application and essay. Supply the appropriate form or forms, as well as stamped, addressed envelopes and a copy of your home address and phone number.

Keep the appointment relatively brief—you're already taking up enough of their time. Give your recommenders a good idea of why you want to go to law school. Play up your good points, of course, but be reasonably humble. If you have a very specific "marketing" image that you're trying to project, let your recommenders in on it—they may want to focus on some of the same points you're trying to stress. But don't tell your recommenders what to write! Don't even give them the impression that you're doing so! Recommenders tend to resent any attempts at manipulation, and may, as a consequence, refuse to write your letter. What recommenders *do* appreciate, however, is some direction as to what you'd like to see.

Keep Your Recommendation Writers on Schedule

Finally, make sure your recommenders know how important it is to complete the letters as early as possible. If they procrastinate, gently remind them that their deadline is approaching and be sure to remind them of the importance of early applications.

Common Questions about Recommendations

Here are other points about recommendations that should be considered.

How Long Should a Recommendation Be?

Like the personal statement, the recommendation should be short and concise. A one-page recommendation is usually sufficient. In any case, it should be no longer than two to two and one-half pages.

Should I Request to Look at the Recommendation?

Easy answer—NO! Almost all schools have a box you check to indicate whether or not you would like to be able to see the recommendation once it's provided to the school. Just say no! If the school believes that the recommender cannot be completely honest for fear of offending the applicant, the school will heavily discount what is written, no matter how laudatory.

Can I Send More Recommendations Than the School Requests?

Be careful. Law schools may request anywhere from one to four recommendations from an applicant (the recent trend is toward fewer recommendations). Invariably, the situation arises in which a student has three good recommendations, but the school only asks for two. Some schools are very specific in their instructions that they will not accept more than the exact number requested. If the application doesn't spell out how the school handles it, call the school and ask to make sure.

Should I Use the Letter of Recommendation Service?

The Letter of Recommendation Service is set up by Law Services as a convenience. Basically, the service allows your recommenders to send letters

YOU OUGHTN'T TO BE IN PICTURES

Don't send videos or pictures of yourself with the application (unless you're specifically asked to). The admissions officers usually aren't terribly interested in what you look and sound like.

to LSAC, who then forwards them to the law schools. Note that the same letter is sent to each school, and so school-specific letters should not be sent through this service. For more information, check out the latest *LSAT/LSDAS Information book*, or contact your target schools to see if they prefer that you use the service.

A Final Check

After you've completed everything and are getting ready to place it in a manila envelope and mail it, make sure you go through one more time and check each document. Law schools frequently receive documents that were intended to go to another law school. With all of this paperwork, it's easy to see how that can happen, and the law schools expect a certain amount of it. However, it can be embarrassing if you've written in your personal statement that ABC Law School is the one and only place for you—and then you accidentally send it to XYZ Law School instead.

APPLICATION CHECKLIST

The three major parts of your law school application:

1. The application form
2. The personal statement
3. Recommendations

The Application Form
- ❏ Working photocopies of applications made
- ❏ Information/addresses/other data gathered
- ❏ Addendums (if any) written
- ❏ Information transferred to actual application
- ❏ Application proofread
- ❏ Final check done

The Personal Statement
- ❏ Theme finalized
- ❏ Readers selected and notified
- ❏ First draft written
- ❏ Self-evaluation made
- ❏ Second draft written
- ❏ Comments from readers received
- ❏ Final draft written
- ❏ Final statement proofread

Recommendations
- ❏ Recommendation writers chosen
- ❏ Recommendation writers on board
- ❏ Informational meeting with recommendation writers conducted
- ❏ Reminders to all recommendation writers sent

❏ **Notice of complete application received**

NOTES

NOTES

NOTES

How Did We Do? Grade Us.

Thank you for choosing a Kaplan book. Your comments and suggestions are very useful to us. Please answer the following questions to assist us in our continued development of high-quality resources to meet your needs.

The Kaplan book I read was: _____

My name is: _____

My address is: _____

_____

My e-mail address is: _____

What overall grade would you give this book? Ⓐ Ⓑ Ⓒ Ⓓ Ⓕ

How relevant was the information to your goals? Ⓐ Ⓑ Ⓒ Ⓓ Ⓕ

How comprehensive was the information in this book? Ⓐ Ⓑ Ⓒ Ⓓ Ⓕ

How accurate was the information in this book? Ⓐ Ⓑ Ⓒ Ⓓ Ⓕ

How easy was the book to use? Ⓐ Ⓑ Ⓒ Ⓓ Ⓕ

How appealing was the book's design? Ⓐ Ⓑ Ⓒ Ⓓ Ⓕ

What were the book's strong points? _____

How could this book be improved? _____

Is there anything that we left out that you wanted to know more about?

Would you recommend this book to others? ☐ YES   ☐ NO

Other comments: _____

_____

_____

Do we have permission to quote you? ☐ YES   ☐ NO

Thank you for your help. Please tear out this page and mail it to:

Dave Chipps, Managing Editor
Kaplan Educational Centers
888 Seventh Avenue
New York, NY 10106

Or, you can answer these questions online at www.kaplan.com/talkback.

Thanks!

KAPLAN 60 · SIXTY · YEARS · OF · BUILDING · FUTURES

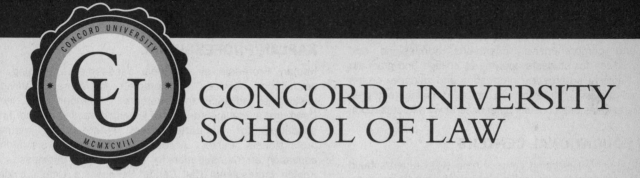

About

Educational Centers

Kaplan Educational Centers is one of the nation's leading providers of education and career services. Kaplan is a wholly owned subsidiary of The Washington Post Company.

TEST PREPARATION & ADMISSIONS

Kaplan's nationally recognized test prep courses cover more than 20 standardized tests, including secondary school, college and graduate school entrance exams and foreign language and professional licensing exams. In addition, Kaplan offers private tutoring and comprehensive, one-to-one admissions and application advice for students applying to college and graduate programs. Kaplan also provides information and guidance on the financial aid process. Students can enroll in online test prep courses and admissions consulting services at www.kaptest.com

Score! EDUCATIONAL CENTERS

SCORE! after-school learning centers help K-9 students build confidence, academic and goal-setting skills in a motivating, sports-oriented environment. Its cutting-edge, interactive curriculum continually assesses and adapts to each child's academic needs and learning style. Enthusiastic Academic Coaches serve as positive role models, creating a high-energy atmosphere where learning is exciting and fun. SCORE! Prep provides in-home, one-on-one tutoring for high school academic subjects and standardized tests. www.eSCORE.com provides customized online educational resources and services for parents and kids ages 0 to 18. eSCORE.com creates a deep, evolving profile for each child based on his or her age, interests and skills. Parents can access personalized information and resources designed to help their children realize their full potential.

KAPLAN LEARNING SERVICES

Kaplan Learning Services provides customized assessment, education and professional development programs to K-12 schools and universities.

KAPLAN INTERNATIONAL PROGRAMS

Kaplan services international students and professionals in the U.S. through a series of intensive English language and test preparation programs. These programs are offered campus-based centers across the USA. Kaplan offers specialized services including housing, placement at top American universities, fellowship management, academic monitoring and reporting, and financial administration.

KAPLAN PUBLISHING

Kaplan Publishing produces books and software. Kaplan Books, a joint imprint with Simon & Schuster, publishes titles in test preparation, admissions, education, career development and life skills; Kaplan and Newsweek jointly publish guides on getting into college, finding the right career, and helping your child succeed in school. Through an alliance with Knowledge Adventure, Kaplan publishes educational software for the K-12 retail and school markets.

KAPLAN PROFESSIONAL

Kaplan Professional provides assessment, training, and certification services for corporate clients and individuals seeking to advance their careers. Member units include Dearborn, a leading supplier of licensing training and continuing education for securities, real estate, and insurance professionals; Perfect Access/CRN, which delivers software education and consultation for law firms and businesses; and Kaplan Professional Call Center Services, a total provider of services for the call center industry.

DISTANCE LEARNING DIVISION

Kaplan's distance learning programs include Concord School of Law, the nation's first online law school; and Kaplan College, a leading provider of degree and certificate programs in criminal justice and paralegal studies.

COMMUNITY OUTREACH

Kaplan provides educational career resources to thousands of financially disadvantaged students annually, working closely with educational institutions, not-for-profit groups, government agencies and other grass roots organizations on a variety of national and local support programs. Kaplan enriches local communities by employing high school, college and graduate students, creating valuable work experiences for vast numbers of young people each year.

BRASSRING

BrassRing Inc., headquartered in New York and San Mateo, CA, is the first network that combines recruiting, career development and hiring management services to serve employers and employees at every step. Through its units BrassRing.com and HireSystems, BrassRing provides an array of on- and off-line resources that help employers simplify and accelerate the hiring process, and help individuals to build skills and find a better job. Kaplan is BrassRing's majority shareholder.

Want more information about our services, products, or the nearest Kaplan center?

1 **Call our nationwide toll-free numbers:**

1-800-KAP-TEST for information on our courses, private tutoring and admissions consulting

1-800-KAP-ITEM for information on our books and software

1-888-KAP-LOAN* for information on student loans

2 **Connect with us in cyberspace:**

On AOL, keyword:"Kaplan"
On the World Wide Web, go to:
www.kaplan.com
www.kaptest.com
www.eSCORE.com
www.dearborn.com
www.BrassRing.com
www.concord.kaplan.edu
www.kaplancollege.com
Via e-mail: info@kaplan.com

**3** **Write to:**

Kaplan Educational Centers
888 Seventh Avenue
New York, NY 10106

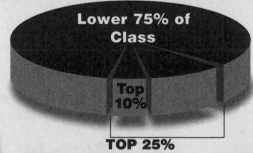